BONHOEFFER AND THE RESPONSIBILITY
FOR A COMING GENERATION

T&T Clark New Studies in Bonhoeffer's Theology and Ethics

Series editors

Jennifer McBride
Michael Mawson
Philip G. Ziegler

BONHOEFFER AND THE RESPONSIBILITY FOR A COMING GENERATION

Doing Theology in a Time Out of Joint

Edited by
Robert Vosloo, Teddy Sakupapa, Ashwin Thyssen,
and Karola Radler

LONDON • NEW YORK • OXFORD • NEW DELHI • SYDNEY

T&T CLARK

Bloomsbury Publishing Plc, 50 Bedford Square, London, WC1B 3DP, UK
Bloomsbury Publishing Inc, 1359 Broadway, New York, NY 10018, USA
Bloomsbury Publishing Ireland, 29 Earlsfort Terrace, Dublin 2, D02 AY28, Ireland

BLOOMSBURY, T&T CLARK and the T&T Clark logo are trademarks of Bloomsbury Publishing Plc

First published in Great Britain 2024
Paperback edition published 2026

Copyright © Robert Vosloo, Teddy Sakupapa, Ashwin Thyssen, Karola Radler, and Contributors, 2024

Robert Vosloo, Teddy Sakupapa, Ashwin Thyssen, and Karola Radler have asserted their right under the Copyright, Designs and Patents Act, 1988, to be identified as Editors of this work.

Cover image: Dietrich Bonhoeffer (1906–45) photographed in the late 1930s.
Photo by ullstein bild via Getty Images

All rights reserved. No part of this publication may be: i) reproduced or transmitted in any form, electronic or mechanical, including photocopying, recording or by means of any information storage or retrieval system without prior permission in writing from the publishers; or ii) used or reproduced in any way for the training, development or operation of artificial intelligence (AI) technologies, including generative AI technologies. The rights holders expressly reserve this publication from the text and data mining exception as per Article 4(3) of the Digital Single Market Directive (EU) 2019/790.

Bloomsbury Publishing Plc does not have any control over, or responsibility for, any third-party websites referred to or in this book. All internet addresses given in this book were correct at the time of going to press. The author and publisher regret any inconvenience caused if addresses have changed or sites have ceased to exist, but can accept no responsibility for any such changes.

A catalogue record for this book is available from the British Library.

Library of Congress Cataloging-in-Publication Data.

Names: Vosloo, Robert, editor. | Sakupapa, Teddy, editor. | Thyssen, Ashwin, editor. | Radler, Karola, editor.
Title: Bonhoeffer and the responsibility for a coming generation : doing theology in a time out of joint / edited by Robert Vosloo, Teddy Sakupapa, Ashwin Thyssen, and Karola Radler.
Description: 1. | London : T&T Clark, 2024. | Series: T&T Clark new studies in Bonhoeffer's theology and ethics | Includes bibliographical references and index.
Identifiers: LCCN 2023059789 (print) | LCCN 2023059790 (ebook) | ISBN 9780567711069 (hardback) | ISBN 9780567711113 (paperback) | ISBN 9780567711076 (pdf) | ISBN 9780567711106 (epub)
Subjects: LCSH: Bonhoeffer, Dietrich, 1906-1945. | Christian sociology. | Contractarianism (Ethics) | Intergenerational relations.
Classification: LCC BX4827.B57 B568 2024 (print) | LCC BX4827.B57 (ebook) | DDC 261–dc23/eng/20240409
LC record available at https://lccn.loc.gov/2023059789
LC ebook record available at https://lccn.loc.gov/2023059790

ISBN: HB: 978-0-5677-1106-9
PB: 978-0-5677-1111-3
ePDF: 978-0-5677-1107-6
ePub: 978-0-5677-1110-6

Series: T&T Clark New Studies in Bonhoeffer's Theology and Ethics

Typeset by Deanta Global Publishing Services, Chennai, India

For product safety related questions contact productsafety@bloomsbury.com.

To find out more about our authors and books visit www.bloomsbury.com and sign up for our newsletters.

To John de Gruchy

In gratitude for

> *living with Bonhoeffer's questions,*
>
> *stirring up conversation across generations,*
>
> *and embodying an inspiring gospel ethos of responsibility and hope.*

CONTENTS

List of Abbreviations   xi
Foreword   xiv
    Nico Koopman

INTRODUCTION   1

PART 1
BONHOEFFER, THE GENERATIONS, AND OUR HERITAGE

Chapter 1
OLD MAN BONHOEFFER: GENERATIVITY, LIFE SPAN PSYCHOLOGY, AND INTERGENERATIONAL ETHICS   7
    Frits de Lange

Chapter 2
"O, POOR JUDAS, WHAT HAVE YOU DONE!": A THEOLOGICAL EXPLORATION OF BETRAYAL   17
    Nadia Marais

Chapter 3
WHAT DOES IT MEAN TO TELL THE TRUTH? BONHOEFFER IN THE DIGITAL ERA   28
    Wolfgang Huber

Chapter 4
GUILT, TRAUMA, RESILIENCE: TRANSGENERATIONAL ASPECTS IN THEOLOGY AND PSYCHOTHERAPY IN CONVERSATION WITH DIETRICH BONHOEFFER AND HANS JOACHIM IWAND   40
    Anne-Katharina Neddens and Christian Neddens

Chapter 5
FACING THE PAST, TAKING RESPONSIBILITY FOR A COMING GENERATION: THE LEGACY OF BONHOEFFER'S TWO "TESTAMENTS"   51
    Gerard den Hertog

Chapter 6
IN THE WAKE: READING BONHOEFFER AT THE DOOR OF NO RETURN   62
    Reggie L. Williams

Part II
BONHOEFFER AND EARTH-HONORING RESPONSIBILITY

Chapter 7
RESPONSIVITY AND RESPONSIBILITY IN THE AGE OF THE ANTHROPOCENE: BONHOEFFERIAN REFLECTIONS ON HOPE IN THE MIDST OF A CLIMATE CRISIS   77
Ulrik Nissen

Chapter 8
HOW IS TODAY'S—AND THE COMING—GENERATION TO GO ON LIVING? BONHOEFFERIAN INSPIRATION FOR AN ECO-THEOLOGY AND AN ECO-ETHICS   89
Carlos Caldas

Chapter 9
BONHOEFFER'S THEOLOGY OF THE BODY AND THE RESPONSIBILITY FOR THE EARTH   99
Gregor Etzelmüller

Chapter 10
TOWARD A THEOLOGICAL ETHIC OF INTERGENERATIONAL RESPONSIBILITY: BONHOEFFER'S CHRIST AS MEDIATOR FOR THE COMING GENERATION   110
Matthew Puffer

Part III
BONHOEFFER, THE POLITICAL, AND SOLIDARITY

Chapter 11
THE POLITICAL MYTH OF CHRISTIAN NATIONHOOD: BONHOEFFER AND THE PUBLIC ROLE OF THE CHURCHES IN ZAMBIA   127
Teddy Chalwe Sakupapa

Chapter 12
RECONCILIATION, FORGIVENESS, AND SCARRING OVER: POLITICAL DIMENSIONS OF MORAL CONCEPTS   141
Ralf K. Wüstenberg

Chapter 13
BEYOND THE DARK NIGHT OF THE SOUL: BONHOEFFER AND JEWS FOR PALESTINIAN RIGHTS   150
Marthie Momberg

Chapter 14
BONHOEFFER'S IDEA OF EUROPE AS AN ANSWER TO THE CRISIS OF VALUES   162
Helena Anna Jędrzejczak

Chapter 15
POLITICO-RELIGIOUS MESSIANISM: A CRITICAL ANALYSIS OF THE BRAZILIAN SITUATION IN CONVERSATION WITH DIETRICH BONHOEFFER   172
Wilhelm Sell and Rudolf von Sinner

Chapter 16
READING BONHOEFFER AMID THE HONG KONG PROTESTS   187
Jason Lam

Part IV
BONHOEFFER, THE CHRIST-REALITY, AND THE LAW

Chapter 17
"THE ONE REALM OF THE CHRIST-REALITY": A CRITICAL EXAMINATION OF A POWERFUL THEOLOGICAL INSIGHT   209
Günter Thomas

Chapter 18
BONHOEFFER'S ETHICS OF RESPONSIBILITY: TRUTH-TELLING, THE LAW, AND THE CHRIST-REALITY   223
Matthias Grebe

Chapter 19
"DEZISION" AS A MODERN VERSION OF DOCETISM: DIETRICH BONHOEFFER'S DISCLOSURE OF THE HERETICAL CONTRAST IN CARL SCHMITT'S THEORY OF STATE   238
Karola Radler

Chapter 20
BONHOEFFER, HUMAN RIGHTS, AND THE NATURAL LAW TRADITION   253
Jens Zimmermann

Part V
BONHOEFFER ON PEACE, HOPEFUL ACTION, AND THE FUTURE

Chapter 21
INTRODUCING BONHOEFFER'S NEWLY FOUND LETTER TO GANDHI   267
Clifford Green

Chapter 22
DIETRICH BONHOEFFER AND STEVE BIKO? TOWARD A POLITICS OF
HOPE AMONG "BORN FREE" SOUTH AFRICANS   278
Dion A. Forster

Chapter 23
BONHOEFFER AND THE HERMENEUTICS OF HOPE: THE QUEST FOR
EXISTENCE AND MEANING   293
Peter Frick

Chapter 24
"MAKE STRAIGHT IN THE DESERT A HIGHWAY": RELATING PRESENT
AND FUTURE IN DIETRICH BONHOEFFER AND WALTER BENJAMIN   306
W. David Hall

Chapter 25
"SEEK THE THINGS THAT ARE ABOVE": BONHOEFFER ON
PERCEIVING AND RESPONDING TO GOD'S ACTION IN HISTORY   314
Kevin O' Farrell

Chapter 26
"A CHURCH FOR THE FUTURE?": DIETRICH BONHOEFFER'S LATE
ECCLESIOLOGY IN CONVERSATION WITH MERCY ODUYOYE, TEDDY
SAKUPAPA, AND VUYANI VELLEM   328
Tim Hartman

SERMON BY THE MOST REV. DR. THABO MAKGOBA   339

List of Contributors   345
Name Index   351
Subject Index   355

ABBREVIATIONS

DBW 1	*Sanctorum Communio: Eine dogmatische Untersuchung zur Soziologie der Kirche.* Edited by Joachim von Soosten. Munich: Chr. Kaiser Verlag, 1986.
DBW 2	*Akt und Sein: Transzendentalphilosophie und Ontologie in der systemantischen Theologie.* Edited by Hans-Richard Reuter. Munich: Chr. Kaiser Verlag, 1988.
DBW 3	*Schöpfung und Fall: Theologische Auslegung zu Genesis 1-3.* Edited by Martin Rüter and Ilse Tödt. Munich: Chr. Kaiser Verlag, 1989.
DBW 4	*Nachfolge.* Edited by Martin Kuske and Ilse Tödt. Munich: Chr. Kaiser Verlag, 1989; 2nd ed., Gütersloh: Chr. Kaiser/Gütersloher Verlagshaus, 1994.
DBW 5	*Gemeinsames Leben/ Das Gebetbuch der Bibel.* Edited by Gerhard Ludwig Müller and Albrecht Schönherr. Munich: Chr. Kaiser Verlag, 1987.
DBW 6	*Ethik.* Edited by Ilse Tödt, Heinz Eduard Tödt, Ernst Feil, and Clifford Green. Munich: Chr. Kaiser Verlag, 1992; 2nd ed., Gütersloh: Chr. Kaiser/Gütersloher Verlagshaus, 1998.
DBW 7	*Fragmente aus Tegel.* Edited by Renate Bethge and Ilse Tödt. Gütersloh: Chr. Kaiser/Gütersloher Verlagshaus, 1994.
DBW 8	*Widerstand und Ergebung.* Edited by Christian Gremmels, Eberhard Bethge, and Renate Bethge, with Ilse Tödt. Gütersloh: Chr. Kaiser/ Gütersloher Verlagshaus, 1998.
DBW 9	*Jugend und Studium, 1918-1927.* Edited by Hans Pfeifer, with Clifford Green and Carl-Jürgen Kaltenborn. Munich: Chr. Kaiser Verlag, 1986.
DBW 10	*Barcelona, Berlin, Amerika, 1928-1931.* Edited by Reinhard Staats and Hans Christoph von Hase, with Holger Roggelin and Matthias Wünsche. Munich: Chr. Kaiser Verlag, 1991.
DBW 11	*Ökumene, Universität, Pfarramt, 1931-1932.* Edited by Eberhard Amelung and Christoph Strohm. Gütersloh: Chr. Kaiser/Gütersloher Verlagshaus, 1994.
DBW 12	*Berlin, 1932-1933.* Edited by Carsten Nicolaisen and Ernst-Albert Scharffenorth. Gütersloh: Chr. Kaiser/Gütersloher Verlagshaus, 1997.
DBW 13	*London, 1933-1935.* Edited by Hans Goedeking, Martin Heimbucher, and Hans-Walter Schleicher. Gütersloh: Chr. Kaiser/Gütersloher Verlagshaus, 1994.
DBW 14	*Illegale Theologen-Ausbildung Finkenwalde, 1935-1937.* Edited by Otto Dudzus and Jürgen Henkys, with Sabine Bobert-Stützel, Dirk Schulz, and Ilse Tödt. Gütersloh: Chr. Kaiser/Gütersloher Verlagshaus, 1996.
DBW 15	*Illegale Theologenausbildung Sammelvikariate, 1937-1940.* Edited by Dirk Schulz. Gütersloh: Chr. Kaiser/Gütersloher Verlagshaus, 1998.

DBW 16	*Konspiration und Haft, 1940-1945*. Edited by Jørgen Glenthøj, Ulrich Kabitz, and Wolf Krötke. Gütersloh: Chr. Kaiser/Gütersloher Verlagshaus, 1996.
DBW 17	*Register und Ergänzungen*. Edited by Herbert Anzinger and Hans Pfeifer, assisted by Waltraud Anzinger and Ilse Tödt. Gütersloh: Chr. Kaiser/Gütersloher Verlagshaus, 1999.
DBWE 1	*Sanctorum Communio: A Theological Study of the Sociology of the Church*. In *Dietrich Bonhoeffer Works*, English Edition. Edited by Clifford Green. Translated by Reinhard Krauss and Nancy Lukens. Minneapolis, MN: Fortress Press, 1998.
DBWE 2	*Act and Being: Transcendental Philosophy and Ontology in Systematic Theology*. In *Dietrich Bonhoeffer Works*, English Edition. Edited by Wayne Whitson Floyd, Jr. Translated by H. R. Rumscheidt. Minneapolis, MN: Fortress Press, 1996.
DBWE 3	*Creation and Fall: A Theological Exposition of Genesis 1-3*. In *Dietrich Bonhoeffer Works*, English Edition. Edited by John de Gruchy. Translated by Douglas Stephen Bax. Minneapolis, MN: Fortress Press, 2004.
DBWE 4	*Discipleship*. In *Dietrich Bonhoeffer Works*, English Edition. Edited by Geoffrey Kelly and John D. Godsey. Translated by Barbara Green and Reinhard Krauss. Minneapolis, MN: Fortress Press, 2001.
DBWE 5	*Life Together/Prayerbook of the Bible*. In *Dietrich Bonhoeffer Works*, English Edition. Edited by Geoffrey Kelly. Translated by Daniel Bloesch and James Burtness. Minneapolis, MN: Fortress Press, 1996.
DBWE 6	*Ethics*. In *Dietrich Bonhoeffer Works*, English Edition. Edited by Clifford Green. Translated by Reinhard Krauss, Charles West, and Douglas W. Stott. Minneapolis, MN: Fortress Press, 2006.
DBWE 7	*Fiction from Tegel Prison*. In *Dietrich Bonhoeffer Works*, English Edition. Edited by Clifford Green. Translated by Nancy Lukens. Minneapolis, MN: Fortress Press, 2000.
DBWE 8	*Letters and Papers from Prison*. In *Dietrich Bonhoeffer Works*, English Edition. Edited by John W. de Gruchy. Translated by Isabel Best, Lisa E. Dahill, Reinhard Krauss, Nancy Lukens, H. Martin Rumscheidt, and Douglas W. Stott. Minneapolis, MN: Fortress Press, 2010.
DBWE 9	*The Young Bonhoeffer: 1918–1927*. In *Dietrich Bonhoeffer Works*, English Edition. Edited by Paul Duane Matheny, Clifford Green and Marshall D. Johnson. Translated by Mary C. Nebelsick and Douglas W. Stott. Minneapolis, MN: Fortress Press, 2003.
DBWE 10	*Barcelona, Berlin, New York: 1928–1931*. In *Dietrich Bonhoeffer Works*, English Edition. Edited by Clifford Green. Translated by Douglas W. Stott. Minneapolis, MN: Fortress Press, 2007.
DBWE 11	*Ecumenical, Academic, and Pastoral Work: 1931-1932*. In *Dietrich Bonhoeffer Works*, English Edition. Edited by Victoria J. Barnett, Mark S. Brocker, and Michael Lukens. Translated by Anne Schmidt-Lange, Isabel Best, Nicolas Humphrey, Marion Pauck, and Douglas W. Stott. Minneapolis, MN: Fortress Press, 2012.

DBWE 12	*Berlin: 1932–1933*. In *Dietrich Bonhoeffer Works*, English Edition. Edited by Larry Rasmussen. Translated by Isabelle Best and David Higgins. Minneapolis, MN: Fortress Press, 2009.
DBWE 13	*London: 1933-1935*. In *Dietrich Bonhoeffer Works*, English Edition. Edited by Keith Clements. Translated by Isabel Best and Douglas W. Stott. Minneapolis, MN: Fortress Press, 2007.
DBWE 14	*Theological Education at Finkenwalde: 1935–1937*. In *Dietrich Bonhoeffer Works*, English Edition. Edited by H. Gaylon Barker and Mark S. Brocker. Translated by Douglas W. Stott. Minneapolis, MN: Fortress Press, 2013.
DBWE 15	*Theological Education Underground, 1937-1940*. In *Dietrich Bonhoeffer Works*, English Edition. Edited by Victoria J. Barnett. Translated by Victoria J. Barnett, Claudia D. Bergmann, Peter Frick, and Scott A. Moore. Minneapolis, MN: Fortress Press, 2012.
DBWE 16	*Conspiracy and Imprisonment: 1940–1945*. In *Dietrich Bonhoeffer Works*, English Edition. Edited by Mark S. Brocker. Translated by Lisa E. Dahill and Douglas W. Stott. Minneapolis, MN: Fortress Press, 2006.
DBWE 17	*Index and Supplementary Materials*. Edited by Victoria J. Barnett and Barbara Wojhoski. Minneapolis, MN: Fortress Press, 2014.

FOREWORD

In the years of our struggle against apartheid in South Africa, many theologians, pastors, religious people, and other concerned citizens abundantly drank from the wells of Dietrich Bonhoeffer. In the almost three decades of building a new democracy, we have continued to engage with the thought, theology, ethics, and example of Bonhoeffer. We were, therefore, glad that the Faculty of Theology and the Beyers Naudé Centre for Public Theology at Stellenbosch University hosted the 13th International Bonhoeffer Congress in partnership with the Department of Religion and Theology of the University of the Western Cape in January 2020.

We are drawn to various themes in the work of Bonhoeffer. The theme of responsible living is a prominent aspect of his person and work that is helpful for us. The 2020 conference and this book, with a selection of the papers read at that conference, focus on responsible living in the light of the question of how future generations are to go living. The title of this book is therefore appropriate: *Bonhoeffer and the Responsibility for a Coming Generation: Doing Theology in a Time Out of Joint.*

Bonhoeffer's work is intergenerational. In the first chapter of this volume, Dutch theologian, Frits de Lange, draws on the notion of generativity used by the famous psychologist, Erik Erikson. Generativity is normally a motive that surfaces in our lives in late adulthood. De Lange shows that, while in prison, Bonhoeffer had the desire to be young, to engage lovingly with his fiancée, and to eventually have a child. On the other hand, Bonhoeffer simultaneously felt old. His awareness that he might be killed imminently by the Nazi regime caused him to experience the urgency that people normally experience closer to the end of their average life span. This urgency is manifested in our concern about what meaning there is to our lives and what legacy we would leave behind for coming generations. The ambivalent coexistence of youthfulness and oldness in Bonhoeffer might explain the intergenerational significance of his work.

Bonhoeffer's work is intercontextual. Authors from different contexts and continents draw on Bonhoeffer's work to contribute to this volume. Challenges and concerns, crises, and cries from different parts of the world are addressed—climate change, political challenges, including the deterioration of democracy, socio-economic inequality, violence, and war in local and global contexts. At the time of finalizing this publication, we are confronted with the unimaginable bloodshed and cruelty in Palestine and Israel.

Bonhoeffer's work is also intersectoral. It impacts church, society, and academy. His ethics of responsibility to future generations nurtures living in hope in all walks of life, as explicitly discussed in various contributions in this book. The South African pastor and theologian, the late Russel Botman, became rector and vice-chancellor of Stellenbosch University in 2007. Drawing on his doctoral work and postdoctoral engagement with Bonhoeffer and educationist Paulo Freire, among others, he developed an epistemology and pedagogy of transformation and hope. Under his leadership, Stellenbosch University prioritized an explicit focus on hope. His hope was not merely a moral principle but also a concrete responsibility. As prominent institutions in society, universities of hope are institutions where the daughter of the farm worker should have the same opportunity to succeed as the son of the farm owner. Hope for Botman was hope in action.

The reflections in this book help us to rediscover and celebrate Bonhoeffer as a reliable guide to realistic hope, to responsive hope, and to resilient hope. Realistic hope rests in the greatest reality of all, namely the real presence of the crucified and resurrected Christ. Responsive hope pays attention to what is going on in the world, to what God is doing in the world, and it participates in God's work in the world. Resilient hope, elastic hope, says circumstances can stress and stretch us, but it shall not break us. By God's grace we shall eventually be more than conquerors. Bonhoeffer guides as to hope that hears the melody of the future and to faith that dances it, also for the sake of those yet unborn, for tomorrow's children.

Nico Koopman
Deputy Vice-Chancellor: Social Impact, Transformation
and Personnel, Stellenbosch University

INTRODUCTION

Dietrich Bonhoeffer was only thirty-nine years old when he was executed on April 9, 1945, by the Nazi regime. We might wonder what an older Bonhoeffer, if he lived to the age of, say, eighty or ninety, would have said about some later events and crises, what texts he would have read or written, and what places he would have travelled to. But this, of course, would be mere speculation. What one can say, though, is that Bonhoeffer was well aware, as Frits de Lange points out in the first chapter in this volume, of the importance of intergenerational processes and the transmission of ideas and values across generations. We can also add that the words and witness of this German pastor and theologian, who died relatively young, proved to be generative and inspirational not only for those who knew him but also for those—including those in later generations and contexts other than his own—who came to "know" him through his writings and the various ways in which his legacy was mediated. One particular way Bonhoeffer's life and thought have been transmitted in an engaging and scholarly manner across generational, geographical, and cultural divides is through the regular International Bonhoeffer Congress meetings, first held in 1971, and since 1976, every four years.

In January 2020, the 13th International Bonhoeffer Congress was hosted by the Faculty of Theology and the Beyers Naudé Center for Public Theology of Stellenbosch University, South Africa, in partnership with the Department of Religion and Theology of the University of the Western Cape. This congress took as its theme the question, "How is the coming generation to go on living?"—a question drawn from Bonhoeffer's remarkable text, "After Ten Years" (written as a Christmas gift for his friends and co-conspirators Eberhard Bethge, Hans von Dohnanyi, and Hans Oster). There we read:

> The ultimately responsible question is not how I extricate myself heroically from a situation but how a coming generation is to go on living. Only from such a historically responsible question will fruitful solutions arise, however humiliating they may be for the moment. In short, it is much easier to see a situation through on the basis of principle than in concrete responsibility. The younger generation will always have the surest sense whether an action is done merely in terms of principle or from living responsibly, for it is their future that is at stake.[1]

1. *DBWE* 8:42.

Bonhoeffer expresses his concern that one should take responsibility not only for one's own personal and communal life but also for the kind of ethos and society one will leave as an inheritance for future generations. In grappling with the question of what it means to take responsibility for future generations, we should also be mindful of the fact that, to quote the South African psychologist Pumla Gobodo-Madikizela, "trauma is passed on intergenerationally in subtle ways through stories of silences, through unarticulated fears and the psychological scars that are often left unacknowledged."[2]

Against this backdrop, the 2020 International Bonhoeffer Congress invited participants to reflect anew on Bonhoeffer's question, "How is the coming generation to go on living?" This question remains pertinent, not the least due to the experience of threats on a global level to socio-political and economic well-being and interreligious solidarity. The question also served as a challenge for dealing with some of the significant sea changes that have taken place since the first truly democratic elections were held in South Africa in 1994, calling in the process for renewed reflection on what a theology and ethics of concrete responsibility entail amid new political, economic, and cultural realities—not only in South Africa but also globally. Several of the essays and conversations at the conference highlighted how climate change and ecological devastation serve as a chilling reminder that the question of how future generations will go on living is linked to the fact that we are living on a planet in jeopardy. Or, as David Tracy poignantly states in his book, *Fragments: The Existential Situation of Our Time: Selected Essays, Volume 1*:

> (A)n individual death is a natural happening in the cycle of life, wherein older generations must leave so that new generations may be born, reproduce, and, in turn, die.... The tragic new fact is that contemporary human beings, for the first time in history, have the ability to end it all by either nuclear or chemical powers, or perhaps by the partly already unstoppable climate change—the major cause of which is our cruel lack of care for future generations.[3]

Shortly after the 2020 Bonhoeffer Congress, the world fell into the grip of the Covid-19 pandemic, and this further exacerbated the general feeling that we are living in "a time out of joint." This phrase, which also serves as this volume's subtitle, reminds us of the famous words in Shakespeare's *Hamlet*: "The time is out of joint—O cursed spite/That ever I was born to set it right." In a lecture, "The Tragedy of the Prophetic and Its Lasting Meaning," which Bonhoeffer gave as a young pastor in November 1928 in Barcelona, he also admits: "Our time is getting out of joint."[4] Bonhoeffer

---

2. Pumla Gobodo-Madikizela, ed., *Breaking Intergenerational Cycles of Repetition: A Global Dialogue on Historical Trauma and Memory* (Opladen: Barbara Budrich Publishers, 2016), 3.

3. David Tracy, *Fragments: The Existential Situation of Our Time: Selected Essays, Volume 1* (Chicago, IL: The University of Chicago Press, 2020), 72.

4. DBWE 10:341.

makes it clear in this address that although the events of the previous decades plunged society into an unprecedented crisis that eroded its sense of stability, people should "show solidarity with the contemporary world in its crisis and hope."[5] The sense that time is out of joint raises the question, how can we resist being paralyzed by events to such an extent that we cannot engage responsibly with the challenges of our time? Following Bonhoeffer, we can point to the vital interconnection between solidarity, hope, and action. Or as Bonhoeffer puts it in his poem, "Stations on the Way to Freedom": "Not in escaping to thought, in action alone is found freedom. / Dare to quit anxious faltering and enter the storms of events."[6]

Something of this spirit of solidarity with the times and the need for action that Bonhoeffer alluded to was evident in the eighty presentations at the 13th International Bonhoeffer Congress, including the keynote addresses by Wolfgang Huber, Nadia Marais, Pumla Gobodo-Madikizela, Terry Lovat, Reggie Williams, and Teddy Sakupapa.

In this volume, we have included twenty-six of the papers from the conference that engage with the life, theology, and legacy of Bonhoeffer as a way of responding to the question of what it means to live responsibly in "a time out of joint," and with the coming generations in view.

Eleven other articles resulting from the congress (by Christoph Barnbrock, Luís Cumaru, Chris Dodson, Ulrich Duchrow, Kevin Lenehan, Katharina Oppel, Martin Pavlík, Jeremy Rios, Alexander Schultze, Joanna Tarassenko, and Aad van Tilburg, respectively) have been published in a special edition of the *Stellenbosch Theological Journal* (*STJ*). These essays are also available online on the journal's website. In addition, several of the congress papers (including those by Lori Brandt Hale, Jennifer McBride and Thomas Fabisiak, Dianne Rayson, and Robert Vosloo) were published in the book, *Dietrich Bonhoeffer, Theology, and Political Resistance*.[7]

In *Bonhoeffer and the Responsibility for a Coming Generation*, we present the various chapters in five parts. The first part, under the heading "Bonhoeffer, the Generations, and Our Heritage," contains chapters by Frits de Lange, Nadia Marais, Wolfgang Huber, Anne-Katharina Neddens and Christian Neddens, Gerard den Hertog, and Reggie Williams. Central to these chapters are themes such as intergenerational ethics, our heritage and betrayal, truth-telling in a digital age, memory and transgenerational trauma, and the inheritance of harmful colonial legacies. The chapters in the second part (by Ulrik Nissen, Carlos Caldas, Gregor Etzelmüller, and Matthew Puffer) express in different yet overlapping ways the plea for an Earth-honoring account of responsibility, and in the process, drawing on insights from Bonhoeffer's theology of the body and his account of (intergenerational) responsibility and hope. Under the heading "Bonhoeffer, the

---

5. Ibid., 326. Cf. Robert Vosloo, "Time Out of Joint and Future-Oriented Memory," in *Reading Bonhoeffer in South Africa after the Transition to Democracy: Selected Essays*, ed. Nico Koopman and Robert Vosloo (Frankfurt, Peter Lang, 2020), 74–6.

6. *DBWE* 8:513.

7. See Lori Brand Hale and W. David Hall, *Dietrich Bonhoeffer, Theology, and Political Resistance* (Lanham, MD: Lexington Books, 2020).

Political, and Solidarity," the chapters in the third part (by Teddy Sakupapa, Ralf Wüstenberg, Marthie Momberg, Helena Anna Jędrzejczak, Wilhelm Sell and Rudolf von Sinner, and Jason Lam) reflect critically on burning political issues and concerns from various contexts around the globe. The chapters in the fourth part (by Günter Thomas, Matthias Grebe, Karola Radler, and Jens Zimmermann), in turn, engage with categories such as "the law," "the state," and "the Christ-reality." The final part opens with a chapter by Clifford Green that introduces and discusses an exciting newly found letter of Bonhoeffer to Gandhi. The other chapters in this part (by Dion Forster, Peter Frick, David Hall, Kevin O' Farrel, and Tim Hartman) focus on themes such as "hope" and "the future." These chapters enter into conversation not only with Bonhoeffer but also with figures such as Steve Biko and Walter Benjamin as well as with the more recent work of some African theologians.

The 2020 International Bonhoeffer Congress opened with a worship service in Stellenbosch, with the Anglican Archbishop of Cape Town Thabo Makgoba as the preacher. His sermon features at the end of the volume. The sermon reflects the concrete challenges of the time, and in response to particular South African realities, it calls for a bold, united witness to the gospel.

As editors, we would like to thank, next to the authors and reviewers of this book, the Bloomsbury editors Jack Curtin, Sophie Beardsworth, Anna Turton, and Akshaya Ravi for their contributions to the production of this book. It is also a privilege that this book can appear in the "T&T Clark New Studies in Bonhoeffer's Theology and Ethics" series, with Jennifer McBride, Michael Mawson, and Philip G. Ziegler as series editors. This series has made an outstanding contribution in recent years to Bonhoeffer scholarship.

We would also like to acknowledge the formatting and editing work done by Marlene Lange during the early stages of this project. And we greatly thank Funlola O. Olojede for her untiring work in editing and preparing the manuscript for publication. We also feel privileged that Nico Koopman, the Vice-Rector for Social Impact, Transformation and Personnel at Stellenbosch University, agreed to write the Foreword to this volume. A former director of the Beyers Naudé Center for Public Theology (and its current chairperson), Koopman, often draws from the wells of Bonhoeffer's thought, and his work and witness in various settings exemplify a future-oriented ethos of responsibility.

The 2020 International Bonhoeffer Congress was not the first International Bonhoeffer Congress held in South Africa. In 1996, the 7th International Bonhoeffer Congress took place in Cape Town, with as its theme Bonhoeffer's self-critical question, "Are we still of any use?" This remains a haunting question, as we grapple with what it means to do theology in a time out of joint. The convener of that conference, John de Gruchy, was also present at the 2020 conference, moderating with his typical insight, wit, and passion a panel session on "How the coming generation is to go on living." As editors, we dedicate this volume to him, in gratitude for his contribution to Bonhoeffer scholarship over many decades and in acknowledgment of how his life and writings continue to inspire a wide variety of people—also across generations.

Robert Vosloo, Teddy Sakupapa, Karola Radler, Ashwin Thyssen

Part 1

BONHOEFFER, THE GENERATIONS, AND OUR HERITAGE

Chapter 1

OLD MAN BONHOEFFER

GENERATIVITY, LIFE SPAN PSYCHOLOGY, AND INTERGENERATIONAL ETHICS

Frits de Lange

Introduction

In this chapter, I interpret Bonhoeffer's concern in his final years for the "coming generation" as an expression of "generativity"—a psychological concept in life course psychology by Erik H. Erikson and developed by subsequent scholars. I consider the concept of generativity helpful in understanding why Bonhoeffer's concern for the future takes the shape of an ethics of intergenerational responsibility. In peaceful times, generativity is supposed to be a psychological motive in people in their late adulthood. But Bonhoeffer was already driven by the same urge in his early thirties.

"Longing to Have a Child"

To make a connection between Dietrich Bonhoeffer, executed at the age of thirty-nine, and gerontology seems far-fetched. But age and chronology often have an accidental relationship—one does not need to be old in order to feel old. The probability of his own imminent death made Bonhoeffer, in prison, feel as if he had left his life behind him.[1]

Bonhoeffer is exceptional, not only because of his precocious adulthood (he completed his dissertation at the age of twenty-one) but also because he felt old so young. In prison, he was haunted by an impossible double bind—he simultaneously had to prepare for a postwar marriage with his fiancée, Maria von Wedemeyer, half his age, and be ready for premature death, when/if the trial turned out wrong. The ambivalence is strikingly voiced in the letter of December 15, 1943, to Bethge in which he openly expresses his longing for privacy with Maria without the military

---

1. Cf. the poem, *The Death of Moses*, in which Bonhoeffer perceives the future world through Moses' "old man's eyes" (*DBWE* 8:534).

restrictions of visiting hours.² On the one hand, he expresses his wish to get married soon after his release, so that they both would actually start getting to know each other—the impatience of a young man in love. On the other hand, his mind is overtaken by despair and the expectation of near death. Old man Bonhoeffer. He openly admits to Bethge, who married earlier in the previous year (May 1943) and was expecting his first child (May 1944):

> Sometimes the age difference also disturbs me again, especially since I have the feeling that I am becoming significantly older here and sometimes think my life is more or less behind me and all I have left to do is to complete my *Ethics*. But you know, in such moments I am gripped with an incomparable longing to have a child and not to vanish without a trace—probably more of an Old Testament wish than a New Testament one.³

The unbearable tension between the expectation of an imminent death and the yearning for a life of young lovers, between the old and the young man Bonhoeffer, is solved and canalized in one single wish—the longing to have a child and not to vanish without a trace.

The concept of generativity as developed in lifespan psychology may elucidate Bonhoeffer's concern for the coming generation, his longing for a child, and his wish to finish his book and clarify the connection between these different desires. Generativity may be defined as the "desire to invest one's substance in forms of life and work that will outlive the self."⁴ However, not explicitly coined as a concept, the desire for generativity is well known in the history of philosophy ever since Plato. In his *Symposium*, Plato speaks about how love strives for immortality. There is a certain age at which human nature is desirous of procreation, and we want to give "birth in beauty, whether of body or of soul." Though it is made concrete in the birth of a child, it transcends biology and the evolutionary survival of our individual genes—"To the mortal creature generation is a sort of eternity and immortality."⁵

Erik H. Erikson was the first to acknowledge and explore the fundamental meaning of generativity within the context of an individual life course. In *Childhood and Society* (first edition 1950), he identifies generativity as the defining psychosocial feature of midlife. It is in the middle-adult years, Erikson maintains, that men and women are most likely to be concerned about the well-being of future generations and involved in various life projects—from parenting to political

---

2. He writes: "Month to month we sit next to each other for an hour as obediently as schoolchildren and are then torn away from each other again. We know next to nothing about each other" (*DBWE* 8:221f.).

3. *DBWE* 8:222.

4. John Kotre, *Outliving the Self: How We Live on in Future Generations* (New York: W.W. Norton & Company, 1984), 10.

5. Plato, cited by Dan P. McAdams, "Generativity in Midlife," in *Handbook of Midlife Development*, ed. Margie E. Lachman (New York: John Wiley & Sons, 2001), 395–443, 398.

action, aimed at generating a positive legacy that will ultimately outlive the self. In the first half of their lives, younger adults are involved in building strong personal identities. They are ego centered, and they have to be. In their final days, close to death and taking stock of life, the question of whether they have lived a meaningful life and which legacy they leave behind comes to the fore.

Generativity then, according to Erikson, is "primarily the concern in establishing and guiding the next generation." Creating offspring and raising children are the prototypical form, but generativity is also exemplified by other kinds of creativity and productivity.[6] In his book, *Gandhi's Truth* (1969), Erikson shows how, as a spiritual leader and a fatherly caregiver for his own people, Gandhi played out his generativity as a public affair, even as he failed to be a good father to his biological children at home.[7] If Erikson was aware of his work and biography, he might also have taken Bonhoeffer as an example of an exceptionally generative person. Though he never had the child he wished for, as a leader in the church struggle and a member of the resistance movement, he had been driven, as he declares in his "After Ten Years," by "the ultimately responsible question not how I extricate myself heroically from a situation but [how] a coming generation is to go on living."[8]

"We Are Merely One Link in the Chain"

Subsequently, Erikson's concept of generativity has been refined theoretically and tested empirically by scholars, whose research enables us to obtain a more accurate understanding of Bonhoeffer's generativity. Two revisions of Erikson's use of the concept are illuminating in this respect:

(1) Erikson's stage model of the life cycle may reflect a postwar American middle-class white male career but cannot stand for generativity as such. Empirical research shows, for example, that a strict connection between late adulthood and generativity is difficult to uphold.[9] Economic conditions, cultural

---

6. Erik H. Erikson, *Childhood and Society*, 2nd ed. (New York: Norton, 1963), 240.

7. Erik H. Erikson, *Gandhi's Truth: On the Origins of Militant Nonviolence* (New York: Norton, 1969). Kotre, *Outliving the Self*, 10–16, distinguishes four different forms of generativity. In *biological* generativity, the generative object is the infant, while in *parental* generativity, the child is initiated into social and cultural traditions. In *technical* generativity, skills are transmitted, but in *cultural* generativity, the adult passes the symbolic system, the "mind" of a culture, on to the next generation.

8. *DBWE* 8:42; cf. Ibid., 50: "To think and to act with an eye on the coming generation and to be ready to move on without fear and worry—that is the course that has, in practice, been forced upon us. To hold it courageously is not easy but necessary."

9. In some research findings, younger adults score even higher on generative commitment than older adults (McAdams, "Generativity in Midlife," 412).

norms, social change, and historical events provide a variety of external contexts for generativity. Gender, race, class/ethnicity, and education result in different styles of generativity. Generativity then is not to be seen as a more or less fixed stage in an individual life course but as a highly *contextual* and therefore *variable* human expression of intergenerational concern.[10] There are perhaps myriad ways to express one's concern for the next generation, other than by taking political courageous action. Bonhoeffer's strong generative consciousness has to be understood against the background of his privileged, educated upbringing of early twentieth-century Germany and cannot serve as a model for generativity as such.

(2) Second, within this diversity and variability, different styles or modes of generativity can be distinguished, according to the distinction between opposing poles of human endeavor made by psychologist David Bakan. *Communal* modes of generativity involve self-sacrificing nurturance and care for others, on the one hand, and *agentic* modes, on the other, encompass creative and/or powerful extensions of the self, as in some forms of leadership, scientific achievement, and so forth. Gender stereotypes would predict that men might express more agentic aspects of generativity, while women show more communal manifestations.[11] To date, however, little research has examined this claim directly. And "many, if not most generative people combine agency and communion in their personalities."[12] With this distinction in mind however, it would be worthwhile to investigate if and how the agentic active style of generativity in Bonhoeffer ("leaving a trace") is balanced by a more communal or kenotic-oriented mode, understanding his death as a sacrifice. In his "After Ten Years," he writes, "It is not external circumstances but we ourselves who shall make of our death what it can be, a death consented to freely and voluntary."[13] This investigation cannot be done here. But a feminist Bonhoeffer reception could gain from reading his work from the perspective of generativity.[14]

Bonhoeffer's upbringing in his particular family made him exceptionally aware of the role of successive generations and the importance of intergenerational

---

10. Cf. also Dan P. McAdams and Ed de St. Aubin, eds., *Generativity and Adult Development: How and Why We Care for the Next Generation* (Washington, DC: American Psychological Association, 1998).

11. Kotre, *Outliving the Self*, 17f.

12. Ibid., 128.

13. *DBWE* 8:51.

14. His explicit wish for a child with his fiancée has been read as the male instrumentalization of Maria for the sake of Dietrich's desires (Diane Reynolds, *The Doubled Life of Dietrich Bonhoeffer: Women, Sexuality, and Nazi Germany* [Eugene, OR: Wipf & Stock, 2016], 356).

processes. The extended family around the parent's home in Berlin cherished the memory of earlier generations and experienced their living together not only synchronically as a caring and nurturing community but also diachronically as a sequence of generations kept together by strains of vicarious responsibility. "I realized you've pushed our family into the next generation," he writes to Bethge after Renate gave birth to his parents' first grandchild.[15] Bonhoeffer's ethical understanding of responsibility as theologically developed in his *Ethics* is strongly marked by this specific intergenerational awareness. In the drama written in Tegel Prison, Bonhoeffer introduces a strange description of how generations in earlier times ideally were related: "Everyone lived only for the other: parents for their children and children so that they would be parents someday, the rulers for the subjects and the subjects for the rulers, one generation for the next and that generation for the one after. But no one—it's truly insane—lived simply and honestly for themselves."[16]

Because of Bonhoeffer's highly developed intergenerational awareness, he intensely experienced the feeling that his own "younger generation" was special because it was haunted by the memory of the First World War. In his lecture, "The Führer and the Individual in the Younger Generation" (Berlin, 1933), he explains that the First World War created a new "young generation," which, not having actively participated in the war, projects its hunger for authority and orientation to a strong leader, a Führer. He does not mention the loss of his brother Walter (1899–1918) at the frontline in 1918 and the trauma it caused his family. Yet, the traumatic experience is palpable in every line. The lecture illustrates Bonhoeffer's keen insight into what generation means—how generations differ, how they follow each other, and how they must try to live together in the postwar German context. He defines generations not in terms of age and offspring but as cohorts "shaped by a particular experience" in their formative years, in his case, the catastrophe of the war.[17] There is an important lesson to be learned here. Bonhoeffer shows how intergenerational relationships are always marked by the wounds of history.

---

15. He writes to Bethge, "On February 3, great-grandparents, grandparents, great-uncles, great-aunts, and young uncles and aunts were newly created. Look what you've achieved—you promoted me, for example, to [the] third generation"! (*DBWE* 8:290). Compare his "Thoughts on the Day of Baptism of Dietrich Wilhelm Rüdiger Bethge" of May 1944 in which he directly addresses his newborn nephew, the little Dietrich: "You are the first of a new generation in our family. Never mind if your coming confuses us a little about our generational relationships, as we suddenly see ourselves moving earlier than expected into the second, third, and fourth generation. It's clear, nevertheless, that you are the eldest, you lead the procession of the next generation, and you will have the incomparable advantage of sharing a good part of your life with the third and fourth generations before you" (*DBWE* 8:383).

16. *DBWE* 7:61.

17. *DBW* 12:268–82, 269. Compare the definition of the Cambridge Dictionary, "*generation*: (1) all the people of about the same age within a society or within a particular

Generations seldom live a full life cycle, as my own baby boom generation had the chance to do in postwar Europe. In most countries, it is not age or a life span, but a war or, as in South Africa, apartheid that is decisive in characterizing and separating generations. Time is contracted or stretched according to political events, rather than along completed life cycles.

In the years 1933-7, the tragedy of the First World War led Germany to a new disaster, which meant that Bonhoeffer's own "younger generation," engaged in the church struggle, quickly got old—old in Bonhoeffer's sense, "shaped by a particular experience," that is, Nazism. On New Year's Eve, December 31, 1937, Bonhoeffer delivered a sermon on Ps. 71:18, "So even to old age and gray hairs, O God, do not forsake me, until I proclaim your might to all the generations to come." He said:

> For some time now we have grown accustomed to the fact that we cannot count on having long periods of time. . . . But time moves on and our text today speaks to us about growing old . . . perhaps we will become gray during this time of struggle for the church, and new generations will bear new burdens on their shoulders. . . . Years and generations pass away, but God's word does not. Indeed, *we are merely one link in the chain*.[18]

Privilege, Sacrifice, Optimism: Bonhoeffer's "Generativity Script"

Bonhoeffer's strong awareness of being "merely one link in the chain" becomes an integral part of what we can call the generativity narrative that he developed in his later writings from prison. Convinced of having "more or less his life behind him," he reviews his life, just as many elderly people do in the face of death. In his research, psychologist Dan McAdams analyzes several life stories and observes that many of them express a late adult's realization that "because I received so much from others it is now my turn to pass it on to whom I leave behind." Accounts like these he calls *generativity scripts*. For some people, they dominate the plot line of their life stories. For others, it is just one scene among others.[19]

McAdams argues that generativity is a configuration of seven psychosocial features. Generativity begins with (1) personal *desires* combined with and structured by (2) cultural *demands*—expectations with regard to how and when to engage in generative behaviors in a given social milieu. Motivated by inner desires and outer demands, adults develop (3) a conscious *concern* for the next generation.

---

family; (2) a period of about 25 to 30 years, in which most human babies become adults and have their own children."

18. *DBWE* 15:25 (italics added). Cf. in the same vein, the *Wedding Sermon from the Prison Cell* in which he writes: "In your love you see only each other in the world; in marriage you are a link in the chain of generations that God, for the sake of God's glory, allows to rise and fade away, and calls into God's kingdom" (*DBWE* 8:83).

19. McAdams, "Generativity in Midlife," 429.

Interacting with desire, demand, and concern are (4) *beliefs* in how worthwhile it will be to invest in the future. A positive belief in the future then may help to translate concerns into concrete (5) *commitments*, and (6) *actions*. Generativity desires, demands, concerns, beliefs, commitments, and actions (1–6) are finally translated into (7) *narratives*, made part of autobiographical stories, which give purpose and unity to one's life. These stories become increasingly central, as one gets closer to death. Generativity narratives defy death in a narrative sense; even though one's own life will end, it will give birth to new beginnings.[20]

Bonhoeffer's review of his life is clearly dominated by a generativity script. Intergenerational ethical responsibility is not one theme among others, but it determines its plot, as is visible especially in "After Ten Years" and in "Thoughts on the Day of Baptism."[21] In his *Account*, quoting Jer. 32:15, as he did earlier in his 1937 New Year's Eve sermon mentioned earlier, he writes that "in the light of the utter deprivation of any future," he and his fellow resisters will have "to think and act with an eye on the coming generation and to be ready to move without fear and worry."[22]

McAdams observes that in generativity scripts of highly generative people, belief in the future is not just a personal conviction but also an essential requirement for the narrative. Generativity requires optimism, even when it is not justified by the facts. Consequently, Bonhoeffer's strong plea for optimism in "After Ten Years" becomes understandable. He admits that given the situation, "it is more sensible to be pessimistic." However, "In its essence optimism is not a way of looking at the present situation but a power of life . . . a power that never abandons the future to the opponent, but lays claim on it."[23] Bonhoeffer's narrative is arranged here according to what McAdams calls a *redemption sequence*: "A bad scene is redeemed, salvaged, made better by that which follows."[24] In the opposite narrative movement coined by McAdams as a *contamination sequence*, an extremely good scene is ruined, spoiled, or sullied by a bad scene that follows it. People with a low generativity score often arrange their life review narrative accordingly. Bonhoeffer however virulently rejects the attitude of people "who believe in chaos, disorder, and catastrophe, perceiving it in what is happening now. They withdraw . . . from the responsibility for ongoing life, for building anew, for the coming generations."[25] Deep pessimism, cynicism, despair, and hopelessness undermine generativity, for they suggest that investments in the future are not likely to bring positive returns. Erikson talks about a "belief in the species"—a faith in the ultimate goodness and worthwhileness of the human enterprise as a necessary attitudinal characteristic

---

20. Ibid., 405–8.
21. *DBWE* 8:37–52; 383–90.
22. Ibid., 50.
23. Ibid., 50f.
24. McAdams, "Generativity in Midlife," 429.
25. *DBWE* 8:51.

for generative behavior.²⁶ Optimism is not a psychological character treat but an ethical obligation.

In Bonhoeffer's "Thoughts on the Day of Baptism,"²⁷ another common feature of life reviews of highly generativity persons, as described by McAdams, becomes visible. With a strong commitment to the future of the next generation, their story often comprises the recognition of early blessings enjoyed in childhood that separates them from others, those less fortuned/fortunate. The blessing stands in sharp contrast to the realization, again in early childhood, that other people suffer. He notes, "The clash between early blessing and the suffering of others sets up a tension in the story and motivates the protagonist to see him- or herself as 'called' or 'destined' to be of good use to other people."²⁸ In this context, we may think of Bonhoeffer's early decision to give catechism lessons to poor youngsters in Berlin-Wedding, a worker's area, in everything the opposite of his own Berlin-Grünewald—a commitment later followed by his engagement with African Americans in the United States, the Jews in Germany, and all those "who see the great events of world history from below, from the perspective of the outcasts, the suspects, the maltreated, the powerless, the oppressed and reviled."²⁹

Bonhoeffer shows that his privileged upbringing creates "a deep-rooted obligation to be guardians of a great historical heritage and intellectual [*geistiger*] tradition."³⁰ Being part of a social and cultural elite group generates a calling, a moral obligation to take responsibility for the well-being of those who suffer—*noblesse oblige*, even when this means that cherished privileges have to be given up, even when ultimately one's life has to be sacrificed. In my view, Bonhoeffer shows a genuine communal style of generativity in writing. "Not in embittered and barren pride, but consciously yielding to divine judgment, we shall prove ourselves worthy to survive [*als lebenstark erweisen*] by identifying ourselves generously and selflessly with the whole community and the suffering of our fellow human beings, (in *weitherziger und selbstlose Teilnahme am Ganzen*)," Bonhoeffer writes.³¹

The idea that being privileged entails a willingness to sacrifice becomes visible on a more theoretical level in Bonhoeffer's analysis of the structure of responsible life.³² It starts, remarkably, with the argument that responsibility is

---

26. Erikson, *Childhood and Society*, 267.
27. *DBWE* 8:383–90.
28. McAdams, "Generativity in Midlife," 431.
29. *DBWE* 8:52.
30. Ibid., 384.
31. *DBWE* 8:389; cf. McAdams, "Generativity in Midlife," 430: "Adult life is full of mistakes, frustrations, and missed opportunities for most people; yet the promise of a new generation is that those same mistakes will not be made again, that frustrations will pass, and new opportunities will be grasped and fulfilled in the generation to come. . . . The discourse on generativity, therefore, is filled with stories about people suffering and making sacrifices in order that the future will be good."
32. *DBWE* 6:257–99.

based on vicarious representative action (*Stellvertretung*). Bonhoeffer refers to relationships in which a person is required to act literally on behalf of others, "for example as a father, as a statesman, or as the instructor of an apprentice."[33] The idea of vicarious representation in the sequel is founded theologically in Jesus Christ, taking responsibility for all humankind and bearing the selves of all human beings. However, when he seeks to exemplify this Christological concept phenomenologically, Bonhoeffer refers first to the intergenerational relationship within the family: "A father acts on behalf of his children by working, providing, intervening, struggling, and suffering for them. In doing so, he really stands in their place."[34] Bonhoeffer's social ethic has been interpreted as conservative and patriarchal, and the way he defends the authority of fatherhood by using the metaphor of above and below offers us some food for thought.[35] However, when not read in categories of social space and power but within the time perspective of the succession of generations, the vicarious representation of children by their parents becomes a powerful generative motive, convincing even egalitarian minds.[36]

The responsibility of those privileged to represent vicariously the less advantaged had already been advocated strongly within the context of the church in Bonhoeffer's dissertation, *Sanctorum Communio*. He describes being there for the other as "the readiness to do and bear everything in the neighbor's place, indeed, if necessary, to sacrifice myself, standing as a *substitute* for my neighbor." Here too, responsibility is phrased in terms of giving of privileges:

> It is apparent that in self-renouncing work for the neighbor I give up happiness. We are called to advocate vicariously for the other in everyday matters, to give up possessions, honor, even our whole lives. . . . The "strong" do not have their abilities for themselves, in order to consider themselves superior to the church-community; they have them "for the common good." (1 Cor. 12:7)[37]

Communal life within the church, according to Bonhoeffer, implies not only living with each other (*miteinander*) and being for each other (*füreinander*) but also vicarious representative action (*Stellvertretung*). Certainly, Bonhoeffer is writing

---

33. Ibid., 257.

34. Ibid., 257–8. Cf. also earlier in the same chapter, "History and Good," in *DBWE* 4:221 in which Bonhoeffer deletes "the mayor, the politician" from his manuscript [Ibid., note 9] and focuses on "the father of a family" who "incorporates the selves of those family members for whom he is responsible."

35. *DBWE* 6:372–6; 391–2; 396–7. Cf. Karl Barth's, *Church Dogmatics* III/4, 22, observation that in Bonhoeffer's doctrine of the mandates, "one cannot entirely shake that little taste of North German patriarchalism."

36. Cf. Robert Bly, *The Sibling Society* (New York: Vintage Books 1996), who argues that in Western egalitarian culture, even the relationships between generations have become horizontal and parents and children relate as peers.

37. *DBWE* 1:184.

about the church here, but it can be argued that he, at that time a twenty-year-old adolescent writing his PhD, and without much ecclesial experience, could not have written these lines without the strong awareness of privileged responsibility maintained within his own family.[38]

Conclusion

In this chapter, I have argued that generativity, understood as the "desire to invest one's substance in forms of life and work that will outlive the self,"[39] is a helpful concept for understanding Bonhoeffer's concern for the coming generation, as ardently expressed in his prison letters.

Though generativity is more or less a common feature in the life course of elderly adults, Bonhoeffer unmistakably was a highly generative person throughout his relatively short life. From his early years onward, he was aware of the fact that generations are "merely one link in the chain" and that intergenerational relationships are marked by the wounds of history. Bonhoeffer's fragmentary life reviews in prison appear to be dominated by what scholars call a "generativity script," typical for highly generative late adults. In this respect, Bonhoeffer was far from unique. With the central themes of privilege, sacrifice, and optimism, Bonhoeffer's generativity script belongs to a common narrative genre.

What makes him extraordinary, however, is his emphasis on the ethical dimension of generativity. Embodying generativity, in Bonhoeffer's view, is not just a sign of individual psychological health, or a more or less expected or admirable stage in the individual life course, but first a moral obligation and a political virtue of generations.

---

38. As I tried to show in my dissertation, *Grond onder de voeten: Burgerlijkheid bij Dietrich Bonhoeffer* (Kampen: van den Berg, 1985), 118–19, vicarious representation continues to be a recurring element in Bonhoeffer's thinking, also outside an ecclesiological framework. It returns, for example, vigorously in the drama he wrote in prison, where Christoph boldly declares to the Major that "for the tiny number of masters [Herren], for the free, the elite, the leaders—for them, love of life and happiness must not be the ultimate standard" (*DBWE* 7:173). Shortly after, the Major responds, "What purpose have you in taking charge, why do you want to lead, why do you want to prepare to bear unhappiness, if not in order to be able to make others happy?" (*DBWE* 7:175). For the societal relevance of Bonhoeffer's explicitly Christological and ecclesial foundation of his ethics of responsibility, cf. Esther D. Reed, *The Limits of Responsibility: Dietrich Bonhoeffer's Ethics for a Globalizing Era* (London: T&T Clark, 2018).

39. Kotre, *Outliving the Self*, 10.

Chapter 2

"O, POOR JUDAS, WHAT HAVE YOU DONE!"

A THEOLOGICAL EXPLORATION OF BETRAYAL

Nadia Marais

Introduction

bibber en beef, die boerebedrieër	tremble, traitor of the people
die wêreld gaan jou haat, my seun	the world will hate you, my son
as jy die waarheid praat	if you speak the truth
gaan hulle jou wil doodmaak[1]	they will want to kill you

In 1994 after apartheid, the South African public holiday, celebrated on December 16 each year, which was called the Day of the Vow, was renamed Reconciliation Day. The Day of the Vow, also called the Day of the Covenant or *Geloftedag*, commemorated the battle that took place in 1838, next to a river that was thereafter named Blood River. A small group of white pioneers was confronted by the local Zulu people of the land they were traveling through, and just before armed conflict, named the Battle of Blood River, ensued, the white Voortrekkers made a vow. If God would give their enemy into their hands, they would commemorate that day as a day of thanksgiving and dedication to God.

The vow does not stop there however, as it has implications for the coming generations. It explicitly refers to the coming generations, as these Voortrekkers also vowed to teach the coming generations to commemorate their victory (despite overwhelming odds against them).[2] On a plaque at the Blood River Monument on

---

1. These lyrics are cited from a popular Afrikaans rock song, entitled "Ek skyn(heilig)," written and performed by the Afrikaans band, *Fokofpolisiekar*, http://www.fokofpolisiekar.za.net/videos/ek-skyn-(heilig).php (accessed January 14, 2020). More information on this band and their music is available on their website: http://www.fokofpolisiekar.za.net/.

2. Much has been written, and there are and have been a number of debates on the historical details of this encounter (including exactly how many Zulu warriors were involved, whether thousands, hundreds, or a handful), but I am less interested in those details than I

which this vow is engraved, the Dutch reads: "onze opkomende geslachten." The wording seems to suggest that this vow is binding for coming generations. The Voortrekkers made this vow not only for themselves but also on behalf of (their) future descendants. Is this how the coming generation is to live?

If this was the end of the scope of this vow, if there had been no lasting legacy and nothing that came of this vow, if it was not celebrated and churches did not actively participate in organizing services in order to commemorate that day and the vow, perhaps it would have faded into history. But that was not possible since this vow to God, this *gelofte*, played a central role in the rise of Afrikaner nationalism, particularly in the 1930s and 1940s, and is therefore not easily dismissible.

In the very years that Dietrich Bonhoeffer lived and struggled with what it meant to inherit his people's history, the words of this vow also lived in the hearts of many people in South Africa. Even now, one could be forgiven for thinking that 1994 and the end of apartheid would also mean a final farewell to this vow and all that it stood for, had been used for, and reminded us of, particularly the rhetorical intention in this story to portray the descendants of the Voortrekkers, namely white Afrikaners, as the chosen people of God who, like the Israelites, were led into the promised land—South Africa—and protected by God. The way the story of Blood River is told, thousands of Zulu warriors died until the river ran red with blood but not a single Voortrekker lost his life.

Recently in 2018, as part of the centenary commemorations of the Battle of Blood River, this vow was adapted into music by a number of well-known Afrikaans artists. The YouTube video has more than a million views.³ In recent years, church dedication services to this vow or covenant seem not to have decreased, but to have even increased. Why? Can it be that coming generations *want* this vow? What exactly *does* the coming generation want? And so there may be in South Africa today, but I suspect not only in South Africa and not only today, ample reason to consider what it means to inherit history.

Do the coming generations have a say in this? What if they (we) opt for betrayal? Suppose future generations choose to opt out of this vow when they are confronted with some of the implications of such a heritage with its highly

---

am in the rhetoric of the vow and its theological implications. Although we have no original transcript of the vow, which was originally in Dutch and later translated into Afrikaans, it is on display in museums such as the Blood River Museum and the Voortrekker Museum.

3. The music video is entitled "Die Gelofte" [*The Vow*] and was made available on October 1, 2018, a few weeks before December 16, 2018, https://www.youtube.com/watch?v=II7Z2ldgaR8 (accessed January 18, 2020). I wrote a column for the church bulletin of the Dutch Reformed Church of South Africa, *Kerkbode*, which included a theological analysis of the theological rhetoric of the vow and it was published with the title, "Geseënd is die vredemakers" [Blessed are the peacemakers] on March 12, 2019, https://kerkbode.christians.co.za/2019/03/12/geseend-is-die-vredemakers/. A number of reactions to this column surfaced, including an invitation to attend a Day of the Vow church service. Most, if not all, of these reactions can be read on https://kerkbode.christians.co.za.

problematic themes of colonialism, war, and violence. What if they—we—choose to inherit history differently? Again, what about betrayal? Or why *not* betrayal? To what exactly do our loyalties bind us?

In this very limited contribution, it will be impossible to deal with this loaded and intimidating topic in its entirety. This contribution is also not intended to trace Bonhoeffer's role within the resistance or to engage in depth with the question of whether Bonhoeffer ought to be regarded as a martyr.[4] Rather, this chapter represents nothing more than an attempt to explore betrayal as a possible expression of an ethics of responsibility and to explore how Bonhoeffer himself may have thought about betrayal—and betrayers.

On Betrayal, Part 1

On March 6, 1996, the *Christian Century* reported that "German politicians, clergy and human rights advocates" requested that Germany's Parliament overturn Dietrich Bonhoeffer's status as a traitor.[5] By August 1997, this was done. "German authorities announced that Dietrich Bonhoeffer was no longer regarded in law as a traitor," writes John de Gruchy.[6] Bonhoeffer's arrest in 1943 and execution in 1945 for his resistance against the Nazi regime earned him the description, "[t]he martyred theologian."[7]

In his book, *Fools, Martyrs, Traitors*, which gives an account of the story of martyrdom in the Western world, Lacey Baldwin Smith makes specific reference to Dietrich Bonhoeffer in his discussion of "martyr-traitors" or "noble traitors."[8] In the chapter titled, "The Debate over Definition," Smith asks important questions about the characteristics of martyrs, as well as the distinctions between heroes,

---

4. In this regard, see for instance, Sabine Dramm's book, *Dietrich Bonhoeffer and the Resistance*, trans. Margaret Kohl (Minneapolis, MN: Fortress Press, 2009). She notes that Dietrich Bonhoeffer's involvement in the resistance was gradual, "a process" or "transition from the informed Bonhoeffer to Bonhoeffer the active participant, from passive to active resistance." The resistance movement against the Third Reich, she argues, involved "an active, personally dangerous intervention with the goal of weakening or ending the regime, and put an end to the National Socialist state." Dramm, *Dietrich Bonhoeffer and the Resistance*, 18–19.

5. See "Ending Bonhoeffer's Traitor Status," *Christian Century* 113, no. 8 (1996): 257.

6. See John W. de Gruchy, "Bonhoeffer's Legacy: A New Generation," *Christian Century* 114, no. 11 (1997): 343–5. De Gruchy, "Bonhoeffer's Legacy," 343, writes that "[t]his somewhat bizarre declaration . . . reminds us that the reception of Bonhoeffer in his native land has by no means been positive, not least because of his act of civil disobedience in participating in the abortive conspiracy to kill Adolf Hitler in 1944."

7. See "Ending Bonhoeffer's Traitor Status," 257.

8. Lacey Baldwin Smith, *Fools, Martyrs, Traitors: The Story of Martyrdom in the Western World* (Evanston, IL: Evanston Press, 1997), 6, 316–36.

martyrs, fools, traitors, and victims. He asks, "Who, then, qualifies as a proper martyr? Does the distinction between the fool, the martyr, and the traitor rest solely in the eyes of the beholder? Are all martyrs heroes and all dead heroes martyrs . . . [Moreover, w]hat is the distinction between a victim and a martyr?"[9] The most difficult distinction by far, he argues, is between a martyr and a traitor though martyrs and traitors share two characteristics: (1) they are alienated from society (their death is "a denial of existing society"), and (2) they are regarded as failures within systems of authority (they have failed to do their duty "in the eyes of officialdom").[10] Yet we are ill at ease in using these two descriptions together, he points out, exactly because we struggle to pinpoint who martyrs are. As Smith notes, history contains a variety of martyrs—"every one of whom is somebody's criminal, traitor, psychopath, murderer, or just plain fool."[11] It is, however, possible to identify two characteristics of martyrs, he argues:[12]

> [A]ll martyrs have two things in common: unlike heroes who are products of a consensus society where the quality and worth of their heroic acts are not in dispute, martyrs tend to be the offspring of a society in conflict with itself; and they are very special kinds of villains—they commit offenses of the mind and of the heart, and only rarely do they perpetrate crimes of the body. Martyrs violate the most revered and treasured abstractions that shape and create a society, giving it its uniqueness and vigor. . . . They strike at ties of loyalty, allegiance, and sense of collective security, while at the same time they defy society's—at least the ruling elite's—definitions of justice, mercy, honor, love and duty.

The boundary between martyrdom and treachery lies terribly close and frequently overlaps, he seems to suggest. If anything, it is a living, breathing distinction; a line that moves in accordance with the particular individual concerned. It is not possible to provide what he calls a "topical analysis" of martyrs, since "martyrs are too aggressively individualistic to be caged and classified."[13] This, too, is the case in his discussion of Dietrich Bonhoeffer. As John de Gruchy notes, the same tension or question, "martyr or traitor?," is evident in Bonhoeffer's legacy: "For some Germans, particularly those in the former German Democratic Republic, Bonhoeffer was a Christian martyr. But for many more he was a traitor who disobeyed authority and undermined the German war effort."[14]

---

9. Smith, *Fools, Martyrs, Traitors*, 4.
10. Ibid., 6.
11. Ibid., 19.
12. Ibid.
13. Ibid., 20.
14. De Gruchy, "Bonhoeffer's Legacy," 343. See also the essay that engages with exactly these questions about Bonhoeffer's death by Eberhard Bethge, "Modern Martyrdom," in Eberhard Bethge, Edited and with an Essay by John W. de Gruchy, *Bonhoeffer: Exile and Martyr* (New York: Seabury Press, 1975), 165. De Gruchy, *Dietrich Bonhoeffer and South*

Martyr. Resistor. Revolutionary. Whistleblower. Informant. Defector. Traitor. Betrayer. These many descriptions of Bonhoeffer raises the question, how did Bonhoeffer himself think about betrayal? How did Bonhoeffer, as a theologian, read the story of betrayers?

"O, Poor Judas, What Have You Done!" On Betrayal, Part 2

In a sermon titled "The Betrayer," preached at Finkenwalde on March 14, 1937, during Lent, Bonhoeffer reflected on Judas' betrayal of Jesus.[15] Bonhoeffer preached this among friends and, as noted in the introduction to the sermon, "Jesus' betrayal by one of his own disciples must have felt particularly horrifying."[16] In a time of increasing distrust and betrayal, the figure of Judas was hardly a comforting figure to behold. In Bonhoeffer's sermon, there is no great sympathy for Judas the betrayer, but perhaps even more significant is the boldness with which Bonhoeffer engages with the reality of betrayal and the figure of a betrayer among friends.

It is to the figure of Jesus that Bonhoeffer returns consistently throughout this sermon. The biblical text is Mt. 26:45-50[17] in which the theme of betrayal is intricately intertwined with friendship. In this account of Judas' betrayal, Jesus calls Judas his friend in the moment of betrayal—a moment that does not escape Bonhoeffer in his reading of the text. Bonhoeffer begins his sermon by pointing out that Jesus' betrayal is not only "one secret" but also the "most profound secret" that Jesus kept from his disciples.[18] This betrayal is crucial to the story of salvation, but it is no less terrible because of it, Bonhoeffer says. Without Judas, without a close friend of Jesus, the enemies of Jesus "can gain no power over him."[19] And so:

Africa, 17–18, agrees with Bethge that "Bonhoeffer's death was that of a martyr because he died on behalf of the weak, despised, and suffering ones, and in so doing affirmed God's love for all in Christ. Moreover, the cause of Bonhoeffer's death and his testimony in dying cannot be separated. His death resulted from his opposition in the name of Christ to the demonic power of Nazism and his struggle to restore a just social order in Germany . . . [Yet] Bonhoeffer's martyrdom is, undoubtedly, even more disturbing because of the circumstances that led to his death. Indeed, he himself was deeply aware that his participation in the conspiracy against Hitler was morally problematic, even though he became convinced that it was necessary in the extreme circumstances facing Germany at the time. Nevertheless, the decision he made to become involved in the plot cannot be separated from his Christian commitment. He certainly did not seek martyrdom, but he did seek to be a faithful witness and understood that this could cost him his life."

15. See Dietrich Bonhoeffer, *The Collected Sermons of Dietrich Bonhoeffer*, ed. Isabel Best, trans. Douglas W. Stott et al. (Minneapolis, MN: Fortress Press, 2012), 185–91.
16. Bonhoeffer, "The Betrayer," 185.
17. Ibid., 186.
18. Ibid.
19. Ibid.

This terrible thing comes about not from the outside, but from the inside. Jesus' path to Golgotha begins with a disciple's betrayal . . . "Betrayed", Jesus says. That is, it is not the world that gains power over him. Instead, Jesus is turned over, surrendered, given up by his own. . . . That is what happens. Jesus is thrown away. The protecting arms of his friends are lowered. . . . Betraying Jesus means no longer intervening on his behalf, means surrendering him to the derision and power of the public, means allowing the world to do with him whatever it pleases, means no longer standing by him. Jesus' own followers deliver him over to the world. That is his death.[20]

The betrayal is a public act. Bonhoeffer notes in his careful rhetorical reading of the text, even though the text makes it clear that this betrayal is unmistakably public—it takes place in front of an audience, a large crowd—Jesus pays no attention to the crowd that accompanies Judas. Jesus also ignores, without exception, the weapons present, "the swords and clubs of the enemy."[21] Those symbols of violence and power, of war and death, are less important than a kiss. The crowd and the weapons they wield fade into the background of the story when those closest to Jesus hand him over to the authorities, Bonhoeffer notes.

Yet we should not miss the suggestion that not only Judas but all of Jesus' disciples fail him—in a myriad of acts—by failing to act, by sleeping, by running away, and by denying Jesus repeatedly. They, all of them and not only Judas, betray Jesus. The disciples are "so completely unprepared," he concludes.[22] This makes it even more remarkable that he attributes to Judas the role of history shaper. Judas' choices shape history for however brief a moment and for even just "a single moment" because "everything, the entirety of salvation and world history, is in the hands of that one person—the betrayer."[23] Judas is "co-responsible for the shaping of history."[24] Judas' choices matter. And Jesus is interested not in the behavior of the mob, the crowd, or even in the disciples but in Judas, who is responsible for shaping history. The interaction between Judas and Jesus takes center stage: "Now our attention focuses on only two people. The disciples and pursuers recede, both failing to do their own work well. Only two do their work properly, namely Jesus and Judas. Who is Judas? That is the question. It is one of the most ancient and haunting questions of Christendom."

What is interesting here is Bonhoeffer's own varied description of Judas. When the disciples recognized Judas, they shuddered—shuddered because none of them had thought any of them was capable of betrayal.[25] Not only did they think it unlikely that another would betray them, but they had each hesitated to accuse a

20. Ibid., 186–7.
21. Ibid., 187.
22. Ibid.
23. Ibid.
24. *DBWE* 8:21.
25. Bonhoeffer, "The Betrayer," 187.

fellow disciple because, for Bonhoeffer, "Each thought his own heart more capable of such a deed than that of the other, the brother."[26] Judas—their betrayer, their brother, their co-disciple, and their friend.[27] The disciples shuddered not because Judas was so different from them, but because he is so familiar—part of their close-knit and intimate community, those chosen by Jesus himself.[28]

But this is not yet, for Bonhoeffer, the worst and most inexplicable part of the betrayal. For Bonhoeffer, Jesus calling, choosing, and loving Judas is what he calls "the real mystery."[29] Jesus loves his betrayer. And yet here Bonhoeffer's sympathy for Judas seems to wear thin—Judas is described as "a devil," "a thief," "an evildoer," "a hater."[30] Jesus chooses, calls, and loves Judas. Judas betrays and hates Jesus.[31] It is however the figure of Jesus to whom Bonhoeffer looks "with enormous consternation." Not only does Jesus choose and call, and love Judas, but also Judas is singled out among the disciples to hold the office of treasurer.[32] There is, remarkably, "[n]ot even the smallest indication that Jesus might have secretly hated Judas."[33]

Jesus not only loved his betrayer but also loved him intimately. Before he discussed the kiss shared between Jesus and Judas, Bonhoeffer identifies other indications of intimacy. Jesus and Judas shared in the communion meal on the night of the betrayal.[34] This—Jesus giving Judas bread—is symbolic of "the most intimate community."[35] As if this is not enough, Jesus spoke to Judas intimately, privately, without the other disciples understanding what was going on. In Bonhoeffer's words, "Only Jesus and Judas knew."[36] Finally, "Jesus and Judas [are also] bound by a kiss," writes Bonhoeffer, for "Jesus and Judas belong together from the outset. Neither lets go of the other."[37]

---

26. Ibid.
27. Ibid.
28. Ibid., 188. Bonhoeffer imagines this in stark terms, as this longer quotation illustrates: "Judas, one of the twelve. We can still sense some of the horror the evangelist must have felt when he wrote these few words. Judas, one of the twelve—what more need be said? . . . Judas' entire, dark secret and at the same time the most profound horror at his deed. . . . It is wholly and completely inexplicable, incomprehensible, and will always remain an utter riddle—and yet it did indeed happen. Judas, one of the twelve, someone who was with Jesus day and night, someone who had followed Jesus, someone who had paid a price, who had had to leave everything behind in order to be with Jesus—a brother, a friend, a confidant of Peter, of John, of the Lord himself."
29. Ibid.
30. Ibid., 188–9.
31. Ibid.
32. Ibid., 188.
33. Ibid.
34. Ibid., 189.
35. Ibid.
36. Ibid.
37. Ibid.

Jesus' path of suffering and torture and death is "opened" by Judas, his betrayer. Bonhoeffer writes that Jesus "loves the person whose betrayal opens up that very path, and indeed, the person who for a brief moment holds Jesus' very fate in his hands."[38] Again and again, Bonhoeffer returns to this question, who is this Judas, the betrayer? For Bonhoeffer, it is remarkable that

> Jesus does not . . . want to let go of Judas. He allows Judas to kiss him. He does not turn him away. No, Judas must kiss him. His fellowship with Jesus must complete itself. Why have you come? Jesus knows full well why Judas came, and yet: Why have you come? And: Judas, is it with a kiss that you are betraying the Son of Man? One final expression of a disciple's love, united with betrayal. One final sign of passionate love, coupled with much more passionate hatred. . . . What a profoundly divided act, this kiss of Judas. Not being able to pull himself away from Jesus, and yet surrendering him. Judas, is it with a kiss that you are betraying the Son of Man?[39]

Yet it is also this very kiss that brings "the path of Judas to its conclusion," which signifies "utter separation" between Judas and Jesus—the end of intimacy, of friendship, of life together, and of *sanctorum communio*. "Who is Judas, who is the betrayer?"[40] Bonhoeffer does not want to let go of this question. At the very end of his sermon, he shares his response to this haunting question with us:

> Christendom has always seen in Judas the dark mystery of divine rejection and eternal damnation. With horror, it has recognized and testified to the seriousness and judgment of God with regard to the betrayer. For precisely that reason, however, it has never looked upon Judas with pride or arrogance; instead, it sings in trembling recognition of its own enormous sin. O, poor Judas, what have you done! Thus do we, too, say nothing more than this: O, poor Judas, what have you done!

However, five years later, Bonhoeffer appears to have softened somewhat in his view of Judas. In his 1942 essay, "After Ten Years," Bonhoeffer again refers to the figure of Judas and the experience of betrayal. Whereas in his 1937 sermon, Bonhoeffer had described Judas' betrayal as "incomprehensible,"[41] in his 1942 essay, Judas' betrayal is hardly incomprehensible anymore. Bonhoeffer does admit however that this betrayal was "once so incomprehensible," and therefore signals a slight but significant change in thinking about the matter.[42] And he does so in a section dealing with "trust":[43]

38. Ibid.
39. Ibid., 190.
40. Ibid.
41. Ibid., 188.
42. *DBWE* 8:46.
43. Ibid., 46–7.

Few have been spared the experience of being betrayed. The figure of Judas, once so incomprehensible, is hardly strange to us. The air in which we live is so poisoned with mistrust that we almost die from it. . . . We now know that to sow and to nourish mistrust is one of the most reprehensible things and that, instead, trust is to be strengthened and advanced wherever possible. For us trust will be one of the greatest, rarest, and most cheering gifts bestowed by the life we humans live in common, and yet it always emerges only against the dark background of necessary mistrust.

Trust is a gift that makes it possible for us to "open up." The ability to "open" toward other people is a crucial element of friendship, argues Bonhoeffer,[44] for such trust is "made possible by friendship."[45] Friendship, in turn, has a twofold effect—it enables "delight in private life" and provides us with "courage for public life."[46] In this essay, it is telling that Bonhoeffer encourages his readers to take care as those "co-responsible" for shaping history. Friendship involves not closing ourselves off or withdrawing from history but entering even more deeply into the circumstances in which we find ourselves and choices we have made.[47]

Conclusion: In Praise of Betrayal?

How does a theological exploration of betrayal help us to consider how the coming generation is to go on living? A crucial question that Bonhoeffer's essay "After Ten Years" confronts us with when we consider history is how did we get here?[48] Theologians including South African theologians, like the former rector of Stellenbosch University, Russel Botman, have also asked: Can Dietrich Bonhoeffer help us in this regard? Indeed, is Bonhoeffer of any use also in South Africa, even today?[49]

---

44. Ibid. Friendship has to do with the recognition that all human beings are worthy of respect. In a section with the title, "The Sense of Quality," Bonhoeffer writes as follows: "We are the midst of the process that levels every rank of society. But we are also at the hour of a new sense of nobility being born that binds together a circle of human beings drawn from all existing social classes. Nobility arises from and exists by sacrifice, courage, and a clear sense of what one owes oneself and others, by the self-evident expectation of the respect one is due, and of the equally self-evident observance of the same respect for those above and those below." Ibid. See also Stanley Hauerwas, *Working with Words: On Learning to Speak Christian* (Eugene, OR: Cascade Books, 2011), 282.
45. Hauerwas, *Working with Words*, 282.
46. *DBWE* 8:47–8.
47. Ibid., 48.
48. Bonhoeffer, "After Ten Years" in *DBWE* 8:35–52.
49. The late South African Reformed theologian, Russel Botman, asked this question in a contribution to the volume, *Bonhoeffer for a New Day: Theology in a Time of Transition*,

Perhaps what reading Bonhoeffer's theological reflections can offer us on betrayal and friendship is a reconsideration of betrayal—not only grand, big acts of betrayal wherein we oppose regimes and systems of oppression but also those many smaller acts, in lesser known deeds and few words, in which we betray those loyalties that undermine the flourishing of those Bonhoeffer calls "the outcasts, the suspects, the maltreated, the powerless, the oppressed and reviled."[50] Betraying those loyalties, those ties that bind, those legacies, those oaths and ancestry, and blood, those vows, those covenants, which ought to be betrayed. Betraying a heritage in order to redeem it. Betraying a heritage for the sake not of "forgetting the past," but for what Eberhard Bethge calls "space to breathe."[51]

Admittedly, Bonhoeffer has few kind words to spare Judas. I would like to think that he softened toward "the betrayer" near the end of his life. However, our reading of his reading of Judas ought not to lose sight of the fact that, for Bonhoeffer, the story of betrayal finds coherence in Jesus. Judas is a truthteller; he does not lie when he betrays Jesus. He does what he sets out to do. Jesus is where he says he will be. Jesus is the one he kisses. Judas does not make a blunder of his betrayal; he is deliberate and calculated. He is not caught out. He does not do more than he set out to do. Even though the whole of salvation history is, but for a moment, in his hands, as Bonhoeffer notes, Judas does exactly what he was to do and nothing more. May we not extend Bonhoeffer's reading to consider, really consider, betrayal—and in the process employ greater charity of interpretation than Bonhoeffer himself perhaps did when he read Judas?

And if we consider, really consider, betrayal, would we not recognize that there may be circumstances that require of us, that call upon us to become "the betrayer?" Are we not those called upon to betray that which ought to be betrayed, not accidentally, without blundering or blustering, but consciously and deliberately, become betrayers or traitors to those cultural values and loyalties that undermine the dignity and flourishing of the most vulnerable in our societies? Where would we be without those Christian traitors—those accused of *hoogverraad, volksverraad,* and *landsverraad*; in short, those who betray, at the highest level, a country and a people for the sake of the lives and dignity, and flourishing of the most vulnerable,

---

ed. John de Gruchy (Grand Rapids, MI: William B. Eerdmans, 1997), 366–72. In the second annual Russel Botman Memorial Lecture, Crain Soudien explored this very question in Botman and Bonhoeffer's respective legacies. The title of his lecture was "'Are We Still of Any Use?' Situating Russel Botman's Thinking on Poverty, Empowerment and Education in Our Contemporary Times," Presented on October 18, 2016, at the Faculty of Theology, Stellenbosch University. http://www.sun.ac.za/english/PublishingImages/Lists/dualnews/My%20Items%20View/cas%202016%20bOTMAN%20lECTURE%20-%20LAH.pdf (accessed January 18, 2020).

50. *DBWE* 8:52.

51. See Eberhard Bethge, "Research—Meditation—Commemoration: Steps to Combat Forgetting," in *Friendship and Resistance: Essays on Dietrich Bonhoeffer* (Geneva: WCC Publications, 1995), 105–11 (108–9, 111).

the oppressed; in the interests of truth, and justice, and mercy, and for the sake of the future, tomorrow's children, the coming generation?

And when we betray those life-denying and injustice-allotting loyalties that bind us; those suffocating ties that would hold us hostage to our dark loves and dark powers; blood and ancestry and oaths that we feel indebted to honor, should our betrayal not be calculated instead of panicked, not be careless but careful, not be accidental but disciplined—a betrayal well thought out? And cannot such betrayals still be earnest, from the heart, and deep because of the very faith and hope, and love we hold for God and our neighbors? Are we not called upon to betray what is sick and sickening in our societies? Should we not betray what is corrupt, what is death dealing, what is war making, and what is violent and exploitative?

Perhaps the coming generation will need more betrayers among us, better betrayers in us, in order for them to live and flourish. Perhaps Judas' path of betrayal is a soteriological opening up that we need to participate in. Jesus' friendship, a friendship that lays its life down for its friends, is not unaccompanied by Judas' betrayal. The betrayer opens up the way of death and, ultimately, contributes to Jesus' opening of salvation and life and flourishing.

Perhaps our betrayals may do such opening up work too.

Perhaps nothing less than betraying what ought to be betrayed may be required to work the seams loose, to take out the stitches, in the deepest parts of ourselves that are tied to blood and ancestry, and oath, to vows and covenants that do not make for the ongoing living and flourishing of the coming generation.

Perhaps, when we consider inheriting history, and all that is good and true, and beautiful, when we consider friendship, justice, grace, and love, we too may need to become "the betrayer."

O, poor Judas, what have you done!

Chapter 3

WHAT DOES IT MEAN TO TELL THE TRUTH?

BONHOEFFER IN THE DIGITAL ERA

Wolfgang Huber

Bonhoeffer on Truth

For several years, I have cherished Bonhoeffer's questions and therefore appreciate that the organizers of the 13th International Bonhoeffer Conference have chosen one of my favorite Bonhoeffer questions as the theme of this congress, that is, "How is the coming generation to go on living"?[1]

This quotation is taken from a text that has been used for a long time as a prologue for *Letters and Papers from Prison*. But it is in fact written in freedom, some months before Bonhoeffer's arrest. At Christmas time in 1942, he wrote an essay with the title "After Ten Years" for his friends Eberhard Bethge, Hans von Dohnanyi, and Hans Oster. In sixteen short reflections,[2] he considered the nearly ten years since Adolf Hitler gained political power in Germany on January 30, 1933. Bonhoeffer reflected on how these years shaped his life and those of his friends and even affected their integrity. He expressed this self-critique in astonishingly clear words in the final part of these original notes under the title, "Are We Still of Any Use?" The small paragraph reads as follows:

> We have been silent witnesses of evil deeds. We have become cunning and learned the arts of obfuscation[3] and equivocal speech. Experience has rendered us suspicious of human beings, and often we have failed to speak to them a true and open word. Unbearable conflicts have worn us down or even made us cynical. Are we still of any use? We will not need geniuses, cynics, people who have contempt for others, or cunning tacticians, but simple, uncomplicated, and honest human beings. Will our inner strength to resist what has been forced on

---

1. *DBWE* 8:37–52, 42.

2. The essay, "The View from Below," in *DBWE* 8:52, was originally not part of "After Ten Years."

3. A better translation of "Künste der Verstellung" could be "arts of dissimulation."

us have remained strong enough, and our honesty with ourselves blunt enough, to find our way back to simplicity and honesty?[4]

As one who was privy to the conspiracy, Bonhoeffer tried to assist his friends to overcome feelings of guilt. In their bid to stop mass murder, they considered killing the dictator. They had sworn an oath to the "Führer" but now were preparing to assassinate him. Bonhoeffer tried to convince them that to thwart Hitler's regime, which has produced countless victims, they needed to follow their conscience and trust in God's grace. But this problem of tyrannicide was not the only conflict in their conscience. There was also another question. How is the integrity of the conspirators affected since they painstakingly had to hide the truth, tell lies, and remain silent observers of brutal crimes while waiting for the right moment to make a move to stop the nightmarish cruelties? "Are we still of any use?" The question of truth underlies this tormenting act of self-examination.

What does it mean to tell the truth? This aspect of Bonhoeffer's existential impasse may relate more closely to our situation than the problem of tyrannicide. The question of tyrannicide clearly shows up in Bonhoeffer's drafts of his ethics, but he also approaches the question of truth with remarkable clarity. His interest is not restricted to the famous construction of the German philosopher Immanuel Kant, who raised the issue of whether I am allowed to lie on reasons of philanthropy when a murderer asks me if his prospective victim hides in my house. In moral philosophy and theology, it was argued that denying the presence of my friend in this case would not be a lie but a false statement to save my friend's life. Kant rejects this distinction because, in his view, there is no appropriate argument to regard as a general rule for violating truth for the benefit of the seemingly higher value of life. Whoever lies commits a crime against the humanity in his or her own person. Lying is a kind of self-violation. Bonhoeffer disagrees with the great philosopher that lying is "self-righteousness of conscience" that escalates "into blasphemous recklessness" and becomes "an impediment to responsible action."[5] In Kant's view, it is not the human being who has a right to truth, but it is the truth which has a right to the human being.[6] But Bonhoeffer differs, saying, "The human conscience is not only bound to principles, but to responsibility." And responsibility means "the entire response, in accord with reality, to the claim of God and my neighbour."[7] He adds that this statement clearly addresses the dilemma of the conspirators—"I come into conflict with my responsibility that is grounded in reality when I refuse to take on and bear guilt out of love for my neighbour." But Bonhoeffer does not use this criterion as a free ticket. The taking on and bearing of guilt are limited by the call to unity with myself. Not only the love for God and the neighbor but also

---

4. *DBWE* 8:52.
5. *DBWE* 6:279f.
6. Eberhard Schockenhoff, *Zur Lüge verdammt?* (Freiburg: Herder, 2000), 99.
7. *DBWE* 6:280.

the unity with oneself—and in this sense the love for oneself—form necessary dimensions of responsibility.

Bonhoeffer had not yet come to a clear conclusion in the summarized reflections on the relationship between responsibility and truth included in the draft of his *Ethics* before he was detained. In jail, he blamed himself for not having finished his *Ethics*[8] and tried to continue his work on at least one point even as a prisoner. This one point was the question of what it means to tell the truth. The essay on this topic was formerly included in *Ethics*, but today, it is found in the volume, *Conspiracy and Imprisonment*.[9] But the relation to *Ethics* is evident. There is only one other text from his time in prison that can also be understood as an additional contribution to his work on *Ethics*, namely a new start to interpreting the Ten Commandments and their ethical relevance.[10]

Bonhoeffer put special effort into his essay, "What It Means to Tell the Truth," which he worked on for at least a month, between mid-November and mid-December 1943.[11] At that time, he had urgent reasons to reflect on the issue. As a detainee awaiting interrogations and afterward his trial, he was directly confronted with the relationship between responsibility and truth. He had reasons to fear that he would be charged with high treason and tried to avoid everything that could be used against him. He gave plausible reasons for his military exemption for "Operation 7," which was initiated to bring a group of Jewish people safely to Switzerland and for the rationale behind his international travels. He tried hard to hide the real reasons for joining the military secret service and to refute as convincingly as possible the allegation that he had evaded military conscription and thus contributed to the so-called "demoralization of the armed forces."[12] His process was announced just when he started working on his essay. So he stopped writing when his trial was called off at short notice after Hans von Dohnanyi fell ill.[13] The personal risks of telling the truth as well as denying it increased dramatically; indeed, it had become a question of life and death.

---

8. *DBWE* 8:181.

9. *DBWE* 16:601–8.

10. "Exposition on the First Table of the Ten Words of God"; *DBWE* 16:633–44. *Ethics* includes an exposition on the Ten Commandments as a confession manual for the confession of the churches' guilt; *DBWE* 6:134–45. The reflection on the first three commandments can be understood as the beginning of a complementary approach to the relevance of the "Ten Words" for ethical responsibility and its theological foundation.

11. He recalls that he had written on the subject on November 18, 1943 (*DBWE* 8:182), refers to it on December 5, 1943 (8:216), and mentions the ongoing work on December 15, 1943 (8:223). So he clearly started writing before November 18 and stopped working on the piece after December 15, 1943.

12. Cf. the series of drafts of letters to the Senior Military Prosecutor, Manfred Roeder, written between June 10, and August 2, 1943; *DBWE* 16:409–27.

13. See Eberhard Bethge, *Dietrich Bonhoeffer: A Biography*, rev. ed. (Minneapolis MN: Fortress, 2000), 810–28.

However, the essay broadens the topic and sees the question of truth as a general human challenge. Bonhoeffer identified several themes he wanted to address—only some of them really got included in the fragmentary essay.[14] Its first words say, "From the moment in our lives in which we become capable of speech, we are taught that our words must be true. What does this mean . . . Who requires this of us?"

The first answer may be that we owe truthful speech to God. But answering this way, we have to realize that God is not a general principle but the "Living One," who calls everyone to a specific place with a specific vocation. Therefore, the reference to God leads to the relationship between those who ask for the truth and those who are asked to tell the truth. This "relevant relationship" includes the question of whether person A has a right to ask question Q from person B. If we reconstruct, for instance, Kant's case of the murderer at the door, who is after my friend, from the perspective of "relevant relationship," it should be evident that the murderer has no right to get an answer. The only serious question is whether B is clever enough to react in a manner which avoids a lie or not. Bonhoeffer maintains that unfair questions very often are addressed to vulnerable people, unfamiliar with situations in which they are compelled to answer questions to which person A has no proper right. He uses the example of a child whose teacher asks openly in the classroom whether it is true that the child's father often comes home drunk. Even under the assumption that this is the case, the child's reaction of denial is more appropriate than a positive answer, because the teacher misuses the public arena to pose a private question that encroaches on the sphere of the family. To distinguish the different spheres and to learn the appropriate use of language for these different spheres is a necessary precondition for dealing responsibly with truth questions.

Truth is relational and therefore situated. Bonhoeffer judges the "usual definition, according to which the conscious contradiction between thought and speech is a lie," as inadequate and contrasts it with a very steep theological definition:

> Lying is first of all the denial of God as God has been revealed to the world. . . . Lying is the negation, denial, and deliberate and wilful destruction of reality as it is created by God and exists in God to the extent that it takes place through words and silence. Our word in union with the Word of God is intended to express what is real, as it is in God, and our silence is to be a sign of the boundary drawn around the word by what is real, as it is in God.[15]

Bonhoeffer is far from a harmonious understanding of reality. It is not "a unified whole but in a condition of disruption and self-contradiction, requiring

---

14. Cf. Dietrich Bonhoeffer, *Zettelnotizen für eine "Ethik,"* ed. Ilse Tödt (Gütersloh: Gütersloher Verlagshaus, 1993), 143–6.

15. *DBWE* 16:607.

reconciliation and healing."[16] He sees telling the truth in tension between conflict and reconciliation. In the end, his question is no longer how can I tell the truth, but how do my words become true? In response, he mentions three criteria: "1) By recognising who calls on me to speak and what authorizes me to speak; 2) by recognising the place in which I stand; 3) by putting the subject I am speaking [of] into this context."[17]

Bonhoeffer's concept of telling the truth may be summarized into six essential features:

1. Truth represents the openness of our world and our human existence before God. We can speak about truth because the divine reality became part of mundane reality. Truthfulness mirrors the respect for God's presence in our world through Jesus Christ.
2. Truth has its place in our "relevant relations" to God, the world, our fellow humans, and ourselves. Truth is relational in itself.
3. Truth is at stake in different speech situations. For these, the difference between the public and the private is of great importance. Respect for truth can only be expected when this difference is taken into account.
4. Truth is not simply the correspondence between facts and statements but is a triple relationship between the real situation, the addressee with his or her questions, and the responder with his or her propositions. Truth is embedded in reality.
5. Truth is related to a conflict-ridden world. To tell the truth means to unmask conflicts in order to open the way to reconciliation. Truth aims for reconciliation.
6. Forgotten truth cannot be part of an open relationship. Forgotten truth cannot contribute to reconciliation. It should therefore be reckoned as part of the essence of truth that is remembered.

Truth in the Digital Era

Whereas some observers argue that digitalization is the main challenge of the present time, others claim that it is climate change. In my view, it is inconsequential to consider any single challenge such as digitalization, climate change, sustainable development, population growth, global migration, or violence in its various forms as our main priority. We live in a complex world and can by no means restrict our awareness to one single issue. But if we ask what makes us to see our time as the beginning of a new era, two propositions are noteworthy. The one describes the new era as the Anthropocene and the other as the digital era. Both

---

16. Ibid.
17. Ibid., 608.

proposals offer specific evidence, but at the same time both are debatable. To date, there is no scholarly consensus on the definition of Anthropocene as a geological era following the Holocene, proposed by Paul Crutzen in 2000 and taken up by a group of Nobel laureates in 2007.[18] But the debate itself demonstrates that the human impact on earth's geology and ecosystem, including, but not limited to, anthropogenic global warming, is growing to an extent that is not only quantitative but also qualitative in character.

Digitalization has relative groundbreaking significance, and there is an obvious but seldom-discussed interrelationship between global warming and digitalization. Globally, the digital sector produces more greenhouse gas emission than air traffic. But the ecological consequences of digitalization are seldom discussed. Its opportunities seem to be overwhelming and without alternative. The critics of social media or the influence of digitalization on the labor market or labor conditions and even the opponents of driverless driving or "autonomous" weapons make use of digital instruments. On a global scale, digitalization is *the* technological innovation of our times, with deeply disruptive consequences.

This technology changed human communication at relative speed as the printing with movable letters more than half a millennium ago. Half a century after the first theoretical concepts about computing with binary codes, digital technologies reached the workplace and even the homes of a continuously growing number of people. Now, through personal computers, tablets, and smartphones, this technology has become omnipresent. The digital divide was overruled not by political or social interventions but by technological innovations. In 1993, only 3 percent of the global technological information capacity was digital, but in 2007, the number had grown to 94.5 percent, and 2002 is seen as the year in which, for the first time, more than half of the globally accessible information was stored in digital forms. Analogous storage of information declined to a minority status. This watershed may be seen as the beginning of the digital era. Since then, the progress of digital communication has become global and accelerated at an astonishing speed, resulting in a remarkable concentration of power and capital in the hands of a few digital giants, whose economic (and political) influence overrules the influence of nearly all states or federations of states on the globe.

The easy and free access to this kind of technology is seen by many as so advantageous that they accept to be monitored by digital platforms and internet firms to an unprecedented extent. This includes using not only their computers, tablets, or smartphones but also bank, credit, or customer cards, which make their actions and transactions checkable and predictable. Most people see great benefit in this quick, easy, and borderless kind of communication, information, action, and transaction that they relegate the risks and ambiguities to a secondary status or ignore them completely. Not only communication in the broad sense of the word but also important fields, such as human labor, consumption, democratic

---

18. See the Potsdam Memorandum in Hans Joachim Schellnhuber a.o., *Global Sustainability: A Nobel Cause* (Cambridge: Cambridge University Press, 2010), 369–72.

or undemocratic public and politic issues, mobility, health, sports, love, religion, science, culture, and war, already are and in the future will be more and more influenced by digitalization, robotics, big data, and artificial (i.e., nonbiological) intelligence. How a technological disruption of such magnitude can be embedded in social transformation is still an open question. But that seems to be one of the decisive issues of our time, and it seems that many people will get lost in this disruption, not only socially but also emotionally and even politically.

But is there a chance of social transformation despite technological disruption? Some people argue that this technological change inevitably includes not only a social but also an anthropological disruption. For example, Ray Kurzweil, the American futurist and Google's director of engineering and the Israeli historian, Yuval Noah Harari, argue that digital technologies together with biotechnological interventions like genome editing will put an end to the era of *Homo sapiens* and open the door to a posthuman age.[19] Luciano Floridi, a philosopher from Italy teaching in Oxford, interprets the transition to the dominance of information and communication technologies as a "Fourth Revolution," characteristic of modern times. The interesting point in this parallel of four revolutions is that every revolution combines a new scientific observation with disillusion, progress with disenchantment. Whereas the revolution of Nicolaus Copernicus showed that humans do not exist immovably at the center of the universe, the revolution of Charles Darwin showed that humans are not naturally detached and diverse from the natural world, and Sigmund Freud's revolution indicated that we humans are not independent subjects entirely transparent to ourselves. And now, in the Fourth Revolution, we have to admit that we are not disconnected agents, but informational organisms ("inforgs"), sharing with biological and engineered agents an environment that is essentially informational ("infosphere").[20] Floridi takes as a symbolic name for this revolution the name of Alan Turing, the inventor of the Turing-Machine and the Turing-Test. Kurzweil, by the way, made a bet that by 2029, the Turing-Test will be rated a success, which means that by this date artificial intelligence would have reached the level of human thinking.

The anthropological change is not a problem of the future, as we already observe a dramatic reductionist change in the understanding of humans. While focusing on the progress of artificial intelligence, we isolate the cognitive capacities of human beings from other aspects of human existence. Therefore, we develop the fear that humans will be overruled by artificial intelligence and its capacity to combine and analyze much more data in a much shorter time than it is possible for the human brain. But we could also draw the opposite conclusion as formulated by the American psychologist Barry Schwartz, who says, "Hands and

---

19. Ray Kurzweil, *The Singularity Is Near: When Humans Transcend Biology* (New York: Viking Books, 2005); Yuval Noah Harari, *Homo Deus: A Brief History of Tomorrow* (New York: Harper, 2016).

20. Luciano Floridi, *The Fourth Revolution: How the Infosphere Is Reshaping Human Reality* (Oxford: Oxford University Press, 2014).

heads are less important, hearts become more important." In times of multiple demographic challenges, of having to accept diversity and to use it creatively, of worldwide migration and manifest needs of integration, services that have to do with counseling, education and training, medical assistance and nursing, conflict management, healing of memories, reconciliation, and integration are needed more than ever before.

Instead of fearing that artificial intelligence will overrule human intelligence, we should critically evaluate the anthropological concept behind this fear. Will a chess computer ever understand why his human counterpart has stronger and weaker days, or why a rugby or soccer team on one day wins against a strong opponent and loses four days later against a much weaker team? We enter the realm of human action only when we accept not only the successes and triumphs but also the failures and mistakes, the vulnerability and finiteness of persons as part of the human condition.

There is no alternative to empathy. We humans belong not only to the species *Homo sapiens* but also to the species "*homo sentiens.*" We are not only rational but also feeling creatures. We are not only "*inforgs*" but also "*empathorgs*" and are not only informational but also empathetic organisms. The fear that artificial intelligence will make humans superfluous because computers deal flawlessly with big data in shortest time, and robots do things more precisely and effectively than humans reduces the human being to a being with a head (comparable to a computer) and a hand (comparable to a robot). Such a view forgets that humans have a heart that helps to deal with the finiteness of one's own life as well as of other human beings. We need a more integral, holistic understanding of the human being. With this purpose in mind, we return to Bonhoeffer and his answer to the question, "What does it mean to tell the truth"?

Theological Challenges and Perspectives

What is the place of truth in the infosphere? There are books on sociological and ethical problems of the digital era, whose indexes show no entry for "truth." The topic does not seem to be of specific interest. There is a growing mistrust in the web because it is misused for the spread of fake news. But the criteria for this criticism can be found easily. The dominant criteria for truth in the infosphere are objectivity on the one hand and authenticity on the other. Objectivity stands for the correspondence between facts and propositions; authenticity stands for the correspondence between one's identity and the kind of self-presentation. The web is full of opportunities for both kinds of truth. People post and find an immense amount of "facts" and an evenly immense amount of authentic explications of one's "true nature and belief."

But there is an obvious tension between these two approaches to truth—the objective and the authentic. To get some clarification, we return to Bonhoeffer's insights on truth with the keen hope that they may be of help for a better understanding of truth in the "infosphere." For that purpose, we follow the six elements in Bonhoeffer's understanding of truth, developed in the first part of this essay.

1. Truth stands for the openness of our world and our human existence to God. We can speak about truth because the divine reality became part of mundane reality. Truthfulness mirrors the respect for God's presence in our world through Jesus Christ.

Compared to contemporary discussions, this first characteristic of Bonhoeffer's understanding of truth seems to come from another planet. What does it mean to speak about God in the digital era? Is God's omnipresence not replaced by the omnipresence of the web, his omniscience by the omniscience of Wikipedia, and his omnipotence by the omnipotence of big data and digital factoring? Is this transfer of the divine predicates to a human project not a good reason why Yuval Noah Harari, one of the most influential gurus of our days, introduces the new species of "*homo deus*," who does not need to respect God's unavailability because everything is in human reach?

But does Harari really speak about humanity as a whole? He admits that the new possibilities to improve the human condition by technological means will benefit only a part of humanity. The poor, the vulnerable, and the marginalized will not make the step from *Homo sapiens* to "*homo deus*." They have quite different problems. The access to education and health and therefore the ability to use properly the benefits of modern technology are, in Harari's view, not available to a considerable part of humankind. Therefore, this part will not be included in the new species of "*homo deus*." The proclamation of the "*homo deus*" includes a farewell to a universalistic ethic that is based on the equal dignity of every human, whether well-known and wealthy or unknown and poor and whether well-educated or not.

Bonhoeffer begins his interpretation of truth by justifying his relating it to God. Today we need to emphasize the link between a universalistic ethic and the acknowledgment of the divine reality that transcends human reach. This correlation forms the center of the Jewish-Christian understanding of every human being as created in the image of God. God's image becomes, as Christianity confesses, visible in Christ as the incarnated, crucified, and risen son of God. In Christ, God becomes present in our world, allowing us to see every human being in his or her relationship to God. This relationship reveals the inviolability or sacredness of humanity in every single person. Technological devices, regardless of how sophisticated they may be, cannot dissolve this relationship. The fact that algorithms can learn and are approaching the idea of artificial intelligence is no reason to change the relationship between humans and digital entities. Only humans have consciousness, empathy, and spontaneous creativity as well as a reflexive understanding of their relation to God as creator, reconciler, and redeemer.

Digitalization includes in its core a theological challenge. The transformation of the "*Cur deus homo*" (as Anselm of Canterbury once reasoned) into the "*homo deus*" formulates this challenge. The understanding of humans as God's corresponding partners leads in another direction—of the relational character of human existence.

2. *Truth has its place in our "relevant relations" to God, the world, our fellow humans, and ourselves. Truth is relational in itself.*

Of course, human beings develop instrumental relationships to things in the world and partially even to other persons. God represents a relation to reality that transcends this instrumental perspective. Therefore, we speak about God's unavailability and his sacredness. By analogy, we learn to see this dimension also in our relation to the world, to other persons, and to ourselves. Hartmut Rosa, a German sociologist and philosopher, points out that our desire to reach out to the world in which we live is not fulfilled as long as we only intend to have power over things and persons. The basic mode of human existence is rather to resonate with or to be mutually responsive to them.[21] This resonance includes, according to Rosa, four central elements. The first is to be affected or touched by a person, but also by a landscape, a melody, and an idea. These persons or things are no longer only instrumental to us but move us internally and call for our reaction. The second element is our response. This has to be an answer; it is not only an echo, but it suggests also a kind of self-efficacy. My answer has to do with me as a person. It includes not only a verbal but also a bodily reaction, maybe in the form of laughter or tears. I myself form a part of the relations with others as with myself, with things, as with God. Resonance has to do with listening as well as being listened to or heard.

Rosa calls the third element transformation. There are several of such transformations. For example, we say that an encounter "made us a different person" and others created a temporary change, while many are in between. But in either case, the experience of resonance changes us, and, in this way, is a lively experience. The feeling of being unable to resonate, perhaps in periods of depression, may therefore lead to situations in which we feel cold or even dead, unrelated to the world around us, and even to ourselves. The fourth and last element has to do with these terrible, unhappy experiences of failing resonance. But it includes also the joyous cases of succeeding resonance. In both forms, we perceive that we have no control over the processes of affection, self-esteem, and transformation. We have to be open to the contingent and the unavailable because that is the risk of, but also the opportunity for resonance.[22]

Following Rosa as well as Bonhoeffer, we arrive at an understanding of relatedness that is not restricted to intersubjectivity but includes the relationship to the world as well as the experience of transcendence. A renewal of the relational understanding of human beings, including the reciprocal understanding of truth is timely. Physical proximity, personal and mutual exchange, in short, analogous communication, continues to be a precondition for the use of digital communication. Analogous communication should set the standard for digital

---

21. Hartmut Rosa, *Resonanz: Eine Soziologie der Weltbeziehung* (Berlin: Suhrkamp Verlag, [2016] 2019); Hartmut Rosa, *Unverfügbarkeit* (Wien-Salzburg: Residenz Verlag, 2019).

22. See the summary of Rosa himself in Rosa, *Unverfügbarkeit*, 38–45.

communication, not the other way around. And the rule should be that we do not publish information about other people and ourselves, about the world, and about God on the web that we would not express in direct communication.

3. *Truth is at stake in different speech situations. For them the difference between the public and the private is of great importance. Respect for truth can only be expected when this difference is taken into account.*

Is digital communication public or private? You may qualify e-mails as private, personal, or confidential, but the system does not guarantee that your messages stay private, personal or confidential. E-mails and other digital platforms are by definition public media; there is no specific space for privacy. The blind copy is one of the symbolic forms that renders privacy an illusion. But many people share issues on the web that belong to the secure realm of privacy. This information is used by the platforms themselves and their algorithms are used most effectively for economic and other purposes. Nowadays, the right to privacy is endangered not only by new forms of autocratic regimes but also by the self-harm of those who own the right to privacy. There is no legal sanction against this self-harm because it happens predictably with the free use of internet platforms or digital networks.

We may think that this is irrelevant compared to the positive fact that we are informed about important global events in real time. We may think that a great vision finally becomes real, namely the vision that was formulated for the first time by the (already mentioned) German philosopher Immanuel Kant, who, in 1795, expressed the hope that the time would come, in which the violation of basic rights in one part of the world would be perceived simultaneously by the rest of the world. Then, he added, the idea of a universal right for all humans on earth as world citizens would no longer be pretentious but would become real. Today, that is technically possible. But practically, this potential is also subject to abuse. As long as we use the web in a way that violates the rights of others as well as our own, then, the web is not yet an instrument for the promotion of the universal human rights of all citizens in the global village. The technological possibilities of our time are used as much to violate human rights as to make these violations known so that they can be overcome.

4. *Truth is not simply the correspondence between facts and statements but is a triple relationship between the real situation, the addressee with questions, and the answerer with propositions. Truth is embedded in reality.*

Even if we understand human existence as relational and responsive, we tend to interpret this relation as a correlation between two poles—facts and propositions, I and you. In the quest for a fuller relational understanding of truth, we should broaden this perspective to (at least) a triple relationship. In their search for truth, partners in dialogue, who (hopefully) have a common topic, should aim to understand reality in its complex character and not only to describe isolated facts correctly. One of the key words in Bonhoeffer's *Ethics* is the term "appropriateness to reality." The search for truth therefore should entail an understanding of reality that helps us to act responsibly within this reality. And different means may be used to accomplish that task, including, of course, the internet.

5. *Truth is related to a conflict-ridden world. To tell the truth means to unmask these conflicts in order to open the way to reconciliation. Truth aims for reconciliation.*

Through South Africa, the connection between "truth and reconciliation" became clear to the whole world, and it demonstrated that reconciliation is one of the most candid tasks set before us as human beings, especially as Christians. However, we do not simply have reconciliation before us as an answer to our non-reconciled world. We also have reconciliation behind us, present in Jesus Christ, through whom the divine reality entered our mundane reality. We know, therefore, that our reality includes not only conflict but also reconciliation. And we are committed to reconciliation because of the equal dignity of all those affected and in remembering the guilt of the past in order to contribute to a better future in which truth becomes a path to reconciliation.

Thus, we should realize that there is no reconciliation without repentance and self-critique, as well as the necessary steps to restore justice. In many parts of the world (including South Africa), corruption tends to devour the fruits of reconciliation. Corruption is indeed one of the most devastating means of denying the truth.

6. *Forgotten truth cannot be part of an open relationship. Forgotten truth cannot contribute to reconciliation. Therefore, it should be reckoned as part of the essence of truth that is remembered.*

For Christians in Germany, 2020 was the year of commemorating not only the death of Dietrich Bonhoeffer seventy-five years earlier on April 9, 1945, but also the trip to the abyss that ended one month after Bonhoeffer's death on May 8, 1945. Dietrich Bonhoeffer stood for another, a better Germany, and his legacy therefore became a source of inspiration and hope. But his own struggle as well as the struggles of his friends and of others could not precipitate the end of the nightmarish atrocities of the Nazi regime and the cruelties of a war that had started six years ago and resulted in the violent death of more than 50 million people. On the way to the memorial dates of April 9 and May 8 this year, we will come across the liberation dates of concentration camps, beginning with Auschwitz on January 27, followed among others by Buchenwald on April 11, and Flossenbürg on April 23, which, together with Schönberg, were the last stations of Bonhoeffer's earthly pilgrimage. As a commitment to his legacy, we know why truth has to be remembered because only then can truth contribute to a resounding, relational life in reconciliation and peace.

Chapter 4

GUILT, TRAUMA, RESILIENCE

TRANSGENERATIONAL ASPECTS IN THEOLOGY AND PSYCHOTHERAPY IN CONVERSATION WITH DIETRICH BONHOEFFER AND HANS JOACHIM IWAND

Anne-Katharina Neddens and Christian Neddens

Introduction

CN:[1] Using an interdisciplinary approach, we wish to draw attention to the importance of transgenerational processes, both in the theological thinking of Dietrich Bonhoeffer and Hans Joachim Iwand and in psychotherapeutic practice today, that is, in relation to guilt, trauma, and resilience.

AN: Pierre Janet, the French pioneer of trauma therapy, knew that those who do not recognize a trauma are forced to repeat or restage it—and so every generation needs its own trauma therapy. Attentiveness to the transgenerational power of guilt and trauma, but also of hidden resources of resilience, is indispensable in both individual and social psychology.

CN: We ask what do we want to pass on to the next generation? How much hurt, inequality, and resentment, but also what resources? What inner attitude in difficulties? What kind of freedom and responsibility? What passion and joy? How much willingness for self-criticism? What acts of atonement and reconciliation? And especially, what hope? A hope for God's creative action in a world come of age?

AN: Transgenerationality began to gain more attention in interdisciplinary *trauma* research, showing that traumatizing experiences of violence and injustice have consequences for upcoming generations, not only for the descendants of the victims but often for those of the offenders as well. Much less focus was given to the aspect of transgenerationality in the research on *resilience*. How can the transfer of faith and virtues affect later generations' inner resources for resilience? Our contribution brings insights from theology into an interdisciplinary conversation with findings from social and individual psychology as well as experiences of

---

1. To ensure that the different perspectives on the topic between medicine and theology are recognizable, the dialogue form has been retained. CN refers to Christian Neddens and AN refers to Anne-Katharina Neddens.

psychotherapeutic-psychosomatic practice in order to illuminate the processes of passing on guilt, trauma, and resilience. Interdisciplinarity is still quite an impassable terrain. Thus, paths of possible discoveries are paved here—in an exploratory way.

CN: Dietrich Bonhoeffer not only had great sensitivity for questions of transgenerational transmission of guilt and hope for the coming generation, but his theology was also interdisciplinary and took into account—although not always in a pronounced way—the psychological and psychiatric knowledge of his time, conveyed through his father Karl Bonhoeffer.[2] Additionally, Bonhoeffer became a key figure in German cultural memory and a symbol of collective resilience. The Remer Trial at the beginning of the 1950s and Hans Joachim Iwand, in particular, played a significant role in shaping that sensitivity. Later, Iwand pushed questions forward that Bonhoeffer left unanswered after his execution on April 9, 1945.[3]

Dietrich Bonhoeffer on Resilience and the "Perpetrator-Introject"

CN: At the end of his "After Ten Years," which he wrote in 1942 for his fellow conspirators, Bonhoeffer asks with shocking frankness whether he and his generation are "still of any use" in the new era. Are not even the victims and the resisters contaminated with the evil seed of Nazi terror? Are they not so internally destroyed that they are no longer useful to a new society?[4]

AN: Looking back on the dictatorship in Chile, Ariel Dorfman asks similarly, "When we leave tyranny behind, what do we do with the consequences of the tyranny that remain in the country and in the psyche and in the sex and in the body of the people themselves?"[5] Like Bonhoeffer, Ariel Dorfman speaks about the all-infecting power of evil deeds that shape societies for generations to come, about powers that invade body and mind and affect how people live together, trust, love, or misuse each other.

What and how Bonhoeffer wrote in 1942 seem to recall the theory of the "perpetrator introjects" that Sándor Ferenczi and Anna Freud employed in the

---

2. As professor of psychiatry and neurology from 1912 to 1938, Karl Bonhoeffer headed the clinic for mental and nervous conditions at the Berlin Charité.

3. Christian Neddens, "Hans Joachim Iwand und Dietrich Bonhoeffer: Kritische Theologen im Dienst der Bekennenden Kirche. Eine biographische und zeitgeschichtliche Skizze," in *Dietrich Bonhoeffer und Hans Joachim Iwand: Kritische Theologen im Dienst der Kirche*, ed. Michael Basse and Gerard den Hertog (Göttingen: Vandenhoeck & Ruprecht, 2017), 13–40.

4. DBWE 8:52.

5. Ariel Dorfman, cited from Elisabeth Lira, "Remembering: Passing Back through the Heart," in *Collective Memory of Political Events: Social Psychological Perspectives*, ed. James Pennebaker et al. (New York: Taylor & Francis, 1997), 232.

1930s.⁶ Those who experienced the abysses of psychological and physical violence through which perpetrators abuse their victims, penetrate their inner life, and destroy their psychological structures, often tend to freeze under the power of this experience, degrade themselves, feel guilty, or even become perpetrators themselves. In this way, the victims remain in the hands of the perpetrators even after the crimes have been committed.⁷

It should not be ignored also that perpetrators often emerge traumatized by their own actions in which they often enough unplanned and unintentionally "get involved," as studies among Vietnam veterans have made clear.⁸ Traumatization is a burden not only to victims and perpetrators but also to their children and grandchildren, as long-term studies have shown.⁹ In "After Ten Years," Bonhoeffer speaks about such transgenerational traumatization and about inner resistance against and sincerity with himself. Research on resilience and self-esteem of people with traumatic experiences is being conducted with increased interest in psychology, psychosomatics, and sociology.¹⁰ Compared with recent research results, Bonhoeffer's personal testimonies from prison shall be examined at this point to identify sources of resilience and their (possible) theological background.

Resistance and Surrender—Steps of Resilience in the Trauma of Imprisonment

CN: Bonhoeffer's letters and fragments from Tegel Prison reveal how he struggles to preserve his freedom, vitality, and activity. Bonhoeffer reads, works, and even tries to write literary texts.

---

6. Sándor Ferenczi, "Sprachverwirrung zwischen den Erwachsenen und dem Kind," *Internationale Zeitschrift für Psychoanalyse* 19 (1933): 5–15; Anna Freud, "Die Identifizierung mit dem Angreifer," in *Das Ich und die Abwehrmechanismen*, ed. Anna Freud (Wien: Internat. Psychoanalyt. Verlag, 1936), 125–39; Mathias Hirsch, "Zwei Arten der Identifikation mit dem Aggressor—nach Ferenczi und Anna Freud," *Praxis der Kinderpsychologie und Kinderpsychiatrie* 45 (1996): 198–205.

7. Angela Kühner, *Kollektive Traumata: Annahmen, Argumente, Konzepte. Eine Bestandsaufnahme nach dem 11. September*, Berghof-Report Nr. 9 (Berlin: Berghof-Forschungszentrum für Konstruktive Konfliktbearbeitung, 2003), 12–17, 37.

8. Robert Jay Lifton, *Home from War: Vietnam Veterans—Neither Victims nor Executioners* (New York: Simon & Schuster, 1973).

9. Dan Bar-On, *Legacy of Silence: Encounters with Children of the Third Reich* (Cambridge, MA: Harvard University Press, 1989).

10. What is meant is a resilience that presents itself simultaneously as responsibility and readiness to intervene—in contrast to a neoliberal type of resilience that focuses solely on adaptation. See, for the criticism, Thomas Gebauer, *Resilienz und neoliberale Eigenverantwortung*, www.medico.de/resilienz-neoliberale-eigenverantwortung-15984 (accessed August 15, 2020).

AN: Medical studies prove that to maintain adaptability and resistance in depressing situations and to preserve inner freedom, some central elements of resilience are required:

(1) stable, supportive relationships within the family and beyond,
(2) a realistically positive self-confidence marked by integrity and dignity,
(3) openness to the future,
(4) creative expression (e.g., through music, texts, pictures), and
(5) a realistic distinction between the possible and the impossible.[11]

CN: In Tegel, Bonhoeffer begins with two autobiographically tinted works—a drama and a novel. Both remain fragments. Bonhoeffer asks about his own roots from which he is suddenly cut off. He attempts to escape the loss of identity in the dehumanization of imprisonment and to bring to life a counter-reality. He writes to Eberhard Bethge, saying, "For me, this confrontation with the past, this attempt to hold on to it and to get it back, and above all the fear of losing it, is almost the daily background music of my life here."[12]

AN: The return to one's own stabilizing roots is an essential step in trauma therapy, as the following example from my own practice shows. A young, non-religious, severely addicted patient decided to have a tattoo hidden on his chest when he lost his beloved grandfather after he had already traumatically lost his parents, who were also non-religious, early in life. Asked what this tattoo [Albrecht Duerer's praying hands] meant to him at the beginning of the therapy, he only answered that it reminded him of his grandfather who would stand on the sideline of the football pitch and watch his grandchild with a rosary in his hand. In the course of therapy, he began to understand how much strength and courage this image of his grandfather gave him, as it provided him with a feeling of being connected to something "bigger" through the piety of his grandfather.

CN: Two of Bonhoeffer's ancestors in particular become points of reference in fictional alienation. First is his highly adored grandmother who opens both the drama and the novel. She stands for courage and for Christian identity in both fragments. She continues to go to church despite the pastor's gossip, and she introduces her grandchildren to the mystery of life and death. When the grandmother is called "the idol of all the grandchildren,"[13] this resonates well with the author's feelings about his own grandmother. The second ancestor in his novel is his great-grandfather, Provost Josias Brake, of whom he writes: "This old orthodox Lutheran pastor had been driven from his pulpit during the age of rationalism, and, when he defied the orders of the authorities and refused to

---

11. The American Psychological Association, *The Road to Resilience*, www.apa.org/helpcenter/road-resilience (accessed January 17, 2020).
12. *DBWE* 8:416. Cf. *DBWE* 7:64f.
13. Ibid., 80.

leave his congregation, he was thrown into prison."[14] It is obvious that Bonhoeffer identified with him in his own imprisonment.

AN: Not dissimilar to Bonhoeffer's literary method, the use of a "resource genogram" in trauma therapy can help to discover transgenerational resources, which are often themselves answers to an earlier generation to traumatization, and which can therefore be the result of *their* "posttraumatic growth."[15] A "resource genogram" aims to raise awareness of a positive "inner attitude" of the ancestors and helps one to adopt it personally, also in the religious-spiritual sense. Thus, the next generation often becomes the topic of therapy. Questions of spiritual legacy arise: "What was credible about what I received? What inner attitude do I want to convey and how can I do this?"

CN: Bonhoeffer's May 1944 letter on the baptism of his godchild, Dietrich Bethge, is an impressive example of the attempt to pass on transgenerational resilience.[16] Hardly any other text conveys Bonhoeffer's thought on the possibilities about future life as powerfully as this one. Self-confidence, piety, and responsibility of the family of origin play a central role, which for Bonhoeffer coincides with the question of restoration of the bourgeoisie from a Christian perspective.

The Remer Trial as Transgenerational Hub

CN: Perhaps Bonhoeffer foresaw that his resistance and his inner attitude in prison might become sources of resilience for an upcoming generation. The resisters had demonstrated that even in the most desperate times, there is still room for action—freedom, albeit limited, for which the individual is responsible. This was shown through the Remer Trial, which attracted widespread publicity in Western Germany because it led to a reassessment of the resistance of July 20, 1944, and thus paved a new path to deal with the past. Otto-Ernst Remer, Major General of the Wehrmacht, was involved in the suppression of the resistance. He was a cofounder of the extreme right-wing Sozialistische Reichspartei and described the resisters of July 20, 1944, as traitors, controlled from abroad. Remer thus did not represent an outsider position. In a survey conducted in 1951, only 38 percent of respondents rated the assassination attempt on Hitler in 1944 positively.[17] The sentence in the Remer Trial created decisive foundations for the anchoring of July 20, 1944, in the historical consciousness of the Federal Republic and changed the public opinion, as shown by a survey, nine months after the trial,

---

14. DBWE 7:87.
15. See Richard G. Tedeschi and Lawrence G. Calhoun, eds., *Trauma and Transformation: Growing in the Aftermath of Suffering* (Newbury Park: SAGE Publications, 1995).
16. DBWE 8:383–90.
17. Anna and Richard Merrit, eds., "Report No. 114, 5 Dec 1951," in *Public Opinion in Semisovereign Germany: The HICOG Surveys (1949–1955)* (Urbana, IL: University of Illinois Press, 1980), 147.

in which 58 percent of respondents indicated that the assassins were not traitors in their eyes.[18]

It was Hans Joachim Iwand who, together with Ernst Wolf, wrote the theological assessment for the trial on the question of whether there is a right of resistance. Like Bonhoeffer, Iwand was one of the formative figures in the *Bekennende Kirche*, and from 1935, head of the East Prussian Preachers' Seminary but at the same time, professor in Göttingen. During the Remer Trial, Iwand acknowledged that Bonhoeffer's resistance had raised a sign of genuine political responsibility.[19] For him, the decisive question was what the past meant for the present and the future. Iwand saw the resistance as a transgenerational source of civil engagement and a beacon of free responsibility. When Iwand took a decisive path of conversion and renewal of the Evangelical Church after 1945, he did so in memory of Bonhoeffer. His legacy became a transgenerational resource of "resilience" for theologians such as Iwand, or in other contexts, Beyers Naudé or John de Gruchy. In Iwand's case, one can certainly speak of "posttraumatic growth," because of his search for ways of spiritual, intellectual, and political renewal in postwar Germany.[20]

Transgenerationality of Guilt—Scarring, Reframing, and Signs of Atonement

Already at an early stage, Bonhoeffer and Iwand faced the confrontation with historical guilt. Bonhoeffer's draft for the Confessing Church at the end of 1940[21] or his unfinished draft of a pulpit pronouncement following the coup (probably from the end of 1942)[22] asserts, "Only in repentance and conversion can we be helped."[23] In the draft of the *Darmstädter Wort* in 1947, Iwand formulated this admission of guilt as a confession and called out the wrong paths of the church in a way that had never been done before in Germany. It was his deepest conviction that for healing to be possible in Germany this devastating trauma of suffering and guilt had to be treated.

AN: Social psychologist, Angela Kühner, notes that it is important for victims who feel complicit regarding their trauma to know who the community

---

18. "Report No. 167, 12 Jan 1953," *Public Opinion in Semisovereign Germany*, 198.

19. Herbert Kraus, ed., *Die im Braunschweiger Remerprozeß erstatteten moraltheologischen und historischen Gutachten nebst Urteil* (Hamburg: Girardet Verlag, 1953), 18.

20. Christian Neddens and Gerard den Hertog, eds., *Über das Zusammenleben in einer Welt: Grenzüberschreitende Anstöße Hans Joachim Iwands (1899-1960)* (Gütersloh: Gütersloher Verlagshaus, 2014).

21. *DBWE* 6:125–36.

22. *DBWE* 16:572–4.

23. Ibid., 573.

blames. Will the perpetrator or perpetrators be convicted? Is the guilt (publicly) acknowledged in some form? What is the public discourse about guilt?[24]

CN: Bonhoeffer and Iwand knew that an admission of guilt could be only a first step—not a final word, and also not reparation. What is explicitly shocking about historical guilt is that there is a "too late" moment there, as Iwand captions it, reading Eugen Kogon's "SS-Staat."[25] But what happens to historical guilt if one cannot "make up" for it? In this context, Bonhoeffer coins the term, "*Vernarbung*" ("scarring of guilt"). A scar closes the open wound but at the same time keeps it visible for all time. And it can tear up again. The question behind the scar metaphor is how a new generation can live with the reality that the war has created. Bonhoeffer thought that only the renunciation of an—impossible—*full* reparation of the injustice that had happened could interrupt revenge and make healing possible. The prerequisite for such a renunciation would be that scarring is made possible, which results from acts of renewal and conversion.[26]

AN: In my psychotherapeutic practice, I encounter patients who intentionally overwrite their wounds, thereby marking them visibly and at the same time placing them in a different context ("reframing").[27] This often finds visible expression in body tattoos as signs of remembrance and commemoration, which in a psychosomatic way contribute to the process of healing. One of my patients had her self-inflicted injuries overdrawn with a trending leaf tattoo. Again, another patient who showed recurring suicidal tendencies had "wwjd" [which stands for "What Would Jesus Do?"] on the inside of her wrist—a reminder not to touch her own life and to relate it to the exemplary life of Jesus.

CN: Talking about "scarring" would be cynical if it would not happen from the victims's perspective.[28] As Bonhoeffer makes clear in his unfinished draft, "The View from Below," only *they* can decide which ways of scarring are bearable for them.

After 1945, Iwand sought a concrete *encounter* with those who had suffered in order to find a new beginning by confessing guilt in the concrete interpersonal situation.[29] In all his efforts at reconciliation, he did not seek to absolve the perpetrators, but rather to let the victims have their say and possibly also justice, because only the victim can decide what is acceptable reparation, as Iwand writes in

---

24. See Kühner, *Kollektive Traumata*, 55.

25. Hans Joachim Iwand, "Ecce homo [A word about Eugen Kogon, Der SS-Staat]," *Die ZEIT*, August 14 (1947): 5, col. 1–3, 1.

26. DBWE 6:143: "To be sure, the guilt is not justified, not removed, not forgiven. It remains, but the wound that it inflicted is scarred over."

27. Nils Greve, "Reframing," in *Techniken der Psychotherapie: Ein methodenübergreifendes Kompendium*, ed. Wolfgang Senf et al. (Stuttgart: Georg Thieme Verlag, 2013), 101–3.

28. DBWE 8:52f.

29. See Hans Joachim Iwand, *Lecture at the Friedensrat in Berlin (East) 1956*, Tape Transcript, Bundesarchiv N 1528/50, 3.

a letter to Lothar Kreyssig with regard to his proposal of an *Aktion Sühnezeichen*.[30] Iwand believed that guilt must be called by name for the sake of those who suffer, so that it can scar. However, he also believed that by *only* accusing the guilty, no real renewal is possible either, because when the guilt is historical, in the irreparable sense, it is like a stone blocking the way. The question is who picks it up rather than pass by it?[31]

The Unexpected Turn

AN: Out of an apparently hopeless situation, a sometimes-surprising turnaround can occur in the therapeutic process, which changes the patient's self-perception and which is sometimes only recognized in retrospect in its full meaning. I remember two pictures painted at the beginning and end of the therapy with a woman who was severely abused as a child. She experienced herself as walled in— without hands to protect herself, without legs to run away, and without a head for consciousness (similar to a dissociative state that people take on in extremely stressful reliving of traumatic experiences). This changed in a very laborious process, in which times of stagnation were to be endured again and again. The last picture surprised the woman, who described herself as non-religious. In her self-portrait—still with a knife in her back—she now suddenly saw a hand coming toward her from the front, "something like . . . as if it could come from heaven," she said.[32]

In my therapeutic work, I have experienced this astonishing phenomenon, namely that in seemingly hopeless therapy processes, something suddenly and unexpectedly opens up. This "unexpected turn," about which there is hardly any literature available to date, seems to me to be a core element of therapeutic work.

CN: Calculating based on an unexpected turn of events played an immense role in Bonhoeffer's and Iwand's lives. Both were convinced that God would create anew. They waited for God's action through his creative word, without idly folding their hands. Even though imprisoned in Tegel and despite his conviction about a non-religious interpretation of biblical concepts and images of God, Bonhoeffer held steadfastly to the idea of an acting, creative God:

> In view of what is coming, I'm almost inclined to quote the biblical δει . . . and feel something of the "longing" of the angels in 1 Pet 1:12, to see how God will

---

30. Letter to Josef Hormádka on June 8, 1959, cited in Jürgen Seim, *Hans Joachim Iwand: Eine Biografie* (Gütersloh: Kaiser Verlag, 1999), 551f.

31. Hans Joachim Iwand, "Antwort: Ein Brief an J. L. Hromádka (1959)," in *Frieden mit dem Osten*, ed. Gerard den Hertog (München: Kaiser, 1988), 199–217, 201.

32. On the frequently neglected perception of religious-spiritual expressions in the therapeutic process, see Norbert Mönter, Andreas Heinz, and Michael Utsch, *Religionssensible Psychotherapie und Psychiatrie* (Stuttgart: Kohlhammer, 2020).

go about solving what seems beyond any solution. I think it has now come to the point where God will arise and accomplish something that we, despite our inner and outer involvement, can only take in with the greatest astonishment and awe. Somehow it will be made plain—for those with eyes to see.[33]

Bonhoeffer and Iwand made a distinction between the penultimate and the ultimate, the second last and the last, between human will and divine action. By so doing, they were able to endure the "unredeemedness" that they experienced and confidently committed themselves to the judgment of God.[34]

AN: To give hope a chance, a trusting therapeutic relationship is crucial.[35] Based on a Christian view of humanity, the patient's spiritual realm is the space where the patient's very own integrity has been violated. At the same time, it is the place where healing can be experienced. During the therapeutic process, the therapist often feels the inner transformation in his or her own inner resonance space. It is as if one enters—one may say—a sacred inner space within a person.

CN: In an early, unpublished lecture, Iwand describes the way to the other as the way to a saint, "adoring and humble," like Anna coming to Mary who conceived by the Spirit of God.[36] Healing only happens in that kind of being-with-others as with saints. In the patience of others, the turnaround becomes possible. I can approach the painful points of life without being injured again. It is nothing other than that I walk those paths holding God's hand, which I otherwise wander through alone, Iwand says. It is only the act of being with the other that turns everything around. God is here, who wants to condemn (Rom. 8:33f.)?[37]

Vicarious: Perceiving, Holding, Naming, and Hoping

CN: For Bonhoeffer, vicarious action is the irreplaceable core in the commitment to or for other people. His motive is the vicarious devotion of Jesus, which makes Jesus perceive, carry, pray, and hope for others.[38]

---

33. DBWE 8:361.

34. See Hans Joachim Iwand, "Meditation über Röm 5,1–11 (1942)," in *Predigtmeditationen, Zweite Folge* (Göttingen: Vandenhoeck & Ruprecht, 1955), 107.

35. See Robert Elliott et al., "Empathy," in *Psychotherapy Relationships that Work: Therapist Contributions and Responsiveness to Patients*, ed. John C. Norcross (New York: Oxford University Press, 2011), 132–52.

36. Hans Joachim Iwand, *Der Weg zum Anderen (1929)*, Bundesarchiv Koblenz, N 1528/268, transcribed by Arnold Wiebel, https://theologie.uni-greifswald.de/storages/uni-greifswald/fakultaet/theologie/ls-sys/Unpublizierte_Quellen/H_J__Iwand_Der_Weg_zum_Anderen.pdf (accessed August 16, 2020), 12f.

37. Iwand, *Der Weg zum Anderen*, 15.

38. DBWE 6:254–9.

AN: In the therapeutic process, there is this vicarious standing up for the other person, too. Four aspects of vicarious action in the therapeutic conversation can be named, which Bonhoeffer also mentions at various points. First, there is the *perceiving* of an activity "of love for the real human being" that "soberly and simply does what is in accord with reality."[39]

Second, there is the *holding* of the other person in the presence of the conversation, which can be seen as *carrying,* that is, to bear the pain with and for your neighbor without there being a solution, a way out or an escape door.[40] Indeed, enduring the pain of the other person can be unbearable for the therapist because it can mean being led into the deepest chambers of suffering and being given roles that may trigger strong defensive reactions within the therapist. Third, it can become necessary to vicariously *name* the pain, the injury, and the perpetrators— to give a name to the "inexpressible" is vicarious for the patient.[41] The fourth aspect concerns vicarious *hope*. Johann Cullberg had pointed out already in the 1970s that the therapist's vicarious hope is a decisive salutogenetic factor for the patient.[42]

CN: For Bonhoeffer, hope is the engine of a faith coming from Easter.[43] Bonhoeffer's *Discipleship* aims at the hope for God's action, which compasses the future and the present.[44] How much the Christian hope is a vicarious hope that also hopes for the coming generations is already made clear in Bonhoeffer's "Baptismal Letter." After 1945, Iwand also rediscovered the power of *hope* for the Christian life and for shaping society. And he describes hope as the opening of a space in which people can live in the righteousness of God.[45]

---

39. Ibid., 238.

40. *DBWE* 4:90: "Suffering must be borne in order for it to pass. . . . God is a God who bears. The Son of God bore our flesh. He therefore bore the cross. He bore all our sins and attained reconciliation by his bearing. That is why disciples are called to bear what is put on them." Iwand was skeptical about Bonhoeffer's ethics of vicarism. Unlike Bonhoeffer, Iwand did not see the church as God's representative. See Hans Joachim Iwand, *Nachgelassene Werke 6: Briefe an Rudolf Hermann*, ed. Helmut Gollwitzer et al. (Gütersloh: Gütersloher Verlagshaus, 2000), 59.

41. Taking the example of the plea for one's enemy, Bonhoeffer describes the dynamics of vicarious naming: "In prayer we go to our enemies, to stand at their side. . . . Now we are taking up their neediness and poverty, their being guilty and lost, and interceding for them before God. We are doing for them in vicarious representative action what they cannot do for themselves" (*DBWE* 4:140).

42. Johann Cullberg, "Krisen und Krisenbewältigung," in *Psychiatrische Praxis* 5 (1978): 25–34. Cf. Chris Feudtner, "Hope and the Prospects of Healing at the End of Life," *Journal of Alternative and Complementary Medicine* 11 (2005): 23–30.

43. *DBWE* 8:49: "What is so liberating about Good Friday and Easter is the fact that our thoughts are pulled far beyond our personal circumstances to the ultimate meaning of all life, suffering, and indeed everything that happens, and this gives us great hope."

44. *DBWE* 4:286f.

45. Hans Joachim Iwand, *Nachgelassene Werke 4: Gesetz und Evangelium*, ed. Walter Kreck (Gütersloh: Gütersloher Verlagshaus, 2000), 117f.

A Coming Generation

The last verse of the Old Testament says, "And he will turn the hearts of fathers to their children and the hearts of children to their fathers" (Mal. 3:24). What could it mean for us, based on Bonhoeffer's concept of being "useful" or Malachi's being "turned" to the next generation? I believe that it is more important than ever to pass on trust—to hope in God's action in our "mature world," which also is vicarious for those who can no longer hope.

AN: I believe that we must not become tired of *asking* the coming generation, what is helpful to you? What spiritual and intellectual resources do you need to meet the challenges of your time? I believe that acts of atonement for the next generation, the children, and their descendants, can bring great comfort. They can promote a sense of deep humanity and "co-responsibility" and a "shared guilt" that supports future action by remembering the past. This makes inner healing possible in terms of not only tangible goals of psychotherapy but also a responsible, sustainable shaping of the future for the coming generations.

An example from my therapeutic practice will illustrate this. Many older patients experience the care for their grandchildren as a compensation and reconciliation for their own or their children's failures. A seventy-five-year-old patient painted two pictures during the therapeutic process—first a withered then a fruitful tree, and described them as follows:

> I used to think that I was completely useless, if not harmful, for my descendants: bad roots, dead branches, no fruits. The most important realization of my life was that it is precisely these my children and grandchildren "from my trunk" with their warmth and love that hold me. They are the ones who keep me alive and for whom I want to live. To know this fills me with gratitude.

Chapter 5

FACING THE PAST, TAKING RESPONSIBILITY FOR A COMING GENERATION

THE LEGACY OF BONHOEFFER'S TWO "TESTAMENTS"[1]

Gerard den Hertog

Introduction

On the first page of "After Ten Years," which Bonhoeffer wrote for his fellow conspirators, Eberhard Bethge, Hans von Dohnanyi, and Hans Oster, and handed over to them by Christmas of 1942,[2] he clearly expresses the relation between *what* was learned and *how* this specific knowledge was acquired: "Indeed, the insights and experiences we have gained and of which we subsequently become aware are only abstractions from reality, from life itself. Yet just as the ability to forget is a gift of grace, so similarly is memory, the repetition of received teachings, part of responsible life."[3]

The last words in this quote refer to what ethics, in Bonhoeffer's view, is about—responsible life. In the paragraph on "Success," he writes, "The ultimately responsible question is . . . how . . . a coming generation is to go on living."[4] Again, the word "responsible" is here linked with "coming generation." First, this link is not atypical, since the choice of "responsibility" as a key term shows that Bonhoeffer frames "reality" in dialogical terms. So, "responsible life" in itself directs our thoughts to the perspective of the generations. It is therefore no wonder that he adds a few lines thereafter, "The younger generation will always have the surest sense whether an action is done merely in terms of principle or from living responsibly, for it is their future that is at stake."[5] Again, this shows that Bonhoeffer writes here from the perspective of the relation between generations. Remarkable in this respect

---

1. The "Two Testaments" are Dietrich Bonhoeffer, "After Ten Years," in *DBWE* 8:37–52 and "Thoughts on the Day of Baptism of Dietrich Wilhelm Rüdiger Bethge," in *DBWE* 8:383–90.
2. *DBWE* 8:37 n.1.
3. Ibid., 37.
4. Ibid., 42.
5. Ibid.

also is the question with which Bonhoeffer concludes "After Ten Years," "Are we still of use?"[6] The question points to the possibility that a certain generation may no longer be fitting to serve in a new time. Here, we read the awkward and moving statements, "We have become cunning and learned the arts of obfuscation and equivocal speech. Experience had rendered us suspicious of human beings, and often we have failed to speak to them a true and open word."[7]

I have offered some details to show how typical the generational perspective is for Bonhoeffer's "After Ten Years," which of course is superfluous, compared to the other "testament" he wrote in the last years of his life, that is, "Thoughts on the Day of Baptism of Dietrich Rüdiger Wilhelm Bethge." So, the question is what makes the relation between the generations so special that it provides an ethical perspective? In the same period of time in which he conceived the "Baptismal Letter," Bonhoeffer wrote to his nephew Hans-Walter Schleicher, who was serving in the military. Bonhoeffer asked him various questions, such as how he experienced life among his fellow soldiers. What did the other soldiers think, and what did they believe? He openly asked his nephew whether his upbringing at home helped him or hindered him from finding his own way. But then he concludes, "After all, the most important question for the future is how we are going to find a basis for living together with other people, what spiritual realities and rules we honor as the foundations for a meaningful human life."[8] Again, the fluent and natural transition from the family perspective to facing the future is remarkable.

Before I take a closer look at the "Two Testaments" (i.e., "After Ten Years"[9] and "Baptismal Letter"),[10] I will briefly consider the concept of generation in Bonhoeffer's other work of that period. When we read Bonhoeffer's letters from prison with "Baptismal Letter" in mind, we find several similar passages that clarify and support his view on the significance of the family, such as in the already mentioned letter to Hans-Walter Schleicher. I restrict this discussion, however, to one letter. On November 18, 1943, Bonhoeffer wrote to Bethge for the first time since his imprisonment, uncensored! And he understandably had a lot to tell. He blamed himself for not having finished his *Ethics*, expressed his longing to share the Lord's Supper with Bethge, mentioned having read the Old Testament two and a half times besides his daily Bible study, and writing an essay on "the sense of time." "Then I began a bold undertaking that I have long had in mind: I began to write the story of a middle-class [bürgerlich] family of our time," which is meant by him as "in brief—a rehabilitation of the bourgeoisie as we know it in our families, and precisely from a Christian perspective."[11] The fact that Bonhoeffer wrote a drama and a play in which the relation between the generations is the

---

6. Ibid., 52.
7. Ibid.
8. Ibid., 409.
9. Ibid., 37–52.
10. Ibid., 383–90.
11. Ibid., 181–2.

core theme shows that this perspective was very real to him. So, there is no question that when Bonhoeffer claims that the novel he worked on was meant as "a rehabilitation of the bourgeoisie as we know it in our families,"[12] we do well to probe the significance of the generation perspective, to look also into the *Fiction from Tegel Prison*, the novel and the drama, and the poetry of course, of which I mention here only *The Death of Moses* of September 1944.[13] These references are enough to show that the generation perspective was very important and present in the prison period, which implies that it is worthwhile to see where and how it sealed his line of thought.

Generation and "Telling the Truth"

In the same letter of November 18, 1943, to Bethge, Bonhoeffer, after mentioning his fiction work, confirms that he is writing an essay on the subject, "What Does It Mean to Tell the Truth?"[14] When Bonhoeffer first mentions this paper in his letter to Bethge, he adds, "and at the moment I am attempting to write prayers for prisoners."[15] This direct sequence suggests that Bonhoeffer's unfinished essay on telling the truth is just about the interviews, about how to justify hiding the truth from the interrogators in order to survive and to give the long-planned attack on Hitler a chance. However, a reading of "What Does It Mean to Tell the Truth?" shows that the interrogations and the conspiracy are definitely not the central theme and even hardly a theme at all. There are no signs in the text itself of wrestling with his conscience or of an attempt at self-justification. The line of thought goes deeper and is about living and walking in the truth.

In his letter of December 5, 1943, to Bethge, Bonhoeffer gives a clear hint about how to interpret his essay: "By the way: 'telling the truth' (about which I wrote an essay) means, in my opinion, to say how something is in reality, that is, with respect for mystery, for trust, for hiddenness. . . . What is concealed may be revealed only in confession, namely, before God."[16] Ten days later, he refers to this essay for the third and last time in his letters and stresses that "telling the truth" is primarily about "the real as it is in God."[17] So, for Bonhoeffer the purpose of writing this letter is to discover what really is at stake in life, or even more basically, what reality is like.

The interpretative hint is confirmed while reading Bonhoeffer's essay. He writes, "Since it is the case, however, that the ethical cannot be detached from reality, the ever-greater capacity to perceive reality is a necessary component of

12. Ibid., 182.
13. Ibid., 531–41.
14. Ibid., 182.
15. Ibid.
16. Ibid., 216.
17. Ibid., 223.

ethical action."[18] Here we find the central theme of his *Ethics*, the first written draft of which was titled: "Christ, Reality, and Good."[19] The question of what the *topos* of "reality" in ethics is and how we deal with it is therefore a central issue. If telling the truth is about finding the entry into reality, then, in his essay, Bonhoeffer does not deal with a particular theme in ethics, but with a basic question of ethics, and from the perspective that "action consists in speaking. What is real is to be expressed in words."[20] In this context, Bonhoeffer speaks about "the living truth between persons."[21]

Bonhoeffer here, as in his *Ethics*, observes and approaches life from the perspective of the orders or mandates, which implies that the word in the family setting is different from the word in the business or public space. Telling the truth is learned through basic upbringing, especially within the family and through intergenerational relationships. It is telling that Bonhoeffer opens his essay by referring to childhood: "From the moment in our lives in which we become capable of speech, we are taught that our words must be true."[22] The child learns to be sincere and open, and not conceal anything. This, however, does not imply that being genuine on the part of the parents is the same the other way around, since the responsibilities differ. The responsibility of the parents is to perform their obligation to the child, which means they have to determine what they do or do not communicate to their child, and most of all, how and why they "tell the truth." From the perspective of this specific relationship, Bonhoeffer approaches other realms of responsibility. What counts here is that it is "pedagogically . . . of the very greatest importance that in some way . . . the parents clarify . . . the differences between these circles of life to their child and make his or her responsibilities understandable."[23] The extent to which the generation perspective here determines his line of thought appears on the very last page of the essay where Bonhoeffer returns to the most authentic and inalienable responsibility of the parents and stresses that "broad judgments as to character fall not to the teacher but to the parents."[24]

We therefore may conclude that Bonhoeffer does not merely deal with a subtheme of *Ethics* or raise a viewpoint he had not yet elaborated on, but rather he refers to ethics from a specific perspective. It is obvious that for Bonhoeffer ethics is about the quest for what is real, that which is learned in everyday life in the family, in the relations between the generations. We should acknowledge that by then the war was nearing its end and that the question of how Germany

---

18. Dietrich Bonhoeffer, "Fragment of an Essay: What Does It Mean to Tell the Truth?," in *DBWE* 16:603.
19. *DBWE* 6:47–75.
20. *DBWE* 16:603.
21. Ibid., 604.
22. Ibid., 601.
23. Ibid., 603.
24. Ibid., 608. Cf. "The family has its own secret that it must keep"; Ibid., 605.

could and should be rebuilt spiritually was pressing. How should the soldiers afterward face their deeds, how would the Hitler Youth find a new perspective, and how should a nation confront itself with the reality of its guilt-laden past, that is, of its reality before God and men? Telling the truth is intrinsically connected with "the ever-greater capacity to perceive reality."[25] In this respect, Bonhoeffer writes:

> What matters is the "right word" for any given circumstance. To discover this is a matter of long, earnest, and continual effort that is based in experience and the perception of reality. In order to say that something is real—i.e., to speak truthfully—one's gaze and thought must be oriented toward how the real is in God, and through God, and toward God.[26]

A similar attitude can be discerned in Bonhoeffer's letter of August 21, 1944, to Eberhard Bethge in which he writes: "We must immerse ourselves again and again, for a long time and quite calmly, in Jesus's life, his saying, actions, suffering, and dying in order to recognize what God promises and fulfills."[27]

Meditation, Worldly Interpretation, and Ethics

The emphasis on "long," "intensely," and/or "quietly" listening and going into is not new in Bonhoeffer's letters. It is already present in his well-known letter about reading the Bible to Rüdiger Schleicher from April 8, 1936,[28] and this emphasis on the Scripture indeed was a specific characteristic of the meditation practice in the seminaries. Here, it appears again, but not in the sense of listening to the Word of God or to the Bible, but to the reality of the life of Jesus—of his saying, actions, suffering, and dying. Of course, we do know the reality of the history of Jesus Christ only from the Bible. It is nevertheless and precisely for this reason that Bonhoeffer expresses himself so strikingly – and at a time the idea of the non-religious interpretation of the Bible in its evidentiality had become clear to him. On July 16, 1944, he writes to Bethge:

> The Bible directs people toward the powerlessness and the suffering of God; only the suffering God can help. To this extent, one may say that the previously described development toward the world's coming of age, which has cleared the way by eliminating a false notion of God, frees us to see the God of the Bible,

---

25. Ibid., 603.
26. Ibid., 607. Also cf. ibid.: "Our word in union with the Word of God is intended to express what is real, as it is in God, and our silence is to be a sign of the boundary drown around the word by what is real, as it is in God."
27. *DBWE* 8:515.
28. *DBWE* 14:166–9.

who gains ground and power in the world by being powerless. This will probably be the starting point for our "worldly interpretation."[29]

The "non-religious interpretation" therefore is a "No" to a false infancy, for on the cross, Christ did not only reconcile us with God but also gave us our responsibility back. "Worldly interpretation" and "coming of age" then do not mean that we leave God or that the "expulsion of God from the world,"[30] as it has become the feature and the "discrediting of religion"[31] is completed. On the contrary, God is recalled from the "edges" of life to its "center," or more correctly, God is found there, where He has always been in Jesus Christ, and from where He fills and determines reality. The "worldly" or "non-religious" interpretation stems from a deep and thorough going into the life, the suffering, and dying of Jesus, and right there it is ultimately about "what God promises and fulfills." He does not as merely a *deus ex machina* manifest Himself in filling the gaps in our lives, but He "waits for and responds to sincere prayer and responsible actions."[32]

Generation and Organization

"You are the first of a new generation in our family."[33] With this opening statement of Bonhoeffer's "Baptismal Letter," the generational perspective is clearly framed.[34] Then Bonhoeffer, together with his young nephew, looks back on the "three houses with which your life is, and [should] remain, inseparably linked,"[35] and is the first to mention the parsonage on the countryside where Eberhard Bethge had grown up. Later in the text, Bonhoeffer contrasts it with city life in the metropoles. He praises the "communal and varied intellectual life" in a village vicarage with its "enduring earthly values."[36] It is unsurprising that a few pages later, Bonhoeffer adds, "I would wish you could grow up in the country."[37] However, he recognizes at once that that would not be the same world in which the little Dietrich's father, Eberhard Bethge, grew up.

I will omit the reflections of Bonhoeffer on the difference between the metropole and the countryside, which follow and return to a rather isolated thesis that

---

29. *DBWE* 8:479f.
30. "Notes I, Tegel, July–August 1944," in *DBWE* 8:490.
31. Ibid.
32. *DBWE* 8:46.
33. Ibid., 383.
34. Cf. what Bonhoeffer writes on February 5, 1944, to Eberhard Bethge, after receiving the message that Bethge's son Dietrich was born: "I realized you've pushed our family into the next generation" (Ibid., 290).
35. Ibid., 384.
36. Ibid.
37. Ibid., 385.

precedes it: "The time when children arrogantly broke away from their parents will be past. The home will draw children back to their parents' care; it will be their refuge where they find counsel, calm, and clarity."[38] What specifically did Bonhoeffer have in mind here? His *Ethics* contains a paragraph, "Natural Life," in which he not only safeguards life from the domination of Nazi ideology but also develops his own new thoughts aimed at renewing Christian ethics by denouncing the wrong view of nature and grace. In the totalitarian society of the Third Reich, the Nazis, in their effort to have a total grip on the life of the people, tried to set up children against their parents, encouraging them to report their parents if they did not proclaim and follow Nazi ideology. Bonhoeffer notes that this was controlled or organized and far from being spontaneous, whereas respect for parents goes without saying.[39] It is remarkable also that the words "organization" and "to organize" feature prominently in his "Baptismal Letter." He speaks about "the bureaucratic organization of almost all aspects of life,"[40] as a characteristic of life in the metropoles, and contrasts it, saying, "Nevertheless, in this time of change, they will gain form having a plot of land under their feet from which to draw strength for a new, simpler, more natural and contented life of daily work and evening leisure."[41] Though Bonhoeffer was aware that rural life should not be idealized romantically and nostalgically, it is clear that he observed the conditions there as fitting for the spiritual rebuilding of Germany.

Bonhoeffer returns to this word "organization/to organize" in the last and most well-known part of "Baptismal Letter." He asks, "Are we moving toward an age of colossal organizations and collective institutions, or will the desire of innumerable people for small, manageable, personal relationships be satisfied?"[42] This seems to be a rhetorical question, but it is not. Again, "Does the one have to exclude the other? Isn't it conceivable that it is precisely the vast scale of world organizations that allow more room for life at the personal level?"[43] Bonhoeffer obviously rejects the nostalgic longing for the past and does not ignore organizations as such, but his main interest is "life at the personal level."

Bonhoeffer addresses Dietrich Bethge directly thus, "You are being baptized today as a Christian. All those great and ancient words of the Christian proclamation will be pronounced over you, and the command of Jesus Christ to baptize will be carried out, without your understanding any of it."[44] Bonhoeffer definitely does not refer to what he then recently characterized as "religion" with those "great and ancient words." No, what I call the generation perspective returns when Bonhoeffer asserts that he and his generation including the young Dietrich Bethge

---

38. Ibid.
39. Cf. ibid., 177.
40. Ibid., 386.
41. Ibid.
42. Ibid., 388.
43. Ibid.
44. Ibid., 389.

are "being thrown back all the way to the beginnings of our understanding."[45] And then he mentions a list of biblical words and theological terms that have grown to be unintelligible, such as "reconciliation and redemption . . . rebirth and Holy Spirit, love for one's enemies, cross and resurrection, what it means to live in Christ and to follow Christ, all that is so difficult and remote that we hardly dare speak of it anymore."[46] Although, with the remarkable exception of "rebirth," these are other words that Bonhoeffer mentions besides those in his letter of some weeks earlier, on May 5, 1944, to Eberhard Bethge[47]. He points again to the very heart of the Christian tradition, saying, "At the moment I am thinking about how the concepts of repentance, faith, justification, rebirth, and sanctification should be interpreted in a 'wordly' way."[48]

Why is a "wordly interpretation" so urgently required? The problem, according to Bonhoeffer, is that we sense in "these words and actions handed down to us . . . something totally new and revolutionary," which "we cannot yet grasp . . . and express."[49] It should be noted that Bonhoeffer traces the "totally new and revolutionary" to "the great and ancient words" of the Christian tradition. However, it remains a question of "sensing," and we recognize the language of the mystery as well as the difficulty of finding words, which formed the theme of the letter on telling the truth. Bonhoeffer illustrates his thoughts by contrasting them with the wandering course of the Confessing Church. There were times she stood firm and confessed clearly and courageously, but there were also moments of blindness to the truth, of compromise, and even cowardice—of not opening her mouth on behalf of the mute. His complaint is that the church "has been fighting during these years only for its self-preservation, as if that were an end in itself. It has become incapable of bringing the word of reconciliation and redemption to humankind and to the world."[50] A church that loses itself in the struggle against time is per definition a church that is lost in "organizing," in trying to get things in control by means of confession, order, structure, and with the consequence that "the words we used before must lose their power." There *is* however an alternative—"prayer and doing justice among human beings."[51] Instead of making efforts at self-preservation, the church should prepare the way of the Lord, which Bonhoeffer had in mind as part of the title of his *Ethics*: "Preparing the Way (*Wegbereitung*) and Entering in."[52] Preparing the Way, however, does not at all imply ignoring all well-reflected action. Bonhoeffer stresses, "All Christian thinking, talking and organizing must

---

45. Ibid.
46. Ibid.
47. Cf. also Bonhoeffer, *Ethics*, 131, where Bonhoeffer, in a context in which he clearly deals with Nazi Germany, mentions "the miracle of a new awakening of faith" as the first thing that "can prevent the final fall into the abyss."
48. Ibid., 373.
49. Ibid., 389.
50. Ibid.
51. Ibid.
52. *DBWE* 16:79.

be born anew, out of that prayer and action."⁵³ This is not organizing in the sense of getting a grip on, but having ourselves renewed.⁵⁴ Bonhoeffer continues the theme of organizing and sees in relation to the church, "every attempt to help it develop prematurely into a powerful organization will only delay its conversion [*Umkehr*] and purification."⁵⁵ The link between "power" and "organization" is striking. When we consider that "[h]uman religiosity directs people in need to the power of God in the world, God as *deus ex machina*," this is exactly the flaw of religion; as such, "only the suffering God can help."⁵⁶ Preparing the way is, therefore, waiting for God, who does not fill the gaps in our lives as a *deus ex machina*, and direct ourselves in penitence and conversion to purification and renewal. In "Baptismal Letter," Bonhoeffer puts it this way:

> It is not for us to predict the day—but the day will come—when people once more will be called to speak the word of God in such a way that the world is changed and renewed. It will be in an new language, perhaps quite nonreligious language, but liberating and redeeming like Jesus's language, so that people will be alarmed and yet overcome by its power—the language of a new righteousness and truth, an language proclaiming that God makes peace with humankind and that God's kingdom is drawing near.⁵⁷

Non-religious Interpretation as Preparing the Way

"After Ten Years" ended with the question of whether Bonhoeffer and his fellow conspirators were still "of use." The concept of generation, which Bonhoeffer had addressed already in this memorandum, receives much urgency here. The "Baptismal Letter" led to the firm hope that the day would come when not just the young Dietrich Bethge but also Bonhoeffer and his generation, who are "being thrown back all the way to the beginnings of [their] understanding,"⁵⁸ can be once more witnesses of the reconciliation and the peace of God with humankind.

---

53. *DBWE* 8:389.

54. Cf. Dietrich Bonhoeffer, "Outline for a Book," in *DBWE* 8:500, "Nature used to be conquered by the soul; with us it is conquered through technological organization of all kinds. What is unmediated for us, what is given, is no longer nature but organization. But with this protection from the menace of nature, a new threat to life is created in turn, namely, through organization itself. Now the power of the soul is lacking! The question is: What will protect us from the menace of organization? The human being is thrown back on his own resources. He has learned to cope with everything except himself. He can insure himself against everything but other human beings. In the end it all comes down to the human being."

55. *DBWE* 8:389f.

56. Ibid., 479.

57. Ibid., 390.

58. Ibid., 389.

Bonhoeffer's firm conviction that the day would come "when people once more will be called to speak the word of God in such a way that the world is changed and renewed" was the hope of a kind of revival in which the generations would face their past and seek a way into the future in repentance and conversion.[59] How does this hope relate to non-religious interpretation? Interestingly, that hope of revival does not emerge only in "Baptismal Letter"; it already appears in the letter of March 27, 1944, to Eberhard Bethge. In this letter, which anticipates the non-religious interpretation, Bonhoeffer contrasts "manag[ing] of dying," either in a "religious" or an agnostic way, with "liv[ing] in the light of the resurrection"[60] of Jesus Christ. Bonhoeffer, furthermore, notes that Easter means that "a new and cleansing wind can blow through our present world,"[61] and with it the power of God's new life. Thus, "If a few people really believed this and were guided by it in their earthly actions, a great deal would change."[62] Bonhoeffer also notes that by the springtime of 1944, the people around him had begun to realize that the defeat of Germany was imminent, and they had become disoriented. He however interprets this positively in the light of Easter: "Unconsciously people are waiting for the word that will unbind them and set them free. But the time probably hasn't yet come when it can be heard. Yet it will come, and perhaps this Easter is one of our last great opportunities to get ready for our future task."[63]

Here, we also hear a word of hope, but with other adjectives than in "Baptismal Letter." However, the terms "unbinding" and "setting free" by no means contrast with "reconciliation and redemption." Rather, they are complementary and enriching. Together they provoke images that inspire and color hope. An awakening such as the one Bonhoeffer looks forward to here is no natural phenomenon that just comes to us fortuitously, neither is it a "religious" ecstasy that takes hold of people's "natural" emotions and feelings, and drags them along—just as National Socialism definitely *also was* a kind of awakening! But it is the new life that comes from the word of God and contains the promise of its power. Therefore, it is crucial that people prepare themselves to proclaim this word. Bonhoeffer obviously counts Bethge among those who are called to do so.

In the same period he wrote "Baptismal Letter," Bonhoeffer started to write on the non-religious interpretation of the Bible and the Gospel, which can be understood as part of the preparation "for our future task." Such secular interpretation aims

---

59. See Heinz Eduard Tödt, "The Disquieting Legacy: Characteristics of Dietrich Bonhoeffer's Theology," in idem., *Authentic Faith: Bonhoeffer's Theological Ethics in Context*, ed. Albert Scharffenorth, trans. David Stassen and Ilse Tödt (Grand Rapids, MI: Eerdmans 2007), 21; idem., "Dealing with Guilt in the Church's Confession and in the Justice System after 1945," in Heinz Eduard Tödt, *Authentic Faith: Bonhoeffer's Theological Ethics in Context*, 249.

60. DBWE 8:333.
61. Ibid.
62. Ibid.
63. Ibid.

at liberating the German society deeply ruined by Nazi ideology and practices from its threatening silence, and opening space for conversation between the generations on what it means to reach out in confession and contrition to the "new and cleansing wind" that blows from Easter into our present world. So, the focus of the non-religious interpretation is definitely not a once and for all farewell to the "great and ancient words" of the Christian tradition. On the contrary, it entails reading the Bible and reality simultaneously in such a way that no "religion" is in between, let alone required, since we "believe in such a way that our lives depend on it."[64]

---

64. Bonhoeffer, "Outline for a Book," in *DBWE* 8:502.

Chapter 6

IN THE WAKE

READING BONHOEFFER AT THE DOOR OF NO RETURN

Reggie L. Williams

Introduction

In 2014, I published a research project on Dietrich Bonhoeffer titled *Bonhoeffer's Black Jesus: Harlem Renaissance Theology and an Ethic of Resistance*, in which I examined critical faith developments that occurred in him as a direct result of his year of postgraduate study in Harlem, New York, in 1930–1. During his time in Harlem, the global Great Depression was ravishing New York. He was a lay leader at the singularly influential Abyssinian Baptist Church, teaching Sunday school to boys and midweek Bible study to women of the church while, simultaneously, the watershed diasporic Black movement that we know today by the name "Harlem Renaissance" was making its indelible mark on history from that same space. Bonhoeffer was there, in New York, finishing his student years amid the convergence of these major historical moments. He was still quite young in 1930–1 (he turned twenty-five in February 1931), and it is apparent that his stay in the United States had a measurable impact on his later resistance to the Nazis.

But New York did not equip him with the hermeneutical key to the problems of white supremacy. Indeed, his trip to Harlem may have made things more acute for him. What he learned in New York troubled him for the rest of his life, specifically, the problem of Christian complicity in racism, which he saw more clearly in his own country when he returned to Germany in the summer of 1931. He found that the content of Christianity in Germany was insufficient to face its most significant problem in recent history—the problem of Nazism. The Australian Bonhoeffer scholar, Clifford Green, recently brought to light direct evidence to that end in a letter Bonhoeffer wrote to Gandhi in 1935. In that letter, Bonhoeffer is clear that he was reaching out to Gandhi for help to reform Western Christianity in ways that he hoped would empower Christians in Germany to stem the tide of Nazi influence and salvage what is left of the faith there. He was looking for help to save the Western Christian project. And with that as his starting point, one might say that his efforts were doomed to fail from the start. For it is in that Western project that several harmful presumptions lay undisclosed and, thus, undisturbed. Bonhoeffer had an intuition about the problems, and he recognized that Western

Christianity suffered from deficits. But rather than reforming the project, what was needed was something entirely new.

Bonhoeffer's fragmentary thoughts from prison about religionless Christianity in a world come of age were, in a way, more of a request for that something new than they were part of his reformist impulse, but he needed more help to follow that new thread of thought to where it was leading him. For that reason, I think it is particularly helpful to read him alongside new fields of thought that were not available to him at the time. This new work reveals that Nazi venom was a direct product of the apologetics that legitimized turning African people into material possessions in the West. The apologetics became an ideology that poisoned Europe, South Africa, the Caribbean, and the Americas. They also animated Nazism, killing millions, including Dietrich Bonhoeffer who became yet another victim of the historical disfiguring of embodied, human life, resulting in large part from harmful European interactions with Africa that proved devastating for Christian social practice. What was needed was not the reform of a disfigured Western Christian project; something fundamentally malevolent needed to be razed, and life together reimagined, anew.

Reading Bonhoeffer in Africa

Thus, there is something imperative to learn from Bonhoeffer's efforts as we read him alongside the fields of Black theology and of religion. It is my goal to offer this reading of him by interacting with a portion of his correspondence with Eberhard Bethge from prison, particularly, because his incarceration by the Nazi government was a moment of concrete association between him and those who were targeted by the regime he opposed. In that opposition, he too was addressing something that predated both him and the Nazis. It is apparent in his prison correspondence that he intuited a problem that his contemporaries did not see. Bonhoeffer had ideas about the problem, but he could not deliver on the solution. I hasten to say what we all know—that his prison letters are not complete, polished works. Indeed, he never meant for them to be published. But what I wish to highlight is that in those unpolished works, he addressed something that not only spoke to his situation but also speaks to our divided, racialized world, today. I would like to engage Bonhoeffer's intuitive discovery in two parts—one as a focus on Christology alongside the insights of a scholar of Black theology and the other as a focus on the problem of religion in dialogue with a scholar of religion. To begin, we need to hear the problem that sets these two parts in motion from the pen of Bonhoeffer, as interpreted by his best friend, Eberhard Bethge.

The Sovereign Subject

The Enlightenment was supposedly the moment when humankind made a departure from self-inflicted immaturity. Our immaturity is marked by the inability to use our own reason without guidance by someone else. These are Bethge's initial reflections on Bonhoeffer's theological discovery in prison. Bethge sees Bonhoeffer accepting a premise from Kant that scholars describe as the turn toward the knowing subject. But the Enlightenment was much more than that. It set in motion several intellectual projects that we have inherited as pre-conscious assumptions about reality. While some of that inheritance is helpful to facilitate progress in sciences that enhance human health and well-being, other Enlightenment projects stabilized suppositions about human life that served as apologetics for domination and cruelty, and subsequently developed into ideological support for some of history's most devastating moments. The trans-Atlantic slave trade was buttressed later by an Enlightenment description of human difference that is more aptly described as financially incentivized anthropology rather than objective biological science. The racial taxonomies of biological anthropology helped justify the very lucrative practice of Europeans acquiring Africans as material property and sending them into the Western world as commodities for sale. That anthropology is a uniquely European description of human beings, overriding all others it encounters in the world to become the language of normalcy, that is, the logic of human hierarchy, which is white supremacy. It was the assembly of an ideological figure, an archetype, who is a white, masculine, autonomous, self-determining sovereign, creator of culture and civilization. Culture and civilization exist nowhere else but in his domain. Everyone's humanity is measured in aesthetic proximity to him, the archetypical figure. The archetype is the animating figure of humanity in the West and is foundational for white supremacy. White supremacy is not primarily driven by hatred, it is driven by longing; longing for a community populated with this idealized type and its appropriate, corresponding, attachments (which is to say that white supremacy is always about more than race. It travels in a gang that includes several other isms and phobias). White supremacy was the ideological bank that funded the racial longing of three overtly racist regimes in the twentieth century—America's Jim Crow South, Nazi Germany, and South Africa's apartheid. One might hope that Western nations would have learned from those tragedies of the twentieth century and moved away from the ideas it derived that inspired unspeakable cruelty. But they have not. The harmful epistemologies that spawned those tragic political moments survived the devastation they unleashed, living on into the present as continued domination and cruelty.

Bonhoeffer's theological project expresses a Christian way of being in the world that many people read as opposition to domination and cruelty. As a pastor and theologian, Bonhoeffer did his work within the field of religion, which was, ironically, one of the key engines mobilizing European ideologies that support domination and cruelty. His early criticism of religion and his later arguments for Christianity without religion in a world come of age are indications of how he read the problem.

As I have stated earlier, I will not only engage Bonhoeffer here, but my interaction with him around those ideas considers historical developments in the European engagements with Africa as a source of what he was struggling to come to terms with in prison. Bonhoeffer recognized that religion was incapable of offering a solution to the problems of harmful ideology in Nazi Germany. It was, in fact, an obstacle rather than a solution. His Christian concept of persons moved theology into social existence and away from the conceptual arena where personhood was captive to abstract epistemologies, leaving it vulnerable to evils like Nazism. It was there, in the social encounter with neighbors during Hitler's regime, that Bonhoeffer's Christ-centered theology diagnosed key Christian failures. And here are the arguments that I will engage with in this chapter. Christianity failed in Nazi Germany for at least these two reasons. First, it was insufficiently, or even erroneously, connected to its Christological source, and second, the way in which the category of religion emerged within modernity had entangled Christianity to its detriment. The result of these two failures was an unhealthy Christian social practice. In order to address the problems that distort Christian social engagement and lead to Christian complicity in political evil, we must come to grips with at least these two failings.

Bonhoeffer's Christological Source

Dietrich Bonhoeffer was a Christ-centered theologian. In his posthumously published *Ethics*, he argued that the reality of God and the reality of the world were reconciled in Christ. In that unfinished set of essays, he further demonstrated how his Christ-centered project rested upon what Eberhard Bethge named *Christokrator*, omnipotence in human suffering and being for others, as opposed to the almighty Lord of history who is unopposed as he does what he wants and is determined by no one.[1] Jürgen Moltmann argues that this concept of God as "the Almighty" was a familiar Nazi description.[2] For Bonhoeffer, responsible life is participation in the life of Christ, in and with *Christokrator*, this being-for-others.

When we get to the prison letters, Bonhoeffer makes further claims about participation in Christ's life and suffering in a world that is no longer immature but has come of age. To do so, to participate in and with Christ, we must make sense of the place of Christ in a world that is no longer in need of a chaperone. Religion is that chaperone that we no longer need; the world is moving toward autonomy. Bonhoeffer says, "What is Christianity, or who is Christ actually for us today? The age when we could tell people that with words . . . is past, as is the age of inwardness of conscience, and that means the age of religion altogether."[3]

Bonhoeffer goes on to say that the religionless Christ is "no longer the object of religion, but something else entirely, truly Lord of the World."[4] The connection

---

1. See Hans Schmidt Smith, Ronald Gregor, ed., *World Come of Age* (Minneapolis, MN: Fortress Press, 1967).
2. See Jürgen Moltmann, *God for a Secular Society: The Public Relevance of Theology* (Minneapolis, MN: Fortress Press, 1999).
3. *DBWE* 8:362.
4. Ibid., 364.

that is made between God and the world in Christ, for Bonhoeffer, is not sufficiently engaged when Christianity is merely a doctrine or practices of piety for individuals. The pious ones separate themselves from the world; they are a privileged community of divinely favored ones, something like a social club where prestige is accorded to members only. The pious ones leave the world to itself, in a religious practice of separation. That arrangement offers no engagement with the real world hence with the incarnate Christ who is reality.

Bonhoeffer uses other words and terms to describe religion, such as individualism, metaphysical, religious *a priori*, and *deus ex machina*, all of which turn an inward gaze in some manner, measuring the religious over and against the world, in a practice of separation. For Bonhoeffer, this will not do. Christianity needs to become worldly, and most scholars understand this as a reference to growing secularism. Yet, I would consider the implications of the location where Bonhoeffer made this theological discovery—in a prison cell. He arrived at this realization while he was a helpless prisoner of the Nazi state, as he was continuing to assess the failures of Christianity in the face of Nazism. Why did it fail? Christianity must engage life together with Christ in the world today, which is to say, in the reality of a suffering world. We cannot do that in religious separation from the world. This claim is not only a religious/secular divide but also a matter of social bonding for a Christ-centered "we." What is at stake here is a better mode of Christian social practice. Christ is not a totem of religious devotion for an assembled community that is separated from the suffering world in safety and piety but the one in and through whom we participate in the sufferings of God in the world.

Reaching beyond Bonhoeffer

While this reading illustrates that Bonhoeffer had his finger on the problem, it also betrays his inability to deliver on the solution that he sought. There is more to the problem, and if we move beyond the tools that Bonhoeffer used for research, while we employ the same concern about Christ as a religious object, we may be able to see a bit more clearly. Christ as an object of religious devotion has led to an erroneous connection to Christianity's Christological source. It is a problem that manifests as a modern iteration of an old Christological heresy. Christ as an object of religion makes it possible to have a perverted devotion that is in line with Nazism. Bonhoeffer's question, "Who is Christ actually for us, today?," highlights this problem.

This objectified Jesus is not a "who" but a "what." It is familiar as an object of religious devotion that aids in broader efforts to organize the Western world's description of humankind. The Swedish naturalist, Carl Linnaeus, writing in the eighteenth century called him "Europeanus." Johan Friedrich Blumenbach called him "Caucasian." These scholars carry out their research within a convergence of science and philosophy. They were important engineers of the modern development of the ideal human as white and male. But theology was also an indispensable tool for the project of making sense of the Western world's concept of the human as white. In modernity, Christianity brought together the assembly of white and human in the figure of Jesus. This is the effect of a historical convergence of ideas from science, philosophy, and theology, which are now fundamental assumptions about human difference. Jesus became an archetype of the human and the catalyst for a hegemonic practice of social connecting.

The Familiar Jesus as a Christological Problem

Without Jesus, as Europeans portrayed him, race as a working ideology of human difference would be impossible. J. Kameron Carter explains:

> The modern racializing of bodies in social space is unintelligible apart from how Christian identity was reimagined during the Enlightenment and how both the content and the disposition animating Christian theology shifted. Christianity was severed from its Jewish roots, lopped off from the people of Israel to facilitate western conquest. Thus, it came to pass that Christianity became the cultural-religious reflex of western existence.[5]

The ideological move that saw Europe rather than Israel as the center of Christianity in the world also gave Jesus a makeover. And embedded within this modern, Western Christology is a race question. As it pertains to the historical body of Jesus, he was a Jew. As it pertains to the Western Christian imperial conquest, he became a concept, an organizing figure of the Occident, and Western property. He is white. The dualism serves to fashion white supremacy as a modern Christological problem.[6] It situates a racial hierarchy within the person of Christ that resembles the early Apollinarian heresy; his body is subordinated to an aspect of him that is understood to be divine. In this modern Christological heresy, Jesus' Jewish body is now located within a scale of racial valuing and subordinated to a Western conceptual, ascendant ideal of him, which is simultaneously signified by a white or Aryan, fetish of cultural longing. Christ, the figure of sacred devotion, is simultaneously a charm of racial ordering and a despised racial other. Concretely, the body is dismissed in place of the spirit.

---

5. Carter J. Kameron, *Race: A Theological Account* (New York: Oxford University Press, 2008), 372.

6. I use the word "dualism" as Kelly Brown Douglas does in her book, *What's Faith Got to Do with It: Black Bodies/Christian Souls*, which refers to dualism as a hierarchy that enables the practices of domination and authoritarianism. Dualisms play favorites, as opposed to a paradox which posits two dissimilar types side-by-side without hierarchy. A body/soul distinction as one finds within a platonic dualism is a hierarchy with a preference. In Christ are a number of paradoxes (e.g., human and divine), none of which must be seen as dominant within him (New York: Orbis Book, 2005).

The Fetish of Human Difference

Seeing Jesus in this way helps to make sense of how Christians lend their support to harmful politics. There is deliberately very little attention given to embodied life. The assertion of Luther's *Theologia Crucis* that Jesus is hidden in the world in suffering and shame is rendered spiritual, and suffering bodies become invisible. Or worse, the disembodied suffering Jesus becomes a political cliché of a majority people, "oppressed for their beliefs," giving sacred license to harmful politics. But the suffering Jesus among us becomes a demand for Christian service when we locate the Christological source for social practice among those who are made invisible in their bodies and harmed in their bodies by policies arranged for the idealized archetype, only. The socially harmed ones are physically pushed out of community and onto the cross, hidden in embodied suffering and shame. Bonhoeffer references this reality when he says, "Human religiosity directs people in need to the power of God in the world, God as *Deux ex Machina*. The Bible directs people toward the powerlessness and the suffering of God; only the suffering God can help."[7] But it is not enough to orient our vision toward the socially marginalized as a location to serve God; we must recognize that the archetype is a manufactured, divinized figure organizing and giving license to the deviant longing that generates suffering. We must undo the connection between white and human that is brought together in the Western anthropological project. Otherwise, we are simply endeavoring to make a benevolent sovereign, turning that same distorting idealized hierarchical figure from violent to kind, which merely redeploys the problem. Bonhoeffer's question, "Who is Christ actually for us today?," points to this problem that early Black scholars and liberation theologians identified in ways that Bonhoeffer could not. Scholars like Albert Cleague, Howard Thurman, Kelley Brown Douglas, Katie Cannon, Sylvia Wynter, Hortense Spillers, Jackie Grant, James Cone, J. Kameron Carter, Willie Jennings, and Eboni Marshall Turman all refer to this problem in one way or another. Bonhoeffer refers to it as the problem of white and Black Christs that was being raised in the United States when he completed his essay "Protestantism without Reformation"[8] in 1939 on returning from his second trip to the United States. Yet he failed to recognize that same white Christ in his own context, as the one Susannah Heschel describes as the *Aryan Jesus*.[9] We cannot make the same mistake. In order to avoid it, we should take heed of the insights afforded to us by reading Bonhoeffer alongside Black theological insights that reveal to us the totem that Jesus becomes with racism, animating popular forms of Christianity that harm the most vulnerable among us.

---

7. *DBWE* 8:479 (emphasis added).
8. *DBWE* 15:438–61.
9. See Susannah Heschel, *The Aryan Jesus: Christian Theologians and the Bible in Nazi Germany* (Princeton, NJ: Princeton University Press, 2010).

Christianity and Religion

In addition to the Christological problem, Bonhoeffer argues that Christianity's failings with Nazism were due to its entanglement with religion. "We are approaching a completely religionless age," he says. "People as they are now simply cannot be religious anymore."[10] Yet, as Bethge and other scholars have indicated, Bonhoeffer does not elucidate those claims enough to offer a clear theory of religion. But he was ahead of his time with what he did say about religion. He was heralding a type of analysis of religion that would find its way into the academy more than twenty years later, placing him well ahead of his time with an investigation of systems of devotion that, to borrow from him, meet others as objects for epistemological consumption, as "I-It" rather than persons for whom I bear responsibility as "I-thou."

Bonhoeffer says, "[O]ur entire nineteen hundred years of Christian preaching and theology are built on the 'religious a priori' in human beings. Christianity has always been a form (perhaps the true form) of religion."[11] As preliminary grounding for his engagement with religion, he argues that the religious *a priori* that justifies the proposition of God's existence prior to empirical evidence is historically foundational for religion. Yet, here again, Enlightenment epistemological projects have significantly influenced our common usage of the word religion in relation to global difference. Bonhoeffer's view of religion opens his analysis onto a broad field of study about people and sacred systems, making it apparent that there is a lot at stake in the use of the term "religion." To probe its significance, we need to look further than Bonhoeffer, into a field where I rely in part on the work of the South African religion scholar, David Chidester, whose research on the study of comparative religion theorizes religion's role in Imperial Europe as a mechanism of control. With Chidester, religion does the work of constructing the epistemic framework of colonialism, which is to say that it is one of the ways of building knowledge about others. Empire includes an academic enterprise, an encyclopedia-making project that serves a practical purpose of intellectually justifying projects of domination. In the process, the ones doing the dominating, European empires, are simultaneously shaped by relations of domination. Another way of saying it is that the metropole invents fields of knowledge production that engage colonial subjects as "it," turning them into objects of knowledge rather than "thou," people to whom they would relate. The object of knowledge cannot really be known, only observed and contemplated, but the subjects in relationship can reveal themselves to us. Religious knowledge of the colonial subject is one of those core fields of observational, contemplative knowledge production. By treating its targets as objects of knowledge production, it serves primarily to create information that clarifies the superiority of the imperial power and the inferior status of the colonial subject. No real contact with colonized people is possible

---

10. *DBWE* 8:362.
11. Ibid., 363.

under these circumstances—knowledge of religion in the practice of comparison serves only to justify subjugation.

The metropole's practice of religious studies included socio-theo-ethical dimensions as indicated by Emile Durkheim, who describes religion as beliefs and practices in relation to the sacred that unify people into a community.[12] The description of how those social cohesions occur determines how they are classified. Imperial descriptions of the beliefs and practices that contribute to social cohesions are done by comparing the white European and the African colonized subject to demonstrate the need for civilizing projects. It is in these comparisons that the terms savage and primitive arise against their polar opposites—civilized and cultured. But the comparison is more of an invention than a description. As Chidester notes, "Europeans discovered African religions, and the discovery often coincided with the colonial containment of particular African populations, as African religious systems were recognized within colonial administrative systems. Analyzing these discoveries, critical scholarship has shown that the invention of African traditional religion was part of a larger imperial project of inventing Africa."[13]

The process of discovery required a narrative of what was discovered. But the narrative could not possibly be objective. The European category of religious studies crafted sacred hierarchies as constituents of cultural narratives to defend their pre-identified ascendancy. This was the practice of the Nazis with Jews, Roma, Sini, and Jehovah's Witnesses, and it was also a very salient colonial practice. With their narratives, they invented the degenerate savage and totem, and fetish worshiping primitive, as counterbalance to the preferable description of their concept of the fully human. They were creating inferior people to legitimize their colonial conquest and subjugation. The religion of the primitive was evidence of an immature people in the early stages of civilization. They could only develop culture and civilization under the parentage of a civilized colonizing people. Gaining religious knowledge of the colonized and soon-to-be colonized served, not as information about new peoples but about those collecting the information. Chidester argues that it was the creation of the "English" or "British," or "Germanic" national identity that relied on the subjugation of others by a process of representing them. Imperial Christianity left no way of knowing the work of God in the world without reference to powerful white men.

This is how religion emerged within modernity, at the same time that anthropology was emerging as a field of study. Religion emerged as a subset of anthropology, and it was mobilized in the assessment of Germany's colonial subjects. Christianity as a religion in Germany fell in step with Nazism; both were guided by practices of comparison for classification, containment, and control. In relation to the Jew, the Roma, and Sinti, and to Jehovah's Witnesses, religion served as justification of "us" and apologetic for practices of cruelty.

---

12. David Chidester, *Savage Systems: Colonialism and Comparative Systems in Southern Africa* (London: University of Virginia Press, 1996), 187.

13. Chidester, *Savage Systems*, 18.

Bonhoeffer asks a question that seems to anticipate this field of study: "How do we go about being religionless worldly Christians? How can we be ecclesia, those who are called out without understanding ourselves as religiously privileged, but instead seeing ourselves belonging wholly to the world?" It is because of these very significant problems with Christ and the category of religion that what goes by the name Christian is fatally sick and incapable of a healthy response to totalitarianism. What would it mean to belong to the world rather than take possession of it? What if the white European had stood alongside the Black African in mutual recognition of dignity and potential for human flourishing rather than the need to dominate and to justify domination? Again, Bonhoeffer makes sense as we imagine that "Christ would then no longer be the object of religion, but something else entirely, truly lord of the world."[14]

Entering Something New

In this analysis, I am admittedly engaging a constructive reading of Bonhoeffer, making his intuition the starting point to take him where he could not go. He was prophetic and brilliant, but he also realized that the internal content of the Christianity he was working with in the West was insufficient for the task laid before them by Nazism. In prison, the term he could think of to refer to the effort to address the problem was religionless Christianity in a world come of age. In 2020, the Bonhoeffer scholar, Clifford Green, made public a letter that Bonhoeffer wrote to Gandhi in 1934, ten years before he began talking about religionless Christianity in a world come of age. In the letter, he says plainly that he is looking for "the way towards a new Christian life in uncompromising accordance to the Sermon on the Mount." Western Christianity is in crisis, and he is reaching outside of the familiar archives for help. I would argue that his intuition is correct. And though our situation in the current rise of Western nationalisms is not as dire as his became, I must quickly highlight that the failures he identified have not gone away. Neither Bonhoeffer nor we can get to the solution by trying to reform what that interaction created nor will we accomplish what is necessary by staying strictly within the Bonhoeffer corpus. Like him and with him, we must do the work of imagining something entirely new.

Christian Response to the Nazis

It goes without saying that there was no unified Christian response in Germany to the Nazis. But one thing can be said for certain; very few Christians were inspired by their beliefs to stand up for their neighbors who were targeted for eradication

---

14. *DBWE* 8:364.

by the Nazis. David Gushee grouped the Christian response into three categories of apathetic bystanders, Nazi-sympathizing perpetrators, and righteous gentiles who put their lives on the line to save lives. It is unclear where Bonhoeffer would fit into these categories. Glen Stassen tried to describe Bonhoeffer as a righteous gentile for his participation in Operation Seven. Bonhoeffer was also among the earliest to name anti-Jewish hatred as a problem for followers of Christ. But most Christians maintained concern for religious propriety that centered a concern for separation between church and government. They did not concern themselves with state violence against fellow citizens, perhaps, because they did not see them as belonging to "us." This was a failure of Christianity.

Deutsche Christen

Susannah Heschel also tells us of another kind of gratuitous Christian response to Nazism that offers a look at Christianity in the crosshairs of Bonhoeffer's analysis. In May 1939, clergy members of the "Institute for the Eradication of Jewish Influence on the German Church" gathered at Germany's historic Wartburg Castle, for a theological project. They were Protestant scholars from among the *Deustche Christen* who sought to offer the Aryan people a Christianity that was suitable for their superior estate. They employed a religious pattern of comparison and clarification, rife with the heretical dualism invoked by the Christological problem of the body of Jesus. Nazi Christians identified the body of the Jew in Europe as a biological pathogen and a danger to the uncontaminated Aryan. In view was a *Völkisch* purity which was a concept committed to an idealized "mankind" as an ethical imperative to guide the organization of humanity by lower and higher value into strata differentiated according to people who were carriers of civilization—a people who have culture and those who do not. To mix the two would be a disaster. Hitler made this rhetoric popular at the beginning of his push for political power in *Mein Kampf* where he described the imperative of racial purity "in a hybridized and negrified world all conceptions of the humanly beautiful and sublime, as well as all conceptions of our humankind would be lost forever. In this world human culture and civilization are inseparably bound up with the Aryan."[15] To negrify, meaning to pollute Aryan purity, is to destroy it, which is an offense of divine proportion. Hilter continued: "He who dares lay a hand upon the highest image of the Lord sins against the benevolent Creator of this miracle and helps in the expulsion from paradise."[16] Accordingly, the Aryan was "the highest image of the Lord" or divine representation of the human ideal, while the Jew is material and flesh. Religion and race are paired as naturally occurring biological realities of human difference, and the White Aryan Christian is given top billing as "the highest image of the Lord."

---

15. George Lachmann Mosse, *Nazi Culture: Intellectual, Cultural and Social Life in the Third Reich* (Madison, WI: University of Wisconsin Press, 2003), 6.

16. Mosse, *Nazi Culture*, 7.

Nazi-sympathizing Christianity and Nazi religion differed on doctrinal matters but spoke the same language of obeisance to the strong leader, *Der Fürher*, and the problem of the Jewish body. The Christian, racist body/soul dualism made Christians sympathetic, as their government set out to eradicate Jewish bodies in Europe to arrange unpolluted living space for the Aryan. That problem was too big to reform.

Conclusion

Christianity's failures in Nazi Germany were the result of centuries-long sick Christian social praxis. Nazi Germany was not the only moment of that kind of failure. German colonial practices were notoriously brutal and hegemonic, decades before they murdered 6 million Jews, Roma, Sinti, Jehovah's Witnesses, queer people, and other undesirables—religious, racial, and otherwise. But a point of origin can be seen on the shores of the African continent. Bonhoeffer claims that a world come of age would no longer support the assumptions of religion that see secularism as encroaching on social maturity resulting from achievements in science and technological advancements that answer questions that were once answered by religion but which are now accessible by human reason. He had a hunch that we must re-calibrate our understanding of what God was doing in the world, by reference to the embodied life of those who were politically targeted. That perspective would have us reckon with the source of the fatal ideas, where the tragic historical justification for transfiguring people into commodities for sale continues to rupture our present social fabric, making it possible to see human beings as refuse or biological contaminants, threatening our hopes for ideal community. In this regard, we must follow Bonhoeffer's early intuition that something more is needed and available beyond the sources of an insufficient Christianity that currently offers no tolerable response to the problems that have taken society by storm, even today.

Part II

BONHOEFFER AND EARTH-HONORING RESPONSIBILITY

Chapter 7

RESPONSIVITY AND RESPONSIBILITY IN THE AGE OF THE ANTHROPOCENE

BONHOEFFERIAN REFLECTIONS ON HOPE IN THE MIDST OF A CLIMATE CRISIS

Ulrik Nissen

Introduction

"You all come to us young people for hope. How dare you! You have stolen my dreams and my childhood with your empty words!"[1] These were the words of Greta Thunberg during the UN Climate Action Summit in New York in September 2019. Thunberg, at the time a Swedish teenager, first became a public figure only a year before, when from August 2018 and the following months she sat silently before the Swedish parliament with a sign saying (in Swedish) "School Strike for the Climate." In the months following, she inspired young people around the world to organize demonstrations against climate change. Thunberg, as a person and as a phenomenon, can be debated (like any other person with such an influence). But it can hardly be questioned that she has been a spokesperson or catalyst for an ongoing change in the public opinion on the necessity of coordinated political action with regard to the climate.

Scientific, philosophical, and theological experts working on these issues have desperately tried to call the public attention to the importance and urgency of the changes in climate on our planet in the last fifty years. Environmental theology or eco-theology traces its more modern origins to the 1970s after the 1967 publication of Lynn White's article on the "Historical Roots of Our Ecologic Crisis."[2] From the beginning of the 1990s and the UN "Earth Summit" in 1992, a similar awareness and subsequent call for a collaborative, political responsibility

---

1. Greta Thunberg, "Greta Thunberg (Young Climate Activist) at the Climate Action Summit 2019: Official Video," United Nations, https://www.youtube.com/watch?v=u9KxE4Kv9A8 (accessed January 7, 2020).

2. Lynn White, "The Historical Roots of Our Ecologic Crisis," *Science* 155, no. 3767 (1967): 1203–7.

for the climate has also been issued in numerous reports by the United Nations. In the last decade, some progress also seems to have been made, but in spite of these continuous efforts, one can sometimes experience disappointment over the insufficient political progress and the "empty words," as Thunberg calls them. The despondency arising from the lack of action beckons hope. How can we maintain hope when one global climate report after another only seems to get worse? Thunberg criticizes the world leaders for their inertness. Clearly, we have to place our hope in the young generation. But if we approach this question more theologically, how can we still speak of hope in a world with very limited progress in the lowering of greenhouse gas emission?[3]

The increased awareness about climate change and the warming of the planet have developed alongside the recognition that the change is caused by humans—it is humanogenic. This awareness is reflected in the geochronological term, the Anthropocene. It is debated when the term became more publicly known, but often the Dutch Nobelist Paul Crutzen is credited with this honor following a conference and an article in the IBGP newsletter in 2000.[4] Since then, the term has become increasingly an accepted label for the geological period, where changes to the earth's surface are caused by human beings. As the term itself is debated, so is the question about when the epoch of the Anthropocene began. More recently, the year 1950 has been proposed.[5] Even if there is a debate on the dating of the Anthropocene, there is an agreement that the term describes a new geological period with a humanogenic impact on the Earth. Consequently, we could claim, from an ethical viewpoint, that this also implies that human beings are challenged with a renewed call for an increased awareness of the responsibility and care for the Earth.

Even though these climate challenges and their causes have attained higher urgency in the seventy-five years after Bonhoeffer, several studies have shown the significance of his theology for our response to these issues.[6] Common to

---

3. Fiona Harvey, "UN Climate Talks End with Limited Progress on Emission Targets," *The Guardian*, https://www.theguardian.com/environment/2019/dec/14/un-climate-talks-drag-on-as-rifts-scupper-hopes-of-breakthrough (accessed January 15, 2020).

4. Paul J. Crutzen and Eugene F. Stoermer, "The Anthropocene," *The International Geosphere-Biosphere Programme (IGBP) Newsletter*, no. 41 (2000).

5. The arguments vary from a period 14,000 years ago with the extinction of large mammals such as the mammoth, over the rise of agriculture between 10,000 and 15,000 years ago, the dawn of the Industrial Revolution, or the dramatic changes and growth appearing after 1945. See John P. Rafferty, "Anthropocene Epoch," in *Encyclopaedia Britannica*, https://www.britannica.com/science/Anthropocene-Epoch (accessed January 8, 2020).

6. Mark S. Brocker, *Coming Home to Earth* (Eugene, OR: Cascade Books, 2016); Larry L. Rasmussen, "Bonhoeffer and the Anthropocene," *Nederduitse Gereformeerde Teologiese Tydskrif* 55, Supplement 1 (2014); *Earth-Honoring Faith: Religious Ethics in a New Key* (Oxford: Oxford University Press, 2013); idem., *Earth Community, Earth Ethics* (Geneva: WCC, 1996); Peter Manley Scott, *A Theology of Postnatural Right*, ed. Sigurd Bergmann,

these, however, is that they are not narrowly conceived as Bonhoeffer studies, but Bonhoeffer is included as a conversation partner in a larger argument about our unity with, dependence on, and responsibility for non-human nature. At the same time, there remains a lacuna to fill. Even in some of the most significant and recent handbooks or companions to Bonhoeffer, the question about our relation to non-human nature or climate issues has no entry of its own.[7] A simple search on the ATLA database for "Dietrich Bonhoeffer and Anthropocene" reveals no results, just as the search for "Dietrich Bonhoeffer and climate."[8] So, if a simple database search is an indication and yet inconclusive, then, it seems justified to contend that we are treading relatively unexplored ground in the search for a Bonhoefferian response to the climate challenges in the age of the Anthropocene. More recent studies by Bonhoeffer scholars such as Dianne P. Rayson and Steven van den Heuvel already embark on this road with comprehensive book-length studies on Bonhoeffer and eco-theology.[9]

The present chapter attempts to go a step beyond the mentioned studies to ask whether we can find in Bonhoeffer an understanding of a biological, social, and spiritual responsivity of the human being, and if so, what does this imply regarding our responsibility to the current climate crisis and does this still enable us to speak of hope? It is widely recognized that Bonhoeffer understands the human as a relational being. Clifford Green's classical work on Bonhoeffer's theology of sociality has played an important role in the recognition of this motif in Bonhoeffer's

---

Studies in Religion and the Environment/Studien zur Religion und Umwelt (Münster: LIT Verlag, 2019); Peter Scott, *A Political Theology of Nature*, ed. Colin Gunton and Daniel W. Hardy, Cambridge Studies in Christian Doctrine (Cambridge: Cambridge University Press, 2003).

7. Philip G. Ziegler and Michael Mawson, eds., *The Oxford Handbook of Dietrich Bonhoeffer* (Oxford: Oxford University Press, 2019); John W. de Gruchy, ed., *The Cambridge Companion to Dietrich Bonhoeffer*, Cambridge Companions to Religion (Cambridge: Cambridge University Press, 1999).

8. If we search for the same combination but with "climate change," we get only one article, whereas with "climate crisis," there is none (ATLA Religion Database search result, January 7, 2020).

9. Dianne Rayson, *Bonhoeffer and Climate Change: Theology and Ecoethics for the Anthropocene* (Lanham, MD: Lexington Press, In press); Steven C. van den Heuvel, *Christocentric Theology and Fundamental Debates in Environmental Ethics*, Princeton Theological Monograph Series (Eugene, OR: Pickwick Publications, 2017). Rayson has also published several articles on Bonhoeffer, the Anthropocene, and eco-theology. See for example, Dianne Rayson, "Bonhoeffer in the Anthropocene: The Climate Crisis and Ecoethics," in *Faith and Politics: Political Theology in a New Key*, ed. Lori Brandt Hale and W. David Hall (Lanham, MD: Lexington Press, 2020); idem., "Earthly Christianity: Bonhoeffer's Contribution to Ecotheology and Ecoethics," *The Bonhoeffer Legacy: An International Journal* 6, no. 1 (2018).

research.[10] Green's focus is primarily on Bonhoeffer's early theology, but we find the theme of sociality and humans as creatures living in bonds of sociality and social responsivity all through Bonhoeffer's writings. This essay is a *first* step in exploring Bonhoeffer's *Creation and Fall* and relatively recent contributions to theological anthropology. It calls for a deep Christological anthropology, which emphasizes the bio-socio-pneumatological relationality and responsivity of the human being under the section, "Whose Are We?" The essay further shows that this responsive understanding of the human being has roots in Bonhoeffer's Lutheran heritage. *Second*, it connects this to Bonhoeffer's understanding of responsibility as the response of life as a whole to the life of Jesus Christ and, primarily, in the light of his *Ethics*. This second part of the essay further argues that the climate crisis calls for a broadening of Bonhoeffer's mandates to include a responsibility for the non-human world. In the *last* part of the essay, the question of hope is addressed briefly. In continuity with Bonhoeffer's wholeness of responsibility, it is argued that the current climate crisis calls for a moral response, which is nourished by a hope that in Christ the future is not absent from the present and how this sustains an understanding of a saturated human reality which gives hope for the future in the midst of a climate crisis.

Whose Are We?

For both Luther and Bonhoeffer, it is pivotal that as created beings we are in a responsive relation to God as our creator.[11] A brief overview of Martin Luther's *Genesis Lectures* will serve as a point of departure for our reading of Bonhoeffer.[12] Already in his comments on the first verses of Genesis, Luther emphasized that God created heaven and earth by his word: "The Father creates heaven and earth out of nothing through the Son, whom Moses calls the Word."[13] The world is created by the word of God, which is Christ himself. For Luther, Christ is present and at work in God's creative work from the beginning. He follows up on this in his exegesis of Gen. 1:3, where the word is emphasized as the means and instrument of God's creative work and notes that this passage points forward to the Johannine understanding of Christ as the word of God (Jn 1:1).[14] The intimate link between creation by the

---

10. Clifford J. Green, *Bonhoeffer: A Theology of Sociality*, rev. ed. (Grand Rapids, MI: W.B. Eerdmans, 1999).

11. A part of the following section is a revised portion of Ulrik Nissen, "Responding to the Word of God and Creation: Ethical Reflections on Genetic Engineering and Responsive Science," in *Liberated by God's Grace: 2017, 500 Years of Reformation: Creation, Not for Sale*, ed. Anne Burghardt (Leipzig: Lutheran World Federation, 2015), 15–22.

12. Martin Luther, *Lectures on Genesis: Chapters 1-5*, ed. Jaroslav Pelikan, vol. 1, Luther's Works (Saint Louis, MO: Concordia Publishing House, 1958).

13. Ibid., 9.

14. Ibid., 16f.

word of God and Christ as this very word is significant for the theological meaning of creation. God calls the world into being by his word, draws the human being into a responding and living relationship, and nurtures this human being spiritually by His word. The Luther scholar, Oswald Bayer, explains that for Luther, creation is fundamentally about the establishment and preservation of community.[15] Creation points forward to justification by faith, and just as the justified sinner responds with gratitude, Luther understands creation as an expression of God's beneficence pointing forward to the ultimate good—the justification by faith in Christ.

This understanding of the intimate relation between creation and Christ is paralleled in Bonhoeffer. The responsive understanding of the relation of the human being, creation more broadly, and God is also found in Bonhoeffer's *Creation and Fall*.[16] He argues that the meaning of creation can only be known through the church. We can never reflect on the meaning of creation from a neutral point, but from the particular place where we have encountered God's beneficence. He states this already in the introduction and later argues that it is hopeless to hypothesize about the origins without an awareness of where we come from.[17] We can only know about the origins of those who live from Christ. The attempt—with the origin and nature of humankind in mind—to take a gigantic leap back into the world of the lost beginning, to seek to know for ourselves what humankind was like in its original state and to identify our own ideal of humanity with what God actually created is hopeless: "Only in the middle, as those who live from Christ, do we know about the beginning."[18]

Further, like Luther, Bonhoeffer emphasizes that creation comes into being from the word of God: "There is no continuum that ties God to, or unites God with, God's work—except God's *word*. God said . . . The only continuity between God and God's work is the word."[19] That the world is created by the word of God implies at least two important things for Bonhoeffer: (1) We can only know the world truly through the word (i.e., Christ), and (2) the world is never independent from the word of God as the will of God. The world is in a constant responsive relation to God. This is reflected both in the human creational relation to God as creator and to fellow human beings:[20]

> To say that in humankind God creates God's own image on earth means that humankind is like the Creator in that it is free. To be sure, it is free only through God's creation, through the word of God; *it is free for the worship of the creator*. For in the language of the Bible freedom is not something that people have for

---

15. Oswald Bayer, *Martin Luther's Theologie: Eine Vergegenwärtigung* (Tübingen: Mohr Siebeck, 2003), 87ff.
16. *DBWE* 3.
17. Ibid., 22.
18. Ibid., 62.
19. Ibid., 40.
20. Ibid., 58f.

themselves but something they have for others. . . . Because freedom is not a quality that can be uncovered; it is not a possession, something to hand, an object; nor is it a form of something to hand; instead it is a relation between two persons. *Being free means "being-free-for-the-other,"* because I am bound to the other. Only by being in relation with the other am I free.[21]

The emphasis on the word of God in both Luther and Bonhoeffer and the response to this word move the focus in the understanding of the human being away from "*who* we are" to "*whose* we are." We are not alone; rather, we stand in a living and responsive community with the triune God as our creator, redeemer, and sanctifier. It is in this living community with God that we are called to respond to and to obey the word and will of God in our relation to God and fellow human beings.

The responsivity as a defining feature of what it means to be a human being also implies that we are not on our own. It is not sufficient to pursue a modernistic account of the individual as autonomous. Rather, we have to maintain that we have the center of our being beyond ourselves and in that sense we are "eccentric beings." We live our lives on borrowed breath; we are not our own creators. David Kelsey makes an extensive argument for this in his theological anthropology, in which he contends that the human being is rightly understood as created, consummated, and reconciled. As created beings, we are living on borrowed breath; as consummated, we are living on borrowed time in anticipation of the eschatological hope; as reconciled, we are living by Christ's death.[22]

If we understand the human being as fundamentally an eccentric being, we move the focus from ourselves to seeking and realizing the will of God. When Bonhoeffer reminds us that we cannot understand creation away from Christ, he is reminding us at the same time of the reality of our lives. There is no reality apart from Christ, as the true understanding of reality is revealed only in Christ. For the Christian, this means that we are called to live our lives in discipleship. We are not called to be the masters of our own or other creature's lives, but to live our lives following Christ and seeking the will of God. When we focus on *whose* we are, we are at the same time asserting that we are servants. We are living our lives with a calling, and we are to respond with faithfulness.

Responsivity of Life as a Whole and a Broadening of the Mandates

The understanding of created life as a responsive life, living in a constant response both to God and fellow creatures, finds a parallel in Bonhoeffer's understanding

---

21. Ibid., 62f. (italics added).
22. David H. Kelsey, *Eccentric Existence: A Theological Anthropology*, vols. 1 and 2 (Louisville, KY: Westminster John Knox Press, 2009). For an emphasis on the special place of human beings in the world, human freedom (in light of the sciences, human evil, and sin), and humanity as a community of men and women, see Hans Schwarz, *The Human Being: A Theological Anthropology* (Grand Rapids, MI: William B. Eerdmans, 2013).

of responsibility. In the section, "History and Good," where the concept of responsibility is most developed in Bonhoeffer's *Ethics*, it is remarkable that his reflections on the question of the good show that we are situated beings—situated in life itself:

> The question about the good always finds us already in an irreversible situation: we are living. . . . We ask about the good not as creators but as creatures. . . . Our question is not what is good as such, but what is good given life as it actually is, and what is good for us who are living. We ask about the good not in abstraction from life, but precisely by immersing ourselves in it.[23]

In other words, we ask about responsibility from within life as something in which we are completely immersed. Subsequently, Bonhoeffer defines responsibility as a response of life as a whole:

> This life, lived in answer to the life of Jesus Christ (as the Yes and No to our life), we call "responsibility" (*Verantwortung*). This concept of responsibility denotes the complete wholeness and unity of the answer to the reality that is given to us in Jesus Christ. . . . Responsibility thus means to risk one's life in its wholeness, aware that one's activity is a matter of life and death.[24]

Part of this emphasis on life as a whole may be due to influence from Wilhelm Dilthey's philosophy of life,[25] but the Johannine understanding of Christ as life also plays a central role. For Bonhoeffer, responsibility is a response to the reality of the life, death, and resurrection of Christ with our whole lives. He sees responsibility primarily as a response, closely tied to the German concept, "*Verantwortung*," which is a concept of responsivity and to the biblical understanding of taking responsibility and answering for Jesus Christ,[26] which again links Bonhoeffer's concept of responsibility with his understanding of the church—and the relation between the church and other mandates.

Bonhoeffer distinguishes four mandates—the church, marriage, culture (or work), and authority (*Obrigkeit*).[27] He understands these mandates in relation

---

23. *DBWE* 6:246–7.
24. Ibid., 254–5.
25. See Ralf K. Wüstenberg, "The Influence of Wilhelm Dilthey on Bonhoeffer's Letters and Papers from Prison," in *Bonhoeffer's Intellectual Formation*, ed. Peter Frick, Religion in Philosophy and Theology (Tübingen: Mohr Siebeck, 2008), 167–74.
26. *DBWE* 6:255.
27. Ibid., 68–75, 388–408; Dietrich Bonhoeffer, "A Theological Position Paper on State and Church," in *DBWE* 16:518–21. The following text on Bonhoeffer's understanding of the mandates is a lightly revised extract from Ulrik Nissen, *The Polity of Christ: Studies on Dietrich Bonhoeffer's Chalcedonian Christology and Ethics*, ed. Brian Brock and Susan F. Parsons, T&T Clark Enquiries in Theological Ethics (London: Bloomsbury, 2020), 86–8.

to Luther's three estates,[28] but in doing so Bonhoeffer emphasizes two important revisions. *First*, the orders are not to be understood as orders of creation. Rather, they are to be seen as "God's orders of preservation that uphold and preserve us for Christ."[29] The orders of preservation are given to preserve life and they are oriented toward Christ and therefore should be open for the preaching of the gospel.[30] *Second*, they rest on a commission upon which they are also conditioned.[31] The theological aim here is to argue for the same—that this commission safeguards these orders from becoming autonomous and that they can only be understood rightly in light of God's commission. This understanding of the commission of the mandates also seems to be in line with his understanding of freedom in *Creation and Fall*. Freedom is given in relation to others.

With regard to the church, Bonhoeffer argues that its commission is to allow "the reality of Jesus Christ to become real in proclamation (*Verkündigung*), church order, and Christian life—in short, its concern is the eternal salvation of the whole world."[32] The mandate of the church thereby reaches into the other mandates—work, marriage, and government—because all of the mandates overlap with one another. The mandate of the church hereby affirms the other mandates as being included in the one Christ-reality.[33] For Bonhoeffer, this does not merely apply to the church in the abstract sense, but it should be seen as affirming the calling of the human being. Bonhoeffer understands the mandates as aiming at the whole person, standing in reality before God. It is in reality in all its manifold aspects that the church bears witness that all the mandates are one in the incarnation of Christ. Thus, "This is the witness the church has to give to the world, that all the other mandates are not there to divide people and tear them apart but to deal with them as whole people before God the Creator, Reconciler, and Redeemer—that reality in all its manifold aspects is ultimately *one* in God who became human, Jesus Christ."[34] Bonhoeffer affirms his Christological approach to reality. Reality and the mandates point to the body of Christ as the reconciliation of God and man. "So here again everything finally flows into the reality of the body of Jesus Christ, in whom God and human being became one."[35]

---

28. DBWE 6:73–5, 16, 547–51. See also Michael Richard Laffin, *The Promise of Martin Luther's Political Theology: Freeing Luther from the Modern Political Narrative* (London et al.: Bloomsbury T&T Clark, 2016), 153–94.

29. DBWE 3:140.

30. Ibid., 139–40; Dietrich Bonhoeffer, "Seminar: Is There a Christian Ethic?," in *DBWE* 11:341; idem., "Primary Report on the Conference of the Provisional Bureau," *DBWE* 11:352–3; idem., "Lecture in Ciernohorské Kúpele: On the Theological Foundation of the Work of the World Alliance," in *DBWE* 11:362–4.

31. *DBWE* 6:389; 16, 519–20.

32. Ibid., 73.

33. Ibid., 72–4.

34. Ibid., 73.

35. Ibid., 74.

At this point also, we can ask whether Bonhoeffer's mandates today call for a broadening of the mandates to include the responsibility for the non-human world. In the section on "The Concrete Commandment and the Divine Mandates" in *Ethics*, Bonhoeffer formulates quite sharply his understanding of the lordship of Jesus Christ as the origin, essence, and end of all the mandates:

> Jesus Christ, the risen and exalted Lord—this means that Jesus Christ has overcome sin and death, and is the living Lord to whom has been given all power in heaven and on earth. . . . The proclamation of Christ is now addressed to all creatures as the liberating call to come under the Lordship of Jesus Christ. . . . It is the lordship of the one through whom and toward whom all created being exists, indeed the one in whom alone all created being finds its origin, essence, and goal.[36]

This seems to be in continuity with *Creation and Fall* in which he argues that we can only speak of creation from Christ. "Only in the middle, as those who live from Christ, do we know about the beginning."[37] If the role of the church is to reach into the other mandates and shed light on their origin, essence, and goal, these mandates must be interpreted through Christ.

Bonhoeffer's reflection on the mandates in *Creation and Fall* emphasizes that they have their end or aim in Christ. Thus, "All orders of our fallen world are God's orders of preservation that uphold and preserve us for Christ. They are not orders of creation but orders of preservation. They have no value in themselves, instead, they find their end and meaning only through Christ."[38] This Christ-oriented understanding of the mandates implies both:

(1) a re-assertion of Christ as the origin, essence, and end of the mandates, and
(2) an emphasis of the deep Christological understanding of the mystery of the Christ-reality that finds a central place in the opening chapter of his *Ethics*.[39]

I have argued elsewhere that this deep Christological understanding of reality draws on a Lutheran understanding of a Chalcedonian mystery of reality which Bonhoeffer also says is expressed metaphorically in the musical expression of the polyphony of life.[40] In a letter to Eberhard Bethge,[41] Bonhoeffer draws on the Song of Songs to explain how the love for God and all other kinds of love are to

---

36. Ibid., 401–2.
37. Ibid., 3, 62.
38. Ibid., 3, 140.
39. Ibid., 6, 47–75.
40. Nissen, *The Polity of Christ*, 39–48.
41. *DBWE* 8:393-5.

be understood as the relation between the *cantus firmus* and other contrapuntal voices, and how this is paralleled in the formula of Chalcedon:

> Where the cantus firmus is clear and distinct, a counterpoint can develop as mightily as it wants. The two are "undivided and yet distinct," as the Definition of Chalcedon says, like the divine and human natures in Christ. Is that perhaps why we are so at home with polyphony in music, why it is important to us, because it is the musical image of this Christological fact and thus also our *vita christiana*?[42]

In his Barcelona lecture from 1929 on "Basic Questions of a Christian Ethic," we also find an allusion to the Song of Songs.[43] There, Bonhoeffer writes: "The earth remains our mother just as God remains our father, and only those who remain true to the mother are placed by her into the father's arms. Earth and its distress—that is the Christian's Song of Songs."[44] So, just as Bonhoeffer uses the Song of Songs to illustrate the deep relation between the love for God and all other kinds of love, he also uses this text to express our deepest unity with and inseparability from the earth as our mother. If we follow Bonhoeffer's understanding of our relation to the earth being so close that we can even call the Earth our mother, and if the relation between the love for God and all other kinds of love is an expression of a deep Christological mystery of reality, how can anything apart from a deep love for the Earth be an expression of a Christian life bearing witness of Jesus Christ? If we follow this line of thought, a call to discipleship today necessarily implicates a call to a responsibility for the earth. It calls for a broadening of the mandates with a divinely commissioned care and responsibility for the earth.

Can We Still Hope in Climate Crisis?

On the question of hope in climate crisis, we are challenged by the lack of progress in political discussion and decision-making. Fear of reduced economic growth or negative impact on employment figures overshadows the much more important goal of taking responsibility for the future of our planet. Thunberg called it "empty words," when the world leaders agree on international treaties and yet repeatedly do not take the necessary steps to reach these goals. Can we still have hope in such a situation?

As Bonhoeffer has shown, life is a mysterious reality, as we are both completely immersed in life and life finds its origin, essence, and goal in Christ. Today we are in a time of crisis due to the climate. When Bonhoeffer gave his Barcelona

---

42. *DBWE* 8:394.
43. Dietrich Bonhoeffer, "Basic Questions of a Christian Ethic, February 8, 1929," in *DBWE* 10:360–78.
44. Ibid., 378.

lecture, it was also a time of immediate political crisis, even if it was of a different kind. In that situation, he still maintained hope, saying, "Human deeds originate in the recognition of God's grace toward humanity and toward each person; those deeds hope in God's grace, which releases us from the crisis of our age."[45] Even though the crisis of Bonhoeffer's age continues to cast its dreadful shadow over our current age, the climate crisis in the Anthropocene age calls for a new response of care and engagement with our earth, our mother. Just as there was reason for despair in the 1930s of Germany, but Bonhoeffer maintained hope, so, we also have to maintain hope, even if we find ourselves challenged by despondency. As Bonhoeffer turned to God's grace for hope, so we can turn to a hope that in Christ all things will be made new.

At this point, we also turn to the section in Bonhoeffer's *Ethics*, where he reflects on the relation between the ultimate and the penultimate.[46] He opens this section with the statement: "The origin and essence of all Christian life are consummated in the one event that the Reformation has called the justification of the sinner by grace alone. It is not what a person is per se, but what a person is in this event, that gives us insight into the Christian life."[47] With these opening remarks, Bonhoeffer alludes to both the distinction and the inner relation between the ultimate and penultimate. The two are different and yet are not to be separated. The ultimate permeates the penultimate, even if at times it may appear at a distance. Later in this section, Bonhoeffer ponders the relation between what he calls the radical and the compromise in Christian life.[48] Whereas radicalism hates time, wisdom, and the real, compromise in contrast hates eternity, simplicity, and the word.[49] Bonhoeffer argues that both solutions tear apart the unity in Christ as incarnated, crucified, and risen. Most Christians find a way between these extremes and maintain a wholeness in the meaning of the Christ-event for Christian life.[50]

Applied to the current debate on Christian life in the Anthropocene, we can say that the present is never separated from the hope that one day all things will be made new. This is a hope we can hold on to, even if at times we struggle to keep it alive. Just as we speak of a hope against hope, with Abraham as an example of such faith (Rom. 4:18), the Christ-event makes it possible in the light of Bonhoeffer's ethics to maintain a hope against all odds, which opens up our lives for a reassured confidence that we are not on our own. We have a reason to hope which gives us a reason to engage in the responsibility for our earth, our mother. This is a hope which calls us to action.[51] It is not a hope which calls us to a kind of quietist

---

45. Ibid., 378.
46. Ibid., 6, 146–70.
47. Ibid., 146.
48. Ibid., 153–9.
49. Ibid., 156.
50. Ibid., 159.
51. For more elaborate arguments on the inner relation between hope, ethics, and motivation for action, see John Webster, "Hope," in *The Oxford Handbook of Theological*

dream for a utopia but rather a hope which nourishes and motivates us in our responsibility for the planet, which we are part of, and where we live our lives in vibrant relations of interdependence with all kinds of living and non-living beings and entities. Here we are called to live our lives as earthly and responsive beings hoping for the day when Christ will be all in all (Eph. 1.8-10).

Ethics, ed. Gilbert Meilaender and William Werpehowski (Oxford, UK: Oxford University Press, 2005), 291–306; Jürgen Moltmann, *Ethics of Hope* (Minneapolis, MN: Fortress Press, 2012).

Chapter 8

HOW IS TODAY'S—AND THE COMING—GENERATION TO GO ON LIVING?

BONHOEFFERIAN INSPIRATION FOR AN ECO-THEOLOGY AND AN ECO-ETHICS

Carlos Caldas

Introduction—the World and the Current Threat of the "Falling Sky"

It is well known that we humans are living in an unprecedented crisis in the *oikos*, that is, our planet, the house we live in. This crisis is due to a vicious circle—the wheel of the economy cannot stop; industries and factories must work incessantly. After all, commerce needs to sell its products. In order to achieve this, having enough raw materials becomes a necessity. These raw materials come from nature; they are extracted from the soil, from the seas, and from the forests. In many cases, the process is destructive, which is illogical, insane even, because in doing so, we are destroying what we need to live. It is like killing the golden goose to get more eggs made of pure gold. But one does not need to be an expert in ecology or economy to conclude that such a policy, guided by an unquenchable thirst for profit, is a form of ecocide, an assassination of the environment.

Two examples will be given of this very dire situation—one from today and the other from yesterday, the recent past. The international media has widely noted and reported the recent fires in the Amazon area in 2019 and, more recently in 2020, in the *Pantanal* region in Brazil.[1] To be fair, deforestation is not merely a

---

1. Jair Bolsonaro, the President of Brazil, has said many times in his campaign and after his election that he is against the preservation of the areas in the Amazon where our Brazilian "First Nations" (as the Canadians call their aboriginal peoples) have been living since time immemorial. And this, Bolsonaro says, is because Brazil needs space to raise cattle in order to export meat to the European Union, to Russia, and to other places. So, in the name of progress and economic development, the Amazonian rainforest should be destroyed. With this motto, "Amazon is ours," Bolsonaro and his followers responded to the criticism of French President Emmanuel Macron, who has been a staunch opponent of Brazil's current policy on the environment.

contemporary problem or a problem of the West. Actually, and sadly, it has always been a problem in human history. For instance, the dramatic history of the *Rapa Nui*, the *Isla de Pascua* (Passover Island), in the very middle of the Pacific Ocean, relates that in the eighteenth century, when the first Europeans "discovered" the island, they found many islanders, descendants of the makers of the famous *moai*, the famous giant stone statues of humanlike figures. But they also found something very strange—there was almost no vegetation, almost no forests, almost no trees. No one knows for sure what took place there that eradicated almost all plant life. Whatever happened there that caused the complete deforestation of the island was by the hands of the locals, not the Europeans. Any naïve and stereotyped notion of greedy capitalist Westerners destroying nature while non-Westerners preserve nature has to be disregarded. In fact, history shows that literally all humans (and not only the Westerners) are to be blamed for the destruction of the environment. The same critique is made by the English philosopher Roger Scruton in his *Green Philosophy* in which he notes that both socialism and liberalism have failed to deal with environmental problems.[2] Scruton coined the interesting neologism *oikophilia*, literally, "love for the house," viz., the planet, the great house, and the home of humankind. One must agree that an attitude of *oikophilia* is desperately needed today as we face very complex challenges such as global warming, the endless problem of the disposal of plastic and garbage (a problem that seems to have no solution), and the rapid increase of deforestation in so many regions on the planet. In fact, the situation has become a nightmare. It is as if we are living in a painting of Hieronymus Bosch.

Some well-intentioned people therefore say, "We must save the planet" or "the planet is in jeopardy." Their intentions no doubt are good. However, the motto "save the planet" is wrong because planet Earth itself is by no means endangered. Human-made destruction is unable to scratch even the surface of the planet. What is in danger is not the planet but we ourselves as humankind. The destruction of the planet and the climate change crisis jeopardize human life as a whole. We, humans, are in danger, not the planet.

The saddening scenario brings to mind what Davi Kopenawa, a Brazilian "shaman" of the Yanomami people of the Amazon area, calls the *falling sky*. According to the traditional beliefs of the Yanomami, the sky itself can fall from the firmament due to the destruction of the earth caused by humanity. Kopenawa narrates in the first person what happens due to the destructive action of *garimpeiros* (prospectors) and lumberjacks—epidemic diseases, pollution of waterways, soil depletion, loss of biodiversity, destruction of cultural heritage, and, finally, destruction of the world itself—this is the falling sky.[3]

---

2. Roger Scruton, *Green Philosophy: How to Think Seriously about the Planet* (London: Atlantic Books, 2012).

3. Davi Kopenawa and Albert Bruce, *The Falling Sky: Words from a Yanomami Shaman* (Cambridge, MA: Belknap Press, 2013).

In fact, the red alert for our planet, or rather, for us humans on this planet, has been issued some decades ago. The alert was issued not only by scientists but also by science fiction literature as well as movies. A good recent example of this is the 2015 movie, *Mad Max: Fury Road*, by Australian filmmaker, George Miller. The warning, "Whoever has ears, let them hear," may sound rather catastrophic, but some theorists say we are about to experience the real possibility of the end of the Anthropocene, the time of the human.

Having such a complex context, the question we now need to ask is how is today's generation to go on living? Is there any inspiration or intuition we can receive from the writings of Dietrich Bonhoeffer for both an eco-theology and eco-ethics? The search for answers to those questions begins with a brief reflection on theology, eco-theology, and eco-ethics. The basic theoretical presupposition of this chapter is that the answer to the proposed questions is, "Yes, it is possible to speak about a Bonhoefferian eco-theology."

Clarifying Concepts—Theology, Eco-theology, and Eco-ethics

To speak about theology, eco-theology, and eco-ethics may sound weird to some readers. This may seem like strange stuff for a theologian. After all, theology is supposed to be a conversation about spiritual matters such as the salvation of the soul and the afterlife "in heaven." With such view of theology, it is helpful to understand first what theology truly is. Traditionally, theology is understood as a critical effort by the community of Jesus' followers to answer the questions presented by their life-situation using Scriptures as the source—*fons et origo*—for such reflection. Theologians speak about the concrete problems of their life-situation and of their faith communities. In ancient times, there were no such problems as climate change and environmental crises, which we witness today. Therefore, theologians of old never spoke about those issues. For centuries, Christians simply had to recite the first words of the Apostles' Creed, "I believe in God, the Father almighty, *creator of heaven and earth*," and/or of the Nicene Creed, "We believe in one God, the Father almighty, *maker of heaven and Earth, of all things visible and invisible*."

But, over time, events such as industrialization and population growth have caused the environment to be increasingly under attack. With the increase in ecological problems, some theologians realized that they had to reflect also on matters of creation, nature, environment, and so on. This is called *eco-theology*. And in our own time, some decades after Bonhoeffer, some Christian thinkers including the German Reformed theologian Jürgen Moltmann and the Brazilian Catholic Leonardo Boff[4] have developed an explicit eco-theology.

---

4. Jürgen Moltmann, *God in Creation: A New Theology of Creation and the Spirit of God* (Minneapolis, MN: Fortress Press, 1993); Leonardo Boff, *Ecology and Liberation: A New*

What then is the role of Dietrich Bonhoeffer in the process of constructing an eco-theology and eco-ethics? Before answering this question, it is important to make an obvious statement—the ecological problem, as we know it today, was non-existent in Bonhoeffer's day. Therefore, a careful hermeneutical approach to Bonhoeffer's theology is necessary; otherwise, we are in danger of "passing the limits," so to speak, by putting our own words in Bonhoeffer's mouth, as if it was possible to find statements in his writings that have to do with our contemporary concerns. It would be rather unfair to seek a reflection like Moltmann's or Boff's in Bonhoeffer's writings. On the other hand, it will be inaccurate to say that Bonhoeffer did not concern himself with the care of creation. In a sermon on John 19 on the Good Friday of 1927 (April 15), Bonhoeffer said in a very touching and beautifully poetical way, "The crown, a wreath of sharp thorns, is pressed upon his forehead. The first drops of blood fall on the earth, upon which he, the love of God, walked. The earth drinks the blood of its creator's beloved Son, who loved it as no one had loved it before."[5] In another surprising passage, Bonhoeffer states, "The earth remains our mother just as God remains our father, and only those who remain true to the mother are placed by her into the father's arms. Earth and its distress—that is the Christian's Song of Songs."[6] Thus, one can say that it is possible to draw some principles from his writings that can guide us in the process of constructing a solid theology of the environment. In other words, the theology of Bonhoeffer contains a promise of both eco-theology and theo-eco-ethics.

If Bonhoeffer were to discuss the theological and ethical responsibility to nature and the environment, that is, advanced theological eco-ethics, it would have been in his commentary on Gen. 2:15, which states, "The LORD God took the man and put him in the Garden of Eden to work it and take care of it."[7] This verse explicitly states, "the first responsibility and task God gave to man was to be a gardener."[8] In *Creation and Fall*, his theological interpretation of the first three chapters of Genesis, Bonhoeffer placed the abovementioned verse in a pericope with Gen. 2:8-17, which he called "The Center of the Earth."[9] His exposition of the pericope is undoubtedly a precious gem that unites Christian piety and academic

---

Paradigm (Maryknoll, NY: Orbis Books, 1995); idem., *Cry of the Earth, Cry of the Poor* (Maryknoll, NY: Orbis Books, 1997).

5. Dianne P. Rayson, "Bonhoeffer's Theology and Anthropogenic Climate Change: In Search of an Ecoethic" (PhD diss., University of Newcastle, Newcastle, 2017), 209.

6. *DBWE* 10:378.

7. New International Version of the Bible (NIV).

8. The author owes this idea of gardening as the first vocation of man to Brazilian theologian Rubem Alves. Unfortunately, it was not possible to locate this quotation due to the extremely fragmentary nature of Alves' work, as he wrote thoughts like this one in hundreds and hundreds of short chronicles, never thinking somehow of systematizing them all.

9. *DBWE* 3:80–93.

scholarship. Bonhoeffer carefully chooses his language—a language which appeals to the imagination:

> How can one speak of the first earth, earth in its youth, except in the language of fantasy [*Märchen*]? God prepares an exceedingly magnificent garden for the human being [*der Mensch*] created with God's own hands. What else would a person from the desert think of here but a land with magnificent rivers and trees full of fruit? Precious stones, rare odors, gorgeous colors surround the first human being. The fruitful land in the distant east, between the Euphrates and the Tigris, of which so many wonderful things were being told—perhaps that was the place, the garden of the first human being. Who can speak of these things except in pictures? Pictures after all are not lies; rather they indicate things and enable the underlying meaning to shine through.[10]

Bonhoeffer was sensible enough not to despise this account of the second narrative of creation in Genesis due to its mythological tone. His concern was, as expressed in the title of the compilation of lectures he gave at the University of Berlin in 1932–3, a "Theologische Auslegung von Genesis 1-3" ("A Theological Interpretation of Genesis 1-3"). Therefore, theology is the north of the compass of Bonhoeffer's reading of the biblical text. He is not concerned with following the steps of the so-called historical-critical method of biblical exegesis, which aims to retell the history of the composition of biblical texts but mostly is a speculative reconstruction that takes unproven hypotheses for granted. Instead of reading the biblical text this way, Bonhoeffer seeks to extract its theological significance. However, the verse that is central to establishing a basis for (any kind of) theo-eco-ethics is not considered in detail by Bonhoeffer, that is, "And Yahweh God took the human being and put the human being in the garden of Eden *to till it and keep it*."[11] His focus was entirely on the theological question of the two trees—the Tree of Life and the Tree of Knowledge of Good and Evil. Thus, he did not advance an ethics of caring for the land from Gen. 2:15. Nonetheless, it is possible to consider a theological eco-ethics based on Bonhoeffer's theology. The next section will present what is generally understood to be an application of Bonhoeffer's theology to environmental ethics.

Christocentric Aspects of Bonhoeffer's Theology as Key to a Bonhoefferian Eco-ethics

The first thing is to remember that Bonhoeffer owes Martin Luther a great debt, as far as the construction of his theology is concerned.[12] Luther makes the person

---

10. *DBWE* 3:81.
11. Ibid., 80 (emphasis added).
12. On the influence of Luther on the thought of Bonhoeffer, the definitive work is Michael P. DeJonge, *Bonhoeffer's Reception of Luther* (Oxford: Oxford University Press, 2017).

of Christ the center of his theology and Bonhoeffer follows Luther to make Christ the *Leitmotif* of his theology. The basic theoretical presupposition of this chapter is that the theology of Bonhoeffer is Christocentric. To draw elements of an eco-theology from his thought however, one always has to keep in mind that Bonhoeffer works in a completely different way from a "gaiacentric" perspective that is used by some defenders of the environment who do not operate a Christian worldview. Thus, from quite a different perspective, a Bonhoefferian eco-theology will not start from nature itself, but from Christ. The creation is important, not because of it *in se*, but because of Christ. According to Steven van den Heuvel, "creation is important because God preserves it to conservate it for Christ."[13]

Another important point in this process of developing a Bonhoefferian theo-eco-ethics is the understanding that in this Luther-inspired tradition, creation is not something done and finished in the past. Creation and preservation walk hand in hand—preservation is *creatio continua*. And in simple events of daily life such as the sprouting of a flower, the birth of a baby, the coming of a new day, the rhythm of the seasons, and the growth of a tree, we experience miracles. Thus, one can conclude that there is goodness in creation. In *Creation and Fall*, Bonhoeffer recalls the words of Jesus, "No one is good, but one, that is God"; and God declares that his creation is good (Genesis 1) not because of itself, but because of God.[14] The Australian Bonhoeffer scholar Diane Rayson states:

> As God considers God's work of creation, God's assessment is that creation is good. God sees that God's work is good; God loves it and upholds it. Bonhoeffer points out that this analysis does not require the presence of evil by way of contrast. Rather, it is a goodness which exists simply by being under God's dominion. This is a crucial point. It has implications for our understanding of creation *qua* creation, its goodness as a given: "God's look sees the world as good, as created—even where it is a fallen world."[15]

So, Christ is the key to a possible Bonhoefferian eco-theology. The Christian idea of incarnation is the very foundation of such a theology. According to Bonhoeffer, "In Christ's incarnation, all of humanity regains the dignity of bearing the image of God."[16] Christ, Bonhoeffer says, is the mediator—*der Mittler*—between God and man, between heaven and earth, between nature and its Creator. The incarnation gives great value to nature and, consequently, to the environment and

---

13. Steven C. van Den Heuvel, *Bonhoeffer's Christocentric Theology and Fundamental Debates in Environmental Ethics* (Eugene, OR: Pickwick, 2017), 93–4.

14. Dietrich Bonhoeffer, *¿Quién es y quién fue Jesucristo? Su historia y su misterio* (Barcelona: Libros del Nopal de Ediciones, 1971), 115.

15. Rayson, "Bonhoeffer's Theology," 117, quotes Bonhoeffer in *Creation and Fall* (*DBWE* 3:45).

16. *DBWE* 4:285.

to the responsibility of the Christian church in the world. Besides, it is necessary to remember that, according to Bonhoeffer, Christ is the center of all reality, because Christ is there for men, for history, and for nature.[17] And the church, the community of the followers of Jesus, is the *Gestalt*, the form of Christ in the world. Christ lived not for himself but for others. As the *Gestalt* of Christ, the church must live for others. In his *Letters from Prison*, Bonhoeffer states: "The Church is the Church only when it is there for others . . . not dominating, but helping and serving. It must tell people in every calling [Beruf] what a life with Christ means, what it means 'to be there for others.'"[18] This Bonhoefferian understanding of the church and its role in the world is clearly Christocentric. Traditionally, Bonhoeffer scholars have used this principle to formulate a social ethics.[19] In fact, it would not be overstated to label Bonhoeffer as a liberation theologian avant la lettre. One cannot deny his great concern for the oppressed and downtrodden of society. Perhaps then, this same Bonhoefferian principle could be used today in an extended way to our care of nature and the environment. In sum, what is suggested here is to apply this Bonhoefferian intuition about the role of the church in the world in a much broader way that includes our care of nature and Earth, and not only of other human beings.

Many conservative Evangelical Christians, especially (but not only) in Latin America, think about the mission of the church only in terms of a "harvest of souls." To them, the only thing that really matters is evangelism. A careful (re)discovery of Bonhoeffer's theology can be a powerful antidote against such a reductionist vision of the responsibility of the community of Jesus' followers in the world. The *Nachfolge* ("discipleship"), following Jesus, has to do also with the care of creation. It is not merely a "spiritual" or "heavenly" matter, as so many Evangelical Christians are prone to think. If one takes seriously the centrality of Christ and the practical implications of the doctrine of the incarnation of the *Logos* in Jesus, one would understand also that taking care of creation is as "spiritual" as evangelization or singing hymns.

There is also another important element in this process of constructing a Bonhoefferian theo-eco-ethic, which is the influence of Luther on Bonhoeffer. It is well known that Bonhoeffer followed Luther very closely on many points of his theology. One of these that could potentially be useful for a comprehension of a theo-eco-ethic inspired by Bonhoeffer is the beautiful notion of *Christus pro me*. Luther builds this Christological notion in a personal and soteriological way. In our own time, we can adapt the notion of *Christus pro nobis* (Christ for us) to include the care for nature in this *nobis* (us), as suggested by Rayson:

---

17. Bonhoeffer, *¿Quién es y quién fue*, 46; Dietrich Bonhoeffer, *Christ the Center* (New York: Harper & Row, 1978), 62.

18. *DBWE* 8:503.

19. Carlos Caldas, *Dietrich Bonhoeffer e a teologia pública no Brasil* (São Paulo: Garimpo, 2016).

> Humans have a particular role in the family which is the biosphere. As Christians, we are bound to Earth and the church-community demonstrates this by being-for-others. This Earth is the new Earth; "There is no planet B" in the words of climate activists. Bonhoeffer's eschatology, such that it is, validates the presence of Christ in the current reality and his intervention in history for the purpose of reconciling the world with God. Standing with and for Earth and her children, between silence and screaming, requires ethical engagement with the problems of the Anthropocene. The costliness of grace goes beyond praying for the kingdom of God; it requires that we stand with the kingdom, with our feet on the ground.[20]

The Christocentric aspect of Bonhoeffer's theology allows him to recognize the amplitude of the redemption Christ brought not only to humans but also to the cosmos as a whole, as the Mediator fulfills the Law and redeems creation.[21] At this point, it is important to add a helpful comment in constructing a theo-eco-ethics from a Bonhoefferian perspective. Even though Bonhoeffer does not explicitly cite Rom. 8:19-23 in his *Christ the Center*, it is possible to conclude that he had this biblical text in mind when he included a reference to nature in his elaboration of the redemption brought to the world by Christ. This "generous soteriology"—a soteriology that encompasses human and non-human creation of God, urgently needs to be understood and taught by the Christian church today. Among Evangelical Conservative Christians, Pentecostals, and non-Pentecostals alike, as well as many Roman Catholics, the tendency is to think only in terms of individual salvation, "You will die and your soul will go to heaven." But a more careful reading of the biblical text will correct such a reductionist understanding of the concept of redemption. Contemporary Bible scholars such as, inter alia, N. T. Wright, have discussed this extensively.[22] It is simply impossible to formulate a sound Christian eco-ethics without a sound (re-)reading of Scriptures that reconstructs our understanding of soteriology and eschatology. In Bonhoeffer's Christology, one can find, *in nuce*, the same understanding that contemporary theologians, like Wright and many others have presented recently. Such environmental stewardship would not be strange to an eco-ethics influenced by the theology of Bonhoeffer. To quote Rayson once more:

> Christ's lordship is not alien to creation but rather is embedded within it, giving it new life through Christ's mercy. He is the living lord of creation, not apart from it but, rather, immanent and sustaining it in a very real way. As Bonhoeffer describes the church as the visible, physical body of Christ, the human participation in Christ, this focal point of creation becomes the tangible, specific

---

20. Rayson, "Bonhoeffer's Theology," 211.
21. Bonhoeffer, ¿*Quién es y quién fue*, 46.
22. N. T. Wright, *Surprised by Hope: Rethinking Heaven, the Resurrection and the Mission of the Church* (Grand Rapids, MI: Zondervan, 2010).

example of what Bonhoeffer understands to be the universal embeddedness of Christ.[23]

Here, as in Bonhoeffer's comment on Gen. 2:15, there is no further elaboration on the practical implications of an eco-ethics derived from the idea of the goodness of creation. But this idea can be a step on the road toward a more responsible and sensible care of creation—creation is good because God looked at it. And we humans were charged with the responsibility to take care of that creation.

Concluding Remarks—Unfinished and Ongoing Challenges

The reflections presented in this chapter will end without a conclusion, for a very simple reason—the current challenges posed by the threats to the environment affecting all men and women of goodwill in this world, unfortunately, are far too many to be solved. Christians, as part of all men and women of goodwill, must and should be especially sensitive to these very difficult problems because they believe that "The earth is the Lord's, and everything in it, the world, and all who live in it" (Ps. 24:1).[24] They also believe that "God saw all that he had made, and it was very good" (Gen. 1:31),[25] and have hope that "in the end" God will restore the original garden (Rev. 22:1-2). Therefore, the care of the environment is a Christian responsibility *par excellence*. Today and much more than any previous time in history, there should be no room for a platonic view of Christian life in the world. A platonic view proposes a binary understanding of body/soul, earth/heaven, and material/spiritual. In Bonhoeffer's theology, one does not find such a simplistic and Manichean comprehension of reality. On the contrary, the strong Christocentric accent in Bonhoeffer's theology emphasizes the responsibility of Christians to the society, and this includes responsibility to the earth as well. The question of how the current as well as the coming generation is to go living must be faced with responsibility. And Dietrich Bonhoeffer can be a trusted guide on this road of an ethical care of the earth, nature, and environment. In Bonhoeffer's words:

> God as such is glorified [*Gott verherrlicht sich*] in the body, that is, in the body that has the specific being of a human body. Humankind created in this way is humankind as the image of God. It is the image of God not in spite of but precisely in its bodily nature. For in their bodily nature human beings are related to the Earth and to other bodies; they are there for others and are dependent upon others. In their bodily existence human beings find their brothers and

---

23. Rayson, "Bonhoeffer's Theology," 75.
24. NIV.
25. Ibid.

sisters and find the Earth. As such creatures human beings of Earth and spirit are "like" God, their Creator.[26]

The discussion presented on these pages may be summarized as follows:

(1) The starting point for an eco-theology inspired by Bonhoeffer's theology is Christ. Bonhoeffer follows Luther's Christological accent in his theology and his ethics;
(2) A Christological approach to ethics must be all-embracing and comprehensive enough to include our care for the environment;
(3) In Bonhoeffer's comments on the second chapter of Genesis in *Creation and Fall*, he seems to gloss over verse 15: "The LORD God took the man and put him in the Garden of Eden *to work it and take care of it.*"[27] But, as stated earlier in this essay, it would be unfair to expect this kind of reflection in Bonhoeffer's day. We can understand the aforementioned verse as a practical principle of our mission as followers of Jesus in the world today;
(4) However, a source of inspiration for a theology and an ethics that cover our responsibility to both our fellow human beings and to the earth and nature can be found in Bonhoeffer's theology.

Finally, but not conclusively, it is helpful to draw on Rayson once more:

> A Bonhoefferian ecoethic is based on contextual, responsible action for the sake of the vulnerable. Bonhoeffer invites participation with Christ, for the sake of our fellow species, which manifests in ethical action to address the problem of climate change. We understand ourselves to be ontologically one with our fellow creatures, which include our Mother Earth, bound together by an intrinsic sociality, and expressed in a kenotic ecology which would characterise Earthly Christianity.[28]

May the Lord grant us wisdom and sensibility not only to formulate an eco-theology inspired by the Christological theology of Bonhoeffer but also to include the responsibility for the rest of creation in our mission.

---

26. *DBWE* 3:176.
27. NIV (emphasis added).
28. Rayson, "Bonhoeffer's Theology," 288.

Chapter 9

BONHOEFFER'S THEOLOGY OF THE BODY AND THE RESPONSIBILITY FOR THE EARTH

Gregor Etzelmüller

In memory of Christof Hardmeier (1942–2020)

Introduction

Climate change reveals the fatal relationship that modern humans have with nature. In the modern era, "humans experience themselves as the ruling subjects of their world, not only the center and reference point of all things, but also the ontological foundation, the first and all-determining being."[1] Human beings treat nature as an object and they understand themselves in contrast to nature rather than situate themselves in nature. This fatal relationship with the earth can be traced back to the Cartesian distinction between *res cogitans* and *res extensa*.[2] People find their self by "reflecting themselves out of this world."[3] *Cogito, ergo sum*. Nature is completely mathematized and thus silenced.

This distinction also affects the human self-perception. Even though the modern *Homo sapiens* has made a distinction between body and nature, it has

---

1. Jürgen Moltmann, "The Alienation and Liberation of Nature," in *On Nature*, ed. Leory S. Rouner, Boston University Studies in Philosophy and Religion 6 (Notre Dame: University of Notre Dame, 1984), 133–44 (133).

2. Cf. Drew Leder, "A Tale of Two Bodies: The Cartesian Corpse and the Lived Body," in *Body and Flesh: A Philosophical Reader*, ed. Donn Welton (Oxford: Blackwell Press, 1998), 117–29 (117–20); cf. Ola Sigurdson, *Heavenly Bodies: Incarnation, the Gaze, and Embodiment in Christian Theology* (Grand Rapids, MI: Eerdmans, 2016), 301–8.

3. Christian Link, *Schöpfung: Ein theologischer Entwurf im Gegenüber von Naturwissenschaft und Ökologie* (Neukirchen: Neukirchen-Vluyn, 2002), 177. Following Viktor von Weizsäcker, Link, *Schöpfung*, 177, rightly criticizes this modern position thus: "Das Bewusstsein wird nicht dadurch konstituiert, dass sich ein zweifelndes Ich (Descartes) aus der Welt herausreflektiert, sondern dadurch, dass ein Ich sich wahrnehmend in der Welt bewegt und in der 'Berührung' mit den Dingen sich selbst erfährt."

not understood the body as an essential part of the human being but rather as the first object of the human self.[4] Drawing on the distinction of *res cogitans* and *res extensa*, body and nature fall into the same category. They do not belong to the thinking spirit but to the material world where they function as disposable objects. However, climate change makes us experience—first-hand through our own bodies—that we are part of nature.[5] Being affected by climate change, we realize that we do not only have a body but that we *are* the body that we have. Climate change is not external to us.

My thesis here is that Dietrich Bonhoeffer's anthropology of the body can contribute to a new attitude toward nature that aims at transforming our typically modern understanding of nature as a disposable object. Since our body is nature, our relationship with the body determines our relationship with non-human nature. Bonhoeffer consistently perceives the human being in its bodiliness/bodily-ness and notes that we as embodied beings are connected with animals—our "brothers and sisters"[6]—and with the earth as our "mother."[7] As embodied beings, we should enjoy the blessings of nature and thus protect nature from a totalitarian grip that reduces it to an object of utility and of commerce. When we become aware that we are always a part of and affected by nature, nature can speak to us and its dignity can be discovered.

Bonhoeffer's Sophisticated Anthropology of the Body

In his early writings and even more in later texts, Dietrich Bonhoeffer put the bodiliness/bodily-ness of the human being at the center of his anthropological reflections.[8] As early as in *Sanctorum Communio*, Bonhoeffer sought a post-idealistic concept of the person and the self. But only since his turn "to the bible" in 1932–3 he developed a viable alternative to the idealistic conception of the human being. In his Berlin lecture, "Creation and Fall," Bonhoeffer developed an anthropology of the body which is in no way inferior to the current *philosophy*

---

4. Cf. Joerg Fingerhut, Rebekka Hufendiek, and Markus Wild, "Einleitung," in *Philosophie der Verkörperung: Grundlagentexte zu einer aktuellen Debatte*, ed. Joerg Fingerhut, Rebekka Hufendiek, and Markus Wild (Berlin: Suhrkamp Verlag, 2013), 9–102 (18).

5. Cf. Gernot Böhme, *Ethik leiblicher Existenz* (Frankfurt am Main: Suhrkamp Verlag, 2008), 120.

6. *DBWE* 3:96.

7. Ibid., 57; cf. *DBWE* 10:378; Larry L. Rasmussen, *Earth Community, Earth Ethics* (Maryknoll, NY: Orbis Book, 1997), 307–13.

8. Cf. Steven C. van den Heuvel, *Bonhoeffer's Christocentric Theology and Fundamental Debates in Environmental Ethics*, Princeton Theological Monograph Series (Eugene, OR: Pickwick Publications, 2017), 119–28; cf. Robert Vosloo, "Body and Health in the Light of the Theology of Dietrich Bonhoeffer," *Religion and Theology*, 13, no. 1 (2006): 23–37.

*of embodiment.*⁹ In contrast to the classical interpretation of Gen. 1:27, which has "almost universally excluded the body from the image" thus encouraging a dualistic worldview,¹⁰ Bonhoeffer argues that the human being "is God's image not in spite of its corporeality but precisely because of it."¹¹ Old Testament research has later confirmed this insight of Bonhoeffer. Today, there is a consensus that the human being is created as a living statue of God, who precisely in and through the bodily behavior represents God in the world.¹²

In his interpretation of Genesis 2, Bonhoeffer anticipates the later thesis of the Old Testament scholar, Hans Walter Wolff, that the ancient Greek as well as the modern concept of soul and body as dualistic entities is alien to the Old Testament.¹³ In his translation of Gen. 2:7, Bonhoeffer does not follow Luther's translation but that of Emil Kautsch. Consequently, Bonhoeffer does not define the human being as a living soul but as a living being. In fact, the Hebrew term *næpæš ḥajjāh* correlates with Bonhoeffer's "humankind's connection with the

---

9. Cf. Francis Varela, Evan Thompson, and Eleanor Rosch, *The Embodied Mind: Cognitive Science and Human Experience* (Cambridge, MA: MIT Press, 1993); Shaun Gallagher, *How the Body Shapes the Mind* (New York: Oxford University Press, 2013); Gregor Etzelmüller, "Verkörperung," in *Entwicklungen der Menschheit: Humanwissenschaften in der Perspektive der Integration*, ed. Gerd Jüttemann (Lengerich: Pabst Science Publishers, 2014), 265–73; Thiemo Breyer, "Philosophie der Verkörperung: Grundlagen und Konzepte," in *Verkörperung als Paradigma theologischer Anthropologie*, ed. Gregor Etzelmüller and Annette Weissenrieder (Berlin: Walter de Gruyter, 2016), 29–50.

10. J. Richard Middleton, *The Liberating Image: The Imago Dei in Genesis 1* (Grand Rapids, MI: Brazos Press, 2005), 88.

11. *DBWE* 3:79.

12. See Nobert Lohfink, "Die Gottesstatue. Kreatur und Kunst nach Genesis 1," in idem., *Im Schatten deiner Flügel: Große Bibeltexte neu erschlossen* (Freiburg et al.: Herder, 1999), 29–48; Bernd Janowski, "Die lebendige Statue Gottes: Zur Anthropologie der priesterlichen Urgeschichte," in *Gott und Mensch im Dialog: Festschrift für Otto Kaiser zum 80. Geburtstag*, BZAW 345/I, ed. Markus Witte (Berlin: Walter de Gruyter, 2004), 183–214; Andreas Wagner, "Verkörpertes Herrschen. Zum Gebrauch von 'treten'/'herrschen' in Gen 1,26–28," *Verkörperung als Paradigma theologischer Anthropologie*, 127–41, 132.

13. Hans Walter Wolff, *Anthropologie des Alten Testaments* [1973], mit zwei Anhängen neu herausgegeben von Bernd Janowski (Gütersloh: Gütersloher Verlagshaus, 2010), 34: *Næpæš* is "das Organ der vitalen Bedürfnisse, ohne deren Stillung der Mensch nicht weiterleben kann." As such, it is not "im Unterschied zum leibliche(n) Leben unzerstörbarer Daseinskern . . ., der auch getrennt von ihm existieren könnte" (47). If the human being is described as *næpæš*, then, he or she is thus not understood as soul but is perceived in his or her embodied vitality, his or her embodied needs; cf. Bernd Janowski, "Die lebendige *naepaes*: Das Alte Testament und die Frage nach der Seele," in *Verkörperung als Paradigma theologischer Anthropologie*, 50–94.

animal world"[14] because the term *næpæš ḥajjāh* is equally applied to both animals and humans (cf. Gen. 1:20,24; 2:7).

Although Bonhoeffer does describe the human being as "body and soul,"[15] he does not pay special attention to the concept of the soul. It is very telling that in the chapter, "The Human Being of Earth and Spirit," the idea of the human being as body and soul is mentioned in the context of the interpretation of the earthliness of human beings.[16] According to Bonhoeffer, therefore, the soul does not possess a special closeness to God's spirit. This understanding corresponds to the view of Apostle Paul. However, Bonhoeffer could have formulated it more precisely, subsequent to Paul: a human being does not "have" a body or "have" a soul; instead, a human being "is" a psychosomatic being, a *sōma psychikon* (cf. 1 Cor. 15:44) [not: body and soul, as Bonhoeffer puts it[17]].[18]

It is impressive that in his interpretation of Genesis 1–2, which is inspired by his Christology and, at the same time, does justice to the Old Testament texts, Bonhoeffer reaches anthropological insights that do not fall short of current interdisciplinary discourses about the proper understanding of the human being. On the one hand, Bonhoeffer emphasizes the "worldliness" and "earthliness" of the human being,[19] which is close to a perspective that describes the evolutionary continuity of humans with the animal world. This interpretation of Bonhoeffer's line of argument in *Creation and Fall* especially makes sense when read in the light of his later critique of the concept of deus ex machina. On the other hand, Bonhoeffer stresses the radical novelty of human existence. He perceives that with the emergence of the human being, "something totally new occurs, with no continuity with what has happened before."[20] The human being is not just an animal with the additional capacity for reason, but in and through his evolutionary development, he is an entirely new being.[21] Bonhoeffer acknowledges both the evolutionary continuity, in which the human being stands and the fact that the

---

14. *DBWE* 3:62.
15. Ibid., 101.
16. Ibid., 76f.
17. Ibid., 77.
18. Bonhoeffer emphasized the connection between human beings and the animal world, and this could have led him to perceive animals, too, as psychosomatic beings. In light of the evolutionary continuity between animals and human beings, he then could have attributed inwardness to animals as well. Consequently, Bonhoeffer would then have to grant the right to bodily joys to animals, too. So, van den Heuvel, *Bonhoeffer's Christocentric Theology*, 144, rightly criticizes Bonhoeffer's view "that human beings alone are capable of experiencing joy."
19. *DBWE* 3:68.
20. Ibid., 57.
21. The philosopher Matthias Jung, *Der bewusste Ausdruck: Anthropologie der Artikulation*, Humanprojekt 4 (Berlin: Walter de Gruyter 2009), 54–61, refers to this phenomenon as "Differenzholismus des Menschlichen."

human being as a whole is something new—and both insights are of theological and ethical importance.

Becoming aware of the evolutionary continuity in which I stand, I realize that "in my whole being, in my creatureliness, I belong wholly to this world; it bears me, nurtures me, holds me."[22] First, from that, it follows that, "The flight from the created work to bodiless spirit, or to the internal spiritual disposition [*die Gesinnung*], is prohibited."[23] There is no "ideal of the spirit's being free from nature."[24] Second, from this fact, a relationship with the world arises that is characterized by gratitude. "The ground and the animals . . . constitute the world . . . without which I cease to be."[25]

Despite outlining the evolutionary continuity of humans with the animal world, it is also vital for any ethics to acknowledge the *differentia specifica* of humankind and to define them as precisely as possible. For Bonhoeffer, the human being is the image of God especially in his sociality—in his "*dependence on the other.*"[26] Starting from the pro-existence of Jesus Christ, in whom God testified his "being for humankind,"[27] the biblical notion that humankind was created male and female leads Bonhoeffer to the understanding of the special sociality of humankind, which distinguishes it from the animals. Thus, via a process of theological reflection, Bonhoeffer gains an insight which is compatible with current interdisciplinary research.

Charles Darwin has pointed out, "that man (*sic*) is one of the most helpless and defenceless creatures in the world." Due to this intrinsic vulnerability of the human being he could/was able to become a social-cooperative being. It should be taken into account that

> An animal possessing great size, strength, and ferocity, and which, like the gorilla, could defend itself from all enemies, would probably, though not necessarily, have failed to become social; and this would most effectually have checked the acquirement by man of his higher mental qualities, such as sympathy and the love of his fellow-creatures. Hence it might have been an immense advantage to man to have sprung from some comparatively weak creature.[28]

Our ancestors were under a selective pressure to trust and help one another. In this way, the human being has evolved to become an extraordinarily cooperative being,

---

22. *DBWE* 3:66.
23. Ibid., 46.
24. Ibid., 66.
25. Ibid.
26. Ibid., 64.
27. Ibid., 65.
28. Charles Darwin, *The Descent of Man, and Selection in Relation to Sex*, with an introduction by John Bonner and Robert M. May (Princeton, NJ: Princeton University Press, 1981), 156f.

as Frans de Waal and Michael Tomasello both emphasize.[29] Every human being is a living creature that cannot be without the other but is "free-for-the-other" because it is "bound to the other."[30] I interpret this insight to mean, as bodily beings, we are always already affected by the suffering of others, and the biblical commandment to love our neighbor calls us to let this natural empathy shape our own actions.[31]

In his interpretation of Genesis 2, Bonhoeffer defines the uniqueness of humankind through the concept of the spirit. Bonhoeffer here always refers to the spirit of God.[32] Thus, "[T]he human body differs from all non-human bodies in that it is the form in which the spirit of God exists on earth."[33] Not that human beings possess something like a spirit, but the promise that the human body will become the temple of the Holy Spirit distinguishes human beings from all their fellow creatures. The human being is "a piece of earth called by God to have human existence."[34] The human being is called to live his human—and not animal—life in a human way.[35] By living his human life humanely, the human body becomes "the form in which the spirit of God exists on earth."[36] According to Bonhoeffer, what it means to live life in a human way can be grasped "in Jesus Christ"[37] thus:

1. To live humanely means to live "from the center of life, and . . . oriented toward the center of life, without [being] . . . at the center."[38] This is why Jesus' preaching focuses on God and his kingdom, but not on himself. Similarly, Genesis 2 locates the tree of life, but not humankind, at the center of the world. In light of the current ecological crises, this means to bid final farewell to an anthropocentric worldview and not continue to understand oneself as being at the center of the world but as embedded into it. Human beings must recognize that "Humankind is derived from a piece of earth. Its

---

29. Cf. Frans de Waal, *The Age of Empathy: Nature's Lessons for a Kinder Society* (New York: Three Rivers Press, 2009); Michael Tomasello, *Why We Cooperate* (Cambridge, MA: MIT Press 2009); Gregor Etzelmüller, "The Lived Body as the Tipping Point between an Evolutionary and a Historical Anthropology," in *Embodiment in Evolution and Culture*, ed. Gregor Etzelmüller and Christian Tewes (Tübingen: Mohr Siebeck, 2016), 205–25.

30. *DBWE* 3:63.

31. Cf. Böhme, *Ethik leiblicher Existenz*, 198: "Das Gebot der Nächstenliebe gebietet nicht einen Affekt zu haben, sondern vielmehr die natürliche Teilnahme an den Leiden der anderen nicht zu verdrängen."

32. Cf. John D. Godsey, *The Theology of Dietrich Bonhoeffer* (London: SCM Press, 1960), 127.

33. *DBWE* 3:78–9.

34. Ibid., 77.

35. Cf. Jens Zimmermann, *Dietrich Bonhoeffer's Christian Humanism* (Oxford: Oxford University Press, 2019), 127.

36. *DBWE* 3:79.

37. Ibid., 73.

38. Ibid., 84.

bond with the earth belongs to its essential being. The 'earth is its mother'; it comes out of her womb."[39] The earth "bears me, nurtures me, holds me."[40]
2. To live humanely means to live for the other.[41] Through Christ, God has testified his "being for humankind."[42] Accordingly, we should be for the other and not rule over the other. That is why the biblical creation mandate rejects the rule of some people over other people by addressing all human beings alike.[43] Genesis 1 implies that it does not correspond with God's will for creation that some groups of people rule over other groups of people that men rule over women. From an ecological perspective, this means if, for example, we give the suppressed voices of the indigenous peoples of Amazonia a chance to speak, we could find a new way to relate to the earth, especially through the voices of these dishonored brothers and sisters.
3. To live humanely means to resonate with the world. Jesus points out the beauty of the flowers, and in his parables, natural processes become transparent for the kingdom of God. According to Bonhoeffer, humankind has lost such relationships of resonance with nature. Therefore, the human being is now "the solitary lord and despot of its own mute, violated, silenced, dead, ego-world [Ichwelt]."[44] Considering the ecological challenges of our time, we should ask how we could learn to listen again to the earth and its wisdom. According to Bonhoeffer, creation teaches us that life is lived in rhythms.[45] But human beings constantly try to combat this wisdom with the help of "technology."[46]

Bonhoeffer's Ethics of the Natural

In his *Ethics*, Bonhoeffer defines the unnatural as "the destruction of the penultimate,"[47] that is, as a fight against the life, which, despite its fallenness, is recognized by God as worthy of being preserved. Bonhoeffer contrasts the

---

39. Ibid., 76.
40. Ibid., 66.
41. Ibid., 63.
42. Ibid., 65.
43. Ibid., 66: Bonhoeffer distinguishes very clearly between human beings and their environment and says of the environment, "Humankind is its lord; humankind has command over it, rules it." Bonhoeffer here uses an expression that is problematic in terms of current ecological debates—that the human being is "free for" the other, but "free from" the world. Ibid. However, the concept of freedom is not mentioned in this biblical passage but is inscribed into it by Bonhoeffer.
44. Ibid., 142.
45. Ibid., 49.
46. Ibid., 48.
47. DBWE 6:173.

unnatural with the natural life—the latter is a way of life that does not simply aim at preserving what is but aims at transforming life toward what has been revealed in and through Jesus Christ.[48] Thus, "the new life . . . breaks ever more powerfully into earthly life and creates space for itself within it."[49] This means that even in our own time in which we are permanently confronted with a humankind alienated from its environment and destroying natural life, a new life and a new ecological attitude can and will emerge.

The Rights of the Bodily Life

A new ecological attitude can emerge when humans perceive and embrace their own bodiliness/bodily-ness. In clear continuity with *Creation and Fall*, Bonhoeffer in his ethics states, "The living human body is always the human person himself or herself."[50] Therefore, the body participates in the dignity of the human being.[51] The bodily life "is not only a means to an end but also an end in itself."[52] Bonhoeffer's appraisal of the body is revolutionary within Protestantism. In his main thesis, "The most primordial right of natural life is the protection of the body from intentional injury, violation, and killing."[53] Bonhoeffer becomes a visionary for the right to physical integrity, which after the Second World War also entered into the German Basic Law. What is more, from the dignity of the body follows the "right to bodily joys."[54] The fact "that the body is an end in itself is expressed within natural life in the joys of the body."[55] Human beings not only have the right to essential things but also have the right to live their bodily life with joy and happiness.[56]

This insight has both juridical consequences and consequences for individual ethics. Human beings not only have the right to accommodation but also have

---

48. Cf. Ibid.: "The natural is that which, after the fall, is directed toward the coming of Jesus Christ."

49. Ibid., 158.

50. Ibid., 214.

51. Zimmermann, *Christian Humanism*, 303: For Bonhoeffer, "the dignity of the person deriving from the divine image shows up phenomenological in the dignity of the body, because personhood is inseparable from embodiment."

52. *DBWE* 6:178.

53. *DBWE* 6:185–6.

54. Ibid., 186.

55. Ibid.

56. This is also true of a Christian life. The human body is supposed to be the temple of the Holy Spirit, but even there, where the Holy Spirit guides human life, life is still to be enjoyed. In an intimate letter to his friend, Eberhard Bethge, Bonhoeffer, *DBWE* 8:184, writes: "You want to live with Renate and be happy, as you have the right to be"; Ibid., 393. Cf. "We need feel no shame as Christians about a measure of impatience, longing, protest against what is unnatural, and a strong measure of desire for freedom and earthly happiness."

the right to such housing in which they "may enjoy the pleasures of personal life in the security of their loved ones and their possessions."[57] We do not do justice to this human right, which can be said also with regard to German refugee accommodations. Human beings have a right to good food and to proper clothing. Because humans by nature are social cultural beings, they not only have the right to essential things but also have the right to live their bodily life with joy and happiness. This is why, according to Bonhoeffer, human beings not only have the right to work but also have the right to "exchange their place of work for another, or [to leave] when they cannot control the amount of their labor."[58]

However, these rights of the bodily life are not only attacked by the state and the economy. More than before, today, we ourselves are in danger of considering our bodies only as objects of service. Instead of providing "the body with the measure of rest and joy"[59] and enjoying breaks and plays, we train our body in order to exploit it even better. In contrast, to exercise the right of one's own body would mean to listen to one's body and to let the body have a say in shaping one's own life. There are several places in the world where the body cannot protest against its working conditions. It is even more shocking that human beings do not listen to their bodies even when they have the freedom and the option to do so. As part of the natural life, a human being should not permanently live against his or her body. Instead, by listening to their own bodies, human beings are guided to a life that suits them. This thought seems unusual to Protestantism, but as Bonhoeffer explains, "through Christ's becoming human we do have the right to call people to natural life and live it ourselves."[60]

Considering that the body is the nature that we are, it becomes clear that in dealing with our own bodies, we simultaneously express our treatment of nature. If we take a mechanistic-exploiting stance toward our bodies, we will even more do so toward the nature that surrounds us. In contrast, if we listen to what the body wants to say, then, our bodies can increase our awareness of the wisdom of nature.

The Enjoyment of Creation

The rigor with which Bonhoeffer understands the human being as an embodied being becomes clear in his ideas about the natural rights of the life of the spirit.

---

57. *DBWE* 6:187.
58. Ibid.
59. Ibid.
60. Ibid., 174. Living a natural life is, however, not synonymous with following every bodily impulse. Life-threatening tendencies are also inscribed into the body, evolutionarily and culturally. This is why listening to one's own body can never be uncritically. Moreover, the rights and the duties of the spiritual life include judging the natural life. But in the process of judging, the body needs to have a say, too. My body potentially wants to tell me what is life-promoting, but I do not attentively listen to my body and so do not understand what my body wants to tell me.

According to Bonhoeffer, the spiritual life is not opposed to the natural-bodily life. The three fundamental practices of the life of the spirit, "judging, acting, and enjoying,"[61] are all embodied practices. Judgments emerge in the interaction between perception and motion. Acting is an embodied activity. What is more, the spiritual life is not "about tempering one's passion"[62] but about consciously letting oneself be affected by the joys of the bodily life. From a theological perspective, Bonhoeffer's claim that there is a right to enjoyment, which God himself guarantees, is revolutionary.[63] Such a perspective is also of the highest importance for environmental ethics.

Bonhoeffer implicitly contradicts the old Augustinian position to enjoy God but to use the world. Instead, he argues that human beings are not only intended to live humanely but also to enjoy their life.[64] By enjoying the gifts of life, humans are in tune with the godly appreciation for creation. They attentively embrace the good that they encounter in a given moment—and appreciate the pleasing moment. The first glass of water in the morning and the sunset in the evening are not taken for granted but are consciously appreciated. The judgment of the creator, "and God saw that it was good," becomes manifest again through the enjoyment of creation.

It is remarkable that Bonhoeffer preserved the skill to enjoy life even when imprisoned in Tegel. In a letter out of the prison, he writes, "There are two wonderful lilac bushes standing on my desk, brought to me by such a kind man . . . I've also lit the big cigar and am enjoying it immensely—thanks very much!"[65] Enjoying creation preserves its character as a gift. Thus, another dimension of the world is revealed, which is disguised by a purely consumption-oriented and exploitative access to the world. To use the world simply means to understand the environment as something that has to be shaped, whereas to enjoy the world allows us to discover what has always already been given to us—an earth, which bears, nurtures, holds, and delights us.[66]

Drawing on the Augustinian distinction of enjoying God but using the world, theology has supported a profiting and exploitative handling of the environment. But discerning the environment only in its practical value fosters a reductionist worldview. The world is thus mathematized and economized. With Bonhoeffer, the intrinsic value of nature as a place of bodily recreation and happiness can be discovered. The mindful enjoyment of the world can lead to a willingness to

---

61. *DBWE* 6:217.
62. *DBWE* 8:394.
63. *DBWE* 6:180.
64. Cf. Oswald Bayer, *Schöpfung als Anrede: Zu einer Hermeneutik der Schöpfung* (Tübingen: Mohr Siebeck, ²1990), 70–2, 157; Michael Roth, *Sinn und Geschmack fürs Endliche: Überlegungen zur Lust an der Schöpfung und der Freude am Spiel* (Leipzig: Evangelische Verlagsanstalt, 2002), 112–50. However, in neither of these works is there direct reference to Bonhoeffer's concept of the right to bodily joys.
65. *DBWE* 8:397.
66. *DBWE* 3:66.

withdraw certain areas of one's environment from a consumption-oriented and exploitative grasp in order to preserve them as places of nature's enjoyment.

Conclusion: Bonhoeffer's Anthropology of the Body as a Path to a New Ecological Attitude

Bonhoeffer's anthropology of the body aims at overcoming the Christian oblivion of and contempt for the body. Thus, the human being is asked to perceive his and her own bodiliness/bodily-ness and accept it as a gift, and Bonhoeffer's anthropology contributes to the liberation of humankind from its captivity through modern dualism. However, this liberation can also benefit the environment. Instead of understanding oneself in contrast to nature, humankind can perceive itself as embedded in its natural surroundings. Thus, human beings understand their connection with the earth and accept it gratefully. They perceive that the powers of creation preserve, heal, and delight them in boundless ways. Before beginning their work, human beings proclaim in Gen. 1:31: "Behold, it was very good."[67]

Humans do not need to optimize the world but have to preserve creation in its fragile beauty and goodness. Where people are willing to interrupt their actions in order to let themselves be affected by the goodness of creation, they perceive themselves as blessed. Thus, the natural surroundings reveal themselves to human beings as worthy to be preserved. In conclusion, Bonhoeffer's anthropology guides us to let our use of the natural goods and landscapes be interrupted by their enjoyment. In this way, we will appreciate our natural environment anew.[68]

---

67. "[B]ehold, it was very good," is the value judgment of the author of Gen. 1:31, who unreservedly adopts "die Wertungsperspektiven Gottes auf seine Schöpfungswerke." With this judgment, the author directly addresses "die jeweiligen Rezipienten der Schöpfungserzählung. Im mimetischen Nachvollzug sollen sie jeweils ihrerseits konfessorisch in dieses begeisterte Gesamturteil des Staunens und der Dankbarkeit einstimmen." Christof Hardmeier and Konrad Ott, *Naturethik und biblische Schöpfungserzählung: Ein diskursivtheoretischer und narrativ-hermeneutischer Brückenschlag* (Stuttgart: W. Kohlhammer, 2015), 154f.

68. I thank my former assistant, Corinna Klodt, for the translation of this essay.

Chapter 10

TOWARD A THEOLOGICAL ETHIC OF INTERGENERATIONAL RESPONSIBILITY

BONHOEFFER'S CHRIST AS MEDIATOR FOR THE COMING GENERATION

Matthew Puffer

"A generation goes, and a generation comes, but the earth remains forever"
—Eccl. 1:4

Introduction

In "After Ten Years," Dietrich Bonhoeffer famously worries that inherited ethical concepts no longer measure up to the task, leaving "little ground beneath [our] feet."[1] Bonhoeffer's efforts to construct a novel theological ethics of responsibility, especially in the 1940–43 period, strive toward a reintegration of moral reflection about being and action and about the individual and society.[2] His ethical project aims to expand agents' perspectives beyond the immediate contexts and direct relationships that often overly narrow or capture the attention of individuals while also giving greater attention to the suffering of marginalized and vulnerable persons—those members of society who occupy "a view from below."[3]

Numerous ancient texts from across the globe were written with a similar aim of expanding the social and moral imaginaries of individuals, forming people who might recognize their obligations to the wider community and indebtedness to generations of ancestors. Such texts include the *Mencius* and the *Xunzi*, Plato's *Republic* and Aristotle's *Politics*, Cicero's *De re publica* and Augustine's *City of God*. And yet, in Bonhoeffer's later writings, he demonstrates less interest in these ancient sources than in the long, slow march of distinctively modern theorists

---

1. *DBWE* 8:38.
2. See *DBWE* 6:47–51.
3. *DBWE* 8:48–52.

who, albeit in different ways, sought to ground political projects and social contracts without recourse to a divine mandate or revelation, *etsi deus non daretur*. He cites Montaigne, Machiavelli, and Grotius, and we might add Locke, Rousseau, or more recent projects by the likes of Rawls, Nozick, Habermas, Nussbaum, Sen, and Sandel.

Most, though by no means all, environmental policies and ethics fall within this modern political tradition, eschewing appeals to transcendent sources and trading instead in a more imminent moral language of rights, contracts, and utility. Meanwhile, an increasingly complex and varied literature has emerged regarding how the present generation should think about, ground, and frame its ecological obligations to future generations. For example, in our newly recognized Anthropocene era, deontologically inclined scholars increasingly ask whether our capacity to affect future generations entails novel duties toward and correlative to the rights claims of future generations. Utilitarian and contractarian scholars might ask whether the present generation ought to optimize or maximize the flourishing of future generations, or whether policy efforts should seek equity between the resource consumption of present and future humans. Such future-oriented inquiries echo difficult questions about moral obligations to present generations affected by past injustices while also raising difficult questions about responsibilities toward alternative potential future generations who may or may not ever exist.[4] In prison, as Bonhoeffer articulated his own questions about the present generation's obligations to "the coming generation," the "wicked problems" of our present ecological crisis were not paramount in his mind, but rather a related, complex set of intertwined moral, political, and social crises arising out of authoritarianism, antisemitism, racism, and militarism run amok.[5] In light of the manifold crises of his time, Bonhoeffer reflected on what social and ethical resources would need to be cultivated by subsequent generations for them to build and sustain a more just world.

In this chapter, I extend and broaden Bonhoeffer's line of questioning to consider how his understanding of Christ as Mediator provides both resources and challenges for thinking about our ecological crisis as it relates to intergenerational ethics. Thus, I draw into conversation several questions Bonhoeffer famously articulates, each of which appears in the posthumously published *Letters and Papers from Prison*. In "After Ten Years" Bonhoeffer poses a basic question about the ethics of future generations, "How is the coming generation to live?" In his

---

4. Importantly, as will be noted, human activity in the present impacts future generations in ways that are disanalogous to how human activity in the past affects present generations such that obligations that obtain between past and present generations are not identical to those between present and future generations.

5. On "wicked problems," see H. W. J. Rittel and M. W. Webber, "Dilemmas in a General Theory of Planning," *Policy Sciences* 4 (1973): 155–69; W. Jenkins, *The Future of Ethics: Sustainability, Social Justice, and Religious Creativity* (Washington, DC: Georgetown University Press, 2013), 20–2, 149–89.

later prison theology, he reiterates the centrality of Christ for our modern context, "Who is Christ actually for us today?" And the titular question of one of his final poems, "Who am I?," is followed by stanzas that direct the reader away from others' perceptions and even one's self-perception in favor of a divinely centered identity.[6] In the next section, I will examine the phenomenology of self-perception in a mirror and further develop, in dialogue with Bonhoeffer, his Christological reflections on human beings' distorted awareness, displaced center, and temporally distended existence. The second section considers how some aspects of Bonhoeffer's Christology, and not others, have been resourced in relation to the ethics of future generations. I also introduce two well-known challenges from intergenerational justice literature, namely the "non-identity problem" and its "repugnant conclusion." The final section will illustrate how Bonhoeffer's account of Christ as Mediator, especially in his Christology lectures and *Discipleship*, offers a provocative and counterintuitive response to the non-identity problem much debated in intergenerational justice discourses.

Who Am I?

Who among us has not looked in a mirror and posed to that image of ourselves the question explored in Bonhoeffer's prison poem, "Who am I?" How am I related to and responsible for the one that I see over there in the mirror? Perhaps most of us, most of the time, give little thought to the phenomenon of mediation in this simple act of apparent self-perception. Whether looking intently or catching a brief glimpse in passing, we may take for granted that we are seeing ourselves. If we pause for a moment to reflect, however, attention to our reflection discloses that we are not really seeing ourselves but rather a distorted image of ourselves. We remind ourselves that a mirror image is, as Bonhoeffer told his London congregation, always both a "mirror- and distorted image [*Spiegel- und Zerrbild*]."[7] The image we see in the mirror is not the image others perceive or that we see in photos but rather a mirror-distorted image with the peculiar effect that horizontal flipping over a vertical axis produces.[8]

We also know that we are not really over there at a distance from ourselves—dis-placed or dis-located to the other side of the mirror. We are not simultaneously both in front of and behind the mirror, self-reflexively viewing ourselves being viewed by ourselves ad infinitum. There is something uncanny about the fact that in order to focus our eyes on ourselves, or rather on this distorted and distant mirror image of ourselves, we cannot focus our eyes on the mirror itself. Rather

---

6. *DBWE* 8:42, 362, 459–60.
7. *DBWE* 13:382.
8. My daughter who is learning to read was wondrously perplexed and deeply concerned recently when she discovered that if she looked in the mirror, the words on her T-shirt were suddenly unintelligible to her.

we must focus behind it, through the looking glass, to a specific place beyond the mirror (where we are not), equidistant to but opposite from our actual position in front of the mirror. The mirror is a mediator in the center between us and the displaced image of ourselves on which we focus. Its nature and position determine it as the mediator and midpoint through and by means of which we are able to recognize the image of ourselves as distorted and dis-placed.

Bonhoeffer also had something of this phenomenon in view as he began his *Ethics*. In the opening paragraph of the initial manuscript composed for his *Ethics*, "Christ, Reality, and the Good," Bonhoeffer calls for a radical shift in perspective from the question of the ethical agent's nature and action to an awareness of the One through whom the agent comes to know reality and themselves. He draws the reader's attention to the distorted understanding that results when one fails to recognize the God-mediated nature of reality: "All things appear as in a distorted mirror [*Zerrbild*] if they are not seen and recognized in God. . . . Awareness of [God's self-revelation in Jesus Christ] is the turning point, the pivot, of all perception of reality as such."[9] One's awareness of Christ as the Mediator is pivotal for a proper perception of reality—of God, the creation, history, oneself, and one's responsibilities to others.

Returning to our illustration and complicating things once more, the physics-minded observer will remind us that the mirror image we see from a distance is also from the past. Self-reflection is inherently temporally distended. Apart from the temporality of consciousness, light's finite speed entails that what we see is not merely a distant, distorted image of ourselves but also a delayed reflection, the photons of which travel the distance from ourselves to the mirror and back over a tiny but measurable lapse of time. In the present, we can see only the past. Only our future selves will ever see what is happening in our present. We might recall at this point the lines from Bonhoeffer's poem, "Who am I? This one or the other? / Am I this one today and tomorrow another? / Am I both at once?"[10] Bonhoeffer was far from the first to contemplate the mystery of continuity, of personal identity through time. He believes that God's self-revelation in Christ mediates human beings' proper perception of all reality as well as of all temporality: "History moves only from this center and toward this center."[11]

In several respects then, who I am in the present is never truly seen by me at all. Rather, who I am now can only be viewed by my future self, when mediated with a mirror distortion, from a slight distance, after a brief delay. The person I see in the mirror is a mediated, distorted, distant, past me. Indeed, "For now we see in a mirror dimly," as the Apostle Paul wrote to the church in Corinth.[12] Light reflecting off of me and my environment at a given moment generates the delayed, distorted, distant image that will be interpreted by my future self, a self whose relationship to

---

9. *DBWE* 4:49.
10. *DBWE* 8:460.
11. *DBWE* 6:58.
12. 1 Cor. 13:12.

my present self is mediated through time and space by the mirror. The mediating mirror provides both the condition of possibility for this self-representation, this relationship of myself to myself, and the means by which the reshaping of the relationship takes place. Below, I further develop the relational, historical, and moral dimensions of Bonhoeffer's understanding of Christ as Mediator, building upon the mirror phenomenon as an imperfect but useful analogy for constructing a Bonhoefferian ethics of intergenerational responsibility. Christ as Mediator is both the condition of possibility for and the one who reshapes human relationality, including the present generation's obligations to past and future generations.

How Is the Coming Generation to Live? Future Generations in Bonhoefferian Environmental Ethics

Environmental scientists were already addressing issues of population growth regularly in the 1960s, but the concept of intergenerational responsibility was not yet a primary concern of governmental policy discourse prior to the UN publication, *Our Common Future*. In 1987, its clarion call was to restructure societies and public policy to promote "development that meets the needs of the present without compromising the ability of future generations to meet their own needs."[13] The intention was clear—the present generation ought not to live in a way that consumes more resources or produces more pollution than would be just, more than one's fair share. Therefore, legislators and other policymakers should incentivize and enforce intergenerational responsibility. In short, people living in the present should not live in a way that is unfair to people who will live in the future.

Affirming such an account of intergenerational responsibility seems intuitive, but translation from formal accounts of justice to their application is fraught with practical difficulties. Not only do ideas of justice and fairness evolve, but scientific, economic, industrial, and technological development and revolutions make it difficult, if not impossible, to predict or plan for fair resource distribution in a single lifetime, never mind across generations. *Our Common Future* was fine as a formal statement about intergenerational justice, echoing *suum quique*—to each their own—but the greater policy challenge involves translating such formal accounts into practical applications that effectively give each generation its due.

Bonhoeffer scholars have a long history of attending to environmental justice concerns, none more so than Larry Rasmussen, and many follow Bonhoeffer's example in bringing theologically informed ethics to bear on practical issues of environmental ethics and policy. Although this chapter focuses on Bonhoeffer's account of Christ as Mediator, it is far from the only resource in Bonhoeffer's theology for thinking about the intersections between intergenerational

---

13. World Commission on Environment and Development, *Our Common Future* (Oxford: Oxford University Press, 1987), 43.

responsibility and environmental ethics. A related concept that has attracted greater attention in Bonhoeffer scholarship is *Stellvertretung*, vicarious representative action or standing in for another.

In recent years, *Stellvertretung* has been put to use in the arena of environmental ethics by Rachel Muers, Steven van den Heuvel, and Rowan Williams, among others. Muers, in particular, foregrounds the unknowability of future generations as a reason to consider them well suited to hold present generations accountable. She writes:

> The unknowability of the future generation—the points that make them . . . so difficult to deal with in many modern ethical theories—fits them to be, from the perspective of the present generation, unbiased judges. We do not know what their interests or partialities will be; we can only know that they will be human. To place oneself before them, as Bonhoeffer does . . . is to confront one's responsibility to "humanity" as a whole.[14]

Muers observes several respects in which future generations are similar to Christ as represented in Scripture—both are presented as "the coming one," "the person of the future," and "the judge" of the present generation.[15] Congruent with Christ's standing in for humanity, the present generation follows Christ by standing in for future generations. Similarly, Van den Heuvel and Williams draw on Bonhoeffer's Christology lectures, *Discipleship,* and *Ethics*, in developing a theological ethic of responsibility based on the concept of *Stellvertretung*, and both attend to Bonhoeffer's claim that Christ as Mediator is *pro me* and *pro nobis*.[16] One concern that none of these scholars examines, but which many philosophers consider a central issue for intergenerational justice, is known as the "non-identity problem." In ways distinct from *Stellvertretung*, Bonhoeffer's account of Christ as Mediator has significant implications for thinking about obligations to future generations, including the non-identity problem and one of its solutions known as the "repugnant conclusion."[17]

The non-identity problem presents a challenge to intergenerational ethics, first, by identifying equivocations in our everyday moral language and intuitions and, second, by undermining traditional forms of moral reasoning and the sort of consistency for which moral philosophy strives. The non-identity problem has to

---

14. Rachel Muers, *Living for the Future: Theological Ethics for Coming Generations* (London: Bloomsbury Continuum, 2011), 106.

15. Muers, *Living for the Future*, 102–26.

16. See Steven van den Heuvel, *Bonhoeffer's Christocentric Theology and Fundamental Debates in Environmental Ethics* (Eugene, OR: Pickwick, 2017), 238–41; Rowan Williams, *Christ the Heart of Creation* (London: Bloomsbury Continuum, 2018), 185–217.

17. Some of the clearest analyses of the complex and interrelated facets of "intergenerational justice," "the non-identity problem," and "the repugnant conclusion" can be found in entries in the *Stanford Encyclopedia of Philosophy* (https://plato.stanford.edu).

do with resolving an apparent paradox to which Derek Parfit returns in a number of thought experiments in his widely acclaimed book, *Reasons and Persons*.[18] Several of the various thought experiments present a case and then modify it slightly to create a second distinct case such that together the two cases serve to highlight an important moral distinction that eludes our everyday language. In many of these cases, there is a choice and a means—a choice between two scenarios involving different degrees of benefits and burdens, and an available means of bringing about either outcome. Parfit introduces such thought experiments, cases, and scenarios in order to explore specific, often overlooked, but morally relevant features of intergenerational ethics that cannot easily be accounted for by standard moral theories.[19] Much like Bonhoeffer's "After Ten Years," Parfit seeks to identify deficient conceptual tools and to replace them with alternatives that are more serviceable. In this sense, both are in search of an intergenerational ethic and practice to resolve the issues that arise when "rusty" inherited forms of moral reasoning confront cases that involve future generations.[20]

In one version of the non-identity problem that is useful for our purposes, Parfit considers two cases. In one case, a pregnant mother has an illness that will cause her child to have a permanent disability unless the mother receives a very simple treatment. In this case, two scenarios between which the mother might choose include (A) receiving the simple treatment so that she will be cured and the child will not have the disability, and (B) not receiving the treatment and welcoming a child with a permanent disability into the world. In the second case, a woman who is not pregnant has an illness for which there also exists a very simple treatment. If this woman becomes pregnant now, before the illness is treated, this will result in her child having a permanent disability. In this second case, two scenarios between which the mother might choose include (A') postponing her pregnancy temporarily until she has received the treatment and recovered from her illness so that her child will not have the disability, and (B') pursuing pregnancy while ill, without treatment, and welcoming a child with a permanent disability.

Using everyday language, one might argue that both women would be justified in taking advantage of the means available to them—a simple treatment in one case and slightly postponing pregnancy during treatment in the other—in pursuit of their child's well-being. The effect of a simple treatment in each case is that the child is relieved of the future burden of a foreseen permanent disability. As

---

18. Derek Parfit, *Reasons and Persons* (Oxford: Clarendon, 1984).

19. Bonhoeffer employs a variety of case-based thought experiments throughout his *Ethics*, especially in the manuscripts, "Natural Life" and "History and Good"; *DBWE* 6:171–298.

20. Bonhoeffer famously critiques traditional ethical theories as "weapons that we have inherited from our ancestors . . . rusty weapons," in the manuscript "Ethics as Formation" from *Ethics*, and he captures these observations about "the world of ethical concepts that we have received" under the heading "Who Stands Firm?," in "After Ten Years"; *DBWE* 6:77–80; *DBWE* 8:38–40.

we noted, each case presents a choice between two scenarios—a child without a foreseen permanent disability or a child with a permanent disability—and a readily available means of pursuing either outcome.

Importantly, however, our everyday moral language elides a potential morally relevant difference between the two cases. The important difference arises from the fact that the woman in the first case is *already pregnant* as she considers *whether* to accept treatment, whereas the woman in the second case is *already ill*, considering *when* to pursue pregnancy. This introduces a non-identity in the second case regarding, and an equivocation with respect to, the meaning of "the child."

Parfit thus draws attention to this specific slippage to which the non-identity problem refers. In the thought experiment's first case, it might seem obvious to most people that it would be better for the child if the pregnant mother undergoes the simple treatment so that the child has no permanent disability. The non-identity problem arises when we try to apply this reasoning to the second case. If the woman who is not pregnant postpones her pregnancy, then the child born to her later (with a different ovum and sperm) is not identical to the child who would have been born had she become pregnant while she was still ill and without the treatment.[21] Thus, from the perspective of the two different potential future children, the alternative is not between existence with or without a disability, but rather between existence with a disability or non-existence for one potential child and between existence without a disability or non-existence for the other potential child. Stipulating that existence, with or without a disability, is preferable to non-existence, it is clearly not in the interest of the potential child with a disability for the woman to wait to pursue pregnancy until she has received the treatment. Consequently, *this* potential child would not be born without a disability. Rather it would never exist at all.

If we describe the two cases using the language of "the child," meaning the child to be born to each mother, then our everyday language fails to attend to a non-identity between two different potential children in the second case and hides from view a significant moral issue for the ethics of future generations. Namely, in situations analogous to the second case, how do we give a compelling account of moral obligations to future generations when it is precisely the decisions and actions of the present generation that will determine which potential future generation comes into existence? If talk of "future generations" in environmental policy discourse does not map onto a determinate child as in the first case but mimics instead the slippage in the second, then, the idea of "future generations" refers not to a determinate population potentially existing in different ecologies but to the distinct potential populations whose existence is mutually exclusive. Application of inherited forms of moral reasoning to this non-identity problem in intergenerational ethics results in what is now known as the "repugnant conclusion."

---

21. We simply note at this point that the thought experiment would seem to stipulate that nothing exists that is analogous to a pre-existent soul constitutive of the child's identity that awaits embodiment at whatever point the woman becomes pregnant.

The various deficiencies of traditional forms of ethics for resolving non-identity cases can be illustrated by an extension of the non-identity problem from the above mother-child cases, which involved historically overlapping individuals, to populations whose existence does not overlap with the present. Parfit's testing of ethical reasoning based on contractarian, rights, and utilitarian theories begins with the following observations about future generations:

> Suppose that we are choosing between two social or economic (or climate) policies. . . . It is not true that whichever policy we choose, the same particular people will exist in the further future. . . . [T]he people who are later born would owe their existence to our choice of one of the two policies. . . . We can plausibly assume that, after one or two centuries, there would be no one living in our community who would have been born whichever policy we chose.[22]

Different policies result not merely in different social arrangements, wealth distributions, and ecological diversity, but also in different persons who will constitute future generations.

From a human rights perspective, the non-identity problem poses a challenge in that the violation of rights in one generation leads both to the very existence of specific people in future generations (who would not otherwise have existed) as well as to the harms inherited and intergenerational injustices suffered. Thus, Andrew Cohen asks, "How can any person have a claim to compensation for a wrong that was a condition of her existence?"[23] The non-identity problem does not assert that there are no victims of past human rights violations, but it draws attention to questions about how future generations that would not have existed apart from specific injustices—for example, the Crusades, the trans-Atlantic slave trade, or the Holocaust—should be understood in relation to the original rights violations.[24] Does it matter that many descendants of those who suffered historical injustices would not exist had those injustices never occurred and, if so, how does it matter? Melinda Roberts observes the counterintuitive nature of the challenge: "People conceived well after the events themselves take place are not, according to the non-identity problem, victims of these events at all, but rather, if anything, their beneficiaries."[25] The implications of this rights-based line of thinking for

---

22. Parfit, *Reasons and Persons*, 361.

23. Andrew I. Cohen, "Compensation for Historic Injustices: Completing the Boxill and Sher Argument," *Philosophy & Public Affairs* 37, no. 1 (2009): 81–102 (81).

24. Jonas argues that human rights offer an appropriate moral grammar for articulating present obligations toward future generations. Hans Jonas, *The Imperative of Responsibility: In Search of an Ethics for the Technological Age*, trans. Hans Jonas and David Herr (Chicago, IL: University of Chicago, 1984), 40–3.

25. Melinda A. Roberts, "The Nonidentity Problem," *The Stanford Encyclopedia of Philosophy*, ed. Edward N. Zalta (Summer 2019 Edition), https://plato.stanford.edu/archives/sum2019/entries/nonidentity-problem/.

political discourse regarding not only obligations to future generations but also reparations to present generations for past injustices, are not difficult to discern.[26]

If a typical reciprocity or rights-based approach to the non-identity problem proves deficient, contractarian approaches do not fare much better. Contractarians "hold that relations of justice can exist only among those who are able to benefit each other,"[27] and they often rely on an explicit voluntary and informed statement of consent either by each party or by a legitimate surrogate, for example, a parent, guardian, or contracted legal representative. Clearly, the contractarian approach faces significant and perhaps insurmountable challenges in a situation where one party, the present generation, must implicitly select one out of several potential future generations with which to enter into a contract. Not only does the second party to the contract not yet exist, but also its coming into existence depends on the present generation's selection of the agreement laid out in the details of the contract. Contractarian theories often rely on surrogacy models where one party is non- or not-yet-competent for the purposes of certain contractual agreements. However, surrogacy in the contractarian model hardly seems a sufficient metaphor for a representative of several mutually exclusive potential future generations whose very existence depends upon the decision of the surrogate.

Another common solution is to propose that what should guide the present generation's actions in relation to future generations should not be determined by the identities of the persons themselves but rather by the state of affairs that would make for the best life for whoever makes up the future generation. This consequentialist or utilitarian approach, however, results in what Parfit and philosophers have considered the "repugnant conclusion." If we consider the identities of the persons who will exist inconsequential and focus instead on the state of affairs that obtain *for whoever* those persons turn out to be, then present-day policymakers must, in turn, identify on behalf of future generations, first, what is meant by "the good" and, second, whether such good should be measured on a

---

26. Consider, for example, how the non-identity problem impinges on the concept of reparations in contemporary social and economic justice discourses. Reparation is comparable to some of what John Rawls had in view in his "principle of redress," what Robert Nozick labeled "rectification of injustice," and what in a post-apartheid South African context is sometimes referred to as "restitution." See John Rawls, *A Theory of Justice* (Cambridge: Belknap, 1971), 100–8; Robert Nozick, *Anarchy, State and Utopia* (New York: Basic Books, 1974), 150–82; T. S. Maluleke, "Justice in Post-Apartheid S.A.: Towards a Theology of Restitution," *Verbum et Ecclesia* 29, no. 3 (2008): 681–96; Sharlene Swartz and Duncan Scott, "Restitution: A Revised Paradigm for the Transformation of Poverty and Inequality in South Africa," Presented at Strategies to Overcome Poverty and Inequality: "Towards Carnegie III" Conference, September 2012, University of Cape Town, Cape Town, South Africa, 1–22; Ta-Nehisi Coates, "The Case for Reparations: A Narrative Biography," *The Atlantic* (June 2014): 54–71.

27. Thomas Hurka, "Future Generations" in *Encyclopedia of Ethics*, vol. 1, ed. Lawrence C. Becker and Charlotte B. Becker (New York: Garland, 1992), 391–4 (393).

population (overall) or individual (the average good per person) basis. Both the overall population good and average per-person good approaches, it turns out, face considerable challenges.

Stipulating that a serviceable account of the good could be arrived at from among the wide range of proposals—from consequentialist to basic goods and capabilities theories—policymakers could seek to bring about the best state of affairs that maximizes good for the human population as a whole. The problem with pursuing the good for an undetermined population is that it will always be better to add another human being to the total number of persons so long as that human being experiences a net positive of the good.[28] Thus, "For any possible population of at least ten billion people, all with a very high quality of life, there must be some much larger number imaginable whose existence, if other things are equal, would be better even though its members have lives that are barely worth living."[29] There is a Malthusian worry here that maximizing overall happiness offers no practical limiting principle. For example, 10 billion people with an average of 100 units of happiness is not justified where 10 trillion people plus one could experience on average 0.1 units of happiness. In short, a theoretical commitment to maximize the total happiness of all lends moral justification to policies that minimize the individual happiness of each person. This "repugnant conclusion" seems unavoidable where the good is maximized on a population level.

A different problem emerges if the consequentialist's "best state of affairs" metric is understood not as total good for the population as a whole but rather as average good for the individuals who make up the population. In this scenario, for any population whose individuals are at a high average-good-per-person, it would not be justified to add individuals whose good-per-person was below that of the society's already high average: "If we add to our state some extra people at a slightly lower (but still very high quality of life), we make the state worse."[30] The mean quality of life for a community, if it can be called such, becomes the sole determinant of which additional persons might be welcomed into or excluded from its population. This conclusion, based on the exclusive criterion of average-good-per-person, like that of the overall good of the population, strikes most observers as similarly repugnant if not more so.

Parfit's point in pursuing these scenarios and testing the adequacy of inherited ethical theories is not merely that the non-identity of future generations, which results from our choices in the present, stresses our everyday moral vocabulary

---

28. Long before Parfit, Sidgwick had observed that "the point up to which, on utilitarian principles, population ought to be encouraged to increase is not that at which the average happiness is the greatest possible, as appears so often to be assumed by political economists of the school of Malthus—but that at which the happiness reaches its maximum"; Henry Sidgwick, *The Methods of Ethics* (London: Macmillan, 1907), 413. Taking the total happiness of the population as a whole as the criterion, Parfit argues, leads to the repugnant conclusion.

29. Parfit, *Reasons and Persons*, 388.

30. Hurka, "Future Generations," 392.

to the breaking point, but also, and more importantly, that modern ethicists need to reconsider whether our moral theories are adequate to address the challenge of articulating our obligations to future generations. Such worries have animated a wide range of responses from philosophers who have considered the gauntlet thrown.[31] For our purposes, we begin by observing that concerns about the adequacy "of ethical concepts that we have received" to cultivate an awareness of our responsibilities to future generations were already familiar to Bonhoeffer, even a decade before he expressed this point so eloquently in "After Ten Years." Already in *Creation and Fall* and subsequently in *Discipleship*, Bonhoeffer begins developing an account of Christ as Mediator that affords a surprising response to the non-identity problem and an innovative grounding for an ethics of intergenerational responsibility.

Who Is Jesus Christ for Us Today? Bonhoeffer's Christ as Mediator of Intergenerational Responsibility

Bonhoeffer's 1933 lectures reflect Christology's entanglement in every aspect of human knowledge, including self-knowledge. Like the mirror, Christ as Mediator (*Mittler*) is "in the center (*Mitte*) between myself and me."[32] Because Christ is the Mediator, Christology is the "invisible, unrecognized, hidden center of scholarship, of the *universitas litterarum*."[33] In these lectures, Bonhoeffer unpacks Christ's mediation as threefold—Christ is at the "center of human existence, history, and nature."[34] First, Christ mediates human existence in the form of God's judgment and justification. In relation to God, human beings exist between law and fulfillment. Since "Jesus himself is God's judgment," God "judges and pardons" humanity's sin in the forgiveness of the cross.[35] Second, Christ mediates history in the dual form of Israel's promised Messiah and of Christ's body, the church: "History lives between promise and fulfilment."[36] As Messiah, Jesus puts an end to the hope of becoming God's people apart from Christ by fulfilling in himself

---

31. See, for example, Hurka, "Future Generations"; Ernest Partridge, "Future Generations," in *A Companion to Environmental Philosophy*, ed. Dale Jamieson (Oxford, UK: Blackwell, 2001), 377–89; idem., "Future Generations," in *Encyclopedia of Science, Technology, and Ethics*, vol. 2, ed. Carl Mitcham (Detroit, MI: Macmillan Reference USA, 2005), 807–10; Holmes Ralston III, *A New Environmental Ethics: The Next Millennium for Life on Earth* (New York: Routledge, 2012), 220–2; John Holt, "Future Generations in Environmental Ethics," in *The Oxford Handbook of Environmental Ethics*, ed. Stephen Gardiner and Allen Thompson (Oxford: Oxford University Press, 2017), 344–54.
32. *DBWE* 12:324.
33. Ibid., 301.
34. Ibid., 324.
35. Ibid., 315, 354.
36. Ibid., 325.

the prophetic hope of Israel. As the church, Christ's body mediates a history that is made between God and the state through the event of the cross that both fulfills and abolishes the law. Third, Christ mediates nature in the form of sacrament as bread and wine, body and blood. For nature that exists as fallen creation, between servitude and its liberation, Christ, its redemption, "is the new creature in the bread and wine, therefore bread and wine are the new creation."[37] In this threefold sense, as the center of human existence, history, and nature, Christ is the Mediator.

In *Discipleship*, Bonhoeffer significantly expands Christ's role as mediator from its soteriological dimensions to include all of human sociality, epistemology, and indeed ontology. Having argued previously that only in Christ are God, world, and human beings rightly recognized as Creator, creation, and creatures, he now foregrounds Christ's role as mediator in these relationships: "[Christ] stands not only between me and God, he also stands between me and the world, between me and other people and things. *He is the mediator* not only between God and human persons, but also between person and person, and between person and reality."[38] Excluding the possibility of unmediated relationships to God, others, and reality, Bonhoeffer rejects as idolatry claims made by German Christians about a revelation apart from Christ in natural and created orders of people, race, blood, and soil, saying, "To be sure, there are plenty of other gods that offer immediate access . . . [However] [e]very unmediated natural relationship, knowingly or unknowingly, is an expression of hatred toward Christ, the mediator, especially if this relationship wants to assume a Christian identity."[39] Here, Bonhoeffer emphasizes that we are to receive and preserve the given realities of the world as mediated by Christ. "Our gratitude for the gifts of creation is offered through Jesus Christ, and our request for the merciful preservation of this life is made for Christ's sake," because in the end:

> There is no knowledge of God's gifts without knowledge of the mediator . . . there is no genuine gratitude for nation, family, history, and nature without a deep repentance that honors Christ alone above these gifts. There is no genuine tie to the given realities of the created world . . . without recognition of the break, which already separates us from the world.[40]

After the Fall, only Christ's mediation enables the preservation of fallen creation to be recognized and received as gift.[41]

---

37. Ibid., 322.
38. *DBWE* 4:94.
39. Ibid., 94–5.
40. Ibid., 96.
41. For more on Christ as Mediator in Bonhoeffer's theology, see Christiane Tietz, "Christology," in *The Oxford Handbook of Dietrich Bonhoeffer*, ed. Michael Mawson and Philip G. Ziegler (Oxford: Oxford University Press, 2019), 150–67; Matthew Puffer,

Consider what these accounts of Christ as Mediator suggest with respect to the non-identity problem. For Bonhoeffer, Christology provides the resources necessary for an innovative response to one of the perennial problems that emerge at the intersection of environmental ethics and intergenerational justice. First, he situates Christ not only at the center of the relation between God and humanity in a soteriological sense but, epistemologically, at the center of all human knowing. Second and equally significant, Bonhoeffer unpacks Christ's mediation existentially, temporally, and ontologically. According to Bonhoeffer, what Christ as Mediator means for our purposes is not that the non-identity problem is done away with but rather that it is expanded to include even those areas of human experience where the problem was deemed not to apply.

Whereas those who wrestle with the non-identity problem take for granted that there is no problem with phenomena that present or identify themselves to us directly in an unmediated sense, Bonhoeffer's claims regarding Christ as Mediator reject the existence of any such unmediated knowledge or encounters. That is, Christ mediates or is at the center of human existence, of history, and of nature such that human beings know God, humanity, and nature, rightly as Creator, creatures, and creation only through Christ's mediation. As a result, Christ as Mediator does not solve the non-identity problem in a manner that gives an account of our obligations to future generations. Bonhoeffer's account of Christ as Mediator does not bring in Christ as a *deus ex machina* who provides unmediated knowledge of which potential future generations will become actualized or realized, nor does Bonhoeffer offer an account of our obligations to potential future generations. Instead, he situates Christ between future generations and us such that Christ becomes the object of our actions *in via*, on the way toward future generations.[42] Importantly, however, Christ is between us and future generations no more and no less than Christ mediates to us knowledge of the present and past, of others and ourselves, of God and the world.

Much as Bonhoeffer in "After Ten Years" and *Ethics* observed that the crisis of National Socialism had thrown all ethical concepts into disarray, leaving little ground beneath our feet, Parfit's non-identity problem demonstrates shortcomings in modern ethical theories regarding obligations to future generations, especially utilitarian, contractarian, and rights-based traditions. Bonhoeffer's identification of Christ as Mediator affords a theological response, though not a solution, to philosophical quandaries about the grounding and specification of our responsibilities to future generations that were likewise left unresolved by modern ethics. As we have seen, at the center and as the mediator of human existence,

---

"Creation" in *The Oxford Handbook of Dietrich Bonhoeffer*, 179–95; and Rowan Williams, *Christ the Heart of Creation* (London: Bloomsbury Continuum, 2018).

42. In this sense Bonhoeffer's Lutheran *genus maiestaticum* has less to do with divine omniscience—by virtue of which God in Christ knows which out of all possible future generations will be actualized—than it has to do with what we might call a divine *omnirelationis* or *omni-mediatoris*—related to but by no means reducible to omnipresence.

history, and nature, Jesus Christ "stands not only between me and God, he also stands between me and the world, between me and other people and things. *He is the mediator* not only between God and human persons, but also between person and person, and between person and reality."[43] By extending this argument about Christ's mediation of present relations to future persons unknown to us but already known to God in Christ, Christ's mediation does not so much solve as exacerbate and amplify the "non-identity problem." This may be cold comfort, but this is clearly the thrust of Bonhoeffer's ethical thought.

Who am I? How is the coming generation to live? Who is Jesus Christ for us today? Bonhoeffer replies: We are those who do not know reality—we do not know ourselves, our neighbors, and certainly, not how the coming generation is to live—apart from Christ who is for us today our Mediator. Bonhoeffer insists that God, history, the world, and we ourselves as well as our responsibilities to others are only rightly known in light of God's self-revelation in Christ. As he would emphasize in the final chapter of his *Ethics*, "Nothing created can be conceived and essentially understood in its nature apart from Christ, the mediator of creation."[44] A Bonhoefferian ethic of intergenerational responsibility begins with this awareness and wagers a free and courageous response on behalf of the poor, vulnerable, and suffering people of present, past, and future generations, all in conformity to Christ's reality as Mediator.

---

43. *DBWE* 4:94.
44. *DBWE* 6:399.

Part III

BONHOEFFER, THE POLITICAL, AND SOLIDARITY

Chapter 11

THE POLITICAL MYTH OF CHRISTIAN NATIONHOOD
BONHOEFFER AND THE PUBLIC ROLE OF THE CHURCHES IN ZAMBIA

Teddy Chalwe Sakupapa

Introduction

In the twentieth century, world Christianity underwent what Dana Robert has described succinctly as "a massive cultural and demographic shift away from Europeans and their descendants towards the peoples of the southern hemisphere."[1] These developments became evident in the context of twenty-first-century Africa in which the abovementioned southward shift led to remarkable transformations of the Christianity of European missionary origins and the proliferation of African independent churches with a Pentecostal character. These transformations have been described variously in terms of widespread pentecostalization and charismatization of Christianity in Africa and are thus indicative of changing ecclesial and theological landscapes in Africa. This is no less true of Zambia where Christianity historically has been "a mosaic of various Christian expressions."[2] Research on changing religious landscapes in Africa has highlighted, among other issues, the political nature of twenty-first-century African Christianities, often debunking arguments that characterize contemporary African Pentecostal Christianity as being apolitical.[3] But how do these developments relate to Dietrich Bonhoeffer (1906–45), a white male European theologian?

The title of this chapter may suggest that this contribution entails a discussion of Bonhoeffer's theology mostly likely in terms of what John de Gruchy has described as the "political appropriation"[4] of Bonhoeffer. While it is indisputable

---

1. Dana L. Robert, "Shifting Southward: Global Christianity Since 1945," *International Bulletin of Missionary Research* 24, no. 2 (2000): 50.

2. Teddy C. Sakupapa, "Zambia," in *Anthology of African Christianity*, ed. Isabel Apawo Phiri et al. (Oxford: Regnum Books International, 2016), 759.

3. Ruth Marshall, *Political Spiritualities: The Pentecostal Revolution in Nigeria* (Chicago, IL: University of Chicago Press, 2009).

4. John W. de Gruchy, "The Reception of Bonhoeffer's Theology," in *The Cambridge Companion to Dietrich Bonhoeffer*, ed. John de Gruchy (Cambridge: Cambridge University Press 1999), 103.

that many aspects of Bonhoeffer's theology, for example, his ethic of responsibility, aspects of his Christological ecclesiology, and his call to costly discipleship do indeed resonate with many of the urgent questions in contemporary discourse on church and politics in African, this chapter is not a wholesale appropriation of Bonhoeffer's theology as a response to the present crisis in the world in general and Africa in particular. Rather, I take John de Gruchy's caution seriously that the true reception of Bonhoeffer's legacy is not a mere repetition of his words but rather "responding to the challenge of what it means to follow Jesus Christ within our own historical context."[5] Therefore, rather than attempt a political appropriation of Bonhoeffer's theology or ask what relevance his theology has for the contemporary African context, I ask what challenges and implications the African context has in relation to Bonhoeffer's theology in general and to the Bonhoeffer scholarship in particular.

This chapter discusses the public role of Christianity in changing ecclesial landscapes in the Southern African country of Zambia. The chapter interrogates the political myth of Zambian Christian nationhood. Structurally, the chapter will begin with brief remarks on Zambia's religiopolitical landscape as a case study and then offer a brief overview of Bonhoeffer's theological reception in Africa. This will be followed by a discussion of recent discourses on the public role of Christianity in Zambia. I will conclude with some thoughts on what I see as opportunities and perils of the reception of Dietrich Bonhoeffer in a contemporary Zambian context.[6]

Politics of the Declaration of Zambia as a Christian Nation

Zambia is the only country in Africa with a widely popularized political myth of Christian nationhood whose origins are traced to the declaration of Zambia as a Christian nation on December 29, 1991, by the country's second Republican President, Frederick Chiluba. The said declaration (hereafter the "Declaration") was first enshrined in the preamble of the 1996 amended constitution and has since been upheld in all subsequent constitutional reviews, essentially on the basis of "Christian demographics and the perceived normative contribution of Christian values"[7] to the Zambian society. The Declaration and its subsequent

---

5. De Gruchy, "The Reception of Bonhoeffer's Theology," 96.

6. While views expressed in this chapter are my own, I wish to thank Prof. Frits De Lange who first introduced me to Dietrich Bonhoeffer's ethics and theology during my studies at the Protestant Theological University in Kampen, Netherlands, between 2011 and 2012.

7. Christian M. Green, "Religious and Legal Pluralism in Recent African Constitutional Reform," *Journal of Law and Religion* 28, no. 2 (2013): 428. Statistics indicate that 95.5 percent of Zambia's population identify as Christian, 0.5 percent Muslim, 0.2 percent other, and 1.8 percent have no religious affiliation. See CSO, "Census of Population and Housing," *Republic of Zambia* (2012): 19.

enshrinement in the preamble of the Zambian constitution sparked intense debate also among churches. The Council of Churches in Zambia (CCZ) and the Zambia Episcopal Conference (ZEC)—now the Zambian Conference of Catholic Bishops (ZCCB)—took a critical stance against the Declaration while the more charismatic Evangelical Fellowship of Zambia largely acquiesced to Chiluba's Declaration. The language and politics of the Declaration have become prominent in Zambian politics recently especially since Edgar Lungu became president of Zambia in 2015. This may be traced to Lungu's 2015 presidential campaign following President Sata's death in October 2014. Being an unlikely candidate to win the 2015 elections not least because of negative media publicity and newspaper editorials commenting on his "drinking problem" (*chakolwa*) and the fact that he had been suspended previously from practicing as a lawyer by the Law Association of Zambia in 2010 after allegedly swindling a client. To counter such negative media publicity, Lungu was portrayed as Sata's anointed successor and his candidacy was branded in Christian rhetoric. He was depicted as a humble man of faith, a man of God, and a man of the people.[8]

In his article, "Christianising Edgar Chagwa Lungu," Chammah Kaunda illustrates the role of social media photography in crafting the Christian image of Lungu. Once Lungu won the elections, he "added a unique semblance to the political rhetoric of Christian nation in radical and ironic ways compared to other presidents after the Chiluba era."[9] Lungu soon began to deploy the Declaration in public discourse to mobilize and frame notions of Christian nationhood and citizenship as well as to use that public albeit questionable Christian identity to distinguish himself from his political opponents who were being projected as being unchristian. Indeed, as Ellis and Ter Haar explain, African politicians "believe that access to the spiritual world is a vital resource in the constant struggle to secure advantage over their rivals in political in-fighting."[10] One may argue that the Christianization of Lungu has almost resulted in the *lungufication* of Christianity in Zambian politics. Christianity has thus been used to achieve all manner of political goals. The intensification of Christian rhetoric in Zambia's public discourse has since become a subject of intense scholarly attention particularly the question of the relationship between religion and politics.[11] These studies suggest

---

8. For example, Alastair Fraser, "Post-Populism in Zambia: Michael Sata's Rise, Demise and Legacy," *International Political Science Review* 38, no. 4 (2017): 456–72. See also Teddy Chalwe Sakupapa, "Ethno-Regionalism, Politics and the Role of Religion in Zambia: Changing Ecumenical Landscapes in a Christian Nation, 2015–2018," *Exchange* 48, no. 2 (2019): 105–26.

9. Sakupapa, "Ethno-Regionalism," 113.

10. Stephen Ellis and Gerrie Ter Haar, "Religion and Politics in Sub-Saharan Africa," *The Journal of Modern African Studies* 36, no. 2 (1998): 175–201.

11. Cf. Austin Cheyeka, "Zambia, a 'Christian Nation' in Post Movement for Multiparty Democracy (MMD) Era, 2011–2016," *International Journal of Humanities and Social Science* 6, no. 7 (2016): 162; Naomi Haynes, "Zambia Shall Be Saved! Prosperity Gospel

that the religious and the political are not treated as separate spheres in most African contexts including Zambia. Both are seen as "systems of ordering power inherent in human society."[12] The political deployment of Christian rhetoric raises significant questions about the relationship between church and state as well as the self-understanding of Christians and churches in their public witness.

This is crucial given that most contemporary Zambian newspaper articles, social media commentary, and posts are punctuated by various complaints about the increasing level of corruption in government, a general distrust of the judicial system, the unbearably high cost of living, the unpredictable and endless power outage, the commodification of higher education, the impotence of the government to address daily challenges, and the hesitation among many including church leaders to speak truth to power for fear of political persecution and, in many cases, the fear of losing the means of survival such as a job or a business. Since Edgar Lungu became President of Zambia, many have noted the waning of "prophetic" Christianity amid a politically driven discourse on Zambia's Christian nationhood. In such a context, Bonhoeffer's pertinent concern expressed in a letter to Eberhard Bethge on April 30, 1944, may well serve as a key to explore the ecclesiological implications of the ambiguous deployment of Christianity in public discourse in Zambia. Bonhoeffer writes, "What is bothering me incessantly is the question what Christianity really is, or indeed who Christ really is, for us today."[13] It is germane to make some remarks about Bonhoeffer's reception in Africa before venturing into a theological discussion of the public role of Christianity in Zambia.

Reception of Bonhoeffer in Africa

A remarkable feature of the scholarship and research on the German theologian, Dietrich Bonhoeffer, is how his theology has been brought to bear on different contexts and social issues. In this regard, the South African theologian, John de Gruchy, has noted the "diversity of Bonhoeffer reception and interpretation."[14] The influence of Bonhoeffer's theology on a number of self-consciously contextual theologies has been widely recognized most notably in a variety of Protestant

---

Politics in a Self-Proclaimed Christian Nation," *Nova Religio: The Journal of Alternative and Emergent Religions* 19, no. 1 (2015): 5–24; Adriaan van Klinken, "Homosexuality, Politics and Pentecostal Nationalism in Zambia," *Studies in World Christianity* 20, no. 3 (2014): 259–81.

12. Ellis and Ter Haar, "Religion and Politics," 195.
13. *DWBE* 8:402.
14. De Gruchy, "The Reception of Bonhoeffer's Theology," 96.

Latin American theologies,[15] some Asian contextual theologies,[16] some liberation theologies in Africa, particularly in the South African context, and more recently in environmental ethics and eco-theology.[17] In South Africa, the influence of Bonhoeffer's theology is arguably considerable as evident in the works of prominent South African theologians, most notably John de Gruchy[18] and several others including Russel Botman, Robert Vosloo, and Nico Koopman. Unarguably, more than any other South African theologian, the scholarship of John de Gruchy has had an incredible impact on the reception of Bonhoeffer's theology and on various interpretations of Bonhoeffer's relevance to the church struggle against apartheid in South Africa.[19] One might argue that among South African Black theologians, the significance of Bonhoeffer may be located in the resonance that his life and theology have with the concerns of Black theology, namely a theology from below that is rooted in the experiences of the oppressed.[20]

However, beyond South Africa, few African theologians[21] have engaged with Bonhoeffer. Reasons for this are mainly contextual. Altmann's observation regarding Bonhoeffer's influence on Latin American theology captures something of what I see as Bonhoeffer's significance in contemporary Zambia. According to Altmann, "Bonhoeffer's theology reveals itself again and again with a potential of inspiring those who seek justice alongside the victims of exclusion, marginalization,

---

15. See Julio de Santa Ana, "The Influence of Bonhoeffer on the Theology of Liberation," *The Ecumenical Review* 28, no. 2 (1976): 188–97. Bonhoeffer's significance in liberation theology may be traced to his Christology, namely a focus on the significance of Jesus Christ to the historical situation in which individuals find themselves.

16. Cf. David Thang Moe, "What Has Dietrich Bonhoeffer to Do with Asian Theology?" *Asia Journal of Theology* 28, no. 2 (2014): 175–202, who underscores the significance of Bonhoeffer's liberative Christology.

17. See Steven Van den Heuvel, *Bonhoeffer's Christocentric Theology and Fundamental Debates in Environmental Ethics* (Eugene, OR: Wipf & Stock Publishers, 2017).

18. John de Gruchy, *Bonhoeffer and South Africa: Theology in Dialogue* (Grand Rapids, MI: Eerdmans, 1984). See also John de Gruchy, *Bonhoeffer for a New Day: Theology in a Time of Transition. Papers Presented at the Seventh International Bonhoeffer Congress* (Grand Rapids, MI: Eerdmans, 1997). This edited volume was the output of the Seventh International Bonhoeffer Congress held in Cape Town in January 1996.

19. Other South African theologians who have reflected on Bonhoeffer's significance in South Africa include the late Russel Botman who wrote a doctoral thesis on Bonhoeffer. See Russel Botman, "Discipleship as Transformation: Towards a Theology of Transformation" (PhD diss., University of the Western Cape, Bellville, 1994).

20. See reflection on Bonhoeffer by Allan Boesak, "What Dietrich Bonhoeffer Has Meant to Me," in *Bonhoeffer's Ethics: Old Europe and New Frontiers*, ed. Guy Christopher Carter (Kampen: Kok, 1991), 21–9.

21. See Elias Bongmba, "The Priority of the Other: Ethics in Africa. Perspectives from Bonhoeffer and Levinas," in *Bonhoeffer for a New Day: Theology in a Time of Transition*, ed. John de Gruchy (Grand Rapids, MI: Wm B. Eerdmans, 1997), 190–208.

discrimination, and oppression, shaping their spirituality and giving strength to their socio-political struggle."[22] The current tone of uncertainty that accompanies commentary on South Africa's economy, the disappointment that young people express regarding what they see as empty slogans of a free and equal South Africa, the rising cost of living, the high rate of unemployment, and the widening levels of inequality highlight ongoing struggles particularly among Black South Africans. The various fall-ist movements and the recent calls for decolonization of higher education including theology and religious studies capture the historical realities. Similar concerns, albeit shaped by a different historical trajectory, characterize what has become a daily struggle for survival in Zambia. Therefore, the question posed in the theme of the thirteenth Bonhoeffer Congress, namely "How is the coming generation to go on living?," is not only timely but also deeply significant for a gathering that is reflecting on the legacy of a theologian who has been described as "one of the most hope-inspiring figures, perhaps the most hope-inspiring figure of modern Protestantism."[23] I now turn to the public role of Christianity in Zambia.

Christianity and Politics in Lungu's Christian Nation

Christianity in Zambia has played a public role since missionary times to which its origins may be traced. Since the Constitution of Zambia as a nation-state, which became politically independent of the British in 1964, the legacy of Western missionaries in the fields of health, education, and social welfare continues to be representative of the overt public role of Christianity in the country. Mission education also played a major role in the rise of African nationalism and subsequently laid a firm foundation for the development of political parties.[24] Born to Malawian parents who served as pioneer missionaries at Lubwa Mission of the Church of Scotland, Zambia's first president, Kenneth Kaunda, often spoke of the church as a "mirror to the nation,"[25] particularly during the first decade of his rule. As such, during Kaunda's era, church-state relations "oscillated between various forms of engagement including resistance, accommodation and collaboration."[26]

---

22. Walter Altmann, "Bonhoeffer in Latin American Perceptions: An Inspiration to Overcome Structures of Injustice?" *Stellenbosch Theological Journal* 2, no. 1 (2016): 13–26.

23. Heinrich Ott, *Reality and Faith: The Theological Legacy of Dietrich Bonhoeffer* (Philadelphia, PA: Fortress Press, 1972), 24.

24. Cf. Austin Cheyeka, "Religion and Political Parties in Zambia," in *The Routledge Handbook to Religion and Political Parties*, ed. Jeffrey Haynes (Abingdon: Routledge, 2019), 275–86.

25. Marja Hinfelaar, "Legitimizing Powers: The Political Role of the Roman Catholic Church, 1972–1991," in *One Zambia, Many Histories*, ed. Jan-Bart Gewald, Marja Hinfelaar and Giacomo Macola (Leiden: Brill, 2008), 127–43.

26. Isaac Phiri, "Why African Churches Preach Politics: The Case of Zambia," *Journal of Church and State* 41, no. 2 (1999): 323–47.

During the 1990s, the so-called three major church mother bodies in Zambia, namely the CCZ, the ZEC (now ZCCB), and EFZ played a conspicuous role in Zambia's transition from a one-party state to multiparty electoral democracy, which marked the end of Kaunda's rule. This return to multiparty democracy in 1991 also witnessed changes in Zambia's religious demographics evident in the proliferation of the so-called Born-Again Christianity. It was in this context of a Pentecostal and charismatic ferment that Zambia's second Republican President, Frederick Chiluba, declared Zambia as a Christian nation on December 29, 1991. As already indicated, the Declaration attained new significance during Lungu's presidential campaigns in 2015. Lungu appropriated the rhetoric of the Declaration in his campaigns and public utterances to affirm Christian nationhood. This public portrayal of Lungu as a Christian or even his Christianization is a subject that deserves separate investigation.[27] It is worth noting here that after winning the 2015 presidential by-elections, Lungu's first year as president was characterized by an ailing economy owing to, among other factors, drought, a poorly performing currency, and high unemployment. Amid such challenges, President Lungu called for a National Day of Repentance, prayer, and fasting on October 18, 2015. Does this suggest something of what Bonhoeffer describes in his *Letters and Papers from Prison*? He writes that religious people "speak of God at a point where human knowledge is at an end . . . or when human strength fails. Actually, it's a *deus ex machina* that they're always bringing on the scene, either to appear to solve insoluble problems or to provide strength when human powers fail, thus always exploiting human weakness or human limitations."[28]

For Bonhoeffer, God is not at the boundaries but the very center of life. For Lungu, however, an interventionist notion of divine action was projected as if God could simply be called upon to intervene drastically and resolve crises and human problems. Ironically, Lungu's appeal to prayer won him the approval of some among the increasingly pentecostalized Zambian constituency. President Lungu subsequently declared October 18 as the official National Day of Prayer and Fasting for all Zambians. Lungu's public image as a Christian was further buttressed by a partisan political group called "Christians for Lungu" that was formed in March 2016, only a few months before the presidential elections. The group's founder, Liya Mutale, a medical doctor, openly campaigned for Lungu. According to Mutale, Lungu deserved the support of Christian citizens given his reaffirmation of the Declaration and his decision to mark October 18 as a National Day of Prayer and Fasting.

Lungu made further pronouncements and decisions that accentuate the politics of the Declaration. In October 2016, he laid the foundation stone at the construction site of the National House of Prayer for All Nations Tabernacle in

---

27. Cf. Chammah Kaunda, "Christianising Edgar Chagwa Lungu: The Christian Nation, Social Media Presidential Photography and 2016 Election Campaign," *Stellenbosch Theological Journal* 4, no. 1 (2018): 215–45.

28. *DWBE* 8:366.

the capital city, Lusaka. Again, in a speech that he delivered on September 4, 2016, at the induction service of Rev. Sydney Sichilima as the new Bishop of the United Church of Zambia (the largest protestant denomination in the country), President Lungu announced plans to create a government Ministry of Religious Affairs. This was subsequently approved by Parliament on October 27, 2016, and a Pentecostal pastor, Rev. Godfridah Sumaili, was appointed as minister for the new Ministry of National Guidance and Religious Affairs (MNGRA). The key functions of MNGRA include the operationalization of the Declaration, interdenominational dialogue, providing guidance on national values, principles and ethics, coordination of public religious celebrations, the preservation of Christian and religious sites, and religious affairs.[29] Recent statements and actions of the Minister for MNGRA begs the question whether the ministry is nothing but the vanguard of state theologies of empire facilitating the political acquiesce of churches in state-led Christian nationalism.[30] Elsewhere, I have offered a case study of how MNGRA may serve as a "force-field" for the polarization of the church's prophetic ministry and therefore complicating Zambia's ecumenical landscape.[31]

Some Pentecostal pastors have openly supported Lungu's Christian nation rhetoric, and some leaders of historic mission churches have been tempted to offer tacit ecclesiastical endorsement of Lungu's "Christian" politics. While a conclusive assessment of the public impact of Christianity in Zambia is not within the purview of this chapter, it may be argued that in general, the advocacy and prophetic stance of the churches have declined during Lungu's tenure as president of the country. His tenure also has had negative implications for institutional ecumenism as there is visibly a competition for voice among the diversity of Christian churches and communities often tailored to support the status quo. Meanwhile, President Lungu and the main opposition leader, Hakainde Hichilema, have continued to frequent church services and other Christian functions and constantly publicize their appearances at such events through various social media platforms.

From the foregoing, I argue that the political deployment of Christian rhetoric and the language of Christian nationhood that underpinned the declaration of October 18 as a day of prayer and fasting, the construction of a National House of Prayer for All Nations Tabernacle, and the creation of MNGRA raise a number of questions. Given that President Lungu is at the center of these initiatives even though he may not be the chief architect of the ideas, in what follows I will speak of the *lungufication* of Christianity in Zambia. Thus, one may ask whether the *lungufication* of Christianity in Zambia is extending the Declaration beyond the

---

29. See Republic of Zambia, "Gazette Notice No. 836 of 2016," *Government Gazette* 52, no. 76 (2016): 941. https://zambialii.org/node/12892 (accessed November 26, 2018).

30. For example, Somizi, a South African openly gay celebrity, was refused entry into Zambia for fear that he would corrupt the Christian morals of citizens in a Christian nation. Zodwa wa Bantu, a South African dancer, was refused entry on similar grounds. Other people who have been refused entry into Zambia include controversial prophets.

31. Sakupapa, "Ethno-Regionalism," 123.

framing of Christian nationhood to making Christianity a de facto state religion. Further, can the state become an actor in religious affairs? And finally, what are the implications of the *lungufication* of Christianity for the public role of the church in Zambia? To reflect on these questions, I will draw on African theologies that engage with the question of the public role of Christianity.

Public Role of Christianity

That the church has a public role in society is assumed by many African theologians not least because of the communal orientations of most African ecclesiologies and theologies. Many also note that theology in Africa has always been related to the social context.[32] This is evident in the respective proposals for a theology of reconstruction offered by Jesse Mugambi and Charles Villa-Vicencio during the early 1990s as well as in the debates which these proposals elicited. Relevant to this essay is the Ugandan theologian Emmanuel Katongole's critique of Mugambi's and Villa-Vicencio's respective proposals. While sharing the view that the church has a public role, Katongole perceptively asks why has "Christianity, despite its overwhelming presence [in Africa], failed to make a significant dent in the social history of the continent?" Katongole's answer to this question is a nuanced portrayal of the inseparability of what the church is (ecclesiology) and the social responsibility of the church (ethics).

Katongole's[33] analysis of how the social responsibility of the church has been understood in African theology identifies three paradigms in the church's quest for social relevance and political performance, namely the spiritual (spiritual formation), the pastoral (social material intervention), and the political (advocacy and mediation). The spiritual paradigm describes an approach to Christian social ethics that privileges the inner transformation of an individual whose new life in Christ leads him or her to recognize that power belongs to God and issues in the formation of "patterns of behaviour." Katongole then describes the pastoral paradigm as focusing on the church's intervention in society in the form of relief services and development services. The third paradigm, namely the political paradigm, indicates that the church has a unique responsibility to ensure justice, human rights, and democracy, among other issues. This third paradigm, Katongole argues, is dominant among ecumenical organizations such as the All Africa Conference of Churches as well as among Roman Catholics. While this neat categorization is useful, an analysis of the programmatic work of churches

---

32. Cf. Bénézet Bujo, *African Theology in Its Social Context* (Eugene, OR: Wipf & Stock, 2006). See also essays in the edited volume by Jesse Mugambi and Laurenti Magesa, *The Church in African Christianity: Innovative Essays in Ecclesiology Theology* (Nairobi: Acton, 1998).

33. Emmanuel Katongole, *The Sacrifice of Africa: A Political Theology for Africa* (Grand Rapids, MI: Wm. B. Eerdmans, 2011).

and ecumenical bodies in Zambia and their public statements and pastoral letters[34] suggests that Katongole's paradigms are not necessarily mutually exclusive. His analysis is nevertheless helpful in assessing the unique contribution of churches to social transformation so that the church is not perceived as just another non-governmental organization.

Thus, following Stanley Hauerwas, Katongole proposes a view of the church as an alternate social expression of the gospel. The church's unique contribution is "imagining the social frames of reference in new and fresh ways grounded in her unique story and calling."[35] In other words, the church is "another form of politics," Katongole asserts. Seeing the church as a socio-political vision, Katongole is of the opinion that the church's "relation to the nation-state cannot be simply one of affirmation or resistance."[36] Accordingly, he critiques what he calls a prescriptive agenda of Christian social reflection preoccupied as it were with "generating recommendations, strategies, and skills to help politics work." Katongole further argues that all three paradigms highlighted above assume a dichotomized view of religion and politics. That is to say, they assign Christianity to the religious domain as if it functions "outside the boundaries of the historical, material, and political processes that shape the social history of Africa."[37] Here, one may add that Bonhoeffer's rejection of a number of dichotomies, including the sacred and the secular, the private and the public, is significant.

As pertinent as Katongole's diagnosis of the limitations of the three dominant paradigms to Christian social ethics Africa is, I find his treatment of the nation-state unconvincing given that the nation-state in Africa has a dubious character. Further, as important as Katongole's attempt to explore how the church in Africa can become a demonstration plot "of a different world right here,"[38] he glaringly overlooks the changing ecclesial landscapes in Africa, characterized by the pentecostalization and charismatization of Christianity. The question of what Christianity really is and most significantly of who Jesus Christ is for us today in Africa cannot be posed without considering at the same time the pentecostalization and charismatization of Christianity, on the one hand, and the credence of the view that Christianity has become an African's religion (Bediako), on the other. In the Zambian context, this is crucial given the overt deployment of Christianity in Zambia's public sphere and the probability that *lungufication* in politics has occurred at a time of rapid pentecostalization alluded to in the introduction.

---

34. For a collection of key statements and documents in this regard, see Joe Komakoma, *The Social Teaching of the Catholic Bishops and Other Christian Leaders in Zambia: Major Pastoral Letters and Statements, 1953–2001* (Ndola: Mission Press, 2003).
35. Katongole, *The Sacrifice of Africa*, 47.
36. Ibid., 121.
37. Ibid., 41.
38. Ibid., 111.

Church and Politics in a Largely Pentecostalized and Charismatized Zambia

While the aim here is not to offer an exhaustive account of the relationship between religion and politics in Zambia, it is worth noting that religion in most African contexts can be seen as both "a mode of apprehending reality"[39] and a practice of mediation. As such, it is not far-fetched to argue as Ellis and Ter Haar do that "it is largely through religious ideas that Africans think about the world today, and that religious ideas provide them with a means of becoming social and political actors."[40] But what may account for the political appeal to religion in Lungu's Christian nation? Given analyses that suggest that both religion and politics are systems of ordering the world even though the spiritual world is perceived as the ultimate source of power in that it impinges on the material world, some argue that politicians seek to have access to the spiritual world as a vital resource in their effort to "secure advantage over their rivals in political in-fighting."[41] As Ogbu Kalu perceptively argues, the interest of African politicians in religion may be attributed to the continuity of a "religious substratum"[42] to African political culture rooted in traditions of the sacralization of power that was prevalent in African traditional societies. In light of the above, theories of clientelism and accounts that depict the relationship between religion and politics merely in terms of the political mobilization of religion as simply another social identity fall short of a comprehensive understanding of the relationship between religion and politics in Africa.

In the case of President Edgar Lungu, a number of questions emerge due to how his appeal to Christianity has been concretized into a particular vision of Zambian Christian nationhood albeit through an ambiguous deployment of Christianity. However, many Zambians, particularly the youth, find it difficult to reconcile the idea of a Christian nation—as deployed in the politics and language of the Declaration—with the reality of poverty, endemic corruption, and political violence. Given the *lungufication* of Christianity in Zambian politics, one wonders whether Christianity has been turned into an idolatrous religion in Zambia. Other challenges have emerged, which call for further reflections on the Zambian churches' ecumenical witness. A few observations may be made in this regard. First, the differing approaches on how to engage the state appear to threaten institutional ecumenism in Zambia. The issue is not about holding divergent views, but it is the motivation and inspiration behind the holding of these views that must be subjected to theological critique. The continued *lungufication* of

---

39. Stephen Ellis and Gerrie ter Haar, "Religion and Politics: Taking African Epistemologies Seriously," *The Journal of Modern African Studies* 45, no. 3 (2007): 387.

40. Ellis and Ter Haar, "Religion and Politics," 4.

41. Ibid., 187.

42. Ogbu Kalu, *African Pentecostalism: An Introduction* (Oxford: Oxford University Press, 2008), 199.

Christianity in Zambian politics has contributed to the strain in ecumenical relations among churches, as some church leaders openly differ in their support of President Lungu's Christian nation agenda or lack thereof. Second, there is a danger of churches being co-opted into partisan political ends, which suggests that Christianity as deployed in Zambia's Christian nation rhetoric may well lead to an idolatrous Christianity that presents a false conception of God and the good. Further, this poses a challenge to the Christian prophetic witness to the reign of God as demonstrated in the ministry of Jesus of Nazareth and the Old Testament prophets. And third, given the pentecostalization of mainline Christianity in Zambia and the growth of Pentecostalism, the so-called mainline churches no longer have a monopoly of what it means to be church since most Pentecostals do not subscribe to creedal notions of ecclesiality that are dominant in traditional ecumenical discourse.

The third point above is critical not least because dominant models of church and state often assume relatively "stable" notions of church. The Zambian case, as elsewhere in Africa, illustrates the point that the pentecostalization and charismatization of mainline Christianity in Africa[43] complicate the dominant and popular understandings of church and church membership.[44] As Bernhard Udelhoven has demonstrated in his analysis of the changing face of Christianity in Zambia, the newer and diverse forms of Christianity in Zambia variously self-identify as ministries, fellowships, or churches[45] and are markedly estranged from creedal traditions of mainline churches and the institutionalized forms of ecumenism. Therefore, given the complexity and diversity of the concrete forms of manifestations of the term church in general and of ecclesial identity in particular, both are becoming elusive in the Zambian context. Does this suggest the provisional nature of the character of what may be termed church? Thus put, I am not suggesting the need for an ideal ecclesiology or what the Roman Catholic scholar Nicholas Healy calls "blueprint ecclesiologies." The problem with blueprint ecclesiologies is that they foster a "curious inability to acknowledge

---

43. See Sakupapa, "Christianity in Zambia"; see also Damaris Seleina Parsitau, "From the Periphery to the Centre: The Pentecostalization of Mainline Christianity in Kenya," *Missionalia* 35, no. 3 (2007): 83–111. See also Cephas Omenyo who speaks of "Pentecost outside Pentecostalism" in his account of the "charismatisation of mainline Christianity" in Ghana, in his book, *Pentecost Outside Pentecostalism: A Study of the Development of Charismatic Renewal in the Mainline Churches in Ghana* (Utrecht: Uitgeverij Boekencentrum, 2006).

44. For a discussion with reference to changing ecumenical landscapes in Zambia, see Teddy Chalwe Sakupapa, "Some African Perspectives on Ecumenical Theology," in *The Routledge Handbook of African Theology*, ed. Elias Bongmba (New York: Routledge, 2020), 210–23.

45. Bernhard Udelhoven, "The Changing Face of Christianity in Zambia: New Churches of Bauleni Compound," *Fenza Documents* (2010): 2–4. https://www.fenza.org/docs/ben/Changing_face--Udelhoven.pdf.

the complexities of ecclesial life in its pilgrim state."[46] These concerns cannot be overlooked by the new generation of African theologians[47] who find themselves building on the foundation of earlier variants of African theology which, as Tinyiko Maluleke observed two decades ago, had "been 'church theology' done by church people for the sake of the church and its missionary task."[48] Contemporary African theology is indeed faced with the challenge of imagining new accounts of being church and asking again what it means to follow Jesus Christ today.

Therefore, in the Zambian context, analysis of church and state relations is not a mere ecclesiological straitjacket. Historically, the term church has been used in the Zambian context to refer to various forms of being church such as local congregations, denominations, and ecumenical church bodies.[49] As highlighted above, the changing ecclesial landscapes in Zambia pose a challenge to idealized notions of being church. Could a reinterpretation of Bonhoeffer perhaps be resourceful in such a context? In Bonhoeffer, the term "church" refers to a historical community, yet one that is established by God. Bonhoeffer's view of the church as a historical community and indeed an empirical reality is apposite in this regard. However, that the empirical church is "the presupposition for theology,"[50] as Bonhoeffer noted in his 1932 lectures, may require a new language given the realities and challenges of being "church" in the Zambian context.

Similarly, Bonhoeffer's Christological conception of the church as the community of the Risen Christ,[51] "Christ existing as church-community,"[52] has significant implications in the Zambian context given how the description of Christ as a man for others suggests that the church is a community of others. As Geffrey Kelly observes, "Bonhoeffer spoke . . . of a 'non-religious Christianity' in which the church would become, like Christ, a community of service to the oppressed, not a sacralised institution eager to preserve its clerical privileges and maintain its powerful hold over spiritually dependent subjects."[53] This close connection between ecclesiology and Christology in Bonhoeffer is pertinent. I argue that Bonhoeffer's

---

46. Nicholas Healy, *Church, World and the Christian Life: Practical-Prophetic Ecclesiology* (Cambridge: Cambridge University Press, 2000), 37.

47. See Teddy Chalwe Sakupapa, "Theology amidst Wickedness: Is African Theology Equipped to Address Intractable Societal Issues?" *Philosophia Reformata* 85, no. 2 (2020): 218.

48. Tinyiko Maluleke, "Half a Century of African Christian Theologies," *Journal of Theology for Southern Africa* 99 (1997): 9.

49. For a thorough discussion of related forms of being church, see Dirkie Smit, *Essays in Public Theology: Collected Essays 1* (Stellenbosch: African Sun Media, 2007), 61–5.

50. *DBWE* 11:290.

51. *DBWE* 1:127.

52. Ibid., 199.

53. Geffrey Kelly, "Prayer and Action for Justice: Bonhoeffer's Spirituality," in *The Cambridge Companion to Dietrich Bonhoeffer*, ed. John de Gruchy (Cambridge: Cambridge University Press, 1999), 249.

notion of existing-for-others, which is most developed in his *Letters and Papers from Prison*, has significant implications for the responsible actions of Christians in society and, in that regard, for the public role of Christianity. Here, Bonhoeffer's earlier articulation of the "sociality of theological concepts," particularly in his dissertation *Sanctorum Communio*, is significant. Such a social understanding of the church may well be relevant in addressing some of the challenges presented by the *lungufication* of Christianity in Zambia, which is born out of the politics and language of the Declaration. Most significantly, while Bonhoeffer's "model" of church and state relations cannot be uncritically appropriated, his categorical insights on the need to critique both church and state are crucial since both have but one Lord.

Conclusion

This chapter discussed the political myth of Zambia's Christian nationhood, analyzing the political deployment of Christianity in Zambia's public sphere and its impact on the waning of the churches' prophetic witness. I argued that the political deployment of Christianity in the politics and language of the Declaration and Zambia's Christian nation rhetoric may well lead to an idolatrous Christianity that presents a false conception of God. The key challenge, therefore, is how the Christian faith and the communities that identify as Christian are to bear witness to Christ in an environment that is increasingly violent and corrupt. If churches and Christians in Zambia do not live up to the demands of the gospel, it may suggest that the Spirit is working beyond the Christian church, its structures, and its institutions. Finally, the chapter cautions against willy-nilly appropriations of church and state models, including Bonhoeffer's Lutheran political theology. It therefore concludes with a question to Bonhoeffer scholarship on the relationship between religion and politics in largely pentecostalized contexts where notions of church have become rather elusive.

Chapter 12

RECONCILIATION, FORGIVENESS, AND SCARRING OVER

POLITICAL DIMENSIONS OF MORAL CONCEPTS

Ralf K. Wüstenberg

Introduction

To speak of reconciliation in the context of politics is controversial. This was as true at the time of Dietrich Bonhoeffer as during the transition to democracy after the fall of the Berlin wall in 1989. A former Minister of Justice in Germany was quoted as saying, "The concept of reconciliation is not useful for the social integration process that we need in Germany."[1] But Anglican Archbishop Desmond Tutu remarked concerning the social upheaval that took place in South Africa after 1990 that, "Without reconciliation there is no future."[2] These divergent perspectives suggest that a different value is placed on the concept of reconciliation when viewed from its own unique politically evolving perspective. The former president of the Federal Republic of Germany, Richard von Weizsäcker, commented: "One can tell from these words on reconciliation that it is a weighty topic and will be with us for a very long time."[3]

It is abundantly clear that reconciliation is a "weighty" theme by virtue of the gravity of the term. Wherever people are at all able to reconcile, it is viewed as nothing less than a remarkable event. Reconciliation is, after all, an extraordinary occurrence and typically unexpected. Hannah Arendt speaks of it in terms of "the wonder of a new beginning."[4] Humans, groups, or nationalities which manage to reconcile have already overcome a guilt-ridden state of alienation, and, in the truest sense, have put it behind them! Through reconciliation, people are able to leap over the shadows of the past and forge a common future together despite

---

1. Cited in Richard von Weizsäcker, *Vier Zeiten: Erinnerungen* (Berlin: Siedler, 1999), 410.

2. Cited in Ralf K. Wüstenberg, *Wahrheit, Recht und Versöhnung: Auseinandersetzung mit der Vergangenheit nach den politischen Umbrüchen in Südafrika und Deutschland* (Frankfurt am Main: Peter Lang, 1998), 125 n.34.

3. Weizsäcker, *Vier Zeiten*, 410.

4. See Hannah Arendt, *Vita activa oder Vom tätigen Leben* (Munich: Piper, 1992), 231–8.

a traumatic past. However, since the concept of "reconciliation" carries so much weight, especially in the Christian tradition, the danger of abuse by political interests is great. Politically charged power relationships can be disguised easily under the banner of "reconciliation" to maintain the status quo, as can be seen by a critical analysis of ways in which the term "reconciliation" was used in political slogans in South Africa in the 1980s.[5] "No reconciliation without justice" was added as a qualifier to the Christian definition of reconciliation in order to prevent its strategic misuse by the apartheid regime. Subsequently, in the 1990s, after the political changes in South Africa, "truth" was added as a qualifier to the definition of reconciliation. "No reconciliation without the truth" was printed on the banners of the South African Truth and Reconciliation Commission.[6] If, for example, I wished to reconcile my own history of injustice, suffering, and persecution during the apartheid period—the coming to terms with the painful past as was the case with numerous victims—then, I at least must know what really happened and I would also want it to be made public.

When it comes to the possibilities for the strategic misuse of the concept of reconciliation, it is striking that in the course of Germany's own process of coming to terms with its past, especially after 1989, the preferred term used for reconciliation was "working out the past" (*Aufarbeitung von Vergangenheit*) rather than "reconciliation" (*Versöhnung*).[7] "Working things out" appeared to be a more apt way of describing the process of mentally resolving the past in such a way that the future would not be burdened by it.

Different terminologies are used by different people to express the idea of dealing with a guilt-ridden past. In some cases, the term "understanding" or even "friendship" is used. For example, one speaks of a German-American understanding (*deutsch-amerikanische Verständigung*) and in East Germany, of German-Russian friendship (*deutsch-russische Freundschaft*). In both cases, the terms used have numerous connotations. Friendship is more than understanding, but understanding is less weighty than reconciliation. In the relationship between Germany and Poland, for example, one hears of German-Polish reconciliation (*deutsch-polnische Versöhnung*), similar to the case of France. Does this terminology imply the acknowledgment of the weight of guilt? Does the term reconciliation also extend to an expression of the depths of the anguish or to the processing of guilt? Is reconciliation the appropriate term, or should we speak of atonement instead, since reconciliation also includes the act of forgiveness? An example here is the relationship between Germany and Israel in which it seems appropriate to

---

5. See Thomas O. H. Kaiser, *Versöhnung in Gerechtigkeit: Das Konzept der Versöhnung und seine Kritik im Kontext Südafrika* (Neukirchen: Neukirchener Verlag, 1996).

6. See Ralf K. Wüstenberg, *Aufarbeitung oder Versöhnung? Ein Vergleich der Vergangenheitspolitik in Deutschland und Südafrika* (Potsdam: Brandenburgische Landeszentrale für politische Bildung, 2008).

7. See Dietrich Bonhoeffer, *Ethik*, ed. Ilse Tödt, Ernst Eduard Tödt, Ernst Feil, and Clifford J. Green (Gütersloh: Gütersloher Verlagshaus, 1992), 134f.; *DBWE* 6.

speak of atonement instead of reconciliation (*Sühne*). It is striking that in 1958, the Synod of the Evangelical Church (EKD) called for "signs of atonement" (*Aktion Sühnezeichen*) in life, not for signs of reconciliation, since Bishop Franz von Hammerstein was convinced that atonement incorporated the perspective of guilt of the perpetrator, while reconciliation in many instances would incorporate a readiness to forgive on the part of the victims.

In one of his fragments on ethics written between 1940 and 1943, titled, "Guilt, Justification, and Renewal" (1941), Dietrich Bonhoeffer wrote that "guilt scars."[8] He then distinguished between political "guilt" and "forgiveness," which "Jesus Christ gives in faith."[9] I would like to ask whether the idea of "scarring over" also conveys the notion of what we understand today as "political reconciliation."[10] According to Bonhoeffer,[11] there is "something similar to forgiveness in the history of internal and external politics of dealings between people." However, this kind of forgiveness is "only a weak shadow of the forgiveness that Jesus Christ gives in faith. Here we have the act of complete atonement for injustices incurred by the guilty; while recognizing that the past cannot be healed by any human power." On the topic of achieving forgiveness in the political sphere, Bonhoeffer says, "Not all wounds can be healed, but it is important not to open new ones." As a condition for such political or "internal-historical forgiveness," he says, "guilt is scarred over so that from force, justice might prevail—from chaos, order; from war, peace. . . . Wherever that is not the case, wherever injustice still reigns unchecked and new wounds are continually opened, then we cannot speak of forgiveness."[12] Bonhoeffer's argument is very dense and, in some places, is assertoric. However, three lines of thought evident in his argument are relevant to the theme of this volume.

Costliness of the Christian Concept of Forgiveness

Bonhoeffer's view of forgiveness sharply contrasts with the strategic misuse of the term in the political sphere. He does not use the term forgiveness lightly but clearly distinguishes the issues when he approaches them from a theological standpoint, that is, informed by Luther's theology.[13] In making his distinctions, he incorporates the legacy of Lutheran theology without falling prey to "thinking in two realms,"

---

8. Ibid., 134f.
9. Ibid., 135.
10. For terminology, see, for example, Wüstenberg, *Aufarbeitung oder Versöhnung?*
11. The following citations are from *DBW* 6:134–6; own translation.
12. Ibid., 135f.; own translation.
13. See Wilfried Härle, "Gott fürchten und lieben: Martin Luther und die Kunst lebenswichtiger Unterscheidungen," in *Nimm und lies! Theologische Quereinstiege für Neugierige*, ed. Ralf K. Wüstenberg (Gütersloh: Güterloher Verlagshaus, 2008), 110–25.

which he observed was the tendency of many Lutheran theologians of his time.[14] For him, there is only one reality—the reality that is reconciled to God in Christ. Ultimate and penultimate things, justification through faith alone, and a life marked by this-worldliness are related. Only the guilty can be justified. However, such interrelatedness is not the same as identity. Forgiveness of sins through grace and political reconciliation where justice is re-instated and guilt is scarred over are very distinct notions. He notes, "Through faith, the church experiences the forgiveness of all sin and a new beginning through grace; in scarring over guilt, people only receive a return to order, justice, and peace."[15] This distinction, however, is underscored by the unique concept of Christian forgiveness. In other words, it is not watered down—even for the sake of political appearances. For Bonhoeffer, forgiveness is not a slow, "gradual process of healing," but a "complete break with guilt and a new beginning . . . in which forgiveness of sins is a gift."[16] With this clear distinction, his concept sharply contrasts with the strategic misuse of the term "forgiveness" in the political sphere.

Estimating Political Possibilities

According to Bonhoeffer, the contrast between internal-historical (i.e., political) forgiveness and Christian forgiveness is evident where the value is placed on what is politically possible. It is not a small thing then that Bonhoeffer attributes "the shadow of forgiveness," for example, to justice resulting from power, order from chaos, and peace from war.[17] To put it another way, can and may more be expected from politics? Can successful political transformation processes be evaluated by other standards than by the categories that Bonhoeffer uses, namely peace, justice, and order? Bonhoeffer subtly introduces places where, in the early ethical debates on peace, the necessity of upholding justice after a war should be emphasized (*ius post bellum*).[18]

---

14. See Bonhoeffer, "Christus, die Wirklichkeit und das Gute," *DBW* 6:40f., and in the same sense, Bonhoeffer, "Die letzten und die vorletzten Dinge"; Ibid., 137–62. See also Ralf K. Wüstenberg, *Bonhoeffer and Beyond: Promoting a Dialogue between Religion and Politics* (Frankfurt am Main: Lang, 2008).

15. *DBW* 6:134; own translation.

16. Ibid.

17. Ibid., 135; own translation.

18. See the publication by the Evangelische Kirche in Deutschland (EKD), ed., *Aus Gottes Frieden leben—für gerechten Frieden sorgen* (Gütersloh: Gütersloher Verlagshaus, 2007), 45–56. The challenge is how to address the issue from the perspective of a peace ethics, in the aftermath of a war between people and countries, when the burden of history surpasses the moral or criminal responsibility of the individual perpetrators. See also Ralf K. Wüstenberg, *The Political Dimension of Reconciliation*, trans. Randi H. Lundell (Grand Rapids, MI: Eerdmans, 2009).

For Bonhoeffer, it was less about the question of the basis for a just war (*ius ad bellum*) or that of waging a just war (*ius in bello*) than it was about the traditional theological argument outlined in the teachings of Augustine and Thomas Aquinas on the topic of a so-called just war.[19] Increasingly, the question of a just postwar peace emerged at the forefront of this thinking, primarily connected with the definition of a "just peace."[20] How can law and justice be reestablished at the end of a totalitarian regime so that, as far as the victims are concerned, injustice does not continue? In addition to the legal institution of amnesty, prosecution, or sanctions other than prosecution (e.g., the elimination of unwanted workers from public offices), moral restitution has, in the view of victims, been valued more highly than judicial and material rehabilitation, as was seen in the work of the Truth Commission.[21] Following Bonhoeffer's argument, political forgiveness that seeks to reestablish justice should not allow forgiveness to be placed on the same level as amnesty for the perpetrator[22] but must also include prosecution as a legal instrument in a theological ethic of justice. Bonhoeffer thus reminds us what is often missing in recent debates on peace ethics, namely the difference in categories (*kategoriale Verschiedenheit*) between morality and legality.[23] Forgiveness is a

---

19. See summaries of the main ideas of Augustine and Thomas von Aquinas in Wolfgang Huber, "Rückkehr der Lehre vom gerechten Krieg? Aktuelle Entwicklungen in der evangelischen Friedensethik," *Zeitschrift für Evangelische Ethik* 49 (2005): 115f., 118f.

20. See Evangelische Kirche in Deutschland (EKD), *Aus Gottes Frieden leben*, 50–6, 57ff. For a critical discussion, see Wolfgang Huber, "Von der gemeinsamen Sicherheit zum gerechten Frieden: Die Friedensethik der EKD in den letzten 25 Jahren," in *Frieden: Einsichten für das 21. Jahrhundert*, ed. Hans-Richard Reuter (Berlin: Lit-Verlag, 2009), 162f., 165–70.

21. During the process of political transition, five options for taking action are distinguished by subject in the so-called "transitional justice" process, each defined according to the character of the transformation (revolution, political compromise, etc.) and the accompanying power relationships that can result: "(1) prosecution of human rights violations; (2) the opposite either in the form of amnesty or letting them be; (3) explanation of past injustices, e.g., through the Truth Commission; (4) restitution for victims, e.g., returning lands, material restitution, legal rehabilitation, and moral rehabilitation; and (5) sanctions apart from prosecution, for example, clearing out public offices, especially police and the military, of affected employees." *Wüstenberg, Political Dimension of Reconciliation*.

22. Thus, Magdalene L. Frettlöh, "Vergebung oder 'Vernarbung der Schuld': Theologische und philosophische Notizen zu einer frag-würdigen Alternative im gesellschaftlichen Umgang mit Schuld," *Evangelische Theologie (EvTh)* 70, no. 2 (2010): 116–29, illustrates the legislation of amnesty of the South African Commission of Truth and Reconciliation.

23. In an objective description of the legal foundation of the first freely elected parliament-instituted South Africa's TRC of 1995, Frettlöh, "Vergebung oder 'Vernarbung der Schuld,'" 128f., mixed the legal institution of amnesty with the readiness to reconcile by former apartheid victims and called "amnesty" "a classic institution of peace forming, reconciling measures" (128; own translation). Frettlöh mistakenly argues regarding the

different category from amnesty or the rule of law because prosecution of the perpetrator or applying amnesty does not mean that forgiveness must necessarily take place on a moral level. One is a legal category (namely amnesty) and the other a moral category (namely forgiveness). In this regard, Bonhoeffer should not only be referred to when it comes to a theological interpretation of the amnesty process by the South African Truth Commission, as Frettlöh[24] suggests, but also in processes of political transformation to democracy where criminal law is applied, as in the German transition after the fall of the Berlin wall in 1989.

Points of Connection between Political and Christian Forgiveness

Bonhoeffer's ethical schema is one of the first attempts to thematize the "forgiveness of guilt" as an instrument of reconciliation in the political life of international communities. His metaphorical term was groundbreaking for peace ethics, when he speaks of a "shadow" that falls over political forgiveness. However, following the tracks of Bonhoeffer, the points of connection may be explored in further depth. I wish to point out the direction in two concluding remarks.

First, Bonhoeffer's position on tying forgiveness to the realm of the church is, I believe, overestimated. Second, in my opinion, his reflections on the symbolic instances of Christian forgiveness within their political dimensions are underestimated for current debates. Bonhoeffer tends to erect two poles, namely politics, on the one hand, and the church, on the other hand—here, the scarring

---

legislation of the TRC. Any mixing of morality and legality, such as Frettlöh presumes in her argument, was ruled out in the conception of the Truth Commission. Individual amnesty, about which the legal expert G. Werle wrote in his legal history of South Africa, is tied to previously established legal rules (e.g., political motive, integrity of the witnesses, or the proportionality of the means). Whether the recipients of amnesty were convicted of serious human rights violations did not depend on the willingness to forgive of the victims, which would be the same thing as mixing morality and legality, and would result in thwarting the principle of just state. There are impressive examples in which this can be seen very clearly. For example, the highly decorated police chief from the days of apartheid received amnesty for horrible methods of persecution, but due to an exception, the moral level of forgiveness from the victim was left out. In the reverse, family members of victims of a Black perpetrator were formally ready to forgive during an amnesty process; the applicant was denied amnesty because he had neglected to comply with previously established criteria (e.g., proportionality of means). See the documentation of both cases (Jeff Benzien und der Familie Siebert) in Wüstenberg, *Aufarbeitung oder Versöhnung?*, 41–5, 32–40.

24. Compare the use of criminal law in the transformation process in Germany after 1989 and its constructivist theological discussion from a legal perspective in Ralf K. Wüstenberg, *Die politische Dimension der Versöhnung: Eine theologische Studie zum Umgang mit Schuld nach den Systemumbrüchen in Südafrika und Deutschland* (Gütersloh: Gütersloher Verlagshaus, 2004), 256–70, 522–39.

over of guilt and the gradual process of normalization; there, the forgiveness of sins and a radical new beginning; here, *immediately* in the Christian sense of a complete break between guilt and healing; there, *gradually* in the political process of healing.

Clearly, Bonhoeffer put a great deal of trust in the church. He thought the church should speak with one voice in the world. It should impart the "concrete commands" of God to the world.[25] Just as God was concretely manifest in His Son, Jesus of Nazareth, so also should the church dare to speak to the world on the subject of terror and war: "Go to war here, or, do not go to war here!" The church should not avoid the issue on principle or through general declarations, or at best, adopt a "qualified silence." As apt and important as the ethical dimension of the church's mission is today, one may also ask whether Bonhoeffer may have underestimated the immanent political dimension of reconciliation. Or, is not Christ also at work where the church is not explicitly present? Designating the church exclusively as the place for acknowledgment of guilt and for reconciliation not only seems questionable in this context but is also incomplete in the context of Bonhoeffer's later ethical considerations regarding the *one* "reality of Christ."[26] He asks, is the incarnation of Christ limited to the realm of the church, "as if there was not also an earthly presence of the raised and ascended Christ outside of the church? To identify the church as the exclusive, earthly form of Christ is to place it the dangerous position of being over-valued and over-extended."[27]

It is evident in several works on the political dimension of reconciliation in South Africa and in Germany that, in theological terms, the contours between the church and the world tend to merge. In the midst of the Truth and Reconciliation Commission (TRC) hearings, one has the impression that *here* is reconciliation; *this* is what reconciliation is. In its political dimension, reconciliation constitutes something more and different than the mere "shadow of forgiveness." It was no different in the victim's testimonials during the 12th and 13th German Parliament's investigative commission on "*Überwindung der Folgen der SED-Diktatur*" (1992–8).[28] Not only is acknowledgment of guilt as well as reconciliation possible in the

---

25. See Bonhoeffer, "Zur theologischen Begründung der Weltbundarbeit," in *Dietrich Bonhoeffer, Ökumene, Universität, Pfarramt 1931–1932* (*DBW* 11), 327–44. The following quotes are from this 1932 presentation (own translations).

26. See also Bonhoeffer, "Christus, die Wirklichkeit und das Gute," *DBW* 6:3161.

27. Frettlöh, *Vergebung oder "Vernarbung der Schuld,"* 120.

28. See, for example, the two-day public hearings of the Inquiry Commission of the 12th session of the German Parliament, which on December 1, 1992, documented in the Berlin Parliament building (Reichstag) the stories of the victims of the SED injustice. Deutscher Bundestag, Enquette-Kommission des 12. Bundestages (1992-4), ed., "Aufarbeitung von Geschichte und Folgen der SED-Diktatur in Deutschland," in *Materialien der Enquete-Kommission,* vol. II, I (Baden-Baden: Nomos, 1996), 111–276. An abbreviated version of the text of the dialogues of the two-day hearings of the Inquiry Commission in Germany can be found in Wüstenberg, *Aufarbeitung oder Versöhnung?*, 92–5.

realm of the church, but also in the midst of political reality—or in the midst of what Bonhoeffer calls "the reality of Christ." The initiators of this reconciliation were not the institutional churches,[29] which, as so-called representatives of the world, supposedly set the reconciliation process in motion. At best, they were church representatives serving in political offices—in South Africa, personalities like Desmond Tutu, the Methodist pastor, Alex Boraine, or the theology professor, Charles Villa-Vicencio, and in Germany, one thinks of pastors like Rainer Eppelmann or Joachim Gauck. In this context, should we not, in line with Bonhoeffer's other arguments, reckon that the church and Christ have something to offer the political sphere on how to live with guilt? And does that also not mean valuing the reality of the world and its inclusion in Christ, something that Bonhoeffer always urged?

Along these lines of argumentation, it appears possible to define the signs of forgiveness within the interpretive horizon of Christian forgiveness and, remaining in the same meta-world as Bonhoeffer, to view the "shadow of forgiveness" as being stronger than the shadows themselves. In this way, clear connections to the Christian concept of forgiveness can be established. Of course, apart from the sacrament of baptism and the Eucharist, there are signs of what Bonhoeffer calls "the ethical sacrament of reality,"[30] which should not be used in all cases in the same way as in the Christian connection. Whereas in the handling of the signs in the Eucharist and baptism, there is immediate clarity of understanding within the congregation—signs of an ethical sacrament of reality remain open to interpretation. Symbolic gestures, such as the clasping of hands between perpetrators and victims on the forum of the TRC, or the mere observation that the hearers themselves express by their very presence—symbolic acts can be interpreted from a Christian perspective, but these interpretations may not be binding for all. For instance, one can make a connection between the greeting and making of peace before the Eucharist embedded in the symbolic reenactment of reconciliation between God and man, and the shaking of hands between victim and perpetrator in an amnesty hearing of the TRC.

Hannah Arendt's title, *The Miracle of Forgiveness*,[31] is validated in connection to Christian theology in the midst of political, religious, and social reality, mediated through language or symbols. In addition to the previous example of South Africa,

---

29. See, among others, Ralf K. Wüstenberg, "Kirche als zivilgesellschaftliche Instanz in Transformationsprozessen: Die deutsche Einigung in vergleichender Perspektive," in *Zwischen Fürsorge und Seelsorge: Christliche Kirchen in den europäischen Zivilgesellschaften seit dem 18. Jahrhundert*, ed. A. Bauerkämper and J. Nautz (Frankfurt am Main: Campus, 2009), 317–30.

30. Bonhoeffer, "Zur theologischen Begründung der Weltbundarbeit," *DBW* 11:334; own translation. See also Ralf. K. Wüstenberg, "Die Wirklichkeit als Sakrament des Gebotes," *Bonhoeffer Rundbrief: Mitteilungen der Internationalen Bonhoeffer-Gesellschaft (ibg)*, sektion Bundesrepublik Deutschland 97 (2012): 13–23.

31. Arendt, *Vita activa*, 231–8.

there are other examples of countries (primarily France and Poland) that should be remembered in this context and, in particular, three significant examples from German history. The representative overcoming of guilt that occurred in Germany was not mediated by the church but through certain non-religious means in the political sphere—by means of language or symbols. One can recall the speech by Richard von Weizsäcker at the 40th anniversary of the end of the Second World War in 1985, the highly symbolic meeting between de Gaulle and Adenauer at the cathedral in Reims, or the bending of the knee by Willi Brandt before the memorial in the Warsaw ghetto in 1970.

Indeed, the boundaries of political reconciliation can be seen wherever there is an intentional effort to establish forgiveness. The opportunity for a politics of reconciliation lies wherever contexts are defined that allow forgiveness to occur in the reality of the political sphere.

Chapter 13

BEYOND THE DARK NIGHT OF THE SOUL

BONHOEFFER AND JEWS FOR PALESTINIAN RIGHTS[1]

Marthie Momberg

Introduction

On reading *Letters and Papers from Prison*, I was struck by Bonhoeffer's loneliness and despair as well as his quest for an alternative to a delusional world. This reading occurred through two lenses—my feelings about my failure to speak up during South Africa's apartheid regime and my turning to scholar-activism decades later as well as insights from research on what motivates South Africans and Israelis who work for Palestinian rights.

Dietrich Bonhoeffer lived at a time of extreme turmoil and destruction when "all ethical concepts" were thrown "into confusion."[2] On April 9, 1945, he was hanged for his role in the resistance movement. The disillusion and devastation of the Second World War gave rise to the founding of the United Nations, and on June 26, 1945, less than three months after Bonhoeffer's death, the Charter of the United Nations pledged to promote "respect for human rights and for fundamental freedoms for all without distinction as to race, sex, language, or religion."[3] To this initial statement of the UN, the Universal Declaration of Human Rights was added in 1948, and subsequently a comprehensive body of laws specifying that "all human beings are born free and equal in dignity and rights" further established a global baseline for human rights.[4]

Notwithstanding the dawn of a new era in which human rights was enshrined in international law, my country's racial segregation was institutionalized on

---

1. This work is based on research supported by the National Institute for Humanities and the Social Sciences (NIHSS) at Nelson Mandela University. The opinions, findings, conclusions, and recommendations expressed are those of the author, and the NIHSS accepts no liability in this regard.

2. *DBWE* 8:38.

3. "The Charter of the United Nations," United Nations, https://www.un.org/en/sections/un-charter/chapter-i/index.html (accessed September 15, 2020).

4. "The Universal Declaration of Human Rights (UDHR)," United Nations, https://www.un.org/en/universal-declaration-human-rights (accessed September 15, 2020).

May 26, 1948. In 1976, when thousands of demonstrating Black students on the streets of Soweto were met by teargas and live ammunition, and when Rev Dr. Beyers Naudé was put under house arrest a year later, I was at university. Many Afrikaners deemed Naudé a traitor at the time, and others stood by passively. That I did nothing to end the systemic injustice in my country is a mistake that I never want to forget or repeat. In 2010, I was shocked to realize my ignorance about Israel's power abuse when a visiting Jewish professor who participated in an evening of lectures, held at Stellenbosch University's Beyers Naudé Centre for Public Theology, made me realize that ignorance. Once again, I had been tacitly supporting the systematic oppression and domination of one group by another.

The State of Israel was conceived as exclusive from the start. Three years after Bonhoeffer was hanged on April 9, 1948, Jewish Zionists from the Irgun paramilitary group killed almost all the inhabitants of Deir Yassin, a Palestinian village near Jerusalem. They raped, severed off body parts to take jewelry, slaughtered a pregnant woman, and shot a girl who tried to rescue the unborn baby. All of this and more were meticulously recorded by a British interrogating officer. The next morning, the head of the International Red Cross delegation in Palestine encountered the young, heavily armed Zionists—men and women—outside Deir Yassin. Some held cutlasses still dripping with blood.[5]

This massacre was not an isolated act of cruelty against unarmed Palestinians, as apologists argue. In the past decades, Israel's New Historians have been challenging the official Israeli view of bravery, blessed by the grace of God in a moral War of Independence, after Israeli government papers were declassified. Although their respective views on the validity of Zionism vary significantly, all conclude that the Deir Yassin massacre and the depopulation of hundreds of Arab villages, towns, and urban areas were part of a master plan to rid historic Palestine of Christian, Muslim, and other Arabs in order to confiscate their land, buildings, money, and natural resources. The New Historians' work shares core themes, including that the Palestinians were killed, displaced, or fled out of fear in a human catastrophe when the Zionist militia had the advantage both in number and in weaponry. Despite their political differences, the historical accounts of Ilan Pappé[6] and Benny Morris,[7] for example, are congruent with that of the Palestinian author Walid Khalidi, who also chronicled the Palestinians' *Nakba* or catastrophe.[8] By the time most of historic Palestine was unilaterally proclaimed as a Jewish-only state in May 1948, more than 80 percent of the Palestinian population were refugees. And although the injustice against the Palestinians was on the agenda of the UN since its inception in 1945, the Palestinian refugees are not yet allowed

---

5. Jonathan Dimbleby, *The Palestinians* (London: Quartet, 1979), 79.
6. Ilan Pappé, *The Ethnic Cleansing of Palestine* (London: Oneworld Publications, 2013).
7. Benny Morris, *The Birth of the Palestinian Refugee Problem, 1947–1949* (Cambridge: Cambridge University Press, 1987).
8. Walid Khalidi, ed., *All That Remains: The Palestinian Villages Occupied and Depopulated by Israel in 1948* (Washington, DC: Institute for Palestine Studies, 1992).

to return to their properties as the UN Resolution 194 recommends. Over the decades, largely due to the vetoing power of the United States, approximately 200 resolutions of the UN Assembly have failed to end or even halt Israel's subsequent acts of killings, land confiscation, resource plundering, and other forms of state violence. Moreover, several reports[9] confirm Israel's apartheid regime, as defined by international law,[10] in respect of the Palestinians.

Zionism is an ideology that aims to transform the transnational and extraterritorial Jewish identity into an exclusivist national identity in order to establish total control over all of historic Palestine.[11] Like Nazism and South African apartheid, Zionism thrives on a cozy relationship between state and religious power, bolstered by militarized violence in its discrimination against people on ethnic, cultural, and religious grounds. It is true that the events of the Holocaust, South African apartheid, and the oppression of the Palestinians are by no means exact replicas of one another. Yet from a perspective of meta-narratives, the dynamics in all three contexts are characterized by the violent enforcement of discrimination to justify imperialist and exclusivist projects. I have argued elsewhere that on this basis, there are indeed grounds for a conversation to deepen scientific and moral understandings of "the underlying dynamics, the consciousness, the world views, the paradigms and the mind-sets that inform oppression, exploitation, domination and dehumanization."[12] This chapter, in turn, explores points of congruence in the lived circumstances and experiences of Bonhoeffer and Jewish activists who campaign for Palestinian rights. The focus here is on their quests for live-giving alternatives to contexts of systemic state violence and discrimination.

---

9. "Occupation, Colonialism, Apartheid? A Re-assessment of Israel's Practices in the Occupied Palestinian Territories under International Law," The Human Sciences Research Council, http://www.hsrc.ac.za/en/research-data/view/4634 (accessed September 30, 2020). "The Question of Palestine," United Nations: Committee on the Elimination of Racial Discrimination, https://www.un.org/unispal/document/auto-insert-193709 (accessed September 16, 2020). John Dugard and John Reynolds, "Apartheid, International Law, and the Occupied Palestinian Territory," *European Journal of International Law* 24, no. 3 (2013): 867–913. "Report of the Special Rapporteur on the situation of human rights in the Palestinian territories occupied since 1967," Richard Falk, United Nations General Assembly, https://www.ohchr.org/EN/HRBodies/HRC/RegularSessions/Session25/Documents/A-HRC-25-67_en.doc (accessed September 30, 2020).

10. "Rome Statute of the International Criminal Court," International Criminal Court, https://www.icc-cpi.int/resource-library/documents/rs-eng.pdf (accessed September 14, 2020).

11. Yakof Rabkin, "Zionism a 'Terrible Enemy' of Jewish people," *Cape Times* (March 10, 2010): 11.

12. Marthie Momberg, "In Search of the Grain: Israel, the Palestinians, South Africa and Germany," *Stellenbosch Theological Journal* 5, no. 3 (2019): 154.

Bonhoeffer's Crisis: What Does It Mean to Be a Christian?

A Shattered Worldview

"The huge masquerade of evil has thrown all ethical concepts into confusion," writes Bonhoeffer in "After Ten Years," which expresses his bewilderment about National Socialism's triumphalist claims of superiority and Christians' uncritical affinity with state power. According to Bonhoeffer, fellow Christians were gratefully "rejoicing in the success of the nation . . . without asking who was paying the price."[13] Being concerned, first and foremost, with the state of Christianity and the church, "the horror," as Bonhoeffer phrased it, is that "evil appears in the form of light, good deeds, historical necessity [and] social justice."[14] He knew that loyalty to the oppressive and exclusive ideology of National Socialism and its belief in homogeneity compromised Christianity to the extent that the integrity of Christianity was at stake. This necessitated a *status confessionis* in the Protestant tradition. At the same time, and ironically, Bonhoeffer struggled to let go of the patriarchal view of life that underscored his well-ordered middle-class existence and his disdain for emancipated women.[15]

In the years of his imprisonment, 1943–5, Bonhoeffer's existential devastation catapulted him into despair. With his ability to assert himself confined to written communication subject to censorship, and his contact with loved ones highly restricted, his sense of entrapment was heightened. The crisis was personal, spiritual, and existential. About a month after his arrest, he wrote about waiting for death, and self-death, "not out of a sense of guilt, but because I am practically dead already." His subsequent efforts to cherish past comforts brought him no relief. The dark night of the soul is associated with the realization that one's worldview and one's old "self" are obsolete and feeling stuck. There is a sense that one cannot live with oneself and in the world the way one used to. There is loss, anguish, grief, nothing to hold on to, and nowhere to go. This departure from an outdated way of being without being able to envision an alternative closes in like a suffocating darkness.

In Search of the Authentic Self

The crumbling of the world to which Bonhoeffer was accustomed and the lack of control over his fate forced him into hitherto unexplored dimensions. After a visit from his fiancée, Maria von Wedemeyer, in May 1944, Bonhoeffer expressed an upwelling of intense longing and grief in his first poem. The emotional and revealing nature of his words displayed a vulnerability and an honesty that he

---

13. Renate Wind, *Dietrich Bonhoeffer: A Spoke in the Wheel*, trans. John Bowden (Grand Rapids, MI: William Eerdmans, 2000), 140.
14. Bonhoeffer, "After Ten Years"; *DBWE* 8:38.
15. Wind, *Dietrich Bonhoeffer*, 69, 161.

had not yet dared to express. Well aware of portraying an image of being ever so centered, stable, serene, and disciplined to others, Bonhoeffer juxtaposed these impressions with his acute inner restlessness. In the poem, "Who Am I?" from July 1944, he spoke of himself as "yearning, sick, like a caged bird, / struggling for life breath," as if strangled in his starvation for nature and kindness.[16] Daniël Louw[17] describes the *cul de sac* of ontological upheaval as a sense of "the death of relationships" through "isolation, rejection, hatred and destructive prejudice." Bonhoeffer did not tumble into this dead end, opting for nihilism, or seeking solace in activism. Rather, he was in search of his undivided self and the nourishment of an integrated life. His quest was for a sense of belonging that transcends the confines of corporeal and earthly dimensions, and he found his answer in his relation with God. "Who Am I?" concludes as follows: "They mock me, these lonely questions of mine. / Whoever I am, thou knowest me; O God, I am thine!"[18]

Metanoia—Undivided Faith

Bonhoeffer's personal shift was radical and transformative, informed by incisive discernment, and extending also to the communal dimensions of his life. His fractured reality eventually opened up space for a more authentic world and life view on what it means to be Christian. In April 1944, he wrote to his close friend Bethge, saying, "What keeps gnawing at me is the question, what is Christianity, or who is Christ actually for us today?"[19] The time when people could use mere words to identify themselves as "religious" is over, he asserted.[20] He was searching for something quite different than the prevailing understanding of "being religious," and Bonhoeffer reflected deeply on Christianity in the context of suffering and public responsibility. "In the last few years," he wrote, "I have come to know and understand more and more the profound this-worldliness of Christianity. The Christian is not a *homo religious* but simply a human being, in the same way that Jesus was a human being."[21] In the words of John de Gruchy, Bonhoeffer's "nonreligious" interpretation of Christianity and the role of the church is not an apologetic undertaking of simply interpreting "Christianity in a new historical context in a new conception or linguistic key—but a fundamental reorientation, or *metanoia*, that leads to an identification with Christ in his sufferings, and therefore to a new way of being the church-community in the world."[22] A month

---

16. *DBWE* 8:459.
17. Daniël Louw, *Icons. Imaging the Unseen: On Beauty and Healing of Life, Body and Soul* (Stellenbosch: SUN Press, 2014), 9.
18. *DBWE* 8:460.
19. Ibid., 362.
20. Ibid.
21. Ibid., 485.
22. Ibid., 26.

later, writing about his godchild's baptism, Bonhoeffer expressed the hope for an altogether "new language, perhaps quite nonreligious, but liberating and redeeming like Jesus's language."[23] Christian "faith," Bonhoeffer asserted, "involves one's whole life. Jesus calls not to a new religion but to life."[24]

Crisis Posed by Zionism: What Does It Mean to Be Jewish?

Many people across the world are uncritical in their views of Israel's relationship to the Palestinians, or they conclude that the issue is too complex to take sides. When I monitored human rights violations in Palestine and Israel in 2011, I met several non-Palestinians, including Jews from Israel and South Africa, who campaign for Palestinian rights. My curiosity about what motivates their activism in the Palestinian struggle inspired an interdisciplinary case study in empirical ethics with twenty-one South Africans and Jewish Israelis. This inductive, exploratory research was informed by a research question and not by any theory or hypothesis. The individual in-depth interviews were guided by a paradigm of inquiry, and I presented the findings thematically and in the form of grounded statements. The twenty-one respondents belonged to different age groups, had different gender orientations, and held different views of religion. Some of the respondents were known to me, others were introduced through mutual contacts, and some agreed to participate in the study after I wrote to them without prior introduction. Of these, fourteen people (three South Africans, ten Israelis, and one person with dual citizenship) identified as "Jewish." Only one of the Jews, a humanist, associated actively with Judaism. The other Jews distanced themselves from Judaism because of the entanglement with Zionism or described themselves as atheist, agnostic, secular, pagan, or spiritual. All agreed that being "Jewish" foremostly implied historical, cultural, and/or civil identities.

A Shattered Reality

Five of the Jewish respondents have never been committed to Zionist ideals or persuaded by Zionist arguments. Not all had detailed knowledge of the oppression from the start, but they sensed the power imbalance which caused the Palestinians to be marginalized and stigmatized simply because they are Palestinian. The other nine Israeli and South African Jews used to embrace Zionism as a benign, socialist project. Like the five who never believed in Zionism, they were raised with sound values. In fact, many volunteered for community work in their youth and several were exposed to and protested against systemic oppression in countries such as South Africa, Argentina, the United States, Vietnam, and Czechoslovakia. Still, they had adopted a wholesale belief in the idea of Israel as an innocent and

---

23. Ibid., 145, 390.
24. Ibid., 482.

quintessential beacon of hope and a historical necessity for the Jewish people after the atrocities of the Holocaust. This premise was based on myths such as "a people without a land for a land without a people" in which Zionism and its Kibbutz movement were portrayed as a socialist utopic society with innocent, courageous Jews who "civilised" a barren land.[25] These activists whose upbringings taught them to have compassion for the other also assumed that Jews had a historical right to all Palestinian land without considering the implications for the people who had been living there for centuries. As a South African woman remarked, "I just thought, we have the right to everywhere, it's all ours. It was very simple really."[26]

There came a time when she and the other former Zionist Jews in the case study could no longer find comfort in societal beliefs. They were sensitized by unexpected encounters that revealed that Israel was not a democracy or a vulnerable victim merely defending itself. They too discovered "the horror" that "evil appears in the form of light, good deeds, historical necessity [and] social justice"[27] upon realizing the widespread propaganda that hides or justifies the rubble of bombed houses, schools, hospitals, roads, and other infrastructure as well as the many deaths, injuries, and displacements. Discovering the gap between their espoused values and Zionism's ethos of superiority, which prioritizes Jewish lives at the cost of Palestinian lives, appalled and unsettled them. Like Bonhoeffer, they were confronted by a ghastly discriminative reality enforced by militarized state power. This challenged their identities, raising questions about their integrity and compelling them to dissect their paradigms, their "selves" and what it means to be Jewish in this world.

Some recalled condensed or sudden insights and conversions, but most experienced gradual awakenings through slow but persistent unlearning, relearning, and making connections in a series of moments over time. The twisted truths and distorted facts, the reality of asymmetric power, and the gap between Zionist sentiments and their assumed values left them feeling betrayed and distraught. An Israeli who discovered the falsehoods about the Israeli military and the country's history exclaimed: "On religious and spiritual and existential levels I don't want to live a lie. I lived a lie growing up and I'm furious about it!"[28] Another person felt despairingly miserable and in turmoil, "upset with the system, with the commanders, the teachers, my parents and everyone. I felt lied to. I felt that everything is a big lie around me. I felt that they turned all of this generation into murderers."[29] The former Zionists expressed their sense of disintegration as the

---

25. Miko Peled, *The General's Son: Journey of an Israeli in Palestine* (Charlottesville, VA: Just World Books, 2012).

26. Marthie Momberg, "Why Activists? A Case-Study into the Self-Perceived Motivations of Selected South Africans and Jewish Israelis in the Palestinian Project" (PhD diss., Stellenbosch University, 2017), 94.

27. *DBWE* 8:38.

28. Momberg, "Why Activists," 113.

29. Ibid.

shattering of walls or barriers, the cracking of a façade, and a point of no return when they realized that the State of Israel did not come into its own through a "miracle" or defend itself against ruthless, irrational Palestinians. Not only did they discover the inaccuracy of these perceptions, but they also realized that Zionism is wholly inappropriate and incongruent with their assumed identities as caring citizens who endorse inclusive human rights, honesty, compassion, justice, and equality. Feeling shocked, disjointed, and catapulted out of their comfort zones into guilt, outrage, and shame, they realized that they had been applying their values inconsistently in their loyalty to Zionism.

Bonhoeffer's words that "'[t]elling the truth' therefore, is not solely a matter of moral character; it is also a matter of correct application of real situations and of serious reflection upon them"[30] ring true in the context of the activists' realization that they had failed to assess the situation critically. Their quests for an alternative to the dislocation between themselves, the reality, and their preference for inclusivity sprang from a longing for authentic, honest, and integrated lives. In a way, they too faced the question, "Who am I?" A former Israeli pilot, for example, reflected on his naïve belief in what he had been told about Israel "because it's easier, it's nicer, it's comforting, it's settling to believe in a system." The realization that he was part of an army, a state, and a social circle "involved in murdering innocent children" however cut "through all the layers of justifications, and compartmentation."[31] He could no longer uphold any of his rationalizations and was thrown into an emotional crisis which prompted him to redefine his identity. In another example, a South African who was nearly sixty-four years old at the time of the interview spoke about what his life really amounts to over and above having a career and a family. His personal crisis surpassed his roles as an ex-Zionist Jew and as a South African. For him, the real issue was about just how far he was prepared to live according to his own truth and principles, since this is "probably the biggest challenge in my life, it always was, and it still is. It's also a reason for being involved in this particular struggle."[32]

The gap between the privileged self and the harsh reality of the Palestinians elicited a deep realization to not turn away from that discrepancy, but to address the injustice as best as they can. Avoiding or turning away from the Palestinian struggle, or recognizing its validity without doing anything about it, was perceived as untenable and also as a disgrace to the self. In other words, the cost of dishonesty and complacency was perceived as higher than that of taking a public stand. These Jews who underwent radical shifts—and everyone else in the case study—affirmed their desire for personal integrity as the core reason for speaking up. To them, having integrity means to be authentic, genuine, and consistent in embodying their values of compassion, justice, equality, and honesty—whether in thought,

---

30. Wind, *Dietrich Bonhoeffer*, 158–9.
31. Momberg, "Why Activists," 106.
32. Ibid., 134.

speech, or action. In short, their understanding of "integrity" is related to life as a whole.

Metanoia—From Zionism to Humanism and Feminism

Bonhoeffer, who was alarmed by "religious people"[33] because of their theological justification of National Socialism and the role of the church, might have understood why several of those Jews who said they are no longer religious nevertheless referred to the Torah and to prophets such as Jeremiah, Isaiah, and Amos. They kept in mind the Judaism of their upbringing that taught them not to dominate or oppress, but to treat opponents, the oppressed, and everyone else the way they wish to be treated. This theological understanding taught them to value every single life, no matter what the person's orientation or ideology is, and to acknowledge and support the struggles of the marginalized.

Yet unlike Bonhoeffer, none of the Jewish respondents found their solution in a relationship with God, but rather in a new hope for a better dispensation and the will to embody their values. This hope is linked to a sense of responsibility to act and, for some also, to transcendence. One person explained that giving up Zionism can leave one in despair and in a downward spiral where "things are toppling on you and you can crash and stay there, or you can get new hope and objectives. And this, this is the empowerment—when you find an alternative hope."[34] It is important to persevere despite challenges, another noted, since:

> This in itself maybe is the definition of religion . . . because we transcend something, you go beyond the reality and you say, okay, you work from an inner—I don't know—power that you cannot sometime[s] understand . . . Maybe some people will say . . . this is God who is in us. I think I would say, no, that is the humanity in us and this human instinct or whatever is there to do the things.[35]

Their transformative changes are also expressed in how they listen and talk. When addressing local and international audiences, a South African Jew, for example, deliberately steers away from "us and them" language that may entrench division and opposition. Instead, she favors a style of joint thinking with her audiences to invite a mutual exploration of a different kind of language. Her style draws on and connects the meta and the micro, and the intersections between feeling and reason, prayer and meditation, to the extent that she shares her own fears and questions, and often feels "naked in public."[36]

---

33. *DBWE* 8:366.
34. Momberg, "Why Activists," 114.
35. Ibid., 122.
36. Ibid., 193.

As with Bonhoeffer, the turnabouts undergone by these activists were radical in both personal relations and in their yearning for shifts in their own communities. All the Jewish respondents were of the opinion that they have a special responsibility precisely because of their Jewishness and a severely compromised collective Jewish identity, whether as a religious, cultural, national, or transnational construct. Their concern is with both right-wing and with left-wing Zionists. They would like to make known that not all Jews condone or excuse Israel's abuses in the name of Jewish security or liberation as asserted by Zionist bodies who claim to speak in the name of all Jews. Indeed, they argue, such a position puts the safety of Jews everywhere at risk. They view Zionism's military and security paradigm as both a response to Jewish fear and a perpetuation of the "fear and siege" mentality which requires a constant "state of emergency" because "everybody is going to throw us into the sea," whether it be the Lebanese, the Hezbollah, the Syrians, the Palestinians, or Iran.[37] As one Israeli exclaimed, "We're spoon-fed fear from the day we're born . . . I think we all deserve to transcend that, to overcome that and to live in a place that doesn't have to be based on that."[38] In an ironic twist, they argued that Israel's militarism and its ethos of othering the Palestinians have become self-destructive. The idea of "living by our sword"—the claim that fighting is the only way that Jewish Israelis can exist—is not sustainable and it leaves the Israeli society "in a terrible state of mind."[39] A woman in her senior years spoke about the danger:

> If you are used to pushing around and screaming at Palestinians, then you sometimes scream at your children, your workers and your wife. . . . People are racist, not only towards Palestinians, but towards everybody. . . . We see a world where everybody hates us. We are the victims of the whole world. That's not very democratic and healthy for the society to see us still as a victim, right? There is also a kind of a distortion of the world-view, because you have to protect yourself as an occupier.[40]

In fact, the Jewish respondents pleaded for help from the international community to help Israel end the occupation of Palestine by putting pressure on the Israeli government "to save this country from ourselves, to save us from ourselves."[41] Especially as Jews, with their history of persecution, they do not want to allow discrimination against another people or claim exceptional treatment for themselves. Thus, they act not only because of the harm done to the Palestinians, but also because of the harm Israel inflicts on itself by being an oppressive state.

37. Ibid., 151.
38. Ibid.
39. Ibid., 152.
40. Ibid., 153.
41. Ibid., 137.

Like Bonhoeffer, they acknowledge the interconnectedness between their ability to face themselves and their community, and the willingness to side with the marginalized. But whereas Bonhoeffer focused on the Jewish question without commenting on the Roma, the disabled, people who are not heterosexual, and others who were persecuted by Nazism or oppressed by patriarchism, the Jewish activists campaign for change with an understanding of a bigger picture that includes other struggles for human dignity in the world. They feel connected to and nourished by a wider circle of like-minded people from different religious orientations with similar values and a shared passion for something much bigger than participating in a particular cause, in a particular location. Their *metanoia* entails a shift from patriarchy and militarism to an inclusive humanist ethos, incorporating feminist values and reaching across national, religious, racial, and gender boundaries. To them, their effort to embody universal values, as opposed to privileging one group over another, is indicative of their own integrity and indeed of Jewish identity itself.

Conclusion

A South African Jew remarked that Germany, Palestine, Israel, and South Africa make visible "under a microscope what so many places in the world experienced which is discrimination, segregation, living as refugees, living precarious lives, being hounded out at any moment, or the threat of that." These countries, she said, strongly bring home "aspects of those experiences that tell us more about what it means to be a human being, or what it can mean, how difficult it is to be a *Mensch* [human]. Why it's easier to swim with the stream, why it's easier to not step out and liberate ourselves."[42]

Neither Bonhoeffer nor the Jewish activists succumbed to the depths of darkness when their former worldviews disintegrated. They may have experienced existential confusion, betrayal, profound loneliness, an acute realization of mortality, and an intense desire for liberating change associated with the dark night of the soul. Yet, they found constructive ways to realign themselves in more authentic ways through the embodiment of their beliefs and values.

How is a coming generation to go on living in a world where authoritarian, dishonest, patriarchal, and xenophobic ideas are admired by enough people to elect leaders who treat gender equality, Black lives, the health of the planet, international law, and science with disdain? In the case of the Palestinians, Christians, Muslims, and others have been denied basic human rights for over seven decades despite the provisions of international law and the espoused values of Christianity and Judaism. Cameron, Bhatti, Duce, Sweeney, and Watkins point out that "discovering the tensions" between the "espoused" theology of a group and their actual practice can lead to a deepening of a commitment to individually and

---

42. Ibid., 147.

group-held values, and to enhanced clarity with respect to action.[43] Bonhoeffer and the activists displayed an intense desire for understanding their place and role on this planet, and when plunged into the depths, they had the courage to face the fallible, vulnerable self along with the ugliness of societal injustices. Their examples point us to a conduct of brutal honesty and an unwavering desire to be committed to ongoing and critical discernment. Through embodied inclusiveness, identities, beliefs, and values can turn from aspirations and projections into concrete expressions of meaning that become the vehicles for what it means to be a Christian or a Jew in this world.

43. Helen Cameron, Deborah Bhatti, Catherine Duce, James Sweeney, and Clare Watkins, *Talking about God in Practice: Theological Action Research and Practical Theology* (London: SCM Press, 2010), 53.

Chapter 14

BONHOEFFER'S IDEA OF EUROPE AS AN ANSWER TO THE CRISIS OF VALUES

Helena Anna Jędrzejczak

Introduction

What is modern Europe, if understood as an idea or a set of ideas? Tony Judt claims that the identity of contemporary Europe is based on the Shoah.[1] This somewhat depressing thesis is the key to the interpretation of both the pre- and postwar ideological heritage of Europe, including those elements which are considered its contemporary crisis in political and media discourses. It is said that currently we are dealing with a new kind of crisis—the crisis of values. Interestingly enough, the notion is shared on various sides of our contemporary ideological and political divides, and most likely, to all of its participants, it means something different. Yet, everyone seems to agree that there is such a crisis of values.

This chapter reflects on European identity and its foundational ideas. First, it discusses briefly the methodology used in the history of ideas and the concept of the crisis on which this text focuses. Second, I present Bonhoeffer's idea of Europe, based mostly on the chapter entitled "Heritage and Decay" in his *Ethics* and focus on the notions of guilt, reconciliation, and forgiveness. Third, I cite the idea of Europe in the thought of Poland's first non-communist prime minister, Tadeusz Mazowiecki, which was based on the interpretation of Bonhoeffer's thought made by post-Vaticanum II Roman-Catholic intellectuals. In the fourth section, I define the contemporary crisis of values. Lastly, I try to seek answers to this crisis in Bonhoeffer's thought.

In this chapter, I employ the methodology of the history of ideas, developed by Arthur O. Lovejoy and fully described in a book titled *The Great Chain of Being: A Study of the History of an Idea*. The second intellectual tradition that is used here is the "Warsaw School (history of ideas)" whose famous representatives include Leszek Kolakowski, Krzysztof Pomian, and Andrzej Walicki. The main assumption of the history of ideas is that ideas matter, and they have histories and consequences. The social and political phenomena could be described as the idea's

---

1. Tony Judt, *Postwar: A History of Europe Since 1945* (Poznań: Rebis, 2008), 934.

background as well as its consequences. As a sociologist and historian of ideas, I infer that if we want to understand social and political phenomena, we have to attend to the afterlife and reception of ideas and—this is specific to the history of ideas—take into account the socio-historical context in which the ideas were developed.[2]

Definition of the Crisis

In order to understand what the contemporary crisis is, it is necessary to revisit the past. The concept of crisis has been observed in European thought for many decades. In his *Vienna Lecture* 1935, Edmund Husserl noted that European nations were sick, and that Europe itself was experiencing profound crisis.[3] German historian and theorist Reinhart Kosseleck, in his extensive essay devoted to the concept of the crisis in the history of European thought, points out that crisis is one of the founding ideas of European identity and that it is rooted in the heritage of the ancient Greek and early Christianity. He writes that "Christians lived in the expectation of the Last Judgement (*krisis = judicum*), whose hour, time, and place remained unknown but whose inevitability is certain."[4] He presents the changes in its understanding and the differences between the French, Anglo-American, and German approaches. I will not summarize Kosseleck's analysis—the key to my chapter is that in the eighteenth century, the concept of crisis was transferred from the area of theology to its secularized version, that is, the philosophy of history, and it became one of the key philosophical categories. Referring to Leibniz, Kosseleck states:

> The concept [of crisis] has now entered into [the] dimension of the philosophy of history that was to become ever more significant in the course of eighteenth century. Through English and French usage and its entry to German language, the concept had expanded into the spheres of internal and external politics . . . and become the key to interpretation [of] the whole course of history and the diagnosis of the epoch.[5]

---

2. See Arthur Oncken Lovejoy, *Wielki łańcuch bytu* [*The Great Chain of Being: A Study of the History of an Idea*] (Gdańsk: Słowo/Obraz Terytoria, 2009).
3. Edmund Husserl, "Philosophy and the Crisis of European Man (Lecture Delivered by Edmund Husserl, Vienna, 10 May 1935)," trans. Quentin Lauer (2008), 22.
4. Reinhart Koselleck and Michaela Richter, "Crisis," *Journal of the History of Ideas* 67, no. 2 (2006): 359; Reinhart Koselleck, "A Few Problems from the History of the Term 'Crisis,'" in *Rozmowy w Castel Gandolfo: O kryzysie* [*Conversations in Castel Gandolfo: On Crisis*], ed. Krzysztof Michalski (Wiedeń-Warszawa: Instytut Nauk o Człowieku / ResPublica, 1986), 59–71.
5. Koselleck, "Crisis," 369.

Bonhoeffer's Idea of Europe—Heritage and Decay

In reference to Europe, Bonhoeffer writes mostly about its heritage, that European states and societies walked away from it. The analysis of selected chapters of *Ethics* enables us to formulate Bonhoeffer's idea of Europe—what it is and was, its underlying ideas and events. In "Heritage and Decay," he describes it as a construct of ideas, created through the ages, mostly on the basis of Christianity. He also shows that Europe has abandoned that heritage, and points to the consequences of that dissociation. Simultaneously, he emphasizes that the unity of the West (i.e., Europe) is not just an idea, but a fact, a historical reality founded on adopting the Christ from Rome:

> It is a historical heritage and, to be sure, a common Western heritage. Jesus Christ has made the West into a historical unit. The decisive turning points in history are of Western dimensions. The unity of the West is not an idea, but a historical reality, which the single source is Christ. The great intellectual movements from then on belong to the whole of the West. Even the wars in the West aim at the unity of the West. They are not wars of extermination and annihilation.[6]

This quote contains two key elements. First, the heritage of Europe is Christ, and second, this heritage is unity. Europe (the West) is not the past in which there are European countries. It is the common history of all countries and nations, which have created it and keep creating it. The heritage is therefore not unique to any one of the European countries. In this fragment, he places Germany together with England and France—countries that had different histories of development but were founded on the same event, which is the adoption of Christianity. Bonhoeffer's reflection therefore pertains to Europe's Christian heritage, which is the basis of building identity, including national identity. Its heritage goes back to antiquity and the Middle Ages—eras in which European Christianity was shaped. He points out that Greek antiquity played a greater role in countries in which the Reformation succeeded than in Roman Catholic ones.

The elements of European heritage stemming from antiquity are foremost Greek philosophy, the Roman law system, and the shape of relations among humans, the state, and the churches. From Rome derives also a substantial preeminence of the state over the nation—the former is a superior category, and it states that individuals should be bound to their state laws, and not to the community, that is, the nation. Lastly, Rome is also associated with the Augustinian theory of just war, which Bonhoeffer pinpoints as one of the building blocks of European heritage.

The "Heritage" is easy to describe, the "Decay," slightly more difficult, as it happens on fewer levels and within a longer time frame. In particular, the decay is a rejection of the heritage. It entails gradual detachment of the earthly realm from Christianity, until it becomes hostile toward it. The consequence is sinking into

---

6. *DBWE* 6:109.

nihilism. Bonhoeffer writes that "The most astonishing observation one makes today is that people surrender everything in the face of nothingness: their own judgement, their humanity, their neighbours. Where this fear is exploited without scruple, there are no limits to what can be achieved."[7] In subsequent paragraphs, Bonhoeffer offers two alternatives to stop the fall into the abyss—"the miracle of a news awakening of faith"; and the power that the Bible calls "the restrainer,"[8] "τὸ κατέχον." Although the second alternative is interesting, especially in combination with Schmitt's notion of "the political," I will discuss only the first.

Europe's walking away from its heritage led to its moral decay. What accounts for it the most is the bringing in of an individual, a human being, to play the role of a part of the entire society. Although, at the onset of the processes that led to it, there is, according to Bonhoeffer, the notion of full freedom of the human being, rejecting Christianity as a constitutive element for countries and societies caused a lapse in personalism—recognizing another person as a human being, together with the person's individualism, needs, and weaknesses. In a group, the individual stops being considered a person—one created in the image of God, for whom Christ sacrificed himself on the cross. That individual becomes merely a speck in the society, which is understood as a whole or an independent entity and therefore irrelevant to others, to bystanders.

The state built on the principles of Christianity would shape the relationships between citizens, members (and not only particles) of the society and thereby foster the building of a community of citizens. What differentiates the approach to the question of statehood based on Christianity from the contemporary to Bonhoeffer, based on a false understanding of freedom and the rejection of European heritage, are love and responsibility—two basic categories designating the relationship between a Christian and another fellow human being.

The Concept of Europe according to Mazowiecki—1970s and 1990s

Tadeusz Mazowiecki was one of the leaders of Polish Roman Catholic anti-communist opposition, and after the collapse of Communism in 1989, he became the first prime minister of independent Poland. He was also a translator and the author of essays dedicated to Bonhoeffer and his thought, which were published in the early 1970s and an advisor to the leaders of workers' strikes who acted in defence of their arrested and tortured participants. To understand the concept of Europe, according to Mazowiecki, a brief historical background is necessary. In 1939, Poland was attacked by Nazi Germany and the Soviet Union. Over 6 million of its citizens were killed, including nearly 3 million Polish Jews. Nazi concentration camps were built on Poland territory that claimed the lives of 2.7 million European Jews. After the war, Poland was under the rule of the Soviet Union (1945–89). As a result of the postwar settlement made by the winning superpowers, Poland lost

---

7. Ibid., 131.
8. *DBWE* 6:131.

much of its Eastern territory to the Soviet Union, and "in exchange," it got lands that earlier belonged to Germany.

In the period of the Second Vatican Council (1962–5) in Poland, there appeared communities of secular anti-communist Catholics—intellectuals working toward democratizing the Polish reality, who combined Christian and leftist ideas with the goal of operating in a peaceful way. They also strived to begin the process of reconciliation with Germany, and one of their inspirations were Bonhoeffer's books, including especially those dedicated to the fault and redemption, and the necessity of spiritual renewal of Europe. Importantly, Mazowiecki stresses this necessity of democratizing Poland where the existing narrative was that the country was solely the victim.

In the chapter, "Guilt, Justification, Renewal," dedicated to the concept of fault and redemption, Bonhoeffer[9] goes from individual fault and the necessity to taking action resulting from the notion that Christ redeemed individual guilt to the question of the guilt of nations and states. He transfers his Christ-centric theology resulting from its ethics on guilt, redemption, and forgiveness to political relations, legal, and political order. He refers to the concept of divine origin of power, but points out that it can become anti-Christian and anti-human. And in such a situation, the fault being both persecution and passivity becomes also the fault of a nation and state defined as political being. Individuals need to acknowledge their fault and begin a new life that strives to follow Christ. In the political context, Bonhoeffer refers to both estrangement of anti-human authority and the necessity for the spiritual renewal of Europe. In the case of the latter, the crucial thing will not be holding one nation accountable for losing the national heritage, but for each nation to take responsibility and acknowledge that it is complicit (albeit in varying degrees):

> The "justification and renewal" of the West can therefore only happen in the restoration of justice, order and peace in one way or another and then by the "forgiveness" of past guilt. This means giving up any illusion that one can, by punishment, undo what has been done . . . Since the guilt of falling away from Christ is a common guilt of the West, however the degree of blame may vary, there can only be a common Western justification and renewal. Every attempt to save the West that excludes one of the Western peoples is condemned to failure.[10]

Like Christians, who take action following the realization of their fault and that Christ sacrificed himself on the cross for them, each nation, acknowledging its fault, needs to work toward reconciliation instead of demanding retribution from those who were at a greater fault.

In the case of Polish-German reconciliation, the influence of Bonhoeffer's thought was substantial. The first gesture was made by the Evangelical Church in

---

9. Ibid., 134–45.
10. Ibid., 145.

Germany, which issued a "Memorandum of the Council of the Evangelical Church in Germany on the Situation of the Expelled and on the Relation of the German Nation to their Eastern Neighbours" (also known as "Eastern Memorandum"), a document, which urged reconciliation and the recognition of the new Polish-Germany border, imposed by the winning superpowers. It was addressed in 1965 through the "Letter of Reconciliation of the Polish Bishops to the German Bishops" in which, although Germany was the aggressor, Roman Catholic bishops wrote: "We extend to you who are sitting here on the benches of the Council, which is coming to an end, our hands and we grant you forgiveness and ask for it."[11] The political context of those words is important. Poland was a communist country, subject to the Soviet Union, and its identity was being built on hatred toward Germany and the Germans, solely blamed for the Second World War.

The next step on the path to reconciliation was an unexpected gesture by the chancellor of the Federal Republic of Germany, Willy Brandt, who during his first postwar diplomatic visit to Poland in 1970, knelt in front of the Monument to the Heroes of the Uprising in Warsaw Ghetto. Similar to the "Letter of the Bishops," this gesture was criticized by Polish authorities. The community around Mazowiecki, however, presented it as an extraordinary act, fitting into the Christian vision of reconciliation and an important step toward spiritual reconstruction of Europe.

The last chapter of postwar reconciliation is the so-called "The Holy Mass of Reconciliation" in Kreisau in 1989. For Bonhoeffer, the spiritual reconstruction of Europe must be founded on confession, forgiveness, and reconciliation. The culmination of those processes in the Polish-German case was this Mass and an unusual sign of peace between Mazowiecki and Helmuth Kohl. Kreisau is a symbolic place. Before the war, it was the property of Grafs von Moltke, during the war, the place of Kreisauer Kreis meetings, and after the war, a village in Poland where German Action Reconciliation: Service for Peace and the Catholic Intelligentsia Club (Mazowiecki's circle) established a Centre for Meetings for European Reconciliation.

According to Mazowiecki, Europe is, above all, a place where mutual faults have been forgiven and reconciled, and citizens are socially aware. In his view, the essential source of identity is Christian personalism, emphasizing the inalienable human dignity. He also points out that responsibility for the state, the church, and another human is borne by every one of us. Christians cannot close their eyes to the suffering of others, nor should they think it is someone else's responsibility to respond (e.g., the state or the institutional church). At the same time, Europe is a Europe of lawful and democratic states conducting responsible politics. Not only are references to Bonhoeffer's biography visible in Mazowiecki's work, but so also is a clear influence of his thought. The concept of reconciliation, personal responsibility, or democracy, described by Bonhoeffer, stems from a similar

---

11. Letter of Reconciliation of the Polish Bishops to the German Bishops (1965), http://polishfreedom.pl/en/document/letter-of-polish-bishops-to-german-bishops (accessed October 5, 2020).

understanding of both Christianity and European heritage. This can be confirmed by Mazowiecki's understanding of history and his description of the aspirations of humanity and each individual:

> The entire human history could be considered as a history of the struggle for human rights. The issue of human rights in the contemporary world, and today's understanding of them, is by no means an ephemeral, seasonal interest. And although there certainly are and will be changes in its configuration, it expresses deeply established aspirations. They do not vegetate on the periphery of human dreams of a conflict-free world, but indicate the direction to achieve a certain universal minimum, and determine the threshold for the realization of a sense of freedom, security and participation.[12]

It can be said that the European heritage has gained another dimension. It has become an acceptance of guilt—a repentance expressed publicly by political leaders and forgiveness in response to it. However, while this "confession" and "forgiveness of guilt" were realized between European countries, there is still a long way to go when it comes to non-European cultures. Following it will be a more complete realization of the heritage.

Contemporary Crisis of Values

At the beginning of this chapter, I mentioned that much is being said about the current crisis of values. Representatives of various ideological orientations speak of it often, while holding extremely different beliefs as to what the said crisis means. In the first part of the chapter, I have outlined the definition of crisis in the European intellectual tradition. Reinhart Kosselleck describes the crisis, with reference to the French lexicon of 1840, as "uncertainty, suffering, trial . . . the premises of which we cannot sufficiently display."[13] Perhaps this short definition best explains the fears of social change.

The description of happenings between 2020 and 2022 appears similar to the definition of crisis cited by Kosseleck. Previous ideological disputes over current social issues of importance to Western societies have receded into the background in the face of the Covid-19 pandemic. Themes, which conservative intellectuals regarded as a contemporary crisis of values, that is, increasing secularization, were replaced by a more or less selfish pursuit of physical survival. It might seem that, once the pandemic ends, the discussion of the "crisis of values" will return to normalcy. However, on February 24, 2022, Russia invaded Ukraine, and Europe, especially the Central-Eastern part, was confronted with the reality of a war it had

---

12. Tadeusz Mazowiecki, "Feel the Freedom," in *The Second Face of Europe* (PL: *Druga twarz Europy*), ed. Tadeusz Mazowiecki (Warszawa: Biblioteka Więzi, 1990), 77.
13. Kosseleck, "A Few Problems," 59.

not experienced for nearly eighty years. The hitherto ideological disputes, reflections by intellectuals on the Just War and Europe's heritage as a space of values, became a contemporary and tangible reality rather than a historical and hypothetical one.

Poland, as the country which shares the longest border with Ukraine (not counting Russia and its dependent Belarus), opened its borders to more than 3 million refugees from war-torn Ukraine. Citizens opened their arms wide to help—as they were commonly called—their Ukrainian brothers and sisters. We witnessed a response to the Gospel of St. Matthew—the hungry were fed, the naked were clothed, the stranger was welcomed warmly. These words seemed to ring out in the mouths of everyone—politicians of every party, millions of Poles volunteering to take in refugees, and hundreds of thousands of those who welcomed them into their homes. In the face of Russia's attack on Ukraine and acts of genocide committed by Russian soldiers, Europe seemed to be reclaiming its ideological heritage. The heritage of the continent, which historically was marked by two totalitarian regimes, obliges us to take special care of the weak so that postwar reconciliation and forgiveness are not only historical gestures but also a commitment to the future. In the case of the war in Ukraine, we managed to fulfill this commitment. At the same time, however, we remain indifferent as states and societies to the suffering of refugees from Africa and the Middle East. They freeze in the cold, being beaten and subjected to a push-back procedure a few dozen kilometers away on the Polish and Lithuanian borders with Belarus (which are also the borders of EU). Their situation touches almost no one. They are dehumanized victims of Putin's struggle against the West—dehumanized by everyone, including the Poles who opened their hearts and homes to the Ukrainians. It is a fight which, on the grounds of humanity, we are losing, not to Putin's regime, but to ourselves.

The attitude of European societies toward refugees from Ukraine and those from the Middle East is radically different. The warm welcome given to the Ukrainians and the indifference or hostility toward the other is easy to explain on sociological grounds and, at the same time, unacceptable on the basis of our ideological heritage. The conviction of the inalienable dignity of human beings seems to be lost when it comes to people who are different from us in terms of race, language, and origin. The world in which we do not see the hungry, the thirsty, or the naked because of some dissimilarities is a world that has rejected the fundamental Christian values.

Bonhoeffer as an Answer to the Contemporary Crisis of Values

Europe, whose heritage Bonhoeffer wrote about in "Heritage and Decay," was primarily a community that offered values, commitment, a desired way of life for people, and right principles for state operation. What happened in Bonhoeffer's time was irreversible, but it did not mean that Christians were exempt from the obligation to work toward the world's well-being. The choices we make today do not have the ancient-tragedy dimension. We are not like Antigone, whose story Bonhoeffer cites. The question is what can we, as Christians, scholars, Bonhoefferers, do today to ensure the spiritual revival of the West, which is again indifferent to suffering? Bonhoefferers as an answer, in part—Christians always ought to take side with their neighbor, the one who is more vulnerable, the one who needs help.

In the narratives of conservative politicians and intellectuals, the crisis of values is defined mainly by secularization and its consequences, especially in the sphere of morality and the decline of the churches in social life. The poor and endangered are supposed to be the churches and the conservatives themselves. However, based on Bonhoeffer's thought, such an account is impossible to justify. The weak is not the church (any church), because it is not a question of who is weak. We are not to defend churches, but people. It is not the post-Enlightenment secularization that leads to failure, but our indifference.

In what way then is Bonhoeffer's thought the answer to this crisis? We need to point out the real problems and direct the attention of societies, politicians, and churches to what is considered a contemporary moral challenge to the Western world. The reflections in Bonhoeffer's "Ethics," showing the decline and departure from heritage, remain a moral compass.

The Second World War ended seventy-five years ago. Over thirty years ago, Communism fell, and Europe again became a community. The heritage of Europe has not changed—both the Christian and the secular. It has been completed through yet another chapter by two totalitarian systems and developed into the concept of a common Europe where totalitarianism should never again occur. But now we are confronted with a cruel war at our borders. Inferring the moral condition of societies from their reaction to the war in Ukraine could give the false impression that Europe has regained its heritage, thanks to it. However, a war never brings out the best in people. A few months of heightened sensitivity to the situation of people like us cannot be proof that the crisis of values involving the disappearance of compassion and concern for the weak has miraculously passed.

Is a real return to heritage possible? Each of us must answer for ourselves as to how we can overcome the crisis of values and to what extent these words of Bonhoeffer's apply to us: "I must acknowledge that my own sin is to blame for of all these things. I am guilty of inordinate desire; I am guilty of cowardly silence when I should have spoken; I am guilty of untruthfulness and hypocrisy in the face of threatening violence; I am guilty of disowning without mercy the poorest of my neighbours."[14]

Tadeusz Mazowiecki, cited earlier, seems to provide some answers. This intellectual, a member of the democratic opposition, and first prime minister of independent Poland, sees the essence of humanity in faithfulness to values. He is convinced that the way to overcome Bonhoeffer's sense of guilt is to reflect on values, to act in accordance with them, or to become aware of one's own helplessness—a thoroughly human trait that makes one turn toward God:

---

14. *DBWE* 6:137.

The turn to the simplest values is a reflex of authenticity. It is not an escape from responsibility and commitment. The need to break through towards these values can always, admittedly, be seen as a luxury distant from real concerns and problems. But such an attempt can also be considered as a necessity . . . as a verification of what I am actually in solidarity with in my "species human being," in my wanting and not wanting, in my disapproval and in my allegiances, in my answer to the question "why." So it can also be understood as an invitation to become aware also of the limits of helplessness.[15]

Is this a satisfactory answer? I do not know. But it offers hope, because it points the way forward, which is to reflect on humanity, the human condition, and the role that each can play in the quest to reclaim our lost heritage.

---

15. Ibid., 13.

Chapter 15

POLITICO-RELIGIOUS MESSIANISM

A CRITICAL ANALYSIS OF THE BRAZILIAN SITUATION
IN CONVERSATION WITH DIETRICH BONHOEFFER

Wilhelm Sell and Rudolf von Sinner

Introduction

Political-religious messianism is not a new phenomenon in Brazil.[1] The government led by Jair Messias Bolsonaro from 2019 to 2022, however, appeared to be a mixture *sui generis* of not only conservatism with religious overtones, considerable popular *evangélico*,[2] but also Catholic and spiritual support, as well as being strongly favored by a neoliberal economic elite. Such religious support is based on long-standing conservative morality of both *evangélicos* and Catholics, combined with—and this is more recent—neoliberal economics. In short, the neoconservatives are morally in tune with politics, with the advances of economic liberalism and of media and technology, but extremely conservative about that which is considered harmful to the soul.

Maurício Moura and José Corbellini highlighted three factors that contributed to the election of Bolsonaro—first, the demoralizing effect of the findings of the so-called Operation "Car Wash" (*operação Lava Jato*), which made the corruption scheme of previous leftist governments as well as other politicians from across the political spectrum public, second, the public security crisis, and third, the use of

---

1. See Marilena de Souza Chauí, "Raízes teológicas do populismo no Brasil: Teocracia dos dominantes, messianismo dos dominados," in *Anos 90: Política e Sociedade no Brasil*, ed. Evelina Dagnino (São Paulo: Brasiliense, 1994), 19–30, 29–30. Translations of quotations from the Brazilian Portuguese into English are all ours, unless otherwise stated. Substantial parts of the text were translated by the Rev. Alexander Busch.

2. *Evangélico* in Brazil includes all denominational and nondenominational forms of Christianity that stem, widely speaking, from the sixteenth-century Reformation. In everyday language, it usually refers to Pentecostals and Neo-Pentecostals, but in the nineteenth and well into the twentieth century, Lutherans were called thus and called themselves *evangélicos*. To indicate this amplitude and diversity, we maintain the Portuguese term.

mobile apps such as WhatsApp as a new platform for political communication, widely used to spread "fake news." The first two factors led people to search for an alternative to traditional politics.³ In what follows, we will examine, first, the *evangélico* landscape in Brazil, situating the currently dominant moral conservatism, combined as it is now with economic neoliberalism. Second, we will interpret the Brazilian situation under the Bolsonaro government as a politico-religious messianism, and third, revisit Dietrich Bonhoeffer's critique of a political messianism of his time. In conclusion, we highlight the importance of Bonhoeffer's Christian humanism for a responsible way of being the church in today's Brazilian society. And this has to mean profound and true respect for human life in all its diversity, not in a way aligned to imposed "Christian principles."

Evangélico-Catholic Conservatism, Economic Neoliberalism, and Bolsonaro's Ascension

The austerity about matters that could defile the soul and the liberal attitude toward the mundane have their historic origin in the influence of Neo-Platonism and Stoicism on Christian ethics, especially sexual ethics. The negative vision of the body as the prison of the soul gave rise to the sexual morality that influenced the whole history of Christianity in some way.⁴ There is a division between that which is trapped and transitory to the sinful world and that which is eternal, the soul, which, for this reason, must be kept as immaculate as possible. This explains why *evangélico, and* also traditional Roman Catholic morality, is much more concerned with issues related to human sexuality, as they are linked to the care of the soul, than issues of social justice, equity, and ideals that strengthen democracy. These are earthly and temporary.

Related to this, however, is the emphasis on material goods and personal comfort as signs of earthly well-being in tune with the status of eternal salvation, which placed many *evangélicos*—on whom is our focus here—in harmony with the logic of the marketplace.⁵ This is how a significant group among *evangélicos*, especially neo-Pentecostals, adapted faith to the lure of neoliberalism. Thus, the goal of faith is restricted to solving the problems caused by the presence of evil in a person's life, problems which prevent him or her from obtaining the material benefits that, through faith, are considered the person's due. It is no coincidence that victory and healing worship services became so popular alongside motivational and self-help

---

3. Maurício Moura and José Corbellini, *A eleição disruptiva* (Rio de Janeiro: Record, 2019), 37–57, 109–33.

4. Urbano Zilles, "A visão cristã da sexualidade humana," *Teocomunicação* 39, no. 3 (2009): 336–50.

5. Manuela Lowenthal Ferreira, "A Moral (Neo)Pentecostal e a ética empreendedora: Sobre a teologia da prosperidade e o impulso para o trabalho," *Diversidade Religiosa* 7, no. 1 (2017): 88–101, 92–3.

preaching. The appropriation of the market logic has made the *evangélico* churches to increase their membership in a traditionally Catholic country thus increasing the importance of their political agenda in Brazilian politics. It is also worth noting that the fight against evil to obtain the benefits of God's kingdom demonstrates the position in the political and economic fields, above all, in the identification of and struggle against evil, not least what is considered socialism and the "Communist conspiracy." Such an idea (stemming especially from the late Olavo de Carvalho's view on "cultural Marxism," which guided the inner government circle—the so-called "hate cabinet") reinforces political polarization and obstructs the democratic debate.[6]

Neo-Pentecostalism unscrupulously expanded the new spirit of capitalism, with a strong presence particularly in the peripheries of Brazil. Thus, what Weber had identified in his analysis of the "Spirit of Capitalism" seems to re-emerge, namely the interpenetration between a religious culture and the expansion of capitalism,[7] but now, in a more aggressive form. In this new form of religiosity, God became the therapist of worldly ills, while lack of success and failure became signs of evil and the devil. The benefits can be gained in two ways—first, by identifying where the evil is and, second, by performing the correct ritual, which invariably implies considerable donations to the church. Meanwhile, the need to assure the "salvation status" and declare victory over "evil," combined with the possibility of experiencing the joys of prosperity, compels a person to accept the necessary sacrifices and adjust to the required limitations and expectations.[8]

By this logic, the outcasts of society, beggars, and all who have failure stamped on their body and way of life are excluded. And there is a logical necessity for this exclusion. The purpose is to heighten the discourse that propels the struggle and the desire for success. In this context, people are encouraged to project the experience of failure onto scapegoats. In religious language, the scapegoats are usually the limitations imposed by the influence of evil spirits (*encostos*). In more secular language, this could be translated as the limitations of the economic politics of the state in favor of a free market with limited labor rights, that is, the obstacles arising from the "bad" influences of social policies and leftist politics. Those who miss their way or give up in the face of failure are entirely responsible for their fate.

---

6. See Alexandre, *E a verdade vos libertará*, 70f.; also https://olavodecarvalho.org/do-marxismo-cultural/ (accessed October 18, 2020); Terrence McCoy, "He's the Rush Limbaugh of Brazil. He Has Bolsonaro's Ear. And He Lives in Rural Virginia," *The Washington Post* online, July 14, 2019, https://www.washingtonpost.com/world/the_americas/hes-the-rush-limbaugh-of-brazil-he-has-bolsonaros-ear-and-he-lives-in-rural-virginia/2019/07/14/4f73dee2-8ac4-11e9-8f69-a2795fca3343_story.html (accessed October 18, 2020).

7. Max Weber, *A ética protestante e o espírito do capitalismo* (São Paulo: Companhia das Letras, 2004), 154.

8. Roberto Torres, "O neopentecostalismo e o novo espírito do capitalismo na modernidade periférica," *Perspectivas* 32, no. 2 (2007): 85–125, 105–17.

In religious language, failure is "lack of faith," and in the secular market language, failure is "lack of will and/or performance."[9]

It is evident that neoliberal rationality, as a way of understanding and acting in the world, which transforms and treats everything and most people as objects and commodities to be traded and/or discarded,[10] was religiously absorbed by many *evangélicos* who altered and reduced the gospel to a simplistic and individualistic code of ethics of moralistic content and form. Its effects on democracy are problematic and of disastrous consequences, especially when strengthened and endorsed by the religious discourses. This is how Bolsonaro obtained power and support for his form of government. In other words, the *evangélico* moral discourse is nothing more than a series of rhetorical maneuvers to establish and maintain the neoliberal economy model.

Indeed, in a configuration that sees an ever-growing influence of *evangélico* churches in a traditionally Catholic country, the country's self-interpretation today is ever more bluntly laden with religious significance, including the task to exterminate "Communism" and "Socialism" with "God" as the guarantee of a highly conservative sexual and family morality that can be combined with a liberal economy and with the extermination of "bandits" by the police or by the so-called good citizens.[11] This poses, evidently, serious dangers. What the political scientist Marina Basso Lacerda calls the "New Brazilian Conservatism" bears many similar characteristics to the "New Christian Right" in the United States under Ronald Reagan. Although this is only part and parcel of a wider and diverse movement of the right, it is this movement that brought Bolsonaro to the presidency.[12] Similarly, social anthropologist Ronaldo de Almeida notes that the movement started in 2013 with the widespread protests against the Dilma Rousseff government around the Confederation's Cup.[13] De Almeida shows that at least four elements characterize their position. They are economically liberal, morally regulative as well as punitive and socially intolerant in terms of security issues.[14] He calls it a "conservative wave"—not without counter forces and indeed creating serious

---

9. See Euler Renato Westphal, *Secularization, Cultural Heritage and the Spirituality of the Secular State* (Paderborn: Ferdinand Schöningh, 2019), 85–6, 99; cf. also chapters 11 and 12 of Rudolf von Sinner, *Public Theology in the Secular State: A Perspective from the Global South* (Zürich: LIT, 2021).

10. Rubens R. Casara, *Estado pós-democrático: Neo-obscurantismo e gestão dos indesejáveis* (Rio de Janeiro: Civilização Brasileira, 2019), 47–57.

11. Cf. Rudolf von Sinner and Euler Renato Westphal, "Lethal Violence, the Lack of Resonance and the Challenge of Forgiveness in Brazil," *International Journal of Public Theology* 12, no. 1 (2018): 38–55.

12. Marina Basso Lacerda, *O novo conservadorismo brasileiro* (Porto Alegre: Editora Zouk, 2019).

13. Ronaldo de Almeida, "Bolsonaro Presidente: Conservadorismo, evangelismo e a crise brasileira," *Novos Estudos CEBRAP* 38, no. 1 (2019): 185–213.

14. Ibid., 185–7.

divisions. Basso identifies these as the upholding of the so-called traditional family, the defence of militarism both internally (by punishing) and externally (by combating Communism) as well as a neoliberal economy with privatization and reduction of state-run social programs and, finally, closeness to Israel. The key aspect that distinguishes this form of conservatism from others is the emphasis on the traditional family, combating gender justice and equality (called "gender ideology"), homoaffective relationships (especially when it comes to marriage), and the decriminalization of abortion—similar to the US mobilization in the 1980s as a reaction against the Equal Rights Amendment that sought to promote family protection legislation.

In Brazil, neoconservative deputies have opposed legislation that would promote the prohibition of corporal punishment of children, references to gender identity and diversity in sexual orientation in educational material, and the program, *School without Homophobia*. Against the latter, they created the idea of *School without a Party*, opposing what they consider leftist "indoctrination" at schools. They further advocate the reduction of the legal age of punishment from eighteen to sixteen, a more rigorous law against drugs, wide access to firearms, and effective impunity to police officers when they kill in action. Many *evangélico* congressmen are themselves members of the armed forces or the police. The impact of the policies, we might add, relate to the fact they mostly also appeal to Catholics (slightly over half of them voted for Bolsonaro) and members of other religions, which form a significant percentage of African Brazilian voters, despite racist and homophobic tendencies present in those policies. Still, the clearest support for Bolsonaro came from *evangélicos*—more than two-thirds of the voters (21.5 million) voted for him in 2018.[15]

"Brazil above Everything, God above Everybody": Bolsonaro's Politico-Religious Messianism

Bolsonaro's motto is "Brazil above everything, God above everybody" (*Brasil acima de tudo, Deus acima de todos*).[16] This is reminiscent of the German national anthem "Germany, Germany above everything, above everything in the

---

15. See the table based on a DataFolha survey carried out on October 25, 2018, quoted by Almeida, "Bolsonaro presidente," 206. While there was a clear reduction in Catholic votes in 2022, *evangélicos* still voted for Bolsonaro in their majority; see Morgan Lee and Mariana Albuquerque, "Com pequena mudança nos votos evangélicos, Brasil elege Lula," *Christianity Today* of November 9, 2022, https://www.christianitytoday.com/news/2022/november/lula-eleicoes-brasil-2022-presidente-voto-evangelicos-pt.html (accessed July 17, 2023).

16. The first part of the motto stems from Bolsonaro's former parachute brigade. This resistance group started to the notion of "Brazil above everything" during the military regime in the 1960s; see https://www.gazetadopovo.com.br/eleicoes/2018/brasil-acima-de-

world" (*Deutschland, Deutschland über alles, über alles in der Welt*) in Dietrich Bonhoeffer's time. With Bolsonaro, the motto took on a strongly religious overtone to appeal to his supporters. To give a religious, indeed messianic, identity to the country and its leadership has been, in different forms, a recurring issue since its so-called discovery and colonization in the 1500s. It was also the responsibility of the crown to cater for religious matters under the patronage system. Contrary to past philosophical views of the messianic as the emergence of transforming forces, which was recently reiterated by authors like Alain Badiou, Slavoj Žižek, and Giorgio Agamben (not least through a productive interaction with biblical authors, namely Paul in the Letter to the Romans), such political messianism is not necessarily seen as fostering transformation.[17] Rather, it invests enormous expectations in a—usually charismatic—leading person, which might bring economic benefits, but remains as authoritarian and clientelistic as Brazil has been, traditionally.

It is clear then that imposing such an agenda, based on rigid principles and strict morality combined with a (neo-)liberal economy on all of society, appeals to large religious groups. The fact that religion plays a role in people's everyday life and in the public sphere is not new. Such roles have been visible in different ways since colonial times. What has developed over decades, however, is the attempts by *evangélico* groups to hold power. While the traditional motto had been "believers don't mingle with politics," in the Constituent Assembly of 1986–7, it started to change to "brother votes for brother."[18] With considerable growth in number, as shown previously, *evangélicos* made their presence felt and forced politicians to seek their support. At the same time, political messianism flagrantly awaits a leadership which, under divine inspiration, would solve the nation's problems. In 2006, one of the foremost researchers of *evangélicos* in politics in Brazil and elsewhere, Paul Freston noted a "messianic" expectation that this *evangélico* candidate will automatically channel God's blessings to Brazil, resolving all problems that afflicted the country. Such messianism is very dangerous, for both country and church. Contrary to what is often said, the last aspect of a person to be converted is "not the wallet but the fascination for power."[19]

---

tudo-conheca-a-origem-do-slogan-de-bolsonaro-7r6utek3uk1axzyruk1fj9nas (accessed March 19, 2019).

17. See, for instance, Josias de Paula Jr., "The Messianic and the Tragic in the Social Theory: Considerations of Left-Wing Thinking," *Política e Trabalho: Revista de Ciências Sociais* 40 (2014): 199–219.

18. Rudolf von Sinner, *The Churches and Democracy in Brazil: Towards a Public Theology Focused on Citizenship* (Eugene, OR: Wipf & Stock, 2012).

19. "Esse messianismo é muito perigoso, para o país e para a Igreja. Ao contrário do que muitas vezes se afirma, a última parte do homem a se converter não é o bolso, é o fascínio pelo poder"; Paul Freston, *Religião e política, sim—Igreja e Estado, não: Os evangélicos e a participação política* (Viçosa: Ultimato, 2006), 10–11.

Bolsonaro's government, however, was the first to identify openly as a religious government. Although Bolsonaro affirmed the secularity on which the Brazilian state is based, he tirelessly repeated that his government is "Christian."[20] As a candidate on the rise in 2018, Bolsonaro declared:

> I am Christian—look at the popular support I am receiving. Is it not unimaginable what is happening? How did I manage this? When I speak about "mission of God," I am thinking: what should be my motto? What will be my brand? Then I went to John 8.32: "and you will know the truth, and the truth will make you free."[21]

Thus, the "Christian faith" is employed as a fundamental key to the administration of the state, similar to the Trump government's position. Like voting for Trump, voting for Bolsonaro meant recovering a conservative Christian influence in Brazilian society, while here it also implies putting it into *evangélico* hands and replacing the traditional Catholic hegemony.[22] At the same time, concerned with "morality and good manners," the *evangélicos* made alliances with Catholic parliamentarians, forming an otherwise unlikely interdenominational dialogue.[23] In this way, Bolsonaro became Brazil's first *pan-Christian* president.[24] Nine months into his tenure, the founder and supreme bishop of the influential Universal Church of God's Kingdom, Edir Macedo, anointed Bolsonaro with oil and said God had chosen him to lead 210 million Brazilians. Therefore, "I make use of all authority that was given to me by God to bless this man, to give him wisdom so that this country will be transformed, that he may make a new Brazil," he declared.[25]

However, the question is which God did Bolsonaro's government appeal to? Who is this God, and on which side is God to be found? The same question had already been asked in Liberation Theology in opposition to the military regime of the 1970s and 1980s. In his regular blog, Leonardo Boff called Bolsonaro's motto "blasphemy" precisely because, in his view, it did not refer to a God of love and mercy but of revenge who also is not committed to life, be it of persons or

---

20. This can be watched on the president's official YouTube channel: https://www.youtube.com/watch?v=4FObF2RiHvE (accessed September 18, 2020).

21. As quoted by Alexandre, *E a verdade os libertará*, 26.

22. Guillermo F. Borda, "A construção de uma *nação cristã* na América Latina," in *Novo ativismo político no Brasil: Os evangélicos do século XXI*, ed. José Luiz Pérez-Guadalupe and Brenda Carranza (Rio de Janeiro: Konrad Adenauer Stiftung, 2020), 131–53 (136–40).

23. Magali do Nascimento Cunha, *Religião e Política*, 149.

24. Freston, *Bolsonaro, populismo*, 372.

25. "uso de toda a autoridade que me foi concedida por Deus para abençoar este homem, para lhe dar sabedoria, para que este país seja transformado, que faça um novo Brasil"; https://politica.estadao.com.br/noticias/geral,bolsonaro-recebe-uncao-de-edir-macedo-e-bispo-diz-que-presidente-vai-arrebentar,70002992132 (accessed January 19, 2020).

of nature.[26] For Bonhoeffer, as is well known, the decisive question was "who is Christ actually for us today?"[27] In Bonhoeffer's time, the choice was between two gods. Is it the god of the *German Christians* who condoned the Nazi regime and its systematic destruction of Jews as well as communists, homosexuals, people with disabilities, and others deemed unworthy to live in an Arian society? Or is it the god who died with the victims in the concentration camps? Although there is no comparison to what happened in Nazi Germany, the gist of the question remains. Today, the question could be asked thus: Is it the god of Bolsonaro, an excluding, punishing, militaristic god that is, among others, insensitive to gender justice, homoaffective relationships, and socially aware movements? Or is it a god that stands at the side of the excluded, promotes human dignity and rights, and recognizes human beings in their diversity?

Bonhoeffer and a Critique of Political Messianism

On June 20, 1931, Bonhoeffer returned to Germany after a period of study and research at Union Theological Seminary. This period was marked by his participation in the Harlem Baptist Church and its struggle for social and racial justice. He then began to teach at the University of Berlin with greater theological sensitivity to social issues in his own context.[28] At the age of twenty-five, Bonhoeffer was also ordained into the pastoral ministry in the *Evangelische St. Matthäus-Kirche in Berlin*. His work switched back and forth between academic teaching and pastoral ministry. What is remarkable during this period is his denunciation of the messianic spirit which became increasingly evident during the Third Reich and the constant concern with theological and philosophical issues that became the basis for the so-called *Positives Christentum*, a strand of Christianity that was used to provide legitimacy for the National Socialist political movement and its depiction as a "divinely ordained cultural redeemer."[29]

During the winter semester of 1932 and 1933, Bonhoeffer lectured on "Creation and Fall," based on the first three chapters of Genesis. He demonstrated his knowledge of all the background research of the historical-critical method in the exegetical task, and, in the wake of the theological heritage of the Protestant Reformation of *theologia crucis*, brought into his classes concise theological responses to his social context. It is likely that the very choice of an Old Testament text is motivated by the political situation in which there was an increasingly

---

26. https://leonardoboff.wordpress.com/2019/03/25/a-blasfemia-de-jair-bolsonaro-que-deus-acima-de-todos/ (accessed January 15, 2020).

27. *DBWE* 8:362.

28. See Reggie Williams, *Bonhoeffer's Black Jesus: Harlem Renaissance Theology and an Ethic of Resistance* (Waco, TX: Baylor University Press, 2014).

29. Ryan Buesnel, "Positive Christianity: Theological Rationales and Legacies," *Religion Compass* 14, no. 7 (2020): e12353, 7.

strong tendency to exclude Semitic texts, besides reflecting on themes such as the *orders of creation*, which belong to the Lutheran theological tradition and were being misrepresented, and which made the political realm a fixed, elevated, and autonomous order from the other orders. Bonhoeffer therefore offered a strong critique of what he calls a "pseudo-Lutheran" theology that gave theoretical support to this theological and political misrepresentation.[30]

In *Creation and Fall*, Bonhoeffer refers to Scripture as the book of the church. In turn, the church acts in the world and interprets Scripture through Jesus Christ. The church also understands the history of creation and its *orders* from and in reference to Christ. Without the mediation of the one who is at the *beginning and the end*, the middle becomes itself *the beginning and the end*. This is humanity's dilemma. As *sicut deus*, humanity will always try to establish something of its own as the regulating principle of reality. Its constant enticement (*Verführung*) is assuming a continuum between creator and creature, which easily results in producing structures and messianic figures that aim to promote what is considered *good*, and in rooting out *evil*. It is for this reason that Bonhoeffer maintains the idea that God creates out of nothing and in freedom. Therefore, everything is created, established, and sustained through his word and the action of the Holy Spirit.[31]

While criticizing the Lutheran concept of *creatio continua*, Bonhoeffer affirms that there is an act of God that does not belong to the *order of creation* but to the *order of preservation*. This emphasis is to avoid any kind of synergism between creator and creature by diluting the "individual spirit" into the "absolute spirit," as Hegel's philosophical idealism asserts. For Bonhoeffer, aspects of this idealism had unfolded in his context within Protestant theology. An example of this is his criticism of Karl Holl and his concept of "religion of conscience."[32] Bonhoeffer affirms the idea of revelation *extra nos*. The human being should not understand the self from within the self but from within Christ in the experience of the church-community, from within his Word. This means that God and God's will cannot be found outside of Christ, as in reliance on conscience and the resulting practice of the law.[33] The feeling of duty and obligation that the conscience can generate and propel the human being to action should not be understood as the voice of God. Even if there is the act of preservation of God by general revelation, this is done through masks (*larvae Dei*) on which the human being has no influence. Besides, the feeling and perception of God's presence in creation after the Fall (Gen. 3:8), as in the case of Adam and Eve, cause a person to use his or her conscience by

---

30. Wilhelm Sell, *Ser humano, ser para a outra pessoa: O significado da antropologia de Dietrich Bonhoeffer para sua ética* (PhD diss., Faculdades EST, São Leopoldo, 2019), 127–33.

31. *DBWE* 3:31–7.

32. Eberhard Bethge, *Dietrich Bonhoeffer: Theologian, Christian, Contemporary*, trans. Eric Mosbacher et al. (London: Collins, 1970), 68.

33. Michael P. DeJonge, *Bonhoeffer's Reception of Luther* (Oxford: Oxford University Press, 2017), 22–3.

becoming a judge and evading the judgment of God. The human being lives trapped in the reality of *good* and *evil*, destiny and tragedy, of the most intimate division within the self and with others.

Therefore, conscience is not the voice of God in the sinful human being but self-defence before God's voice. The voice of God, which reveals his presence, comes when God, through God's word, calls the individual and asks him or her the question, "Where are you?" (Gen. 3:9). God calls human beings out of their hiding place, their own conscience. And it is there, standing before God, that they find themselves naked, disconnected, disjointed, and, on recognizing their condition, flee from the existential situation justifying their condition and guilt by accusing the other person and the situation that led them to evil. Eve considered the "flesh of his flesh, bone of his bones," a perfect creation of God, but introduced deceit, saying, "she gave me the fruit and I ate it" (Gen. 3:12). So, amid all the accusations, the guilt falls on the creator himself, and Adam and Eve no longer recognize God's call as grace.[34]

For Bonhoeffer, when human conscience as a kind of internal capacity is regarded as an immediate place of divine revelation, the radicality of sin is ignored. In this view, Christ is no longer the mediator between God and human beings. Rather, his incarnation is considered the beginning of an internal process in humans toward the capacity for self-justification. The question then is how does this understanding of humanity lead to religious discourses that openly endorse a project of totalitarian power? Even though politics belongs to the realm of reason and is part of general revelation, it is distorted because of messianic discourses that claim a kind of specific revelation as the incarnation of the good and as representing the divine will. Before this, theology can only expose its personal responsibility to the church and its civil responsibility to the world when it understands sin primarily as guilt and a human tragedy that affects the human being in totality, essentially, and existentially, making him or her to be *cor curvum in se*.[35]

Bonhoeffer, in some other instances, reflects on the role of the church in the face of Adolf Hitler's Third Reich and its blatant political messianism. In *The Nature of the Church*, Bonhoeffer states that the church's critique of the state must begin by listening to the gospel. Its political vocation is based on the gospel. For Bonhoeffer, the church is simply not the body that calls itself church or that recites creeds, consecrates bishops, or that preaches Luther's doctrine of justification. The church is humanity newly created by Christ through his death and resurrection. The church is the new humanity, the new society that is under Christ's lordship, and is determined to highlight this new reality. Thus, "*Christ is not the founder* of a new religion and religious community. He is the Redeemer, *the foundation* of the church, *not the founder* . . . Christ is the new humanity. Christ is simultaneously the foundation and beginner and fulfiller of the church."[36] For this reason, this

---

34. *DBWE* 3:119–22.
35. Sell, *Ser humano*, 49.
36. *DBWE* 11:301.

new humanity in Christ is the church which, through the action of the Holy Spirit, actualizes and represents Christ's presence in the world, time and time again.

In this way, the church is not formed by individuals who share the same piety derived from a common desire, as suggested by Schleiermacher, but the church is the action and concretization of Godself who moves toward God's creation.[37] However, the church too is under the sign of sin. This means that it is not some sort of "purity" that dignifies the church, but the one who is its foundation, Jesus Christ. For this reason, the church does not promote an escape from the world, but it assumes its worldliness as a vocation, becoming the presence of the God who became human. Since Jesus Christ is the foundation and sustains all reality, his presence through the church also sheds light on the state. Still, this does not mean that the church has the authority to interfere in the affairs of the state since the state is established by God as a critical warning that God did not give the church the power of the sword. Rather, "Its sword is [the] word and [the] prayer. Thereby it serves the state. When it is threatened by the state, it fights against the state. It will not try to govern the state. [The] goal is the proclamation of the lordship of Christ over the whole world in faith and [in the] word."[38]

The same point is made in a lecture given at the end of 1932 during a devotional retreat at the Protestant Institute of Continuous Education for Women, under the title *Thy Kingdom Come!* There, Bonhoeffer argued that praying "Your kingdom come" means praying for the kingdom of God to be established on earth.[39] Both the church and the state are forms of God's kingdom on earth. Their relationship is mutual and necessary. In Bonhoeffer's view, the kingdom of God on earth, as a penultimate reality, takes two forms—the church and the state. Both are related and cannot be isolated even though they must be distinguished in their function. The kingdom of God takes shape in the church in so far as the church witnesses to the miracle of God's new creation. The kingdom of God takes shape in the state in so far as the state preserves the order of the old creation:

> Thus the Church witnesses to the overcoming of the power of death by the miracle of the resurrection; the state upholds the order of the preservation of life. In the church the power of loneliness is overcome by the miracle of confession and forgiveness and the creation of a new community; in the state the given orders of society, marriage, family, people, are preserved in the world of the curse. In the church the thirst of the egocentric man for his own self is overcome by the proclamation of the cross and resurrection of Christ and is transfigured into a loving thirst for the other, namely, for God and the brother [sic]; in the state thirst of man, which may bode good or evil for others, is ordered and

---

37. Wilhelm Sell and Carlos Caldas, "Vocação política da igreja em tempos sombrios: Denúncia de Dietrich Bonhoeffer ao Messianismo Político," *Protestantismo em Revista* 46, no. 1 (2020): 50–63, 57.

38. *DBWE* 11:332.

39. *DBWE* 12:285–97.

restrained by responsible authority. From this it becomes clear, therefore, that the church limits the state and the state limits the church. Both of them must remain cognizant of this mutual limitation and bear the strain of existing side by side without overstepping the boundary between them.[40]

Bonhoeffer argues that the church should not aspire to take over the power of the state, as governance is carried out based on the dictates of the church. Likewise, the state should not have religious and soteriological aspirations, since its function is to maintain order and to manage well the public resources for the good of all. Therefore, it is only possible to pray for the coming of the kingdom of God in a full and ultimate form when in a penultimate form one is submissive to what was inaugurated in the incarnation, death, and resurrection of Christ, that is, submissive to the God who came and took over what belongs to God. The two kingdoms represent God's dual activity and are thus related.[41] They signify the activity of God, as preserver and redeemer, in which the state and the church play important roles.

For Bonhoeffer, the problem with *pseudo-Lutheranism* was the interpretation of the two kingdoms as completely distinct, so that the idea of *Volk* ("the people") could be interpreted as an *order of creation*. On the one hand, the church passively endorsed the unscrupulous actions of the Nazi state by assuming that the *temporal kingdom* has total autonomy from the church (*Eigengesetzlichkeit*), thus autonomy from the government of God in Christ. As such, the church loses its relevance to earthly reality. On the other hand, the temporal kingdom is governed not only by reason but also by a religious subjectivity of hope centered around a "messenger" from God who would fulfill his will for the sake of the *Volk* ("the people"). This messianism does not tolerate the tension of the simultaneity between good and evil present in creation after the Fall. On the contrary, it insists on a dichotomy between good and evil. Good has only one side, and so does evil. Therefore, identifying the one who "incarnates" the good exposes the one who is the representation of evil and to be resisted. Thus, even murder could be "sanctified" as a pleasant offering for the "good" of the people.[42]

---

40. Ibid., 108.
41. In *Thy Kingdom Come!*, Bonhoeffer cites only the state as the temporal kingdom. However, at other times, especially in his *Ethics*, he expands and groups the mandates into family, culture, and government. DeJonge recalls that, in Bonhoeffer, the two kingdoms are not reduced to a doctrine of church and state, because the latter is not the only agent of preservation in the temporal kingdom (the family is another), and the church as an institution has a place not only in the spiritual kingdom but also in the temporal kingdom. Michael P. DeJonge, *Bonhoeffer on Resistance: The Word against the Wheel* (Oxford: Oxford University Press, 2018), 37–8; cf. *DBWE* 6:68–74.
42. Sell and Caldas, *A vocação política da igreja*, 61.

Conclusion—Bonhoeffer's Christian Humanism as an Inspiration for Today

We have tried to show that Brazil has been facing a theologically charged political situation in which the president is attributed with messianic qualities that make a political as well as a theological critical discourse and argument as difficult as is necessary. We compared the situation to Bonhoeffer's critique of political and theological support of Nazism and considered some of the rich theological resources he has to offer in this regard, while reading Luther against his contemporary "pseudo-Lutheranism." In conclusion, we further appropriate some aspects of Bonhoeffer's theology that seem helpful in the present situation, as we seek to situate faith and religion in society, namely Bonhoeffer's humanism, deeply rooted in Christ's incarnation, death on the cross, and resurrection.

As found in Bonhoeffer's famous poem, "Christians and Heathen," to stand by God in God's suffering is what distinguishes Christians from heathens.[43] There is no external, judging distinction, nor is God's love withdrawn from heathens. No clarity is given as to who is in and who is out, who is wrong and who is right. This is a position that makes it possible to be a Christian in the real world, which is marked by profound ambiguity. Lutheran theology has expressed this through the *simul iustus et peccator*.[44] It is important to note that this does not excuse responsibility for wrongdoing. On the level of human practice, there is sin, which is different from just action, and should be denounced as such. Responsibility for poverty and oppression is not evenly distributed. What is common, however, is the living under the power of sin, which creates an inescapable situation and, which structural aspects, such as Liberation Theology, have always maintained. Christians know about this situation brought about by Adam, the first human, and from there have, as one could call it, a "confessional" mistrust in themselves and others, inasmuch as all, including the believers, are subject to the power of sin. Rather than seeking to escape such ambiguity by artificially clarifying it, with clearcut distinctions, firm answers, and stark judgment, this infuses humility, realism, and hope.

A second point is to maintain in a fruitful tension between the calling and claim of Christ over humanity and a deep respect for humans, whether they are

---

43. For further details, see Rudolf von Sinner, "The Ethics of the Penultimate in a Situation of Ambiguity: A Possible and Relevant Interpretation of Bonhoeffer in Brazil Today," *Stellenbosch Theological Journal* 2, no. 2 (2016): 77–91.

44. See Luther's lectures on Romans, here on Rom. 4:7, LW 25:260: "Now, is he perfectly righteous? No, for he is at the same time both a sinner and a righteous man; a sinner in fact [*in re*], but a righteous man by the sure imputation and promise of God that He will continue to deliver him from sin until He has completely cured him. And thus he is entirely healthy in hope [*in spe*], but in fact he is still a sinner; but he has the beginning of righteousness, so that he continues more and more always to seek it, yet he realizes that he is always unrighteous."

Christian or not. While there is a clear call from God who in Christ experienced vicarious suffering, in Bonhoeffer, there is profound respect for and a statement of love for human beings as they really are. The goal is conformity with Christ, but it is precisely in this that human beings become truly human. Thus, "Human beings become human because God became human. But human beings do not become God."[45] Although God in Christ comes into human life, the difference between God and human beings is not blurred, taking seriously and preserving human beings as such. It is, also in line with Bonhoeffer's ethics, not the task of such conformity to impose "so-called Christian principles" directly on the world. This is a central point because it sees God acting through those conformed to Christ in the world, in solidarity with one another and with the world, without imposing their principles on others. In *History and the Good I*, Bonhoeffer states that this conduces to a situation of a dangerous and always endangered freedom:

> To act out of concrete responsibility means to act in *freedom*—to decide, to act, and to answer for the consequences of this particular action *myself* without the support of other people or principles. Responsibility presupposes ultimate freedom in assessing a given situation, in choosing, and in acting. Responsible action is neither determined from the outset nor defined once and for all; instead, it is born in the given situation.[46]

A third element is eschatological. Through the tension between the penultimate and the ultimate, Bonhoeffer helps us to both affirm unequivocal action in the world and endure a real, ambiguous situation in which there is no escape into false purity. Responsible decisions are to be made in freedom, within ambiguity, tension, and often a lack of clarity. Responsibility for such a decision cannot be delegated, and sometimes means opting for the lesser of two evils, even to incur guilt. Again, the world as it is, but in view of what it is to become, is the proper place where the Christian is placed and Christ is present through his church. "If the ultimate is their justification, the penultimate must be that their condition should be truly human," the movement Church and Society in Latin America (*Igreja e Sociedade na América Latina, ISAL*, 1961–73), for which Bonhoeffer was an important reference, affirms.[47]

Bonhoeffer explains that the ultimate is what the Reformation called the justification of the sinner by grace through faith alone. The basis of new life is the life, death, and resurrection of Christ, which beyond faith creates love and hope. Justification is the ultimate in a qualitative sense, that is, there cannot be anything that goes beyond God's mercy. It is the last word also in the sense of time, as "It is always preceded by something penultimate, some action, suffering, movement,

---

45. *DBWE* 6:95.
46. Ibid., 221.
47. Júlio de Santa Ana, "The Influence of Bonhoeffer on the Theology of Liberation," *The Ecumenical Review* 28, no. 2 (1976): 192–4.

volition [*Wollen*], defeat, uprising, entreaty [*Bitten*] or hope."[48] Bonhoeffer offers two "extreme" solutions that, after all, try to do away with the relation and the tension between the ultimate and the penultimate. In what he calls the "radical" solution, one forgets about the penultimate and only sees the ultimate. And in the solution of "compromise," the penultimate is accorded its own right and is detached from the ultimate. Although there is some truth in both solutions, the first one sees God only as judge and redeemer, the other sees God only as creator and preserver. In this way then, "faith in God is broken apart." As Bonhoeffer states, "There is earnestness neither in the idea of a pure Christianity in itself nor in the idea of man [*sic*] as he is himself; there is earnestness only in the reality of God and the reality of man which became one in Jesus Christ."[49] All dimensions of Christ have to be held together—God's love in the incarnation, God's judgment in the crucifixion, God's will for a new world in the resurrection. Thus, coherence and tension, fullness and brokenness have to be held together. Whoever dedicates himself or herself to the ultimate cannot flee from the penultimate in all its ambiguity.

Given these theological insights from Bonhoeffer, what about the place and responsibility of the church in society? While the participation of religious persons, groups, and churches in the public sphere is welcome and, indeed, necessary, it has to exercise its responsibility in the sight of God, oriented by a deep respect and love for human beings. And this has to mean profound and true respect for human life in all its diversity, not according to imposed "Christian principles." To maintain both aspects and hold them together such that they are not separated but also not confused is, in our view, one of the greatest assets of Bonhoeffer's theology, and one that we find extremely helpful today. The present religiously overladen government in Brazil reflects a theology that fails to recognize both God as incarnate in Jesus Christ and human beings as adult, mature citizens in a world "come of age." Bonhoeffer's Christian humanist challenge should be heard.

---

48. *DBWE* 6:83.
49. Ibid., 87.

Chapter 16

READING BONHOEFFER AMID THE HONG KONG PROTESTS

Jason Lam[1]

Introduction—Reading Bonhoeffer in Smog-Filled Hong Kong

When I began writing this chapter at the end of November 2019, the protests in Hong Kong had been going on for half a year. The siege on two university campuses by the police would soon be coming to an end, the landslide victory of the pro-democracy camp in the election of the Hong Kong district councils was widely taken as a referendum of the citizens, and the US government was about to pass the "Hong Kong Human Rights and Democracy Act." The political participation of Hong Kong churches was becoming more marked than at any point in history.[2] In mid-October 2019, an article entitled "Hong Kong's Spiritual Battle" about the involvement in the movement and the position of Hong Kong clergy and lay Christians appeared in *The Wall Street Journal*.[3] Due to the obvious involvement of the church, many people in this secular city suddenly found that the religious or spiritual dimension cannot be ignored even in a modern society. The whole situation presented an opportunity to dialogue with Dietrich Bonhoeffer, not only because he had participated in the anti-Nazi movement during his lifetime, but also because he had thought deeply about issues concerning what he later coined

---

1. An earlier version of this chapter was published in *Studies in World Christianity* 27, no. 2 (2021): 170–93. It is adapted here with permission.

2. For an account by a historian, cf. Ying Fuk-tseng, "Zhengzhi yu Zongjiaode Jiujie" [The Entanglement between Politics and Religion], Unpublished essay delivered at the Fifteenth International Academic Conference on the History of Cultural Exchange: Religion, Reason and Passion, held at Fu-jen Catholic University in Taipei on November 8–9, 2019. For an overview of past relations between the Hong Kong church and the state, cf. Beatrice Leung and Shun-hing Chan, *Changing Church and State Relations in Hong Kong, 1950–2000* (Hong Kong: Hong Kong University Press, 2003); Ka-Shing Ng, "Rethinking the Political Participation of Hong Kong Christians," *Social Transformations in Chinese Societies* 13 (2017): 37–55.

3. Jillian Kay Melchior, "Hong Kong's Spiritual Battle," *The Wall Street Journal*, October 17, 2019, https://www.wsj.com/articles/hong-kongs-spiritual-battle-11571351877 (accessed October 19, 2019).

"religionless Christianity."[4] This is also related to the development of his thought on Christology and ecclesiology. A contextual reading in the secular city of Hong Kong may provide therefore an opportunity to reflect on Bonhoeffer's thought.

Many people in Hong Kong developed interest in Bonhoeffer's life and thought before the protests began in June 2019.[5] This is, needless to say, primarily due to his participation in anti-Nazi resistance and even the plot to assassinate Hitler. Civil disobedience has been a thorny topic among Hong Kong residents in recent years, and it is unsurprising that Christians and theologians began to seek inspiration from Bonhoeffer. It is even more interesting that some Hong Kong writers, including those from the religious, the academic, and even the popular sectors, regardless of their religious orientation, have found relevant inspiration in Bonhoeffer. On the surface, this is hardly surprising—Bonhoeffer was also read among resistance fighters in South Africa, in several South American countries, and even in South Korea.[6] The case of Hong Kong, however, is different in that only 10–12 percent of the total population are Christians. Christianity has never prominently shaped the region's ethical landscape.[7] Apart from being inspired by his participation in the resistance movement and consequent martyrdom as a pastor and theologian, some people outside the church in Hong Kong, as we will see, are drawn to Bonhoeffer's concept of "religionless Christianity" and related ideas. Moreover, as mentioned earlier, the churches in Hong Kong played a significant role during the recent protests. This situation contrasts sharply with the German experience of resistance under the Nazi regime. The contextual reading of Bonhoeffer both inside and outside the church may also shed some light on why Christianity has been disproportionately involved in Hong Kong's pro-democracy movement.

First-generation Bonhoeffer scholars were responsible for compiling mainly a comprehensive view of his thought rather than merely delivering a romantic reading of his life. The second-generation scholars not only focused on his late thought but also addressed the relationship between his theology and philosophy as well as social science and the humanities. The third-generation scholarship today has probed these questions more deeply,[8] especially among scholars from

---

4. "Religionless Christianity" appeared only once in the famous letter written by Dietrich Bonhoeffer dated April 30, 1944; *DBWE* 8:364.

5. For a survey of Chinese intellectuals' interest in Bonhoeffer, see Jason Lam, "Why Chinese Intellectuals Are Keen on Reading Bonhoeffer? Bonhoeffer Perceived as a Public Theologian in the Chinese Context," *The Bonhoeffer Legacy: Australasian Journal of Bonhoeffer Studies* 5, no. 2 (2018): 37–45.

6. For a survey of these few places, see the related works in Peter Frick, ed., *Bonhoeffer and Interpretive Theory: Essays on Methods and Understanding* (Frankfurt: Peter Lang, 2013).

7. Having said this, we must also state that the influence of Christianity in Hong Kong has significantly outsized its population. For an overview, see the works cited in n. 2.

8. This three-generation perspective is cited from Adam C. Clark and Michael Mawson, "Introduction: Ontology and Ethics in Bonhoeffer Scholarship," in *Ontology and Ethics:*

non-Christian cultural backgrounds. Some have even brought resources from their own cultures into dialogue with Bonhoeffer's ideas. This is one of the aims of this chapter, which will also expand on themes from Bonhoeffer's thought. Therefore, in what follows, I will describe first the Hong Kong situation in 2019, especially the conditions after the extradition to China bill was introduced by the government, and the response of the churches. This will help to articulate the relevance of Bonhoeffer's thought and seek inspiration from it. Secondly, in relation to the emergency situation in Hong Kong, I will reflect on several important concepts on how Bonhoeffer transformed from a seeming "pacifist" into a member of the anti-Nazi movement. These include willingness to take on guilt, free responsibility, and so on. Next, the roles of some important figures in the Hong Kong pro-democracy movement who are interested in Bonhoeffer will be examined.[9] They are unaffiliated to the institutional church and thus provide us a good opportunity to examine why Bonhoeffer's thought can truly gain "this-worldly" acceptance through their contextual readings. It is just this line of questioning, however, that may bring about another set of questions inherent in Bonhoeffer's thought. What is the church? Is Christian "religion" still necessary in a "world come of age"? These questions not only make Bonhoeffer's thought appealing but also challenge traditional theology. The situation in Hong Kong offers us a chance to review his thought in line with these crucial questions.

Hong Kong Churches and the Anti-Extradition Bill Protests

Since early June 2019, large-scale protests have taken place in Hong Kong, some of which eventually led to violent clashes between the protesters and the police. The catalyst was clearly the government's introduction of an extradition to China bill that would establish a mechanism for the transfer of alleged criminals from Hong Kong to Mainland China.[10] Previously, local law offers protection against such extradition before the controversial National Security Law was introduced on June 30, 2020. Since most citizens do not trust Beijing's legal system, the

---

Bonhoeffer and Contemporary Scholarship, ed. Adam C. Clark and Michael Mawson (Eugene, OR: Pickwick, 2013), 2–13.

9. Two figures in focus are Joseph Lian and Chan Kin-man; cf. Joseph Lian (Lian Yi-zheng), "Lun Liusi de Shenxue Yiyi" [The Theological Significance of June 4th Crackdown], *Stand News*, June 4, 2019, https://www.thestandnews.com/politics/%E8%AB%96%E5%85%AD%E5%9B%9B%E7%9A%84%E7%A5%9E%E5%AD%B8%E6%84%8F%E7%BE%A9/ (accessed December 11, 2019); Au Ka-lun, "Chen Jianmin Zhongwen Daxue Zuihou yike Quenwenzigao" [The Full Script of Chan Kin-man's Last Lecture in CUHK], *Hong Kong In-Media*, November 29, 2018, https://www.inmediahk.net/node/1060933 (accessed December 12, 2019).

10. The official name of the bill is "The Fugitive Offenders and Mutual Legal Assistance in Criminal Matters Legislation (Amendment) Bill 2019."

proposal aroused such heated debate that some even feared the collapse of the "One country, two systems" principle.[11] As has been the case in other instances of social upheaval, the views of the churches in Hong Kong differ widely. Apart from a few organizations and denominations, most churches did not make any clear statement on the crisis. Some even instructed their clergy not to make any political comments in preaching and public speaking in order to avoid further bifurcation following the emergence of the Umbrella Movement five years earlier.[12]

As the debate became heated, however, some Christians initiated signed petitions against the government to withdraw the bill, using names like "a group of Christians from a certain denomination." Some of these petitioners belonged to the more conservative wing of the church. Subsequently, millions of people took to the streets in protest, but the government continued to ignore their demands. This resulted in a series of violent conflicts with the police in different districts. Many local churches opened their buildings to provide rest and shelter for the protesters, while some clergy offer additional support by joining the frontline protesters. In most cases, they did not declare their own political affiliations, but stated that they were just providing pastoral care for the crowd, hoping to lessen the conflicts. But for some people, the support offered moral legitimacy to the protests. Consequently, some pro-Beijing media outlets published negative comments on the churches in Hong Kong. Apart from the usual strategy of linking them to hostile foreign influence and picturing them as agents of infiltration, smear tactics were employed against the churches. For example, one reporter wrote that the CIA controlled about 300–500 influential Hong Kong Christians and, through them, gained access to the leaders and key members of the churches. The reporter went on to write that over 80 percent of the Protestant and Catholic churches in Hong Kong were not true churches but organizations embracing political objectives.[13] According to some pro-Beijing newspapers, providing refuge to protesters by the churches amounted to shielding rioters, and they accused some religious organizations and church folks of poisoning youngsters by condoning violence.[14]

---

11. As a theological chapter, this chapter will not offer a detailed analysis and interpretation here. For academic reviews, cf. Martin Purbrick, "A Report of the 2019 Hong Kong Protests," *Asian Affairs* 50, no. 4 (2019): 1–23; Francis L. F. Lee, Samson Yuen, Gary Tang, and Edmund W. Cheng, "Hong Kong's Summer of Uprising: From Anti-Extradition to Anti-Authoritarian Protests," *The China Review* 19, no. 4 (2019): 1–32.

12. Ying Fuk-Tseng, *Zongguo fu? Bentu xi! Shenfun Rentong de Shizijia* [China? Local! The Cross of Self-Identity] (HK: Inpress, 2016), 118–38.

13. Hui Jian, "Zhengzhi Jiaogun de Xianggang Zongjiao shi zenmo zuo de" [How the Religion of Hong Kong Operates by Political Cudgel], http://m.cwzg.cn/politics/201908/50906.html?page=full (accessed December 23, 2019). It is quoted also in Ying, "Zhengzhi yu Zongjiaode Jiujie."

14. "Zheque Shengun dui Xianggang de Duhai, Chaochu ni xiangxiang" [The Scourge to Hong Kong by These Religious Swindlers Is Beyond Your Imagination], https://news.sina

Since the Umbrella Movement began, churches in Hong Kong have been pressured to distance themselves from political events. Needless to say, most were not influenced by the malicious lies, and their activities remained unaffected. During the early stages of the protests, some pastors even hosted prayer meetings on the streets and sang hymns with the crowd. Many people saw and were touched by the videos of protesters chanting, "Sing Hallelujah to the Lord," together in the street.[15] Nevertheless, the level of violence kept rising and even peaceful protests were later dispersed by a brutal police force. In some incidents, protesters and passersby were beaten by the police and gangsters. Thus, some Christians, pastors, and churches began to ask what their roles should be in such a situation of escalating violence. There was no easy answer, of course. *The Wall Street Journal* article mentioned earlier reported a simple but difficult question a young Christian asked his pastor, Daniel Chan: "Can I throw bricks?"[16] This was by no means a question driven by sentiment but by a sense of responsibility by those facing oppressive regimes. In some situations, we know that the frontline protesters not only put up bricks on the streets but also threw Molotov cocktails and employed other weapons.

But if government had no reasonable responses to peaceful protests and the police employed unreasonable force to disperse and arrest people, then, was it appropriate to practice civil disobedience and even (defensive) violence? Another pastor, Mike Chan, pointed out that this question was raised not by only ordinary citizens; young Christians in particular believed that they had undeniable moral responsibility to fight injustice by participating in the protests. However, when asked for concrete and comprehensive guidance on this difficult question, he found himself at a complete loss.[17] In short, whether achieving justice by breaking the law should be considered a genuine option is a controversial question among Christians as well as the rest of the people of Hong Kong.

When it became evident that the government had no intention of effectively resolving the political conflict and had even tried to use violence as a way of breaking the people's will, a local renowned ethicist, Lo Ping-cheong, professor at Hong Kong Baptist University, used the theory of war to examine the

.cn/gn/2019-09-19/detail-iicezzrq7053837.d.html?from=timeline (accessed December 23, 2019). It is quoted also in Ying, "Zhengzhi yu Zongjiaode Jiujie."

15. Verna Yu, "'Sing Hallelujah to the Lord' Becomes the Unofficial Anthem in Hong Kong," *America: The Jesuit Review*, July 8, 2019, https://www.americamagazine.org/politics-society/2019/06/18/sing-hallelujah-lord-becomes-unofficial-anthem-hong-kong (accessed December 3, 2019). For a theological reflection on this event, cf. Jason Lam, "Christonomy in a World Come of Age: The Vision and Actualisation of Bonhoeffer's Christian Ethics," *Phronema* 35 (2020): 79–83.

16. Melchior, "Hong Kong's Spiritual Battle."

17. Ibid.

persistent movement of protests.[18] Although Ping-cheong's position may require substantiation to become a plausible paradigm, the ambivalent scenario in Hong Kong resembles, to a certain degree, Bonhoeffer's experience in the 1930 and 1940s. Besides that the government tried to use violence to solve political problems, the churches are also being pressured to take sides; some are accused of not being patriotic or of committing treason. Nonetheless, the history of Hong Kong is unique, and churches and Christians, who distance themselves from this novel form of government propaganda, have developed a new alertness and protective attitude in the face of the pressure.[19] The general vigilance in the population against pro-state propaganda contrasts with the situation in Germany leading up to and during the Second World War. Hong Kong Christians are more ready to align themselves with the Confessing Church in their political stance contra some actions of the government. But the move from alertness in the midst of self-protective caution to open participation in the protests is neither straightforward nor easy; it requires justification. And because of the contested situation, Bonhoeffer's life and thought have been studied and deeply admired as a significant reference point in Hong Kong. This has been observed since the rise of the Umbrella Movement. Hong Kong's citizens have similar questions on responsibility as those asked by Bonhoeffer, who wrestled with the right relationship between thought and action, and went as far as participating in the plot to assassinate Hitler. Thus, his influence in Hong Kong has extended beyond the church. Some recent contextual readings of Bonhoeffer may also help us to examine and develop his late thought in an emergency situation.

The Church's Presence and Struggle in an Emergency Situation

There are gray areas in all expressions of social activism. Due to their conservative Chinese cultural background, many Christians in Hong Kong are attracted to the evangelical tradition. As a result, most churches in Hong Kong have rarely been socially or politically active in the past. In addition, as the Christian community in Hong Kong is relatively small, churches tend not to focus too much on social affairs in order to minimize division. Therefore, the active role of the churches this time around is all the more remarkable, as they believe that the government ignored the voices of many citizens and whole communities. The public utterance of Rev. Joseph Ha, auxiliary bishop of the Catholic Church, reflects the view of many clergy. "Where our sheep are, there the pastors should be," he said[20] While

---

18. Lo Ping-cheung, "Xianggang Neizhan shi ruhe xingchen de?" [How Did Hong Kong's Civil War Begin?], *Stand News*, July 15, 2019.

19. Since the Cultural Revolution, many people immigrated to Hong Kong to escape the persecution of the Communist Party. Hong Kong Christians thus have long been aware of the attitude of the Communist Party toward the churches.

20. Quoting Yu, "Sing Hallelujah to the Lord."

many Christians have participated in the movement, the protesters, regardless of their religious affiliation, tend to be viewed as sheep to be cared for in the eyes of the city's Christian clergy. Reading against Bonhoeffer's early thought, this approach of viewing people as sheep is correct and appropriate. The church's action on behalf of the community at large invites people to experience the presence of Christ, as "Christ existing as church-community" (*Christus als Gemeinde existierend*), a key concept that has attracted prolonged discussions on the theologian's early works.[21]

As mentioned earlier, in the early stages of the protests, prayer meetings were hosted by church members and believers on the streets during which they chanted, "Sing Hallelujah to the Lord," along with the crowds. Many Christians said they felt empowered by a pervasive sense of God while non-Christian demonstrators also reported that they were touched by a feeling of love and peace through the singing of the hymn.[22] But as the violent clashes between the protesters and the police continued, this peaceful condition gave way to increasing unrest. How can Christ be present in this situation? People have begun to seriously ask themselves whether or not they, as committed Christians and disciples of Jesus, are justified in opting for more aggressive actions such as taking up arms. This question not only concerns the moral legitimacy of a particular action but also addresses the issue of whether the individual Christian and the church should be present at the frontlines of the protests once nonviolent opposition is no longer an option.

During a prayer meeting held at the end of October 2019, Bishop Ha urged believers to keep the peace while participating in the protests, as "Many people think that because our opponents provoke us and don't respond to us, we have the right to harbour hatred and anger. But Hong Kong Christians, even in their resistance, have the responsibility to remain nonviolent."[23] Even though he actively participated in the protests, Ha, being a priest, hesitated to endorse more "radical" actions. Putting some of the motivations for radical action into perspective, another pastor who stood with the protesters, Rev. Yuen Tin-yau of the Methodist Church, asked, "Who was it that used violence? Who rioted? I believe it was the government who used its power to crush the powerless citizens of Hong Kong."[24] Yuen seems to imply that the violence used by the protesters was merely defensive, and that these young people should not be labeled rioters. Rather, any violent

---

21. The key literature includes *Sanctorum Communuio* (*DBWE* 1) and *Act and Being* (*DBWE* 2). Significant secondary literature includes Clifford J. Green, *Bonhoeffer: A Theology of Sociality* (Grand Rapids, MI: Eerdmans, 1999); Charles Marsh, *Reclaiming Dietrich Bonhoeffer* (Oxford: Oxford University Press, 1994); Michael G. Mawson, *Christ Existing as Community* (Oxford: Oxford University Press, 2018).

22. Yu, "Sing Hallelujah to the Lord."

23. Quoted from Verna Yu, "As Protests Continue in Hong Kong, Beijing's Criticism of Churches Grows Louder," *America: The Jesuit Review*, December 13, 2019, https://www.americamagazine.org/politics-society/2019/12/13/protests-continue-hong-kong-beijings-criticism-churches-grows-louder (accessed December 14, 2019).

24. Quoting Yu, "Sing Hallelujah to the Lord."

action on their part should be tolerated in view of the disproportionate violence of the police. Clearly, there is no easy way to reach a fair judgment. This ethical dilemma has led some to reflect on Bonhoeffer's participation in the anti-Nazi movement and eventual role in the assassination plot against Hitler.

Coincidentally, it was around the same time at the end of October 2019 that the Protestant churches in Hong Kong hosted a series of public lectures entitled, "The Church in Smog: Lectures on Church and State." On October 26, the topic was "Between Peace and Protest: Reconsider the Mission of the Church from Bonhoeffer's Theological Ethics." According to a news report, over 200 people attended the lectures.[25] The speaker, Rev. Prof. Lee Man-yiu, a young Bonhoeffer scholar from Hong Kong's Alliance Bible Seminary, introduced the theologian's life and thought from a historical perspective, based on Bonhoeffer's own writings. Lee contends that Bonhoeffer's Christian ethics was primarily concerned with how to conform to the revelation of a God-for-us. The church should therefore focus on the following three relationships: (1) personal union with Christ; (2) the union of the church with others; and (3) the influence of the church on the world through the four mandates (which are interconnected) so as to bring about the values of the kingdom of God. Lee believes that the church's mission is to preach the gospel in everyday life. When the message of the gospel is obscured or hindered as in times of socio-political unrest or upheaval, the church has the responsibility to remove the hindrances and protect the society. The question arises, however, of where legitimate and responsible action begins and ends. This is an important question Hong Kong Christians grappled with at that time. Lee argues that Bonhoeffer never offered a clear verdict on the question of what constitutes ethically responsible action in a crisis situation. He draws his conclusions from an early text by Bonhoeffer entitled, "Basic Questions of a Christian Ethics."[26]

Nevertheless, because Bonhoeffer did not aim at offering some timeless or universal principles but a concrete ethics, Lee's understanding is reasonable and coheres with Bonhoeffer's thought overall. Lee *did* stress Bonhoeffer's admonition to the church to remain peaceful, rational, and nonviolent in its protest, but when asked about the underground organizations, his answer was ambiguous. He also noted that while Bonhoeffer knew of and abetted the assassination plot, he might not be considered an active participant. It seems Lee was eager to distinguish between Bonhoeffer (and Hong Kong Christians by extension) and the so-called radicals who have joined the protest movement. To me, Lee's interpretation does not offer the most accurate depiction of Bonhoeffer's thought and actions.[27] Apart

---

25. Chen Baitun, "Pan Huohua Shenxue yu Heping Kangzhen de Zaisi" [Bonhoeffer's Theology and Rethinking of Peaceful Fight], *Christian Times*, October 28, 2019, https://christiantimes.org.hk/Common/Reader/News/ShowNews.jsp?Nid=160048&Pid=102&Version=0&Cid=2141&Charset=big5_hkscs (accessed December 11, 2019).

26. DBWE 10:359–78.

27. It is true that Bonhoeffer withdrew from the Confessing Church during this period. But it may have been a tactical move combined with practical and theoretical consideration

from leading to potential misunderstandings, it hardly provides an insightful response to the ethical dilemma faced by Hong Kong Christians in the ambivalent situation. I am certainly not saying that we can find answers to questions in Bonhoeffer such as whether protesters may or may not throw bricks. Interpreting his ideas as answers to the situation is obviously a far more complicated process than discovering simple binaries or giving a straightforward "Yes" or "No" answer. Besides, answering questions in the context of a postlecture Q&A is perhaps not the best setting to elaborate on that complexity.[28]

Incidentally, the first Chinese commentary on Bonhoeffer's *Ethics* was published at the end of 2018. The essay by Dr. Huang Ying offers a thorough analysis of Bonhoeffer's peace ethics,[29] a topic that has stimulated many debates.[30] While I will not review her arguments in detail here, I wish to highlight her treatment of so-called emergency situations (*Grenzfälle*) during wartime, which functions as an interpretive key in her essay on Bonhoeffer's transition from his earlier works to a modified approach in his *Ethics*. Simply speaking, when at war, the state is no longer able to fulfill its mandate of protecting the lives of the citizens, and the church can hardly enhance peace by proclaiming the message of faith. In such a situation, citizens should consider their right to protest and the responsibility to promote peace.[31] It seems then that Lee is justified in distinguishing between the church and the underground movements. However, this formal bifurcation is exactly the point Bonhoeffer criticized in his *Ethics* about the two kingdoms' perspective from a pseudo-Lutheranism.[32] At its heart lies the issue of the conflict within one's conscience in individual decision-making. For Bonhoeffer, however,

---

in the situation. Cf. *DBWE* 16:517; see also ch. 15 of Renate Wind, *Dietrich Bonhoeffer: A Spoke in the Wheel*, trans. John Bowden (Grand Rapids, MI: Eerdmans, 1992).

28. For a more comprehensive analysis of Bonhoeffer's "The Church and the Jewish Question (1933)" and beyond, cf. Christiane Tietz, "'The Church is the Limit of Politics': Bonhoeffer on the Political Task of the Church," *Union Seminary Quarterly Review* 60 (2006): 23–36.

29. Huang Ying, "Chaoxiang Heping de Maoxian" [Venture Toward Peace], in *Jiedu Panhuohua Lunlixue* [Interpreting Bonhoeffer's *Ethics*], ed. Andres Tang (HK: VWLink, 2018), 131–57.

30. For a recent case, see the conversation between Clifford Green and Larry Rasmussen on Green's review of Rasmussen's book, *Dietrich Bonhoeffer: Reality and Resistance*, *Conversations in Religion and Theology* 6, no. 2 (2008): 155–73. Matthew Puffer has added his comments recently. Matthew Puffer, "Three Rival Versions of Moral Reasoning: Interpreting Bonhoeffer's Ethics of Lying, Guilt, and Responsibility," *Harvard Theological Review* 112, no. 2 (2019): 160–83.

31. Huang, "Chaoxiang Heping de Maoxian," 148–9; cf. *DBWE* 6:272–5; also cf. Matthew Puffer, "The 'Borderline Case' in Bonhoeffer's Political Theology," Christ College Faculty Publications 50, https://www.academia.edu/4069411/The_Borderline_Case_in_Bonhoeffer_s_Political_Theology (accessed January 2, 2020).

32. *DBWE* 6:56–60, 417–18.

an individual did not live an atomic life in isolation from others; the conscience was often a sinful consciousness limited by the ego, while the liberation by Christ was experienced in the acceptance of guilt.[33] In this process, discernment in a conflict situation leading to the question of whether or not one is willing to take on guilt becomes the focus. It may also shed light on the dilemma faced by Hong Kong protesters when they consider taking actions that violate the law.

Returning to the early 1940s Germany, the overall aim of the anti-Nazi movement was to overthrow the regime. But how? For Bonhoeffer and some conspirators, removing Hitler was a pragmatic necessity, but others might disagree. As a theologian and pastor, Bonhoeffer certainly understood the ethical issues involved and did not make light of it, as reflected in his *Ethics*. Is this not similar to the question posed by Hong Kong Christians, "Can I throw bricks"? Interestingly, Bonhoeffer had gone beyond the issue of moral legitimacy of a particular action and participated in the plot to assassinate Hitler. He even raised the issue of one's free responsibility in such a situation. We cannot deny that free responsibility is one of the most controversial concepts in Bonhoeffer's theological ethics, and it is closely related to the concept of accepting guilt. Both must be understood in relation to his Christology. This leads to another notion—that of Christ's vicarious representation (*Stellvertretung*)—and confronting the difference between human action and that of Christ. According to Christine Schließer, besides that human action does not bear salvific relevance, the more original difference is found between Christ's sinlessness and humans' original sin. Nevertheless, in Bonhoeffer, as she convincingly demonstrates, we find the "relative sinlessness" of humans in their acceptance of the guilt of others through responsible action. In this situation, humans have no genuine choice between accepting guilt and maintaining innocence. While obsessing only over his or her personal blamelessness, an individual may incur even more guilt. This is a reflection of the fact that we are bound by God's commandments to love God and our neighbors.[34] Bonhoeffer admitted that relative sinlessness could only be vindicated before humans in the process of taking on guilt in responsible actions. Before God, we can only rely on his grace and forgiveness.[35] This insight may also speak to the struggle faced by Hong Kong protesters. Like Bonhoeffer's involvement in the assassination plot, many Hong Kong Christians found themselves entangled in the struggle to participate in actions that violate the law, but saw those as necessary means to attaining justice.

Schließer further points out that Bonhoeffer never offered a clear definition of guilt, especially whether guilt was the result of an active or passive action,

---

33. Huang, "Chaoxiang Heping de Maoxian," 150–3; *DBWE* 6:432.

34. Christine Schließer, *Everyone Who Acts Responsibly Becomes Guilty: The Concept of Accepting Guilt in Dietrich Bonhoeffer—Reconstruction and Critical Assessment* (Neukirchen-Vluyn: Neukirchener, 2006), 170–1.

35. *DBWE* 6:282.

which made it difficult to ground it in Christology.[36] This is precisely the point that attracted scholarly interest for decades and marked a significant distinction between scholars who regarded Bonhoeffer's thought as evolving and those who did not. Puffer went as far as to describe "History and Good [2]" as a short-lived thought experiment in *Ethics*.[37] I consider the abovementioned theoretical analysis by and large correct and appropriate, although further exploration is still required.[38] Nonetheless, in reality, this kind of objective and detached analysis is not always the most helpful. In the case of the question, "Can I throw bricks?," contextual factors may vary significantly. Thus, it is difficult to offer a general response, which is precisely why Bonhoeffer subscribed to a concrete ethics. Each real situation entails risk (*Wagnis*), and thus his life and thought have served as inspiration for Hong Kong. Perhaps we must admit in the end that this reasoning is just a rational discussion in this world, which is fragmentary and imperfect, especially in complicated ethical situations. Although Bonhoeffer never had the chance to complete his own theological system, his striking insight into the ethical dilemmas still haunts us. In his words, "We have lived too much in our thoughts; we believed that by considering all the options of an action in advance we could ensure it, so that it would proceed of its own accord. We learned too late that it is not the thought but readiness to take responsibility that is the mainspring of action."[39] This is relevant not only to the Germany of Bonhoeffer's time but also to Christians today in "a world come of age," particularly in Hong Kong at a time of turmoil.

Non-Religious Christian Interpretation of Discipleship

Although non-believers would not be concerned too much about ethical issues like breaking the commandments and accepting guilt, achieving justice by violating the law is also a controversial topic in society. This topic was heatedly debated after the Umbrella Movement emerged in Hong Kong. In 2019, the issue even became more complicated and many people sought a convenient solution. Readers of Bonhoeffer outside the church may offer us important food for thought,

---

36. Schließer, *Everyone Who Acts Responsibly*, 189–91.
37. Puffer, "Three Rival Versions of Moral Reasoning."
38. There are several excellent works in this regard, which cannot be explored here, including Matthew Puffer, "Election in Bonhoeffer's *Ethics*: Discerning a Late Revision," *International Journal of Systematic Theology* 14 (2012): 255–76; Jeremy K. Kessler, "Bonhoeffer on Law-Breaking: A Reassessment of the Ethical Exception to the Divine Command," in *Ontology and Ethics: Bonhoeffer and Contemporary Scholarship*, ed. Adam C. Clark and Michael Mawson (Eugene, OR: Pickwick, 2013), 102–17; Joshua A. Kaiser, *Becoming Simple and Wise: Moral Discernment in Dietrich Bonhoeffer's Vision of Christian Ethics* (Eugene, OR: Pickwick, 2015).
39. *DBWE* 8:387.

especially with regard to his late works, which discuss the "world come of age," a world experienced as if God does not exist and which requires a non-religious interpretation. Can this scholar-pastor's controversial action and concept truly obtain this-worldly acceptance?

Before the large-scale protests broke out in Hong Kong in the summer of 2019, several intellectuals outside the church had begun to take note of Bonhoeffer's life and thought. This was plausible since Bonhoeffer himself was deeply interested in non-Christian thinkers such as Mahatma Gandhi. Bonhoeffer was drawn to nonviolent revolution, even to the point of wanting to visit India. Thus, these Hong Kong intellectuals not only became interested in his thought and practice in relation to the anti-government movement, they even went as far as publishing their theological reflections. One of them is Joseph Lian (Lian Yi-zheng), a prolific writer for newspapers who has lectured in many universities and was once employed as a consultant of the government's Central Policy Unit. On June 4, 2019, he published an article entitled, "The Theological Significance of the June 4th Crackdown." Lian admitted that he was a Christian when he was young. But as an adult, he has only been a "sincere non-stake holder" in the church and the Christian faith.[40] In relation to the topic of this chapter, the most interesting point is that Lian introduced Bonhoeffer in a newspaper column published in *Hong Kong Economic Journal*. In the piece, he explicated the concept of civil disobedience and considered the movement, Occupying Central with Love and Peace.[41] In that short piece, Lian introduced the political and theological situation of Germany during Bonhoeffer's time and Bonhoeffer's participation in the plot to assassinate Hitler. Furthermore, he analyzed two possible reasons why Bonhoeffer violated the principle of nonviolence and observing the law. First, the church should not only save those who suffer due to government's unreasonable acts but should also try to stop the rolling of the evil wheel with her little effort. Secondly, when the law is not effective in emergency situations, one has no other choice but to break it. It is still a kind of guilt; but participating in evil is even worse than taking on this guilt. This is exactly the point Bonhoeffer tried to make with the concepts of free responsibility and the acceptance of guilt, as explained earlier.

---

40. Lian, "Lun Liusi de Shenxue Yiyi."

41. Joseph Lian, "Jiju Xinyang yu 'Zhanzhong' hegan? Jianjie Panhuohua" [What Is Christian Faith to Do with "Occupying Central"?], *Hong Kong Economic Journal*, October 10, 2019, https://www1.hkej.com/dailynews/commentary/article/694414/%E5%9F%BA%E7%9D%A3%E4%BF%A1%E4%BB%B0%E8%88%87%E3%80%8C%E4%BD%94%E4%B8%AD%E3%80%8D%E4%BD%95%E5%B9%B2%EF%BC%9F%E2%80%94%E7%B0%A1%E4%BB%8B%E6%BD%98%E9%9C%8D%E8%8F%AF (accessed December 11, 2019); "Occupying Central with Love and Peace" is a closely related but yet different movement from the "Umbrella Movement." For a brief account with historical explanation, see Edmund W. Cheng and Wai-yin Chan, "Explaining Spontaneous Occupation: Antecedents, Contingencies and Spaces in the Umbrella Movement," *Social Movement Studies* 16, no. 2 (2017): 222–39.

When Lian proposed these concepts, Hong Kong was still at the stage of thinking about the concept of civil disobedience and the legitimacy of the Occupying Central movement. But he understood Bonhoeffer's concept of the disciples breaking the commandments and was even sympathetic to the burden of Christians participating in Occupying Central. During the social upheavals of 2019, not many churches in Hong Kong declared their political position, but many Christians joined the protests. We believe that many encountered the same struggle, as reported by *The Wall Street Journal*. Now a "non-believer" can understand his or her heavy load after reading Bonhoeffer and even understand his concepts of breaking the commandments and taking on guilt. It seems that in the Christ-reality (*Christuswirklichkeit*), non-religious interpretation can break down the wall of the institutional church, such that those outside the church can understand Bonhoeffer's key concepts.

Chan Kin-man, a former associate professor at the Sociology Department of the Chinese University of Hong Kong (CUHK), is another noteworthy activist. He is the only one who is not affiliated to any church among the three initiators of the Occupying Central movement.[42] For many years, many students have asked Chan if he was a Christian. In his last public lecture delivered in CUHK, he offered a Bonhoefferian answer, "I can only say, I am a man of faith but without religion."[43] He took early retirement from the university precisely because he participated in the Occupying Central movement and kept his promise to surrender himself to the police, even if this meant a prison sentence. The result, as widely expected, was imprisonment for sixteen months.[44] Before Chan went to prison, he knew from some former prisoners that one was allowed to read books there. He immediately ordered some books, including Eric Metaxas' *Bonhoeffer: Pastor, Martyr, Prophet, Spy*.[45] To his own surprise, Chan finished the bulky volume before his imprisonment.[46] However, Chan had known about Bonhoeffer's works for a long time. He said that he was a churchgoer when he was an undergraduate, but he found the pulpit message no better than "chewed tallow," until he read

---

42. For the participation of Hong Kong Christians in the movement, see Shun-hing Chan, "The Protestant Community and the Umbrella Movement in Hong Kong," *Inter-Asia Cultural Studies* 16 (2015): 380–95; Nancy Ng and Andreas Fulda, "The Religious Dimensions of Hong Kong's Umbrella Movement," *Journal of Church and State* 60 (2017): 377–97; Justin K. H. Tse and Jonathan Y. Tan, ed., *Theological Reflections on the Hong Kong Umbrella Movement* (New York: Macmillan, 2016).

43. Au, "Chen Jianmin Zhongwen Daxue Zuihou yike Quenwenzigao."

44. The charges were "conspiracy to public nuisance" and "incitement to public nuisance." He was released on March 14, 2020.

45. Eric Metaxas, *Bonhoeffer: Pastor, Martyr, Prophet, Spy* (Nashville, TN: Thomas Nelson, 2010).

46. Au, "Chen Jianmin Zhongwen Daxue Zuihou yike Quenwenzigao." Unfortunately, Chan did not tell us how his reading of Metaxa's work had affected him.

Bonhoeffer's *Letters and Papers from Prison*.[47] The first job Chan got after finishing his undergraduate studies was a post in a community center run by a church where everyone was a Christian. During the interview for the post, he was asked whether he was a Christian. He answered, "In my understanding a Christian is a humanist. Can you accept this answer?" We may find this to be another Bonhoefferian response. Chan was employed as the only so-called Christian in that center, who was not a "churchgoer." And he admitted that his answer came from Bonhoeffer's saying, "To be fully human."[48]

Clearly, that was Chan's first encounter with Bonhoeffer and even with genuine Christian faith. But how did that affect his later practices? In the Umbrella Movement, one of the most circulated slogans is "I want true universal suffrage!" Chan thought that in Bonhoeffer's time it corresponded to "I want the true church!" It is because the mainstream German churches at that time were standing on the wrong side, like a person on a train trying to run toward the opposite direction—it would be in vain even if the person tries hard to run in the backward direction on the corridor. Based on this understanding, Chan believed that the faith of the true church that Bonhoeffer was sketching would not adhere to the church building, liturgy, clergy, and the like. He believed that the clue for the "true church" lies in the question concerning the Jews: Do you stand with them? When the Jews are persecuted, what would the Christian do?[49] Similarly, Chan understood how Bonhoeffer and his own generation walked on the path of protest. This is not too surprising. What is most striking, however, is how he perceived Bonhoeffer after the plot to kill Hitler failed, and this happened especially when Chan was preparing to go to prison after the Umbrella Movement:

> Bonhoeffer is marvellous. If I had been him, I'd have felt very upset. I admire him. The devil did not die in the explosion. But he still kept his faith.
>
> I think that if Hitler had been blown up that time, there'd be another Hitler, since the Nazis were still powerful at that time. They would have said that it was a conspiracy attacking them and put another Hitler in place.
>
> Dear friends, we cannot control time. We can only do the things we think are correct. Only after the Nazi party was defeated in the war, was Nazism truly destroyed along with radical nationalism in Germany. There is a time for

---

47. Chan Kin-man, "Qiuhou Suanzhang zhong du Yuzhongshu" [Reading Prison Writings during the Settling of Old Account], *Stand News*, January 12, 2015, https://www.thestandnews.com/politics/%E7%A7%8B%E5%BE%8C%E7%AE%97%E8%B3%AC%E4%B8%AD%E8%AE%80%E7%8D%84%E4%B8%AD%E6%9B%B8/ (accessed December 12, 2019).

48. Au, "Chen Jianmin Zhongwen Daxue Zuihou yike Quenwenzigao," citing *DBWE* 8:480.

49. Ibid.

everything. There is no need to ask ourselves why our action failed? Why is the bad guy still boasting? There is a time for everything.[50]

In other words, Chan thought that the participation and decision of true faith did not lie in the present success or failure, but whether one could live according to the values of faith. He quoted Bonhoeffer's famous saying, "Every Christian must be fully human by bringing God into his [sic] whole life, not merely into some spiritual realm."[51] In view of the present situation, Chan comments:

> From the letters and hymns [Bonhoeffer] wrote in prison we see him thinking that Christians should commit themselves to this world to practice faith. The church should abandon her comfort and privilege, and have courage to practice the values different from the secular world, and standing with those who are suffering. Bonhoeffer requested believers to ask the question: In this time and space, who is Jesus? That is to say, what stand would Jesus take in the present situation? After reading this book, friends who are Christians you may ask yourselves: Who looks closer to Jesus? Is that Paul Kwong, Peter Koon, Daniel Ng or Joseph Zen, Yiu-ming Chu, Benny Tai?[52]

For non-churchgoers like Lian and Chan, their struggle does not lie in participating or not participating in some concrete actions even if it is appropriate to achieve justice by violating the law. They might think that grappling with these questions at this time makes one to lose focus. Applying Bonhoeffer's ideas to the Hong Kong situation means, if one can practice free responsibility but insist on maintaining his or her innocence, then, it means being indifferent to the suffering of the protesters who are brutally beaten in one's presence. To criticize the protesters then would be to commit the error of blaming the victim. However, it is not to say that no discernment is needed in an emergency. The discernment is not according to some universal principles, but it enables one to participate in the Christ-reality on a deeper level in order to shape a this-worldly life of following Jesus.[53] This approach may be closer to Bonhoeffer's Christological ethics, which is discerning how one can become a disciple, a form of life shaped by Christ in a world come of age, as if God does not exist.[54] The non-churchgoers show us that they can understand

---

50. Ibid. Chan's reading of the then German political situation is different from Bonhoeffer's in the sense that removing Hitler from power may not affect the overall aim of overthrowing the Nazi regime.
51. Ibid.
52. Chan, "Qiuhou Suanzhang zhong du Yuzhongshu"; the two groups mentioned in the last sentence belong to the pro-establishment and pro-democracy camps, respectively.
53. This is a complex issue which cannot be dealt with in this chapter. See, specifically, ch. 2 of Kaiser, *Becoming Simple and Wise*, 20–55.
54. No doubt, in a concrete situation, the most difficult discernment to exercise is whether the situation is a borderline case (*Grenzfall*). Some interpreters note that this can

Bonhoeffer's non-religious interpretation, such that they can participate in social movements as the disciples of Christ and without regret. This seems to be a beautiful thing though we understand that there are always gray areas in such discernments. In the last section, I will point out that this may also invite questions asked by Bonhoeffer himself in his late works, even to the point of threatening the formation of his own thought at the core of which the relation between Christ and the church lies.

Conclusion—Shaping the Christ-Reality in the Penultimate World

From the earlier cases of interpreting Bonhoeffer in present-day Hong Kong, we find that his Christo-universal perspective of viewing the world can gain this-worldly acceptance.[55] As Larry Rasmussen points out in his interpretation of *The Letters and Papers from Prison*, "'To be a Christian is . . . to be a human'; but what makes a Christian a Christian and a human a human is 'participation in the sufferings of God in the worldly life.'"[56] Therefore, we also find from Bonhoeffer's late works that conformity with Christ (*Gleichgestaltung*) and action in accordance with reality are among his most important concerns. The former seems to aim at Christians while the latter is also relevant for non-believers. But because the one and only reality is the Christ-reality, which is made possible through the reconciling work of God in Christ,[57] this universality is used to combat what Bonhoeffer called pseudo-Lutheran ethics, which neatly divided reality into two realms. Therefore, he did not really suggest two types of ethics. In line with the genuine Lutheran version that he interpreted, the two kingdoms are not only parallel realms but work together to bring about the reign of God.[58] This way of treating reality as the ultimate means avoiding a binary thinking for ethics and theology. But for traditional confessing Christians, the most challenging point was expressed by Bonhoeffer himself:

> The questions to be answered would be: What does a church, a congregation, a sermon, a liturgy, a Christian life, mean in a religionless world . . . How do we

---

be a common or everyday occurrence; cf. Robin Lovin, *Christian Realism and the New Realities* (Cambridge: Cambridge University Press, 2008). This point can also be considered central to Bonhoeffer's thought in transiting from *Ethics* to his prison theology. Cf. Kessler, "Bonhoeffer on Law-Breaking."

55. Larry Rasmussen, *Dietrich Bonhoeffer: Reality and Resistance* (Louisville, KY: Westminster John Knox, 2005), 16.

56. Ibid., 18; quoting *DBWE* 8:480.

57. Rasmussen, *Dietrich Bonhoeffer*, 23.

58. On this issue, cf. Lam, "Christonomy in a World Come of Age"; Ulrik Becker Nissen, "The Christological Ontology of Reason," *Neue Zeitschrift für Systematische Theologie und Religionsphilosophie* 48, no. 4 (2006): 460–78.

go about being "religionless-worldly" Christians, how can we be ἐκκλησία, those who are called out, without understanding ourselves religiously privileged, but instead seeing ourselves as belonging wholly to the world . . . In a religionless situation, what do ritual and prayer mean? Is this where the "arcane discipline," or the difference . . . between the penultimate and the ultimate, have new significance?[59]

It is true that people outside the church like Chan may have no difficulty understanding Bonhoeffer's views. Since Chan declares that he himself is a man of faith without religion, we may call him a "religionless Christian," in Bonhoeffer's words. This seems to be a beautiful thing for Bonhoeffer lovers. But consequently, the urgent questions quoted earlier would arise, as people ask about the role of the church in this world. This is not only a pastoral concern but may even become a threat to the Bonhoeffer's whole idea. "Christ existing as church-community" is a key concept and even the foundation of his early works. But this concept vanishes in his later thoughts and we may say that this formula of Christ's presence is replaced by "Christ existing as the world."

In the abovementioned Chinese commentary on Bonhoeffer's *Ethics*, Thomas Tseng (Tseng Nien Yueh) from the Methodist Graduate School in Taiwan also sensed this difficulty. He pointed out that since Christ became part of the structure of this world, Christology can include this-worldliness in human experience. But as Bonhoeffer included the world in the Christ-reality, his concept of the church loses the function of differentiating the world-reality from the Christ-reality.[60] Christiane Tietz's analysis of the relationship between Christ and the church in Bonhoeffer's early works may be useful here. She points out carefully that "Christ existing as church-community" did not mean that Christ only existed as church-community and nowhere else. Therefore, the church-community was no more and no less than just one mode of being of Christ.[61] This view may help to ease the tension inherent in Bonhoeffer's entire thought process, but the question of whether the presence of the church in this world is still meaningful becomes crucial.

In the same Chinese commentary on *Ethics*, Barry Cheung's (Cheung Man Chung) cautious reading points out that although "Christ existing as church-community" disappeared from Bonhoeffer's late works, it did not imply that Bonhoeffer dismissed the role of the church. In the important piece, "Ethics as

---

59. DBWE 8:364–5.

60. Thomas Tseng (Tseng Nien Yueh), "Panhuohua Lunlixue Daodu" [Guided Reading to Bonhoeffer's *Ethics*], in Tang, ed., *Jiedu Panhuohua Lunlixue*, 94, 100.

61. Christiane Tietz, "Bonhoeffer on the Ontological Structure of the Church," in *Ontology and Ethics*, 40–1. In another article, she considers further the issue of religious pluralism; cf. "Bonhoeffer's Strong Christology in the Context of Religious Pluralism," in *Interpreting Bonhoeffer: Historical Perspectives, Emerging Issues*, ed. Clifford J. Green and Guy C. Carter (Minneapolis, MN: Fortress, 2013), 181–96.

Formation," Bonhoeffer mentioned that incarnation was the important foundation of formation. But before the ultimate comes, there would only be a small group found in the church of Christ. Therefore, Bonhoeffer talked about the formation of the church according to the form of Christ:[62]

> So the church is not a religious community of those who revere Christ, but Christ who has taken form among human beings. The church may be called the body of Christ because in the body of Jesus Christ *human being per se*, and therefore all human beings, have really taken on. The church now bears the form that in truth is meant for all people . . . It is solely the form of Christ that matters, not any form besides Christ's own. The church is the human being who has become human, has been judged, and has been awakened to new life in Christ . . . The church's concern is not religion, but the form of Christ and its taking form among a band of people.[63]

Seen this way, the position of Christ is of course prior to the church in reality. It is because only Christ rather than the church as a salvific institution can offer a special ontological status to those who are being formed. This is the result of the revelation of God's action in love instead of a concrete ontological construct. Nevertheless, the role of the church is irreplaceable. It is not because the church is an institution of grace in this world, but because through it, humans can experience the grace of Christ as the one for others. In the end, Tietz states, "the structure of the *with-each-other*, the action of the *for-each-other*, and the encounter with the other as a loving I are all only possible within the church and through faith."[64] It could be the reason that Bonhoeffer, in his later works, asked for a religionless Christianity and his ecclesiology was under his strong critique of church and religion.[65]

Returning to the real world, we may still ask, can this grace be granted outside of the (institutional) church? Or putting it differently, if someone finds this miracle of grace in life, should he or she be seen as having already lived in the "church"? It follows that the concept of "church" should be reconsidered and not be limited merely to a visible historical institution. Rather, it is a reality that can be experienced widely by all in the reconciling grace, which means Bonhoeffer's concept of the "middle" (*Mitte*) must center more on Christ than on the church. And our imagination of the "church" (as a visible human community) must be

---

62. Barry Cheung (Cheung Man Chung), "Lunlixue zhongde Jiaohui Lunlixue" [Church Ethics in *Ethics*], in Tang, ed., *Jiedu Panhuohua Lunlixue*, 162–3.

63. *DBWE* 6:96–7.

64. Tietz, "Bonhoeffer on the Ontological Structure of the Church," 40–1.

65. Kirsten Busch Nielsen, "Community Turned Inside out: Dietrich Bonhoeffer's Concept of the Church and of Humanity Reconsidered," in *Being Human, Becoming Human: Dietrich Bonhoeffer and Social Thought*, ed. Jens Zimmermann and Brian Gregor (Eugene, OR: Pickwick, 2010), 93.

broadened.⁶⁶ To some degree Bonhoeffer's view may help explain why Christianity seems to have played a significant role in recent pro-democracy movements though most churches are not directly involved.

If we return to the Hong Kong situation, I believe that Bonhoeffer would approve the act of the pastors standing with the frontline protesters, and might even tolerate some of the protesters' violent actions. This is not a judgment based on any political orientation, but it corresponds with the idea of making Christ present in the world. It echoes what Rev. Wu Chi-wai said during an early prayer meeting, "We hoped to bring the presence of Christ there. We saw our roles as peacemakers placed between protesters and police to calm emotions."⁶⁷ And when the protests had reached a more radical point, professor Kung Lap-yan from CUHK labeled the protesters as a Messianic community in a public lecture at Southern Methodist University in the United States in October 2019.⁶⁸ He noted that the church as a Messianic community should be characterized by inclusiveness, forgiveness, truth, and unity, and should provide an alternative to political identity for the people. This view comes close to the late Bonhoeffer, as noted earlier, and we may say that Kung tried to identify the protesters as a "religionless Christian church." Although the protests have led to some chaotic and even anarchic situation in Hong Kong, there was unity and solidarity among the oppressed. They demanded an imminent penultimate judgment, and the protesters acted like suffering messiahs under the rule of a modern form of *Pax Romana*. This is not to say that the church must completely agree with what they (or other political camps) have done. For Bonhoeffer, all ethical discernment should be handled in light of the concrete situations rather than just relying on some once-off and universal principles. Instead, it is more important to demonstrate concretely the love of Christ to others.⁶⁹ This echoes Bishop Ha's statement that "Even though the government did

---

66. This could be part of the reason that Bonhoeffer mentioned "arcane discipline" in the previous quotation. Under the "worldly" situation, traditional religious language may be misunderstood and it may be better to keep silent about God. But this is too vast a topic to be explored here. The understanding of the "church" in Bonhoeffer's thought was also debated earlier in Chinese literature; cf. Jason Lam, "The Significance of Bonhoeffer's Thought for the Recent Discussion within Sino-Christian Theology," *The Bonhoeffer Legacy: Australasian Journal of Bonhoeffer Studies* 3, no. 1 (2015): 37–56.

67. Yu, "Sing Hallelujah to the Lord."

68. Kung Lap-yan, "Hong Kong Protest: A Messianic Movement?," Lecture Delivered on October 22, 2019 at the Southern Methodist University, Dallas, TX, USA, https://www.youtube.com/watch?v=hiFp2jkDkKA (accessed December 24, 2019).

69. To a certain extent, there is some parallel between non-church Hong Kong protesters and the non-Catholics in Poland during and after the collapse of the communist government. Cf. Joel Burnell, *Poetry, Providence and Patriotism: Polish Messianism in Dialogue with Dietrich Bonhoeffer* (Eugene, OR: Pickwick, 2009).

many things that we don't like and were very wrong, we cannot demonize them because this is [against the demands] of our faith."[70]

During the Hong Kong protests, some analysts believe that the Christian presence, including the statements issued by various church members and churches, urging the government to retract the proposed extradition law, had changed the views of many non-believers in Hong Kong, who used to see Christianity as politically conservative and out of touch with society.[71] Needless to say, in concrete situations, there still exist gray areas in this social movement, and one can hardly regard them all as divine actions. Nevertheless, Bonhoeffer's struggle and reflection in the period of the anti-Nazi movement gives Hong Kong people, especially Christians, an important reference point for ethical discernment in uncertain times. The situation and the Hong Kong pro-democracy movement also give us an opportunity to examine Bonhoeffer's important concepts in greater depth. Their contextual readings in Hong Kong shed light on the late works of Bonhoeffer—why he had tried to explore a this-worldly and even a non-religious perspective beyond the institutional church. The concept of the presence and reconciling work of God in Christ as depicted and witnessed by Bonhoeffer can find resonance among Hong Kong people in spite of their religious affiliation during this period of unrest and upheaval.

---

70. Quoting Yu, "Sing Hallelujah to the Lord."
71. Ibid.

Part IV

BONHOEFFER, THE CHRIST-REALITY, AND THE LAW

Chapter 17

"THE ONE REALM OF THE CHRIST-REALITY"

A CRITICAL EXAMINATION OF A POWERFUL THEOLOGICAL INSIGHT

Günter Thomas

Introduction

There are no two realities, but *only one reality*, and that is God's reality revealed in Jesus Christ in the reality of the world. Partaking in Christ, we stand at the same time in the reality of God and in the reality of the world. The reality of Christ embraces the reality of the world in itself. The world has no reality of its own independent of God's revelation in Christ. It is a denial of God's revelation in Jesus Christ to wish to be "Christian" without being "worldly," or [to] wish to be worldly without seeing and recognizing the world in Christ. Hence there are not two spaces (*Räume*), but only *the one space of the Christ-reality* (*Christuswirklichkeit*), in which the reality of God and the reality of the world are united . . . This is all about the realization (*Wirklichwerden*) of the Christ-reality in the contemporary world that it already embraces, owns, and holds. There are not two competing spaces standing side by side and battling over the borderline . . . Rather, the whole reality of the world has already been drawn into and is held together in Christ. History moves only from this center toward this center.[1] Before God, there is no autonomous realm; instead, the law of God revealed in Jesus Christ is the law of all earthly orders.[2]

For that reason,

---

1. See *DBW* 6:58. In some cases, the translation needs some correction. In particular, the translation of "*Raum*" as "realm" misses a crucial aspect in Dietrich Bonhoeffer's argument and his suggested shift in meaning. The page references in the text refer to the English and German edition of *Ethics*. This chapter focuses exclusively on *Ethics* (*DBWE* 6) and *Ethik* (*DBW* 6). To correct tensions and to iron out theological wrinkles, which are due to Bonhoeffer's theological development, is far too tempting when texts from other periods are pulled in. This holds particularly true in the case of the doctrine of the two kingdoms.

2. *DBW* 6:364, *DBWE* 6:362.

The church does not have a twofold word, the one general, rational, and grounded in natural law and the other Christian—that is, it does not have one word for unbelievers and another for believers . . . The church also does not have a twofold commandment at its disposal, one for the world and one for the congregation. Instead, its commandment is the one commandment revealed in Christ, which it proclaims to the whole world.[3]

The Explosive Claim

The whole world is the one realm of the Christ-reality. This is the explosive claim that Dietrich Bonhoeffer put forth in 1940–1 in one of his drafts for his *Ethics* in the section on "Christ, Reality, and the Good." Looking back in 2020, after eighty years, this must be seen as a bold, forceful, profoundly influential, and thoroughly transformative claim. Indeed, his claim that there is just one Christ-reality embracing the whole world lies at the heart of most conceptions of public theology.

Is Bonhoeffer's claim valid? Is it prophetic? Is it problematic or even wrong? Is it an absurd claim in the good or the bad sense of the term? Is it, at least in hindsight, plainly stupid? Without any question, Bonhoeffer's insight, which is shared by many, opened the door to a new political ethic—support of the social welfare state and concern for the structurally disadvantaged and oppressed. It did build a bridge to traditions of the social gospel as well as to liberation theologies. It paved the way for a new coalition of churches and progressive forces in Western societies. It taught generations that moral and political progress can go hand in hand, that Christian stewards and political liberationists can march side by side. This one Christ-reality allowed quite a few Christians to see Socialists and Marxists as fellow travelers or even "brothers in arms."[4]

In all actions and coalitions, the church has only an epistemic privilege with respect to an ontological fact: "The church of Jesus Christ is the place (*Ort*)—that is, the space (*Raum*)—in the world, where the reign of Jesus Christ over the whole world is to be witnessed and proclaimed."[5] In short, "The world stands

---

3. *DBW* 6:403, *DBWE* 6:399.

4. The tremendous impact of Dietrich Bonhoeffer's thinking is outlined by Matthew D. Kirkpatrick, *Engaging Bonhoeffer: The Impact and Influence of Bonhoeffer's Life and Thought* (Minneapolis, MN: Fortress Press, 2016); Clifford Green and Thomas Tseng, eds., *Dietrich Bonhoeffer and Sino-Theology* (Taoyuan: Chung Yuan Christian University, 2008); Nico Koopman and Robert Vosloo, *Reading Bonhoeffer in South Africa after the Transition to Democracy* (Frankfurt am Main: Peter Lang, 2020).

5. *DBW* 6:49, *DBWE* 6:63. The translation is changed. The German term "*bezeugt*" should not be translated as "demonstrated" but as "witnessed." This insight into the universal impact of the Christ-event is already emphasized in Bonhoeffer's dissertation: "In Christ humanity is drawn into community with God, just as in Adam humanity fell . . .

in relationship to Christ whether the world knows it or not."⁶ Nevertheless, the question that has been on the table since Bonhoeffer (and others) promoted this Christological universalism is how much can the world with all its structures and processes be moved into the direction of Christ—if the goal of this indivisible Christ-reality "is called the kingdom of God"?⁷ Are there limits to any Christ-supported social engineering and improvement of the world? Theologically phrased, to what extent can the orders of reconciliation be pushed in the direction of redemption? What do we need to do if "the will of God is nothing other than the realization of the Christ-reality among us and in our world?"⁸

Not only are these questions relevant in the ivory tower of academic discourse, the answers to them also are tearing apart liberal Western churches. One should not forget that Bonhoeffer's claim is deeply counterintuitive for anyone standing outside the highly committed theological circle and watching the daily news. Without any doubt, it strongly foregrounds the challenge of theodicy. It calls for explication and justification. Thus, Bonhoeffer's far-reaching claim requires navigation skills for those who operate as churches and Christians in this Christ-reality. Bonhoeffer is quite clear—the traditional way of looking at the world in relation to two realms is still so powerful that one needs "to break the spell of this conceptual framework."⁹ What is required, according to Bonhoeffer, is a radical reorientation. To envision, however, the thorough theological disruption offered by Dietrich Bonhoeffer in terms of the perception of the world outside the realm of the church, we need to revisit the hotly discussed topic of the "two kingdoms."

Unplugging All Versions of the Doctrine of Two Kingdoms

Whether Bonhoeffer is drawing on traditional Lutheran ethics was fiercely debated among the German-speaking Bonhoeffer scholars of the 1970s and 1980s.¹⁰ During the previous decade, especially in the English-speaking world,

---

the new humanity is entirely concentrated in the one single historical point, Jesus Christ"; *DBWE* 1:146, *DBW* 1:91.

6. *DBWE* 6:68, *DBW* 6:54.
7. *DBWE* 6:53, *DBW* 6:38.
8. *DBWE* 6:74, *DBW* 6:61.
9. *DBWE* 6:58.
10. Clifford Green denies the connection but James Burtness, who sees a transformation from spatial to temporal imaginations, clearly notes it. See Clifford J. Green, "Soteriologie und Sozialethik bei Bonhoeffer und Luther," in *Bonhoeffer und Luther*, ed. Christian Gremmels (München: Christian Kaiser, 1983), 93–128; James H. Burtness, "Als ob es Gott nicht gäbe: Bonhoeffer, Barth und das lutherische finitum capax infiniti," in *Bonhoeffer und Luther*, ed. Christian Gremmels (Munich: Christian Kaiser, 1983), 167–83. Ulrich Duchrow, however, tried to uncover Martin Luther's original intention and saw this mirrored in Bonhoeffer's changes of the tradition.

we saw an intensified debate about whether Dietrich Bonhoeffer abandoned the Lutheran doctrine of two kingdoms, he properly reinstated it or he transformed and reinterpreted it.

For Martin Luther, the theology of two realms is not first and foremost an ethical theory, but primarily a theological answer to the question, who rules the world and by what means? And who rules the church? According to Luther, the agent operating in hidden ways in history, ruling through the law, and ordering violence is the hidden, and eventually unknown, God.[11] In stark contrast, it is Christ who rules and works in the church through his spirit and the word of the gospel. The teaching of the two kingdoms addressed the theodicy issues in a world saturated with violence and stupidity and, on the other hand, sketched out the specific work of the spirit and the redeemer in the realm of the church. At the core of the doctrine of two kingdoms are not distinctive types of human actions, but different types and agents of divine action—the unknown God of history vis-á-vis Jesus Christ.

Bonhoeffer does abandon the very idea of different types of agents—Christ belongs to the whole world.[12] To be precise, Christ is not only a possibility but a reality for the world.[13] In the whole Christ-space, all human beings are "living a new life in the power of the resurrection."[14] Of course, Bonhoeffer also explicitly rejects the modernized versions of the two-kingdom doctrine in which notions of a dual-agency were combined with the modern observation of a diversity of autonomous value-spheres, which are in tension with religion's high moral claims. Bonhoeffer targets the resulting idea of "*Eigengesetzlichkeit*" (relative autonomy). In fact, it was Luther's dual-agency that opened the door to the theological fusion of orders of creation and modern "*Eigengesetzlichkeit*." The assumption of a dual-agency not only limits the impact of Christ but also paves the way for destructive and dehumanizing political ethics. For Christians following Bonhoeffer, this separation of the two realms is a highway to irresponsibility.

Nonetheless, Bonhoeffer's proclamation of the one realm of Christ leaves many problems unaddressed. What Christ is at work in the domains of deadly

---

11. Martin Luther, *Ausgewählte Werke: Daß der freie Wille nichts sei. Antwort D. Martin Luthers an Erasmus von Rotterdam* (München: Christian Kaiser, 1962), for an interpretation, see Thomas Reinhuber, *Kämpfender Glaube: Studien zu Luthers Bekenntnis am Ende von De servo arbitrio* (Berlin: de Gruyter, 2000); also Oswald Bayer, *Martin Luther's Theology: A Contemporary Interpretation* (Grand Rapids, MI: Wm. B. Eerdmans, 2008).

12. There remain strands of thought in Bonhoeffer's writings, which still point to the classical Lutheran notion of a God of history in disguise. The core idea behind the trope, "resistance and submission" refers to fate whose author can only be the incomprehensible God "behind" the revelation in Christ. See *DBWE* 8:334.

13. In his dissertation, Bonhoeffer already paradoxically stated that, "The will of God is . . . a reality that wills to become real ever anew in what exists and against what exists." *DBWE* 6:74, *DBW* 6:61.

14. *DBWE* 6:159, *DBW* 6:150.

competition, fight, and triumph over the weaker forces? What is the status of reason, and in particular contextual reason(s), in society's various spheres? What deserves to be preserved, at least in the light of the Christ-event, and what ought to be radically transformed? If in Christ the one world was reconciled with God and one Christ-realm is created, and if in the event of the resurrection the new creation of the world started, how much can the world be changed in the direction of redemption? How much of humanity present in Christ can be realized in today's political, economic, and other sub-systems of society?[15] Left-wing interpreters of Dietrich Bonhoeffer give substantially different answers than right-wing interpreters. While the manifest temptation of the classical Lutheran doctrine of two kingdoms was leaning toward political conservatism, the manifest living temptation of the one Christ-realm appears to be illusionary optimism, religious enthusiasm, and childish political cheerfulness.

The central thesis here is that most of Bonhoeffer's *Ethics* can be interpreted as a laboratory where he experimented with a whole set of possible navigation tools for the one Christ-space. The various tools do not seamlessly fit together like jigsaw pieces but partially overlap, are partly in tension, and ultimately, create empty spaces in between. But we should keep in mind Bonhoeffer's signpost warning. If the churches strive "to combat this or that kind of worldly evil . . . this is a continuation of the medieval idea of crusade."[16] Thus, Bonhoeffer's six tools can be divided into two different boxes—those in the first box can primarily be used to discover *order, continuity, and stability* in the Christ-space. The tools in the second box are to be used more for *transformation, change, disruptive interventions*. If one would use a temperature model, the tools in the first box *cool down* moralism, while those in the second one *heat up* moralism at the risk of hypermoralism.

Christ-Based Perspectivism (Incarnation, Cross, and Resurrection)

Toolbox II: Transformation, Change, Disruptive Interventions

The reality of Christ in God's revelation needs to be differentiated. Both the creation and the kingdom of God are present only in Christ. In Christ, the world needs to be seen in three perspectives, namely in the incarnation—in God

---

15. In the most elementary formulation, "The point of departure for Dietrich Bonhoeffer's concrete ethics is the theological question of how the reality of God revealed in Jesus Christ can take form in human life in the world"; *DBWE* 6:409. For a lucid analysis of the corresponding Puritan program, see Michael Walzer, *The Revolution of the Saints: A Study in the Origins of Radical Politics* (Cambridge, MA: Harvard University Press, 1965), which opens with the remark of the puritan, Stephen Marshall, "you have great works to do, the planting of a new heaven and a new earth among us, and great works have great enemies."

16. *DBWE* 6:355, *DBW* 6:357.

becoming human—the world is honored and appreciated; in the cross, the world is judged and corrected; and in the resurrection, the world is made anew. Similarly, life needs to be seen in a threefold way. It is "created, reconciled, and redeemed."[17]

In short, "In Jesus Christ, Incarnate, Crucified and Risen, humanity has become new."[18] And "Humanity still lives, of course, in a world of death but is already beyond death. Humanity still lives, of course, in a world of sin, but we are already beyond sin. The night is not yet over, but day is already dawning."[19] Nevertheless, this compact Christ-event still needs to be differentiated into three analytical perspectives.[20] But we are challenged to solve a puzzle—what elements, processes, and structures are honored and confirmed? Which ones need to be criticized, and which represent the dawning daylight, the eschatological daybreak? What elements of darkness remain before the appearance of the new heaven and earth?

Christ's Mandates

Toolbox I: Order, Continuity, and Stability

Bonhoeffer's proposal of the divine mandates grounded in Christ seeks "to contribute to renewing and reclaiming the old concepts of order, estate, and office."[21] Many interpreters consider the proposal of two mandates grounded in Christ a truly two kingdoms rule. However, this is a misconception which misses Bonhoeffer's revolutionary insight and dismissal of a dual divine agency. Regardless of the number of mandates, Bonhoeffer notes that they do not stand side by side like freestanding, independent pillars. If one imagines for a moment the three mandates of family, economy, and the state as vertical structures, the church lives as a horizontal structure intersecting all the others. The church proclaims God's commandment:

> The commandment of Jesus Christ, the living Lord, sets created being free to fulfill its own law, that is the law inherited in it from its origin, essence, and goal

---

17. *DBWE* 6:251, *DBW* 6:250.

18. *DBWE* 6:92, *DBW* 6:78. Unfortunately, the English translation misses the subtle point of the German original: "In Jesus Christus, dem Menschgewordenen, Gekreuzigten und Auferstandenen, ist die Menschheit neu geworden"; *DBW* 6:78, in *DBWE* 6:91: "In Jesus Christ, the one who became human was crucified and is risen; humanity has become new." Bonhoeffer emphasizes how humanity became anew first and foremost *in Jesus Christ*, that is to say, through the three distinct yet related processes: incarnation, cross, and resurrection.

19. *DBWE* 6:92 (own translation), *DBW* 6:79.

20. The perspectives can also be found in the section on "The Concrete Commandment and the Divine Mandates" (*DBWE* 6:399ff., *DBW* 6:403ff.) and in "Ultimate and Penultimate Things" (*DBWE* 6:149ff., *DBW* 6:140).

21. *DBWE* 6:390, *DBW* 6:394.

in Jesus Christ . . . To be sure, the commandment of Jesus Christ rules church, family, culture, and government . . . Jesus Christ's claim to rule as it is proclaimed by the church simultaneously means that family, culture, and government are set free to be what they are in their own nature as grounded in Christ.[22]

Contrary to a long-standing tradition (not the least represented by Max Weber), Bonhoeffer vividly rejects the assumption of conflicting autonomous spheres of culture because, such an interpretation "casts a dark glow of tragic heroism"[23] on life. And yet it remains unclear how much these mandates can be transformed in light of Jesus Christ. For some Christians, it implies the marriage of gays and lesbians; for others, this is the signature of sin and destruction to the order of marriage. How can we describe the vector, speed, direction, reach, and intensity of transformation? What is the signature of a mandate under the rule of Christ over against the rule of the Creator? In 1941, Bonhoeffer had clearly moved beyond the idea that the orders only preserve for the new creation. He wanted more—the ability to reflect the resurrection.

Radical Actualism

Toolbox II: Transformation, Change, Disruptive Interventions

Since his Habilitation, *Act and Being*, a theologically formatted philosophical actualism, pervades Bonhoeffer's theology. His ethics of responsibility is also saturated with actualist motifs, which bring a permanent moment of liquefaction into the one Christ-space. In doing what is necessary and grasping concrete responsibility, this actualist motif, reaching out to the moment, is found. Bonhoeffer's emphasis on free responsibility also takes up the motif. If ethical speech is not "timeless and placeless ethical discourse,"[24] then, it is temporally transient, bound to specific "persons, times, and places."[25] After all, it is crucial "at the given place to consider reality and do what is necessary."[26] As Bonhoeffer points out, "in the given situation, it is necessary to observe, weigh, evaluate, and decide."[27] This "given situation" exists in the moment of decision—in freedom and a relative distance to the given. The radical actualism is accompanied, even

---

22. *DBWE* 6:402, *DBW* 6:406.
23. *DBWE* 6:252, *DBW* 6:251.
24. *DBWE* 6:371, *DBW* 6:373.
25. *DBWE* 6:372, *DBW* 6:374.
26. *DBWE* 6:268, *DBW* 6:267. The proper translation of the German "to do in the given place what is necessary in view of reality" captures much more the enormous tension between the actualist action and what is necessary in view of reality.
27. *DBWE* 6:268, *DBW* 6:267.

based on dynamic personalism. "Life is not a thing, an essence, or a concept, but a person."[28]

Reason, Appropriateness to Reality, and Relative Autonomy (Eigengesetzlichkeit)

Toolbox I: Order, Continuity, and Stability

According to Bonhoeffer, action in the Christ-space should be adequate to reality. Like a *basso continuo*, the conviction runs through the ethics that even in the one Christ-space, there must be no "principled rebellion against the status quo, in the name of some ideal higher reality."[29] Despite all polemics against an "*Eigengesetzlichkeit*," Bonhoeffer surprisingly emphasizes that responsibility in the Christ-space is not "to impose a foreign law on reality."[30] Especially in the context of his remarks on the "possibility of the word of the church to the world,"[31] Bonhoeffer resolutely opposes the idea of specifically Christian solutions to problems, and pleads for a specialized competence and, in fact, for the recognition of "a relative autonomy (*Eigengesetzlichkeit*)."[32] Since in Christ creation is also accepted and appreciated, Bonhoeffer takes up motifs of creaturely goodness and positive rationality.

Ultimate and Penultimate

Toolbox II: Transformation, Change, Disruptive Interventions

In the famous chapter, "Ultimate and Penultimate Things," Bonhoeffer develops a strong transformative model for the Christ-space. Already, the explicit emphasis on the unity of faith, love, and hope[33] aims at a transformation of the world with the "possibilities . . . of the living God."[34] This "liquefaction" of reality occurs between the extremes of destruction or abandonment of the penultimate and a constant practice of compromise seeking adaptation. It is, for Bonhoeffer, a dynamic process and, arguably, progress: "The new life breaks ever more powerfully into earthly life and creates space for itself within it."[35] The messianic motif of preparing the way also implies a profound transformation in the Christ-space. It is about "concrete

---

28. *DBWE* 6:249, *DBW* 6:249.
29. *DBWE* 6:261, *DBW* 6:261.
30. *DBWE* 6:261, *DBW* 6:260.
31. *DBWE* 6:352ff., *DBW* 6:355ff.
32. *DBWE* 6:362, *DBW* 6:364.
33. *DBWE* 6:148, *DBW* 6:139.
34. Ibid.
35. *DBWE* 6:158, *DBW* 6:150.

interventions in the visible world,"[36] in which the "coming of Christ" takes place.[37] However, even in this context, Bonhoeffer offers an important provision and does not lose sight of the goal that "we *as human beings* can and should live a 'good' life in given orders."[38] He is deeply convinced that "every radical Christianity . . . is impossible in view of the reality of Jesus Christ and Christ's coming into the world."[39]

The Vitality of Life

Toolbox I: Order, Continuity, and Stability

A much less transformative approach that exposes and openly affirms dynamic structures of reality is found in Bonhoeffer's attempt at a Christological grasp of natural life. "Created, reconciled, and redeemed" life is allowed to unfold. The Christ-space is filled with vital processes that are constitutive for life. Undoubtedly drawing on insights from the philosophy of life and partly reminiscent of Friedrich Nietzsche, Bonhoeffer attempts to develop a Christologically structured understanding of life.[40] Thus, he vehemently emphasizes "the Yes to what is created, to becoming to growth, to flower and fruit, to health, to happiness, to ability, to achievement, to value, to success, to greatness, to honor, in short, the Yes to the flourishing of life's strength."[41] In Christ, the "Yes" and the "No" to the dynamics of life are united so that a vitalist ethic does not come to stand alongside a Jesus ethic. In this turn to the vital forces of life, Bonhoeffer apparently wants to retrieve aspects for the Christ-space that had been discussed in theology within the framework of creation theology. In Christ, this "Yes" is always dialectically accompanied by a "No" and, according to Bonhoeffer's thesis, the dynamics of life are united. Against a religious fascination with the limits and truncated edges of life and against a "flat-footed moralizing and homespun pedagogical approach to all of life," Bonhoeffer demands that the "ethical" refers to the "center and richness of daily life."[42]

---

36. *DBWE* 6:164, *DBW* 6:156.
37. *DBWE* 6:164, *DBW* 6:157.
38. *DBWE* 6:165, *DBW* 6:158.
39. *DBWE* 6:168, *DBW* 6:160f.
40. For an analysis of Bonhoeffer's critical, but indeed also positive, references to Friedrich Nietzsche, see the classic study by Peter Köster, "Nietzsche als verborgener Antipode in Bonhoeffers 'Ethik'," *Nietzsche-Studien* (Berlin: de Gruyter, 2016), 367–418.
41. *DBWE* 6:251, *DBW* 6:251.
42. *DBWE* 6:368, 389, *DBW* 6:371.

The Crisis of the Christ-Space—Three Ways Out, a Dead-End Street and Two Alternatives

Whether it is the actualism of the command, the understanding of life as being its own physician, the vision levelling the hills in preparation for the penultimate, or the formation of Christ's mandates, all of Bonhoeffer's attempts to navigate the Christ-space have one feature in common—the powerful presence of Christ. Indeed, Christ's presence is presupposed by all the navigation tools presented in *Ethics*. Except for a few limitations and questions already in *Ethics*, the undercurrent of Bonhoeffer's tools is the notion of powerful divine presence. This common feature of powerful presence is and was the basis for a strong theo-political optimism in theologies and on the churches' side. Following Bonhoeffer's emphasis on the one Christ-space, the idea of powerful presence looms in the background of many theological mindsets.

However, the world as the Christ-space is not filled with the irresistible presence of the merciful, peaceful, and forgiving Christ. And, we should remember the presence of Christ in the one Christ-space is not conditional—it does not depend on moral acts nor on the witness of the church. For Bonhoeffer, this presence is first and foremost not a task that needs to be taken up by Christians, but it is a given reality. This is Bonhoeffer's Christ-ontology—at least at the time he wrote the *Ethics* fragments.

So, where do we stand eighty years after Bonhoeffer? The moral lament in theology about the state of the world and the hypermoralism of many "liberal" churches reveals that both theology and the churches are in despair. The one Christ-space is not filled with Christ but should be filled with Christ by acts of righteousness, mercy, love, and works that favor human rights. It is a possibility which urgently needs to be turned into reality by human beings and their actions. Consequently, the optimistic hope of the long "Jürgen Habermas period," as one might call it, turns into a time of desperate hope, driven by anger and anguish, the possibility of violence, and a readiness to declare exceptional states even in constitutional democracies. The moral optimism of much public theology and activism is a thin veneer on a thick board composed of dystopia, illusion, real misery, and, not the least, rapidly shrinking church membership in all strands of Christianity worldwide, which put political activism at the center of their mission. This situation must be acknowledged self-critically without any sense of triumph and any false contentedness. Because of the living Christ, a new quietism out of despair cannot be an option.

The longing for political impact, relevance, and change in this world often fall into the temptation of using religion to paint our political ambitions. The theo-political optimism of the last decades, which absorbed so much of Bonhoeffer's idea of the one Christ-space, is in a deep crisis. The number of those putting democracy into question is growing from both angles, left and right. The one Christ-space appears to be filled with resistance, sin and stupidity, corruption and questionable self-interests, power politics and misuses of morality, wrongheaded idealism, and cynical power politics in need of clear limitations.

Again, where are we today? How do we get out of the crisis of the Christ-space? When I visit parishes, talk to ministers, and read what colleagues in the field of theology are writing, one route out of this crisis frequently taken is to say in a heroic posture—God in Christ is only present in our human moral acts. There is no God at all, independent of our actions and our imagination. In my judgment, this is a dead-end street for these branches of Christianity. For Protestantism, it is, at least in the long run, a suicidal endeavor.[43] I take it as a sign of Bonhoeffer's theological sensitivity and genius-prophetic insights that it did not take him eighty years to recognize the questionable implications of his navigation tools. Most theological proposals, which can be found in Bonhoeffer's *Letters from Prison*, need to be interpreted as Bonhoeffer's responses to his earlier notion of powerful presence. Bonhoeffer's later answer emphasizes the weak God who is pushed not only out of Jerusalem to Golgotha but out of the world.

The notion of powerful presence can be called into question in two ways, both of which were touched on by Bonhoeffer himself. A powerful presence can be transformed into a weak presence. This is the main road that Bonhoeffer later took, though it is hardly ever understood by many of his followers. The church's weakness and the weakness of the theological semantics correspond to the fundamental weakness of Christ. Jürgen Moltmann and many others followed this lead.[44] And yet, the theologies of the presence of the weak Christ are still theologies of presence.

There is another way of modulating the notion of powerful presence—powerful absence. Following a short hint by Bonhoeffer himself, we need to explore absence, to understand Christ and our times. "[B]ut there will be those who pray and act for justice and wait for God's own time"—not night watchers but daybreak managers waiting for the aurora.

One hint Bonhoeffer himself left can be found in his statement, which became a free-standing aphorism: "but there will be those who pray and act for justice and wait for God's own time."[45] Interestingly enough, this short sentence is mostly

---

43. For a more detailed argument leading to his judgment, see Günter Thomas, *Gottes Lebendigkeit: Beiträge zur Systematischen Theologie* (Leipzig: Evangelische Verlagsanstalt, 2019).

44. The theological phenomenon of lament becomes a litmus test for the doctrine of God. Not only classical theism, but also a radical theology of God's co-suffering in weakness simply makes lamentation turn out to be meaningless. For this, see Günter Thomas, "Theodicy and Lament: Implications for Conceiving God," in *Theodicy and Protest: Jewish and Christian Perspectives*, ed. Beate Ego, Ute Gause, Ron Margolin, and Dalit Rom-Shiloni (Leipzig: Evangelische Verlagsanstalt, 2018), 199–214.

45. *DBWE* 8:390. The recently published and, so far, only comprehensive study of this aphorism assumes that in the short version, "im Beten und im Tun des Gerechten unter den Menschen" the just [*des Gerechten*] is indeed a *genetivus subjectivus*. The doing of the just is then the doing of the justified human being. "Es wird Menschen geben, die beten und das Gerechte tun und auf Gottes Zeit warten," this longer version of the aphorism, consisting

quoted in the abbreviated form, "through prayer and in doing justice," and the third part, "wait for God's own time," is left out. In addition, the particular ambivalence of "Tun des Gerechten" is not taken into account. "Tun des Gerechten" can mean "doing of acts of justice" but more likely "the doing of the just/justified person." The emphasis on "waiting for God's own time" has far-reaching implications that directly speak to our time. This shift from the distinction of power/weakness to absence/presence opens the conceptual space for a theology of God's differentiated absence and presence.

Let me sketch with very broad brushstrokes the crucial aspects of such a theology that takes God's temporal absence seriously. "Waiting for God's own time" implies a fundamental absence of God in our current time. Even if we experience and confess God's presence in the church now, the world, the Christ-space, there is a coming presence that marks the current presence as an absence. Besides, the particular absence of God in our time is not a static one. It does not lead to the celebration of God's death or a disengaged acceptance of God's absence. The very act of waiting points to a dynamic of absence and presence. Waiting for God's own time points to an absence that will be filled with presence. To pray and act for justice is framed by this third act of active waiting, which is both encouraging and limiting. Waiting is eminently active waiting and longing. When the acts of waiting are forgotten, the manifest temptation of the church is to engage in moral crusades. To wait because God is waiting is a real challenge. It can lead to temptation. In all prayer and all actions, we wait for Christ to fill the Christ-space. "To wait for" means to accept limits. This waiting even limits the world responsibility of Christians. "Waiting for God's own time," Christians acknowledge their limitations in making Christ present in the one Christ-space. The presence of Christ cannot be realized only by acts for justice. The absence can be overcome only by God him- or herself. It is an absence that human activities cannot solve but only the passionately living God. Whoever is waiting for someone is drawing a distinction between oneself and another agent.

The tension between the "act for justice" and the "waiting for God's own time" opens not only a conceptual but also an experiential "space" in which both hope and longing but also lament need to be negotiated. The absence of God's time is a reason for hope and a reason for lament. Suppose we translate the temporal image of "waiting for God's time" into the spatial image of the Christ-space. In that case, we would need to explore the notion of relative emptiness and relative fullness due

---

of three parts, itself implies a *genitivus objectivus*. The English translation of Bonhoeffer's *Ethics* excludes the possibility of a *genitivus subjectivus* without further comment and speaks of "through prayer and in doing justice among human beings" and of "people who pray and do justice and wait for God's own time"; *DBW* 8:436, *DBWE* 8:390. See Nicole Herrmannsdörfer, *Beten, Tun des Gerechten und Warten auf Gottes Zeit. Gott und Welt in der Theologie Dietrich Bonhoeffers* (Leipzig: Evangelische Verlagsanstalt, 2020), 121–60. Herrmannsdörfer's emphasis on the *genitivus subjectivus* goes against the mainstream of Bonhoeffer interpretation at this point—in my opinion, with good reasons.

to God's absence and inbreaking presence through the spirit. In terms of agency, the distinction between our acts for justice and God's own time points to God's own agency distinct from others. This is why Christian hope as hope in someone can transcend human hope in something or for a future state of the world.

When we look back to Bonhoeffer's rejection of the double agent in the doctrine of two kingdoms, the trope of "waiting for" offers a third option beyond the indeterminate God of history (as *deus absconditus*) and the resurrected Christ. God is not acting in every event in space and time.[46] Many events in this world and the Christ-space cannot be attributed to any underdetermined God, neither a *dark* God nor to Christ. Nonetheless, the absence is not plain absence. Whoever is "waiting for" experiences an absence. Christ's particular presence in the church and the world makes his partial but painful absence present. As we say in every celebration of the Lord's Supper, "until he comes" (1 Cor. 11:3). So, the absence of Christ is intensely experienced in the presence of the spirit; hence, "*Maranatha*" (1 Cor. 16:22; Rev. 22:20).

The critical concept implied in the "waiting for God's time" is God's patience. Christ's patience is ambivalent, not only benevolent. We are experiencing God's patience in all aspects of the Christ-event—in the incarnation, God honors a natural world where any integrity and systemic balance also imply violence and destruction—long before the advent of human beings. As Bonhoeffer points out in his late letters, it is God's patience that allows humans to bring Christ to the cross, to bring him into the twilight of sacrifice and victimization. God's vulnerability in Christ is part and parcel of God's waiting. Even more, it is God's patience that spreads the reality of the new creation, allowing it to grow and radiate so slowly into this world. If the world is new in Christ, humanity is created anew, why do we have to wait so long?

In light of the present state of the world, God's patience needs justification. Eighty years after the letters from prison, we could dare to say the weak God alone cannot help—the weak God on the cross, no excuse of/by God for the present power of sin and stupidity, exploitation, and violence. But the patience of the risen Christ is equally challenging. So, in order to sustain hope here and now, lament and the search for God's justification must find a place in our theology and the rationale for our social action.[47] We are not just waiting for God's time. We also wait for God's own vindication of his patience. The public protest of Christians

---

46. Within the framework of Bonhoeffer's theology, the notions of *submission* and *fate* need further exploration. As already mentioned, a great tension opens up here between the radically Christological passages of the *Ethics* and the later (!) hints in the *Prison Letters* to the necessary discovery of a Thou in the working of fate.

47. For an emphasis on spirituality in dealing with this aphorism, see Nico Koopman, "How Do We Live Responsibly? Dietrich Bonhoeffer and the Fulfilment of Dignity in Democratic South Africa," in *Reading Bonhoeffer in South Africa after the Transition to Democracy*, ed. Nico Koopman and Robert Vosloo (Frankfurt am Main: Peter Lang, 2020), 41–56, 53ff.

against God's patience should be—and this seems contradictory only at first sight—an essential element in the recovery of credible speech about God in the present. Against all philosophical, theological, and social-ethical programs of excusing God, Christians who are indeed "waiting for" pray with Christ himself, saying, "And lead us not into temptation, but deliver us from evil."

While Christians are waiting, a powerful and dangerous temptation is to confuse the necessary prayer of lament with one's moral lament and perfectly legitimate complaints about the world's state. The widespread gesture of anger and indignation at the world tends to obscure the core of Bonhoeffer's insight that even before we arrive and act in this pain-ridden world, this world is already a Christ-space, whether it is filled with divine power, with weakness, with emptiness, or with traces of the spirit of Jesus Christ. To resist this powerful temptation, Christians pray and celebrate in every worship service the promises of God, the very promises in which they charge God simultaneously with lament and often with silent anger.

A Concluding Remark

Dietrich Bonhoeffer's powerful theological insight into the one Christ-space is not open to revision. In retrospect, after eighty years of reception history, it needs clarification and specificity. The one Christ-space is a theological solution, which at the same time has created and is creating many new problems. This, as the laboratory of Bonhoeffer's *Ethics* clearly shows, Bonhoeffer himself saw quite clearly.

What I call for in our political and ecclesial situation is a paradoxical theological intervention. In waiting for God to speak and act, we might practice a balance of patience and impatience in the practice of world responsibility that does not destroy our churches and democratic institutions but appropriately enriches social and spiritual life. Such a practice is a form of active waiting for the daybreak of the living Christ's final appearance in our one worldly Christ-space.

Chapter 18

BONHOEFFER'S ETHICS OF RESPONSIBILITY
TRUTH-TELLING, THE LAW, AND THE CHRIST-REALITY

Matthias Grebe

Introduction

One of the key themes in Dietrich Bonhoeffer's *Ethics* is responsibility[1] (*Verantwort-ung*), which he defines as the Christian life lived in "answer to the life of Jesus."[2] This chapter examines the twofold structure of this ethics of responsibility, which Bonhoeffer calls "life's *bond* to human beings and to God."[3] It is within this bond which constitutes the freedom of human life and provides the framework for responsible life in the form of *Wirklichkeitsgemäßigkeit* (accordance with reality) and *Stellvertretung* (vicarious representative action), that human responsibility can flourish.[4] In order to deepen our understanding of Bonhoeffer's ethics of responsible living, two complex ethical matters will be investigated here, namely "truth-telling" and "fulfilling the law," with a view to answering the following questions: "What is truthful speech?" and "What is responsible human action?" We shall see that Bonhoeffer's understanding of ethics is grounded in his concept of sociality, and is both contextual and relational.

Bonhoeffer's own life cannot be separated from his theological thought, especially when it comes to truth-telling and fulfilling the law—two aspects of responsible life which highlight the reconciliation between God and the world in Christ. Consequently, after a brief outline of Bonhoeffer's ethics of responsibility, the chapter will begin *in medias res* with a biographical sketch of the theologian's time in Tegel, followed by a closer look at the two ethical matters.

---

1. See especially *DBWE* 6. Cf. Larry Rasmussen, "The Ethics of Responsible Action," in *The Cambridge Companion to Dietrich Bonhoeffer*, ed. John W. de Gruchy (Cambridge: Cambridge University Press, 1999), 206–25.

2. *DBWE* 6:254.

3. Ibid., 257 (italics added). See Mt. 22:37-40 for the double command to love one's neighbor and God.

4. See Ibid., 257: "Responsibility is based on vicarious representative action" [*Stellvertretung*].

In a "post-truth" society filled with accusations of fake news, political manipulation of social media, and even impeachment trials, the subject of truth-telling and responsible action is more relevant than ever. This chapter therefore stresses the significance of Bonhoeffer's attempt to tackle the *Zeitgeist* in word and action, and reaffirms it for the twenty-first century too. His thoughts on discipleship and responding to Christ's call as well as his fragmentary piece of discourse ethics on the topic of truth-telling are shown to be equally relevant today as they were in Tegel Prison in 1943.

The Nature of Ethics

At the risk of my life, I give an account and thus take responsibility for what has happened through Jesus Christ . . . I take responsibility and answer for Jesus Christ, and with that I naturally also take responsibility for the commission I have been charged with by him. (1 Cor. 9:3)[5]

Yet for Bonhoeffer, this responsibility also extends to other human beings, since responsibility is both the "basic answering (*Ver-antwort-ung*) of a person to life itself" and the "fundamental response of one's own life to life as constituted in and by relationship."[6] Thus, the Christian takes responsibility for his or her own life and simultaneously also for other human beings before Christ.[7]

Bonhoeffer sees the foundation of ethical behavior as located in the Christ-reality, in which the reality of the world and the reality of God have been reconciled.[8] He particularly expounds this thought in *Ethics* where in the section on "History and Good" he discusses the concept of *das Wirklichkeitsgemäße*—accordance with reality.[9] This represents a pivotal point in his ethics—that in the reconciliation of Christ, God and the world have a qualitative new relationship.[10] From the perspective of Christ's *Stellvertretung*, his reconciling work, Bonhoeffer's theology shows that both *truth* and *reality*—the question of truthful speech and the question of responsible human action in accordance with reality—are interdependent and always linked to the question of God. As Bonhoeffer maintains, the reality of the

---

5. Ibid., 255f.
6. Rasmussen, "The Ethics of Responsible Action," 219.
7. See *DBWE* 6:256.
8. Bonhoeffer writes: "Whoever confesses the reality of Jesus Christ as the revelation of God confesses in the same breath the reality of God and the reality of the world, for they find God and the world reconciled in Christ"; *DBWE* 6:48.
9. See Bonhoeffer's remarks on "accordance with reality," in *DBWE* 6:222–4, 261–4.
10. See Christiane Tietz-Steiding, "Lebendige Wahrheit—wirklichkeitsgemäße Lüge: Zu einem Aufsatzfragment Dietrich Bonhoeffers," in *Lügen und Betrügen: Das Falsche in der Geschichte von der Antike bis zur Moderne*, ed. Oliver Hochadel and Ursula Kocher (Köln: Böhlau Verlag, 2000), 279.

world can only be understood within the reality of God.[11] Christian ethics therefore is about the "reality of God that is revealed in Jesus Christ,"[12] about "becoming real" (*Wirklichwerden*).[13]

Reality encapsulates both truth-telling and keeping God's commandments and must therefore correspond to Jesus the reconciler. If it is the Christocentric nature of his thought, which gives shape to Bonhoeffer's ethics of moral action—seeing human beings as dependent on the other for selfhood and seeing Christ in the other, a particular identification with the weak and oppressed—then Bonhoeffer's vision and basic conception of telling the truth and keeping God's commandments can be understood as emerging from his concept of sociality, which becomes the "key to its ethical implications."[14]

Bonhoeffer in Tegel

On November 18, 1943, after long months of *Anfechtungen*,[15] without worship, confession, or the Lord's Supper, and haunted by resignation and melancholy ("*acedia*"–"*tristitia*"), Bonhoeffer writes to his friend Eberhard Bethge to inform him that he has written,[16] among other things, "an essay on the subject, 'What does it Mean to Tell the Truth?'"[17] By now, Bonhoeffer is seven months at the military prison in Tegel, held on suspicion of conspiracy to overthrow the *Führer*, a plot in which he and several members of his family were co-conspirators.

Almost two thousand years earlier, another man encountered his own severe *Anfechtungen*, this time in the Garden of Gethsemane, only to be asked a cynical question about truth by a jesting Pilate (Jn 18:38). We will return to this later. But for Bonhoeffer, the question of truth was no joking matter. It was during these early months at Tegel that he was regularly subjected to long interrogations by *Oberkriegsgerichtsrat* (Senior Military Prosecutor) Manfred Roeder about his role in the resistance and the plot against Hiter, "while simultaneously exchanging encoded messages with his family so that he knew what could be safely disclosed and what needed to be concealed to protect the conspiracy and individual

---

11. Tietz-Steiding, "Lebendige Wahrheit." See also *DBWE* 6:47: "Since ethical thinking in terms of realms is overcome by faith in the revelation of ultimate reality in Jesus Christ, it follows that there is no real Christian existence outside the reality of the world and no real worldliness outside the reality of Jesus Christ."

12. *DBWE* 6:33.

13. Ibid., 34.

14. Ned O'Gorman, "'Telling the Truth': Dietrich Bonhoeffer's Rhetorical Discourse Ethics," *JCR* 28 (November 2005): 236.

15. *DBWE* 8:187.

16. See ibid., 180. Cf. *DBWE* 6:273f., 366, where Bonhoeffer discusses the significance of the *Grenzfall* and the *Grenzereignis*.

17. *DBWE* 8:182.

conspirators."[18] Writing about the topic while being interrogated meant that it was no mere academic exercise, but part and parcel of his quite unique and concrete situation. Without doubt, Bonhoeffer was among the first in Germany to "recognize that the ascension of Hitler to power constituted a political problem of the first order, and not just one having to do with the church."[19] And now at Tegel, Bonhoeffer was faced with the *Grenzfall* situation (borderline case) between life and death. Should he "truthfully" admit to Roeder his involvement as a double agent in the plot, thereby risking not only his own life but those of many others, or should he deceive him when answering the questions? The internal struggle of this moral dilemma is depicted powerfully in his essay on truth-telling.

Bethge, in his biography of Bonhoeffer, paints Bonhoeffer's situation at Tegel as a series of "successful efforts to conceal the true facts."[20] His friends and family "helped him weave an intricate net of camouflage."[21] The fact that Bonhoeffer wrote his essay during this time reveals "something of the true background of that study," and highlights his awareness "of his dilemma, and that he did not seek to pretend or hide anything from himself," Bethge maintains.[22] However, Bonhoeffer's deception and concealment only lasted until July 20, 1944, when the "true facts" of the conspiracy came to light after a failed attempt to assassinate Hitler.

Bonhoeffer's Ethics of Truth-Telling

Bonhoeffer famously gives the example of a teacher, who in front of the entire class, asks a child whether it is true that his father is an alcoholic. Though it is the case, the child denies it.[23] Bonhoeffer asks whether what the child does constitutes a lie or not, raising questions about how lying and truth should be defined. Bonhoeffer explains:

> One could call the child's answer a lie; all the same, this lie contains more truth— i.e., it corresponds more closely to the truth—than if the child had revealed the father's weakness before the class. The child acted rightly according to the

---

18. Nancy Berlinger, "What Is Meant by Telling the Truth: Bonhoeffer on the Ethics of Disclosure," *Studies in Christian Ethics* 16, no. 2 (2003): 82.

19. Barry Harvey, *Taking Hold of the Real: Dietrich Bonhoeffer and the Profound Worldliness of Christianity* (Eugene, OR: Wipf & Stock, 2015), 273.

20. Eberhard Bethge, *Dietrich Bonhoeffer: A Biography*, rev. and ed. V. J. Barnett, trans. E. Mosbacher (Minneapolis, MN: Fortress Press, 2000), 799.

21. Ibid.

22. Ibid., 813. According to Bethge, Bonhoeffer's notes show that the initial drafting of the essay took place from April to June 1943, at the time when he was interrogated by Roeder.

23. See *DBWE* 16:606.

measure of the child's perception. Yet it is the teacher alone who is guilty of the lie.[24]

He goes on to say that telling the truth means "different things, depending on where one finds oneself. The relevant relationships must be taken into account. The question must be asked whether and in what way a person is justified in demanding truthful speech from another."[25] "How does my word become true?," he asks, answering his own question with the following:

1) By recognising who calls on me to speak and what authorizes me to speak;
2) By recognising the place in which I stand;
3) By putting the subject I am speaking about into this context.[26]

Despite all appearance, these three statements do not sum up a "principle" or method of procedure for Bonhoeffer. Instead, what they reveal is that the "ability to tell the truth rests on faculties of perception and relation, the ability to judge where one stands in relation to audience, context, subject matter, and ultimately a social and political network."[27] Furthermore:

> The single word is always a portion of an entire reality that seeks expression in the word. Depending on the person to whom I am speaking, the person who is questioning me, or what I am discussing, my word, if it seeks to be truthful, must vary. A truthful word is not an entity constant in itself but is as lively as life itself. Where this word detaches itself from life and from the relationship to the concrete other person, where "the truth is told" without regard for the person to whom it is said, there it has only the appearance of truth but not its essence.[28]

Truth-telling is therefore contextual and relational, as it depends on the specific situation and is always "relative to where one stands."[29] For example, the "truthfulness of the child toward parents is by its very nature something different from that of parents toward their child,"[30] and telling the truth must therefore "be learned."[31] Furthermore, since "'lies' are the destruction of and the enmity against the real as it is in God; whoever tells the truth cynically is lying."[32] The child lies in order not to expose the father's weakness, thereby preserving the family's integrity.

---

24. Ibid.
25. Ibid., 602.
26. Ibid., 608.
27. O'Gorman, "Telling the Truth," 242.
28. *DBWE* 16:605.
29. O'Gorman, "Telling the Truth," 238.
30. *DBWE* 16:602.
31. Ibid., 622.
32. *DBWE* 8:223.

Likewise, the political prisoner deceives the interrogator in order to safeguard the lives of his co-conspirators.

Is Bonhoeffer drawing a comparison here between the child before the teacher and the *Doppelagent* (double agent) before the *Oberkriegsgerichtsrat*? Bearing in mind that his essay was "subjected to the censorship of the Tegel prison hierarchy"[33] at a time when he was "deliberately deceiving prison examiners and writing elaborate and dissembling letters"[34] to Roeder, the relatively innocent example of the child-teacher scenario becomes all the more profound in terms of what it says about political resistance in Nazi Germany. Writing this piece led Bonhoeffer to the "recognition that the essence of lying is found much deeper than in the contradiction between thought and speech,"[35] as Augustine had famously put it. In fact, the "usual definition, according to which the conscious contradiction between thought and speech is a lie, is completely inadequate."[36] It appears that for Bonhoeffer, truth is more than simply naming facts, and that there are cases when even the negation of facts can be truthful. Thus, facticity and truth are apparently not identical to him.[37] So Bonhoeffer argues, "It is questionable whether it makes sense to generalize and extend the concept of lying . . . in such a way that it coincides with the concept of a formally untrue statement."[38]

Infamously, however, Immanuel Kant regarded truth-telling as a duty (*Pflicht*), which we are obligated to carry out. For Kant, it was impermissible to lie under any circumstances. And prior to the Tegel fragment on truth-telling, Bonhoeffer had already queried Kant's understanding of lying in *Ethics*.[39] Kant, according to Bonhoeffer, had argued that "if asked by a murderer whether my friend, whom he was pursuing, had sought refuge in my house, I would have to answer honestly in the affirmative,"[40] as I would be obligated to do so and not lie. The possibility of a person's harm by my truth-telling does not, for Kant, "have any bearing upon the

---

33. O'Gorman, "Telling the Truth," 242.
34. Ibid., 237.
35. *DBWE* 16:608.
36. Ibid., 606.
37. See Christiane Tietz, "Eine Korrespondenztheorie besonderer Art. Dietrich Bonhoeffers Wahrheitsbegriff im Horizont traditioneller Bestimmungen von Wahrhaftigkeit und Lüge," in *Bonhoeffer—Rundbrief: Mitteilungen der Internationalen Bonhoeffer-Gesellschaft. Sektion Bundesrepublik Deutschland*, 78 (Oktober 2005): 9.
38. *DBWE* 16:607.
39. See *DBWE* 6:279f.
40. Ibid., 280. Kant writes: "For if you had told the truth to the best of your knowledge, then neighbors might have come and apprehended the murderer while he was searching the house for his enemy and the deed would have been prevented" ("On a Supposed Right to Lie from Philanthropy," 612f.). Immanuel Kant, "On a Supposed Right to Lie from Altruistic Motives," in *Critique of Practical Reason and Other Writings in Moral Philosophy*, 346–50; *DBWE* 6:279 n.130.

principle."[41] In this way, Kant's treating of truthfulness "as a principle" had led to a "grotesque conclusion" and "self-righteousness of conscience that has escalated into blasphemous recklessness and become an impediment to responsible action."[42]

These examples not only reveal that truth deeply mattered to Bonhoeffer but also that, for him, "far more significant than offering a 'theory of truth' is . . . an account of what it means to be truthful."[43] It does not inevitably mean that some kind of hierarchy of values underpins the moral decision-making—saving a life is of greater value than telling the truth—which would only create a principle or moral system, but it is more likely that Bonhoeffer means that "the ethical cannot be detached from reality, [because] the ever-greater capacity to perceive reality is a necessary component of ethical action."[44] There might be something to say here about Weber's distinction between "Ethics of responsibility" and "Ethics of moral conviction."[45] Arguably, Kant advocated the latter and Bonhoeffer the former. But to think in these categories would work against what Bonhoeffer wants to achieve with his ethics, as again this could potentially reduce ethics to a "static basic formula."[46]

The key concept in his essay on truth-telling is that truth is *alive*, and in this way truth-telling becomes an expression of the real in words. Since for Bonhoeffer, God is not a "general principle" but "the Living One" revealed in Christ, the *what* question of truth is answered only by the *who* question. This becomes the prerequisite to his answer of the question of truth-telling[47]—truth and lie must be seen from within his concept of sociality, always depending on *who* is speaking to whom. It is the person who stands behind what is said, which "makes it into a lie or the truth."[48] Ultimately, for Bonhoeffer, a lie is a "contradiction of the word of God as it was spoken in Christ."[49]

---

41. Berlinger, "What Is Meant by Telling the Truth," 85.

42. *DBWE* 6:279f.

43. Stanley Hauerwas, "Bonhoeffer on Truth and Politics," *Conrad Grebel Review* 20, no. 3 (2002): 45.

44. *DBWE* 16:622.

45. Bonhoeffer's use of the term *Verantwortung*, "responsibility," is similar to Weber's concept of *Verantwortungsethik*, "ethics of responsibility," which Weber introduced into the discussion of ethics in 1919 (see Weber, "Politics as a Vocation"). However, Bonhoeffer not only emphasizes that one pay attention to the consequences of one's actions, but also at the same time the element of caring for the other. See also Bonhoeffer in *Sanctorum Communio* on "the ethical concept of the person" and "responsibility"; *DBWE* 1:50.

46. *DBWE* 6:220.

47. See Tietz-Steiding, "Lebendige Wahrheit," 275.

48. *DBWE* 16:608.

49. Ibid.

A Covenantal Approach

Bonhoeffer's approach to truth-telling, as part of responsible living within the bond of life, is contextual and relational. It could be summarized as *covenantal* since the "obligation to tell the truth is bounded by the particular relationship we have to the person with whom we are speaking."[50] Telling the truth "means something different according to the particular relation in which we stand."[51] In this light, truth-telling is not only a contextual reality but also a *covenantal* reality, which indicates that it is always "tied to the obligations that exist by virtue of the kinds of relationships we have with others."[52] Thus, we can say that Bonhoeffer had no *covenant*-relationship with Roeder—or for that matter with the Nazis—and did therefore not see himself as obliged to disclose to Roeder the full facts.

Bonhoeffer's Ethics of Responsible Action

Given that the "subject matter of a Christian ethics is God's reality revealed in Christ,"[53] "what matters is participating in the reality of God and the world in Jesus Christ today."[54] Therefore, any discussion of ethics needs to rest on a solid soteriology because it is from the *Stellvertretung* and reconciliation achieved in Christ that we understand "reality," "truth," and "responsible action." The atonement not only helps us to make sense of reality but also sheds light on truth-telling as well as on responsible living, as in Christ we are faced with a new reality that shatters all our existing *Arbeitshypothesen* (working hypotheses) about God.

This calls for a closer look at the doctrine of God and God's own truth-telling and fulfilling the law through the lens of the reconciling work of Christ—from Gethsemane to Golgotha. The way God acts in the Passion and the atonement sheds light on the *who* question and on responsible living in word and action—on truth-telling and fulfilling the law.

Christ's Stellvertretung as Ransom

Considering the events prior to Jesus' death on the cross, it is apparent that just as Joseph is sold for the price of a slave and handed over to the Gentiles, so too is Jesus sold and handed over to the Roman soldiers in Gethsemane. During the

---

50. Glen H. Stassen and David P. Gushee, "Truthtelling," in *Kingdom Ethics: Following Jesus in Contemporary Context* (Downers Grove, IL: IVP, 2003), 384.
51. Ibid.
52. Ibid.
53. *DBWE* 6:49.
54. Ibid., 55.

Passover meal, he drank from the cup of suffering, a symbol that features heavily in both stories, and knows that eventually evil will be turned into good, as in the story of Joseph (Genesis 50).[55]

Even though Jesus had predicted the necessity of his death on a number of occasions, at Gethsemane, the *Anfechtungen* and the fear of the Passion, and being handed over to the Gentiles for torture and death are now written on his forehead as he sweats blood. In the past, Jesus had explained to his disciples that the Son of Man must suffer many things and be rejected by the elders, chief priests, and teachers of the law (Mk 8:31), that he would be condemned to death and handed over to the Gentiles, who would mock, spit on him, flog and kill him (Mk 10:33f.), and that he would give his life as a ransom for many (Mk 10:45), and after three days would rise again (Mk 9:31). The ransom passage in Mk 10:45 has prompted many questions in atonement debates. To whom is the ransom paid—to God, to the devil, or to the law itself?

To think of ransom here in terms of the demands of a kidnap misses the point. Instead, we must consider the Jewish concept of the law and the *kopher* (the ransom payment), which has nothing to do with kidnapping. Whereas "no one thinks the kidnapper's demands are legitimate, it is necessity, not justice, that obliges us to pay them,"[56] Jesus' death as a ransom sacrifice needs to be viewed within the cultic-legal system of the ancient Israelites. The *kopher*, the ransom payment, was part of the legal system of Israel (Exod. 21:30) and was demanded by the law. According to Jeremiah, it was demanded as "the ransom money for the firstborn, for slaves to be set free, for ground and land, [and] for life forfeited."[57] The term "ransom" in Mk 10:45, *lytron*, is used twenty times in the Septuagint for this kind of ransom payment and carries the wider meaning of substitutionary offering and freedom from slavery. Furthermore, whereas kidnap victims are innocent, human beings are both victims enslaved by sin and active doers of sin, guilty before the law and as such condemned to death. Jesus becomes a servant—Paul even says "slave"— in order to release those who are under a curse, enslaved by sin and therefore condemned in front of the law.

But how does Christ fulfill the law and its demands? How does he free those who stand condemned by the law? What is the relationship been the law, Christ's death on the cross, and responsible living? And what does Bonhoeffer mean when he says that Christ "became a breaker of the law"?[58]

---

55. Bonhoeffer writes: "I believe that God can and will let good come out of everything, even the greatest evil"; *DBWE* 8:30.

56. Gordon Graham, "Atonement," in *The Cambridge Companion to Christian Philosophical Theology*, ed. Charles Taliaferro and Chad Meister (Cambridge: Cambridge University Press, 2010), 126.

57. Joachim Jeremias, *New Testament Theology, Volume 1: The Proclamation of Jesus* (London: SCM, 1972), 292.

58. *DBWE* 6:278.

Fulfilling the Law

Christ himself said that he came to fulfill the law (Mt. 5:17). It is the elders and the chief priests who symbolically and probably unknowingly pay the price of the law to set Jesus free from the hands of sinful humanity (Judas). And a transfer of ownership takes place as Judas hands Jesus over to the soldiers to become the *doulous theou* and die as a ransom. The same way that "manumitted slaves were 'reassigned' from the service of a human master to the service of a divine master,"[59] Jesus now encapsulates both—he is the *doulous theou* in that he becomes the servant of all.

Ultimately however, this handing over, *paradidomi*, must be seen as an act of self-surrender (Jn 10:17-18), as Jesus willingly drinks from the cup in order to obey the Father's will and redeem "the many" from the final judgment. Jesus' willingness to offer his own life for the many is the inner core of his messianic mission.[60] He understood his "witness and his approaching death in the light of the tradition already given to him in Isaiah about the (vicariously suffering) Servant of God. He understood the suffering laid upon him as an event in which God's will was fulfilled."[61] The central message of Mk 10:45 is that the Son of Man does not represent equivalent material value in exchange but instead offers his own *nefes* as a *kopher* (see Exod. 21:30).

Bonhoeffer picks up on Mt. 5:17 to show how Christ "puts the law of the Old Covenant into force."[62] He answers the question of whether the Christian owes allegiance to Christ or the law. For Bonhoeffer, discipleship involves being *bound* to the person of Jesus but not without a simultaneous allegiance to the law since Christ has fulfilled the law and carries out the will of God in complete unity. It is in this way, by being bound to Christ that "Christ binds his disciples to the law,"[63] and the law becomes a new commandment. Bonhoeffer sums up this *covenantal* approach to the law by saying that "there is no fulfilment of the law without communion with God; there is also no communion with God without fulfilment of the law."[64] Regarding the law and its demands, therefore, Bonhoeffer warns us of "blind legalism." And on the subject of the Sermon on the Mount, he claims that:

---

59. John A. McGuckin, "St. Gregory of Nyssa on the Dynamics of Salvation," in *T&T Clark Companion to Atonement*, ed. Adam J. Johnson (London: T&T Clark, 2017), 166.

60. Peter Stuhlmacher, *Reconciliation, Law, and Righteousness: Essays in Biblical Theology* (Philadelphia, PA: Fortress Press, 1986), 25.

61. Peter Stuhlmacher, "Isaiah 53 in the Gospels and Acts," in *The Suffering Servant: Isaiah 53 in Jewish and Christian Sources*, ed. B. Janowski and P. Stuhlmacher (Grand Rapids, MI: Eerdmans, 2004), 153.

62. *DBWE* 4:116.

63. Bonhoeffer, "Discipleship," 116.

64. Ibid., 117.

[Jesus] fulfills the law; that is what he says about himself. Therefore it is true. He fulfills it to the last letter. By his fulfilling it, "everything is done" which is needed for the fulfillment of the law. Jesus will do what the law requires; therefore, he will have to suffer death. For he alone understands the law as God's law.[65]

On the other hand, Israel misunderstood the law by idolizing it and legalizing God.[66] Bonhoeffer explains that, "when the Jews equated God and the law, they did it in order to get God into their power with the law. God was dissolved into the law and was no longer Lord over the law."[67] Jesus however "validates anew the law as God's law. God is the giver and Lord of the law, and it is fulfilled only in personal communion with God."[68] Jesus shows that "the law itself is not God; nor is God the law, as if the law had replaced God. That is how Israel misunderstood the law."[69] Thus, Bonhoeffer sums up the "grotesque" misunderstanding of the law:

> Jesus, the Son of God, who alone stands in full communion with God, renews the validity of the law by coming to fulfill the law of the Old Covenant. Because he was the only One who did that, he alone could truly teach the law and how it is fulfilled. The disciples would know and understand this when he told it to them, because they knew who he was. The Jews could not understand it as long as they did not believe him. That was why they had to reject his teaching of the law as blasphemy against God or, rather, against God's law. Thus, for the sake of God's *true law*, Jesus had to suffer at the hands of the advocates of the *false law*. Jesus died on the cross as a blasphemer, as a transgressor of the law, because he put into force the *true law* against the misunderstood, *false law*.[70]

We read in Romans 7 that in order to be released from the law and its requirements, one party must die: "You also died to the law through the body of Christ, that you might belong to another, to him who was raised from the dead." Jesus understood the law and its requirements and had this in mind when he said he would become a ransom. What this means is that because he did what he did in obedience to the will of the Father and out of love for humanity, the law and its demands had no right to punish or sentence him to death. The *false law*, as Bonhoeffer explains, could not convict Jesus, as he upheld and fulfilled the *true law*. It is in this light that we should understand Bonhoeffer's comment that "for the sake of God and human beings Jesus Christ became a breaker of the law: he broke the law of the Sabbath in order to sanctify it, out of love for God and human beings."[71]

---

65. Ibid.
66. Ibid., 117.
67. Ibid.
68. Ibid.
69. Ibid.
70. Ibid., 117f. (italics added).
71. *DBWE* 6:278.

Christ fulfills the law by living a responsible life that is obedient to the will of God. By becoming the *Stellvertreter* of all, by becoming guilty on behalf of all, he changes reality for all:

> The figure [*Gestalt*] of the reconciler, of the God-man Jesus Christ, steps into the middle between God and the world, into the center of all that happens. In this figure is disclosed the mystery of the world, just as the mystery of God is revealed in it. No abyss of evil can remain hidden from him through whom the world is reconciled to God. But the abyss of the love of God embraces even the most abysmal godlessness of the world. In an incomprehensible reversal of all righteous and pious thought, God declares himself as guilty toward the world and thereby extinguishes the guilt of the world. God treads the way of humble reconciliation and thereby sets the world free.[72]

Ultimately, the profound irony permeating the atonement with regard to truth-telling and responsible living is that when Christ became humanity's ransom and gained her freedom, he did so through precisely the means by which the devil (or evil) was seeking to destroy him. As evil sought to destroy Jesus, starting with Judas' betrayal, the false verdict of blasphemy and law breaking, and Pilate's wrongful conviction of him to death, the trickster was tricked by precisely his own trickery. By condemning the sinless one, evil and all its lies and deception ran full force against the living truth and reality of God incarnate and by doing so, engaged in self-destruction.

We must also emphasize that God's *allowance* of evil is quite distinct from his *approval* or even his *causation* or *determining* of evil. The maxim from the story of Joseph, "What you meant for evil, God used for the Good, to save many lives (Gen. 50:20)," also applies to Jesus' vicarious representative action. Although he betrayed Jesus for 30 shekels of silver—the price of a slave's freedom (Exod. 21:31)—Judas' plan to harm him is turned through God's wisdom into the greatest blessing for the whole world. As Bonhoeffer points out, "Christ and Christ's adversary the devil are mutually exclusive opponents, but in such a way that even the devil, unwillingly, must serve Christ, and, willing evil, must ever again do good, so that the kingdom of the devil is always only under the feet of Christ."[73]

Conclusion

Bonhoeffer was no "armchair" theologian. His life influenced his work, and his work impacted the way he lived his life. It comes as no surprise then that Bonhoeffer's discourse on ethics is "strongly contingent and situation dependent"[74]

---

72. Ibid., 83.
73. Ibid., 65.
74. O'Gorman, "Telling the Truth," 225.

and, as we saw, shaped by a Christocentric theological ontology. What this essay has highlighted is that "Bonhoeffer's Christological social ontology is the basis for his discourse on ethics" and that "responsible speech and actions depend upon seeing things from below," which lead "to an insistence on a dynamic and complex concept of the real."[75]

Furthermore, for Bonhoeffer, the foundation of ethics is Jesus Christ, as it is in and through Christ that the reality of God has entered the world and reconciled God and the world. With regards to truth-telling, Bonhoeffer was very critical of any "ethical theory" that would fail to confront evil directly. He also thought that not acting amounted to condoning evil. A person cannot preserve moral purity by withdrawing from conflicts, for this is morally irresponsible. For example, in his own life and through his analysis of the passion and death of Christ, Bonhoeffer showed that everyone who lives responsibly invariably becomes guilty and needs to accept this sort of guilt.[76] Ethics, for Bonhoeffer, rests on responsible human action in any given situation, and reliance on a theory destroys the whole enterprise of Christian ethics. Ultimately, in a *Grenzfall* situation, an individual ought not to "apply a principle that eventually will be shattered by reality anyway, but to discern what is necessary or 'commanded' in a given situation."[77]

Christ's silence in the face of his accusers and oppressors reveals something about the wisdom of God. We have seen that even though he dies according to the law as one accursed by God, Jesus fulfills the law since, as Bonhoeffer highlighted, it is the *false law* that his accusers are trying to uphold, and therefore in this specific context, it is a wrong verdict. This means that Jesus was not a blasphemer neither did he break the law of God. Therefore "Death," the last enemy (1 Cor. 15), had to let him go, as witnessed in the resurrection. In an ethics of responsibility, this means that the action of the responsible person has to be in "accord with reality," which springs from the vicarious representative action of Christ and the reality of the world's reconciliation with God as witnessed in Christ. It is in being united with Jesus Christ in a *covenantal bond*, "who sets the conscience free for

---

75. Ibid., 237.

76. See *DBWE* 6:282 where Bonhoeffer writes: "Those who in acting responsibly take on guilt—which is inescapable for any responsible person—place this guilt on themselves, not on someone else; they stand up for it and take responsibility for it. They do so not out of a sacrilegious and reckless belief in their own power, but in the knowledge of being forced into this freedom and of their dependence on grace in its exercise. Those who act out of free responsibility are justified before others by dire necessity [not]; before themselves they are acquitted by their conscience, but before God they hope only for grace." See also Christine Schliesser, *Everyone Who Acts Responsibly Becomes Guilty: The Concept of Accepting Guilt* (Louisville, KY: Westminster John Knox Press, 2008).

77. *DBWE* 4:221. While imprisoned in Tegel, Bonhoeffer expressed his reservation against truthfulness as a "principle"; see *DBWE* 8:157f.

the service of God and neighbour,"⁷⁸ that the freed conscience aligns itself with responsible action.⁷⁹

Telling the truth and carrying out responsible action require being bound to Christ because once Christ has become the believer's conscience, "the origin and goal of my conscience is not a law but the living God and the living human being as I encounter them in Jesus Christ."⁸⁰ What Bonhoeffer aims to communicate is the deeper truth about the responsibility and reality entailed in a life with Christ, which necessitate seeing questions about the nature of truthful speech and responsible human action in light of (1) the "unifying center"⁸¹ of the Chalcedonian formula— "the unity of the reality of God and the reality of the world established in Christ."⁸² In Christ, all human reality is assumed, and thus "it is ultimately only in and from Christ that it is possible to act in a way that is in accord with reality,"⁸³ and (2) the concept of conscience, expressed through the dual allegiance to both God and to neighbor. Only when "Jesus Christ has become my conscience"⁸⁴ do I live responsibly and "in accord with reality, to the claim of God and my neighbour."⁸⁵

From Bonhoeffer's perspective of the Christ-reality, there is a correspondence between truth-telling and fulfilling the law. Just as the one who "tells the truth cynically is lying,"⁸⁶ so too are those who fail to respond to Christ's call and have "dispensed themselves from following Jesus, who referred them back to the law"—they do not have "this better righteousness," and will therefore "not enter the kingdom of heaven."⁸⁷ For Bonhoeffer, an allegiance to the law detached from Christ, who lives in communion with God, would only mean a "disrupture of all bonds instead of being bound to him."⁸⁸ Christ-reality becomes the lens through

---

78. *DBWE* 6:279. For Bonhoeffer, "service of God and neighbor" is always responsible action, which is demonstrated by "the responsible taking on of another's guilt."

79. Ibid. Bonhoeffer writes: "The freed conscience aligns itself with the responsibility."

80. Ibid., 278.

81. Ibid. "Where Christ, true God and true human being, has become the unifying center of my existence, conscience in the formal sense still remains the call, coming from my true self, into unity with myself."

82. Ibid., 44.

83. Ibid., 224.

84. Ibid., 278.

85. See further ibid., 280: "I come into conflict with my responsibility that is grounded in reality when I refuse to become guilty of violating the principle of truthfulness for the sake of my friend, refusing in this case to lie energetically for the sake of my friend—and any attempt to deny that we are indeed dealing with lying here is once again the work of a legalistic and self-righteous conscience—refusing, in other words, to take on and bear guilt out of love for my neighbor. Here, as well, a conscience bound to Christ alone will most clearly exhibit its innocence precisely in responsibly accepting culpability."

86. *DBWE* 8:223.

87. *DBWE* 4:116.

88. Ibid., 118.

which we understand truth-telling and the fulfillment of the law, which is more than simply naming facts and living without sin. If a lie is a "contradiction of the word of God as it was spoken in Christ,"[89] then, breaking the law contradicts the way Christ lived a responsible life for God and neighbor. Ultimately, to tell the truth and fulfill the law, it is the *covenantal* notion of being bound to Christ that is required.[90]

---

89. *DBWE* 16:608.

90. Thanks are due to the Deutsche Forschungsgemeinschaft (DFG) for supporting my research fellowship and project on theodicy and Dietrich Bonhoeffer, including my attendance at the International Bonhoeffer Congress in 2020. This chapter was written in close conversation with my good friend Javier Garcia, who left us far too soon when he passed away just eighteen months after the Congress. It is with fond memories of our time spent together in South Africa that I dedicate this chapter to Javier.

Chapter 19

"DEZISION" AS A MODERN VERSION OF DOCETISM
DIETRICH BONHOEFFER'S DISCLOSURE OF THE HERETICAL CONTRAST IN CARL SCHMITT'S THEORY OF STATE

Karola Radler

The Problem of the Contrast

The theologian Dietrich Bonhoeffer's early 1933 claim that the heresy of *Docetism* had reemerged "though in a different form"[1] does not only assess the heretical nature of particular Protestant theologies, but it can be read also as a forceful rejection of the structural basis of the jurist Carl Schmitt's theory of state known as *Dezision* or Decisionism. In his 1922 book, *Political Theology*,[2] Schmitt, a professor of jurisprudence, located the problem of the juristic form of the modern state in "the contrast [*Gegensatz*] between subject and content of a decision, and the self-significance of the subject"[3] in an attached sense of personality and independence. In his search for solution, he developed and applied his sociological method of comparing the social structures of historic ages with the prevailing ideas of those eras. He concluded that Decisionism, the representation and implementation of sovereign decisions, fitted the demands that the secular period placed on the form for a state. A decade later in his 1933 lecture on *Christology*,[4] Bonhoeffer insisted that the church must reject as a form of negative Christology any theology that is grounded in a contrast (*Gegensatz*)[5] between idea and appearance, between

---

1. *DBWE* 12:336.
2. Carl Schmitt, *Political Theology: Four Chapters on the Concept of Sovereignty*, trans. Georg Schwab, 1985 (Chicago, IL: University of Chicago Press, 2005).
3. The original reads, "In dem Gegensatz von Subjekt und Inhalt der Entscheidung und in der Eigenbedeutung des Subjekts liegt das Problem der juristischen Form"; Carl Schmitt, *Politische Theologie*, 8th ed. based on the 2nd ed. (Berlin: Dunker & Humblot, 2004), 40; own translation.
4. *DBWE* 12:299–360, *DBW* 12:279–348.
5. *DBWE* 12:335; my own translation, replacing the translation in the official *DBWE* series of the German word *Gegensatz* as "opposition" with the more fitting word "contrast."

substance and individuality, and specifically the heresy of *Docetism*.[6] In view of salvation history, he reckoned that this heresy would remain as long as the philosophical presupposition about idea and appearance remains.[7] Bonhoeffer's analysis unfolded following his discussion of contemporary authors[8] who had positively assessed Schmitt's friend-enemy distinction in its relation to life and the Tree of Knowledge of the Creation story,[9] and had expressed interest in Schmitt's turn to dogma and theology.[10] The structures that Bonhoeffer's critique of a re-emerging, though altered, *docetic* heresy exposes in Schmitt's theory of state remain foundational issues for contemporary renegotiations of the distribution of power between populist personalities and democratic state structures.

Schmitt—the Structural Foundation for a Decisionist Modern State

In his 1928 *Verfassungslehre* (Constitutional Theory), Schmitt considered the modern state, which had developed in Germany during the nineteenth century and had become concretely manifest in the constitutional Weimar state of his time, to be seriously flawed due to its compromises and concomitant competitive nature regarding parliamentary and presidential leadership[11] as well as the attempted integration of liberalism and democracy.[12] Having already in the early years of the Weimar Republic diagnosed the problem as being located in the form of the state of the modern age, he responded by devising a methodological solution to the ongoing controversy on methods.[13] He applied his method of a "sociology of . . . concepts"[14] to the institutional form he detected in the structure of the Roman Catholic Church and theorized that combining this form with an analogy to the church's juristic spirit could solve the institutional problems of the state in a secular age.

---

6. Ibid., 338.
7. Ibid., 335–6.
8. *DBW* 12:169–73.
9. Wilhelm Stapel, *Der Christliche Staatsmann: Eine Theologie des Nationalismus*, 2nd ed. (Hamburg: Hanseatische Verlagsanstalt, 1932), 169–70.
10. Alfred de Quervain, *Das Gesetz des Staates: Wesen und Grenze der Staatlichkeit* (Berlin: Fuche, 1932), 13, 66 n.2.
11. Carl Schmitt, *Verfassungslehre*, 10th ed. (Berlin: Dunker & Humblot, 1989), 28–36, 338–53.
12. Carl Schmitt, *The Crisis of Parliamentary Democracy*, trans. Ellen Kenney (Cambridge, MA: MIT Press, 1985; Paperback, 1988).
13. Michael Stolleis, *A History of Public Law in Germany 1914–1945*, trans. Thomas Dunlop (Oxford: Oxford University Press, 2004), 139–45.
14. Schmitt, *Political Theology*, 44, specifically differentiates his "sociology of concepts" from a "sociology of juristic concepts." This difference he attributes to Max Weber's tracing of particular legal fields to theories developed by trained legal specialists.

Schmitt, convinced that his sociology of concepts provides the singular possibility for achieving scientific results, attached to his method a quality that transcends juristic conceptualizations, which are focused on only limited, immediate, practical interests.[15] Despite being generally in tune with the historicism of his intellectual context, attaining methodological results with his sociology of concepts rested on a particular view of history. Although he had launched already in his 1922 *Political Theology*[16] an understanding of history with his sociology of concepts in mind, he complemented and extended this view in his 1929 essay, "The Age of Neutralizations and Depoliticization."[17] For Schmitt, history is a forward moving trajectory on which a line-up of epochs is located each of which has a central domain of meaning and a matching elite. In response to conflict, the elite of each age's central domain creates a central idea which depoliticizes and neutralizes the conflict. But almost immediately new conflict arises and prompts the development of a new domain, elite, and idea for a new age. On the forward moving trajectory of history, this dynamic happens in a repetitive succession. With his sociology of concepts, Schmitt aimed at discovering "the basic, radically systematic structure" of the ages. Consequently, he investigates methodically the conceptual social structures and characteristic states of consciousness of the various epoch's respective domains and elites.[18] From this comparison, he infers that the social construction of a historical-political reality always finds a conceptual juristic structure that corresponds to the distinctive consciousness for its particular era.

Schmitt claims that his sociology of concepts revealed that "sovereignty" in the seventeenth century had found its basic, radically systematic structure in the institution of the monarchy which, in turn, corresponded to the general Western European consciousness of that time. The historical-political reality of the time found a juristic form "whose structure is in accord with the structure of metaphysical concepts."[19] Then monarchy was self-evident to that epoch's consciousness as democracy would be to a later epoch. He concludes that an epoch's metaphysical image of the world structurally has the same form as the political organization of that age because this form is easily understood as the appropriate one.[20] Thus, the presupposition of his radical conceptualization, attained through developing and applying a sociology of concepts, pushes into the metaphysical and theological[21] because it aims to establish sociological evidence

---

15. Ibid., 45.
16. Ibid., 46–8.
17. See the essay titled, "The Age of Neutralizations and Depoliticization," in Schmitt, *The Crisis*, 80–96.
18. Schmitt, *Political Theology*, 45.
19. Ibid., 46.
20. Ibid., 45–7.
21. Ibid., 46.

"of two spiritual but at the same time substantial identities."²² Therefore, a juristic structure of sovereignty demands that the historical-political status of the form corresponds to the consciousness of the epoch.

In his 1923 booklet, *Römischer Katholizismus und politische Form*²³ [*Roman Catholicism and Political Form*], Schmitt presents the juristic form that was in accordance with and could control the conflicts of the historical-political reality of the modern age. He asserts that in a secularized juristic form, the Roman Catholic Church provides a model for the modern state's demands for a basic, radically systematic structure of sovereignty and its decisionist, personalist character.²⁴ After monarchy and democracy, this matched the intellectual consciousness of the new modern age because the intellectual sphere had moved through a process of secularization from transcendence to immanence²⁵ which had made possible the transfer of the systematic structure of theological concepts into jurisprudential concepts and the theory of state. Conversely stated, this meant that "all significant concepts of the modern theory of state are secularized theological concepts."²⁶ For example, a transcendent God had turned into an immanent ruler, the miracle into the exception, and the omnipotent invisible person into the modern lawgiver. Also, the positive laws of the state acted now as *deus ex machina* and the loss of legitimacy signified a situation *ex nihilo*.²⁷ Applied to his contemporary political context of the failing processes of the Constitution amid civil unrest, economic calamity, and governmental infighting, this meant that the legitimacy of the Weimar state had vanished and given birth to a creative new political will and idea, emanating with a transformative decision from *ex nihilo*.²⁸

The process of secularization and the applied sociology of concepts meant, for Schmitt, that the institutional rationality of the Roman Catholic Church was not only transferrable to the modern state but also that as heir of Roman jurisprudence and with the pope insisting on being the papal state's sovereign,²⁹ it provided a new form for the state. In the contemporary age, due to the church's jurisprudential invention of the office of the pope, the pope stands between the church and the papal state and is tasked in personal, direct authority from Christ to represent the idea of God to the world.³⁰ The pope personifies an idea in the world similar to God's becoming man in historical reality for the purpose of mediating in Christ the idea of God to the world. The pope, the official representative, makes the

---

22. Ibid., 45.
23. Carl Schmitt, *Römischer Katholizismus und politische Form*, 5th ed. (Stuttgart: Klett-Cotta, 2008).
24. Schmitt, *Political Theology*, 48.
25. Ibid., 49–50.
26. Ibid., 36.
27. Ibid., 36, 38, 65–6.
28. Ibid., 32, 52.
29. Schmitt, *Römischer Katholizismus*, 31.
30. Ibid., 24.

invisible Christian idea visible.[31] Therefore, representation means that a publicly present being makes an invisible being existentially visible.[32] Just as in Christ so also in an official representative the idea was "becoming human" (*Mensch werden*), that is, divinity becomes personified in a human being.[33] Despite the successive changes in the office's occupants, the formal superiority over the material matters of human life that is bestowed on the representative office of the pope prevents it from becoming impersonal. Rather, the holder of the office carries a certain dignity that is grounded in Christ's personal mandate and the high value of the represented principle. The pathos of public authority and the represented inherent juristic spirit give the office holder a concrete personality.[34] This particular dignity of the personality in public office sets representation apart from any *Stellvertretung* of private law[35] in which a person of only limited authority simply acts in place of someone else.[36] The idea that the dignified personality of public office represents, according to Schmitt, is a unified idea conveying a content analogous to the Roman Catholic Church's *complexio oppositorum*, which unifies in dogma oppositional thought.[37] Overall, applying his sociology of concepts in combination with the theory of a transfer of transcendental substance into immanent jurisprudential secular content leads Schmitt to confer on a dignified official personality special significance and to let a personified jurisprudential-political idea become publicly represented in worldly reality. A subject of personality and an idea's content merge in deified official significance.

In the socio-political upheavals of his context of the 1920s, Schmitt intended to solve with his theory of state the issue of the Weimar Constitution's alternative types of leadership[38] in which parliamentary legislation conflicted with presidential commands by decree, that is, in which the form-principle of parliamentary responsibility contrasted with trust in a leader. He envisioned unifying these two form-principles.[39] This meant, for Schmitt, combining the parliamentary representation of a political program, developed either prior or subsequent to elections, with the basic democratic demand of an identity of the

---

31. Cf. Carl Schmitt, "The Visibility of the Church: A Scholastic Consideration," in *Roman Catholicism and Political Form*, trans. and annotated G. L. Ulmen (Westport, CT: Greenwood Press, 1996), 50, 52, 53.

32. Schmitt, *Verfassungslehre*, 209.

33. Schmitt, *Römischer Katholizismus*, 32, 36.

34. Cf. ibid., 24, 31, 36.

35. Ibid., 36; Schmitt, *Verfassungslehre*, 208–9.

36. Paras 164 to 181 *Bürgerliches Gesetzbuch* [Civil Code], Bundesministerium der Justiz und für Verbraucherschutz, https://www.gesetze-im-internet.de/bgb/BGB.pdf (accessed March 30, 2018).

37. Schmitt, *Römischer Katholizismus*, 11–12, 14.

38. Schmitt, *Verfassungslehre*, 342.

39. Ibid., 276.

ruler and the ruled, of the governed and those governing.[40] This objective could be accomplished by unifying representation and identity in an official leader[41] who embodies a political idea that was either developed post-election or consisted of an independent, personal program.

By 1933–4, in the context of the early National Socialist state, Schmitt rationalized that his institutional form for the modern state, developed on the basis of his sociology and transfer of concepts, was a type of jurisprudential thinking that fitted the decisionist *Führer*-state.[42] In such a state, a personality who authorizes the self to the significant position of a leader in a dignified office[43] could unite the two form-principles of legislative representation and responsibility, on the one hand, and trust, command, and identity, on the other hand. This official personality would represent the political program, the National Socialist idea, to an existential people who was of identical substance; a substance of national homogeneous equals, who, however, do not need to be of universal equal nature.[44] Once the homogeneity of the people, determined by differentiating between friend and enemy,[45] was joined to the formal institutions which were synchronized (*gleichschalten*)[46] to the leader, a form-identity with one final, absolute human figure, one *Gestalt*, would be achieved. This unconditional, personified identity, this unity of idea and form in the figure of a dignified, official representative personality, would provide a sovereign of self-significance as the basis for decisions on the time of action and the extent of authority.[47]

40. Carl Schmitt, Preface to the Second Edition (1926) of *The Crisis*, 14–16.

41. Schmitt, *Verfassungslehre*, 205.

42. Schmitt added this institutional type of juristic thinking to his previously identified impersonal normative and decisionist types in 1934. He understood the institutional type as superior to any decisionist type and denounced positivism as a degenerate decisionist type. However, after the *Röhm*-Putsch in mid-1934, in which he barely escaped with his life, Schmitt abandoned his idea that the National Socialist "revolutionary" idea became the foundational jurisprudential institutional essence (*Sinn*) for a new constitution. Instead, he turned to justifying the violence from an anti-Semitic attitude; Carl Schmitt, Preface to the Second Edition (1934) of *Political Theology*, 8; Carl Schmitt, *Über die drei Arten des rechtswissenschaftlichen Denkens*, 3rd ed. (Berlin: Duncker & Humblot, 2006).

43. Cf. Schmitt, *Politische Theologie*, 40.

44. Cf. Schmitt, *The Crisis*, 9–13.

45. Carl Schmitt, *The Concept of the Political*, trans. George Schwab, ex. ed. (Chicago, IL: University of Chicago Press, 1995; reprint 2007), 26; Schmitt, *Verfassungslehre*, 389.

46. Schmitt was one of the major contributors to the *Reichsstatthaltergesetz* (Act of Reichgovernance) which synchronized the provinces to the Reich. In April 1933, Schmitt declared that this Act was the new constitutional law; Carl Schmitt, *Das Reichsstatthaltergesetz* (Berlin: Heymann, 1933).

47. For Schmitt, the one with the highest non-derivative power "decides whether there is an emergency as well as what must be done to eliminate it." Schmitt, *Political Theology*, 6–7;

Overall, in Schmitt's vision of sovereignty and *Dezision* (Decisions), a dignified personality in the position of an official representative, a secularized pope-figure, embodies a superior, unified political idea in analogy to the dogma uniting *complexio oppositorum* of the Catholic Church for the purpose of overcoming the contrast between content, the idea, and subject by decisively establishing its own significance at a self-determined moment in time and with self-authorized jurisdiction.

Bonhoeffer—the Contrast within Negative Christology

Bonhoeffer perceived the 1933–4 efforts to extend to the ministry of the church the legislation that expelled civil servants of Jewish ancestry from public office as targeting the spiritual independence of the Protestant Church. For him, such an endeavor not only contested the continuity of God's Word in the church but also, most of all, amounted to persecution which necessitated a firm rejection without compromises. Interfering with the affairs of the church by synchronizing the church's constitution to the state's form posed a *status confessionis* in which "too much" law of the state presented a legalistic intrusion that robbed the "Christian faith of its right to proclaim its message."[48] This situation reminded Bonhoeffer of the intra-Lutheran period of the sixteenth century when a dispute *in casu confessionis* arose and was settled. Then the *Formula of Concord* had ascertained that matters of the gospel such as preaching, confession of faith, and theology always remained under the church's authority, independently of interferences from the state authorities. However, the external, usually indifferent matters of *adiaphora*, such as the order and practice of the church, permit compromises, except in times of persecution when they become more than just indifferent matters.[49] For Bonhoeffer, the state's demand of synchronization went beyond a matter of *adiaphora*. Thus, he joined the public discourse[50] on the limitations that state and church provide to each other[51] and theologically processed the developing political situation with a Christology that included a focus on the negative Christology of the heresy of *Docetism*.

Carl Schmitt, *Staat, Bewegung, Volk: Die Dreigliederung der politischen Einheit* (Hamburg: Hanseatische Verlagsanstalt, 1933), 41–2.

48. DBWE 12:364–6.

49. Michael DeJonge, *Bonhoeffer on Resistance: The Word against the Wheel* (Oxford: Oxford University Press, 2018), 91.

50. Karola Radler, "The Leibholz-Schmitt Connection's Formative Influence on Bonhoeffer's 1932–33 Entry into Public Theology," *Stellenbosch Theological Journal* 4, no. 2 (2018): 693.

51. DBWE 12:326–7, 294.

19. *"Dezision" as a Modern Version of Docetism*   245

Already in his 1927 *Sanctorum Communio*,⁵² which was originally inspired by the institution of the Roman Catholic Church,⁵³ Bonhoeffer had analyzed the Protestant Lutheran Church under the conditions of the Weimar Constitution's novel abolition of an official state-church.⁵⁴ Although prescribing to churches the juristic form of a corporation of public law, the Constitution left unclear the extent as to which the state retained its powers of supervision over the Protestant Church's legal and economic capacity regarding activities in the private law sector.⁵⁵ The general legal opinion understood the Constitution as guaranteeing the church's independent status which, at a minimum, excluded state interferences in the internal affairs of filling ecclesiastical positions or in spiritual matters of faith and dogma.⁵⁶

Bonhoeffer, analyzing the situation of the Lutheran Church within the parameters set by the Weimar Constitution concluded that despite being a public corporation the church was foremost a communal institution *sui generis* that centered spiritually on the person of Jesus Christ and is therefore to be characterized as "Christ existing as church community."⁵⁷ In the structurally collective form of *sui generis*, the empirical church was legally grounded in a novel combination of the already existing sociologically based juristic forms of community, society, and a federation of authentic rule with hierarchical structure.⁵⁸ For satisfying the demand that an association's capacity is built on a legal analogy to a person, Bonhoeffer

---

52. *DBWE* 1 was written in 1927 and published in 1930.

53. Bonhoeffer's 1924 diary confirms his fascination with the Roman Catholic Church; *DBWE* 9:82–109.

54. Article 137, para. 1 Weimar Constitution, in *Die deutschen Verfassungen des 19. und 20. Jahrhunderts*, ed. Horst Hildebrandt, 11th enl. ed. (Paderborn: Ferdinand Schöningh, 1979), 102.

55. "Religionsgesellschaften erwerben die Rechtsfähigkeit nach den allgemeinen Vorschriften des bürgerlichen Rechts" (Religious communities acquire their legal capacity according to the regulations of the civil law) and "Die Religionsgesellschaften bleiben Körperschaften des öffentlichen Rechts, soweit sie solche bisher waren" (The religious communities remain corporations of public law insofar as they have been such previously); Article 137, para 4 and 5 Weimar Constitution, in Hildebrandt, *Verfassungen*, 102.

56. Gerhard Anschütz, *Die Verfassung des Deutschen Reichs vom 11. August 1919: Ein Kommentar für Wissenschaft und Praxis*, 10th ed. (Berlin: Stilke, 1929), 550–1, 556–7.

57. *DBWE* 1:121; this description of the church is used throughout *Sanctorum Communio*. For a specifically Lutheran analysis of Bonhoeffer's use of the concept of person, see Michael P. DeJonge, *Bonhoeffer's Theological Formation: Berlin, Barth, and Protestant Theology* (Oxford: Oxford University Press, 2012), 83–100.

58. *DBWE* 1:264, 266. Green also has noted: "ultimately Bonhoeffer argues that the structural, sociological distinctiveness of the church consists in the fact that it *combines* characteristics of *Gemeinschaft, Gesellschaft,* and *Herrschaftsverband*"; Clifford J. Green, *The Sociality of Christ and Humanity: Dietrich Bonhoeffer's Early Theology 1927–1933* (Missoula, MT: Scholars Press, 1972), 94 n.46; emphasis in the original.

centered the collective institution of the church on the spiritual capacity which the person of Jesus Christ extends to the church-community.

From the position of a Protestant Church grounded in a collective as well as personal-spiritual characterization, Bonhoeffer warned about adopting a political attitude of dutiful, unconditional obedience to the messianic idea of a leader who uses dominance and his personality to forge a collective extreme individualism.[59] Idealizing and charging this human leader with ultimate hope would not only dismiss the centrality and significance of the person of Jesus Christ, but would dissolve also social structures and communal reciprocal responsibility. Obedience within the church as well as within the state was owed to God, and faith is not a guarantee of obedience as it was the case in the Catholic Church.[60] Demanding the synchronization of the institution of the Lutheran Church to this glorified messianic figure of the leader and his political idea of persecuting by exclusion meant stretching with too much law beyond matters of indifferent *adiaphora* into internal spiritual matters that were defined by faith in the person of Jesus Christ.

With the state not being the sole "place of holiness,"[61] Bonhoeffer in his early 1933 lecture on *Christology* turned to forms of negative Christology, including the heresy of *Docetism*,[62] which provide undeniable, indispensable limitations for assertions about Christ. The limitations test in a negative way efforts to comprehend "the incomprehensibility of the person of Jesus Christ."[63] In *Docetism* which, according to Bonhoeffer, continued to be present in his time,[64] the idea of God and God's incarnation in Christ are abstracted from each other. In this heretic "distinction between idea and appearance,"[65] Christ's humanity is conceptualized as God's means of talking to human beings. Christ's incarnation, God's human nature, is turned into the appearance of God in the sense of "becoming human" (*Mensch werden*)[66] that excludes "the essence of God's nature."[67] The appearance of the Godhead in history is only incidental and the idea is the substance, that is, Christ is the carrier of religious ideas in the form of religious personality.[68] Without the incomprehensibility of the humanity in the incarnated God, God would not be truly human but would remain an idea.[69] By eliminating Christ's

---

59. Cf. *DBWE* 12:277–8.

60. Cf. ibid., 277.

61. See the book by Bonhoeffer's brother-in-law, Gerhard Leibholz, *Die Auflösung der Liberalen Demokratie in Deutschland und das autoritäre Staatsbild* (Munich: Duncker & Humblot, 1933), 74.

62. *DBWE* 12:331–8; *DBW* 12:315–22.

63. *DBWE* 12:331–2.

64. Ibid., 333.

65. Ibid., 338.

66. Cf. ibid., 334.

67. Ibid., 332.

68. Ibid., 335, 336.

69. Ibid., 337.

human nature, individuality, that which constitutes the person, disappears too. Most of all, negating Christ's human nature in this way prevents redemption itself; that is, prevents freeing the human being to live as an individual person.[70]

Thus, the heresy of *Docetism* forestalls redemption by differentiating between human nature and the individuality of a person. And the most dangerous version of *Docetism* involves, according to Bonhoeffer, turning God's appearance in Jesus into a principle of necessity in which Christ is the necessary form, the needed *Gestalt*, for the idea to appear in history.[71] In an understanding of history as the carrier of meta-historic religious ideas, Christ appears simply as the representative (*Vertreter*) who embodies such an idea in history.[72] God's humanity as a necessary derivative of God misses and reduces the incomprehensibility of His true humanness to an idea of the human being.[73] Instead, God was not merely realizing a human principle but truly "became human" (*Mensch geworden*) in an event within history. Therefore, "[e]verything depends on Jesus' existence in history."[74]

With redemption being conditioned on the real existence of Jesus Christ in this world, Bonhoeffer asserted that the historic form of Jesus was subject to the dual aspects of history and faith. The existence of Jesus in history must be understood from the perspective of God's eternity and God's resurrection.[75] From rereading the story of creation in the book of Genesis,[76] Bonhoeffer saw history not as a linear trajectory but as a rather circular movement from God to God, which revolves around the Tree of Knowledge and the Tree of Life, around the fall into sin and God's grace in Jesus Christ. Human history thus lives between promise and fulfillment with Christ as its boundary and middle.[77] The Fall tells the "history of humanity with God,"[78] and is the "event at the beginning of history, before history, beyond history, and yet in history."[79] By eating from the Tree of Knowledge, which turned out to be the tree of death, the human being fell into

---

70. Ibid., 334.
71. Ibid., 337.
72. *DBW* 12:320.
73. *DBWE* 12:337.
74. Ibid., 336.
75. Ibid., 331.
76. In the winter of 1932/33, Bonhoeffer taught the course, "Creation and Sin," at Berlin University and it was published in 1937 as "Creation and Fall: A Theological Exposition of Genesis 1-3," *DBWE* 3.
77. *DBWE* 12:325; Instead of translating the German term "*Mitte*" as "center," as in the official translations of the *DBWE* series, I opted for the direct translation, "middle." This allows for a spatial as well as a temporal meaning in the sense of "middle of time and place," and relates immediately to the term "*Mittler*" (mediator), which Bonhoeffer uses in relation to Christ's *Stellvertretung* on the cross.
78. *DBWE* 3:72.
79. Ibid., 782.

the life of death in Adam.⁸⁰ In the Adam-event of the Fall, Adam's dominion changed from the Garden of Eden to the world,⁸¹ and thus did also change the identity as the earth's ruler. As *sicut deus*, like God, the now deified human being absorbed God's right over life and death and acted out of own resources⁸² and an unlimited ego.⁸³

However, the Fall foreshadowed the Christ-event of the cross in which the Tree of Life and the Tree of Knowledge were transposed from the Garden of Eden to the middle⁸⁴ of the reality of time on earth, into the history of this world. At this decisive moment in time, Christ becomes the new center of human existence, history, and nature.⁸⁵ The cross holds the tension between curse and promise,⁸⁶ God's incarnation and Jesus' crucifixion, God's divinity and His humanity. In this extraordinary moment of the tension between God's decision and Jesus' *Stellvertretung*⁸⁷ for humanity, transcendence meets immanence. In the light of a this-worldly existence, Jesus the incarnated God "'became human' [*Mensch geworden*] as we became human."⁸⁸ Here, the reality of the person of Jesus Christ calls a new creation to life⁸⁹ by changing with a simple and direct act of faith⁹⁰ once again the identity of the human being.⁹¹ The human being is con-formed (*gleichgestalten*)⁹² from being like God, *sicut deus*, to before and with God, to aligning to the form (*Gestalt*) of the God-human Jesus Christ. In the middle of historic time, God offers redemption through faith in Christ and fulfills his promise of

---

80. *DBWE* 1:107–9.
81. Cf. *DBWE* 3:83, 89.
82. Ibid., 113.
83. Returning in the 1940s to this topic, Bonhoeffer asserted that the conscience of the natural human being who knows about good and evil is the ego's attempt to justify itself to God; *DBWE* 6:277.
84. See n. 77.
85. *DBWE* 12:324–7.
86. *DBWE* 3:131–6.
87. The *DBWE* series translates the German term "*Stellvertretung*" as "vicarious representative action." However, in the course of the nineteenth century's constitutional developments in German jurisprudence, the concept of public representation and the private law's concept of *Stellvertretung* acquired a different meaning and function. Because the English language does not have an equivalent term for *Stellvertretung* without taking recourse to the word "representation" in one form or another, I maintain Bonhoeffer's *Stellvertretung* to prevent any confusion between the political term and the private law term. For example, Schmitt clearly differentiates between both terms; see n. 35.
88. *DBWE* 12:353; emphasis and German translation added.
89. Cf. *DBWE* 3:92; 6:158; 12:316.
90. *DBWE* 12:259.
91. Cf. *DBWE* 10:406–7.
92. *DBWE* 6:94, 322.

restoring human life, all human beings,[93] to the wholeness of life in Christ.[94] Thus, in the reality of Christ's cross is revealed God's Word of promise for upholding and reconciling humanity, and it continues to exist as permanent presence in the proclamation of the church in the middle of historic time.[95]

However, faith in the instance of the cross is one of subjectivity and at the same time a moment without future and past.[96] For Bonhoeffer, this moment in which nothingness is present differs from the moment of *ex nihilo*, which belongs to God alone and describes the "utterly unique"[97] primeval beginning. *Ex nihilo* is a formless, empty, deep dark nothing that waits on God and exists only in God's action of creation.[98] In God's thinking, in complete freedom,[99] He summons His good creation out of nonbeing and prevents it from falling back into nonbeing by willing to uphold and preserve it.[100] Therefore, the reality of every moment is from God. And fallen, sinful humankind, stuck in the "anxiety-causing middle"[101] of history, is unable to think beyond this beginning *ex nihilo*. Humankind neither knowing the end nor the beginning, but coming from the beginning and compelled to move to the end,[102] mistakes in an ultimate attempt at explaining its philosophical thinking as the beginning of a creative nothingness.[103] Instead, God's *creatio ex nihilo* is the absolute beginning of theology beyond which no human being can venture with creativeness, philosophical reasoning, or reflection.

For Bonhoeffer, due to the interconnection of the intentionality of God's promise from beyond time with the fact of the cross within history, that is, the connection of the Tree of Knowledge that leads to spiritual death with the tree of new life in Christ, Jesus Christ cannot be reduced to a "transient bearer of eternal values and ideas."[104] Instead, only in direct and simple faith in God's decision and promise can be heard the incarnation's tension of the incomprehensibility of God's divinity and humanity. This ultimate mystery of the One who "became human," the incarnated humiliated One on the cross, is the One of divinity, humanity, and the content of the Word. As Bonhoeffer clarifies, this is what is captured in the *Formula of Concord*'s two states of Jesus Christ, the state of humiliation (*status*

---

93. *DBWE* 1:120–1.
94. Ibid., 124.
95. Cf. ibid., 153.
96. *DBWE* 6:128.
97. *DBWE* 3:34.
98. Ibid., 37.
99. Ibid., 32, 38.
100. Cf. ibid., 42–3, 45, 76.
101. Ibid., 30.
102. Ibid., 28.
103. Ibid., 33.
104. *DBWE* 10:457.

exinanitionis) and the state of exultation (*status exaltationis*),[105] and in the concept of identity of substance,[106] which tells of Christ's person being God's revelation.[107]

Bonhoeffer's analysis of the heresy of *Docetism* and his assertion of the Trinity revises his late-1920s view of faith as presenting a point of contact for "the personalities of God and of man,"[108] of God's "self-revelation of personality,"[109] and of faith as an idea directed toward the primacy of God's authority over against the content of His Word.[110] Bonhoeffer's thoughts on authoritative personality and on content being secondary to authority gave way to the Word, standing under God's decision and being revealed in the *Gestalt* (form) of Christ who con-forms (*gleich-gestalten*) the human being. The Trinity dissolves any differentiation between God's Word, the content, which is incarnated in Jesus Christ's divine-human nature, the subject, and with it any thoughts of substance as interchangeable idea, the negation of individuality in human nature, and God's appearance as personality. Because, as Bonhoeffer affirmed in the early 1940s in his *Ethics*, the revealed Word in Jesus Christ is the reality as such, the Real One;[111] the Word exists and is thus present in the world. The presence in history of the Three-in-One of God, Jesus, and the Word clarifies the impossibility of representing God's Word as an idea because, for Bonhoeffer, only that which is not present can be represented.[112] Instead, the divine miracle of "the one who is present"[113] reveals God's redemptive Word of reconciling all human beings of faith to the Trinitarian God in the God-human's *Stellvertretung* on the cross.

Understanding the negative Christology of the heresy of *Docetism* makes comprehensible the idea that the incomprehensible mystery of the Incarnation presents the limitation to abstracting the substance, the content, of God's Word from an appearance in history of God's human existence in the form (*Gestalt*) of Jesus and his redemptive *Stellvertretung*. With God's Word of salvation from beyond time but existing in the reality of time in the person of Christ as the spiritual core of the church, a human personality, a leader of a state cannot visibly represent to the world in his human appearance a political idea analogous to God's Word and existence.

---

105. Ibid., 12:345–7.

106. Ibid., 350.

107. Ibid., 351. Bonhoeffer also referred to Luther's position that the one nature of Jesus' divinity and humanity prevents a deified human being; DBWE 12:346–7.

108. DBWE 10:459–60.

109. Ibid., 456.

110. Such early thoughts, although published in 1932, go back to Bonhoeffer's university writings of the 1920s, "Concerning the Christian Idea of God"; DBWE 10:451 n.1.

111. DBWE 6:49, 263.

112. DBWE 12:318.

113. Ibid., 322.

The Inherent Heresy of the Contrast

Bonhoeffer as well as Schmitt set out to assess and define the intellectual and institutional situation of the church and the state, respectively, and their relation to each other within modernity and under the parameters of the Weimar Constitution. Parallel to the changing political conditions toward an authoritarian, increasingly totalitarian, political leadership, Bonhoeffer's theology developed in diametrical opposition to Schmitt's jurisprudentially corroborated ideology. While Bonhoeffer moved from an ideological moment in time to a divinely manifested redemptive history, Schmitt moved in the reverse direction from a model and method of a religiously underpinned theory of history to an ideology for his immediate context. In his theological efforts, Bonhoeffer used the semantic tools of setting the "*gleich-gestalten*" (con-forming) of humanity to Christ's form over against Schmitt's "*gleich-schalten*" (synchronizing) of citizens to institutional form. Bonhoeffer redirected Schmitt's thought of the "*Mensch werden*" (becoming human) of an idea in historical reality to God as "*Mensch geworden*" (became human) in an event in the middle of worldly reality. And the meaning of the word "*Gestalt*" (form) is moved from Schmitt's juristic form of the institutional leader to the form of Jesus Christ.

Bonhoeffer as well as Schmitt located the problem of their time in the relation of content to subject but in reverse functions. Schmitt needed their abstraction from each other for making the self-significance of the sovereign possible and rationalized this separation with analogies to theology and the Roman Catholic pope and office. Bonhoeffer, however clarified that theology makes this abstraction impossible. This impossibility of a separation carries through into the reality of the present world due to faith, not in a self-assuming sovereign but in Christ's continued presence in the church and in the rational comprehension of faith in His incomprehensible mystery.

For Bonhoeffer, the negative Christology of the heresy of *Docetism* functions as a test for the positive Christology of the Incarnation and the Trinity and thus for repudiating any form of abstracting an idea or content from appearance as it was already pronounced in the *Formula of Concord* and in the attached concept of identity of substance. And *Docetism* reveals the heresy within the ideology of the context of his time which Schmitt masqueraded as a political theology. The *docetic* abstraction between idea and appearance is repeated in the separation of a political program, understood in analogy to a Christ-idea and consolidated in a dogmatic *complexio oppositorum*, from a human subject of dignified personality who is deified through an analogy to a Christ-authorized pope and his office for the purpose of representing and saving with sovereign decisions a synchronized identity of a select group of people. Bonhoeffer argues that an official representative who places the self into a significant position cannot heal a contrast between content and subject with the decisive implementation of an idea at a self-determined moment in time. The contrast cannot be unified with a human decision *ex nihilo* that creates and acts on a new idea, political program, or an ideology in a situation of nothingness in the switch between domains and elites on a forward moving trajectory of history, as Schmitt's theory states. Rather, true unity comes, according to Bonhoeffer, through differentiating God's decision *ex nihilo* from the situation of the redemptive nothingness on the cross. This healing redemption God had promised and already provided for from beyond time and human history and fulfilled in the middle of history with the only one of significance, Jesus Christ.

Recognizing the heresy of *Docetism* within his contemporary context preserves for Bonhoeffer the question of "who" over the question of "how."[114] Schmitt's "how" of model and method which includes analogy, idea, personality and representation, and his demand for exclusion in a synchronized church endanger confessing the "who," the person of Jesus Christ and his redemptive, unifying *Stellvertretung*, and therefore amount to a persecution beyond the usually indifferent state of the matters of *adiaphora*. Confessing the unity of idea and appearance in the reality of the God-human Jesus Christ as the only person of significance uncompromisingly overrides any interaction between subject and content that is forcibly achieved by the decisions of a self-significant politician. Bonhoeffer's insistence that in "every abstract doctrine of God and in every concept of redemption, there is at bottom the same presupposition, namely, the contrast (*Gegensatz*) between idea and appearance"[115] underlines the perpetual need of remaining aware of the dangers of the abstracted contrast wherever an absolutized state official claims a position *sicut deus*. Bonhoeffer argues that the structural contrast beneath Schmitt's secularized theory of transposed theological assumptions contains a fundamental theological error. Being mindful of the abstracted contrast between content and subject that was already embedded in the heresy of *Docetism* sharpens the awareness of any hidden danger posed by rising populism and nationalism.

---

114. Ibid., 323, 353.

115. Ibid., 335; own translation of the German word *Gegensatz* as "contrast." See n. 3 above.

Chapter 20

BONHOEFFER, HUMAN RIGHTS, AND THE NATURAL LAW TRADITION

Jens Zimmermann

Introduction

One of the most remarkable features of Bonhoeffer's later theology is his recovery of *the natural* in the *Ethics* fragment "Natural Life."[1] This topic is essential to the development of Bonhoeffer's theology because it demonstrates his continuing exploration of the Incarnation's radical ramifications for an appreciation of life in the world.[2] When assessing the development of his theology, commentators commonly stress the uniqueness of Bonhoeffer's interest in the *natural*, for a Lutheran—or even a Protestant—theologian. Moreover, Protestant Bonhoeffer scholars also point out that in contrast to Roman Catholic theology, Bonhoeffer derives the creational dynamics of the natural from Christology rather than from natural law. Eberhard Bethge represents this view with his conclusion that "Bonhoeffer opened the way for a rediscovery (so rare on Protestant soil) of a theology of the 'natural,' but one derived, not from the *analogia entis* as in Roman Catholic theology or from natural law, but from the doctrine of justification and Christology."[3]

In this chapter, I aim to show that Bonhoeffer's recovery of the natural is not "so rare on Protestant soil," neither does it contrast as sharply with Catholic thought as Bethge implies. In fact, Bonhoeffer's recovery of the natural is part of a broadly shared interest in this topic among Protestants and Catholics in Europe, from the 1930s onward, who explored natural law and human rights in order to reestablish a humane, law-based, secular society on Christian principles after the atrocities of the First and the Second World Wars. My point is not to diminish Bonhoeffer's unique contribution to natural theology and human rights but to pinpoint more

---

1. *DBWE* 6:171–218.

2. See Jens Zimmermann, *Dietrich Bonhoeffer's Christian Humanism* (Oxford: Oxford University Press, 2019), 291–329.

3. Eberhard Bethge, *Dietrich Bonhoeffer: A Biography* (Minneapolis, MN: Fortress Press, 2000), 719.

precisely the nature and context of his contribution. I will try to accomplish this goal in two steps—first by contextualizing Bonhoeffer's recovery of the natural within the broader conversation about natural law among Catholic and Protestant intellectuals in the 1930s and 1940s. This broader view will demonstrate that Bonhoeffer is by no means the only Protestant theologian working on natural law and human rights in his time. Rather, Bonhoeffer's efforts correspond to a larger, international revival of natural law by Catholic and Protestant thinkers who sought to establish a secular social order for postwar Europe based on a Christian foundation. The central anthropological component of this foundation was the dignity of the human person as a spiritual being and the recovery of natural law theory as common ground for universal human rights. In a second, much briefer part, I will touch on two unique contributions of Bonhoeffer to the Protestant side of this larger project on human rights in the trans-war period.

Rise of Christian Human Rights

My contextualization of Bonhoeffer within the broader history of human rights discourse relies heavily on the recent work of the historian Samuel Moyn. In his book *Christian Human Rights*, Moyn shows that the language integral to the 1948 UN Declaration of Universal Human Rights is a Christian invention of the 1930s and 1940s. In making this argument, Moyn opposes two common historical mistakes about the origin of human rights. The first misreading is the secularist claim that universal human rights resulted from the victory of secular liberalism over Christianity. He also rejects a second misinterpretation made by Christians who claim human rights as an organic, progressive development from medieval to modern Christianity. Correcting both the secularist and organicist[4] Christian reading of history, Moyn shows that modern human rights language originated when politically alert Christians saw the need for shoring up universal human rights against the rising communist and fascist regimes during the early twentieth century. Catholic theologians like Jacques Maritain led the way by combining a personalist conception of human dignity with natural law theory to establish inviolable human rights. Moyn argues that this relatively recent Christian origin of human rights language is often conveniently ignored: "Forgotten now, the spiritual and often explicitly religious philosophy of the human person was the conceptual means through which continental Europe initially incorporated human rights—and, indeed, became the homeland of the notion for several decades."[5]

---

4. An organicist view of history claims that human rights were already fully contained within Christian thought and just had to be drawn out over time. A secularist account depicts the development of human rights as a departure from or watering down of religious convictions.

5. Moyn, *Christian Human Rights* (Philadelphia, PA: University of Pennsylvania Press, 2015), 67.

Of course, the correlation between natural law and human rights has a long history from Greek Stoic thought to its adaptation and transformation in the early Christian church, from claims for religious freedom during the Protestant Reformation all the way to Thomas Jefferson's "inherent and inalienable rights" of every human being as created equal by God.[6] However, in none of these constructs does the dignity and equality of the human person play the central role it occupies before, during, and just after the Second World War. Only around the 1930s do we begin to see language of personhood used as a foundation for human dignity and rights. This new development was the response of Catholic and Protestant Christians to the political disasters of the twentieth century, which they blamed on the West's departure from Judeo-Christian metaphysics and anthropology. For Christian thinkers like Romano Guardini and Jacques Maritain on the Catholic side as well as George Bell, Emil Brunner, and Bonhoeffer on the Protestant side, communist and fascist totalitarian regimes were consequences of the secular liberalist ideal of human autonomy. In their view, unmooring the self from a personal God and disregarding the principles within creation required for human flourishing explained not only the failure of secular liberalism to control the excesses of individualism, technology, and capitalism, but also the rise of totalitarian communist and fascist regimes. The Christian response to this failure of modernity then was to revive an anthropology that emphasized personal dignity with its attendant human rights. Only Christian personalism, they argued, could achieve a proper balance between individuality and community.

The first official use of this human rights language occurred in the encyclical, *Mit brennender Sorge* [*With Burning Concern*], which Pope Pius XI addressed to German bishops who had complained about Hitler's violation of the concordat. Pius warns that the Nazis, in their nationalist obsession, disregarded "the basic fact that the human being as a person possesses rights he holds from God," which should never be sacrificed for the greater good of society.[7] The Nazis also overlooked the fact that "the real common good ultimately takes its measure from man's nature, which balances personal rights and social obligations."[8] Trampling

---

6. See here the critical cultural history of human rights by Lynn Hunt, *Inventing Human Rights: A History* (London: W.W. Norton, 2007). Hunt's point is that these rights were not so evident after all but required social experience and practices for their development. Hans Joas makes a very similar point in his recent study, *The Sacrality of the Person: A New Genealogy of Human Rights* (Washington, DC: Georgetown University Press, 2013). Curiously, Hunt's brief foray into modern human rights developments completely leaves out the decades of Christian development Moyn documents as crucial for the modern human rights language and personalism that shaped the UN Declaration. On this, see Hunt, *Human Rights*, 196–210.

7. Pope Pius XI, *Mit brennender Sorge*, Libreria Editrice Vaticana, §30, https://www.vatican.va/content/pius-xi/en/encyclicals/documents/hf_p-xi_enc_14031937_mit-brennender-sorge.html.

8. Pius XI, *Mit brennender Sorge*, §30.

on human rights in the name of the common good, Pius concludes, will end up destroying society because the divinely ordained purpose of true community is to enable the best possible human development of each person.[9]

In a subsequent anti-communist encyclical, Pius draws on natural human rights to argue against the failed anthropology of secular humanism responsible for the rise of totalitarian regimes. In other words, the idea of modern human rights is unthinkable without the kind of cultural analysis of a "Christian occident" Bonhoeffer offers in the *Ethics* fragment "Inheritance and Decay." The Protestant Reformers' insistence on freedom of conscience had intensified the Judeo-Christian insight of individual rights against coercion by church or state, but this freedom was then secularized by the French Revolution, which in turn gave rise to two distortions of these rights, namely rationalist individualism and totalitarian collectivism.[10]

Bonhoeffer was familiar with this kind of historical analysis from his reading of the historian Gerhard Ritter (1888–1967), whose work Bonhoeffer consulted when writing *Ethics* and who was himself an important figure in the Kreisauer circle working for a postwar social order. German thinkers like Karl Jaspers, Romano Guardini, and Bonhoeffer's British friend George Bell offered similar assessments,[11] and Bonhoeffer certainly could have gleaned an analogous interpretation of modern culture from his reading in the 1930s of the premier philosopher of natural law and human rights, Jacques Maritain. Maritain's book on Christian humanism (which Bonhoeffer owned and apparently read), translated as *Die Zukunft der Christenheit* (1938), combines natural law theory with a personalist view of the human being to advance a this-worldly Christianity that promoted Christian humanism for secular society in a world that had come of age.

Maritain's work was not decisive for German Christians,[12] but was quite influential for the Anglo-American theologians with whom Bonhoeffer had been in contact since his time as youth secretary of the ecumenical movement. As the intellectual historian Terence Renaud has shown, the ecumenical Protestants who gathered at the famous Oxford Conference of 1937 and whose efforts resulted in forming the World Council of Churches at Amsterdam in 1948 were integral to shaping the language of the UN Declaration. According to Renaud, ecumenical

---

9. Ibid., §35.

10. *DBW* 6:115. All translations from the German text are my own.

11. A very similar cultural analysis is offered in the 1940 book by George Bell, *Christianity and World Order* (London: Penguin, 1941).

12. See Heinz Hürten, "Der Einfluß Jacques Maritains auf das politische Denken Deutschlands," *Jahrbuch for Christliche Sozialwissenschaften* 26 (1985): 25–39. Hürten argues that the translation of Maritain's *Integral Humanism* appeared at a time "when the domestic and foreign political situation was not conducive for a discussion of his ideas in public. To what extent they were discussed in secret is hard to determine"; Ibid., 34. We know, however, that Bonhoeffer and especially his friend, Franz Hildebrand, were familiar with this book.

Protestants like Bonhoeffer's friend, George Bell, who was a leading voice in the Oxford meeting, offered a crucial response "to the mid-century crisis of man: a theological anthropology that linked individual human persons together in community with each other and with a transcendent universal principle, God."[13] Natural law, human dignity based on a Christian view of personhood, and human rights laid the theological foundation for the anthropology that undergirds our current human rights discourse. Bonhoeffer was well familiar with this conversation.

An important link between the ecumenical recovery of natural law and the German Protestant conversation about natural law and human rights is the work of Emil Brunner whose personal attendance of the Oxford Conference was also of great influence. From his earliest embrace of dialectical theology, Brunner pursued personalism and Christian natural law theory to oppose, well before Bonhoeffer,[14] the abstract anthropologies of idealism together with modern individualism. Brunner's insistence on the need for natural law provoked strong opposition from Karl Barth. In their famous exchange on the topic of natural theology in 1934, Brunner argues that the political situation demands Protestantism's recovery of "theological thinking which tries to account for the phenomena of natural life."[15]

Brunner concedes to Barth that the doctrine of natural theology bears in it the potential for dangerous and destructive outcomes. Roman Catholicism falsely equated natural law with nature, a natural revelation accessible to reason. The result is an "*unrefracted theologia naturalis* . . . a self-sufficient rational system," a crystal clear book of natural moral law, entirely accessible to a human rationality that is unimpeded by sin.[16] He also admits that in the nineteenth century, a distorted understanding of natural theology had allowed the church to slide into liberal Protestantism and that Barth's sharp opposition of nature and grace had served as an important "counterweight to dangerous aberrations" of such strictly cultural Christianity.[17] Moreover, under the contemporary Nazi rule, once again, "a false theology derived from nature," namely the nationalist

---

13. Terence Renaud, "Human Rights as Radical Anthropology: Protestant Theology and Ecumenism in the Transwar Era," *The Historical Journal* 60, no. 2 (2017): 493–518, 517.

14. Brunner defends Christian personalism as early as 1924 in Emil Brunner, *Mysticism and the Word* (*Die Mystik und das Wort*, Tübingen: Mohr, 1924).

15. Emil Brunner, "Nature and Grace," in *Natural Theology: Comprising "Nature and Grace" by Professor Dr. Emil Brunner and the Reply "No!" by Dr. Karl Barth*, trans. Peter Fraenkel (London: Centenary Press, 1937), 20.

16. "But in Roman Catholicism, the *lumen naturale* is co-extensive with nature itself. Or, to put it differently: the *theologia naturalis* is for the Reformers dialectical, for Roman Catholicism undialectical. . . . Thus, natural knowledge is freed from the twilight that lies upon it in the doctrine of the Reformers. There is no antinomy in it [Roman Catholic natural theology]. A dichotomy has taken the place of the antinomy"; Brunner, "Nature and Grace," 46.

17. Ibid., 59.

theology of the German Christians, was "also at the present time threatening the Church to the point of death."[18] Yet in this case, Brunner argues, Barth's nature-grace opposition turns out to be counterproductive because his uncompromising rejection of any creational basis for ethics deprives Christians of a platform for public reasoning about the common good and social responsibility.[19] Therefore, Brunner concludes that "it is the task of our theological generation to find the way back to a true *theologia naturalis*," as the ground for public ethics[20]. This is exactly Bonhoeffer's argument for recovering the natural—Protestantism has allowed nature to "sink into the night of sin,"[21] thereby cutting itself off from the shared ground of natural life with its inherent principles for human flourishing. Without such common ground for public ethics, Christians in a secular society have no publicly recognizable argument against inhumane policies and practices.[22]

Brunner also anticipates the path Bonhoeffer takes in his *Ethics* to recover the natural, namely the natural law theory of Luther and Calvin. Brunner argues that the Reformers taught a Christologically grounded natural law theory in which the principles of creation had been obscured by sin and had "been made known afresh by Christ as ordinances of creation."[23] Hence, Brunner claims (as does Bonhoeffer) that nature is not an open book of revelation about human identity, but it requires interpretation in light of Christ—more precisely, in light of Christ's revelation of who we are in relation to God. Brunner argues that Calvin and Luther believed that divine ordinances like marriage or the state were not simply restraints required by human sinfulness, but they positively reveal creational principles about our interdependent, communal nature.

Brunner's subsequent theological works[24] all explored in detail natural law, personalism, and human rights, including the basic principle of distributive justice "to each his own" (*suum cuique distribuere*) that was also central to Bonhoeffer's recovery of natural rights.[25] In fact, at the time Bonhoeffer was writing his *Ethics*, Brunner was also composing a detailed account of Protestant natural law and

---

18. Ibid. In his response, Barth, of course, claimed Jean Calvin's position as his own.
19. Ibid., 58–9.
20. Ibid., 59
21. *DBW* 12:164
22. Brunner, "Nature and Grace," 59–60.
23. Ibid., 39. The Reformers, he concludes, had a *dialectical* natural law theory in which even Christian civic laws were *at best* an approximation to the truth.
24. *Der Mittler*, 1927 (Christology); idem., *Gott und Mensch: Vier Untersuchungen zum personenhaften Sein*, 1930; idem., *Der Mensch im Widerspruch*, 1937 (theological anthropology); and idem., *Das Gebot und die Ordnungen: Entwurf einer protestantisch-theologischen Ethik*, 1932 (Christian ethics).
25. Brunner also read Bonhoeffer's work, as shown by a reference in *Das Gebot und die Ordnungen* (*The Divine Imperative*) to Bonhoeffer's personalist and relational conception of the human subject in *Act and Being*: "On this point compare the instructive work of

human rights, which was published in 1943 as *Gerechtigkeit* [*Justice and the Social Order*].[26] In this work, Brunner continues to argue for "orders of creation" that are not merely negative restraints to curb evil but positive principles commensurate with human nature as created by God. Aware of its abuse by German Christians, Brunner hangs on to the problematic term "orders of creation" because he believes that the term "orders of preservation" (the term Bonhoeffer eventually adopts) reduces such orders to restraints for evil rather than good creational dynamics proper to human nature as created by God.[27]

In short, my first point is that Bonhoeffer's recovery of natural law and human rights is not in itself unique at all—it is part of a larger conversation among many leading Christian thinkers of his time.[28] From one of Bonhoeffer's letters, dated March 7, 1940, we know that this conversation included Bonhoeffer's brother-in-law, the constitutional lawyer Gerhard Leibholz. Leibholz wrote his dissertation on natural law in Fichte and was working on an article that supports relating civic law to Christian natural law when Bonhoeffer wrote the letter.[29] In this letter, Bonhoeffer continues a previous conversation with Leibholz on natural law and indicates his interest in moral principles found in creation.[30] He takes up the point Brunner had already isolated as the central problem of Protestant natural law ethics—how does one relate natural rights discernible within creation to biblical revelation without relativizing either? How does one safeguard the integrity of

---

Dietrich Bonhoeffer *Act and Being*, 1931"; Emil Brunner, *Das Gebot und die Ordnungen: Entwurf einer protestantisch-theologischen Ethik* (Zürich: Zwingli Verlag, 1939), 586 n.5.

26. Emil Brunner, *Gerechtigkeit: Eine Lehre von den Grundgesetzen der Gesellschaftsordnung* (Zürich: Theologischer Verlag Zürich, 1943).

27. He admits, however, that institutions like the state are ambivalent in this respect. They may be necessary "orders of preservation" (*Erhaltungsordnungen*) to curb not only evil but also "orders of creation" (*Schöpfungsordnungen*) or a divine mandate (*göttliche Stiftung*). See Brunner, *Gerechtigkeit*, 85–6.

28. Notes from Bonhoeffer demonstrate that the topic of natural law, as reflected in the Decalogue and therefore bridging the moral frameworks of church and state, was central to the rebuilding of Germany as envisioned by the Freiburger Kreis in which Bonhoeffer was involved. Bethge cites the following headings Bonhoeffer noted for his thoughts about the circles' discussions: "Economic questions: Eucken, von Dietze, Bauer, Karrenberg. Law of the State inside Decalogue, God and State outside Europe . . . Asmussen, Ritter, Luther. God and justice: fundamental and human rights . . . [v. Simson] Böhm-Jena natural law, Mensing, criminal law, State-Church. The Jews. Education. The Church's proclamation to the world. The Word of God and counsel. The basis of right. Existence of the Church in the world. Perels"; Bethge, *Dietrich Bonhoeffer: A Biography*, 776.

29. See the correspondence between George Bell and Leibholz in *An der Schwelle zum gespaltenen Europa: Der Briefwechsel zwischen George Bell und Gerhard Leibholz 1939–1951* (Stuttgart: Kreuzverlag, 1974), 114.

30. It is significant that the letter was written at the time Bonhoeffer was composing his *Ethics*.

the natural, on the one hand, and the necessity of divine revelation for true self-knowledge because of the Fall, on the other hand?[31] As Bonhoeffer puts it, "so, on the one side: relativization of the revelation; on the other: relativization of the historical, the norms of creation. Both, however, must be avoided. That in my opinion is the crucial issue, and that is how the problem is posed at present."[32]

Bonhoeffer's Unique Contributions to Natural Law and Human Rights

This problem takes me to Bonhoeffer's unique contribution to natural law theory and human rights. Long after the war, the tension between natural law and revelation continued to haunt the debate between two Protestant camps. The first camp, including thinkers like Brunner and Bonhoeffer as well as Thomists like Josef Pieper, leaned toward a Roman Catholic understanding of natural law, defined as creational dynamics commensurate with nature as created by God. For this group, the natural, understood as good but fallen creation with inherent dynamics for human flourishing, yielded substantial insights into human rights and ethics that were dim reflections of divine realities. As is well-known, Bonhoeffer here followed, more or less, Josef Pieper's Thomistic view that "what is good is commensurate with reality" because God created the world.[33] Thus, "moral imperatives" should be derived from reality itself—without, however, equating nature with the Good.[34]

The other camp, represented by thinkers like Helmut Thielicke (who took part in the Confessing Church's discussions about postwar social foundations), argues that the Roman Catholic position did not take the distortive effects of sin within creation seriously enough. True human identity and virtues are revealed only in Christ and therefore cannot be deduced from fallen creation by sinful human beings. For Thielicke, the idea of natural law is at best a "heuristically provisional" position required for holding human laws accountable to a higher standard that transcends communal laws. Otherwise, one would have no way of countering Nazis who claimed their genocide was perfectly legal in Germany.[35]

---

31. More specifically, how does one relate distributive justice to the divine justification that forgives everything on a personal level? How do we relate, in Brunner's terms, "justice of faith" to "worldly justice"? Brunner, *Gerechtigkeit*, 17.

32. *DBW* 15:298; *DBWE* 15:301.

33. Josef Pieper, *Die Wirklichkeit und das Gute* (München: Kösel Verlag, 1949), 79–80.

34. Pieper, *Die Wirklichkeit*, 81: "So auch muß die Betrachtung des Guten als des 'Wirklichkeitsmäßigen' nicht bis zu der letzten und absoluten Norm hinaufdringen, wenn nur nicht die endliche Wirklichkeit selbst für diese absolute Norm gehalten wird."

35. See Helmut Thielicke, *Being Human, Becoming Human: An Essay in Theological Anthropology*, trans. Geoffrey W. Bromiley (New York: Doubleday, 1984), 168. Thielicke rightly interprets Bonhoeffer's statement that modern Christians should live as if God did not exist to mean that they can rely on an implicit order in creation. However, Thielicke seems less confident than Bonhoeffer that universal natural rights can be deduced from this

In light of these two camps, one stressing revelation, the other stressing the importance of substantive natural rights, let me conclude by noting briefly how Bonhoeffer addresses this problem. Bonhoeffer's solution is the ultimate-penultimate relation—Bonhoeffer's *first* unique contribution to natural law theory. Based on the Pauline and the Johannine traditions, Bonhoeffer defines reality as unified in Christ.[36] Within that unity, he defines the natural as fallen creation, as the penultimate, in its openness toward its ultimate redemption by Christ in whom new humanity and new creation are already accomplished. As he puts it, "The natural is that which, after the fall, is directed toward the coming of Jesus Christ. The unnatural is that which, after the fall, closes itself off from the coming of Christ."[37]

Bonhoeffer thus manages to retain Barth's revelational focus on Christ while also maintaining the relative integrity of the natural. What about the effects of sin on reason that worried Thielicke? Bonhoeffer affirms the ability of natural, fallen reason to discern the "content" of the natural as "the form of preserved life that comprises humanity as a whole."[38] As part of fallen creation, reason has no ability to deduct salvific knowledge of God from nature. Yet because reason *is* part of the divinely affirmed *natural*, fallen reason is able to perceive reality as something given rather than constructed and to discern being the "foundational will" for the preservation of life.[39] In granting fallen reason the power to discern creational directives for human flourishing, Bonhoeffer establishes the natural as common ground for public moral reasoning. In terms of the greater Christian tradition, Bonhoeffer's working out of the cosmic ramifications of the Incarnation thus moves him close to a position of classic Catholic moral theology where "grace does not destroy" nature[40] and where principles for the preservation and flourishing of humanity, principles inherent in life itself, allow us to discern fundamental human rights.[41] Natural life, Bonhoeffer argues, is a gift from God, from which natural

---

order. Like Bonhoeffer, Thielicke speaks of orders of preservation of a penultimate creation held over by God until its renewal. Unlike Bonhoeffer though, he stresses the inherent evil of human beings that make these orders necessary. Thielicke's erudite disquisition on natural law is well worth recovering for recent debates on this topic. See Helmut Thielicke, *Theologische Ethik*, vol. 1, 4th ed. (Tübingen: Mohr Siebeck, 2022 [1971]), 610–707.

36. I refer here to Bonhoeffer's well-known view that there is only "*the one realm of the Christ-reality [Christuswirklichkeit], in which the reality of God and the reality of the world are united*"; *DBWE* 6:58.

37. Ibid., 173.

38. Ibid., 166.

39. Ibid., 168.

40. See Jacques Maritain, "Christianity and Democracy," in *Christianity and Democracy and the Rights of Man and the Natural Law*, trans. Doris C. Anson (San Francisco, CA: Ignatius Press, 1986 [1942 and 1943]), 113.

41. René Marlé, *Bonhoeffer: The Man and His Work* (New York: Newman Press, 1968), 100. However, Bonhoeffer also retains the Protestant reservation that "the church knows

rights flow to each person. From these natural rights flow the obligation of justice, of giving each person his or her own, as demanded by each concrete life situation.[42] Here the classic principle of natural justice, "to each his or her own," obtains its "relative legitimacy" in acknowledging the priority of natural rights over any positive law.[43] The ultimate ground of this penultimate natural principle is when, at the last judgment, "Christ through the Holy Spirit will give each his own."[44]

Conclusion

I conclude with the briefest reference to Bonhoeffer's *second* unique contribution to natural law theory, namely the fact that a fundamental set of human rights—personal property, personal freedom, and personal dignity—that is irreducible to economic value derives from the embodied nature of human existence.[45] Other major proponents of human rights at this time like Brunner or Maritain pay lip-service to the embodied nature of the human spirit, but none of them equals Bonhoeffer in grounding human rights in the body.[46] Bonhoeffer divides natural

---

no other relation to the world as through Jesus Christ; that is, not based on a natural law (*Naturrecht*), or reason (*Vernunftrecht*), or universal human right, but *solely* commencing from the gospel of Jesus Christ results the proper relation of church to the world"; *DBW* 6:358. The basic structure of Christian reasoning—and here Bonhoeffer remains resolutely Barthian—"proceeds not from the world to God, but from God to the world goes the path of Jesus Christ and thus the path of all Christian thought"; *DBW* 6:358. Bonhoeffer also championed the same reservation about orders of creation in his draft of the Bethel Confession (1933); none of these orders of preservation (*Erhaltung*), "of the sexes, of marriage, of family, of nation, of property (work and economy)," has "intrinsic value but they refer solely to the end which God will bestow on mankind, the new creation in Christ"; *DBW* 12:375.

42. As part of his anti-Kantian rhetoric, Bonhoeffer makes a special point of the ontological priority of rights over duties. A similar point is made in Catholic human rights discourse. Josef Pieper views human rights as rooted in life itself (like Bonhoeffer), and Jacques Maritain regards rights and duties as correlatively arising from the nature of personhood: "The same natural law which lays down our most fundamental duties, and by virtue of which every law is binding, is the very law which assigns to us our fundamental rights" because "we are enmeshed in the universal order"; Maritain, "Christianity and Democracy," 107.

43. *DBW* 6:175.

44. Ibid., 176.

45. Ibid., 183–91.

46. Maritain's list of fundamental rights is as follows: "the right to existence and life; the right to personal freedom or to conduct one's own life as master of oneself and of one's acts, responsible for them before God and the law of the community; the right to the pursuit of the perfection of moral and rational human life; the right to the pursuit of eternal good

rights into rights of bodily and spiritual life (*leibliches* and *geistliches Leben*). He only had time to cover the right to bodily life, which he declares to be "the very foundation of all natural rights and therefore of extreme importance."[47] Since human beings will retain their body into eternity,[48] the right to bodily life and physical joy is God-given and sacred. On these grounds, Bonhoeffer rejects not only forced sterilizations and the murder of handicapped patients implemented by Hitler's euthanasia program (1939–41) but also suicide and abortion.[49]

As Helmut Thielicke has rightly observed, natural law always becomes a hot topic when we experience a crisis of human identity, when human persons become objectified and lives are sacrificed for the "greater good" of politics or economics. Under these circumstances, aging, handicapped, or sick bodies become a burden. This was the case in the 1930s and 1940s, when Bonhoeffer's interest in natural law was broadly shared by many reflective Christians. Given our current uncertainty about human identity for reasons too numerous to list here, interest in natural law is once again on the rise in our time, and Bonhoeffer's reflections on this topic remain as relevant as ever.

(without this pursuit there is no true pursuit of happiness); the right to keep one's body whole; the right to private ownership of material goods, which is a safeguard of the liberties of the individual; the right to marry according to one's choice and to raise a family which will be assured of the liberty due it; the right of association, the respect for human dignity in each individual, whether or not he represents an economic value for society—all these rights are rooted in the vocation of the person (a spiritual and free agent) to the order of absolute values and to a destiny superior to time"; Maritain, "The Rights of Man and the Natural Law," in *Christianity and Democracy*, 116.

47. *DBW* 6:179. Bonhoeffer's emphasis on the body can be seen as early as in his Genesis lectures of 1932.

48. "The human being is an embodied being [*leibliches Wesen*] and remains so into eternity. Bodily nature and being human belong inseparably together"; Ibid., 180.

49. Bonhoeffer applies the same right to life to his prohibition of abortion: "Killing the fruit [of new life] in the womb is a violation of the right to live God granted to the becoming life"; Ibid., 203.

Part V

BONHOEFFER ON PEACE, HOPEFUL ACTION, AND THE FUTURE

Chapter 21

INTRODUCING BONHOEFFER'S NEWLY FOUND LETTER TO GANDHI

Clifford Green

Introduction

The International Bonhoeffer Congress meeting in Stellenbosch in January 2020 was a fitting occasion to present publicly the newly found Dietrich Bonhoeffer's letter to Mahatma Gandhi. In 2019, we celebrated the 150th anniversary of Gandhi's birth. After studying law in Britain, Gandhi began his career of resisting colonialism and racism by means of civil disobedience in South Africa. In South Africa, too, Gandhi engaged in dialogue and critical debate with Christian missionaries, among whom he found a lifelong friend in Charles Freer Andrews, an English Anglican priest with deep Quaker connections.

Julius Rieger, a German pastor colleague in London, understood Bonhoeffer's motives in writing to Gandhi, saying, "He was drawn as though magnetically by a man like Gandhi, who thought more highly of the Sermon on the Mount than most Christians and who, by means of passive resistance, had achieved his political aims against a first-class world power."[1] The magnetism Rieger describes suggests that Bonhoeffer's strong desire to visit Gandhi is both older and deeper than the common opinion that he wanted to learn more about Gandhi's nonviolent resistance methods to use against Hitler. Not surprisingly, the resistance topic is indeed in the letter but within a much larger framework. This 1934 letter, I believe, is a window into his mind at the time, touching on a range of topics found throughout his works in the next decade to the *Ethics* and the theology of the prison letters. Actually, the Bonhoeffer-Gandhi story is not fully understood until one begins with Bonhoeffer's undergraduate reading and discussion of Gandhi at Tübingen in 1924–5, and until we study the Gandhi books Bonhoeffer was reading during the next decade.

---

1. Julius Rieger, "Contacts with London," in *I Knew Dietrich Bonhoeffer: Reminiscences by His Friends*, ed. Wolf-Dieter Zimmermann and Ronald Gregor Smith (New York: Harper & Row, 1966), 96. See also Hans Pfeifer on Rieger and Bonhoeffer, *DBWE* 10:42 n.183.

In this introduction, however, we must focus on the letter itself. In volume 13 of the Dietrich Bonhoeffer Works, we find letters recommending Bonhoeffer to Gandhi from his friend, C. F. Andrews, and from Bishop George Bell—Bonhoeffer refers to both of them in his own letter. Even more pertinent, the Bonhoeffer Works contain a letter from Gandhi himself, dated November 1, 1934, inviting Bonhoeffer and a companion to come and stay with him in his ashram; it is obviously a reply to a letter from Bonhoeffer. Finally, eighty-five years later, we now have Bonhoeffer's own letter to Gandhi.

For the privilege of introducing the text of Bonhoeffer's letter to scholars and the public, I am very grateful to Ramachandra Guha, the distinguished Indian historian. He was the first to reveal the location of Bonhoeffer's letter in the Gandhi archives of the Nehru Memorial Museum and Library, New Delhi. Indeed, he quotes from the letter in his recent monumental biography, *Gandhi: The Years That Changed the World, 1914–1948*.[2] When this volume was published in 2018, Guha was in the United States giving lectures and interviews. After reading an interview in which he quoted from the Bonhoeffer letter,[3] I immediately wrote him, requesting a copy. He replied promptly, kindly sent me a scan of the original, and requested that I send him anything I wrote about Bonhoeffer's letter. The letter with my notes was first published digitally in *The Journal of Ecclesiastical History* on April 9, 2020, the seventy-fifth anniversary of Bonhoeffer's death; later it was published in the print volume.[4]

Here, we can only offer an introduction to the letter, quoting and summarizing the key points, and then noting some other Bonhoeffer texts related to these topics. Readers of this chapter can also consult the complete text of the letter in either the online or the printed version in the *Journal*. But the key topics are outlined later.

Critique of Western Society

European countries, including Germany, are in a distressing situation. In Germany, a "deep spiritual need" underlies the economic and political confusion. Whereas

---

2. Ramachandra Guha, *Gandhi: The Years That Changed the World, 1914–1948* (New York: Knopf, 2018), 470–2, 948 n.8. This is Volume Two of a three volume biography.

3. Guha, *Gandhi*, 470–2. Guha also speculates about what might have happened had Bonhoeffer actually visited and learned from Gandhi in his ashram. "Could Bonhoeffer then have returned to Germany and mobilized his fellow Christians in a non-violent resistance movement against the Nazis . . . Could a popular movement have crystallized around the figure of a Gandhi-inspired Bonhoeffer, awakening the conscience not merely of his fellow Germans but of democrats around the world, forcing the other European powers and America to intervene much before they did, forestalling the horrific loss of life in the Second World War? . . . [H]ad Bonhoeffer apprenticed with Gandhi in 1934, it might—just—have influenced social and political history as well." Ibid., 538–9.

4. *The Journal of Ecclesiastical History*, 72, no 1 (2021): 113–21.

"Europe and Germany are suffering from a dangerous fever and are losing both self-control and the consciousness of what they are doing,"[5] looming war will bring "spiritual death" to Europe.

Critique of the Western Church

"Only true Christianity can help our Western peoples to a new and spiritually sound life." Thinking people are disappointed by organized Christianity which is not communicating the healing power of "Christ's message." A fundamental regeneration is needed, for "Christianity must be something very different from what it has become in these days." With war looming, "a truly spiritual living Christian peace movement" is needed.

Karl Barth's Retrieval of Reformation Theology and Its Limit

Karl Barth, the greatest of German theologians, was teaching "the great theological thoughts of the Reformation anew, but there is no-one to show us the way toward a new Christian life in uncompromising accordance with the Sermon on the Mount." Bonhoeffer looked up to Gandhi for help "in this respect." "Western Christianity must be reborn on the Sermon on the Mount." This is the "crucial point" of Bonhoeffer's letter to Gandhi. Western Christians need to learn from Gandhi what "realization of faith means,"[6] especially "a life devoted to political and racial peace."

Disappointment in America

Having travelled widely in Europe, living and working in different cities, Bonhoeffer wrote from London, noting that he "went to the USA to find what I was looking for—but I did not find it."

Learning from Gandhi "the Meaning of Christian Life"

Now his request to spend some time with Gandhi in his ashram is expressed in the strongest terms: "I do not want to accuse myself of having missed the

---

5. Where a quotation has no footnote, the quote is from Bonhoeffer's letter. DOI:https://doi.org/10.1017/S0022046920000093

6. Bonhoeffer wrote to Gandhi in English, and his phrase "realization of faith" is rather Germanic. He means making faith real in life—faith which is not just an idea, a belief, but faith which is existential and lived, a trust and commitment that is embodied in action. Wolfgang Huber's translation of Bonhoeffer's letter into German translates his English with the phrase "Wirklichwerden des Glaubens." Wolfgang Huber, "Einige Zeit im Ashram verbringen," in *Zeitzeichen*, April 12–14, 2020.

one great occasion in my life to learn the meaning of Christian life, of real community life, of truth and love in reality." Indeed, it is extraordinary that Bonhoeffer expects "to learn the meaning of Christian life" from the Hindu Gandhi. But so great is his desire to know Gandhi's movement that he writes, "I should be willing to bring any sacrifice whatever" for this purpose. This is surely the most unpredictable statement in the whole letter. After this brief overview of Bonhoeffer's self-introduction to Gandhi, it is helpful to acknowledge various writings, many in the early 1930s, in which he makes similar points as in the letters and sermons.

Bonhoeffer's Critique of Western Society and the Western Church

Bonhoeffer began his petition to Gandhi because of "the most distressing situation" in Europe, particularly, in Germany. Surely, this alludes to the Nazi regime, then twenty months in power when Bonhoeffer wrote. And just a few months before Bonhoeffer's letter, part of the Protestant Church had marked this crisis with the Barmen Declaration in May 1934. But this "situation," says Bonhoeffer, has troubled him for "a long time," possibly even for a decade since his undergraduate years.[7] "But now things have advanced so far."

Four years earlier, more than two years before Hitler came to power, Bonhoeffer had given an Armistice Day sermon in New York on November 9, 1930. It was a theological assessment of Germany and the First World War. Rejecting the charge of solely blaming Germany for the war, Bonhoeffer concluded that the war was "a judgment of God upon this fallen world, and especially upon our [German] people. Before the war we lived too far from God, we believed too much in our own power, in our almightiness and righteousness." For Bonhoeffer, the fundamental issue was deeper than war guilt; "Germany's complacence, in her belief in her almightiness, in the lack of humility and faith in God and fear of God.... [T]his is the meaning of the war for Germany: we had to recognize the limits of man and that means: we discovered anew God in his glory and almightiness, in his wrath and his grace."[8] Bonhoeffer ended with the appeal, which we hear again in ecumenical speeches like the one at Fanø, namely "one of the greatest tasks for our church [is] to strengthen the work of peace in every country and in the whole world. It

---

7. It is worth noting that in his 1927 doctoral dissertation, *Sanctorum Communio*, Bonhoeffer included a section on "Church and Proletariat," much to the chagrin of his advisor Reinhold Seeberg. Critical of the bourgeois empirical church he was familiar with, Bonhoeffer wrote: "The proletariat has turned its back on the church.... The gospel must be proclaimed concretely in history," addressing issues of capitalism, socialism, "the growth of militaristic and bureaucratic giant states," and industry "that treats people and labor like machines"; *DBWE* 1:271-4.

8. *DBWE* 10:582, 583.

must never more happen that a Christian people fights against a Christian people, brother against brother, since both have one Father."⁹

While Gandhi's invitation letter to Bonhoeffer was making its way from India to England, Bonhoeffer was preaching a Reformation Day sermon to his London congregation on November 4. His text was 1 Cor. 13:13.¹⁰ The church that exalts faith alone, higher than any other, "must be even greater in its love."¹¹ First, Bonhoeffer argues, the church must recognize "a degeneration that has threatened Protestantism since its beginnings. . . . For the message that faith alone [*sola fide*] saves and redeems has become hardened, a dead letter, because it has not been kept alive by love."¹² A "faith" that does not practice the reconciling will and teaching of Christ is not faith; it is hypocrisy. Authentic faith is always embodied in action and enacted by love.

In this sermon, Bonhoeffer spelled out essentially the same point made in a letter to Reinhold Niebuhr three months earlier, on July 13. Arguing from the same fundamental perspective, he said to Niebuhr, "It is high time to bring the focus back to the Sermon on the Mount, to some degree on the basis of a restoration of Reformation theology, but in a way different from the Reformation understanding. . . . The new church that must come into being in Germany will look very different from the opposition church of today."¹³ Bonhoeffer then mentioned that he was planning to go to India quite soon "to see what Gandhi knows about such things and what there is to learn there. I am just now waiting for a letter and an invitation from him."¹⁴ He also told Niebuhr that he was working on "some writing about the question of the Sermon on the Mount."¹⁵

---

9. Ibid., 583–4.

10. "And now faith, hope, and love abide, these three; and the greatest of these is love" (1 Cor. 13:13); *DBWE* 13:392.

11. *DBWE* 13:392.

12. Ibid. See Bonhoeffer's letter from Tegel to his parents on Reformation Day in 1943: "One wonders why consequences had to arise from Luther's action that were exactly the opposite of those he intended"; *DBWE* 8:172. In fact, he had already answered his own question in *Discipleship*, where he commented on the "word of the justification by grace alone" because "false use of the same statement can lead to the complete destruction of its essence"; *DBWE* 4:51. In other words, "faith" which is not embodied in acts of obedient love is not the faith of discipleship.

13. *DBWE* 13:183–4.

14. Ibid., 184. Since this statement came three months *before* Bonhoeffer wrote his own letter requesting an invitation, we can safely assume it alludes to the letter of recommendation C. F. Andrews had written to Gandhi on May 14, 1934; see Guha, 470, 948 n.6. This letter has not yet been recovered but we know it is in the New Delhi archive. See also Larry L. Rasmussen, *Dietrich Bonhoeffer: Reality and Resistance* (Louisville, KY: Westminster John Knox, 2005), 213–17.

15. *DBWE* 13:184. This is writing for *Discipleship*. See also the remarks about the Sermon on the Mount in his April 28, 1934, letter to Irwin Sutz; Ibid., 135–6.

Bonhoeffer's Visit to the United States and His Disappointment

It has become commonplace to say that Bonhoeffer's 1930-1 experience at Union Seminary and Abyssinian Baptist Church was formative—transformative, perhaps, even a "conversion," as some would have it—and this in spite of his severe criticisms of theology at the seminary and of preaching in the white churches.[16] But in his letter, Bonhoeffer bluntly states, "I went to the USA to find what I was looking for—but I did not find it."[17] Then he mentioned why he really must visit Gandhi—it would be "the one great occasion in my life to learn the meaning of Christian life, of real community life, of truth and love in reality." His "great desire" was to know Gandhi's movement, and for this, he was willing to make "any sacrifice whatever." Strong words indeed!

How literally should we take this blunt "I did not find it" conclusion about what Bonhoeffer was looking for? Does that sum up his whole experience at Union Seminary and Abyssinian Church? Other letters suggest otherwise. In prison, he looked back thirteen years and recalled his discussions with Jean Lasserre about learning to have faith.[18] In 1936, closer to 1931, Bonhoeffer's very revealing letter to Elizabeth Zinn spoke of experiencing a "great liberation" due to the discovery of the Bible and especially the Sermon on the Mount. It was "a change that transformed my life and set its course in a new direction . . . I discovered the Bible. . . . The Bible, especially the Sermon on the Mount liberated me" from being "my own master," "wild and untamed," ambitious and vain. Now "the church and the ministry became my supreme concern" and "Christian pacifism . . . suddenly came into focus as something utterly self-evident."[19] Since this commitment to church and ministry and to "Christian pacifism" took root in New York in 1931, we must add a very pertinent insight derived from Gary Dorrien's book on the Black Social Gospel,[20] namely the preaching of Adam Clayton Powell Sr. at Abyssinian Baptist

---

16. Along with the important insights about Bonhoeffer and the Harlem Renaissance, the strongest claims are found in Reggie L. Williams, *Bonhoeffer's Black Jesus: Harlem Renaissance Theology and an Ethic of Resistance* (Waco, TX: Baylor University Press, 2014), involving Bonhoeffer's Christology, theology of the cross, and resistance to racism.

17. That was not the first time Bonhoeffer made such a statement. In his very depressed 1930 Christmas letter to Rößler, a fellow student and pastor in Berlin, he wrote: "my hope of finding Heb. 12.1 fulfilled here has been bitterly disappointed"; *DBWE* 10:261. By referring in the text to being "surrounded by so great a cloud of witnesses," I assume Bonhoeffer expected the "witnesses" to exemplify authentic Christianity rather than representing the sort of faults he described in the churches in Germany.

18. *DBWE* 8:486.

19. Ibid., 14:112-13; see also the Editor's Introduction in *DBWE* 10:37-8. Note that, among the important points in this letter, Bonhoeffer explicitly speaks of *Christian* pacifism, not just "pacifism," as though the meaning of pacifism was self-evident.

20. Gary Dorrien, *The New Abolition: W.E.B. Du Bois and the Black Social Gospel* (New Haven, CT: Yale University Press, 2015).

Church in Harlem. Because this is an important new insight, the summary is quoted at some length:[21]

> There Adam Clayton Powell Sr. was preaching "that enemy-love, non-retaliation, and forgiveness were the very heart of the gospel . . . to follow Jesus, Powell urged, one had to take up the costly, fellow-suffering discipleship of the Sermon on the Mount." Like Bonhoeffer, who was reading reports on Gandhi in Harry Ward's course and making practical plans to visit him in India,[22] "Powell lionized Gandhian nonviolent resistance to oppression." And Powell, like Bonhoeffer, held the Spirituals in high regard, taking his Abyssinian singers to anti-war rallies where they would sing, "I'm gonna lay down my sword and shield, down by the riverside . . . I ain't gonna study war no more." Therefore we must conclude that discussions with Lasserre and Powell's preaching reinforced each other.

Actually, the discussions at Union involved not only Lasserre but certainly also Erwin Sutz, and probably Albert Franklin Fisher and Paul Lehmann.[23]

Bonhoeffer told Gandhi he did not find what he was seeking in the United States, but elsewhere he also spoke autobiographically of his "great liberation," inspired by the Bible and especially the Sermon on the Mount, his commitment to the church and ministry, and to Christian pacifism. How are we to explain these two reports? Obviously, Bonhoeffer experienced a decisive personal development. But he was seeking a "host of witnesses" that he did not find. This phrase surely does not describe a personal experience; it really must refer to the predominant church at large, namely white Protestantism, which was in its heyday in the first

---

21. The following paragraph is quoted from Clifford Green, "Bonhoeffer's Christian Peace Ethic: Conditional Pacifism, and Resistance," in *The Oxford Handbook of Dietrich Bonhoeffer*, ed. Michael Mawson and Philip G. Ziegler (Oxford: Oxford University Press, 2019), 347. The many phrases in single quotes are from Dorrien, *The New Abolition*, 437–42.

22. Clifford Green, "Bonhoeffer's Courses and Ethics Readings at Union Theological Seminary 1930/31," in *Dietrich Bonhoeffer Jahrbuch 3, 2007–2008*, ed. Victoria J. Barnett, Sabine Bobert, and Ernst Feil (Gütersloh: Gütersloher Verlagshaus, 2008), 45–59. In February and March of the Spring semester, Bonhoeffer read eighteen *New York Times* articles on Gandhi's negotiations with Britain on independence for India.

23. Bonhoeffer's summary of his conversation with Jean Lasserre about learning to have faith in *Letters and Papers from Prison* (*DBWE* 8:541–2) has heretofore eclipsed the name of another participant, Erwin Sutz. But Bonhoeffer kept up the conversation with Sutz, for example, in his letter of April 28, 1934. The topics remain the same—the Sermon on the Mount, *keeping* the commandments, *following* Christ, the meaning of faith. Very pertinent to the Gandhi letter is this statement: "*Following* Christ—what that really is, I'd like to know—it is not exhausted by our concept of faith"; *DBWE* 13:136. In other words, "*sola fide*" is not just a belief, an idea, but a trusting embrace of grace expressed in following Jesus—the marriage of faith and obedience responding to the call and command of Jesus yields discipleship.

half of the twentieth century. He told Gandhi that the church in Germany was bourgeois and had alienated the proletariat, that it lacked humility and faith in God, and that it was not communicating Christ's message. He found much the same in America.

Bonhoeffer's Critique of Karl Barth's Theological Renewal

Bonhoeffer's praise of Barth is unstinting. He is the greatest of the key theologians in Germany, and Bonhoeffer is happy to be his disciple and friend. Barth and others have revived "the great theological thoughts of the Reformation." But something is missing, something Bonhoeffer regards as essential: "There is no-one to show us the way towards a new Christian life in uncompromising accordance with the Sermon on the Mount." Bonhoeffer seeks Gandhi's help on this central point.

Two years later at Finkenwalde, Bonhoeffer wrote a long letter to Barth explaining why he had not written to him in three years: "Basically the entire period was an ongoing, silent dispute with you, which is why I had to remain silent for a while. Primarily it involved questions concerning the interpretation of the Sermon on the Mount and the Pauline doctrine of justification and sanctification."[24] Bonhoeffer further told Barth that while engaging these questions arising from Scripture and still working on these issues for his book, *Discipleship*, he frequently found that he "was probably moving away from what you yourself think about these questions."[25] Bonhoeffer had already made this point to Niebuhr, saying, "It is high time to bring the focus back to the Sermon on the Mount, to some degree on the basis of a restoration of Reformation theology, but in a way different from the Reformation understanding."[26]

This critical praise of Barth is similar to a judgment Bonhoeffer made in his Tegel theology. There, he wrote in April 1944, ten years later, that Barth was the first to begin the critique of religion, and that was his great strength. But he did not take the necessary next step to interpret biblical and theological concepts as a worldly, religionless Christianity, a regenerated Christianity for a culture that had "come of age." So, Barth's great promise turned up to be a "restoration" and "a positivism of revelation," as Bonhoeffer's most famous polemical phrase puts it.[27]

The same pattern of praise and critique of Barth could already be found much earlier in *Act and Being*. To Bonhoeffer, it is as if Barth's "*ganz andere*" God and the revelation "perpendicularly from above" never quite managed to make a landing on earth. On the contrary, Bonhoeffer argues, God's freedom in revelation is not

---

24. *DBWE* 14:252–3.
25. *DBWE* 14:252.
26. Ibid., 13:183–4.
27. *DBWE* 8:363–4; see also on Barth, ibid., 373, 429. Note that this is about the problem of "the Western form of Christianity"; Ibid., 363.

being free *from* the world and humanity in divine aseity. The true divine freedom is "that God freely chose to be bound to historical human beings . . . God is not free *from* human beings but *for* them. Christ is the word of God's freedom. God *is present . . . graspable in the Word* within the church."[28] Bethge describes this propensity of Bonhoeffer as his quest for concreteness.

Moving on now from the postdoctoral dissertation of 1930, we find another relevant comment about Barth in Bonhoeffer's April letter to his Swiss friend from Union Seminary, Erwin Sutz.[29] His topic was the Sermon on the Mount and resistance to National Socialism. Bonhoeffer wrote, "National Socialism has brought about the end of the church in Germany." He predicted that the present opposition would give way to a very different kind of opposition, namely "resistance 'to the point of shedding blood.'"[30] This resistance will be "simply suffering through in faith . . . it is my belief—perhaps it will amaze you—that it is the *Sermon on the Mount*[31] that has the deciding word on this whole affair. I think that Barth's theology . . . [has] delayed recognition of this a little while, but . . . certainly also made it possible." In other words, Barth's theology of revelation certainly leads to costly resistance to National Socialism, but it does not articulate a mode of Christian resistance derived from the Sermon on the Mount.

Where Bonhoeffer is coming from is clear. He asks Sutz how he preaches about the Sermon on the Mount. Then, he describes his own approach—that he tries to "keep it infinitely plain and simple, but it always comes back to *keeping the commandments and not trying to evade them. Following* Christ [*Nachfolge Christi*]—what that really is, I'd like to know—it is not exhausted by our concept of faith."[32] This is doubtless an allusion to a corrupt view of *sola gratia, sola fide* that Bonhoeffer mercilessly satirizes in the writing for *Discipleship* that he had been working on for a couple of years. Those who believe in this sort of cheap grace and perverse faith which justify sin think like this:

> In all things the Christian should go along with the world and not venture . . . to live a different life under grace from that under sin! The Christian better not rage against grace or defile that glorious cheap grace by proclaiming anew a servitude to the letter of the Bible in an attempt to lead an obedient life under the commandments of Jesus Christ![33]

---

28. *DBWE* 2:90–1, 170.
29. Ibid., 13:134–6, April 28, 1934.
30. Heb. 12:4.
31. Bonhoeffer's italics.
32. Bonhoeffer's italics. In the book *Nachfolge*, faith and obedience have an intimate and inseparable unity, analogous to Chalcedon's Christological formula of unity, yet distinct in the divine-human Christ.
33. *DBWE* 4:44.

Sermon on the Mount: Gandhi and Bonhoeffer on Peace

Bonhoeffer and Gandhi were both strong advocates of peace, and they both held the Sermon on the Mount in high esteem—it had made Christian pacifism "self-evident" to him, Bonhoeffer wrote. So, the peace issue is important in his letter, though he did not compare his own position on peace and resistance to Gandhi's. He obviously knew though, that in philosophy and in practice, Gandhi was committed to nonviolence as a consistent principle. For Gandhi, *ahimsa*, nonviolence, is the supreme law.[34] That was not Bonhoeffer's form of pacifism, as the testimony of his friends Hildebrandt and Bethge confirms, and as I have argued elsewhere. Here is a brief summary of the salient points of Bonhoeffer's position, which I contend—with Bethge and Hildebrandt—and which is best described as conditional pacifism:[35]

1. Bonhoeffer's position is a Christian theological peace ethic.
2. The theological foundation is not nonviolence as the fundamental principle.
3. The peace ethic is rooted in his theology—Christology (cf. *Discipleship*), Scripture (especially the Sermon on the Mount), and doctrine, especially ecclesiology.
4. The peace ethic default is nonviolence, but it is not a "fundamental pacifism" (Bethge, Hildebrandt).[36]
5. Bonhoeffer did not abandon his peace ethic to work for the resistance conspiracy.

---

34. *Gandhi on Non-Violence*, Selected Texts from Mohandas K. Gandhi's *Non-Violence in Peace and War*, ed. Thomas Merton (New York: New Directions, 1965), 38. In its positive aspect, *ahimsa* is equivalent to love; see Charles F. Andrews, ed., *Mahatma Gandhi: His Own Story* (New York: Macmillan, 1930), 61 n.2. In *Gandhi on Non-Violence*, 38, he writes: "Jesus lived and died in vain if He did not teach us to regulate the whole of life by the eternal law of love."

35. Clifford Green, "Bonhoeffer's Christian Peace Ethic, Conditional Pacifism, and Resistance," in *The Oxford Handbook*, 347.

36. Eberhard Bethge, *Dietrich Bonhoeffer. Theologe—Christ—Zeitgenosse: Eine Biographie*, 9th ed. (Gütersloher: Gütersloher Verlagshaus, 2005), 161, 190: "bedingte Pazifismus," (conditional pacifism) and "grundsätzlich Pazifist" (fundamental pacifist); cf. Eberhard Bethge, *Dietrich Bonhoeffer*, rev. ed. (Minneapolis, MN: Fortress Press, 2000), 127, 153. In a 1985 interview, Hildebrandt agrees with Bethge that, "It was never a pacifism unqualified and held to in principle." See Clifford Green, "Hauerwas and Nation on Bonhoeffer's 'Pacifism: A Literature Overview'," *The Bonhoeffer Legacy* 3, no. 1 (2015): 10. Hildebrandt, a lifelong pacifist, maintains that he would "stay with Gandhi." See Holger Roggelin, *Franz Hildebrandt: Ein lutherischer Dissenter im Kirchenkampf und Exil* (Göttingen: Vandenhoek und Ruprecht, 1999), 264.

Gandhi and the Meaning of Christian Life

Having begun his letter to Gandhi with the diagnosis of the "deep spiritual need" of Western Christianity, Bonhoeffer concludes by offering to make "any sacrifice what-ever" to know Gandhi's movement: "I do not want to accuse myself of having missed the one great occasion in my life to learn the meaning of Christian life, of real community life, of truth and love in reality." What is "the meaning of Christian life"? Is Bonhoeffer asking Gandhi to teach him the basics of Christianity, as if his studies during the previous decade had taught him nothing? No, his concern is with "Christian life"—an idea and phrase he uses often—as "real community life," "truth and love in reality," and "realized [i.e., lived] faith."

What is required is a "fundamental regeneration" of organized Christianity in the West—"Western Christianity must be reborn on the Sermon on the Mount." Karl Barth is right in teaching anew the theology of the Reformation, but this must entail more than "great theological thoughts"—it entails "a new Christian life in uncompromising accordance with the Sermon on the Mount." And, as he had written to Niebuhr, "It is high time to bring the focus back to the Sermon on the Mount, to some degree on the basis of a restoration of Reformation theology, but in a way different from the Reformation understanding."[37]

Bonhoeffer wants to learn from Gandhi insights and practices that bear on the Christian life, centered on the Sermon on the Mount. He is looking for a fundamental regeneration of organized Christianity, a rebirth no less. It is not for nothing that he praises Barth as reviving *Reformation* thinking nor is it accidental that he tells Niebuhr that the Sermon on the Mount must be understood differently from the *Reformation*. Ever since his 1932 "Christ and Peace" lecture[38] in which he first published his key ideas about *Discipleship*, Bonhoeffer became occupied with the Sermon on the Mount which he went on to expound in hundred pages of his *Nachfolge*. What he seeks from Gandhi is a new way, a new form of Christian life. These references to the Reformation surely bring with them thoughts of Martin Luther.

What is it that embraces both Bonhoeffer's critique of the Western church and culture and his desire to learn from Gandhi "the meaning of Christian life"—real community life, truth and love in reality, "realized" faith, and "life devoted to political and racial peace"? Reading the letter as a whole, Bonhoeffer seems to be reaching for a vision of a New Reformation.

---

37. *DBWE* 13:183–4.
38. *DBWE* 12:258–62.

Chapter 22

DIETRICH BONHOEFFER AND STEVE BIKO?

TOWARD A POLITICS OF HOPE AMONG "BORN FREE" SOUTH AFRICANS

Dion A. Forster

Introduction

While preparing for the Bonhoeffer conference that was held in Stellenbosch in 2020, I was wrestling with the notion of a strident and realistic hope for the future. I grappled with notions of hope that were shaped by my reading of two persons—Steve Biko and Dietrich Bonhoeffer. Later in this chapter, I shall discuss the notion that South Africa is "coming of age" as a democracy even though after the end of political apartheid in South Africa in 1994, many of the evils of that system have intensified in our social, political, and economic life.

What kind of hope could inform, shape, and engage our *polis* or common life, indeed, our "life together"[1] in South Africa? While our context is particular, it is not unique in the world or unique in history. With this in mind, I reflect on the contributions of two young persons who lived in different historical periods, had different life experiences, and held divergent worldviews. Yet, they do seem to have some coherent concerns for justice and the realization of true humanity even for the coming generations. The first is Dietrich Bonhoeffer, the Confessing Church pastor, theologian, and opponent of the evils of German National Socialism in the 1930s and 1940s. He asked, "How can life be assured for the coming generations?"[2] The other is Steve Bantu Biko, the South African anti-apartheid activist and Black Consciousness leader in the 1960s and 1970s. In an interview entitled *Our Strategy for Liberation* and elsewhere in his work, Biko reflects at length on how young Black women and men brought new impetus, energy, and focus to the struggle for liberation in the student uprisings of 1976 and beyond.[3]

---

1. *DBWE* 5.
2. *DBWE* 8:138–9.
3. Steve Biko, *I Write What I Like: Selected Writings* (Chicago, IL: University of Chicago Press, 2002).

Both Biko's and Bonhoeffer's lives were cut short by violent and totalitarian political actors while they were still young. At the age of thirty, Biko died in prison in apartheid South Africa on September 12, 1977, while Bonhoeffer died in prison at the age of thirty-nine in Nazi Germany on April 9, 1945. Their deaths can be related to the values they held, the views they espoused, and their respective forms of activism for liberation and transformation. So the question to consider is: *Can Bonhoeffer and Biko offer us any resources for a politics of hope for the "born free" generation of South Africa?*

The final part of my reflective enquiry is marked by the use of that highly contested phrase, the "born free generation." I will discuss this contention in some detail later. However, at this point I simply note that its use elicits the historical location of the political hope that I seek in both Bonhoeffer and Biko, namely that it is intended to be a politics of hope for the future of the generation of South Africans who were born after 1994, after the end of political apartheid and the transition to democratic rule.[4]

Before we get to that last point, which considers some resources from Bonhoeffer and Biko for a politics of hope for the "born free" generation, let us first return to South Africa's past in order to gain insight into how the history of colonialism and apartheid perpetuates a loss of hope for the future among young South Africans. The emphasis on past, present, and future in this chapter is important as we shall see.

The State of the Nation—"Most Apartheid" South Africa

South Africa remains a deeply wounded society. Almost three decades after the end of political apartheid, the lived reality of the majority of young, Black South Africans does not differ that much from the experiences of racial enmity, poverty, and spatial separation that their historical forebears experienced growing up first under colonialism and later under apartheid rule. South Africa has a predominantly young population, the average age of its citizenry being 27.6 years. Shockingly, 55.5 percent of the population live below the international poverty line of less than $2 per day, and unemployment sits at 29.1 percent. South Africa also remains the most economically unequal society in the world.[5] What is of particular concern is that the injustices of white privilege and Black subjugation

---

4. See Nico N. Koopman and Robert Vosloo, *Reading Bonhoeffer in South Africa after the Transition to Democracy: Selected Essays*, vol. 7, International Bonhoeffer Interpretations (IBI) 7 (Berlin: Peter Lang, 2020).

5. Aryn Baker, "Inequality Is Widening around the World. Here's What We Can Learn From the World's Most Unequal Country," *Time Magazine*, 2019, https://time.com/longform/south-africa-unequal-country/; Paula Armstrong, Bongisa Lekezwa, and Krige Siebrits, "Poverty in South Africa: A Profile Based on Recent Household Surveys," *Matieland: Stellenbosch Economic Working Paper* 4, no. 8 (2008); "Poverty Is so Extreme in SA that Even Lower Middle Class Area Looks Rich," *TimesLIVE* 2019, https://www.timeslive.co.za/

remain evident in the economic and spatial inequalities between Black and white South Africans. The average South African household income is R930 (US$64) per month, while white South Africans earn on average three times more than Black South Africans.[6] White South Africans, less than 10 percent of the population,[7] dominate the ownership of land (72 percent of private land),[8] while Black South Africans, who constitute 89 percent of the population, own only 26 percent of private land.

The social economist, Sampie Terreblanche, notes that on average, white South Africans have never been as prosperous as they became in the years since the end of political apartheid.[9] Achille Mbembe, an African philosopher and political scientist, notes that young Black South Africans are expressing their political, social, and economic discontent by turning to a politics of identity (pitting the races against one another), a generational politics (in which young people increasingly distrust older generations of activists and liberation leaders as "sellouts"), and a politics of impatience (where young people seek rapid and significant transformation by revolution rather than social evolution).[10]

Dealing with the consequences of colonialism and apartheid, while transforming society from benefiting a privileged few to meeting the needs of the many, has proven to be a slow and complex task.[11] The 2016 and 2017 #FeesMustFall protests

news/south-africa/2019-05-03-poverty-is-so-extreme-in-sa-that-even-lower-middle-class-areas-looks-rich/ (accessed December 16, 2019).

6. "Whites Earn Three Times More than Blacks: Stats SA," *TimesLIVE*, https://www.timeslive.co.za/news/south-africa/2019-11-18-whites-earn-three-times-more-than-black-people-stats-sa/ (accessed January 21, 2020).

7. Staff Writer, "South Africa's White Population Is Still Shrinking," https://businesstech.co.za/news/government/260219/south-africas-white-population-is-still-shrinking/ (accessed January 21, 2020).

8. "Blacks Own the Least Land—Report | Cape Times," https://www.iol.co.za/capetimes/news/blacks-own-the-least-land-report-13145254 (accessed January 21, 2020).

9. Sampie Terreblanche, *Verdeelde land: Hoe die oorgang Suid-Afrika faal* (Cape Town: Tafelberg, 2014).

10. Achille Mbembe, "Passages to Freedom: The Politics of Racial Reconciliation in South Africa," *Public Culture* 20, no. 1 (2008): 5–18; Achille Mbembe, "Achille Mbembe on the State of South African Political Life," *Africa Is a Country* (blog), September 19, 2015, http://africasacountry.com/2015/09/achille-mbembe-on-the-state-of-south-african-politics/ (accessed December 16, 2019).

11. Cf. Dion Angus Forster, "Translation and a Politics of Forgiveness in South Africa? What Black Christians Believe, and White Christians Do not Seem to Understand," *Stellenbosch Theological Journal* 14, no. 2 (2018): 77–94; Dion A Forster, "A Social Imagination of Forgiveness," *Journal of Empirical Theology* 1, no. 32 (2019): 70–88; Dion A. Forster, *The (Im)Possibility of Forgiveness? An Empirical Intercultural Bible Reading of Matthew 18:15-35* (Eugene, OR: Wipf & Stock, 2019).

against economic inequalities and economic injustice in higher education,[12] the spate of racial slurs on social media,[13] and the re-racialization of society through identity politics[14] show just how fractured and divided South African society is. The nation remains unreconciled and unjust. Young people, in particular, experience the utter hopelessness of the slow violence of poverty, racism, and spatial injustice. They are losing hope for the future.[15] One could question the use of the phrase, "post-apartheid" South Africa. Indeed, in a political sense the apartheid system has ended. While persons have the "right to have rights," the rights themselves have not been realized in their everyday lives.[16] I have claimed elsewhere that statistics show that far from living in a "post-apartheid" South Africa, we live in "most-apartheid" South Africa.[17]

Language matters—it can witness to the truth and communicate it with clarity and intent. Or, it can be used to "perpetuate a deceptive and dangerous story" of untruth and the unreal.[18] The ignorant employment of half-truths and untruths in South African politics and theology has contributed to the loss of confidence in important terms and concepts such as hope, reconciliation, transformation, and forgiveness. We have inadvertently made them too "thin" to be credible. In this sense, a great deal of the hope that is offered by theologians, ecumenical and religious leaders, and even politicians is politically inadequate to answer the question of what kind of hope can ensure fullness of life "for the coming generations."[19] Let us therefore turn to this generation—the so-called born free generation.

---

12. Basani Baloyi and Gilaad Isaacs, "#FeesMustFall: What Are the Student Protests about? CNN.Com," *CNN*, October 28, 2015, http://www.cnn.com/2015/10/27/africa/fees-must-fall-student-protest-south-africa-explainer/index.html (accessed December 16, 2019).

13. A. M. Makhulu, "Reckoning with Apartheid: The Conundrum of Working through the Past—An Introduction," *Comparative Studies of South Asia, Africa and the Middle East* 36, no. 2 (2016): 260; Artwell Nhemachena, "Rhodes Must Fall: Nibbling at Resilient Colonialism in South Africa," *Journal of Pan African Studies* 9, no. 4 (2016): 411–16; Kate Surmon, A. Juan, and V. Reddy, "Class over Race: New Barriers to Social Inclusion," *HSRC Review* 9258 (2016): 1–2.

14. Mbembe, "Achille Mbembe on the State of South African Political Life."

15. Sharlene Swartz, James Hamilton Harding, and Ariane De Lannoy, "Ikasi Style and the Quiet Violence of Dreams: A Critique of Youth Belonging in Post-Apartheid South Africa," *Comparative Education* 48, no. 1 (2012): 27–40.

16. Seyla Benhabib, *The Rights of Others: Aliens, Residents, and Citizens* (Cambridge: Cambridge University Press, 2004), 50.

17. Cf. Jaco Botha and Dion A. Forster, "Justice and the Missional Framework Document of the Dutch Reformed Church," *Verbum et Ecclesia* 38, no. 1 (2017): 2 n.7.

18. Lovelyn Nwadeyi, *Our #storiesmatter—Lovelyn Nwadeyi*, Youth Day Lecture 2019 (Stellenbosch University, 2019), https://www.youtube.com/watch?v=KKO7CsOa03o.

19. *DBWE* 8:138–9.

Troubling Generational Identity—"Born Free" as a Problem

The majority of South Africa's young population who were born after 1994 have been labeled the "born free" generation.[20] This was a well-intentioned although somewhat naïve claim. Since political apartheid ended in 1994, these young people were supposedly born into a form of freedom that their forebears had not experienced since settlers first arrived at the Cape in 1652. Those forebears faced massive dispossession of land and resources, as they were enslaved and dehumanized, and their freedoms and opportunities were stripped from them. The #RhodesMustFall and #FeesMustFall protests clearly show that this generation have deep questions about the nature and extent of the freedom and the specific freedoms that are ascribed to them by virtue of their birth. Indeed, by the time they came of age at twenty-one (in 2015), the promised freedoms of the "new" South Africa had not been realized.[21]

As stated, while this generation has the "right to have rights," the enactment of those rights has not been realized in any significant and transformative manner.[22] What seems to be most painful for young South Africans is not only that their oppressors retain the undeserved privileges of colonialism and apartheid but also that they feel a sense of betrayal from the former leaders of the struggle for liberation who now occupy the seats of power in government and the economy. A high profile #RhodesMustFall student, Ntobo Sbo Qwabe, said in 2016, "Older black people who want to silence us on the basis that they fought against apartheid need to shut the f*** up!!! We are here because you failed us! So please!"[23] His statement expresses the deep frustration that little has changed in the three decades after the end of political apartheid. It lays the blame in large measure on those who are now in power. "We are here because of you," he said. It is these "older people" who "fought against apartheid" that optimistically spoke of the younger generation as the "born free" generation. At a Youth Day lecture, commemorating the students who were slain in the 1976 Soweto Massacre, Lovelyn Nwadeyi, a

---

20. Robert Mattes, "The 'Born Frees': The Prospects for Generational Change in Post-Apartheid South Africa," *Australian Journal of Political Science* 47, no. 1 (2012): 133–53; Joleen Steyn Kotze and Gary Prevost, "Born Free: An Assessment of Political Identity Formation and Party Support of South Africa's First Post-Apartheid Generation," *AfricA Insight* 44, no. 4 (2015): 142–68.

21. Cf. Baloyi and Isaacs, "#FeesMustFall"; Lisa Grassow and Clint Le Bruyns, "Embodying Human Rights in #FeesMustFall? Contributions from an Indecent Theology," *HTS Theological Studies* 73, no. 3 (2017): 1–9.

22. Cf. Benhabib, *The Rights of Others*; Seyla Benhabib, *Dignity in Adversity: Human Rights in Troubled Times* (Hoboken, NJ: John Wiley & Sons, 2013).

23. Cited in Dion Forster, "Why the 'Loss of Faith' in Heroes like Mandela May not Be Such a Bad Thing," *Sunday Times*, November 3, 2016, http://www.timeslive.co.za/sundaytimes/stnews/2016/09/29/Why-the-'loss-of-faith'-in-heroes-like-Mandela-may-not-be-such-a-bad-thing (accessed January 7, 2020).

student activist and one of the leaders of #FeesMustFall at Stellenbosch University said:

> I completely and unequivocally reject the term "born free," because this is a term that perpetuates a deceptive and dangerous story about the reality of South African youth. Phrases like "born free" and "rainbow nation," amongst others, have come to find comfort in the mediocre lexicon that we have entertained since the end of apartheid in South Africa . . . I've experienced these words as tools for silencing, silencing and diminishing the genuine grievances of young people, and particularly young South Africans of colour. I also think that the process of meaning making that is associated with this ideology of "born free-ism" and "rainbow-ism" is one of the most insidious and powerful attempts at whitewashing the complexities of the struggle for liberation in this country.[24]

Nwadeyi is right! Just as we need to question the uncritical use of the phrase post-apartheid, we also need to trouble and disrupt the use of the phrase born free. What happens when we label a whole generation of persons as "free" by virtue of the date of their birth? We politicize the act of their birth, and indeed we politicize the very existence of unsuspecting children. By linking freedom to the date of one's birth, we perpetuate the lie of freedom where there is none. This is an act of linguistic and historical dishonesty, and as Nwadeyi contends, a perpetuation of ongoing injustice.[25] Surely, we do not have the right to impose a label, particularly an untrue label that denies the suffering and daily lived reality of the majority of young South Africans? As Nwadeyi notes, "It is part of perpetuating a false narrative that disguises the terror, the violence, the deliberateness, and the logic of erasure, that is [sic] core to the formation of the story of modern South Africa at various points in this 25-year long journey after 1994."[26] So, I would contend that we dispense with the myth of the "born free" generation and rather speak of freedom for the "coming" generation—that we approach the notion of hope for this coming generation as a future-oriented task with a history that must be truthfully acknowledged and addressed through present action.

A Politics of Hope for the Coming Generation?

Both Dietrich Bonhoeffer and Steve Bantu Biko formed part of a younger "generation" (a similar age to today's so-called born free generation) when they engaged in their work for liberation and transformation. I intend to glean some resources from their experiences that may be of value for a politics of hope for the coming generations.

24. Nwadeyi, *Our #storiesmatter*.
25. Ibid.
26. Ibid.

It is a complex task to relate credibly the contributions of Bonhoeffer and Biko to one another. I wish to be clear that I do not claim that Bonhoeffer and Biko share a common history or a common worldview. However, a case can be made that they shared some coherent commitments to the building of a more just and humane world, which would secure the future of coming generations. It is in this sense at least that we can see some coherence between these two important historical figures. They both lived in challenging times. Both were deeply reflective on the nature of what constitutes the good and the just. As a result of their reflection each became active and transforming agents in history in their respective contexts. Moreover, both were willing to live for ultimate truth and justice, even to the point of giving up their lives. Of course, I am not the first person to undertake such a task. There are many fine examples of approaches to the value, significance, and importance of their respective contributions.[27] I would like to focus on a few points that emerged and that could be identified as characteristics of a politics of hope for the coming generation.

A Tri-Directional Orientation in History

A contemporary of Biko's and cofounder of the Black Consciousness movement Barney Pityana says that Biko, through his thought and work, "gave birth to a society that could shape its own future."[28] One view of hope is that it is directed toward the future—a tomorrow that will be better than today.[29] However, future-oriented hope cannot be removed from the past or the present. For example, in some ways, life in South Africa is better today than it was when Biko was alive in the 1970s. South Africans have far greater political rights today than they did during Biko's lifetime. Yet, as we have noted, the right to have rights and the enactment of those rights are not synonymous. Hope does not only have a future, it also has a clear link to the past and a foundation in the present. This is the first aspect of a politics of hope for the coming generation that I would like to highlight, namely a historical consciousness that takes account of the past, the present, and the future.

For Biko, this meant, among other things, untangling and deconstructing the dehumanizing psychological consequences of colonialism and apartheid that reified whiteness and demonized blackness. Biko writes:

---

27. Cf. Thyssen Ashwin, "A Church for Others? Queering the Ecclesiology of Dietrich Bonhoeffer" (MTh. Thesis, Stellenbosch: Stellenbosch University, 2020), https://scholar.sun.ac.za:443/handle/10019.1/107896.

28. C. W. Du Toit, *The Legacy of Stephen Bantu Biko: Theological Challenges* (Pretoria: University of South Africa, Research Institute for Theology and Religion, 2008), 2.

29. Michael Mawson and Philip G. Ziegler, *The Oxford Handbook of Dietrich Bonhoeffer* (Oxford: Oxford University Press, 2019), 221.

> the most potent weapon in the hands of the oppressor is the mind of the oppressed. Once the latter has been so effectively manipulated and controlled by the oppressor as to make the oppressed believe that he is a liability to the white man, then there will be nothing the oppressed can do that will really scare the powerful masters. Hence thinking along lines of Black Consciousness makes the black man see himself as a being, entire in himself, and not as an extension of a broom or additional leverage to some machine. At the end of it all, he cannot tolerate attempts by anybody to dwarf the significance of his manhood. Once this happens, we shall know that the real man in the black person is beginning to shine through.[30]

The project of Black Consciousness is the untangling of the lies that were told about and to Black persons throughout (South) Africa's history. In untangling and deconstructing these lies from the past, the goal in the present is the construction of a new future. This task is primarily to be undertaken by Black persons. Yet, as Cobus van Wyngaard points out, in the process of Black Consciousness, there is also the possibility of the "inversion of a dominant white progressive logic."[31] The intention is Black liberation but, as a consequence, white persons may also come to be liberated from their prejudices.

Of course, Bonhoeffer's context was different from Biko's and so were his sources. Rather than an ideological struggle, Bonhoeffer engages history, and so hope and its ethical requirements, from an explicitly theological perspective. Yet as the following quotation illustrates, this is not an "otherworldly" passivity that waits on salvation from elsewhere:

> The ultimate question that responsible people ask themselves is not, how can I extricate myself heroically from the affair? But, how is the coming generation to live? It is only in this way that fruitful solutions can arise, even if for the time being they are humiliating. In short it is easier by far to act on abstract principles than from concrete responsibility. The rising generation will always instinctively discern which of the two we are acting upon. For it is their future which is at stake.[32]

Here, we see the construction of a historical consciousness that also relates the past, the present, and the future. The future is inextricably linked to the choices one makes in the present, and present choices cannot be divorced from the actions and choices from the past. John de Gruchy summarizes this tension in history between theology and action by noting that the core questions that Bonhoeffer

---

30. Biko, *I Write What I Like*, 69.
31. Cobus Van Wyngaard, "In Search of Repair: Critical White Responses to Whiteness as a Theological Problem: A South African Contribution" (PhD diss., Amsterdam and Pretoria, Free University and University of South Africa, 2019), 117.
32. *DBWE* 8:138–9.

seeks to address in his work and life are, "What does it mean to be human, who am I, is there room for God, and how will future generations live?"[33] Who I am, my understanding of humanity, and my willingness to work alongside God determine what the future will look like. This is beautifully captured by Bonhoeffer who claims that "God is the beyond in the midst of our lives."[34] Indeed, Bonhoeffer was acutely aware of the crisis that he and his contemporaries faced. He understood what led to his reality. Yet, he also recognized that the resolution of the crisis was not solely up to him and his contemporaries. It did not depend only on their work and agency. Like Biko, he engaged in critical reflection on the causes and symptoms of the prevailing crisis. He understood that they emerged from culture, religion, values, and commitments in history. Like Biko, Bonhoeffer regarded the situation of his time as "out of joint" with its intended historical trajectory, as Robert Vosloo puts it.[35] The past had led to a present reality that was disjointed with God's intended future. Bonhoeffer writes:

> It almost seems to me as if we must come to terms with it over the long haul, to live more deeply out of the past and the present—and that means out of gratitude—than from any vision of the future. On the other hand, one notices how strongly human life desires to live from the future, more than from anything else.[36]

There is a subtle reprimand in this statement—it is easy to lose historical consciousness and give over one's present responsibility if one desires to live in the future without a present commitment and the courage to change and work for change.

Biko and Bonhoeffer both recognize that hope is often derived from a hopeful view of the future. Yet, true hope also comes from understanding and discerning the past in order to deal with the present (in concrete political action), in order to secure the hope for the future. Bonhoeffer says:

> all of us feel obliged to take a position ourselves, to evaluate, to enter into, and to participate in the struggle and crisis of contemporary movements. . . . We are twentieth-century people and, like it or not, must come to terms with that fact; indeed, even more, we should have so much love for this contemporary world of ours, for our fellow human beings, that we should declare our solidarity with it in its crisis as in its hope.[37]

---

33. John W. de Gruchy, *Bonhoeffer's Questions: A Life-Changing Conversation* (London: Lexington Books, 2019), 175.

34. In Robert R. Vosloo, "Bonhoeffer, Transcendence, and the 'Turn to Religion,'" in *Culture and Transcendence: A Typology of Transcendence*, ed. Wessel Stoker and W. L. van der Merwe (Leuven: Peeters, 2012), 45–61.

35. *DBWE* 10:341.

36. *DBWE* 16:11, 113–14.

37. *DBWE* 10:326.

A problem that we face at present is the de-politicization of hope, making it only a future ideal or a past memory. This removes it from concrete action and "decision" (as Bonhoeffer puts it) or "consciousness" in the present (as Biko puts it). A politics of hope for the coming generation requires a tri-directional historical focus—critically discerning the past and actively engaging the present, while holding on to a realistic hope for the future. Bonhoeffer asserts that in taking a position and participating in contemporary crises, we focus not only on this current reality that is shaped by our past but also on the future by being in "solidarity with it in its crisis as in its hope."[38]

Of course, we have to respond to our community in proximate time and space, that is, our contemporaries in history and our fellow human beings with whom we share this current and common life. There is hardly any disagreement on this among activists and theologians in South Africa. We have a responsibility to respond with courage and justice to the realities of our context. Yet, Biko and Bonhoeffer also remind us that we also have a responsibility toward persons who are *not* proximate to us in time and space. This takes on at least three forms. First, we have to ask how we relate to persons who no longer exist (the past). How will we live our lives today so that we undo the injustices of our past? Second, as already noted, we must relate to persons with whom we currently exist (in the present). Third, we also have to ask how we build ethical relationships of responsibility with persons who do not yet exist (the future). In Wolfgang Huber's words, "the liability for the future affects our present actions."[39]

Thus, a politics of hope for the coming generation entails working for freedom from the injustices of our past, and it requires responsibility to work for freedom in the present and enacting freedom for the future. Indeed we are already judged not only for what we did in the past but also for what we do in the present by our future. Both Biko and Bonhoeffer seem to understand the importance of this tri-directional focus on history in fostering a politically adequate hope for the future.

Taking Responsibility in Action

Another correspondence that I identify in Biko and Bonhoeffer was their willingness to take responsibility for change in concrete action—what some might term "activism" in contemporary terms. Political hope requires action. However, as we shall see, their understanding of what calls forth an appropriate action differs, as does their understanding of what constitutes worthy action. For Biko, action requires bodily presence:

---

38. Ibid.
39. Wolfgang Huber, "Towards an Ethics of Responsibility," *The Journal of Religion* 73, no. 4 (1993): 579.

In order to achieve real action you must yourself be a living part of Africa and of her thought; you must be an element of that popular energy which is entirely called forth for the freeing, the progress and the happiness of Africa. There is no place outside that fight for the artist or for the intellectual who is not himself concerned with, and completely at one with the people in the great battle of Africa and of suffering humanity.[40]

What Biko advocates is both a physical and a psychological underpinning for true, liberative, and transformative action. He espouses not some sort of ideal—a thought experiment, a hypothesis, if you will. Rather, he advocates for persons who will be "completely at one with the people in the great battle of Africa and of suffering humanity." It is a radical and deep solidarity that requires bodily presence and ongoing transformative action. In a slightly different way, Bonhoeffer also relates responsible action to location, saying, "Only the one whose ultimate standard is not his reason, his principles, conscience, freedom, or virtue; only the one who is prepared to sacrifice all of these when, in faith and in relationship to God alone, he is called to obedient and responsible action."[41] However, neither Bonhoeffer nor Biko negates the importance of discernment, of reflection, of wisdom, and of understanding. Both of the above quotations show that they see a teleological intent to thoughtful reflection, namely responsible action.

What is different about the nature of action in Bonhoeffer and Biko is that in Biko, the action is validated and given its authenticity in relation to a specific people (suffering humanity), a place (Africa), and a specific battle (the liberation of Africa). For Biko, action is primarily a response to the negation of one's humanity and the historical injustices that go hand in hand with such a negation. History is a first order category that requires a response in action. The goal of action is the liberation of self and others for a future in which flourishing and true humanity are possible. This is a worthy and admirable goal.

While Bonhoeffer is also deeply tied to his context and deeply committed to the wholeness of humans and societies, his measure of the validity and appropriateness of action stems from it being a response to God's call. He says of a responsible person, an activist if you will, "[s]uch a person is the responsible one, whose life is nothing but a response to God's question and call."[42] For Bonhoeffer, history is a second order category that is placed under the authority of God. The action of the person is to become a co-participant with God in directing the course of history toward wholeness, regardless of personal success, well-being, or acclaim. Thus, "The one who allows nothing that happens to deprive him of his co-responsibility for the course of history, knowing that it is God that placed it on him, will find a

---

40. Biko, *I Write What I Like*, 33.
41. *DBWE* 8:37.
42. Ibid.

fruitful relationship to the events of history, beyond fruitless criticism and equally fruitless opportunism."[43]

For Biko, the politics of hope in action is related to particular historical persons, circumstances, and places, and it seeks to secure a better future for those persons and their descendants. For Bonhoeffer, on the other hand, the politics of action is specifically related to a faithful response to God's call to take co-responsibility for God's intended future for humanity and creation—while it is historical, it is first of all eschatological. He expressed aspects of such sentiments, asking, "For those who are willing to take responsibility, the ultimate question is not 'How can I come out of this event with honour?' but rather 'How can the life of the next generation be assured?' Only from this historically responsible question can fruitful solutions arise, even if they might seem initially humble."[44]

From the Personal to the Structural

The next area in which I believe both Biko and Bonhoeffer can contribute to a politics of hope for the coming generation is through their respective emphasis on moving from a singular focus on the personal to a broader and more encompassing focus on the structural aspects of life. The agency to shape one's own future is surely one of the most important aspects of a politics of hope for the coming generation. However, a crucial question is not only what such a future looks like but also for whom will it be shaped.

Both Biko and Bonhoeffer challenged Christians and Christianity to address internal structural heresies and external structural and political social intentions. In relation to internal structural concerns, Bonhoeffer focuses on the capturing of the German Church by Nationalism, but for Biko, it was the capturing of the Southern African Church by whiteness and colonialism. In keeping with their respective worldviews, they approached these deficiencies and aberrations in Christianity in different ways. For Biko, Black identity played a central role in unshackling Christians and Christianity from whiteness and the abuse of whiteness that were formalized through structurally violent policies and persons during colonial and apartheid eras. He writes, "No nation can win a battle without faith, and if our faith in our God is spoilt by our having to see Him through the eyes of the same people we are fighting against, then there obviously begins to be something wrong in that relationship."[45] As a Southern African Catholic, Biko was rightly critical of the shape, identity, culture, and theologies of missionary Christianities and their colonial aims and occident. In Biko's view, "Christianity can never hope to remain abstract and removed from the people's environmental problems . . . Black Theology therefore is a situational interpretation of Christianity. . . . In other

---

43. Ibid., 42.
44. Ibid., 138–9.
45. Biko, *I Write What I Like*, 59–60.

words, it shifts the emphasis from petty sins to major sins in a society, thereby ceasing to teach the people to 'suffer peacefully.'"[46]

Here, one can see a commuting between internal structural issues and external political concerns. Recognizing that many young Black persons were leaving Christianity because it was captured by whiteness, Biko noted: "These are topics that black ministers of religion must begin to talk about seriously if they are to save Christianity from falling foul with black people, particularly young black people. The time has come for our own theologians to take up the cudgels of the fight by restoring a meaning and direction in the black man's understanding of God."[47]

Central to Biko's idea of transforming the structural elements within the church is the understanding that a certain kind and quality of persons are crucial to the kind of transformation that would liberate Black South Africans. We find this expressed in two ways. First is his constant use of the South African Students Association's (SASO's) cry, "Black man [sic] you are on your own!"[48] Structural transformation could not be realized through white liberalism or colonial Christianity. It would only be achieved through the transformation of the minds and lives of Black Africans. Anything else was simply a naïve form of slavery or subjugation, teaching people to "suffer peacefully."[49] He admonished Black South African clergy and Christians, "that God is not in the habit of coming down from heaven to solve people's problems on earth."[50] For Biko, the hope for the future lies both in the correction of the psychosocial errors of the past and the ideologically informed activity of Black persons in the present moment.

Bonhoeffer's view was also not devoid of criticism of the church and of religion in his time and context, as he called for a Christocentric, "religionless Christianity."[51] Behind this much misunderstood and even abused concept is a framing question, "What is bothering me incessantly is the question what Christianity really is, or indeed who Christ really is, for us today?"[52] For Bonhoeffer, the central issue is not first and foremost the role of the Christian or the church in addressing structural concerns for the future. Rather, as Urbaniak points out, Bonhoeffer poses a Christological question, "What shape does Christ take in the world?" This question has ecclesiological implications: "How does the church, the community of disciples founded in Christ's name, make itself manifest in the midst of the world come of age?"[53] Here, we return again to Bonhoeffer's claim that "God is the

---

46. Ibid., 59.
47. Ibid., 59–60.
48. Ibid., 91.
49. Ibid., 59.
50. Ibid., 61.
51. *DBWE* 8:279.
52. Ibid.
53. Jakub Urbaniak, "From Religionless Christianity to Immanent Grace: Bonhoeffer's Legacy in Badiou," *The Journal of Religion* 94, no. 4 (October 2014): 458.

beyond in the midst of our lives."⁵⁴ In Bonhoeffer's perspective, obedient action is obedience to God, first and foremost. Indeed, Bonhoeffer was a strong advocate for making decision in the now, that is, human agency.⁵⁵ Yet, the decision is made in relation to the will and person of God in the world and in history. Human agency is central to transformation yet such agency is to come in response to God who is already working in the world.

In his doctoral dissertation on Bonhoeffer, the late South African theologian, Russel Botman, argues for transformation as human responsibility in response to the will of God.⁵⁶ Dirkie Smit, coined the phrase, "hopeful agency" to describe this cooperative missiological relationship between God and humanity.⁵⁷ What Bonhoeffer advocated, Botman described, and Smit characterized as "hopeful agency," took seriously the point that true hope for the future comes from the God who calls us into the future. It is active hope in the midst of a current struggle that can be traced to historical sin. Bonhoeffer notes that the "question is not how I extricate myself heroically from a situation but how a coming generation is to go on living."⁵⁸ This requires that the Christian take "each day as if it were the last and yet living it faithfully and responsibly as if there were yet to be a great future."⁵⁹ It is the God who is incarnate in Christ, becomes part of, and is for this world who ushered in this-worldly hope. Smit sums up Botman's interpretation of Bonhoeffer's "hopeful agency" as follows:

> The fact that it was a this-worldly hope meant for him that it should not lead to idle waiting and become a form of escapism, but rather that it should inspire concrete actions, practical engagement in the fullness of life, hopeful agency in the utterly serious realities of the penultimate. . . . The fact that it was an empowering hope was for him of great importance . . . he refused to be held captive by the past—with its legacies, divisions, hurt and bitterness. . . . The fact that it was a modest and self-critical hope meant for him that these transformation processes—all these attempts to make history for the coming generation—remains provisional and penultimate.

---

54. Cited in Vosloo, "Bonhoeffer, Transcendence, and the 'Turn to Religion.'"

55. Karola S. Radler, "Decision in the Thought of Dietrich Bonhoeffer and Carl Schmitt: A Comparative Study" (Mth. Thesis, Stellenbosch: Stellenbosch University, 2019), 126–36, https://scholar.sun.ac.za:443/handle/10019.1/107319.

56. H. Russel Botman, "Discipleship as Transformation? Towards a Theology of Transformation" (PhD diss., University of the Western Cape, Bellville, South Africa, 1994).

57. Dirkie Smit, "'Making History for the Coming Generation': On the Theological Logic of Russel Botman's Commitment to Transformation," *Stellenbosch Theological Journal* 1, no. 2 (2015): 607–32.

58. *DBWE* 8:42.

59. Ibid., 51.

Like Bonhoeffer, Botman contends that our work is never the final word in history. We are co-creators of the future, by God's invitation. But we are not our own salvation. So, while both Bonhoeffer and Biko advocate for a move from the personal to the structural, their approach to human agency is one of the major differences between them. Biko emphasizes the agency of persons as a primary means toward historical transformation into the future. Bonhoeffer, on the other hand, sees human agency as a response-ability in relation to God's ongoing work for justice and the restoration of all creation in history. In spite of these differences, both emphasize the importance of concrete action to deconstruct injustice for the sake of a better future.

Conclusion

In this chapter, I have sought to answer the question, *Can Bonhoeffer and Biko offer us any resources for a politics of hope for the "born free" generation of South Africa?* I have argued that they can. Each of them, sometimes in similar and sometimes in different ways, offers us some insights and guidance. They both help us to see that history matters (past, present, and future), and that our generation has both responsibility and agency in the present and so should take responsibility for the future. This can be done by addressing the past with concrete and courageous action in the present.

Finally, we should move from the personal to the structural in order to secure a future in which the coming generation can live. Perhaps, as Bonhoeffer reminds us, what is needed is the willingness to listen, to listen to God and to the coming generation:

> The first service one owes to others in a community involves listening to them. Just as our love for God begins with listening to God's Word, the beginning of love for others is learning to listen to them. God's love for us is shown by the fact that God not only gives God's Word but also lends us God's ear. . . . We do God's work for our brothers and sisters when we learn to listen to them.[60]

So, let us listen to the coming generation and acknowledge that they are not yet free. But let us also not give up hope for the future since both Bonhoeffer and Biko lived and, indeed, died for a better future for coming generations. Learning from them allows us to respond concretely to the God who is freedom, who is inviting us to live and work with courage and commitment today for the flourishing of coming generations. This could form the foundation of a politics of hope for the future.

---

60. *DBWE* 5:75.

Chapter 23

BONHOEFFER AND THE HERMENEUTICS OF HOPE

THE QUEST FOR EXISTENCE AND MEANING

Peter Frick

> Sehnsucht, Erwartung,
> Hoffnung also
> brauchen ihre Hermeneutik.
>
> —Ernst Bloch[1]

Introduction

Is our generation or the coming one in the most precarious situation ever, regarding the prospect of hope, peace, and a future for global well-being? Historically, there were various times and places when people felt that *their* future was hopeless. One such place of hopelessness was Berlin in February 1945. On Saturday February 3, the city suffered the heaviest air attacks in its history and was reduced to rubble. At that time, Bonhoeffer was imprisoned in the Gestapo Security Office in the Prinz-Albrecht Strasse, just a few days before he would be transported to Buchenwald Concentration Camp. In the same month, my then sixteen-year-old father was also in Berlin, and he saw with his own eyes the devastation of the city. Decades later, he told me how utterly hopeless the devastation left him as a teenager. Only a few months later in August 1945, the world witnessed another human disaster of unimaginable proportions when the A-bomb devastated Hiroshima. Such large scale and instant mass destruction from just one weapon had never before been experienced. It opened up the world of destruction to a scale of sheer insanity. And recently, we have witnessed the unprecedented global Covid-19 pandemic, another reason to question a hopeful and bright future. Still, just as both Berlin and Hiroshima slowly rose from the ashes, so did my father who was able to establish a life of faith, love, and hope.

For me, as a postwar child and as most teenagers in the 1970s, I believed that humanity had reached its lowest point in history with the Holocaust and that from

---

1. Ernst Bloch, *Das Prinzip Hoffnung*, vol. 1 (Frankfurt: Suhrkamp Verlag, 1959), 5.

there on, we human beings had learned our lesson. Humanity would slowly regain its goodness, I thought, and progress toward the virtues we now call equality, dignity, respect, inclusivity, diversity, and so on. I was mistaken. Rwanda happened. And why do we still have a long list of tyrants running various governments around the world? To this day I still ask myself, is it realistic to assume that Auschwitz and Hiroshima were the low points of civilization and that one day the world will be a better and just place? After all, the Berlin Wall fell unexpectedly and apartheid came to an end, at least officially, both without bloodshed.

The question addressed in this chapter is how can we (theologians, educators, parents, pastors) speak of hope and a future for our world without sounding cheap, naïve, and merely optimistic? Drawing on Dietrich Bonhoeffer, Ernst Bloch, and Jürgen Moltmann, I will proceed as follows—first, to examine the dynamic of hope as a Christian virtue; second, to discuss how hope is an existential marker of human existence; and third, to suggest how hope may function as a social and political catalyst for the future.

Grounding Hope Theologically

Hope is one of the foundational convictions of the Christian tradition. If there is no hope, there would be no Christian faith. Thus, it is a curious fact that it is *not* Jesus who is the protagonist of hope. Jesus never employed the noun "hope" (ἐλπίς), and only once in Lk. 6:34 does the verb "to hope" (ἐλπίζετε) appear, but even in that instance, it may have been a Lucan redaction.[2] Still, the idea of hope is of course deeply embedded in the Hebrew Bible. One needs only to read the Psalms, for example, David's prayers, to get a sense of the centrality of hope. How then did hope get into mainstream Christian teaching?

It was through the apostle Paul. In the oldest Christian document, 1 Thessalonians, it took Paul only three verses before he speaks of the "steadfastness of hope in our Lord," a hope he specifies at the end of the letter as the "hope of salvation" (1 Thess. 5:8). In Romans, Paul says that Abraham was "hoping against hope" (4:18) because he and Sarah were definitely past the age of childbearing. In Rom. 8:24-25, the apostle speaks with conviction that "in hope we were saved. Now hope that is seen is not hope. For who hopes for what is seen? But if we hope for what we do not see, we wait for it with patience." And in Rom. 15:3, Paul even characterizes God himself as "the God of hope." Moreover, as we all know, in Paul's famous hymn on the excellence of love in 1 Cor. 13, he places hope on the level of

---

2. It is very likely that Lk. 6:34 is either a Lucan composition or draws on pre-Lucan tradition; cf. I. Howard Marshall, *Commentary on Luke*, New International Greek New Testament Commentary (Grand Rapids, MI: William B. Eerdmans, 1978), 263. At any rate, the greater prevalence of the semantic domain "to hope, hope" in Acts suggests that Luke could have inserted the verb "to hope" in Lk. 6:34. See also Joseph A. Fitzmyer, *The Gospel According to Luke (I-IX)*, The Anchor Bible 28 (New York: Doubleday, 1981), 640.

faith and love. And according to the Acts of the Apostles, Paul had to stand trial before the Emperor because of the hope of the resurrection (24:15; 26:6). In sum, for Paul, hope not only operates in our present world,[3] but it also has a decidedly eschatological ring. Perhaps no other verse in the Pauline corpus expresses this better than 1 Cor. 15:19-20: "If for this life only we have hoped in Christ, we are of all people most to be pitied. But in fact Christ has been raised from the dead, the first fruits of those who have died."

Like Paul himself, Bonhoeffer takes for granted the centrality and significance of the eschatological fulfillment of hope. In a 1938 sermon, Bonhoeffer preached on the Pauline verse "we boast in the hope for the future glory" (Rom. 5:2).[4] He declares, "God's right and victory on earth *have begun*, and will become eternal glorious peace."[5] Similarly, in *Discipleship*, Bonhoeffer remarks that in the resurrection of Christ, "imperishable hope *now opened*,"[6] namely hope for the eternal future. It is crucial to note that Bonhoeffer does not say "hope is now realized," but he says "hope now opened." It is clear that Bonhoeffer subscribes to an eschatological view of partial fulfillment. While our hope will be completely fulfilled only in the life to come, the beginning of that ultimate fulfillment is here on earth. We know that Bonhoeffer consistently stresses the human connectedness to the earth, a life that is deeply rooted in the earthly realities of our everyday lives, an idea that he called *Diesseitigkeit*.[7]

In other words, Bonhoeffer is keenly aware of the biblical-theological two-sidedness of hope. On the one hand, there is the eschatological dimension of the future fulfillment of all hope in the coming life with Christ. But on the other hand, there is the immanent aspect of a hope that is inextricably linked to our lives here on earth, in the here and now. And yet, we must not understand a theology of hope as if the transcendent outplays the immanent or as if the immanent swallows up the transcendent. They are different aspects of the one teaching on Christian hope. Bonhoeffer wants to keep the two together when he says in the same sermon mentioned earlier that hope, though in faith, is grounded in God himself. In short, if we have "this great hope in God . . . then everything is won. Do we no longer have it? Then everything is lost."[8] "Everything," Bonhoeffer says, is equally won or lost unless we believe that both heavenly and earthly hopes are grounded in God.

Moltmann captures this dynamic between hope in Christ and hope on this earth very aptly: "Thus in the Christian life faith has the priority, but hope has the

---

3. Hebrews 6:18-19 says we are "strongly encouraged to seize the hope set before us," a hope that is "a sure and steadfast anchor of the soul."

4. Cf. *DBWE* 15:471–6, "Sermon on Romans 5:1–5."

5. Ibid., 473 (emphasis added).

6. *DBWE* 3:146 (emphasis added).

7. On Bonhoeffer's love of the earth and *Diesseitigkeit*, cf. Peter Frick, "Friedrich Nietzsche's Aphorisms and Dietrich Bonhoeffer's Theology," in *Understanding Bonhoeffer*, ed. Peter Frick (Tübingen: Mohr Siebeck, 2018), 78–104 (101–4).

8. *DBWE* 15:475.

primacy. Without faith's knowledge of Christ, hope becomes a utopia and remains hanging in the air. But without hope, faith falls to pieces, becomes a fainthearted and ultimately dead faith."[9] In other words, precisely because of Christ and the resurrection hope does our earthly hope not hang in the air but is grounded in real life. For the purpose of this chapter, however, I focus on the immanent aspect of hope.

Regarding hope as an earthly good in his sermons during the years in London (1933–5), Bonhoeffer repeatedly and eloquently speaks of hope. He asks how can we "talk about peace and love . . . about a new world and a new humanity?"[10] The short answer, he proposes, is that hope is rooted in our faith, for "faith that has no hope is sick." Hence, Bonhoeffer dares us "to hope so unconditionally that our loving hope can empower others."[11] A decade later, in his Christmas message of 1942, "After Ten Years," in spite of the downward spiral of his own life in Nazi Germany, Bonhoeffer still has not given up hope. In fact, he claims that "no one ought to despise optimism as the will for the future"[12] because healthy optimism is the "power of hope when others resign."[13] When Bonhoeffer himself faces an increasingly hopeless situation, he holds firm to a healthy and realistic optimism that he calls hope. For Bonhoeffer, hope is grounded in faith, as we said, but such grounded hope is not simply the psychological side of a theological doctrine.

Grounding Hope Existentially

As human beings, we desire hope to be real, to be tangible, to be part of our everyday existence. In this regard, it is not coincidental that there are two post-Second World War monographs on the subject of hope that gained instant popularity. The first is the work of the Jewish philosopher Ernst Bloch, who had written the famous *Das Prinzip Hoffnung* [*The Principle of Hope*],[14] while in exile in New York during the war. The second book is by Jürgen Moltmann, who started his path to academic fame with the publication of the monograph, *Theology of Hope*, first published in 1965. It is telling that both Bloch and Moltmann took their disciplines by storm in that they employed the term "hope" in the titles of their works. While the word "hope" does not immediately suggest a philosophical topic, it is much closer to Christian theology. However, it seems that the success of these two books has to do with the fact that hope was lost during the Holocaust and that

---

9. Jürgen Moltmann, *Theology of Hope*, trans. James W. Leitch (London: SCM Press, 1967), 20.
10. *DBWE* 13:394.
11. Ibid., 386.
12. *DBWE* 8:51.
13. Ibid., 50.
14. Ernst Bloch, *The Principle of Hope* (Cambridge, MA: MIT Press, 1977). Apparently, the title of the English version was originally meant to be *The Dreams of a Better Life*.

that loss lasted well into postwar reconstruction attempts. It is also not a surprise that Moltmann's *Theology of Hope* was a great success in Latin America where in the 1960s Liberation Theology was about to receive its first major impetus with Gustavo Gutiérrez's *A Theology of Liberation* in 1968.[15] Gutiérrez, not unexpectedly, draws both on Bloch and Moltmann.[16] The soil was ripe for the power of hope to put down new roots in Europe and South America.

But why do we human beings desire a life of hope? What is it in us that makes us people of hope? Even as Christians, we confess that the resurrection of Jesus Christ is the foundation of all hope, both here on earth and in the life to come in the future. But where and how, exactly, do we as human beings experience the reality and content of hope? Moltmann is quite right that the notion of future "must mean ontological possibility and anthropological freedom."[17] But how can we claim an ontological foundation that includes an anthropological freedom in our exercise of hope?

In his habilitation, *Act and Being*, the young Bonhoeffer daringly rewrote the Cartesian dictum *cogito ergo sum* into *sum cogito ergo* and thereby, with Heidegger, assigns priority of being over thinking.[18] For Bonhoeffer, an epistemological premise now became an ontological foundation. Bonhoeffer agrees with Heidegger against Descartes that being has priority over thinking or to put it in plain language, our human existence is the basis of our thinking and not the other way round. To assign priority to ontology is further to claim that human existence is structured in a specific way, in the way that we call "human," or in philosophical language, we speak of the ontological structures of being human. In order to understand the relevance of these ontological structures to our discussion of hope, let us take a short detour into Heidegger, a step that Bonhoeffer did not make.

Heidegger maintains overtly that the "concept of 'meaning' is one which is ontologico-existential in principle,"[19] and that "meaning is an *existentiale* of Dasein,[20] not a property attaching to entities, lying 'behind' them."[21] By this he asserts that our search for a meaningful life is not something that we eventually discover or find interesting, among many other things. Meaning is not something

---

15. Gustavo Gutiérrez, *A Theology of Liberation: History, Politics, and Salvation*, trans. Sister Caridad Inda and John Eagleson, rev. ed. (Maryknoll, NY: Orbis Books, 1988).

16. Gutiérrez, *A Theology of Liberation*, 123–6.

17. Jürgen Moltmann, "Hope and Planning," in *Hope and Planning*, ed. Jürgen Moltmann, trans. Margaret Clarkson (London: SCM Press, 1971), 181.

18. *DBWE* 2:71.

19. Martin Heidegger, *Being and Time*, trans. John Macquarrie and Edward Robinson (New York: Harper and Row, 1962), 193. For an excellent study of Heidegger vis-á-vis Bonhoeffer, see Stephen Plant, "'In the Sphere of the Familiar.' Heidegger and Bonhoeffer," in *Bonhoeffer's Intellectual Formation*, ed. Peter Frick (Tübingen: Mohr Siebeck, 2008), 301–27.

20. See Heidegger, *Being and Time*, 27, n.1, for an explanation of "Dasein."

21. Ibid., 193.

that is a mere option among many other opportunities in life, but "meaning is that wherein the intelligibility of something maintains itself."[22] For Heidegger, "*only Dasein can be meaningful [sinnvoll] or meaningless [sinnlos]*" because Dasein is always a "disclosedness of Being-in-the-world."[23]

In other words, Heidegger claims that the ontological-existential structure of our being is the basis and reason for the quest for a meaningful existence. The human quest for meaning is part of the basic ontological-existential structure of human existence; it is an *a priori* reality, *the* distinguishing feature of personhood as such. In short, every person who has existence, who lives, who is a human being, desires a meaningful life. To claim that the search for meaning *is* our ontological structure entails that we do not have to motivate ourselves to think we desire a meaningful life. Every single human being desires automatically, unknowingly, consciously, and subconsciously a meaningful life, irrespective of age, gender, geography, education, personality, economics, status, etcetera. Interestingly, from a psychological perspective, Viktor Frankl, Holocaust survivor and founder of the third Vienna School of Psychoanalysis (after Freud and Adler), anchored his so-called logotherapy precisely in the human quest for meaning. Frankl claims that logotherapy "focuses on the meaning of human existence . . . [because] the striving to find meaning in one's life is the primary motivational force in man."[24]

To take one crucial step beyond Heidegger and beyond Bonhoeffer, I would like to suggest that our desire for hope is likewise grounded in our ontological-existential structure of being human. While Heidegger does not explicitly speak of hope as *existential*, he seems to imply just that when he says that "what is decisive for the structure of hope as a phenomenon, is . . . the existential meaning of hoping itself."[25] That is to say, meaning and correspondingly hope are part of the innermost core of our human makeup. Without hope, it is impossible to live a meaningful life or in existential terminology, an authentic Dasein. Here then lies the clue to what Moltmann calls the "ontological possibility and anthropological freedom." We really do not have to motivate ourselves to desire a meaningful and hopeful life. There is freedom in us, in every human being, which nearly automatically, unknowingly, consciously, and subconsciously empowers us to seek meaning, understanding, and hope. It is *a priori*, or in the language of Heidegger, hope can be characterized as *Existenzial* (existential).[26] Most importantly therefore, the desire for hope has, as its starting point, an ontological reality of possibility that

22. Ibid.
23. Ibid.; original emphasis.
24. Viktor E. Frankl, *Man's Search for Meaning: An Introduction to Logotherapy*, 4th ed. (Boston, MA: Beacon Press, 1992), 104.
25. Heidegger, *Being and Time*, 395–6.
26. Cf. Friedrich Beisser, "Hoffnung. IV. Dogmatisch," in *Religion in Geschichte und Gegenwart*, ed. Hans D. Betz, Don S. Browning, Bernd Janowski, and Eberhard Jüngel (Tübingen: Mohr Siebeck 2008), 1826.

can be exercised[27] because of our equally ontological possibility for freedom. We are free to desire hope. This is true, for every person, irrespective of age, gender, geography, education, personality, economics, status, etcetera, strives to find meaning in life. To express it differently, existence that seeks meaning or existence that seeks understanding—this is our basic human ontological and existential structure. Moltmann puts it aptly by modifying Anselm of Canterbury's definition of theology ("faith seeking understanding") to "hope seeking understanding" (*Spes quaerens intellectum*).[28]

Living Hope Existentially

While hope is ontologically grounded in human freedom, the experience of hope is not only eschatological but also one of existential experience. We will now turn to this second dimension.

Hope Is Tangible

Let us return to Moltmann briefly. Moltmann fully supports "the demand made by Barth and Bonhoeffer that the 'lordship of Christ' must be consistently testified and presented all the way to the very heart of secular reality."[29] For Moltmann, this means that "the theologian is not concerned merely to supply a different *interpretation* of the world, of history and of human nature, but to *transform* them in expectation of a divine transformation."[30] This last statement is of course vintage Karl Marx but claimed by Moltmann for his Christian view of eschatology. Moltmann's argument is valid but in my view, the lordship of Christ is not exhausted in the transformation of what he calls "secular reality." Bonhoeffer has clearly and, in my view, successfully demonstrated that it is more appropriate to speak of reality as *one* reality, namely the reality that comprises both what we would call secular and sacred reality. Suffice it here to say that, for Bonhoeffer, reality (*Wirklichkeit*) in its totality is constituted, centered, and fulfilled in Jesus Christ. If so, it follows that there is no reality that is *not* part of the one divine reality revealed in Christ:[31]

---

27. Cf. Hans-Georg Gadamer, *Wahrheit und Methode: Grundzüge einer philosophischen Hermeneutik. Hermeneutik I*, GW 1, 5th ed. (Tübingen: J.C.B. Mohr, 1986), 355: "Das Wesen der Hoffnung ist . . . eine so klare Auszeichnung der menschlichen Erfahrung."

28. Jürgen Moltmann, *Theology of Hope*, trans. James W. Leitch (London: SCM Press, 1967), 36.

29. Moltmann, *Theology of Hope*, 83.

30. Ibid., 84.

31. Cf. "The world has no reality of its own independent of God's revelation in Christ"; *DBWE* 6:58.

> There are not two realities, but *only one reality*, and that is God's reality revealed in Christ in the reality of the world. Partaking in Christ, we stand at the same time in the reality of God and in the reality of the world. The reality of Christ embraces the reality of the world in itself. The world has no reality of its own independent of God's revelation in Christ. It is a denial of God's revelation in Jesus Christ to wish to be "Christian" without being "worldly," or [to] wish to be worldly without seeing and recognizing the world in Christ. Hence there are not two realms, but only *the one realm of the Christ-reality* [*Christuswirklichkeit*], in which the reality of God and the reality of the world are united.[32]

It is important for our purpose to recognize that hope must be part of this one reality or *Christuswirklichkeit*. We cannot have hope and experience hope outside of the reality of our world. As the word "reality" implies, it is the sphere of the real. That implies that a hope that is merely an abstract idea is no hope at all. But sadly, hopelessness can also be part of this one reality.

Hope Is Transformative

But hope in the one reality of our world and Christ, that is to say, "real hope," must move beyond the real to the tangible, the transformative. How then can hope become an existential experience and transformative for us and the world? Let us return to Viktor Frankl whose experiences at Auschwitz are of course at the extreme end of the spectrum of life, but whose basic ideas expressed in logotherapy illustrates how hope is transformative. Frankl recounts that those inmates who were losing hope and giving up were the ones who would inevitably die. The loss of hope was indeed so powerful that it had far-reaching impact on the immune system and therefore literally over life and death.[33]

Though Frankl's experiences illustrate the extreme of losing hope, they nonetheless clearly point to the positive and transformative aspects of the power of hope. Even in dire circumstances, the holding on to hope is so powerful that both the body and the mind are transformed and invigorated with life. And herein lies precisely the transformative element of hope—it gives life. It gives life because it is tied to meaning. In other words, when hope is anchored in meaning, both are a vehicle toward life.

Hope Is Existentially Lived

In order to experience hope, we must seek a life that values understanding and meaning, and that lays claim to the freedom to be filled with hope. And that hope,

---

32. *DBWE* 6:58. On the postmodern condition and the unifying reality of Jesus Christ, cf. Michael Trowitzsch, "Jesus Christus: Wahrheit der Kirche, Einheit der Wirklichkeit—oder: Bonhoeffer und die Postmoderne," in *Über die Moderne hinaus: Theologie im Übergang*, ed. Michael Trowitzsch (Tübingen: Mohr Siebeck, 1999), 159–73.

33. Cf. Frankl, *Man's Search for Meaning*, 84.

in short, must be exercised. In other words, hope grounded in both God and our ontological structures must be tangible hope. We could also say that hope is never just passive but always active. Hope does not just sit back and wait for its easy and miraculous fulfillment. Moltmann rightly remarks that "the most serious objection to a theology of hope . . . arises from the religion of humble acquiescence in the present."[34] It is indeed a dangerous thing to be falsely humble and just hope in God quietly and do nothing for the things we hope for. It is an art both to place our hope in God and at the same time be active toward its realization. This is true not only for the individual believer but also for the church as a whole.

Bonhoeffer's teaching on the ultimate and penultimate things in his *Ethics* are of highest importance here. Bonhoeffer argues that "the essence of the gospel does not consist in solving worldly problems, and also that this cannot be the essential task of the church. However, it does not follow from this that the church would have no task at all in this regard. *But we will not recognize its legitimate task unless we first find the correct starting point.*"[35]

But what is the correct starting point? For Bonhoeffer, it is that the church addresses the world and its problems and "defines a space" within which faith "is at least not made impossible . . . [that] there is at least no *offence* that hinders faith."[36] So, Bonhoeffer argues that the task of the church is not primarily and ultimately in actions of social justice, but in relating to the world with "the effect of *preparing the way* for the coming of Jesus Christ."[37] In Bonhoeffer's distinction between the ultimate and penultimate things, he claims that "the coming of grace"[38] is the ultimate. God's grace is ultimate because it is the last and final act in the divine-human drama. In his own words, "the entry of grace is the ultimate";[39] it is, in other words, the eschatological fulfillment of hope. Bonhoeffer further explains that "the condition in which grace meets us is not irrelevant . . . because we can make it hard for ourselves and others to come to faith."[40] He does *not* say that everything we Christians do must—or even can—always lead to faith, or that all our actions should always have faith as its ultimate goal. But Bonhoeffer does say that there is "immeasurable responsibility"[41] placed on Christians with respect to the penultimate reality of our world. "The hungry person needs bread," he reminds us, "the homeless person needs shelter, the one deprived of rights needs justice, the lonely person needs community, the undisciplined one needs order, and the slave needs freedom."[42] All of this entails that the acts in the penultimate realm are

---

34. Moltmann, *Theology of Hope*, 26.
35. *DBWE* 6:356; original emphasis.
36. Ibid., 360.
37. Ibid.
38. Cf. ibid., 160–6.
39. Ibid., 163.
40. Ibid., 162.
41. Ibid., 163.
42. Ibid.

"a matter of concrete intervention in the visible world," that is to say, they must be "visible deeds."[43] Whether we engage in acts of social justice as a church[44] or as individuals, these acts in the penultimate realm will necessarily turn out to be acts of hope. Bonhoeffer never calls them directly actions of hope, but I would argue that this is what they become.

The reason we can substantiate such a claim has to do with the effects of penultimate actions. They lead to "being human,"[45] to becoming "human again,"[46] or "to an entirely new way of being human."[47] When something good happens to us, "the conditions that are part of being human"[48] are registered on the ontological level, namely in the sense that we find understanding, meaning and correspondingly hope in our being. This is exactly what happens when we practice actions in the penultimate realm. These are experienced by both the agent and the recipient as signs of hope. When the hungry person can eat, when the homeless person has shelter, when the marginalized receive their rights, when poverty is structurally lessened, then, there is hope, and with it, we experience "a new way of being human," a *hopeful* way of being human.

Hope Includes Otherness

To take the thought of being human one step further, we note that many times our hopes are directed toward better conditions, experiences, and relationships. In almost all of these situations, it is the case that the fulfillment of hope critically includes other persons. Moltmann makes the intriguing statement, long before the discourse about "the other" and "otherness" became popular and politically correct, that "hope presupposes the otherness of the other and his [and her] freedom."[49] What he means by this is that in relation to the other, hope is not something that derives "out of my own powers" but rather something that "another person places at my disposal."[50] In other words, my own hope is contingent on the other person being there—for me. Put differently, because the fulfillment of hope lies essentially outside of myself, I need to rely on someone else, precisely on "the other."

---

43. Ibid., 164.

44. Cf. ibid., 361. The church must be concerned with "worldly questions, and in certain earthly conditions. There are, for example, certain economic or social attitudes and conditions that hinder faith in Jesus Christ, which means that they also destroy the essence of human beings and the world. It can be asked, for example, whether capitalism, or socialism, or collectivism are such economic systems."

45. Ibid., 165.
46. Ibid., 166.
47. Ibid., 167.
48. Ibid., 160.
49. Moltmann, "Hope and Planning," 180.
50. Ibid., 180–1.

Bonhoeffer repeatedly speaks of "the other."[51] He claims that "the other can be experienced by the I only as You, but never directly as I, that is, in the sense of the I that has become I only through the claim of a You."[52] Here, Bonhoeffer asserts that the formation of the I, my own self, is always in relation to the You, precisely "the other." The I is never completely independent from the You. In relation to hope, this entails that the fulfillment of my hope most often depends on the other. This is not to say that my I, myself, is always completely dependent on the You, but it does mean that the You always impinges in some way on the I, or in Bonhoeffer's words, "the You sets the limit for the subject."[53]

In relation to the fulfillment of hope, it seems to me that we may place Bonhoeffer and Moltmann in a constructive dynamic. Moltmann's insistence that "the otherness of the other" requires "his [and her] freedom"[54] is the positive side of Bonhoeffer's position that the other constitutes "my limit." In other words, precisely because "the other" is free in his or her behavior, the freedom of the other may in fact become my limit when I do not agree with the acts of the other. In effect, the freedom of the other may stand in the way of the fulfillment of my hope. This raises a precarious question. What is more significant, my unconditional acceptance of the other or the fulfillment of my hope?

Hope—Learnable but Fragile and Fragmentary

Whether we can prioritize the fulfillment of our hope over against the freedom of the other is a complex question that defies any simplistic answer. Rather than trying to deal abstractly with this existential question, let us now point to a few important issues to consider when we desire the fulfillment of our hope.

First, as Bloch reminds us, "es kommt darauf an, das Hoffen zu lernen" [it is decisive to learn the art of hoping].[55] But how do we learn the art of hoping in a world that demolishes such expectancy on a daily basis? According to Bloch, "hope needs its own hermeneutic."[56] Bloch assumes, without saying so explicitly, an ontological foundation of hope. He says that hope is the "Grundzug des menschlichen Bewußtseins" [the basic principle of human consciousness]. He further assumes that hope has, as correlate, what he calls a "noch unabgeschlossene Daseinsbestimmtheit," meaning, "a not yet finished element of our human existence." To put all this in positive terms, Bloch argues that our hermeneutic

---

51. Cf. my essay, "The Art of Tolerance: Insights from Bonhoeffer and Levinas," in *Polyphonie der Theologie: Verantwortung und Widerstand in Kirche und Politik. Festschrift für Andreas Pangritz zum 65. Geburtstag*, ed. Matthias Grebe (Stuttgart: W. Kohlhammer, 2019), 161–74.

52. *DBWE* 1:51.

53. Ibid.

54. Moltmann, "Hope and Planning," 180.

55. Bloch, *Das Prinzip Hoffnung*, vol. 1, 1.

56. Ibid., 5: "Sehnsucht, Erwartung, Hoffnung also brauchen ihre Hermeneutik."

of hope should take hope seriously given both our ontological and psychological dispositions that seek present and future fulfillment. And because of these dispositions we as human beings can understand hope. Thus, Bloch speaks of "begriffene Hoffnung" [understandable hope].[57] The aspect that makes hope precisely an exercise in *learned* and *understandable* hermeneutics is deliberately learning to *think* of hope as a basic human constituent and therefore acting in a manner that seeks hope and its fulfillment. Put differently, Bloch seems to suggest that hope is not just a little bonus to human life, but a basic intellectual and emotional part of it. We are. Therefore, we hope. We *can* choose to hope!

We encounter the full force of Bloch's ideas only when we consider its reverse, namely the absence of hope. In his own words, "die Hoffnungslosigkeit ist . . . das Unaushaltbarste, das ganz und gar den menschlichen Bedürfnissen Unerträgliche" [hopelessness is the most unbearable, that which goes entirely against our human needs].[58] A life without hope, a life characterized by hopelessness, according to Bloch—and to Frankl, as noted earlier—is that which diminishes life more than anything else. A person may face practically unbearable physical and mental challenges, but hopelessness is the most severe. It pulls the foundation for life itself from under our feet.

Second, even though we can learn the art of a hermeneutic of hope, the fulfillment of hope will always remain fragile and fragmentary. Moltmann is well aware of the fragile nature of hope when he acknowledges that hope is not only "a fragmentary knowledge forming a prelude to the promised future" but also a "source of restlessness and torment."[59] As human beings, we will always be caught in that fragile pendulum between the realization and the disappointment of our hopes. When our hopes are realized, we are filled with joy; but when they are frustrated, we are ever so coldly reminded that no matter how hard we try, the ultimate fulfillment of our hopes is not grounded in ourselves. The ultimate fulfillment of our hope lies in the hands of God. Even if it does not help us many a times we desire the fulfillment of our hopes, it remains part of the fragile nature of hope to agree with Moltmann that "Christian hope is resurrection hope."[60]

Conclusion

In one of his many exegetical notes from Finkenwalde, Bonhoeffer says, "*content of hope, strength.*"[61] Given the irrevocable downward spiral in Bonhoeffer's life, it is remarkable that he displayed what we may call the strength of hope. Even though he died, or more correctly he was murdered, he held out to the very end.

---

57. Ibid.
58. Ibid., 3.
59. Moltmann, *Theology of Hope*, 33.
60. Ibid., 18.
61. *DBWE* 15:355.

Like Frankl, he exemplified with his life that when hope is tied to a life that has meaning, then, there is no defeat. And when we realize that earthly hope is fragile and fragmentary, then, there is no despair.

Vaclav Havel, the former Czech writer, dissident and head of state, once said, "Hope is not the conviction that there will be a happy end, but the assurance that what we do makes sense, even if it does not have a good ending."[62] When Bonhoeffer's short life was ended by the Nazis, it was exactly as Havel had said. It was not that Bonhoeffer's life had a happy ending, not at all. But his life remains a model for us because it made sense even though it did not have a happy ending. He remains an inspiration for us to learn to hope and make hope a foundational hermeneutic for life.[63] For Bonhoeffer, "hope [was] not a reflex rebounding from defeat but a reflection of theophany."[64] It is not the end of life that matters, but how we live it in the strength of faith, love, and hope.

---

62. *Der Spiegel*, a feature on right-wing populism and extremism, Spring 2019.

63. I am following the hermeneutical position of Gadamer, *Wahrheit und Methode*, 270–83.

64. John Howard Yoder, "To Serve Our God and to Rule the World," in *The Royal Priesthood: Essays Ecclesiological and Ecumenical*, ed. Michael G. Cartwright (Grand Rapids, MI: Eerdmans 1994), 138, cited in Kyle Gingerich Hiebert, *The Architectonics of Hope: Violence, Apocalyptic, and the Transformation of Political Theology* (Eugene, OR: Cascade Books, 2017), 128.

Chapter 24

"MAKE STRAIGHT IN THE DESERT A HIGHWAY"

RELATING PRESENT AND FUTURE IN DIETRICH BONHOEFFER AND WALTER BENJAMIN

W. David Hall

Introduction

Dietrich Bonhoeffer and Walter Benjamin were contemporaries. Both were German. Both witnessed the rise of fascist populism in Germany and in Europe in general. Both were openly critical of that fascism and, eventually, both were its victims—Benjamin in 1940, while attempting to cross the Pyrenees to escape the German invasion of France where he was in exile and Bonhoeffer in 1945 at Flossenbürg concentration camp where he was hanged as a conspirator against Hitler. There are then several interesting historical reasons for comparing these two figures.

However, those who know both might suggest that there is very little with which to link them, philosophically and ideologically. For instance, their perspectives on the role of the state and the rule of law are quite divergent. Bonhoeffer, arguing from a Christian Lutheran position, claimed that the state exists alongside the church as part of God's ordained order for the world. The state performs the critical function of preserving the created order through the coercive force of law, a function made necessary by the fallen, guilty state of unredeemed humanity. As such, the state has legitimate authority and must be obeyed so long as it performs its function within proper limits of the law, even if the state becomes superfluous after the ultimate redemption of humanity. For Benjamin, a secular Jew interested in Kabbalah and an avowed anarcho-Marxist materialist, a legitimate state authority or just order of law is unthinkable. State institutions and the coercive force of law hinder the establishment of just relations between individuals. The state exercises no preservative function, but an entirely alienating one; the force of law is not necessitated by the guilty condition of humanity—the law is the cause of that guilty condition through the imposition of a mythical violence that declares humanity irredeemable. This is a significant divergence indeed, as Bonhoeffer and Benjamin seem to argue from diametrically opposed positions.

Nonetheless, this chapter proposes a significant point of convergence in their ideas—a similar conception of the relationship between history and temporality—

and seeks to enact a conversation around this convergence. Bonhoeffer and Benjamin are both critical of a particular conception of history, one that Benjamin calls historicism. Both offer similar alternative conceptions—Bonhoeffer most explicitly in the essay "Ultimate and Penultimate Things," Benjamin in the posthumously published fragment, *On the Concept of History*. Both thinkers seek to provide a perspective from which to judge the meaning of the present by linking it with a moment or moments in the past. That perspective aims to orient human responsibility in the present toward a more just future. For both, the actual achievement of that future lies just outside the scope of human responsibility in a "messianic" event; thus, responsible human action represents a sort of "preparing the way" for the coming messianic reign. In tracing the contours of this convergence, I will show first that Benjamin's historical materialism provides a sort of philosophy of history that is helpful for understanding Bonhoeffer's claims about history and time in "Ultimate and Penultimate Things." Second, as much as they may have diverged philosophically and ideologically, the central concern for both Bonhoeffer and Benjamin was the manner in which concrete human responsibility is tied up with the question of how, in Bonhoeffer's words, "a coming generation is to go on living." Lastly, Benjamin's ideas lend an interesting perspective on the connections between Bonhoeffer's claims in "Ultimate and Penultimate Things" and his later explorations in *Letters and Papers from Prison*. I will conclude tentatively with the suggestion that the convergence with Benjamin offers possibilities for reclaiming Bonhoeffer in a radically different context than his own.

Time and History

Let me begin by explaining what I mean by the terms "time" and "history." By time, I refer to the temporal structure of human existence—the brute fact that human life takes place within and is bounded by time. By history, I refer to the meaningful articulation of that temporal existence. History aims to interpret, that is, explain and understand time as it relates to the human condition. There are many possible ways to conceive history, and a viable account is a central concern of both Benjamin and Bonhoeffer.

Benjamin was critical of a conception of history, dominant in both bourgeois liberal and Marxist Social Democratic circles. This conception, which he labeled "historicism," understands temporality as progressive movement toward a utopian future and history as the scientific discipline that charts the course of cause and effect leading to the inevitable accomplishment of that future. Benjamin found this account untenable on several levels. It is *ontologically untenable* because it presents human existence in vulgarly naturalistic terms, as a mere chain of cause and effect where all is inevitable. As such, this progressive view of history reduces time to a homogenous medium, a causal nexus for the unfolding of necessity, emptying past and present of any significance. It is *existentially unappealing* because it robs individuals of the ability to judge the meaning of temporal existence since the significance of events can only be interpreted in light of a yet-to-be-accomplished future. Human beings must live *in* time and thus lack any position from which to judge past events or respond to current exigencies (if indeed, it is even meaningful to speak of responsibility in the causal nexus of homogenous, empty time). But most importantly, from Benjamin's perspective, progressive history is deeply *morally problematic* because it is the history of the victorious, and here it is worth pausing to quote him at length:

> With whom does historicism actually sympathize? The answer is inevitable: with the victor. And all rulers are the heirs of prior conquerors. Hence, empathizing with the victor invariably benefits the current rulers. . . . Whoever has emerged victorious participates to this day in the triumphal procession in which current rulers step over those who are lying prostrate. According to traditional practice, the spoils are carried in the procession. . . . There is no document of culture which is not at the same time a document of barbarism. And just as such a document is never free of barbarism, so barbarism taints the manner in which it was transmitted from one hand to another.[1]

Historicism is the historical documentation of the victors, the silencing of the vanquished, and the legitimation of the *status quo* in the name of "progress."

There is no way to ground the kind of revolutionary praxis Benjamin sought on this understanding of progressive historicism. What is needed is an entirely different perspective, one that he called "historical materialism." The historical materialist aims to "brush history against the grain" in order to lay open the revolutionary potential of the present. He accomplishes this by linking the present with a moment in the past. That resurrected past moment then serves as a "dialectical image," which brings the flow of time to a standstill much as a photograph freezes a particular moment into an image. The dialectical image allows a vision of the present, not as a transition to the next moment in the world historical process, but as a "constellation saturated with tensions."[2] The present is no longer a homogenous bit of empty time but *Jetztzeit*, "time filled full by now-time."[3] Benjamin takes as an example of such a transformation the adoption of the ancient Rome by the French revolutionaries as an image for the goals of the Revolution:

> Thus, to Robespierre ancient Rome was the past charged with now-time, a past he blasted out of the continuum of history. The French Revolution viewed itself as Rome reincarnate. It cited ancient Rome exactly the way fashion cites a bygone mode of dress. . . . The same leap into the open air of history is the dialectical leap Marx understood as revolution.[4]

---

1. Walter Benjamin, "On the Concept of History," in *Selected Writings: Volume 4, 1938–1940*, ed. H. Eiland and M. Jennings (Cambridge, MA: Harvard University, 2003), 391–2.
2. Ibid., 396.
3. Ibid., 395.
4. Ibid.

In bringing time to a standstill, in shocking the moment into a constellation saturated with tensions, in blasting open the continuum of history, the historical materialist reveals the present as a *kairos* pregnant with possibilities.

In short, in the idea of progressive historicism, Benjamin saw a threat to human agency. By robbing the past of any decisive significance, progressivism deprives agents of any meaningful perspective on the present and any effective influence on the future. In articulating his alternative historical materialism, Benjamin sought to restore possibilities for a better future by linking the present with a decisive moment in the past. The dialectical image of the past reinvests the present with the sense of a task, a call to human responsibility for a better future, a revolutionary potential that Benjamin called "weak messianic power," a notion which I will return to later.

While Bonhoeffer did not criticize progressive historicism directly, he did offer a similar diagnosis of the temporal meaninglessness that threatened his contemporary situation, most notably in the essay "Heritage and Decay." Speaking of the loss of a sense of historical heritage introduced by modernity, Bonhoeffer writes:

> Faced with the abyss of nothingness, the question about a historical heritage that we must make our own, use in the present, and pass on to the future is snuffed out. . . . The burden of yesterday is shaken off by glorifying shadowy times of old; the task of tomorrow is avoided by talking about the coming millennium. Nothing is fixed, and nothing holds us. The film, vanishing from memory as soon as it ends, symbolizes the profound amnesia of our time. . . . There is no personal destiny and therefore no personal dignity.[5]

Without a sense of heritage lacking some anchor in the past, humanity had become temporally unmoored, in Bonhoeffer's assessment. The cure for this historical rootlessness therefore was a reclamation of the heritage of the Reformation faith in God's redeeming activity in Christ. From the Reformation perspective, the ultimate event of God's becoming human in Jesus Christ shatters the abyss of meaninglessness. Bonhoeffer asserts:

> [T]he length and breadth of human life are concentrated in one moment, one point; the whole of life is embraced in this event. . . . The dark tunnel of human life, which was barred within and without and was disappearing ever more deeply into an abyss from which there is no exit, is powerfully torn open; the word of God bursts in.[6]

This event is *qualitatively ultimate*. It is God's final and decisive judgment on reality, but it is also *temporally ultimate* and in relation to this temporally ultimate

---

5. *DBWE* 6:128–9.
6. Ibid., 146.

time, the present is revealed in all its richness and meaning as "penultimate," as the time before and leading up to the "ultimate."

It is worth pausing to explore the temporal structure of this ultimate event. In a somewhat paradoxical way, we must see it as a past event; it has happened. The ultimate is announced in the incarnation, crucifixion, and resurrection, which are historical, for Bonhoeffer, even if not in a straightforward way. The present is understandable as penultimate only to the degree that it is viewed from the perspective of this past event. As such, it is a dialectical image in Benjamin's sense of the term; Christ's coming crystalizes the present into *kairos*. At the same time, the ultimate is yet to come; the ultimate redemption of humanity will only be achieved when the penultimate comes to an end, and here the scope of human responsibility is set in relief. Proper human responsibility in and toward the penultimate is bounded by two extremes—radicalism, which seeks to bring about the ultimate through the destruction of the penultimate, and compromise, which too readily resigns itself to the worldliness of the penultimate. Both positions are extremes in that each, in its own way, seeks to sunder the necessary connection between ultimate and penultimate, which renders the present meaningful. Radicalism devalues the penultimate in seeking the ultimate; compromise ignores the demands of the ultimate in caring for the penultimate. Proper human responsibility is a matter of preparing the way for the ultimate *in* the penultimate.

Human Responsibility as "Preparing the Way"

For Bonhoeffer, responsible human existence, synonymous with genuine Christian life, is a matter of living in the penultimate in the manner of waiting for the ultimate, for Christ's final return and God's final judgment and restoration. Thus, "Only Christ brings us the ultimate . . . still, or rather therefore, we are not deprived of, or spared from, living in the penultimate. The penultimate will be swallowed up by the ultimate, yet it retains its necessity and its right as long as the earth endures."[7] It is not in the scope of human responsibility to bring about the ultimate. Christ must come to us. We cannot bridge the gap from our end—to attempt to jump the gap or even bridge it from the human side is the way of radicalism. At the same time, our waiting is not passive observance of the penultimate. Rather, respecting the penultimate for the sake of the ultimate, responsible action prepares the way for Christ's coming: "It is . . . a commission of immeasurable responsibility given to all who know about the coming of Jesus Christ. The hungry person needs bread, the homeless person needs shelter, the one deprived of rights needs justice, the lonely person needs community, the undisciplined one needs order, the slave needs freedom."[8] Preparing the way means making the penultimate ready for Christ's ultimate return. And this endeavor means, among other things, adopting

---

7. Ibid., 167–8.
8. Ibid., 163.

Bonhoeffer's oft quoted view, learning "to see the great events of world history ... from the perspective of the outcasts, the suspects, the maltreated, the powerless, the oppressed and reviled, in short from the perspective of the suffering."[9]

We should hear some deep resonances with Benjamin's historical materialist perspective at this point. For both, any morally legitimate vision of the present, any responsible action toward the future, must privilege the perspective of history's victims. However, Benjamin's own perspective would likely have appeared as a secular version of radicalism to Bonhoeffer. As a Marxist, Benjamin saw the *status quo* as an economically unjust system for which revolutionary praxis was the only genuinely responsible human action. As an anarchist, Benjamin viewed any state administered rule of law as a form of bondage that must be shrugged off in the name of freedom and justice. From Benjamin's perspective, Bonhoeffer's Lutheran justification of state authority would have appeared as a version of bourgeois conformism.

Nonetheless, even here at the point of greatest difference between the two, there is another, somewhat surprising, point of convergence. Benjamin's political radicalism was not a simple secular ideology. He viewed the Marxist goal of a classless society not as a historical reality but as the event that brings history— the process driven by class conflict—to an end. Anything short of complete accomplishment is merely a revolutionary reversal, the replacing of one oppressive regime with another equally oppressive regime and the continuation of the history of conquest. The completion of the Marxist project is, from Benjamin's perspective, only conceivable as a messianic event. In the end, the goal of complete justice lies outside the scope of human responsibility. Benjamin makes this quite explicit in his *Theological-Political Fragment*:

> Only the Messiah himself completes all history, in the sense that he alone redeems, completes, creates its relation to the messianic. For this reason, nothing that is historical can relate itself, from its own ground, to anything messianic. Therefore, the Kingdom of God is not the telos of the historical dynamic; it cannot be established as a goal. From the standpoint of history, it is not the goal but the terminus.[10]

For Benjamin, the coming of the Messiah is the religious counterpart of the secular, political aim of the classless society. The messianic reign of justice is a sort of dialectical image of the completion of the Marxist project. Human responsibility is limited to what he calls "weak messianic power," a capacity to recognize and act upon "a conception of the present as now-time shot through with splinters

---

9. *DBWE* 8:52.

10. Walter Benjamin, "Theological-Political Fragment," in *Selected Writings: Volume 3, 1935–1938*, ed. H. Eiland and M. Jennings (Cambridge, MA: Harvard University, 2002), 305.

of messianic time."[11] From this perspective, every second is "the small gateway through which the Messiah might enter."[12] But the Messiah must enter, and we must wait and prepare the way for that entrance.

The Potential of a Merely Religious Christianity

I want to conclude by briefly marking one last, critical difference between these two thinkers, which is, at the same time, a rather paradoxical point of convergence—the function of theological concepts in secular existence. I will touch lightly on this topic and draw some tentative conclusions without fully developing the ideas. Indeed, I suppose that any conversation on this topic must remain tentative and open-ended given the incomplete and fragmentary nature of the sources we have to draw from.

Benjamin was fundamentally a secular thinker, a Marxist anarchist for whom revolutionary transformation of the political realities of his time was the principal focus. However, he found secular political ideas inadequate to articulate how such transformation might proceed or what such a transformed existence might look like. He adopted theological concepts from his own Jewish background to think past this impasse. As such, Benjamin put theological concepts in the service of a wholly secular, political project. He moved toward the theological from the secular.

Bonhoeffer, on the other hand, was a Christian theologian, and he remained so to the end. His worldview was shaped wholly by the Christian belief that God became human in order to redeem a fallen world incapable of saving itself. However, he began reinterpreting the meaning of this revelatory event in a "world come of age," that is, a world for which God was no longer "a working hypothesis"[13] and in which religious faith was quickly becoming intellectually indefensible. This interpretation of his historical context led Bonhoeffer to look for another, more comprehensive understanding of Christian existence:

> Being a Christian does not mean being religious in a certain way, making oneself into something or other (a sinner, penitent, or saint) according to some method or other. Instead it means being human, not a certain type of human being, but the human being Christ creates in us. It is not a religious act that makes someone a Christian, but rather sharing in God's suffering in the worldly life. . . . There is nothing about a religious method; the "religious act" is always partial, whereas "faith" is something whole and involves one's whole life. Jesus calls us not to a new religion but to life . . . [I]f one wants to speak of God "nonreligiously," then one must speak in such a way that the Godlessness of the world is not covered

---

11. Benjamin, "On the Concept of History," 397.
12. Ibid.
13. *DBWE* 8:478.

up in any way; but rather precisely to uncover it and surprise the world by letting light shine on it.[14]

In "a world come of age," God commands us to live our lives in a wholly worldly manner. Bonhoeffer therefore approached the secular from the theological.

In concluding, I suggest that Bonhoeffer's proposal for Christianity in "a world come of age" is untenable in our context, and it requires a corrective in the direction of Benjamin. Bonhoeffer's proposal is not tenable for several reasons. First, Bonhoeffer's claim that the world has come of age is, at the very least, premature. Far from existing in a world where God is no longer a working hypothesis, our world seems to be reverting to a childish existence where the most simplistic forms of the God-hypothesis are the order of the day, and this simplistic "child-like faith" is called upon to defend the most absurd positions. Second and related with the idea of religionless Christianity, Bonhoeffer hoped to address what he saw as the rise of secularism and the seeming irrelevance of religious claims in a world for which religion was no longer the intellectual center. Our historical context is characterized by the reemergence of a kind of religiously dogmatic absolutism that functions not as an intellectual center but as a point from which to challenge any intellectual pursuits whatsoever, a perspective that refuses to turn a critical eye on the human past, a position that dismisses any well-founded but unwelcomed predictions about the human future. Third, the loudest voices in this reemergence of dogmatism are frequently the defenders of Christianity against forces of "secularism" and "cultural Marxism." Christian forms of absolutism are neither more prevalent nor worse than other forms; they are nonetheless plentiful and destructive and so, I argue that Christianity has lost the intellectual and moral high ground that Bonhoeffer attributed to it.

In short, the last thing we need is a Christianity that refuses to see itself as merely religious. The last thing we need is a Christianity (or Islam, or Hinduism, or nationalism, or what have you) that asserts itself as the voice of God to a godless world. What is needed is the courage of epistemic humility, the willingness to see our theological statements as conceptual constructs, hermeneutical lenses—even useful fictions—that help us to link the present with the past so that we can act responsibly toward the future. This, it seems to me, is the potential of a "merely religious" Christianity, a Christianity humbled by Benjamin's materialist messianic perspective.

14. *DBWE* 8:480, 482.

Chapter 25

"SEEK THE THINGS THAT ARE ABOVE"

BONHOEFFER ON PERCEIVING AND RESPONDING TO GOD'S ACTION IN HISTORY

Kevin O' Farrell

Introduction

What do we mean when we speak of discerning the signs of the times? There is broad agreement that the task of discernment is left for each generation, but understanding what it entails varies. A number of prominent approaches can be used to elucidate this task. Some seek to comprehend the present moment by looking for parallels and analogies in past situations and contexts—the past becoming the lens for understanding the present. In this approach, history has a cyclical or repeatable character, an assumption common to ancient Greek notions of history and time. Others seek to comprehend the present in orientation to the future. The present becomes a historical index for anticipating what is to come as a forewarning or a necessary step in a historical process. The future becomes the standard and referent for understanding the present, often assuming a progressive or immanent teleology to history. Whether the past or the future orients one's discernment, both approaches typically assert that the *telos* of this task is action. They agree that primarily what is required is not comprehension but responsive decision since history is oriented to action and even originates in action. The impetus in both is the perception of the moment that culminates in responsiveness to its demands.[1]

Bonhoeffer notably maintained the urgency of this task, arguing that one's attitude to history is not primarily interpretative but one of decision.[2] In contradistinction to the foregoing approaches, however, I wish to explore how

---

1. For a summary of these approaches and their emergence, see Jacob Taubes, *Occidental Eschatology*, trans. David Ratmoko (Stanford, CA: Stanford University Press, 2009); Karl Löwith, *Meaning in History* (Chicago, IL: Chicago University Press, 1949); Louis Dupré, *The Enlightenment and the Intellectual Foundations of Modern Culture* (New Haven, CT: Yale University Press, 2004).

2. Dietrich Bonhoeffer, "Concerning the Christian Idea of God," *DBWE* 10:458.

Bonhoeffer orients a perception of the times not by looking to the past (assuming a repeatability to history) or to the immanent and foreseeable future but by seeking the things that are above. Bonhoeffer frequently suggests that how one perceives and acts in the present derives from eternity where the ascended Christ reigns. In his 1943 manuscript fragment, "On the Possibility of the Church's Message to the World," Bonhoeffer laments the church's failure to speak directly to the "concrete situation" with a "concrete directive." He notes that such a word is available to the church from a unique Christian "vantage point" that "has something specific to say about worldly things." And yet this vantage point is not reducible to moral proclamation or political program since it originates from an entirely different plane. Christ's "word is essentially determined not from below but from above, it is not a solution [*Lösung*] but redemption [*Erlösung*]." The Word from above speaks to his ascended and exalted state, "standing beyond the human problematic."[3] Bonhoeffer's assumption is that the unique perspective of a Christian reading of history is based on Christ's ascended position in eternity.

This chapter expands on how Bonhoeffer's account of the ascended Christ frames and contextualizes present readings of history.[4] The chapter proceeds in two stages. In the first part, I elucidate the oft unarticulated logic of ascension that is crucial to Bonhoeffer's account of Christ's disclosure of the moment and its disruption of prevailing modes of interpreting history. In the remainder of the chapter, I turn to Bonhoeffer's June 1932 sermons on "seeking the things that are above" in Col. 3:1-4 in order to explicate further how Christ's ascended state bolsters a perceptive reading of history and responsive action today.[5] Through this exposition, I show that, for Bonhoeffer, Christ's ascended state undoes accounts of history that disable perceptiveness of the moment, it liberates the forgotten histories of the oppressed from destruction and commodification, and it reorients and enables perceptiveness and responsiveness to Christ's adventitious action in history. The result is a sketch of how the ascended Christ undoes false modes of reading history and empowers responsivity to God's action in history today.

Logic of Ascension

It is true that Bonhoeffer infrequently mentions the ascension. Most references to it occur in passing, and it is often subsumed into the crucial event of Christ's

---

3. Dietrich Bonhoeffer, "On the Possibility of the Church's Message to the World," *DBWE* 6:353–4.

4. Lowe describes contextualization thus: "The accustomed business of the mind is to place or contextualize things, to label and handle them. But occasionally it happens that we ourselves are contextualized—placed in an unfamiliar setting that exceeds and relativizes us. It is this event that I propose to call contextualization"; Walter Lowe, "Why We Need Apocalyptic," *Scottish Journal of Theology* 63, no. 1 (2010): 48.

5. *DBWE* 11:450–65.

resurrection.[6] Nevertheless, its importance emerges with the most concentrated attention in Bonhoeffer's 1940 "Reflection on the Ascension" and in his sermons that directly pertain to the theme.[7] The relevance of the ascension to Bonhoeffer's theology, however, is not limited to these explicit references but is constitutive of Christological presence and disclosure epitomized in Bonhoeffer's frequent references to Christ's Word coming from above, which undercuts the systems and modes of thought that characterize the present age.

There are obvious echoes to the theology of crisis when Bonhoeffer refers to the irruptive Word that comes from above, capturing the way that God's liberation becomes "the overturning or rupture of all systems" determined by sin.[8] While summarizing Barth's theology of crisis, Bonhoeffer explains that in the Word of Christ, "all human order and ranking is subverted, for God's new order has been established, which is contrary and beyond all human understanding."[9] The encounter with the divine Logos becomes the judgment of the human Logos, leading to a forfeiture of moral or rational paradigms to narrate history by acknowledging the new reality that God initiates from there.[10] There is a clear Barthian and Kierkegaardian accent to these themes though, unlike Kierkegaard and Barth, Bonhoeffer speaks less of the juxtaposition of eternity and time and instead speaks primarily of Christ's presence or inbreaking from above. In his 1932 "What Is the Church," for instance, Bonhoeffer remarks:

> With the proclamation of the commandments and grace of God, the church finds itself at the boundary [*Grenze*], at the boundary of human possibilities that has now been broken through from above. However, in speaking of breaching

---

6. Whenever Bonhoeffer makes a brief reference to the ascension, it is usually to stress (1) how Christ and the church resist mystical identification (*DBWE* 1:140; *DBWE* 4:22); (2) the presence of the Spirit in the church (*DBWE* 1:152; *DBWE* 4:210, 218); (3) Christ's continual intercession for the church (*DBWE* 5:132; *DBWE* 14:805); and (4) Christ's exalted state in the heavens with the Father (*DBWE* 11:303; *DBWE* 14:766, 805). There are instances also that Bonhoeffer refers quickly to the "resurrection and ascension" as one event with two dimensions (*DBWE* 14:798; *DBWE* 15:516). As Bonhoeffer suggests in his "Reflections on the Ascension," the only difference between resurrection and ascension is the mode of appearance and thus the Bible does "refer to the resurrection of Jesus as the decisive act of salvation without mention of the ascension" (*DBWE* 16:477–8).

7. "Reflection on the Ascension," *DBWE* 16:476–81. The two most pertinent sermons are Bonhoeffer's 1933 Ascension Day sermon on 1 Peter 1:7b–9 (*DBWE* 12:468–71) and his homiletical exercises on Acts 1:1-11 in Finkenwalde (*DBWE* 14:468–71).

8. Judith Wolfe, "The Eschatological Turn in German Philosophy," *Modern Theology* 35, no. 1 (2019): 56.

9. Dietrich Bonhoeffer, "The Theology of Crisis and Its Attitude toward Philosophy and Science," *DBWE* 10:464.

10. There is an apocalyptic logic to this movement. See Phil Ziegler, "Dietrich Bonhoeffer: An Ethics of God's Apocalypse," *Modern Theology* 23, no. 4 (2007): 579–94.

this boundary, this worldly order, the church . . . knowingly points to these laws, these worldly orders, the destruction [*Zerstörung*], and obliteration of which it is empowered to witness by God.[11]

Bonhoeffer's appeal to God's irruptive Word from above usually has one of two senses. The first sense speaks to Christ's origin and unity with the Father. It is from this unity that the Incarnate Christ, during his earthly ministry, spoke in a way that surpassed the finite paradigms and divisions that characterize human thought.[12] The second and more frequent sense speaks to Christ's revelatory presence today, and it is here that the logic of ascension reveals its importance for a narration of God's activity in history. When speaking to the continued reception and proclamation of Christ's Word from above, Bonhoeffer shifts to describing "above" as Christ's eternal reign. But following the Lutheran logic of Christological thinking that begins from the Incarnation, Christ's eternal status can only be the culmination of the "Christ-event," affirming that the One who speaks today from eternity is always the Incarnate, Crucified, and Resurrected One who came into history and is now ascended at the end of history.[13]

The importance of the ascension in narrating God's activity in history is twofold. First, it affirms the indirectness of God's activity and word today. While the identity of the God who acts remains the Resurrected One, the indirect mode of appearance stresses the asymmetry between historical events and God's activity, since God's activity originates from a different plane that has judged finite accounts of good or divine action.[14] Second, it narrates Christ's eternity as the eschaton since Christ's eternal reign is the judgment and culmination of history at the end of history—his present voice comes from the future and interrupts the present. As transcribed from his lectures, "The Nature of the Church," Bonhoeffer declares, "For Christ has ascended, eschatological!"[15] In his 1935 lecture, "Contemporizing New Testament Texts," Bonhoeffer further speaks of Christ disclosing and determining the present by his emergence from the *eschatos* that is heterogeneous to the present: "*the present is determined externally* rather than internally . . . is determined instead by that which approaches us externally, by that which approaches, by the future. The present is determined primarily not by the past but by the *future*, and this

---

11. Dietrich Bonhoeffer, "What Is the Church," *DBWE* 12:264–5.

12. See, for instance, Dietrich Bonhoeffer, "On the Possibility," *DBWE* 6:352; "God's Love and the Disintegration of the World," *DBWE* 6:312–13.

13. This is not a denial that eternity can speak to Christ's origin, but only that the "above" speaks first and primarily to the ascension. There is no possibility of speaking of the *logos asarkos* but only of the God who took on flesh. On the difference between the Reformed and Lutheran Christological concerns in relation to Barth and Bonhoeffer, see Rowan Williams, *Christ the Heart of Creation* (London: Bloomsbury, 2018), 169–99.

14. Dietrich Bonhoeffer, "The Character and Ethical Consequences of Religious Determinism," *DBWE* 10:440–4.

15. Dietrich Bonhoeffer, "The Nature of the Church," *DBWE* 11:302.

future is Christ, is the Holy Spirit. The criterion of the authentic present resides outside that present itself."[16] Or, as Bonhoeffer remarks in his "Reflection on the Ascension," "That which is future is present, and the present already past. In this way we live in the power of Christ's ascension."[17] The perception of the present and its demands depends upon a disclosure that originates beyond history with the ascended Christ who stands at the end of history. What emerges is that the ascension is not merely a dogmatic statement about Christ's status; it is rather a confession that directs human perception of and response to the present. It is in this this way that one "seeks the things that are above" (Col. 3:1-4).[18]

Necessity of Experience and Disabling the Philosophy of History

Bonhoeffer's June 1932 sermons on Col. 3:1-4 capture the importance of a perceptive reading of history. Bonhoeffer exudes the urgency of the theology of crisis in these sermons, pressing against the prevailing domestication of the gospel in a postwar era that bolstered the nationalist readings of history that assisted the imminent rise of National Socialism.[19] Bonhoeffer perceives a correspondence between the widespread "methods" of reading history that he encountered and the societal numbness to God's claim and irruptive action in history. This is one of the central claims of Bonhoeffer's first sermon on "seeking the things that are above." Bonhoeffer opens the sermon with a criticism of the "modern" listener, who confesses the truth of the claim, "I have been raised with Christ" but does not experience its reality in day-to-day life.[20] He maintains that a veil has covered their eyes, making them blind to the power and presence of Christ's victory in history: "Now it lies over us like a punishment that we must stand before these words with blind eyes and deaf ears, completely at a loss about what they should mean and what we should do with them in our lives."[21] Bonhoeffer blames this "blindness" on two different but interconnected approaches to the historical moment. The first approach invokes God's name to baptize the pursuit of national interests as expressions of the universal will of

---

16. Dietrich Bonhoeffer, "Contemporizing New Testament Texts," *DBWE* 14:417.
17. Dietrich Bonhoeffer, "Reflection on Ascension," *DBWE* 16:481.
18. "The ascension of Jesus has transposed us into the heavenly places (Eph. 2:6) and thereby orients our gaze toward heaven (Col. 3:1)." Bonhoeffer, "Reflection on Ascension," *DBWE* 16:481.
19. The timing of the sermons are important given that only a month later, "nearly 38 per cent of the German electorate voted for Hitler's party"; Eberhard Bethge, *Dietrich Bonhoeffer: Theologian, Christian, Contemporary*, trans. Eric Mosbacher et al. (London: Collins, 1970), 177.
20. *DBWE* 11:451f.
21. Ibid., 456.

God in history.[22] Through the appeal to God, a government claims that God's providential activity manifests itself in and through the activity of the nation. In an indirect attack on the Papen government, Bonhoeffer argues that what is visible in the invocation is not the universal will of God unfolding in history but only "our irrepressible craving for freedom and our own will—to do in the name of God what *we* want, in the name of the Christian worldview to play off one nationality against another and stir them up to conflict with one another."[23] The name of God only functions to bolster readings of history that enact *violence* in seeking one's self-determined end.[24] The second approach looks to scientific Experts for Solution to the historical crisis, trusting in the expert to expunge "all instability" from the world in order to "bring order in our chaos."[25] The approach suggests that modern methods can control the future, overcoming and subduing the chaos of history. The hope is that "this longed-for salvation" will come through the scientific method that "push[es] forward in all areas of our human life."[26] Bonhoeffer's critique simply states that experience reveals the illusions of this approach; history is uncontrollable, resisting even the best organizing methods. Its atheistic methodology further offers no hope once the promise of method is lost since it conceives of history as having no *telos*—history becomes the compound of "empty time" that offers no promise in itself: "Our future looks at us with hollow eyes."[27]

Whereas both approaches are distinct, Bonhoeffer lumps them together because they both collapse heaven into earth thus debilitating perceptiveness of God's Word that originates from beyond history. In the first approach, the divine will becomes perspicuous and enacted in national history. Behind this approach is the immanentization of eschatology and providence common to post-Enlightenment philosophies whereby the "semiotic relation between present and the eschaton" common in Hebrew and Christian eschatologies "is displaced by system-immanence."[28] Eschatology thus becomes the teleology of "universal history" and

---

22. "One went one's way in complete freedom, the name of God harmlessly backing one up and the earthly well-being of human beings in view"; Ibid., 452.

23. Ibid., 454. On the denial of a visible progression history, see the August draft of the Bethel Confession: "We reject the false doctrine that would see within the world a gradual development taking place that will culminate in the new world. . . . We reject any version of the doctrine of the thousand-year reign [Reich] that clearly seeks to interpret certain historical events as the beginning of Christ's visible reign on earth"; *DBWE* 12:424.

24. Odo Marquard, *Farewell to Matters of Principle: Philosophical Studies* (Oxford: Oxford University Press, 1989), 120–4.

25. *DBWE* 11:453.

26. Ibid.

27. Ibid., 454.

28. Wolfe, "The Eschatological Turn," 57.

providence becomes the immanent historical process that completes it.[29] In this approach, the eschatological end of history eventually takes a nationalist turn since the end comes providentially through the German people with all events being interpreted in light of their imminent destiny. Indeed, it was common to think during the era that Germany's loss in the First World War were the mere birth pangs that would precede the coming glory of the Third Reich (whose appellation intentionally echoes the coming third age of the Holy Spirit in Joachim).[30] In the second approach, the universe possesses the secrets for overcoming historical chaos by creating one's desired future. Reality is reduced to a closed system of its immutable laws of nature that determine all incidents, threatening the very possibility of freedom.[31] As Agamben suggests, modern scientific methods build upon the paradigm of astrology whereby one looks to the stars to comprehend and participate in their fate.[32]

Bonhoeffer perceives that the result of this shared collapsing of heaven into earth is that it leads to a serious *mistrust* of one's immediate experience and to a numbness to historical encounter that grants perception of the present. The religious appeal of the first approach becomes an ideology that can explain all historical phenomena in advance; no experience can disrupt what is already certain, namely the divine will enacted by regional powers. As Hannah Arendt notes, "Ideologies always assume that one idea is sufficient to explain everything in the development from the premise, and that no experience can teach anything because everything is comprehended in this consistent process of logical deduction."[33] The scientific method of the second approach likewise works to undermine "immediate" experience, recasting it in light of real knowledge gained through empirical testing. Experience is reframed as the result of method, which casts immediate suspicion on all encounter that eludes its prior findings. The result of both approaches is that historical events are no longer able to confront and irrupt one's perception, leading to the veil over the eyes and the corresponding numbness to Christ's presence and activity today. Individuals become deadened to their time and to God, standing under God's judgment.

The question is thus posed, how can one experience and see again? Bonhoeffer is unflinching that only a divine incursion that simultaneously shatters and renews

---

29. On these points, see Löwith, *Meaning in History* and Dupré, *The Enlightenment*. Cf. also Immanuel Kant, "Idea of a Universal History with a Cosmopolitan Purpose," in *Political Writings*, ed. Hans Reiss (Cambridge: Cambridge University Press, 1991), 41–54; G. W. F. Hegel, *Lectures on the Philosophy of World History*, trans. H. B. Nisbet (Cambridge: Cambridge University Press, 1975).

30. Wolfe, "The Eschatological Turn" 66.

31. Dupré, *The Enlightenment*, 25.

32. Giorgio Agamben, *Infancy and History: On the Destruction of Experience*, trans. Liz Heron (London: Verso, 2007), 20.

33. Hannah Arendt, *The Origins of Totalitarianism* (London: Penguin Random House, 2017), 617.

is sufficient if one is to perceive what is meaningful in history. One must die and be resurrected in encounter. Such an event is irreducible to historical processes or scientific method; it is utterly adventitious and overwhelming. It originates in eternity with the ascended Christ who addresses people today, setting minds to seek the things that are above. For if it originates in the immanence of historical processes, it would become once again "pious, edifying human thoughts" that are incorporated into the prevailing ideologies.[34] The experience of Christ's message must break the sinful trains of thought if a new perception and orientation to history emerges where one can seek the things that are above. One must experience and orient oneself to God's eternal message in the ascended Son to perceive the meaning of historical events. Whereas the possibility and necessity of this renewal supersede immanent possibility, Bonhoeffer insists it is trustworthy and sure since Christ declares God's *desire* to set captives free, and thus it is the surest basis for renewed perception and experience of Christ in history. Bonhoeffer notes:

> [These] are God's thoughts, they cannot remain hidden from us in eternity. . . . He himself will tear away the veil that now lies over his holy words; he himself will open our astonished eyes for that glory, for it is true that we have died with Christ but have also been raised with Christ, that our true life is that which is now and always hidden with Christ in God.[35]

It is the only sure ground that allows for genuine experience of the moment where one is liberated and empowered to read history anew.

Preservation of Below in the Ascended Christ

One might question the focus on the ascended Christ when Bonhoeffer's more consistent emphasis is the crucified Christ who disparages and reveals the false pretensions of ideological readings of history. This is one of the great insights of liberation theologies that identify Christ crucified, not with the oppressor but with the oppressed. The viewpoint from below is certainly necessary, affirming the need to narrate histories and historical processes in service to human activity that participates in the liberating movement of God for the world. Indeed, the ascended Christ is always the crucified and resurrected Christ who has been raised on high. Nevertheless, Bonhoeffer provides two reasons in these sermons for the emphasis on the ascended Christ, particularly his ability to preserve the view from below as hopeful.

First, the ascended God liberates the forgotten histories of the oppressed. Bonhoeffer surveys "visible life" at the end of the second sermon, observing the blatant and pervasive violence that marks history. History is sheer contingency,

---

34. *DBWE* 11:456f.
35. Ibid.

bestowing fortune on some and endless tragedy on most others, for "Our visible life flows away like a dream and often like a curse."[36] The powers of this age exacerbate the situation, oppressing and condemning the histories of the other in establishing their own "universal" history. This destines the lives of many to "forgotten history," narrating history solely from the perspective of the powerful.[37] The crushing force of visible life undermines any false sentimental hopes for a crisis-free life or for a destined overcoming of evil in this age. Bonhoeffer is resistant to the idea that history tilts toward justice. Rather, "The visible world strides brutally and heartlessly and violently past all of this."[38] The only hope is the hidden presence of our new life with the ascended Christ, which awaits culmination in the *eschaton*. Christ is building our life—our "true life"—in eternity, hidden away from the violent processes of history in the ascended Christ.[39] The effect of this confession is not a detachment from historical processes. Rather, it empowers resistance that can simultaneously confess the seeming ineffectiveness of much resistance as well as that God does not overlook or forget *this* foolish resistance fo the world. One can hope against hope that sometimes God does effect change in the least of these, that resurrection power becomes visible in a punctuated moment—as a glimmer—even when history's violence carries on.

Second, the ascended Christ resists the commodification of the oppressed by the privileged and the powerful of this age. Earlier in the second sermon, Bonhoeffer addresses the prominence of a conservative ethos in the church, asking, "Must it be that Christianity, which began in such a tremendously revolutionary way long ago, is now conservative for all time? That each new movement must forge a path for itself without the church, that time after time the church does not see what has actually happened until twenty years after the fact?"[40] The fear is that the church has an unavoidably conservative perception of the world that subsequently misses the significance of the historical moment but only follows the trends once the revolutionary movement becomes victorious or normalized. This danger is paradigmatically present in Bonhoeffer's own theology. Although Bonhoeffer advocated for the viewpoint from below in "After Ten Years," he had not yet learned this by experience but only by imagination and empathy.[41] The view from below is more trustworthy when Latin American and Black liberation

---

36. Ibid., 464.

37. See Theses VI and VII of Walter Benjamin, "Theses on the Philosophy of History," in *Illuminations*, trans. Harry Zohn, ed. Hannah Arendt (New York: Mariner Books, 2019), 198–200.

38. *DBWE* 11:465.

39. Ibid., 465f.

40. Ibid., 459.

41. Though it is included in the critical edition of *Letters and Papers from Prison*, it was written before Bonhoeffer's imprisonment; *DBWE* 8:37–52.

theologians advance it than when Bonhoeffer does.[42] The danger intensifies when the conservative ethos of Bonhoeffer's later political thought emerges, which prioritizes law and order over a revolutionary ethos from below.[43] The danger is that when considering protest movements, one can maintain sympathy for those that protest while prioritizing the preservation of order and culture (*Bildung*). The danger, in other words, is that the unique perspective and witness of the oppressed is only affirmed as long as it becomes sufficiently malleable to the given paradigms thus being incorporated into the view from above that is understood sociologically. What many consider to be a liberating encounter can become what Esther Reed calls a "spectacle" that subsumes liberating historical movements into the present univocal logic—it gives the appearance of change while maintaining the present state of affairs.[44] Like Bonhoeffer, one thus reads and participates in historical movements, declaring them liberating while missing how they become subverted by and ultimately incorporated into the very historical processes that ultimately benefit the privileged.

The ascended Christ affirms that the encounter with the oppressed is not sufficient in itself. For the encounter to affect and disrupt one's perception of the oppressed, the ascended Christ, who supersedes the totalizing logics of the day as the crucified and risen one, must make his appeal in and through the oppressed—himself effecting a subjective break that generates a new politics. One must maintain the priority of God's Word that shatters us through the neighbor; this is the surest hope for historical movements to effect and catch a glimpse of Christ's reconciling and resurrecting power in history:

> And this truth of God would take us captive, would bind and be an obligation to us, would bond us together, person to person. If we come together with some [religious slogan], then we still come in our unbroken human pride, then we never really find one another; then we never really meet each other, then we always talk past each other. . . . For it is simply impossible for us to give up our demands that seem so justifiable. But if we come together as the crucified and risen ones of Jesus Christ . . . then we will find one another, then we would look into one another's eyes and would recognize one another completely new, as we are recognized by God.[45]

---

42. The two most notable examples are Gustavo Gutiérrez, *The Power of the Poor in History*, trans. Robert R. Barr (New York: Orbis Books, 1983); James H. Cone, *A Black Theology of Liberation* (New York: Orbis Books, 1986).

43. "According to Scripture there is no right to revolution"; Dietrich Bonhoeffer, "A Position Paper on State and Church," *DBWE* 16:525.

44. Esther Reed, *The Limit of Responsibility: Dietrich Bonhoeffer's Ethics for a Globalizing Era* (London: T&T Clark, 2018), 40–5.

45. *DBWE* 11:455–7.

The Moment of Perception and the Confession of Action

In the exposition of Bonhoeffer's June 1932 sermons, the focus has fallen thus far on the irruption of history in the ascended Christ who reigns in eternity, leaving unanswered the question, how does the ascended Christ inform a "positive" reading of history? From these sermons, an answer begins to emerge. On the one hand, Bonhoeffer maintains that the form of Christ orients and reveals the character of historical processes. Christ is present in history and he directs the reading of history through the pattern of his own activity as the incarnate, crucified, and resurrected One.[46] As Bonhoeffer suggests in "Ethics as Formation," Christ's threefold form is present and becoming real in history, directing human perception and activity in the here and now.[47] On the other hand, Bonhoeffer stresses in these sermons that the pattern of Christ's activity refuses objectification or reduction to a hermeneutical lens for reading history since its emergence remains beyond the boundaries of human understanding and method. In the middle of the second sermon, Bonhoeffer confesses that the simultaneous activity of Christ that kills and makes alive cannot be deduced through reason since its origin is beyond the boundaries of our understanding. It is hidden in eternity in the ascended Christ. This is not problematic for Bonhoeffer, since:

> Christ came into the world not so that we should understand him but so that we should cling to him, so that we should simply let him pull us into the unbelievable event of the resurrection, so that we simply have it said to us, said to us in all its incomprehensibility: You have died—and yet you have been raised! . . . Right next to each other the completely contradictory; right next to each other, just the way the two worlds, our world and the world of God, are right next to each other.[48]

In this confession, Bonhoeffer stresses that death and resurrection are not two moments in a dialectic.[49] Both are utterly adventitious. Resurrection is not the negation of death but the surprising eruption of life. Death and life, Bonhoeffer contends, belong together but this is only possible "if one could see through God's own eyes."[50] The various moments of the Christ-event are present but they

---

46. This pattern can be seen in the text of Col. 3:1-4, which shows that one's past is marked by crucifixion and resurrection ("I have died and been raised with Christ"), the present is marked by ascension ("my life is hidden with God"), and the future by the eschatological final judgment ("my life will be revealed in glory").
47. Dietrich Bonhoeffer, "Ethics as Formation," *DBWE* 6:76–102.
48. *DBWE* 11:464.
49. As Bonhoeffer notes in "Creation and Fall," "There is absolutely no transition, no continuum between the dead Christ and the resurrected Christ, but the freedom of God"; *DBWE* 3:35.
50. *DBWE* 11:461.

both exceed the finite moment, finding their fullness and unity in eternity in the ascended Christ. The only adequate response to God's activity is decision—to cling to him in action.

The stress on the ascension of Christ then suggests that the primary orientation of Christian reflection on history is not about historical processes (important as those are) but moments or events that initiate or disrupt historical processes, eliciting responsive action in the hope of Christ.[51] In such moments, the form of Christ, which is often obscured, emerges with intense clarity, revealing the finitude and pretensions of visible history in judgment (crucifixion) as well as the unexpected newness that emerges in historical action (resurrection). These moments become beacons in history that reveal how resurrection power can emerge unexpectedly in and through the frailty of human activity, bolstering future acts of faith. In Bonhoeffer's famous 1942 letter to his fellow co-conspirators, "After Ten Years," he speaks in a creedal formulation in the eighth subsection, using the phrase "I believe" (*ich glaube*) four times. It is the only place in the letter he speaks in this idiom, and this has led Kai-Ole Eberhardt to argue that this is the theological center of the letter.[52] The subsection is titled, "Some Statements of Faith on God's Action in History":

> I believe that God can and will let good come out of everything, even the greatest evil. For that to happen, God needs human beings who let everything work out for the best. I believe that in every moment of distress God will give us as much strength to resist as we need. But it is not given to us in advance, lest we rely on ourselves and not on God alone. In such faith all fear of the future should be overcome. I believe that even our mistakes and shortcomings are not in vain and that it is no more difficult for God to deal with them than with our supposedly good deeds. I believe that God is no timeless fate but waits for and responds to sincere prayer and responsible actions.[53]

As in the sermons on Colossians, Bonhoeffer's orientation here is confession rather than comprehension, and it is this confession that propels responsible action in the moment that he experienced being "without ground under his feet."[54] The moment

---

51. Robert Vosloo has reflected well on how Bonhoeffer's theology bolsters a responsible reading of history and the legacy of historical processes. See Robert Vosloo, "Dietrich Bonhoeffer's Reformation Day Sermons and Performative Remembering," *Theology Today* 74, no. 3 (2017): 252–62; and Robert Vosloo, "Time out of Joint and Future-Oriented Memory: Engaging Dietrich Bonhoeffer in the Search for a Way to Deal Responsibly with the Ghosts of the Past," *Religions* 8, no. 42 (2017): 1–9.

52. Kai-Ole Eberhardt, "Das Geheimnis des Waltens Gottes in der Geschichte: Providenz und Ethik in Dietrich Bonhoeffers Glaubenssätze von 1942," *Kirchliche Zeitgeschichte* 31, no. 1 (2018): 221–44.

53. *DBWE* 8:46.

54. Ibid., 38.

taught him above all else that history is determined not by human activity but by divine activity that originates from above, and that God nevertheless delights in using the finitude of human activity for his good in history. As Bonhoeffer says in "History and Good [1]", "Free action, as it determines history, recognizes itself as ultimately God's action, the purest activity as passivity. Only in this perspective is it possible to speak now of good in history."[55]

Conclusion

The singular focus on Christ's ascension has elicited less a hermeneutic for the reading of history than the negation of historical narrations that either overlook God's activity in the moment of encounter or quench the histories of the oppressed that assert their historical vision. The focus has been on the irruption of history that originates beyond history rather than the fulfillment of history by the Christ who became human in history. There is a notable risk of imbalance in this one-sided emphasis on the ascension over the other moments of the Christ-event; the risk where God's "No" is arbitrarily separated from God's "Yes" to history.[56] Nevertheless, the risk has been worth venturing since it exposes the gap between human representations of history—even ones structured by incarnation-crucifixion-resurrection—and the unity of history preserved in the *eschaton* beyond human purview, awaiting final disclosure. The one-sided emphasis on the ascended Christ has accentuated that history is neither perspicuous nor a seamless garment. Rather, history is a fallen creature characterized by fragmentation, gaps, and what Bonhoeffer terms "times that are out of joint," within which individuals look for signs of God's activity and promise.[57] It has likewise accentuated that the irruption of history is, in the idiom of Barth's *Römerbrief*, "a work of clearance by which room is made in this world for that which is beyond it."[58] Individuals are thus made attentive to this irruptive presence, confessing that capturing a glimpse of history's form emerges not through method but by recognizing God's incursion when it flashes at that moment brimming with divine activity.[59] It is through this orientation to and confession of the ascended Christ that historical action is freed from the determination of historical processes for free decision in

---

55. "History and Good [1]," *DBWE* 6:226.

56. As Bonhoeffer says in "Heritage and Decay," "God's Yes and God's No to history, as we understand it in the incarnation and crucifixion of Jesus Christ, bring a lasting and irremovable tension into every historical moment"; *DBWE* 6:104.

57. Dietrich Bonhoeffer, "Church and World I," *DBWE* 6:347. On this point, see Robert Vosloo, "Bonhoeffer, Our Contemporary? Engaging Bonhoeffer on Time, the Times, and Public Theology," *The Bonhoeffer Legacy: An International Journal* 5, no. 2 (2018): 19–36.

58. Karl Barth, *The Epistle to the Romans*, 6th ed., trans. Edwyn C. Hoskyns (Oxford: Oxford University Press, 1975), 39–40.

59. See Thesis V of Benjamin, "Theses on the Philosophy of History," 198.

responsiveness to God's prior and pervasive activity in our lives. As Bonhoeffer remarks in another sermon:

> The most profound insight, however, emerges only when we consider that not only does the world have its time and its hours, but our own life also has its time and its hour of God, and that behind the times of our own life God's traces become visible, that beneath our own paths lie the deep shafts of eternity, and every step generates a faint echo from eternity. If we but understand the deep, pure form of these times and how to represent them in the way we conduct our own lives, then we will encounter God's holy presence in the midst of our own time.[60]

---

60. "Sermon on Romans 12:11c," *DBWE* 10:530.

Chapter 26

"A CHURCH FOR THE FUTURE?"

DIETRICH BONHOEFFER'S LATE ECCLESIOLOGY IN CONVERSATION
WITH MERCY ODUYOYE, TEDDY SAKUPAPA, AND VUYANI VELLEM

Tim Hartman

Introduction

Of the many titles used to describe Dietrich Bonhoeffer—theologian, writer, professor, activist, conspirator, and martyr—rarely is prophet used. Yet, at Tegel Prison in the spring and summer of 1944, a prophet was what he became as he wrote letters to Eberhard Bethge about a "world-come-of-age" and a "religionless Christianity." As a manifestation of this so-called New Theology,[1] Bonhoeffer sketched an "Outline for a Book,"[2] saying, "I would like to write an essay—not more than one hundred pages in length—with three chapters: 1. Taking stock of Christianity; 2. What is Christian Faith, really?; 3. Conclusions."[3] Bonhoeffer's zeal for this project was demonstrated in that he diverted his attention from his *Ethics* and letter writing to work on the manuscript, and then, instead of sending off the manuscript for safe-keeping, kept it with him as one of his few possessions when he was transferred to the Gestapo prison in October 1944.[4] While only the "Outline" survived, Bonhoeffer left a number of interpretive clues through his life and writings, which point to his ideas of a new ecclesiology. Surprisingly, much scholarly attention has been given to his early ecclesiology in *Sanctorum Communio*, which was written when he was only twenty-one. As a result, many

---

1. The "New Theology" letters were written to Bethge in April–August 1944: April 30, May 5, May 29, July 16, July 18, July 21, as well as "Thoughts on the Baptism of Dietrich Bethge" from May, and "Outline for a Book" in August. See "The New Theology" in Eberhard Bethge, *Dietrich Bonhoeffer: A Biography—Theologian, Christian, Man for His Times*, rev. and ed. Victoria J. Barnett (Minneapolis, MN: Fortress Press, 2000), 853–91.
2. *DBWE* 8:499–504.
3. Ibid., 499.
4. Larry Rasmussen, with Renate Bethge, *Dietrich Bonhoeffer: His Significance for North Americans* (Minneapolis, MN: Fortress Press, 1990), 57.

have missed the main thrust of Bonhoeffer's late or mature ecclesiology as expressed in fragments in his *Ethics* and *Letters and Papers from Prison*.[5]

While Bonhoeffer's ecclesial insights have been lauded in the increasingly secularized societies of Europe and North America,[6] this chapter asks the question, what might Bonhoeffer's ecclesiology offer in twenty-first-century Africa where the Christian faith is growing exponentially? And conversely, what might contemporary African understandings of the church offer to twenty-first-century readers of Bonhoeffer? The argument of this chapter unfolds in three stages. First, drawing on *Ethics* and *Letters and Papers from Prison*, this chapter explores Bonhoeffer's late ecclesiology by tracing his Christological move from the "man for others" to "Church for others" in a "world come of age." As German Protestants turned toward resistance (and away from alliances with the Nazi state), a new ecclesial self-understanding emerged for Bonhoeffer. Second, while there is no such thing as a monolithic African ecclesiology (in part because African Christianities are diverse and varied in beliefs and practices), by turning to three African theologians, certain distinctive similarities and some stark differences with Bonhoeffer's late ecclesiology can be identified. The ecclesiological insights of Mercy Oduyoye of Ghana, Teddy Sakupapa of Zambia, and the late Vuyani Vellum of South Africa will be discussed. The chapter concludes by considering possible multiple learnings from this side-by-side cross-contextual ecclesiological engagement and proposes potential collaborative learnings.

Close Reading of Bonhoeffer's Late Ecclesiology—From Christology to Ecclesiology or the "Church for Others" Follows "Man for Others"

Originally a mere four pages in Bonhoeffer's own handwriting, the penultimate paragraph of his "Outline for a Book" offers these "Conclusions":

> The church is the church only when it is there for others. As a first step it must give away all its property to those in need. The clergy must live solely on the freewill offerings of their congregations and perhaps be engaged in some secular vocation. The church must participate in the worldly tasks of life in the community—not dominating but helping and serving. It must tell people in every calling what a life with Christ is, what it means "to be there for others" . . . the church's word gains weight and power not through concepts but by example.[7]

---

5. Most recently, the fifteen-page entry on ecclesiology in *The Oxford Handbook of Dietrich Bonhoeffer* discusses Bonhoeffer's prison writings in less than one page. See Tom Greggs, "Ecclesiology," in *The Oxford Handbook of Dietrich Bonhoeffer*, ed. Philip G. Ziegler and Michael Mawson (New York: Oxford University Press, 2019), 225–40.

6. Indeed, Greggs, "Ecclesiology," 225, refers to Bonhoeffer as "an ecclesial thinker above all else."

7. *DBWE* 8:503, 504.

The emphasis of these conclusions is on the orientation of the church. The church is to focus outward—toward the world, toward others. The church's primary concern is not itself, but others. The church and its clergy are not to be concerned with accumulating money, property, or power. Instead, through solidarity with others, the church (as an institution and as individuals) is to live for, to help, and to serve others. Bonhoeffer arrived at these ecclesiological conclusions based on his Christological reflections that Jesus Christ is a "human being for others,"[8] which formed chapter 2 of the Outline. Repeating the phrase "for others" five times in just a few sentences, Bonhoeffer articulated an understanding of a God, who fundamentally is *for others*. "Jesus only is there for others."[9] God then is not an object of abstract belief but an encounter with Jesus Christ. For Bonhoeffer, humanity is not to seek a "religious" relationship with the highest or most powerful but rather by participating in the being of Jesus, humanity gains new life by "being there for others."[10] This Christological understanding of Christ as the "human being for others" was not new in Bonhoeffer's thought, but his understanding began to take on a new emphasis as he reflected on who Jesus Christ is for a "world come of age."[11] Bonhoeffer was moving toward an outward orientation characterized by action *for others*. He was not advocating a vague motif of love or even simple encouragement to love one another. Bonhoeffer's understanding of "being for others"—both Christ as the "man for others" and the church "existing for others"—are genuinely theological categories.[12] To grasp Bonhoeffer's ecclesiology, the Christological understanding of Jesus Christ as the "man for others" necessitates that all who seek to follow Christ must live for others.

"The Church on the Defensive" and a Turn to Resistance

Against the inward, self-preserving pull of all human institutions, Bonhoeffer boldly asserted an outward orientation for the church. The motivation for his

8. Ibid., 501.
9. Ibid.
10. Ibid.
11. According to Bethge, "The phrase 'being for others' had occurred already in *Act and Being* and in the Christology lecture. The concept of faith as being drawn into the vicarious being of Christ had been included in *Discipleship*, only now [in *Letters and Papers from Prison*], instead of the judging element, the world-preserving one emerges much more encouragingly"; Bethge, *Dietrich Bonhoeffer*, 890.

12. Jürgen Moltmann writes, "In *Ethics* and in his last letters from his prison cell at Tegel, Bonhoeffer could call this vicarious action 'Being for others' (Christ the man who lives for others). This has been widely misunderstood in a moralistic sense as general humanitarian love. But here (in *Sanctorum Communio*, 156) where the idea first occurs in his earliest writings, its strictly Christological basis is obvious. Vicarious representation is not a moral possibility or norm"; Jürgen Moltmann and Jurgen Weisbach, *Two Studies in the Theology of Bonhoeffer*, trans. Reginald Fuller (New York: Scribner's, 1967), 44.

"Outline" was his negative assessment of the church in the 1930s Germany which he described as a "Church defending itself. No risk taking for others."[13] Bonhoeffer had witnessed how the Confessing Church, which was formed by pastors unwilling to participate in the nazification of the German Church in the 1930s, had fizzled out by 1940. More than that, Bonhoeffer believed that the church had abandoned its calling. He wrote in *Ethics*:

> The church confesses that it has not professed openly and clearly enough its message. . . . The church was mute when it should have cried out, because the blood of the innocent cried out to heaven. The church did not find the right word in the right way and at the right time. . . . The church has looked on while injustice and violence have been done, under cover of the name of Christ.[14]

The church, as Bonhoeffer knew it, had failed not only to change German politics but even to be faithful to itself, to God, and to its calling. The Confessing Church had become a church-for-itself (protecting the gospel and its confessions), instead of a church-for-others. "The '*Kirchenkampf* (church-struggle) was about the freedom of the church to be the church," writes South African theologian John de Gruchy, "not about the freedom of the church to speak and act on behalf of the Jews and other victims of Nazi terror."[15] These failures of the church and the seeming impossibility of working *through* the church to change the German state or to rescue individuals led Bonhoeffer to seek another avenue to live out "being for others" personally by joining the *Abwehr* (resistance).[16] As a "theologian in resistance," Bonhoeffer chose, in response to Christ, his own act of "free responsibility" to those whom the church had failed. Through his actions, Bonhoeffer attempted to do what the church did not. Participating in these political duties liberated him for a new theological beginning.

---

13. Ibid., 500.
14. *DBWE* 6:138
15. John W. de Gruchy, "*Sanctorum Communio* and the Ethics of Free Responsibility," in *For All People: Global Theologies in Contexts: Essays in Honor of Viggo Mortensen*, ed. Else Marie Wiberg Pedersen, Holger Lam, and Peter Lodberg (Grand Rapids, MI: W.B. Eerdmans, c. 2002), 107.
16. Sabine Dramm articulates the pedestrian manner in which Bonhoeffer joined and participated in the resistance—Bonhoeffer "did not develop any finished and systematic theology of resistance. [He] was not the theologian of the resistance. He was a theologian in resistance. Nor did he act, as it might be, out of any distinct political theory. During one of their last meetings in the spring of 1945, Hans von Dohanyi said to his wife, 'When all is said and done Dietrich and I didn't do the thing as politicians. It was simply the way a decent person had to go'"; quoted in W. Meyer, *Unternehmen Sieben* (Frankfurt am Main: Hain, 1993), 458. See Sabine Dramm, *Dietrich Bonhoeffer and the Resistance* (Minneapolis, MN: Fortress, 2009), 239.

An Outline for Ecclesiology

Written after the collapse of the Confessing Church and during his participation in the conspiracy, *Ethics* offers insight into the sparse "Outline." In *Ethics*, Bonhoeffer was already thinking that "This space of the church does not, therefore, exist just for itself, but its existence is already always something that reaches far beyond it."[17] The movement of the church in the outward direction is clarified on the next page: "The church can only defend its own space by fighting, not for space, but for the salvation of the world. Otherwise, the church becomes a 'religious society' that fights in its own interest and this has ceased to be the church of God in the world."[18] For the church to be the church, it cannot fight for itself but for "the salvation of the world." The goal and purpose of the Church are to enact "the love of God really lived in Jesus Christ."[19] The church had to be careful not to "fall unavoidably into those programs of ethical or religious world-formation"[20] but to constantly keep its focus "from below, from the perspective of the outcasts, the suspects, the maltreated, the powerless, the oppressed and reviled, in short from the perspective of the suffering."[21] While the focus must be on the suffering, Bethge reminds his readers that Bonhoeffer still held a deep love for the community gathered for worship. In addition, justice must always be connected to the pursuit of righteousness and flow from prayer and community. "Justice," for Bonhoeffer, was not merely an abstract ideal but an earthly reality of "taking responsibility" for others. The future of the church in this new era required a worshiping community centered on Jesus Christ that is sent out to participate in righteous action for others.

The Church in a "World-Come-of-Age"

Bonhoeffer's vision for the church of the future, as contained in the "Outline," shows that even in a world-come-of-age, Jesus Christ remains at the center of all theological reflection. An "Encounter with Jesus Christ"[22] is the only way to know who God is. Further, it is "the Crucified One"[23] who is to be encountered; this Jesus who is the "human being for others." Thus, for Bonhoeffer, all theological reflection begins and is centered in Jesus Christ. Yet, there is a hint in the "Outline" that Christian theology needs to be rethought for the present era. He even wrote about a "revision of the question of 'confession'; revision of apologetics."[24] If the questions about the era change, then, the response of the church must also change. Bonhoeffer foresaw that established ecclesial institutions will fight to keep

---

17. *DBWE* 6:63.
18. Ibid., 64.
19. Ibid., 83.
20. Ibid., 97.
21. *DBWE* 8:52.
22. Ibid., 501.
23. Ibid.
24. Ibid., 504.

whatever power and influence they can, even if it means forfeiting their spiritual calling. The clergy will use "clerical tricks" to retain religion as a sector of life. The non-religious may be closer to following God than the religious themselves. "The tragedy," writes Larry Rasmussen, "is that the church will be the strongest opponent of the rediscovery of Christianity in its nonreligious biblical roots and will be the ablest opponent of its own conversion."[25] Instead of using what the world has to offer to strengthen the church, Bonhoeffer feared that the church would lash out at the world. He therefore saw "the attack by Christian apologetics on the world's coming of age as . . . pointless . . . ignoble . . . [and] unchristian."[26] The church no longer held a privileged position in society therefore sharing influence with others, churches must chart a new course.[27]

As Bonhoeffer demonstrated through the actions he took, living out the theological questions is, in itself, an act of theological reflection. As current generations "come-of-age" in their understanding of Christian faith and practice, they are seeking new forms and expressions of theology, community, and worship.[28] There is an inherent tension between facing outward the suffering and the outsider and offering comfort, refuge, and safety to those disoriented by the world today. Bonhoeffer took stock of the state of Christianity, investigated the real meaning of Christian faith, and offered his conclusion—the measure of the church will be whether it follows Jesus Christ to exist for others.

On African Ecclesiologies

A dozen years after Bonhoeffer's death in 1945, African peoples began gaining independence from European colonial rule. As colonial officials and missionaries returned home to Europe, many thought that the Christian faith would shrivel on the continent. While Christianity has been receding in Europe and North America (in terms of both influence and number of adherents), it is growing exponentially in the Global South. Some empirical data are telling. In 1910, 66 percent of Christians worldwide lived in Europe and North America. In 2010, 61 percent of Christians worldwide lived in the Global South (63 percent of Africans are Christians).[29] While the number of Christians worldwide has quadrupled over the

---

25. Rasmussen, *Dietrich Bonhoeffer*, 65.
26. DBWE 8:427.
27. Literature on the "missional church" attempts to chart such a new course. See David Bosch, *Transforming Mission* (Maryknoll, NY: Orbis Books, 1991); Lesslie Newbigin, *The Gospel in a Pluralist Society* (Grand Rapids, MI: Eerdmans, 1989); Darrell Guder et al., *The Missional Church* (Grand Rapids, MI: Eerdmans, 1998).
28. Some examples were found in the emerging church movement in the United States. See Tony Jones, *The New Christians* (San Francisco, CA: Jossey-Bass, 2008); Eddie Gibbs and Ryan Bolger, *Emerging Churches* (Grand Rapids, MI: Baker Academic, 2005).
29. For more on this demographic shift and its importance for theological reflection, see Tim Hartman, *Theology After Colonization: Bediako, Barth, and the Future of Theological Reflection* (Notre Dame: University of Notre Dame Press, 2020), 20.

past century to 2.2 billion, the proportion of the world population that is Christian has remained constant at about one-third. In a dramatic change that few people saw coming, there are now nearly twice as many Christians in the Global South as in the Global North. This tremendous growth happened *after* the missionaries left Africa. The end of colonization and Christendom offered new opportunities for African ecclesiologies to depart from colonial models.[30]

Insights from African theologians have demonstrated the need for African Christian thought to turn away from the dominating influence of European Christianity and toward authentic, indigenous, African understandings of the Christian faith. At first informally and now explicitly, many African theologians seek to decolonize theology. Their reasoning is inherently postcolonial and offers surprising connections with Bonhoeffer's postmodern moves toward a less institutional and more "other-centered" church. Further, the dramatic increase in charismatic-Pentecostal expressions of the Christian faith in Africa point toward the attention paid to the spirit-world in a way that might push Bonhoeffer further than his comfort zone. Whereas Bonhoeffer discussed the connection between the church and the Holy Spirit in *Sanctorum Communio*, he seemed only to assume the role and presence of the Spirit in his later ecclesiology. The Holy Spirit establishes the church in whatever form. As Tom Greggs writes, "The reality established by the Spirit is a reality in which the church exists for the sake of the world."[31] Though some African Christians may want to introduce Bonhoeffer to charismatic expressions of the Spirit, the presence of the Spirit in the church was a foundation of Bonhoeffer's ecclesiology. If he had lived to write the book based on his "Outline," he would have been pressed for more explicit engagement with the Holy Spirit.

Unlike Western European theological loci, African ecclesiology is typically not a separate, distinct, topic of reflection.[32] But compared to other doctrines, such as Christology, comparatively little has been written on the doctrine of the church by African theologians.[33] Further, "in Africa the majority of ecclesiological works, and theologies as a whole, are written by Catholic theologians."[34] There are notably

---

30. Hartman, *Theology After Colonization*, 8.
31. Greggs, "Ecclesiology," 234.
32. Teddy Sakupapa, "Ecumenical Ecclesiology in the African Context: Towards a View of the Church as *Ubuntu*," *Scriptura* 117, no. 1 (2018): 1–15 (1).
33. One prominent example is theologian Kwame Bediako of Ghana, who sees the church as a presence in the world and then seeks to get the church and its members to free their thinking from colonial categories. His interest lies in questions of theology and identity rather than ecclesiology. See Kwame Bediako, *Theology and Identity: The Impact of Culture on Christian Thought in the Second Century and Modern Africa* (Oxford: Regnum, 1992); Kwame Bediako, *Christianity in Africa: The Renewal of a Non-Western Religion* (Edinburgh: Edinburgh University Press, 1995).
34. Stephanie A. Lowery, *Identity and Ecclesiology: Their Relationship among Select African Theologians* (Eugene, OR: Pickwick Publications, 2017), 177.

fewer ecclesiological works by Protestant African theologians.³⁵ Due in part to the significant work of African Roman Catholic theologians, "the most common ecclesiological model in Africa appeals to family, variously defined."³⁶ These various definitions cause the author of the essay on "African Ecclesiologies" in the *Oxford Handbook of Ecclesiologies* to conclude that "One cannot define an African ecclesiology."³⁷ Instead, the *Oxford Handbook* entry seeks rather "to describe the nature of churches in Africa and show how they are distinct from other forms of the church outside Africa."³⁸ African ecclesiological categories are different than the ecclesiological categories used in Europe and North America.

One commonality among the few writings on ecclesiology by African theologians is that they "are all searching for new language, new structures, and new narrative of being church in Africa which can bring about authentic and integral human and cosmic flourishing in Africa."³⁹ The hope of these African theologians is that the power of God can meet the physical and spiritual needs in their nations and communities. *How* African theologians seek to navigate these questions and challenges in each of their own contexts demonstrates the diversity of the African continent and the vast potential of ecclesiological possibilities based on the Scriptures. However, many Africans, including African theologians, are much too busy *being* the church by serving others to pull back and talk *about* or write *about* the Church. In this way, many African churches are enacting a vision similar to that of Bonhoeffer's church-for-others, as both respond to the New Testament and the moving of the Holy Spirit—even if the Africans are not aware of Bonhoeffer's specific insights.

For African theologians within Christian traditions with a European heritage (Anglican, Presbyterian, Methodist, Roman Catholic, Moravian, etc.), the concept of church is assumed, often in an unreflective manner. Even as African theologians seek to decolonize readings of Scripture and theological thought, the forms of church that are inhabited remain fixed. In a sense, there is an attempt to put new wine into old wineskins. Bonhoeffer's key insight in his "Outline for a Book" was that a "new" church was needed for a world come of age. His late theological insights could not be held within the established churches of the 1940s Germany with their legacy of Christendom. The churches of Africa often find themselves in similar situations. African ecclesial innovations may not easily fit within colonial, European, denominational boundaries.

In this regard, Mercy Amba Oduyoye, a Ghanaian Methodist theologian, offers an alternate view with a clear exposition of her vision of the church and its mission.

---

35. Lowery, *Identity and Ecclesiology*, 167.
36. Ibid., 177.
37. Stan Chu Ilo, "Method and Models of African Theology," in *Theological Reimaginations: Conversations on Church, Religion, and Society in Africa*, ed. Agbonkhianmeghe E. Orobator (Nairobi: Paulines Publications, 2014), 615–38, 619.
38. See Ilo, "Method and Models of African Theology," 619.
39. Ibid., 619.

She states, "The vision I have of the church is quite simply this: It should be a community that demonstrates to Africa how variety and diversity may become a blessing. In other words, it should pick up the traditional African communal principles, enhance them with the good news of Jesus Christ, and enable caring communities to develop and thrive."[40] Oduyoye appeals to traditional African principles and values to call for a church in Africa that will be built on local grassroots theologies to work for justice for all, including overcoming cultural evils, such as patriarchy. In her view,

> The mission of the future church is to respond to all the poverties of humanity, and there is none so poor as the one who does not feel any need. . . . The church of the future should make people feel the need to talk about justice, peace, and sharing, and not only to talk or advocate but also to practice the demands of the good news of Jesus Christ.[41]

The future of the church will be "a community of good news"[42] for all peoples.

Zambian theologian Teddy Sakupapa goes further to assert: "The church in Africa cannot be truly church if it does not engage with the existential needs of God's people on the continent and in creation as a whole."[43] For Sakupapa, ecclesiology and ethics must be held closely together in order for a community of faith to be an active presence.[44] He believes that the church in Africa is "a complex reality that defies any simple description."[45] Thus, he articulates a view of the church as an "*ubuntu* community,"[46] which is characterized by inclusion and interdependence.[47] In a striking similarity to Bonhoeffer, Sakupapa argues that the church must exist for those outside it, beyond its "walls," to include those who are not Christians and the entire created order.[48]

Reformed theologian Vuyani Vellum criticized his fellow South African theologians, including Desmond Tutu and Allan Boesak, for offering underdeveloped ecclesiologies since they claimed that the "church must be a visible sign of the presence of the Lord in the struggle for liberation," without specifying the form of the church, the nature of the church, or the content of

---

40. Mercy Amba Oduyoye, "The Church of the Future, Its Mission and Theology," *Theology Today* 52, no. 4 (1996): 494–505, 498.
41. Oduyoye, "The Church of the Future," 499.
42. Ibid., 505.
43. Sakupapa, "Ecumenical Ecclesiology," 13.
44. Ibid., 1.
45. Ibid., 4.
46. Ibid., 10.
47. Ibid., 11.
48. Ibid.

the mission of the church.[49] In contrast, Vellem notes "that the discussion of the concept 'church' in South Africa is difficult outside the conundrums of colonialism and thus the 'before' and 'after' of colonialism, regardless of the changes that might have taken place."[50] In South Africa as well as across the continent more broadly, "the reflection on black ecclesiological discourse [is] a response to black Africa's negative encounter with the European ecclesiology."[51]

Vellem's ecclesiological conviction is that "the more there is change, the more things stay the same."[52] What he means is "that if there is democratic dispensation in South Africa, it is more likely that the church stays the same . . . the more there is an upsurge of the gospel of prosperity, the postmodernist culture, for example, the more the church that oppressed the poor stays the same."[53] For Vellem, the attempts by the church to preserve itself and to maintain the *status quo* go beyond programmatic decisions. Rather, "Our focus is the church that is a response to the denial of African identity, the denial of African history and the totalising violent logic of ontological denial of black Africans by the Western Eurocentric categories and their historical formulations of ecclesiology specifically."[54]

Vellem claims that even though South Africa was granted its independence from Britain in 1910, became the Republic of South Africa by leaving the Commonwealth in 1961, and elected a democratic government in 1994, "From the perspective of Black Theology of liberation the pervasive spirit or fetish of Settler and Missionary Models of ecclesiology is still dominant even to this day despite attempts to deal with [them]."[55] Contemporary South Africa is postcolonial and the lived experience of many South Africans is rooted in a colonial legacy. As long as the church (and individual congregations) remain in their spheres (racially, socially, politically), the church constitutionally cannot be prophetic.

We should recall that for Bonhoeffer, the church cannot be the church unless it is facing outward. Bonhoeffer wrote that "the Church of Jesus Christ is the place, in other words the space in the world, at which the reign of Jesus Christ over the whole world is evidenced and proclaimed."[56] For Vellem, the church cannot be the church in Africa until it is unshackled. "In a nutshell," Vellem writes, "the church must be unshackled from the colonial legacy and its pervasive trauma that

---

49. Vuyani S. Vellem, "Unshackling the Church," *HTS Teologiese Studies/ Theological Studies* 71, no. 3 (2015): 1–5, 4.

50. Vellem, "Unshackling the Church," 2.

51. Ibid.

52. Ibid., 1.

53. Ibid., 2.

54. Ibid. There is an overlap here with Bediako's work on theology and identity, though on this point Vellem pushes further ecclesiologically.

55. Ibid., 5.

56. *DBWE* 6:63.

remains a ferocious residue in South Africa post-1994."[57] Vellum enumerates four shackles binding the church and preventing its flourishing.

First, in spite of the transition to democracy in South Africa in 1994, Vellem notes that "the pigmentocratic structures" continue to define and divide congregations and denominations based on skin color.[58] Second, Vellem calls on his fellow South African Christians to stand on their own feet and not to borrow ecclesiologies or theologies from others, but to contextualize the Christian faith for themselves. Third, the South African church must reject capitalism as a means of salvation and resist capitalism as a means of oppression of the poor. Fourth, South African churches must not think that they are free from these three dangers—pigmentocratic structures, being used for cultural and theological domination, and complicity with capitalist exploitation.

For the church to be a church for others, the church must also be a church for itself, that is, a church of and for Jesus Christ; not a church yoked to culture or power, or an economic system. This is the overlapping vision for the church shared by Bonhoeffer, Oduyoye, Sakupapa, and Vellem—the church for others, an unshackled church.

---

57. Vellem, "Unshackling the Church," 5.
58. Ibid.

SERMON BY THE MOST REV. DR. THABO MAKGOBA, ANGLICAN ARCHBISHOP OF CAPE TOWN, AT THE OPENING SERVICE OF THE 13TH INTERNATIONAL BONHOEFFER CONGRESS HELD AT THE STELLENBOSCH UNITED CHURCH (JANUARY 19, 2020)

[29]The next day John saw Jesus coming toward him and said, "Look, the Lamb of God, who takes away the sin of the world! [30]This is the one I meant when I said, 'A man who comes after me has surpassed me because he was before me.' [31]I myself did not know him, but the reason I came baptizing with water was that he might be revealed to Israel." [32]Then John gave this testimony: "I saw the Spirit come down from heaven as a dove and remain on him. [33]And I myself did not know him, but the one who sent me to baptize with water told me, 'The man on whom you see the Spirit come down and remain is the one who will baptize with the Holy Spirit.' [34]I have seen and I testify that this is God's Chosen One." (Jn 1:29-34)

May I speak in the name of God who is Creator, Redeemer, and Sustainer? Amen.

Fellow students of the Gospel, sisters and brothers in Christ, good evening! And to those who have travelled here from afar, welcome to our country! It is a great honor for me to speak at this Thirteenth International Bonhoeffer Congress, hosted and organized here in Stellenbosch and at the University of the Western Cape.

You will find, I hope, as scholars in your particular field that our welcome is especially warm. This is because Dietrich Bonhoeffer was one whose theology was centered on the fact that through Christ the world and God are reconciled, one who presented a suffering God and one who was disillusioned by the weakness of the church in challenging the status quo—one who, for all these reasons and more, has inspired and continues to inspire Christians in South Africa. Our excitement at you bringing your conference here this year reflects our reverence and deep gratitude for the life and witness of this extraordinary Christian and human being.

I have to admit being nervous about addressing such a distinguished and expert audience on what Bonhoeffer has meant to us and, as I will argue, what Bonhoeffer should continue to mean to us. Just looking at our own John de Gruchy, I question what I can say that is of value to you. As the British say, me telling all of you about Bonhoeffer is a bit like teaching one's grandmother to suck eggs. But let me put that nervousness behind me and tell you why, as a practitioner of our faith on the coalface, as one exposed daily to the everyday challenges, problems, and opportunities experienced by ordinary South Africans, I believe that Dietrich Bonhoeffer's theology can indeed help us to discern, as your conference theme says, "How the coming generation is to go on living."

Let me say at the outset that—as I have said in Stellenbosch before—I speak simply as one who is a Christian and remains a Christian because our faith begins with a young Palestinian on a donkey. I expressed it this way in a memoir I have written about my ministry to Nelson Mandela in his last days: "[S]ince Roman times we have perverted the Word and the mission of Jesus Christ, and its message about what God is up to in our world. Over the centuries we've allowed ourselves to be pointed to imperial agendas. Christ's message has been attached to national flags, to military might and to the AK-47."[1] To that I could add, Christ's mission was perverted by the German Christians of the 1930s and 1940s and by those who found theological justification for apartheid. However, as I continued in my memoir, "But that is not the Gospel. Christianity is not imperialism. Christianity is not colonialism." To that, I would also add, Christianity is not National Socialist ideology. Christianity is not apartheid. For me, my own life and faith experience, including all I know and have read about Dietrich Bonhoeffer, tell me that, and I quote again from my memoir:

> Christianity is how do I love my neighbour as myself and as others. The man who links us to God is he who enters Jerusalem a nonentity, riding a borrowed donkey. He is humble and he is marginalised but his message of love and simplicity is powerful; powerful enough to challenge the perversion of common humanity that empire engenders.[2]

You all no doubt are aware of the areas in which South Africans identify with Bonhoeffer's ideas:

- Of how the concept of a *status confessionis*, retrieved by Bonhoeffer, became central to the South African Reformed churches' rejection of apartheid in the 1980s.[3]
- Of how Bonhoeffer's willingness to join a plot against Hitler's life resonated in the South African debate of whether taking up arms against the apartheid regime was justified.

---

1. Thabo Makgoba, *Faith and Courage* (London: SPCK, 2019), 188.
2. Ibid [It is also from Makgoba, Faith and Courage, 188].
3. Piet Meiring, "Bonhoeffer and Costly Reconciliation in South Africa: Through the Lens of the South African Truth and Reconciliation Commission," *Verbum et Ecclesia* 38, no. 3 (2017): a1559; John de Gruchy cited in Nico Koopman, "Bonhoeffer, South Africa and Global Contexts," in *The Oxford Handbook of Dietrich Bonhoeffer*, ed. Michael Mawson and Philip G. Ziegler (Oxford: Oxford University Press, 2019), 412.

- Of how strongly South Africans have identified with Bonhoeffer's contrast of "cheap grace" with "costly grace." As John de Gruchy has written, "This contrast, perhaps more than anything else in Bonhoeffer's writings, provided the language we . . . have so often used to distinguish between the costly reconciliation of restored justice, and cheap reconciliation without justice."[4]
- And you have heard of our explorations of how Bonhoeffer's emphasis on, as Nico Koopman has described it, "the communal character of humanity" can help us renew and enhance *ubuntu*.[5]

But what I want to highlight here is the relevance of Bonhoeffer's work on forgiveness to "how the coming generation is to go on living." You don't have to visit South Africa for very long today, especially on university campuses, to learn that for many, forgiveness and reconciliation have become discredited concepts. Nelson Mandela is seen as having sold out to white interests and having failed to take those oppressed under apartheid into the Promised Land. In response, I have argued that when Mandela began negotiations to usher in democracy, our country was at war, our liberation armies had no prospect of imminent victory and if we had not compromised by reaching a negotiated settlement, the civil war would have intensified. As a result many of those now criticizing their parents' generation would probably not have been alive to do so.

But that doesn't take away from the fact that we have one of the most unequal societies in the world today. The analyst and writer Moeletsi Mbeki has calculated that only 12 percent of South Africans of working age earn more than 800 US dollars a month. Of the rest, 38 percent are blue-collar workers earning less than that. And 50 percent—half of those of working age—comprise the unemployed and what he calls the "underclass." That is an unsustainable situation. And although we can blame our government for many failures, we also have to acknowledge that a large part of the problem is that our society has indulged in what Bonhoeffer refers to as "the preaching of forgiveness without requiring repentance." Apartheid was a sin, but too many of those who implemented it or benefitted from it have tried to get away with "cheap grace" and with holding on to the privileges which the transfer of wealth across generations endows them with.

Listen to these words of Dietrich Bonhoeffer, quoted by Gregory Jones in his book, *Embodying Forgiveness*:

> [T]he preaching of forgiveness must always go hand in hand with the preaching of repentance, the preaching of the gospel with the preaching of the law. Nor can the forgiveness of sin be unconditional—sometimes sin must be retained. It is the will of the Lord himself that the gospel should not be given to the dogs. He too held that the only way to safeguard the gospel of forgiveness was by

---

4. John de Gruchy, *Being Human: Confessions of a Christian Humanist* (London: SCM Press, 2006), 150.

5. Koopman, "Bonhoeffer," 416.

preaching repentance. If the Church refuses to face the stern reality of sin, it will gain no credence when it talks of forgiveness. Such a Church sins against its sacred trust and walks unworthily of the gospel. It is an unholy Church, squandering the precious treasure of the Lord's forgiveness.[6]

As you meet this week to reflect on Bonhoeffer's life, his work and his theology and ponder on ways in which generations to come can fulfill his dream of a society that is Christ-like, I appeal to you, please help us. Please help South Africa at this critical time in our history. We need you, our theologians, to help confront the stern reality of sin in our society. We need you to help us preach repentance. We need you to help us work out what that means in practical steps so that we transform our society to fulfill the vision of Jesus promised in John's Gospel, "I came so that you may have life and have it in abundance."

Will you help us do that?

Allow me to conclude this focus on Dietrich Bonhoeffer by weaving in the core of the lessons set down in our lectionary for today. How do we describe our identity in Christ and what are the values that characterize our lives and witness? The humility of John the Baptist, his clarity in pointing others to Christ and his witness to who Christ was and is for us today set before us a vital example that we are called to account before God for how we live out our faith. And Paul's message to the spiritually arrogant Corinthians is relevant to us if we are to speak with confidence and authority to erring followers of Jesus today. Like Isaiah, we are called to acknowledge our inadequacy and recognize the power of being able to draw on God's strength as we embark on his mission to restore the world.

What is our clear message today? Does God's message of salvation ring true against unjust structures, arrogant leaders, and spiritually inept and arrogant churches? In our current context in South Africa, I believe we as church leaders are called to challenge church and society to come out in active opposition to the forces of greed and what we call "state capture" in order to prevent our country from sliding into economic ruin. In my Christmas sermon, I said I hoped 2020 would be the "year of the orange jumpsuits," the year in which those who drove our country to the brink of disaster would start going to prison. In the coming weeks, we hope that in his annual State of the Nation Address, our president, President Ramaphosa, will give us a clearer vision of how he intends to deal with the erring politicians and civil servants as well as the business people who corrupted them, who as we speak are engaging in a fight back to try to defeat our efforts to root out corruption.

Let us all renew our vocations and like John give a bold, united witness and testify that Jesus is the Lamb of God who takes upon himself the sin of the world; that we did not know him, nor have we seen him but we nevertheless believe in

---

6. Bonhoeffer, *The Cost of Discipleship*, 324, quoted in L. Gregory Jones, *Embodying Forgiveness: A Theological Analysis* (Grand Rapids, MI: Williams B. Eerdmans, 1995), 20.

him and seek to be in alignment with and intimate with him in our prophetic ministry.

Congratulations on the successful preparations for this 13th International Bonhoeffer Congress, and I wish you the best of times together.

God loves you and so do I. Amen.

CONTRIBUTORS

Carlos Caldas received his doctorate in religious studies from the São Paulo Methodist University. Besides his position as a lecturer at the Postgraduate Department of Religious Studies at the Pontifical Catholic University of Minas in Belo Horizonte, Brazil, he is also an associate researcher at the Faculty of Theology and Religion at the University of Pretoria. His publications include *Dietrich Bonhoeffer e a teologia pública no Brasil* (2016) and "Mad Max and Dietrich Bonhoeffer: Two Views on the Future of the World" in the journal *The Bonhoeffer Legacy* (2020).

Frits de Lange is professor emeritus of ethics at the Protestant Theological University Groningen, the Netherlands. He is also extraordinary professor in Systematic Theology and Ecclesiology at the Theological Faculty of Stellenbosch University. His publications include *Waiting for the Word: Dietrich Bonhoeffer on Speaking about God* (2000) and *Loving Later Life: An Ethics of Aging* (2015), among others.

Gerard den Hertog is professor emeritus in systematic theology at the Theological University Apeldoorn, the Netherlands. He is an ordained pastor in the Christelijke Gereformeerde Kerken. His publications include the chapter "Schöpfung, Sünde, Kreuz und Nachfolge Christi. Die Suche Emanuel Hirschs und Dietrich Bonhoeffers nach einer konkreten und wirklichkeitsgemäßen Ethik im Vorfeld des 'Dritten Reiches'" in the book *Anstoß des Kreuzes. Aufbrüche im 20. und 21. Jahrhundert. Konzeptionen radikalen Christseins* (2021) and *Dietrich Bonhoeffer: Levenswijsheden* (2023).

Gregor Etzelmüller is professor of systematic theology at the Institute of Protestant Theology, Osnabrück University. He is an ordained pastor of the Protestant Church of Baden (Germany). His publications include *Gottes verkörpertes Ebenbild: Eine theologische Anthropologie* (2021) and *Migrationskirchen: Internationalisierung und Pluralisierung des Christentums vor Ort* (with Claudia Rammelt, 2022).

Dion A. Forster is professor of public theology in the Department of Beliefs and Practices, at the Faculty of Theology, Vrije Universiteit Amsterdam. He is also a research associate in the Department of Systematic Theology and Ecclesiology at the Faculty of Theology, Stellenbosch University. He is an ordained minister in the Methodist Church of Southern Africa and a Research Fellow at Wesley House, Cambridge. His recent publications include *The (Im)possibility of*

Forgiveness? (2019) and *African Public Theology* (edited with Sunday Agang and Jurgens Hendriks, 2020).

Peter Frick is professor of religious studies at United College (formerly St. Paul's University College) at the University of Waterloo, Canada. His main research interest focuses on the intersection of theology, continental philosophy, and biblical studies. His most recent books are *Understanding Bonhoeffer* (2017) and *Understanding Paul: The Existential Perspective* (2023).

Matthias Grebe is centre lead of St. Mellitus College, Chelmsford, and Lecturer in theology at St. Mellitus College, London. An ordained priest in the Church of England, he is associate vicar of St. Edward, King and Martyr in Cambridge, and the Church of England's Adviser for European Church Relations for the Council for Christian Unity at Lambeth Palace. He serves on the committee of the International Bonhoeffer Society (German Language Section) and his current research focuses on Bonhoeffer and theodicy. His latest publications include *Bonhoeffer and Christology: Revisiting Chalcedon* (2023) and the *T&T Clark Handbook of Suffering and the Problem of Evil* (2023).

Clifford Green is executive director of the Dietrich Bonhoeffer Works English Edition and he edited several of the volumes in the series. He is a former professor of theology at Hartford Seminary and is the author of *Bonhoeffer: A Theology of Sociality* ([1972] 1999). He is also the editor, with Michael P. DeJonge, of *The Bonhoeffer Reader* (2013).

W. David Hall is the W. George Matton professor of philosophy and religion at Centre College. His research focus ranges from religious and philosophical hermeneutics to post-theisms to political theology. His publications include *Paul Ricoeur and the Poetic Imperative: The Creative Tension Between Love and Justice* (2007), *Dietrich Bonhoeffer, Theology, and Political Resistance* (with Lori Brandt Hale, 2020) and most recently *How to Think Philosophically* (2024).

Tim Hartman is associate professor of theology at Columbia Theology Seminary, near Atlanta, Georgia. He has published *Theology After Colonization: Bediako, Barth, and the Future of Theological Reflection* (2020) as well as essays in *Modern Theology*, *Black Theology* and *Stellenbosch Theological Journal*. He is also an ordained pastor in the Presbyterian Church.

Wolfgang Huber was professor in systematic theology and social ethics in Marburg and Heidelberg. He served from 1994 till 2009 as bishop of Berlin and was for six years president of the Protestant Church in Germany. Following Heinz Eduard Tödt, he was the spokesperson of the editorial board for the German edition of Dietrich Bonhoeffer's works. He is an honorary professor at Stellenbosch University and at the Humboldt University in Berlin. His many publications include *Dietrich Bonhoeffer: Auf dem Weg zur Freiheit* (2021).

Helena Anna Jędrzejczak has a PhD in sociology and is a member of the editorial board of the weekly magazine *Liberal Culture*. She works at the Educational Research Institute in Warsaw, Poland. She writes about the relationship between religion and politics. Her scholarly interests include German political theology and the work of Dietrich Bonhoeffer.

Nico Koopman is professor of public theology and ethics and vice-principal for Social Impact and Transformation at Stellenbosch University. He is an ordained pastor in the Uniting Reformed Church in Southern Africa. His publications include *Reading Bonhoeffer in South Africa after the Transition to Democracy: Selected Essays* (with Robert Vosloo, 2020).

Jason Lam is senior lecturer in Christian thought at Melbourne School of Theology and senior research fellow at Australian College of Theology. His research interests include theological and philosophical hermeneutics, modern Christian thoughts, and contextualization of theology. His recent publications include *Moltmann and China: Theological Encounters from Hong Kong to Beijing* (edited with Naomi Thurston, 2023) and *The Use of the Bible in the Chinese Context* (editor, 2023).

Thabo Makgoba is the Anglican archbishop of Cape Town and president of the South African Council of Churches. With degrees in science, applied psychology, and educational psychology, he served as a lecturer, a psychologist, and a priest before being elected a bishop. He has published his PhD thesis as *Workplace Spirituality in a South African Mining Context* (2012), as well as an autobiographical account *Faith and Courage: Praying with Mandela* (2017). He is chancellor of the University of the Western Cape and the recipient of honorary doctorates from institutions in South Africa, Canada, and the United States.

Nadia Marais is senior lecturer in systematic theology at Stellenbosch University in South Africa. She is ordained in the Dutch Reformed Church of South Africa and is a Mandela Rhodes Scholar. She co-edited *Reconceiving Reproductive Health* (2020) and *Sexual Reformation?* (2022). Her most recent book is *Homo Florens? Cultivating Grammars of Salvation* (2023).

Marthie Momberg is a research fellow in systematic theology at Stellenbosch University. She has postgraduate qualifications in theology, literature, and education and is interested in the dynamics between identity, ethics, and public life. Her recent publications include *21 VOICES from Israel and South Africa: Why the Palestinian Struggle Matters* (2023). She also serves on the Theology Committee of Kairos for Global Justice.

Christian Neddens is professor in systematic theology at the Lutherische Theologische Hochschule, Oberursel, Germany. He is an ordained pastor in the

Independent Evangelical-Lutheran Church and president of the Hans Iwand Stiftung. His publications include *Politische Theologie und Theologie des Kreuzes* (2010), *Hans Joachim Iwand on Church and Society, Opened by the Kingdom of God* (2023) and *Anstoß des Kreuzes: Kreuzestheologische Aufbrüche im 20. und 21. Jahrhundert* (2021).

Anne-Katharina Neddens is a doctor for internal medicine and psychosomatics. She is the medical director of a clinic for psychosomatic medicine (Vogelsbergklinik Grebenhain) and president of the Akademie für Psychotherapie und Seelsorge. She is a lecturer in practical theology at the Lutherische Theologische Hochschule in Oberursel, Germany.

Ulrik Nissen is associate professor in ethics and philosophy of religion at the Department of Theology, Faculty of Arts, Aarhus University. He is also an ordained priest in the Evangelical Lutheran Church in Denmark. His recent publications include *The Polity of Christ: Studies on Dietrich Bonhoeffer's Chalcedonian Christology and Ethics* (2020) and a Danish book on the relation between responsibility and love in Christian ethics, *Kærlighedens Ansvar: Grundlag og områder for kristen etik* (2022).

Kevin O'Farrell is director of Theological Education and Engagement for the Joni Eareckson Tada Disability Research Center at Joni and Friends. He is author of *Dietrich Bonhoeffer and a Theology of the Exception* (2024). He completed his doctorate in divinity at the University of Aberdeen.

Matthew Puffer is associate professor of humanities and ethics at Christ College, Valparaiso University. He is the co-chair of the Bonhoeffer: Theology and Social Analysis Unit at the American Academy of Religion and he co-edited *Comparative Religious Ethics: Critical Concepts in Religious Studies*, four volumes (2016). He has published on Bonhoeffer in *Harvard Theological Review*, *International Journal of Systematic Theology*, and chapters for edited volumes.

Karola Radler is currently a post-doctoral research fellow in theology and jurisprudence at the Beyers Naudé Centre for Public Theology and a research associate in systematic theology at the Faculty of Theology, Stellenbosch University. She had a prior career as a judge in Frankfurt am Main, Germany. She holds law degrees from Germany, and a master's degree and a doctorate in theology from Canada and South Africa respectively. Her work has been presented and published internationally, including in Canada, Germany, Australia, Sweden, the United States, and South Africa.

Teddy Chalwe Sakupapa is senior lecturer in the Department of Religion and Theology at the University of the Western Cape in South Africa, where he teaches ecumenical studies and social ethics. Originally from Zambia, his research traverses the fields of ecumenical studies, systematic theology and social ethics, decoloniality, African theology, and the history of Christianity in Africa on which he has published several articles and book chapters. He is an ordained minister in the Presbyterian tradition. His recent publications include "Tracking the Decolonial in African Christian Theology: A Southern African Perspective on Mission from the Margins as a Decolonial Mode of Mission" (*International Review of Mission*, 2023).

Wilhelm Sell has a PhD in systematic theology from Faculdades EST in Brazil. He is an ordained pastor of the Evangelical Church of the Lutheran Confession in Brazil (IECLB) and is currently doing post-doctoral research in public theology and social ethics at the Faculty of Evangelical Theology of the Humboldt University in Berlin, Germany.

Günter Thomas is professor of systematic theology at Ruhr University Bochum and research associate at the Faculty of Theology, Stellenbosch, South Africa. He is an ordained pastor of the Württemberg Church in Germany, co-investigator of the Enhancing Life Project, and chairperson of the annual International Karl Barth Conference in Switzerland. His publications include *Gottes Lebendigkeit: Beiträge zur Systematischen Theologie* (2019), *Im Weltabenteuer Gottes leben: Impulse zur Verantwortung der Kirche* (2020), and *Chaos und Erbarmen: Gesundheit und Krankheit in Karl Barths Theologie* (2023).

Ashwin Thyssen is a junior lecturer in church history and church polity at the Faculty of Theology, Stellenbosch University. He is a ministry candidate in the Uniting Reformed Church in Southern Africa. Recently he co-edited *Queering the Prophet: On Jonah, and Other Activists* (with Julie Claassens, Steed Davidson, and Charlene van der Walt, 2023).

Rudolf von Sinner is professor of systematic theology at the Pontifical Catholic University of Paraná at Curitiba, Brazil, where he heads the Graduate Programme in Theology and also teaches in the Graduate Programme on Human Rights and Public Policies. He is an extraordinary professor in the Faculty of Theology, Stellenbosch University, South Africa. His main areas of research are public theology and ecumenism and interreligious dialogue. Among his publications are *The Churches and Democracy in Brazil* (2012) and *Public Theology in the Secular State* (2021).

Robert Vosloo is professor in systematic theology at the Faculty of Theology, Stellenbosch University. He is an ordained pastor in the Dutch Reformed Church and also the director of the Bonhoeffer Unit hosted in the Beyers Naudé Centre for Public Theology, Stellenbosch University. His publications include *Reforming Memory: Essays on South African Church and Theological History* (2017) and *Reading Bonhoeffer in South Africa after the Transition to Democracy: Selected Essays* (with Nico Koopman, 2020).

Reggie L. Williams is professor of Christian ethics at McCormick Theological Seminary in Chicago, Illinois. He is the author of *Bonhoeffer's Black Jesus: Harlem Renaissance Theology and an Ethic of Resistance,* which was selected as a Choice Outstanding Title in theology, in 2014 (revised edition, 2021). His research interests are Black arts, Black studies, Black theology, Black church studies, and ethics. He is a board member of the English Language section of the International Dietrich Bonhoeffer Society, of the Society for the Study of Black Religion, and a former board member of the Society for Christian Ethics.

Ralf K. Wüstenberg is chair for systematic and historic theology at Europa-University Flensburg and the director of the European Wasatia Graduate School for Peace and Conflict Resolution on campus. He is also a senior research associate in the Von-Hügel-Institute at St. Edmund's College in the University of Cambridge. His monographs in English include *Conflict Resolution through Reconciliation* (2024), *Islam as Devotion: A Journey into the Interior of a Religion* (2019), and *A Theology of Life: Dietrich Bonhoeffer's Religionless Christianity* (1998).

Jens Zimmermann is professor of theology at Regent College, Vancouver, Canada, and director of the Centre for Humanity and the Common Good (houstoncentre.org). His publications include *Hermeneutics: A Very Short Introduction* (2015), *Bonhoeffer's Christian Humanism* (2019), and *Human Flourishing in a Technological World: A Theological Perspective* (2023).

NAME INDEX

Abraham 87, 294
Adam 180-1, 184, 248
Adenauer, Konrad 149
Adler, Alfred 298
Agamben, Giorgio 177, 320
Almeida, Ronaldo de 175
Altmann, Walter 131
Amos 158
Andrews, Charles Freer 267-8
Anselm, of Canterbury 36, 299
Aquinas, Thomas von 145
Arendt, Hannah 141, 148, 320
Augustine 110, 145, 228

Badiou, Alain 177
Bakan, David 10
Barth, Karl 257, 269, 274-5, 277, 299, 316, 326
Basso Lacerda, Marina 175-6
Bayer, Oswald 81
Bediako, Kwame 136
Bell, George 255-7, 268
Benjamin, Walter 306-13
Bethge, Dietrich Wilhelm Rüdiger 44, 52, 57, 59
Bethge, Eberhard 7-8, 11, 26, 28, 43, 51-3, 55, 58, 60, 63-5, 69, 85, 130, 154, 225-6, 253, 275-6, 328, 332
Bethge, Renate 11
Biko, Steve Bantu 278-9, 283-4, 286-90, 292
Bloch, Ernst 294, 296-7, 303-4
Boesak, Allan 336
Boff, Leonardo 91-2, 178
Bolsonaro, Jair 172-3, 175-9
Bonhoeffer, Karl 41
Boraine, Alex 148
Bosch, Hieronymus 90
Botman, H. Russel 25, 131, 291-2
Brake, Josias 43

Brandt, Willy (Willi) 149, 167
Brown Douglas, Kelly 68
Brunner, Emil 255, 257-60, 262

Calvin, John 258
Cameron, Helen 160
Cannon, Katie 68
Carter, J. Kameron 67-8
Chan, Daniel 191
Chan, Kin-man 199-201, 203
Chan, Mike 191
Cheung, Barry (Man Chung) 203
Chidester, David 69-70
Chiluba, Frederick 128-9, 133
Chu, Yiu-ming 201
Cleague, Albert 68
Cohen, Andrew I. 118
Cone, James 68
Copernicus, Nicolaus 34
Corbellini, José 172
Crow, Jim 64
Crutzen, Paul J. 33, 78
Cullberg, Johann 49

Darwin, Charles 34, 103
David 294
de Gaulle, Charles 149
de Gruchy, John 19-20, 45, 127-8, 130-1, 154, 285, 331, 339, 341
Descartes, René 297
Dilthey, Wilhelm 83
Dohnanyi, Hans von 28, 30, 51
Dorfman, Ariel 41
Dorrien, Gary 272
Duerer, Albrecht 43
Durkheim, Emile 70

Eberhardt, Kai-Ole 325
Ellis, Stephen 129, 137
Eppelmann, Rainer 148
Erikson, Erik H. 7-9, 13

Ferenczi, Sándor 41
Fisher, Albert Franklin 273
Frankl, Viktor E. 298, 300, 304–5
Freston, Paul 177
Frettlöh, Magdalene L. 146
Freud, Anna 41
Freud, Sigmund 34, 298

Gandhi, Mahatma 198, 267–74, 276–7
Gauck, Joachim 148
Grant, Jackie 68
Green, Clifford J. 62, 71, 79–80
Greggs, Tom 334
Grotius, Hugo 111
Guardini, Romano 255–6
Guha, Ramachandra 268
Gushee, David P. 72
Gutiérrez, Gustavo 297

Ha, Joseph 193
Habermas, Jürgen 111, 218
Hammerstein, Franz von 143
Harari, Yuval Noah 34, 36
Hardmeier, Christof 99
Hauerwas, Stanley 136
Havel, Vaclav 305
Healy, Nickolas 138
Hegel, Georg Wilhelm Friedrich 180
Heidegger, Martin 297–8
Heschel, Susannah 68, 72
Heuvel, Steven van den 79, 94, 115
Hichilema, Hakainde 134
Hildebrandt, Franz 276
Hitler, Adolf 28–9, 44, 53, 55, 65, 72, 181, 188, 192, 194, 196, 198, 200, 226, 255, 263, 267, 270, 306, 340
Holl, Karl 180
Huber, Wolfgang 287
Husserl, Edmund 163

Isaiah 158, 232, 342
Iwand, Hans Joachim 40–1, 45–9

Janet, Pierre 40
Jaspers, Karl 256
Jefferson, Thomas 255
Jennings, Willie 68
Jeremiah 158, 231
John 80, 83, 92, 178, 261, 339, 342

John the Baptist 342
Jones, Gregory 341
Judas 21–7, 232, 234
Judt, Tony 162

Kalu, Ogbu 137
Kant, Immanuel 29, 31, 38, 64, 228–9, 262
Katongole, Emmanuel 135–6
Kaunda, Chammah 129
Kaunda, Kenneth 132
Kautsch, Emil 101
Kelly, Geffrey 139
Khalidi, Walid 151
Kierkegaard, Søren 316
Kin-man, Chan 199
Kogon, Eugen 46
Kohl, Helmuth 167
Kolakowski, Leszek 162
Koon, Peter 201
Koopman, Nico N. 131, 341
Kopenawa, Davi 90
Koselleck, Reinhart 163, 168
Kreyssig, Lothar 47
Kühner, Angela 45
Kurzweil, Ray 34
Kwong, Paul 201

Lap-yan, Kung 205
Lasserre, Jean 272–3
Lee, Francis L. F. 190
Lee, Man-yin 194–5
Lee, Morgan 176
Lehmann, Paul 273
Leibholz, Gerhard 259
Leibniz, Gottfried Wilhelm 163
Lian, Joseph (Yi-zheng) 198–9, 201
Locke, John 111
Louw, Daniël 154
Lovat, Terry 162
Lungu, Edgar Chagwa 129–30, 133–4, 137
Luther, Martin 43, 68, 80–2, 84–5, 93–5, 98, 101, 140, 143–4, 180–1, 184, 202, 211–13, 244–6, 253, 258, 277, 306, 311, 317

McAdams, Dan P. 12–14
Macedo, Edir 178
Machiavelli, Niccolo 111
Malachi 50

Maluleke, Tinyiko. S.   139
Mandela, Nelson   340–1
Maritain, Jacques   254–6, 262
Marx, Karl   174, 299, 306–8, 311–13
Matthew   169
Mazowiecki, Tadeusz   162, 165–8, 170
Mbeki, Moeletsi   341
Mbembe, Achille   280
Metaxa, Eric   199
Miller, George   91
Moltke, Graf von   167
Moltmann, Jürgen   65, 91, 219, 294–9, 301–4, 330
Montaigne, Michel de   111
Morris, Benny   151
Moura, Maurício   172
Moyn, Samuel   254
Muers, Rachel   115
Mugambi, Jesse   135
Mutale, Liya   133

Naudé, Beyers   45, 151
Ng, Daniel   201
Niebuhr, Reinhold   271, 274, 277
Nietzsche, Friedrich   217
Nozick, Robert   111
Nussbaum, Martha   111
Nwadeyi, Lovelyn   282–3

Oduyoye, Mercy Amba   329, 335–6, 338
Oster, Hans   28, 51

Papen, Franz von   319
Parfit, Derek   116–19
Paul   102, 113, 177, 231, 261, 274, 294–5
Pieper, Josef   260
Pilate, Pontius   225, 234
Ping-cheung, Lo   191–2
Pityana, Barney   284
Pius XI   255–6
Plato   8, 97, 110
Pomian, Krzysztof   162
Powell Sr., Adam Clayton   272–3
Puffer, Matthew   197

Qwabe, Ntobo Sbo   282

Ramaphosa, Cyril   342
Rasmussen, Larry L.   114, 202, 333

Rawls, John   111
Rayson, Dianne P.   79, 94–6, 98
Reagan, Ronald   175
Reed, Esther D.   323
Remer, Otto-Ernst   41, 44–5
Renaud, Terence   256
Rieger, Julius   267
Ritter, Gerhard   256
Robert, Dana L.   127
Roberts, Melinda A.   118
Robespierre   308
Roeder, Manfred   225–6, 228, 230
Rosa, Hartmut   37
Rousseau, Jean-Jacques   111
Rousseff, Dilma   175

Sakupapa, Teddy Chalwe   329, 336, 338
Sandel, Michael   111
Sarah   294
Sata, Michael   129
Schleicher, Hans-Walter   52
Schleicher, Rüdiger   55
Schleiermacher, Friedrich   182
Schließer, Christine   196
Schmitt, Carl   165, 238–43, 251–2
Schwartz, Barry   34
Scruton, Roger   90
Sen, Amartya   111
Sichilima, Sydney   134
Smit, Dirkie   291
Smith, Lacey Baldwin   19
Spillers, Hortense   68
Stassen, Glen H.   72
Sumaili, Godfridah   134
Sutz, Irwin   273, 275
Sweeney, James   160

Tai, Benny   201
Ter Haar, Gerrie   129
Terreblanche, Sampie   280
Thielicke, Helmut   260–1, 263
Thunberg, Greta   77–8, 86
Thurman, Howard   68
Tietz, Christiane   203–4
Tomasello, Michael   104
Trump, Donald   178
Tseng, Thomas (Nien Yueh)   203
Turing, Alan   34

Turman, Eboni Marshall   68
Tutu, Desmond   141, 148, 336

Udelhoven, Bernhard   138
Urbaniak, Jakub   290

Vellem, Vuyani S.   337–8
Villa-Vicencio, Charles   135, 148
Vosloo, Robert   131, 286

Waal, Frans de   104
Walicki, Andrzej   162
Ward, Harry   273
Watkins, Clare   160
Weber, Max   174, 215
Wedemeyer, Maria von   7, 153

Weizäcker, Richard von   141, 149
White, Lynn   77
Williams, Rowan   115
Wolf, Ernst   45
Wolff, Hans Walter   101
Wright, N. T.   96
Wu, Chi-wai   205
Wyngaard, Cobus van   285
Wynter, Sylvia   68

Ying, Huang   195
Yuen, Tin-yau   193

Zen, Joseph   201
Zinn, Elizabeth   272
Žižek, Slavoj   177

SUBJECT INDEX

above   15, 122, 176, 274, 315–18, 321, 326
   view from above   323
absence   219–21, 304
absolute   180, 243, 249
abstract   65, 84, 246, 252, 257, 285, 289, 300, 330, 332
abstraction(s)   20, 51, 83, 251
abuse(s)(d)   38, 42, 142, 151, 159, 259, 289, 290
abyss(es)   39, 42, 165, 234, 309
Abyssinian Baptist Church   62, 272–3
acceptance   168, 189, 196, 198, 202, 220, 303
accidental   7, 26–7, 277
accountable   115, 166, 260
achievement(s)   10, 73, 217, 307
acknowledge(d)   8, 45–6, 54, 138, 160, 166, 170, 218, 220, 270, 283, 292, 341–2
acknowledgment   36, 142, 147
act   13, 15, 22, 24, 29, 48, 112, 142–3, 151, 158–9, 167, 170, 180, 185, 187, 205, 219–20, 222, 232, 235–6, 248, 283, 285, 301, 311, 313, 331, 333
Act and Being   215, 274, 297
activism   150, 154–5, 192, 218, 279, 287
adaptation   216, 255
adiaphora   244, 246, 252
admission of guilt   45–6
adulthood   7, 9
advantage(d)   103, 116, 129, 137, 151
affiliation(s)   190, 193, 206
affirm(ed)(s)   84, 133, 157, 178, 180, 185, 217, 250, 261, 317, 323
Afrikaner(s), Afrikaans   18, 151
"After Ten Years"   9–10, 13, 19, 24–5, 28, 41–2, 51–2, 59, 110–11, 114, 116, 121, 123, 153, 170, 224, 229, 322, 325

age   7–8, 11–12, 34, 43, 57, 65, 69, 79, 87, 155, 176, 179, 239–41, 274, 279, 283, 294, 298–9, 316, 320, 322, 341
   come of age   40, 55–6, 63–5, 71, 73, 186, 189, 197–8, 201, 256, 274, 278, 282, 290, 312–13, 328–30, 332–3, 335
agency   10, 214, 221, 286, 289, 291–2, 309
agenda(s)   136, 138, 151, 174, 177, 340
agent(s)   34, 110, 113, 190, 212, 220, 284, 302, 309
   dual/double agent   212, 221, 226, 228
agnostic   60, 155
algorithms   36, 38
alien   96, 101
   alienated   20, 106, 274
   alienation   43, 141
allegiance(s)   20, 171, 232, 236
Almighty   65, 91
   almightiness   270
alternative(s)   33, 35, 58, 100, 111, 116–17, 150, 152–3, 157–8, 165, 173, 205, 242, 307, 309
ambiguity, ambiguities   33, 184–6
   ambiguous   130, 137, 185, 194
America, American   9, 34, 95, 131, 142, 163, 185, 188, 256, 274, 297, 322, 329, 333, 335
amnesty   145–6, 148
analogia entis   253
analogy(ies)   37, 114, 239, 244–5, 251–2, 314
   analogous   33, 37, 117, 242, 250, 256
ancestor(s)   43–4, 103, 110
   ancestry   26–7, 244
Anfechtungen   225, 231
anger   193, 218, 222
Anglican   141, 267, 335

anguish   142, 153, 218
answer(s)   31, 35, 37, 39, 44, 73, 83, 91,
    135, 154, 162, 170-1, 184-5, 191,
    194-5, 199-200, 211-13, 219,
    223-4, 226, 228-9, 232, 281, 292,
    296, 303, 308, 324
  answering   31, 83, 92, 195, 223-4,
    226-7
anthropocene   32-3, 78-9, 87, 91, 96,
    111
anthropology(ies)   64, 70, 80, 82, 100,
    109, 255-7
  anthropological   34-5, 68, 100, 102,
    254, 297-8
apartheid   12, 17-18, 64, 119, 131, 142,
    145-6, 150, 152, 278-84, 289, 294,
    340-1
apologetic(s)   63-4, 70, 154, 332-3
apostle(s)   91, 102, 113, 294-5
appearance(s)   134, 144, 214, 222,
    227, 238-9, 246-7, 250-2, 317,
    323
arrest   19, 28, 151, 153, 165, 191
arrogant(ly)   24, 57, 342
Aryan   67-8, 72-3
ascended   67, 70, 147, 315, 317-18,
    321-6
ascension   226, 315-18, 325-6
assassinate   29, 188, 192, 196, 198, 226
  assassination   44, 89, 194, 196
association   63, 129, 245, 290
assumption   31, 162, 212, 215, 314-15
atonement   142-3, 230
atrocities   39, 156, 253
attitude   13, 40, 44, 55, 90, 100, 106, 109,
    169, 173, 192, 246, 314
audience(s)   22, 158, 227, 339
Augustine   110, 145, 228
  Augustinian   108, 164
authentic   35, 54, 154, 157, 160, 245,
    271, 298, 318, 334-5
  authenticity   35, 171, 288
authoritarian   160, 177, 251
  authority(ies)   11, 15, 20, 83, 166,
    178, 182-3, 241-4, 250, 288, 306,
    311, 342
autonomous   33, 64, 82, 84, 180, 209,
    212, 215
  autonomy   65, 183, 255

  relative autonomy
    (*Eigengesetzlichkeit*)   212, 216
awakening(s)   60, 156, 165
awareness   11-12, 16, 32, 44, 77-8, 81,
    107, 112-13, 121, 124, 226, 252

baptism   44, 148, 155
  Baptismal Letter   49, 52, 56-7, 59-60
  Day of Baptism   13-14, 52
Baptist churches   62, 179, 191, 272, 342
Barmen Declaration   270
became human (*Mensch geworden*)   84,
    182, 185, 247-9, 251, 312, 326
become human, becoming human
    (*Mensch werden*)   185, 204
becoming real (*Wirklichwerden*)   225,
    324
behavio(u)r(s)   14, 22, 101, 224, 303
being human   297-8, 302
  living being(s)   88, 101
being-for-others (*füreinander*)   65, 96
  being for humankind   103, 105
  being-free-for-the-other   82
  existing-for-others   140
  man for others   139, 329-30
belief(s)   13, 35, 68, 70-1, 90, 153, 155-7,
    160-1, 168, 270, 275, 312, 329-30
believers   177, 184, 193, 197, 201-2, 206,
    210
belonging   71-2, 154, 203
below   14-15, 114, 120, 131, 235, 279,
    315, 323, 332
  view from below   46, 110, 321-2
Berlin   11, 14, 93, 100, 141, 146, 179,
    293-4
betrayal(s)   18-19, 21-7, 160, 234, 282
  betrayed   22, 25-7, 156, 223-4
  betrayer(s)   19, 21, 26-7
Bible   52, 55, 60-2, 68, 81, 96, 100, 165,
    194, 272-3, 275, 294
biography   9, 167, 226, 268
birth   8, 11, 13, 94, 241, 267, 282-4, 320
  rebirth   58, 277
Black Africans   290, 337
  Black consciousness   278, 284-5
  Black theology   63, 131, 289, 337
blasphemer   233, 235
  blasphemous   29, 229
  blasphemy   178, 233-4

blessing(s)   14, 100, 177, 234, 336
blindness   58, 318
blood   17–18, 26–7, 92, 122, 151, 231, 275, 331
bodily(ies)   37, 97, 101, 104, 106, 108, 263, 287–8
   bodiliness/bodily-ness   100, 106, 109
   bodily life   106–8, 263
bond(s)   80, 105, 223, 230, 235–6, 323
bound   23, 29, 72, 82, 96, 98, 104, 164, 196, 215, 232, 236–7, 275
   boundary(ies) (*Grenze*)   20, 31, 133, 136, 149, 160, 183, 247, 316–17, 324, 335
bourgeois   174, 307, 311
   bourgeoisie (*Bürgertum*)   44, 52–3
Brazil   89, 172–4, 176–8, 184, 186
   Brazilian   90–1, 173–6, 178
Britain   267, 337
   British   70, 132, 151, 256, 339
brothers   97, 100, 105, 169, 210, 292, 339

calling   14, 23, 82, 84, 95, 136, 184, 329, 331, 333
capital   33, 134
   capitalism   174, 255, 338
care   9, 10, 25, 50, 57, 78, 86–7, 97–8, 169, 173, 190, 193, 285
   careful(ly)   22, 27, 92–3, 95–6, 203, 332
   caring   11, 93, 157, 310, 336
casu confessionis   244
catalyst   67, 77, 189, 294
catastrophe   11, 13, 151
category(ies)   15, 65, 70–2, 100, 144–6, 163–5, 229, 288, 330, 335, 337
Catholic Church(es)   192, 239, 241, 244–6
   Catholic theologians   254, 334–5
   Catholicism   241, 257
   Catholics   96, 135, 166, 172, 176, 253
century(ies)   10, 19, 33, 64, 66, 73, 90–1, 118, 127, 156, 163, 224, 239–40, 244, 254–5, 257, 274, 286, 329, 334, 340
Chalcedon   86
   Chalcedonian formula   86, 236
   Chalcedonian mystery   85
chaos   13, 143–4, 319–20

character(ized)   14, 33, 36, 38, 54, 57, 103, 108, 127, 133, 136, 138, 152, 157, 205, 241, 245, 291, 298, 304, 313–14, 324, 326, 330, 336, 341
characteristic   19–20, 175, 284
charismatic   129, 133, 177, 334
charismatization   127, 136, 138
child(ren)   8–9, 11, 15, 27, 31, 42, 47, 50, 54, 57, 96, 116–18, 157, 159, 176, 226–8, 283, 293, 313
   childhood   8, 14, 54, 77
choice(s)   22, 25, 51, 69, 116–18, 120, 179, 196, 198, 285
Christ
   risen Christ   139, 221
   raised and ascended Christ   147
   risen son of God   36
Christ existing as church-community   139, 193, 203, 245
Christ the center   94
Christendom (*Christenheit*)   22, 24, 256, 334–5
Christmas   28, 51, 296, 342
Christocentric   94–7, 225, 235, 290
Christology   63, 67, 96, 102, 112, 115, 121, 123, 139, 188, 196–7, 203, 238, 244, 246, 251, 253, 276, 329, 334
   negative Christology   238, 244, 246, 250–1
Christ-reality (*Christuswirklichkeit*)   199, 209, 300
Christ-space   212–13, 215–22
church struggle (*Kirchenkampf*)   9, 12, 131, 331
church-community   15, 96, 154, 203, 246
citizens   38, 72, 133, 157, 165, 167, 169, 175, 186, 187, 189, 191–3, 195, 251
   citizenship   129, 155
city   56, 110, 134, 187–8, 293
civil disobedience   188, 191, 198–9, 267
civilization   64, 70, 72, 294
   civilized   70, 156
class   9–10, 52, 153, 226, 267, 311
clergy   19, 72, 187, 190, 192–3, 200, 290, 329–30, 333
climate   77–80, 86–7, 96, 118
   climate change   32, 77–8, 90–1, 98–100
cogito, ergo sum   99, 297

collective 20, 41, 159, 245–6
  collective institution(s) 57, 246
  collectivism 256
colonial 69–70, 73, 177, 289–90, 333–5, 337
  colonialism 19, 69, 267, 279–80, 282, 284, 289, 337, 340
  colonization 177, 334
command 57, 218, 243
commandment(s) 30, 85, 104, 196–7, 199, 210, 214–15, 225, 232, 275, 316
commission 84, 142, 145–7, 224, 310
commitment(s) 13–14, 39, 48, 120, 160, 169, 171, 272–3, 284, 286, 292
commodities 64, 73, 175
common good 15, 255–6, 258
communal 10, 14–15, 56, 135, 154, 245–6, 258, 260, 336, 341
communion 10, 23
  communion with God 232, 233, 236
Communism 165, 170, 175–6
  communist(s) 162, 165–7, 174, 179, 254–6
compassion 156–7, 170
complexio oppositorum 242, 244, 251
complicity 62, 65, 338
  complicit 45, 166
comprehension 95, 97, 251, 314, 325
  comprehensive 13, 79, 98, 150, 188, 191, 312
compromise(s) 58, 87, 186, 216, 239, 244, 310
  compromised 153, 159, 341
concentration camp(s) 39, 165, 179, 293, 306
concept of sociality 223, 225, 229
confessing 46, 252, 326
confessing Church 45, 58, 192, 202, 260, 278, 331–2
confession(s) 45, 53, 58, 61, 167–8, 182, 225, 244, 262, 318, 322, 324–6, 332
conform(ed) (*gleich-gestalten*) 185, 194, 248
  conformity 124, 185, 202
congregation(s) 44, 112, 139, 148, 202, 210, 271, 329, 337–8
conquest 67, 70, 311
conscience 29, 53, 65, 180–1, 195–6, 229, 235–6, 256, 288

conscious(ly) 12, 14, 26, 31, 64, 108, 130, 228, 298
consciousness (*Bewußtsein*) 10, 36, 47, 113, 152, 196, 240–1, 269, 278, 284, 287, 303
  Black consciousness 278, 284–5
  historical consciousness 44, 284–6
conservatism 172–3, 175–6, 213
  conservative(s) 15, 95–6, 168, 170, 172, 175, 178, 190, 192, 206, 322–3
conspiracy 29–30, 53, 174, 200, 225–6, 276, 332
  conspirator(s) 29, 41, 51, 59, 196, 225–6, 228, 325
constitution 128–9, 132, 241, 244–5, 251
  constitutional(ly) 128, 218, 239, 259, 337
consumption 33, 69, 108–9, 111
content(s) 62, 67, 71, 175, 238, 242, 244, 249–52, 261, 297, 304, 336
contextual 10, 98, 130–1, 188–9, 192, 197, 206, 213, 223, 227, 230, 239
  contextual theologies 130–1
continent(al) 73, 135, 169, 254, 333, 335–7
continuum 81, 180, 308–9
contrast(s) (*Gegensatz*) 14, 31, 56–7, 60, 87, 94, 101, 105, 107, 109, 143–4, 188, 192, 212, 238, 242, 244, 251–3, 337, 341
conversion(s) 40, 49, 61, 79, 91, 111, 152, 254, 257, 259, 307, 312
correspondence 32, 35, 38, 63, 236, 287, 318
corrupt(ed) 27, 140, 275, 342
  corruption 39, 130, 137, 172, 218, 342
costly 128, 273, 275, 341
council 129, 166–7, 256
courage 25, 43, 162, 201, 286–7, 292, 313
  courageous(ly) 10, 58, 124, 156, 292
creatio continua 94, 180
creation 70, 80–2, 84–5, 91–8, 105, 108–9, 113, 122–4, 134, 180–3, 213, 216–17, 239, 249, 255, 258–62, 289, 292, 336
  creational 81, 253, 258–61

new creation   122, 182, 213, 215, 221, 248, 261–2
order(s) of creation   84–5, 180, 183, 212, 259
Creation and Fall   80–1, 84–5, 92, 94, 98, 100, 102, 106, 121, 179–80
creator(s)   36, 64, 72, 80–4, 91, 94, 98, 108, 122–3, 180–1, 186, 215, 292, 339
creature(s)   8, 35, 80, 82–3, 85, 98, 103–4, 122–3, 180, 326
creed(s)   91, 181
crisis, crises   71, 79–80, 86–7, 89–91, 104, 111, 123, 128, 133, 153, 157, 162–3, 165, 168, 170, 172, 190, 194, 218–19, 257, 263, 270, 286–7, 316, 318–19, 322
cross   56, 58, 68, 121–2, 151, 165–6, 182, 184, 221, 230–1, 233, 248–50, 252, 306, 329
crowd   22, 190–1
crucified   36, 87, 214, 217, 321, 323–4
  crucified One   332
  crucifixion   186, 248, 310, 325
cruel(ty), cruelties   29, 39, 64, 70, 151, 170
culture(s)   34, 64, 70, 72, 83, 137, 168, 174, 189, 215, 256, 274, 277, 286, 289, 308, 323, 337–8
  cultural   9, 14, 26, 41, 67, 70, 90, 107, 127, 152, 155, 159, 174, 179, 189, 192, 256–7, 313, 336, 338

dark   24–5, 27, 151, 153, 160, 215, 221, 249, 309
  darkness   160, 214, 253
Dasein   297–8
data   34–6, 79, 333
death(s)   7–10, 12–13, 20, 22, 24, 27, 30, 39, 43, 53, 82–3, 85, 129, 150, 153, 156, 181–5, 214, 220, 226, 230–5, 247–9, 258, 268–9, 300, 324, 333
decay   162, 164–5, 169, 256, 309
decision(s)   14, 86, 119, 133, 185, 195, 201, 215, 229, 238, 241, 248–52, 287, 291, 314, 325–6
  decisionism   238
  decisionist   241, 243

decision-making   86, 195, 229
decisive(ly)   12, 34, 44–5, 49, 164, 179, 248, 251, 256, 273, 298, 303, 309
deed(s)   23, 26, 28, 41, 55, 87, 153, 156, 302, 325
dehumanization   43, 152
  dehumanized   169, 282
  dehumanizing   212, 284
deliberate(ly)   26, 31, 68, 158, 228, 304
demand(s)   12–13, 68, 140, 190, 206, 217, 231–3, 238, 241–2, 244–5, 252, 257, 299, 310, 314, 318, 323, 326
  demanded   205, 231, 262
democracy   133, 135, 141, 146, 156, 167, 173, 175, 187–9, 205–6, 218, 239–41, 278, 338, 341
  democratic   33, 159, 167, 170, 174, 222, 239, 242, 279, 307, 337
denial   20, 31, 209, 300, 337
denomination(s)   134, 139, 190, 335, 338
dependent   97, 139, 169, 225, 234, 303
descendants   18, 40, 50, 90, 118, 127, 289
desire(s)   8, 13, 16, 37, 57, 157, 160–1, 170, 174, 182, 267, 270, 272, 277, 296–9, 303–4, 321
despair   8, 13, 87, 150, 153, 158, 218, 305
destruction   31, 90, 105, 150, 179, 215–16, 221, 227, 234, 293, 310, 315, 317
  destructive   89, 90, 154, 159, 212, 257, 313
deus ex machina   56, 59, 66, 102, 123, 133, 241
development(s)   32, 55, 62, 64, 66, 89, 102, 114, 127, 132, 135, 164, 188, 209, 240, 253–6, 273, 320
  develop(ed)   7–8, 11–12, 34, 36–7, 59, 64, 70, 78, 83, 86, 100, 112, 114, 138–9, 140, 162–3, 170, 177, 188, 192, 217, 242–3, 251, 336
devil   23, 174, 200, 231, 234
devotion   48, 66–7, 69
dialogue   63, 112, 134, 178, 187, 189, 267
die(d)   18, 25, 96, 179, 200, 232–3, 279, 292, 295, 300, 304, 321, 324
  dying   21, 55–6, 60
difference(s)   8, 32, 38, 56, 64, 67, 69, 72, 117, 145, 185, 196, 203, 311–12

digital 32–8
  digitalization 32–4, 36
dignity 26, 36, 39, 43, 71, 94, 100, 106, 150, 160, 167, 169, 179, 242, 254–5, 257, 262, 294, 309
  dignified 242–4, 251
dilemma(s) 29, 180, 194–7, 226
disability(ies) 116–17, 179
discernment(s) 154, 161, 196, 201, 202, 205–6, 288, 314
disciple(s) 21–3, 128, 193, 199, 201, 231–3, 274, 290
  discipleship 82, 86, 95, 224, 232, 273, 276
Discipleship (Nachfolge) 49, 112, 115, 121, 122, 274–5, 277, 295
discrimination 132, 152, 159–60
disobedience 188, 191, 198–9, 267
dis-placed, displaced 112–13, 151, 319
disruption 31, 34, 211, 315
dissertation 7, 15, 140, 259, 275, 291
diversity 10, 35, 118, 130, 135, 138, 173, 176, 179, 186, 212, 294, 335–6
divine 14, 24, 32, 36, 39, 48, 67, 72, 85–6, 111, 113, 166, 177, 181, 206, 212, 214, 218, 222, 232, 250, 258–60, 275, 299, 301, 316–17, 319–20, 326
divinity 242, 248–9
division(s) 158, 173, 176, 181, 192, 291, 317
  divide(ed)(s) 24, 33, 63, 66, 84, 162, 202, 213, 262, 338
Docetism 238–9, 244, 246–7, 250–2
doctrine(s) 66, 95, 181, 212–13, 221, 230, 252, 253, 257, 274, 276, 296, 334
dogma 239, 242, 244–5
  dogmatic(s) 251, 313, 318
domain(s) 64, 136, 212, 240, 251
domination 57, 64, 69, 71, 151–2, 338
  dominating 69, 95, 329, 334
drama 11, 43, 52–3, 301
dualism 67, 72–3, 109

earth 38, 77–8, 80–1, 85–7, 90–100, 102, 104–5, 108–9, 183, 214, 248, 274, 290, 295, 297, 310, 319–20
  earthly 56, 60, 88, 98, 106, 147, 154, 164, 173, 183, 209, 216, 295–6, 305, 317, 332

Easter 49, 60–1
ecclesia 71
  ecclesial 16, 127–8, 136, 138–9, 222, 329, 332, 335
  ecclesiastical 134, 245, 268
ecclesiology(ies) 128, 135, 138–9, 188, 204, 276, 328–30, 332–7
  African ecclesiology(ies) 329, 334–5
  ecclesiological 130, 139, 290, 329–30, 334–5
ecology 89, 98
  ecological 33, 91–2, 104–6, 111, 118
economy 89, 107, 132–3, 175–7, 214, 262, 282
  economic 9, 33, 38, 86, 89, 115, 118, 172–4, 177, 198, 213, 241, 245, 262, 268, 278, 280–1, 338, 342
ecumenical 134–9, 256–7, 270, 281
education 10, 35–6, 130, 132, 182, 281, 298–9
election(s) 129, 133, 187, 242–3
elite(s) 14, 172, 240, 251
embodiment 101, 160
  embodied 63, 68, 73, 100, 107–8, 161–2, 271
  embodying 16, 157, 341
emergency 159, 201
  emergency situation(s) 189, 192, 195, 198
empirical 9, 69, 139, 155, 245, 320, 333
encounter(s)(ed) 37, 46, 64–5, 81, 108, 123, 151, 156, 199, 204, 225, 236, 304, 316, 318, 320–3, 326–7, 330, 332, 337
end in itself 58, 106
  means to an end 106
enem(y)(ies) 17, 21–2, 58, 103, 235, 239, 243, 273
Enlightenment 63–4, 67, 69
  post-Enlightenment 170, 319
environment 34, 89–92, 94–5, 97–8, 106, 108–9, 113, 140
  environmental 77, 90–1, 96, 111, 114, 117, 289
  environmental ethics 93, 108, 114–15, 123, 131
equality 157, 160, 176, 255, 294
  equal 36, 39, 120, 132, 150, 176, 243, 255

Subject Index

era(s) 32–6, 41, 99, 111, 129, 132, 150, 164, 238, 240, 289, 318, 320, 332
eschatology 96, 299, 319
   eschatological 82, 185, 214, 289, 295, 299, 301, 317, 320
   eschaton 317, 319, 322, 326
essence 13, 32, 39, 85–7, 170, 214, 216, 227–8, 246, 301
eternal 24, 173, 249, 295, 317, 321
   eternal salvation 84, 173
eternity 8, 87, 247, 263, 315–17, 321–2, 324–5, 327
Ethics 8, 11, 30, 52, 54, 57, 58, 65, 80, 85, 87, 105, 113, 115, 123–4, 162, 164, 170, 185, 195–7, 203, 211, 213, 218, 222–4, 228, 250, 253, 256, 258, 267, 301, 328–9, 331–2
ethics
   Christian ethic(s) 57, 86, 173, 194, 225, 230, 235
   environmental ethics 93, 108, 114–15, 123, 131
   ethic of responsibility 115, 128
   ethical 11, 13–14, 16, 30, 35, 52–4, 70, 71, 78, 92, 96–8, 103, 110–11, 113, 115, 118, 120–1, 123–4, 144, 146–8, 150, 153, 188, 194–7, 205–6, 212, 215, 217, 222–5, 229, 285, 287, 332
Europe 12, 63, 67, 69, 72–3, 162–70, 253–4, 269–70, 297, 306, 329, 333, 335
   European(s) 63–4, 67, 69–71, 90, 127, 162–5, 167–9, 240, 268, 333–5, 337
evangelical 45, 95–6, 129, 143, 166–7, 175, 192
event(s) 10, 12, 14, 38, 47, 87, 91, 94, 118, 122, 134, 141, 152, 164, 191, 213, 221, 230, 232, 247, 251, 289, 307–12, 315, 317, 320–1, 324–5
   Adam-event 248
   Christ-event 87, 213–14, 221, 248, 315, 317, 324, 326
evil(s) 28, 41, 65, 93–4, 153, 156, 173–4, 180–3, 185, 198, 213, 222, 231, 234–5, 259, 278, 322, 325, 336
ex nihilo 241, 249, 251–2
exception 22, 58, 241
exclusion 131, 174, 246, 252

exclude(d)(s) 57, 101, 120, 174, 179–80, 245
exclusive(ly) 117, 119–20, 136, 147, 151, 153, 234
existence 32, 34, 36–8, 65, 67, 69, 97, 102–4, 112, 117–23, 153, 247–8, 250, 262, 283, 294, 296–9, 303, 307, 310, 312–13, 332
exist 34, 64, 111, 117–19, 121, 159, 198, 201, 206, 230, 249, 287, 332–3, 336
existential 29, 153, 156, 160, 181, 243, 294, 297–300, 303, 336
existing as church-community 139
expectation(s) 8, 12, 163, 174, 177, 299
experience(s) 11–12, 16, 24–5, 28, 37, 40, 42, 47, 50–2, 55, 78, 91, 94, 99–100, 120, 123, 131, 144, 152, 160, 174, 180, 188, 192–3, 203–4, 220–1, 263, 272–3, 278–9, 281, 283, 297, 299–300, 302, 318–22, 337, 340
experienced 11, 42, 47–8, 52, 156, 160, 169, 185, 196, 198, 204, 221, 273, 279, 282–3, 293, 302–3, 325, 340
external(ly) 10, 100, 143, 163, 179, 184, 244, 289–90, 317
extraordinary(ily) 16, 103, 141, 167, 248, 270, 339

facts 13, 32, 35, 38, 156, 226, 228, 230, 237
failure(s) 20, 35, 50, 65–6, 71–3, 166, 170, 174–5, 201, 255, 315, 331, 341
fail(ed) 9, 20, 22, 28, 52, 62, 65–6, 68, 90, 103, 133, 135, 152, 157, 200–1, 226, 235–6, 256, 282, 331, 341
faith 13, 27, 40, 49, 58, 81, 87, 91, 129, 140, 143–4, 155, 165, 173, 175, 178, 182, 184–6, 195, 198–204, 206, 216, 240, 244–51, 260, 269–77, 288–9, 293–6, 299, 301, 305, 309, 312–13, 325, 328–9, 333–4, 336, 338, 342
   faith alone (*sola fide*) 144, 185, 271, 275
fall 122, 132, 165, 180, 183, 247–8, 260–1
   Creation and Fall 80–1, 84–5, 92, 94, 98, 100, 102, 106, 121, 179–80
false 23–5, 29, 55–6, 138, 140, 165, 170, 185, 218, 257, 283, 315, 321–2

family 10–11, 15–16, 31, 43–4, 52, 54, 56, 96, 122, 157, 175–6, 182, 214–15, 225–7, 262, 335
father(s) 9, 15, 31, 41, 50, 56, 80, 86, 91–2, 226–7, 232–3, 271, 293, 317
fear(s) 13, 30, 34–5, 43, 86, 130, 151, 158–9, 165, 168, 231, 270, 322, 325
feeling(s) 8, 11, 29, 35, 37, 43, 60, 150, 153, 156–8, 180, 193
fiancée 7, 153
Fiction from Tegel Prison 53
figure(s) (*Gestalt*) 21, 23–5, 41, 45, 64, 67–8, 77, 86, 90, 132, 180, 189, 234, 243–4, 246, 256, 284, 306
flourish(ing) 26–7, 71, 111, 217, 223, 255, 258, 260–1, 288, 292, 335, 338
followers of Jesus 22, 72, 91, 95, 98, 342
for-each-other (*füreinander*) 15, 204
forgiveness 121, 142–9, 162, 166–9, 182, 196, 205, 273, 281, 341–2
  forgiveness of guilt 146, 168
  political forgiveness 144–6
formation 135, 202, 204, 218, 283, 303, 324, 332
Formula of Concord 244, 249, 251
foundation(s) 44, 52, 94, 99, 132–3, 139, 181–2, 203–4, 224, 235, 239, 254–5, 257, 260, 263, 276, 284, 292, 297, 303–4, 334
freedom(s) 28, 40, 42–4, 81–2, 84, 107, 150, 165, 168, 180, 185, 215, 223, 231, 234, 249, 255–6, 262, 274–5, 282–3, 287–8, 292, 297–303, 310–11, 319–20, 331
French 40, 163, 168, 256, 308
friend(s) 21–3, 27–9, 31, 39, 63, 154, 200–1, 225–6, 228, 239, 243, 256–7, 268, 274–6
  friendship 21, 24–7, 142
Führer 11, 29, 225, 243
fulfillment 121, 233, 237, 247, 295, 301–4, 326
  fulfilled 37, 232–3, 252, 295, 299
  fullness 186, 220, 281, 291, 325
fundamental 8, 67, 108, 150, 154, 169, 178, 219–20, 224, 252, 261–2, 269–71, 276–7
future 7–8, 13–14, 18, 27, 34, 39, 43–5, 49–52, 60, 80, 86, 111–21, 123–4, 141–2, 169, 221, 249, 278–9, 281, 283–97, 304, 307–9, 311, 313–15, 317–20, 325, 332, 336

garden 93, 97, 225
  Garden of Eden 92–3, 98, 248
gender 10, 155, 160, 176, 179, 298–9
generations 8, 10–13, 15–18, 40–1, 49–52, 54, 60–1, 110, 114–21, 123–4, 210–12, 278, 280–1, 283–4, 286, 292, 333, 341–2
  born free generation 279
  coming generations 13, 17–18, 49–50, 278, 281, 283–4, 292
  intergenerational 7, 10–11, 13, 15–16, 54, 111–18, 121, 123–4
  transgenerational 40–2, 44–5
generativity 7–10, 12–14, 16
Genesis 80, 92–4, 98, 101–2, 104–5, 179, 231, 247
German 11, 19–20, 29, 37–8, 41, 61, 72–3, 83, 91, 106–7, 130, 142, 146–7, 149, 163, 166–7, 176, 188, 200, 211, 244, 255–9, 267, 269–70, 278, 289, 306, 320, 329, 331
  German Christians 122, 179, 256, 258–9, 340
  Germany 10, 12, 14, 28, 39, 44–5, 54, 57, 60, 62, 64–5, 70–1, 73, 87, 141–2, 147–9, 160, 164–7, 176, 179, 192, 196–8, 200, 226, 228, 239, 260, 268–71, 274–5, 279, 296, 306, 331, 335
gift(s) 25, 51, 108–9, 122, 144, 261
global(ly) 32–3, 38, 62, 69, 78, 150, 293, 333–4
  Global South 333–4
  global warming 33, 90
goodness 13, 97, 109, 216, 294
  the good 83, 108, 119–20, 138, 181, 183, 210, 234, 260, 284, 336
  good and evil 93, 181, 183
Gospel 40, 84, 136, 140, 169, 175, 181, 194, 210, 212, 244, 272–3, 301, 318, 331, 337, 339–42
government 63, 72–3, 84, 130, 133–4, 151, 159, 172–5, 178, 183, 186–7, 189–93, 198, 205–6, 215, 282, 319, 337, 341

Subject Index

grace 27, 29, 51, 57, 87, 96, 144, 151, 181, 185, 196, 204, 247, 257, 261, 270, 275, 301, 316, 341
   cheap grace 275, 341
   costly grace 341
   sola gratia 275
grandchild(ren) 11, 42–3, 50
gratitude 50, 81, 103, 122, 286, 339
Greek 101, 163–4, 255, 314
guidance 64, 134, 191, 292
guilt 29, 39–41, 45–7, 49–50, 55, 141–4, 146–9, 153, 157, 162, 166, 168, 170, 181, 185, 189, 196–9, 234–5, 270
   guilty 42, 47, 143–4, 170, 227, 231, 234–5, 306

happiness 15, 106–8, 120, 217, 288
health(y) 16, 34, 36, 64, 71, 159–60, 217, 296
   healing 32, 35, 45–6, 48, 50, 252, 269
heart(s) 18, 20, 23, 27, 35, 50, 58, 169, 195, 210, 273, 299
heaven 47, 80, 85, 91, 94, 96–7, 214, 236, 290, 319–20, 331, 339
heresy 66–7, 238–9, 244, 246–7, 250–2
heritage 14, 18, 26, 80, 90, 162–6, 168–71, 179, 309, 335
hermeneutic(s) 303–5, 326
   hermeneutical 62, 313, 324
heroes 19–20, 167
   heroic(ally) 9, 20, 219, 285, 291
hidden 40, 43, 68, 121, 212, 234, 252, 321–2, 324
history 8, 11, 14, 16, 18–20, 22, 25–7, 55, 62, 65, 83, 90, 93, 95–7, 113–14, 121–4, 135–6, 142–3, 149, 156, 159, 162–4, 168, 173, 180, 185, 187, 192, 197, 209, 212, 221–2, 224, 239–40, 246–52, 254–5, 268, 278–9, 283–9, 291–3, 299, 306–8, 311, 314–22, 326
   end of history 317–18, 320, 322–6, 337, 342
   historical 10, 14, 17, 44–7, 62–4, 67, 69, 73, 77, 93, 114, 118, 127–8, 132, 136, 139, 143–4, 151, 153–6, 163–5, 169, 179, 194, 204, 240–1, 251, 254, 256, 260, 275, 278–9, 283–9, 291–3, 306–15, 317–26, 337
   history of ideas 162–3
   irruption of history 324, 326
Holocaust 118, 152, 156, 293, 296, 298
hope 27, 35, 38–41, 48–50, 59–60, 64, 77–80, 82, 86–8, 97, 121–2, 132, 155–6, 158, 171, 183–6, 218, 220–1, 246, 278–9, 281, 283–7, 289–305, 319, 322–3, 225, 335, 339, 342
   Christian hope 49, 221, 295, 304
   hopeful 286, 291, 293, 298, 302, 321
   hopelessness 13, 281, 293, 300, 304
humanism 173, 184, 256
humanity 29, 36, 48, 50, 64, 72, 81, 87, 90, 94, 115, 121, 123, 158, 165, 168–71, 180–2, 184, 213–14, 221, 232–4, 246–9, 251, 261, 275, 278, 286, 288–9, 291, 293–4, 296, 306, 309–10, 330, 336, 340–1
   human action(s) 35, 196, 212, 223–4, 235–6, 307, 311
   human being(s) 14–15, 28–9, 34–7, 39, 49, 52, 58, 64, 69, 73, 78–82, 84, 93, 95, 97–9, 100–9, 112–13, 120–3, 150, 154, 160, 165, 169, 171, 179–81, 185–6, 204, 212, 217–18, 220–1, 223–5, 231–3, 236, 242, 246–7, 249–50, 255–6, 263, 275, 286–7, 294, 296–8, 304, 308, 312, 325, 330, 332, 339
   human body 97, 104, 106
   human dignity 160, 167, 179, 254–5, 257
   human nature(s) 8, 79, 86, 100, 246–7, 250, 259, 299
   human person(s) 106, 122, 124, 254–5, 257, 263
humankind 15, 36, 58–9, 63, 66, 73, 81, 90, 97, 101, 103–6, 109, 249
humble 48, 129, 234, 289, 301, 340
humility 184, 270, 274, 313, 342
hypothesis(es) 93, 155, 230, 288, 312–13

idea(s) 14–15, 36–8, 47, 55, 63–4, 67, 73, 94, 97, 102, 107, 114, 117, 134, 137, 142–3, 155, 159–60, 162–4, 166, 174, 176, 180, 183, 186, 188–9, 195, 201, 203, 205, 212–13, 215–16, 218, 238–44, 246–7, 249–52, 256, 260, 277, 290, 294–5, 300, 304, 306–7, 309, 312–13, 320, 322, 328, 340

ideal(s)   66-7, 72-3, 81, 103, 138, 155, 173, 216, 255, 287-8, 332
  Idealism   180, 218, 257
  idealized   57, 64, 68, 72, 139
identity(ies)   9, 35, 43, 67, 70, 112-13, 115-24, 129, 137-8, 144, 152, 155-7, 159-64, 167, 176-7, 205, 241-4, 248, 250-1, 258, 260, 263, 280-1, 289, 317, 337, 342
  non-identity problem   112, 115-19, 121, 123-4
image(s)   36, 43, 47, 60, 72, 81, 86, 101, 112-13, 129, 133, 154, 220, 240, 308-11
  image of God   36, 94, 97, 103, 165
impact   33, 62, 78, 86, 131, 134, 140, 176, 212, 218, 300
imprisonment   30, 43-4, 52, 153, 199
incarnation   84, 94-5, 147, 181, 183-4, 186, 204, 213, 221, 246, 248-51, 253, 261, 310, 317
  incarnate(d)   36, 66, 87, 186, 214, 234, 246, 248-50, 291, 317, 324
incomprehensibility   246-7, 249, 326
  incomprehensible   24-5, 234, 250-1
independence   87, 151, 238, 244, 333, 337
  independent   34, 81, 127, 132, 165, 170, 209, 214, 219, 243, 245, 303
individual(s)   8, 10-11, 16, 20, 40, 44, 66, 82, 96, 106, 110, 118, 120, 135, 155, 160, 164-6, 168, 175, 180-2, 193, 195-6, 225, 235, 239, 246-7, 250, 255-7, 301-2, 306-7, 320, 326, 330-1, 337
  individualism   66, 165, 246, 255-7
  individualistic   20, 175
  individuality   239, 247, 250, 255
inequality   40, 132
influence   33, 62, 63, 72, 77, 95, 130-1, 166-7, 173-5, 178, 180, 190, 191, 194, 257, 309, 333-4
injustice(s)   27, 40, 46, 111, 118-19, 142-3, 145, 151, 157, 162, 191, 279, 281, 283, 287-8, 292, 331
insight(s)   11, 35, 40, 51, 63, 68, 87, 101-4, 106, 140, 150, 156, 186, 192, 196-7, 210, 214, 217, 219, 222, 256, 260, 272-3, 277, 279, 321, 327, 329, 332, 334-5
inspiration   91, 98, 137, 177, 188-9, 197, 305
institution(s)   57, 139-40, 145, 204, 222, 240, 243, 245-6, 306, 330, 332
  institutional   134, 137, 239, 241, 243, 251, 334
  institutional church(es)   148, 167, 189, 199, 204, 206
integrity   28-9, 43, 48, 106, 153, 156-8, 160, 221, 227, 259, 261
international   86, 89, 146, 150-2, 158-60, 254, 267, 279
interpretation(s)   26, 36, 56, 58, 60, 101-2, 104, 130-1, 148, 162-3, 175, 183, 194, 198, 202, 215, 256, 258, 274, 289, 291, 299, 312
  non-religious interpretation   47, 55-6, 60-1, 154, 198-9, 202
  theological interpretation   92-3, 146
intervention(s)   33-4, 96, 135, 213, 217, 222, 302
invisible, *see* visible
Israel   67, 121-2, 142, 151-2, 155-7, 159-60, 176, 231, 233, 239
  Israeli(s)   34, 150-1, 155-7, 159
  Israelites   18, 231

Jew(s)   14, 67, 70, 72-3, 155-61, 165, 179, 200, 233, 306, 331
  Jewish   30, 36, 67, 72-3, 151-2, 155-6, 158-60, 195, 231, 244, 296, 312
joy(s)   40, 106-8, 174, 263, 304
  enjoyment   108-9
judge(s)   31, 115, 121, 181, 186, 227, 307-8
  judged   204, 214, 287, 317
judgment(s)   14, 24, 48, 54, 108, 121, 181, 186, 194, 205, 219, 232, 260, 270, 274, 309, 310, 316-17, 320, 325
justice   20, 27, 39, 46, 58, 102, 107, 114, 119, 123, 131, 135, 141-5, 157, 166, 176, 179, 191, 196-7, 201, 219-21, 231, 258-9, 262, 278, 284, 287, 292, 301, 310-11, 322, 332, 336, 341
  intergenerational justice   112, 114-15

social justice   153, 156, 173, 301–2
justification(s)   53, 58, 70, 73, 81, 87,
    120–1, 143–4, 157–8, 166, 181, 185,
    192, 211, 221, 253, 274, 311, 340
  justified   13, 79, 81, 116, 120, 144,
    193, 195, 220, 227, 340

kingdom(s)   96, 104, 182–3, 234, 236
  kingdom of God   59, 96, 105, 174,
    178, 182–3, 194, 211, 213, 311
  two kingdoms   183, 195, 202,
    211–14, 221
  two realms   143, 202, 211–12, 300
knowledge   41, 51, 69–70, 121–3, 133,
    155, 178, 260–1, 296, 304, 320

land   17, 57, 93, 151–2, 156, 231, 280,
    282
  Promised Land   18, 341
landscape(s)   37, 109, 127–8, 134, 136,
    139, 173, 188
language   31, 58–9, 64, 73, 81, 93, 111,
    115–17, 129, 134, 139–40, 148–50,
    155, 158, 163, 169, 174–5, 197–8,
    254–6, 281, 335, 341
law(s)   19, 96, 106, 121–2, 129, 145–6,
    150, 152, 153, 157, 160, 164, 176,
    180, 189, 191, 196–8, 201, 206,
    209–10, 212, 214, 216, 223, 230–7,
    241, 244–6, 259, 262–3, 267, 276,
    306, 311, 317, 320, 323, 341
  fulfilling the law   223, 230, 236
  law of God   209, 235
  natural law   210, 253–63
  natural moral law   257
leader(s)   9, 11, 62, 73, 78, 86, 130, 134,
    138, 160, 165, 168, 190, 242–3, 246,
    250–1, 278, 280–3, 342
  leadership   10, 177, 251
legacy(ies)   9, 18, 20, 26, 39, 44–5, 128,
    132, 143, 291, 335, 337
legitimacy   179, 190, 193, 196, 199, 241,
    262
  legitimate   119, 194, 222, 231, 301,
    306, 311
letter(s)   7, 16, 33, 42, 44, 47, 49, 52–3,
    55–60, 62–3, 65, 71, 85, 108, 130,
    136, 167, 177, 201, 221, 228, 233,
    259, 267–72, 274–7, 294, 325, 328

*Letters from Prison/Letters and Papers
    from Prison*   28, 52, 95, 111, 133,
    140, 150, 200, 202, 219, 307, 329
liberalism   90, 172, 239, 254–5, 290
  liberal   173, 175, 177, 211, 218, 257,
    307
liberation   39, 109, 122, 159, 178–9, 196,
    272–3, 280, 282–3, 285, 288, 314,
    336–7, 341
  liberating   59, 61, 85, 155, 160, 321,
    323
  liberation theologians   68, 95, 323
  liberation theology(ies)   131, 178,
    184, 210, 297, 321, 337
lies   29, 93, 191, 202, 227, 234, 285
  lying   29, 31, 226–8, 236
limit(s)   92, 165, 171, 183, 211–12, 217,
    220, 270, 303, 306
  limitation(s)   133, 136, 174, 183, 218,
    220, 244, 246, 250
listen(ing)   37, 55, 107, 158, 181, 292, 341
lives   9, 15, 26, 31, 47, 54, 56, 59, 61, 72,
    82–3, 87–8, 120–1, 156–7, 160, 165,
    181, 195, 214, 228, 234–6, 247, 263,
    279, 281, 284, 286–7, 290–1, 295,
    298, 313, 318, 322, 327, 342
  Christian life   49, 71, 84, 86–7, 97,
    202, 223, 269–70, 272, 274, 277,
    295, 310
  common life   278, 287
  life cycle   9, 12
  life together   24, 63, 66, 278
  natural life   57, 106–7, 217, 253,
    257–8, 261
living   9, 11, 15, 20, 25, 27, 28, 51–4, 64,
    73, 80–3, 85, 88, 96–7, 101, 104,
    106, 114, 118, 120, 130, 132, 156,
    159–60, 184, 212–14, 216, 218, 220,
    222, 223, 230–1, 234, 236–7, 269,
    281, 288, 291, 299, 307, 310, 333,
    340–1
  Living One   31, 229
longing   7–8, 47, 52, 57, 64, 67–8, 153,
    157, 218, 220
Lord   58, 65, 71–2, 85, 92, 96, 98, 105,
    140, 191, 193, 214, 233, 294, 336,
    341
  Lord's Supper   52, 221, 225, 342
  Lordship   85, 96, 181–2, 299

loss   11, 43, 90, 153, 191, 241, 279, 281, 296, 300, 309, 318, 320
love   8, 20, 23–4, 27, 29–30, 34, 41, 49, 50, 58, 85–6, 90, 92, 103–4, 165, 178, 184–6, 193, 196, 198, 204–5, 216, 218, 233–4, 270–3, 277, 286, 292–6, 305, 330, 332, 340
Lutheran(s)   43, 80, 85, 140, 144, 172, 180, 184, 211–13, 244, 253, 306, 311, 317
  Lutheran Church   245–6
  Lutheran theology   143, 180, 184
  Pseudo-Lutheranism   183–4, 195

mandate(s)   54, 80, 83–6, 105, 111, 194, 195, 214–15, 218, 242
manuscript   113, 315, 328
marriage   7, 12, 83–4, 176, 182, 215, 258, 262, 273
martyr(s)   19–21, 199, 328
  martyrdom   19–21, 188
master(s)   82, 151, 232, 272, 285
material   63–4, 72, 97, 100, 135–7, 145, 173, 176, 232, 242
meaning   8, 47, 81, 85, 87, 93, 117, 161, 231, 240, 251, 270, 272–3, 277, 283, 290, 297–300, 302–3, 305, 307, 310, 312, 321, 333
  meaningful   9, 52, 203, 297–8, 307–10, 321
  meaningless(ness)   298, 309
media   38, 89, 129, 172, 190
  social media   33, 129–30, 134, 162, 224, 291
mediation   112, 121–4, 135, 137, 180
mediator (*Mittler*)   94, 96, 111–15, 121–4, 181
  pro me   95, 115
  pro nobis   95, 115
member(s)   9, 66, 72, 110, 120, 146, 165, 170, 176, 189, 190, 193, 206, 225
  membership   138, 174, 218
memory   11, 35, 41, 45, 51, 287, 309
men   8, 10, 55, 72, 95, 97, 105, 151, 278
Mensch   93, 160, 242, 246–8, 251
mercy   20, 27, 96, 170, 178, 185, 218
message(s)   38, 194–5, 199, 225, 232, 244, 269, 271, 274, 296, 315, 321, 331, 340, 342

messiah(s)   121, 311–12
  messianic   177, 179–81, 184, 205, 216, 232, 246, 307, 309, 311–13
  messianism   172–3, 177, 181, 183
method(s)   44, 93, 146, 179, 227, 238–40, 251–2, 267, 312, 318–21, 324, 326
middle   8–9, 52, 81, 85, 90, 153, 164, 169, 180, 204, 234, 247–52, 324
military   7, 30, 52, 156, 159, 178, 225, 340
mind(s)   8, 10, 15, 20, 35, 52, 57–8, 81, 90, 94, 96, 111, 114, 152, 158–9, 213, 228, 233, 240, 267, 278, 284, 290, 300, 321
ministry(ies)   134, 138, 179, 244, 272–3, 317, 340
miracle(s)   70, 94, 148, 157, 165, 182, 204, 241, 250
mirror(s)   32, 36, 112–14, 121, 132
mission   95, 98, 132, 135, 147, 178, 194, 218, 232, 335–6, 340, 342
  missionary(ies)   127, 132, 139, 267, 289, 333–4, 337
model(s)   9–10, 119, 138, 140, 151–2, 175, 213, 216, 241, 305, 334–5, 337
modern   34, 36, 66–7, 77, 99–101, 109–11, 115, 121, 123, 132, 162, 187, 205, 212, 238–9, 241, 243, 254, 256–7, 283, 318–20, 334
  modernity   65, 67, 70, 251, 255, 309
moment(s)   8, 21–2, 24, 26, 29, 31, 46, 53–4, 58, 62–4, 73, 108, 112–13, 156, 160, 214–15, 244, 248–9, 251, 290, 307–9, 314–15, 318, 321–2, 324–6
moral   14–16, 29, 80, 110–11, 114–17, 120–1, 145–6, 151–2, 157, 165, 170, 173, 175, 190–1, 193, 196, 210, 212, 218–20, 222, 225–6, 229, 235, 257, 259–61, 313
  morality   145, 170, 172–3, 175, 177–8, 218
mother   86–7, 92, 98, 100, 105, 116–18, 133
motif(s), motive(s)   7, 15, 48, 79, 215–16, 267, 330
  motivation(s)   137, 193, 330
movement(s)   9, 13, 62, 132, 150, 156, 164, 175, 179, 185, 187–200, 202,

205–6, 246, 247, 269–70, 272, 277, 284, 286, 307, 321–3, 332
murderer(s)   20, 29, 31, 156, 228
mystery   23–4, 43, 53, 58, 85–6, 113, 234, 249–51
myth   128, 140, 283

narrative(s)   12–13, 16, 70, 93, 152, 166, 170, 335
nation(s)   54, 55, 78, 122, 128–9, 132–4, 136–8, 140, 150, 153, 163–4, 166–7, 262, 281, 283, 289, 319, 335, 342
   national   70, 133–4, 152, 159–60, 164, 166, 176, 189, 243, 318–19, 340
   nationalism(s)   18, 71, 130, 132, 134, 200, 252, 289, 313
   nationhood   13, 128–30, 133–5, 140
National Socialism   19, 60, 123, 153, 158, 179, 243, 275, 278, 318, 340
natural   34, 52, 57, 60, 104–5, 108–9, 122, 151, 221, 253, 256–63
   natural law (*see* law(s))
   natural life (*see above* lives)
   natural theology (*theologia naturalis*)   153, 257–8
nature   35, 57, 81, 89–92, 94–100, 103, 105, 107–9, 113, 118, 121–4, 127, 138, 153–4, 179, 181, 215, 224–5, 227, 236, 238–9, 243, 246–8, 250, 254–5, 257–62, 282, 288, 304, 312, 317, 320, 335–6
   human nature   8, 86, 246–7, 250, 259, 299
   non-human nature   79, 100
Nazi(s)   19, 39, 41, 57, 61–3, 65, 70–3, 165, 179, 187–9, 194, 196, 200, 206, 230, 255, 257, 260, 270, 305, 331
   Nazi Germany   64–5, 73, 165, 179, 228, 279, 296
   Nazi state   66, 183, 329
   Nazism   12, 21, 62–3, 65–6, 69–72, 152, 160, 184, 200
neighbor(s), neigbour(s)   15, 27, 29, 49, 65, 104, 124, 165, 167, 170, 196, 236–7, 323, 340

obedience   233, 246, 291
   obey   82, 232

object(s)   65–6, 69, 71, 82, 99–100, 107, 123, 175, 330
objective(s)   35, 64, 70, 158, 190, 197, 243
obligation(s)   14, 16, 54, 110–11, 114–17, 119, 160, 169, 180, 230, 255, 262, 323
offering(s)   64, 183, 194, 229, 231, 277, 329, 333, 336
office(s)   23, 145, 148, 214, 241–2, 244, 251, 293
ontology   122, 218, 235, 297
   ontological(ly)   98–9, 123, 154, 204, 210, 262, 297–9, 301–4, 307, 337
opponent(s)   13, 33, 129, 158, 193, 278, 333–4
opportunity(ies)   33, 35, 37, 60, 128, 149, 187–9, 206, 298, 334, 340
opposition   21, 63–4, 134, 158, 165, 170, 178, 193, 251, 257–8, 271, 275, 342
   opposite   13–14, 34, 133, 145, 200
oppressed   14, 26–7, 68, 95, 131, 139, 158, 160, 205, 210, 225, 284–5, 311, 315, 321–3, 326, 332, 337, 341
oppression   26, 132, 151–2, 155, 184, 273, 338
optimism   12–14, 16, 213, 218, 296
order(s)   58, 84, 143–4, 166, 180, 182–3, 213–15, 226, 244, 254, 256, 259, 288, 301, 306, 310, 313, 316–17, 319, 323, 336
   order(s) of creation (*see* order(s))
   order(s) of preservation (*see* preservation)
organization(s)   56–7, 59, 72, 135–6, 190, 194
orientation(s)   11, 135, 155, 158, 160, 168, 176, 188, 205, 314, 321, 325–6, 330
origin(s)   44, 73, 77, 81, 85–7, 127–8, 132, 166, 169, 173, 214, 236, 254, 317, 324
   original   28, 81, 97, 118, 196, 268
others   10, 12–15, 28, 32, 37–9, 48, 64–5, 69–70, 82, 84, 95–7, 104, 112–13, 115, 122–4, 131, 139–40, 151, 154–5, 160, 165, 167, 176, 179, 181–2, 184–5, 194, 196, 204–5, 211, 214–15, 219, 221, 226, 230, 274, 283, 288, 292, 296, 301, 314, 322, 329–33, 335, 338, 340, 342

pacifism 272–3, 276
paradigm(s) 135–6, 152, 155–6, 159, 192, 316–17, 320, 323
parent(s) 11, 15, 43, 54, 57, 119, 132, 156, 227, 294, 341
participation 65, 72, 96, 98, 168, 179, 186–8, 192, 194, 198, 201–2, 332
  participant(s) 162, 165, 194, 288
past 26, 39, 43–5, 50, 55, 57, 60, 65, 89, 94, 111, 113–14, 118–19, 123–4, 141–3, 151, 153, 163–4, 166, 177, 192, 231, 249, 279, 284–7, 290–4, 307–9, 312–15, 317–18, 322–3, 334
pastor 43, 64, 134, 148, 188, 191, 193, 196, 199, 267, 278
  pastoral 135–6, 179, 190, 203
patience 48, 221–2, 294
patient(s) 43, 46, 49–50, 263
peace 39, 59, 143–6, 148, 166–7, 193–5, 198, 269–70, 276–7, 293, 295–6, 336
  peaceful(ly) 7, 166, 191, 193–4, 218, 290
Pentecostalism 138, 174
  Pentecostal 127, 133–4, 334
  Pentacostals 96, 138, 173
  Pentecostalization 127, 136, 138
penultimate 30–2, 48, 87, 105, 144, 182–3, 185–6, 202–3, 205, 216, 218, 261–2, 291, 307, 310, 329
people(s) 7, 9–10, 12–14, 17–18, 22, 25–6, 28, 30–1, 33–5, 38–9, 41–2, 47–9, 52, 55, 57, 59–60, 63–5, 67–70, 72–3, 77, 81, 84, 90, 95, 105, 107, 109–10, 114, 117–18, 120–2, 124, 127, 129, 132–3, 139, 141–4, 152, 154–6, 158–60, 165, 169–70, 173–5, 179, 182–3, 185, 187–8, 190–1, 193–4, 197, 203–6, 243, 251, 269–71, 280–3, 285–6, 288–90, 293, 295, 297, 320–1, 329, 333–4, 336, 342
perception(s) 47, 55, 99, 108, 112–13, 180, 211, 227, 314–15, 318, 320–4
persecution 130, 142, 159, 166, 244, 252
person(s) 9, 14–16, 22, 24, 29, 31, 35–7, 48–9, 54, 65, 67, 69, 77, 82, 84, 87, 90, 93, 100, 106, 110, 113, 115–16, 118–20, 122, 124, 156, 158, 165, 174, 177–8, 180–1, 186, 200, 215–16, 220, 224, 227, 229–30, 232, 235, 241–2, 245–8, 250, 252, 254–7, 262–3, 278, 281, 283–5, 287–92, 298–9, 301–2, 304, 310, 323
  human person(s) (*see* humanity)
  personal 9, 12–13, 30, 33, 37–8, 42, 57, 95, 106, 113, 153–7, 159, 167, 173, 181, 194, 196, 233, 241–3, 246, 255, 257, 262, 273, 288–9, 292, 309
personalism 165, 167, 216, 255, 257–8
personality(ies) 10, 148, 238–9, 242–4, 246, 250–2, 298–9
phenomenon, phenomena 47, 60, 77, 112–14, 123, 157, 162–3, 172, 298, 320
philosophy 8, 29, 66–7, 83, 90, 100, 115, 163–4, 188, 217, 254, 276, 307
  philosopher(s) 29, 34, 37–8, 90, 115, 119, 121, 256, 280, 296
  philosophical(ly) 77, 123, 163, 177, 179, 180, 215, 222, 239, 249, 296–7, 306–7
planet 36, 77–8, 86, 88–91, 96, 160–1
Poland 142, 149, 162, 165–7, 169–70
  Polish 142, 165–7, 169
police 175–6, 187, 189–91, 193–4, 199, 205
policy(ies) 68, 89, 111, 114, 117–18, 120, 174, 176, 198, 258, 289
politics 68, 110, 128–9, 133–4, 136–8, 140–1, 143–4, 146, 149, 163, 167, 172–4, 177, 181, 218, 263, 279–81, 283–4, 287, 289, 292, 323, 331
  political theology 140, 238, 240, 251
  politician(s) 19, 129, 137, 169–70, 172, 177, 252, 281, 342
poor 14, 24, 27, 36, 124, 170, 336–8
population(s) 32, 70, 91, 114, 117–18, 120, 188, 192, 279–80, 282, 334
positive 9, 13, 31, 38, 44, 120, 216, 241, 251, 259, 262, 300, 303, 324
possibility(ies) 36, 38, 44, 52, 91, 114, 122, 142, 144, 174, 212, 216, 218, 228, 240, 285, 297–9, 307, 309, 315–16, 320–1, 335
poverty 137, 184, 279, 281, 302
power(s) 13, 15, 21–2, 27–8, 33, 37, 40–2, 49, 56, 58–60, 72, 85, 109,

130, 133, 135, 137, 142–4, 151–3,
  155–6, 158, 165–6, 175, 177, 181–4,
  193, 212, 218, 220–2, 226, 233, 239,
  245, 261, 267, 269–70, 282, 296,
  297, 300, 302, 309, 311, 318, 320,
  322–3, 325, 329–33, 335, 338, 342
 powerful   10, 15, 59, 70, 95, 139, 200,
  211, 218–19, 222, 283, 284, 300,
  322, 330, 340
 powerless(ness)   14, 26, 55–6, 68, 193,
  311, 332
pray(ing)   43, 48, 96, 182, 219–20, 222
 prayer   56, 58, 133–4, 158, 182, 191,
  193, 203, 205, 220, 222, 225, 332
presence   29, 32, 36, 49, 94, 96, 135,
  147–8, 173–4, 177, 180–2, 193, 201,
  203, 205–6, 218–21, 249–51, 287–8,
  316–18, 320, 322, 326–7, 334, 336
preservation   58, 81, 84–5, 94, 122, 134,
  180, 182, 259, 261–2, 323
 order(s) of preservation   84–5, 180,
  259
president   128–30, 132–4, 137–8, 141,
  178, 184, 342
principle(s)   29, 31, 51, 92, 95, 98, 120,
  134, 147, 157, 165, 169, 173, 177,
  180, 185–6, 190, 194, 198, 201, 205,
  227, 229, 235, 242–3, 247, 253, 255,
  257–9, 261–2, 276, 285, 288, 296–7,
  303, 336
prison   7, 11–12, 30, 42, 44, 52–3, 63–6,
  71, 108, 111–12, 173, 199–201, 221,
  224–5, 228, 267, 272, 279, 328, 342
private   25, 31–2, 38, 136, 141, 145, 280
privilege(s)   12, 14–16, 135, 139, 201,
  210, 268, 279, 282, 311, 341
 privileged   10, 14–16, 66, 71, 157, 203,
  280, 322–3, 333
proclamation (*Verkündigung*)   36, 57,
  84–5, 182, 212, 249, 315–17
progress   33–4, 64, 78, 86, 210, 216, 288,
  294, 308
 progressive   210, 254, 285, 307–9, 314
project(s)   8, 11, 36, 62–5, 67–70, 72,
  110–11, 152, 155, 174, 181, 254,
  285, 311–12, 328
promise(s)   55–6, 60, 92, 104, 121, 199,
  222, 247–9, 274, 319, 326
 Promised Land   18, 341

prophetic   71, 122, 130, 134, 138, 140,
  210, 219, 337
protest(s)   107, 175, 187–95, 198–200,
  205–6, 221, 280, 282, 323
 protesters   189–91, 193, 195–6, 201,
  205
Protestant(s) (*evangelisch*)   13, 72, 130,
  153, 179–80, 182, 190, 194, 238,
  244–6, 253–60, 270, 335
 Protestantism   68, 106–7, 132, 219,
  257–8, 271, 273
psychology   7–8, 40, 42
 psychological   7, 14, 16, 41–2, 284,
  288, 296, 298, 304
public   9, 17, 22, 25, 31–2, 34, 38, 44, 46,
  54, 71, 77, 114, 128–30, 132–6, 140,
  142, 145, 154, 157–8, 172, 183, 190,
  192, 194, 199, 205, 221, 242, 244–5,
  258, 261, 268
 public sphere   136, 140, 177, 186
 public theology   151, 210, 218

race(s)   10, 64, 67, 72, 122, 150, 169, 280
 racial   64, 67, 72–3, 150, 160, 179,
  269, 277, 279, 281
 racism   62, 68, 111, 267, 281
radical   87, 102, 113, 129, 147, 154, 157,
  159, 186, 193, 200, 205, 211, 215,
  217, 240, 253, 288
raised   147, 233, 295, 318, 321, 324
reality (*Wirklichkeit*)   21, 29, 31–2, 36–9,
  43, 46, 49, 51, 53–6, 61, 64–6, 68,
  80, 82–6, 95–7, 113, 122, 124, 137,
  139, 144, 148–9, 154, 156–8, 164,
  166, 168–9, 180–6, 197, 202, 204,
  209, 212, 215–18, 221, 223–5, 227,
  229–30, 235–6, 248–52, 260–1, 270,
  272, 277, 279, 283, 286–7, 298–301,
  309, 311, 316, 318, 320, 332, 334,
  336, 340–2
 accordance with reality
  (*Wirklichkeitsgemäßheit*)   202,
  223–5
 Christ-reality
  (*Christuswirklichkeit*)   54, 84–5,
  199, 201–3, 209–11, 236, 300
 God's reality   209, 230, 300
 reality of Christ   147–8, 209, 213,
  300

reality of God   65, 113, 186, 209, 224–5, 230, 234–6, 300
realization (*Wirklichwerden*)   12, 14, 50, 66, 153, 157, 160, 166, 168, 209, 211, 269, 278, 301, 304
realm(s)   35, 38, 48, 54, 143, 146–8, 164, 180–1, 201–2, 209–13, 225, 300–2
reason(s)   18, 24, 29–30, 36, 55, 63–5, 73, 87, 97, 102, 115, 131, 157–8, 173, 180–3, 198, 204, 213, 220, 257, 261–2, 288, 293, 298, 302, 306, 311, 321, 324, 339
reconciliation   17, 32, 35, 39–40, 46, 50, 58–60, 84, 141–4, 146–9, 162, 166–7, 169, 211, 223–4, 230, 234–5, 281, 341
  reconciled   39, 65, 82, 144, 167, 213–14, 217, 224, 234–5, 339
  reconciler   36, 84, 225, 234
redemption   13, 24, 58, 60, 96, 122, 166, 211, 213, 247–8, 252, 261, 306, 310, 315
  redeem(ed)   13, 26, 166, 214, 217, 232, 312
  redeemer   36, 82, 84, 179, 181, 183, 186, 212, 339
Reformation   68, 87, 164, 179, 185, 255, 269, 271, 274, 277, 309
regime(s)   19, 26, 29, 38–9, 63–5, 142, 145, 150, 152, 169, 178–9, 188, 191, 196, 254–6, 270, 311, 340
relations   32, 37, 54, 69, 88, 119, 124, 132, 138–40, 159, 164, 166, 306
  relationship(s)   7, 11, 15–16, 30–2, 36–7, 43, 48, 54, 57, 69, 81, 99–100, 103, 105, 110, 113–14, 122, 129–30, 137, 140, 142, 152, 154–5, 158, 165, 176, 179, 182, 188, 192, 194, 203, 211, 224, 227, 230–1, 287–9, 291, 302, 306, 330
religion 34, 56–7, 59, 61, 63–6, 69–73, 129, 135–7, 140, 150, 155, 158, 177, 180–1, 184, 189, 199, 203–4, 218, 274, 286, 290, 301, 312–13, 333
  religionless 65, 69, 71, 202, 205
  religionless Christianity   63, 71, 188, 204, 274, 290, 313, 328
religious   43–4, 47, 55–6, 59–61, 66–7, 69–70, 72–3, 127, 130, 132–7, 139, 148–9, 152, 154, 156, 158–60, 172–8, 181–3, 186–8, 190, 193, 198–9, 202, 206, 211–13, 217, 246–7, 254–5, 281, 320, 323, 330, 332–3
  non-religious   59–60, 154–5, 333
renewal   37, 45–7, 59, 143, 166, 321
repentance   39, 45, 58, 60, 122, 133, 168, 341–2
representation   15, 72, 114, 183, 196, 238, 242–3, 252
representative (*Vertreter*)   119, 132, 149, 241–4, 247, 251, *see also* vicarious representative action *and Stellvertretung*
resistance   19, 42–5, 62, 132, 136, 188, 193, 218, 225, 228, 267, 273, 275–6, 322, 329, 331
  resistance movement   9, 150, 188
resource(s)   40, 44–5, 50, 111, 114, 123, 129, 137, 151–2, 183–4, 189, 248, 279, 282–3, 292
respect   32, 36, 38, 57, 150, 173, 184–6, 269, 294, 301
response(s)   24, 29, 32, 37, 71–3, 78–80, 82–3, 87, 112, 121, 123–4, 128, 159, 168–9, 189, 191, 195, 197, 200, 219, 224, 240, 255, 257, 288–9, 291–2, 318, 325, 331–2, 337, 341
responsible   9, 14, 22, 25, 44, 50–1, 65, 69, 112, 167, 173–4, 183, 185, 188, 223, 230, 285, 288–9, 307, 310–11
  responsible action(s)   29, 56, 98, 140, 185, 194, 196, 223–4, 229–30, 236, 288, 310–11, 325
  responsible life   14, 51, 65, 223–4, 237
  responsibly   31, 51, 235–6, 291, 313
responsive   37, 80–2, 88, 314–15, 325
responsivity   79–80, 82–3, 315
resurrection   58, 60, 83, 181–6, 212–15, 235, 247, 295–7, 304, 310, 316, 322, 324–6
  Resurrected One   317, 324
revelation   111, 113, 122, 124, 180–1, 194, 204, 209, 213, 250, 257–61, 274–5, 300
revolution   34, 198, 256, 280, 308
  Fourth Revolution   34
  French Revolution   256, 308
  revolutionary   21, 58, 106, 108, 214, 308–9, 311–12, 322–3
righteousness   29, 49, 59, 218, 229, 236, 270, 332

rights 38, 107, 111, 118–19, 123, 150, 152, 155, 174, 176, 179, 255–6, 258–9, 261–3, 281–2, 284, 301–2, 310
  human rights 19, 38, 118, 135, 150, 155, 157, 160, 168, 187, 218, 253–62
risk(s) (*Wagnis*) 30, 37, 83, 159, 197, 213, 224, 326, 331
Roman 164, 230, 241, 340
  Roman Catholic 138, 162, 164–5, 167, 173, 239, 241–2, 245, 251, 253, 260, 335
rule 29, 38, 105, 132–3, 146, 165, 205, 214–15, 245, 257, 279, 306, 311, 333
  ruler(s) 11, 241, 243, 248, 308

sacred 48, 67–70, 136, 263, 299, 342
sacrifice(s) 10, 14–16, 174, 221, 231, 270, 271, 277, 288
salvation 21–2, 26–7, 84, 91, 96, 173–4, 239, 250, 285, 292, 294, 319, 332, 338, 342
Sanctorum Communio 15, 24, 100, 140, 245, 328, 334
scholar(s) 7, 9, 16, 63–4, 66, 68–9, 71–2, 79, 81, 94–6, 101, 111, 114–15, 138, 150, 169, 188, 194, 197–8, 211, 253, 268, 339
  scholarship 70, 93, 115, 121, 128, 130–1, 140, 188
science(s) 34, 64, 66–71, 73, 91, 160, 188
scripture(s) 55, 91, 96, 115, 180, 274, 276, 335
secular 60, 66, 136, 155, 166, 170, 174–5, 187–8, 201, 238–9, 242, 253–6, 258, 299, 306, 311–12
sermon(s) 12–13, 21, 24, 92, 202, 270–1, 295–6, 315–16, 318, 321–2, 324–5, 327, 342
  Sermon on the Mount 71, 232, 267, 269, 271–7
significance 52–3, 69, 78, 93, 131, 133, 175, 198, 203, 224, 238, 242–4, 246, 251–2, 284–5, 295, 307–9, 322
silence 31, 61, 96, 147, 170, 235, 282
sin 24, 85, 118, 121, 144, 170, 181–2, 184, 196, 214–15, 221, 231, 237, 247, 257–8, 260–1, 275, 291, 316, 339, 341–2
  sinner 81, 87, 185, 312

situation(s) 9, 13, 29, 31–2, 37–8, 43, 46–7, 63, 71, 83, 86–7, 89–91, 117, 119, 157, 166–7, 169–70, 173, 179, 181, 184–5, 187–9, 191–8, 201, 203, 205–6, 215, 218, 222, 226–7, 234–5, 241, 244–5, 251–2, 257, 262, 268, 270, 286, 291, 293, 296, 302, 309, 314–15, 322, 335, 341
social 10, 12, 14–15, 33–4, 40, 45, 63, 65–8, 70, 79–80, 95, 103, 107, 110–11, 118, 129–30, 132, 134–7, 140, 141, 148, 153, 156–7, 163, 168, 170, 173–6, 179, 188, 190, 192, 199, 202, 206, 210–11, 221–2, 224, 227, 235, 238, 240, 246, 254–6, 258–60, 272, 278, 280–1, 289–90, 294, 301–2, 307
  Socialism 60, 90, 123, 153, 158, 174–5, 275, 278, 318
  sociality 79–80, 98, 103, 122, 140, 223, 225, 229
society 8, 20, 41, 49, 57, 61, 73, 95, 97, 110, 120, 128, 130, 135, 140, 156, 159, 165, 173–4, 177–9, 181–2, 184–7, 194, 197, 206, 213, 224–5, 253, 255–6, 258, 279–81, 284, 290, 311, 332–3, 341–2
sociology 42, 199, 243
  sociology of concepts 239–42
solidarity 171, 185, 205, 286–8, 330
son 17, 80, 92, 147, 321
  Son of God 36, 233
  Son of Man 24, 231–2
soul(s) 8, 73, 91, 95–7, 101–2, 153, 160, 172–3
South Africa(n) 12, 17–18, 25, 39, 63, 69, 130–2, 141–2, 146–8, 152, 155–8, 160, 167, 188, 278–81, 283–4, 287, 290–2, 329, 331, 336–42
  South Africans 132, 150, 155, 279–80, 282–4, 290, 337, 340–1
space(s) 15, 26, 38, 48–9, 54, 61–2, 67, 73, 106, 114, 154, 169, 201, 209–10, 212–13, 215–22, 287, 301, 332, 337
speak 5, 17, 28, 32, 36–7, 52, 58–60, 78–9, 85, 87, 91–3, 100, 105, 130, 133–4, 141–3, 147, 150, 159, 168, 178, 196, 220, 222, 227, 283, 294, 297–9, 308, 312, 314–15, 326, 331, 339–40, 342

speaking 32, 54, 157, 190, 195, 211, 227, 229–30, 309, 316–17
sphere(s) 31, 130, 136, 140, 143–4, 148–9, 163, 170, 177, 186, 212, 215, 241, 300, 337
spirit 67, 98, 100, 102–4, 107–8, 140, 174, 179–80, 212, 221–2, 239, 242, 262, 334, 337, 339
   Holy Spirit 58, 104, 180, 182, 262, 318, 320, 335, 339
   Spirit of God 48, 104
spiritual 9, 44–5, 48, 50, 52, 57, 68, 79, 91, 95, 97, 103, 108, 129, 135, 137, 153, 155–6, 166–7, 169, 172, 187, 201, 222, 241, 244–6, 249–50, 254, 263, 268–9, 277, 333, 335
Stellvertretung 15, 115, 196, 223–4, 230, 242, 248, 250, 252, *see also* vicarious representative action
story(ies) 14, 18–19, 21–2, 26, 52, 136, 169, 231, 234, 239, 247, 267, 281, 283
structure(s) 12–14, 42, 58, 140, 180, 203–4, 211, 214, 217, 223, 238–41, 245–6, 262, 297–9, 301, 307, 310, 335, 338, 342
   social structures 238, 240, 246
struggle 9, 12, 20, 29, 58, 87, 129, 131–2, 155, 157, 168–9, 174, 179, 196, 199, 201, 206, 226, 278, 282–3, 285–6, 291, 331, 336
   church-struggle (*Kirchenkampf*) 331
subjects 11, 34, 69–70, 99, 139
suffering(s) 14–15, 24, 45, 49, 55–6, 65–6, 68, 104, 110, 124, 142, 154, 167–70, 184–5, 201–2, 205, 231–2, 269, 273, 275, 283, 288, 311–12, 332–3, 339
symbol(s) 22, 41, 148–9, 231
   symbolic 23, 34, 38, 146, 148–9
synchronization 244, 246
   synchronized (*gleich-schalten*) 243, 244, 251–2
   synchronizing 244, 251
system(s) 20, 26, 38, 69–70, 130, 137, 156–7, 164, 170, 177, 189–90, 197, 213, 229, 231, 257, 278, 281, 300, 311, 319–20, 338

teaching(s) 34, 51, 62, 145, 179, 212, 233, 269, 271, 277, 290, 294–5, 301, 339
technology(ies) 33–4, 36, 105, 172, 255
temporal(ly) 112–13, 123, 183, 215, 220, 307, 309–10
temptation 213, 218, 220, 222
tension(s) 8, 14, 20, 32, 35, 160, 183–6, 203, 212–13, 220, 248–9, 260, 285, 308–9, 333
testament 52, 335
   New Testament 8, 317, 335
   Old Testament 8, 50, 52, 101–2, 138, 179
theologian(s) 25, 45, 68, 91, 96, 131, 135, 139, 144, 188, 254, 256, 269, 274, 281, 287, 290, 294, 323, 329, 334–6, 342
theory(ies) 41, 69, 115–16, 118–21, 123, 137, 155, 164, 191, 212, 229, 235, 238–9, 241–2, 251–2, 254, 256–8, 260–2
Third Reich 57, 179, 181, 320
together 11, 20, 23–4, 34, 39, 41, 45, 52, 56, 60, 63, 66–8, 98, 116, 141, 164–5, 186, 191, 202, 209, 213, 257, 278, 319, 323–4, 336
totalitarian 57, 100, 145, 169–70, 181, 251, 255–6, 279
tradition(s) 14, 58, 61, 94, 111, 123, 137–8, 142, 153, 161–2, 168, 180, 192, 210, 215, 232, 261, 294, 335
   traditional(ly) 70, 90–1, 95, 115, 118, 137–8, 145, 173–8, 189, 202, 211, 308, 336
traitor(s) 17, 19–21, 26, 44–5, 151
transcendence 37, 158, 241, 248
   transcend(s) 8, 36–7, 154, 158–9, 221, 240, 260
transformation(s) 8, 34, 36–7, 48, 127, 135–6, 144, 146, 177, 213, 215–16, 255, 279–81, 283, 290–2, 299, 308, 312
trauma 11, 40–1, 43–5, 337
treatment 107, 116–17, 136, 159, 195
tree(s) 50, 90, 93–4
   tree of death 247
   Tree of Knowledge 93, 239, 247–9
   Tree of Life 93, 104, 247–9

trial(s)   7, 30, 41, 44–5, 168, 224, 295
trust   24–5, 29, 41, 50, 53, 103, 147, 189, 242–3, 342
  mistrust   25, 35, 184, 320
truth   9, 17, 27, 29–32, 35–9, 53–5, 58–9, 130, 135–7, 142, 145–7, 157, 178, 186, 204–5, 223–30, 234–7, 270, 272, 277, 281, 284, 318, 323
  truthful   31, 223–4, 227–9, 236
  truthfulness   32, 36, 227, 229

ubuntu   336, 341
ultimate   13, 48, 81, 87, 137, 144, 183, 185–6, 202–4, 216, 246, 249, 261–2, 284–5, 288–9, 295, 301, 304, 306–7, 309–10
United Nations   29, 78, 150
United States   14, 62, 68, 152, 155, 175, 205, 268, 272–3
unity   13, 29–30, 79, 83, 86–7, 164, 205, 216, 232, 236, 252, 261, 317, 325–6
universal   29, 38, 97, 150, 160, 168, 178, 194, 200–2, 205, 243, 254, 257, 318–19, 322
upheaval(s)   141, 154, 190, 194, 199, 206, 242
utilitarian   111, 118–19, 123

values   26, 56, 128, 134, 155–8, 160–2, 168–71, 194, 201, 229, 249, 279, 286, 300, 336, 342
vicarious representation   15, 196
  represent vicariously   15
vicarious representative action (*Stellvertretung*)   15, 115, 196, 223, 234–5
victim(s)   20, 29, 40–1, 45–6, 63, 118, 131, 142–3, 145, 148, 156, 159, 166, 169, 179, 201, 231, 306, 311, 331
victory   17, 173–4, 187, 254, 295, 318, 341
violation(s)   29, 38, 106, 118, 155, 255
violence   19, 22, 32, 40, 42, 72, 137, 152, 170, 190–4, 212, 218, 221, 281, 283, 306, 319, 321, 322, 331
  violent   27, 39, 68, 140, 152, 189–90, 193, 205, 279, 289, 322, 337
virtue(s)   16, 40, 141, 230, 260, 282–3, 288, 294

visible   13–14, 36, 46, 91, 96, 160, 167, 177, 204, 217, 242, 302, 319, 321–2, 325, 327, 336
  invisible   68, 91, 121, 241–2
vow(s)   17–18, 26–7
vulnerable   26, 31, 36, 65, 68, 98, 120, 124, 156, 161, 170

waiting   29, 59–60, 153, 219–22, 271, 291, 310
war   11–12, 19–20, 22, 27, 34, 39, 46, 54, 143–5, 147, 151, 164–5, 167–70, 191, 195, 200, 254, 260, 269–70, 273, 296, 341
  postwar   7, 9, 11–12, 45, 145, 162, 165, 167, 169, 254, 256, 260, 293, 297, 318
  World War(s)   11–12, 106, 149–50, 167, 170, 192, 255, 270, 296, 320
weak   103, 143, 169–70, 219, 221, 225, 309, 311
  weakness   113, 219–20, 222, 226–7, 339
West   63–4, 71, 90, 164, 166, 169, 277
  Western   19, 44, 62–4, 66–8, 71, 132, 164, 166, 168, 170, 210–11, 240, 269, 277, 334, 337, 339
who am I   112–13, 124, 154, 157
wholeness   80, 83, 87, 249, 288
will of God   81–2, 211, 232, 234, 291, 319
wisdom   87, 98, 105, 107, 178, 234–5, 288
witness(es)   28, 59, 70, 73, 84, 86, 91, 130, 137–8, 140, 182, 218, 232, 273, 318, 323, 339, 342
  witnessed   133, 169, 206, 210, 235, 293, 306, 331
woman, women   8, 10, 47, 62, 97, 105, 116–17, 151, 153, 156, 159, 182, 278
word   28, 31, 33, 46–7, 51–2, 54–5, 57–8, 60, 69, 80–2, 87, 180–2, 185, 210, 212, 216, 224, 227, 230, 249–51, 275, 292, 296, 300, 315–17, 329, 331, 340
  Word of God, God's word   12, 31, 55, 59–60, 80–2, 229, 237, 244, 249–50, 275, 292, 309, 319, 323
work(s)   8–10, 15–16, 22, 27, 30, 42–3, 47, 52–3, 57, 63–4, 69–71, 79–81, 83–4, 92, 94, 98, 103, 107, 109,

135–6, 145, 147, 151, 155, 158, 166, 169, 179, 193, 195, 198, 202–4, 206, 212, 218, 224, 230, 234, 256, 258, 267, 270, 276, 278, 283–7, 292, 326, 334–6, 341–2
world come of age   40, 63–4, 71, 73, 189, 197–8, 201, 290, 312–13, 328–30, 332, 335
worldliness   102, 182, 310
   this-worldliness   144, 154, 203
worldly   56, 66, 71, 174, 202–3, 209, 213, 222, 242, 251, 274, 300–1, 312–13, 315, 317, 329
   this-worldly   189, 198, 201, 206, 248, 256, 291, 317
worldview(s)   94, 101, 104, 108, 153, 279, 284, 289–90, 312, 319
worship   81, 173, 222, 225, 332–3

young   7–8, 11, 43, 56–7, 59, 62, 77–8, 132, 151, 191, 193–4, 198, 278–83, 290, 297
youth   55, 93, 137, 155, 256, 282–3

Zionism   151–2, 155–9

www.ingramcontent.com/pod-product-compliance
Lightning Source LLC
Chambersburg PA
CBHW071239300426
44116CB00008B/1102